A LIBERAL CHRONICLE IN PEACE AND WAR

A Liberal Chronicle in Peace and War

Journals and Papers of J. A. Pease, 1st Lord Gainford, 1911–1915

Edited by
CAMERON HAZLEHURST
and
CHRISTINE WOODLAND

Great Clarendon Street, Oxford, OX2 6DP,
United Kingdom

Oxford University Press is a department of the University of Oxford.
It furthers the University's objective of excellence in research, scholarship,
and education by publishing worldwide. Oxford is a registered trade mark of
Oxford University Press in the UK and in certain other countries

Published in the United States of America by Oxford University Press
198 Madison Avenue, New York, NY 10016, United States of America

British Library Cataloguing in Publication Data
Data available

Library of Congress Control Number: 2022944967

ISBN 978–0–19–288705–4

Printed and bound in the UK by
Clays Ltd, Elcograf S.p.A.

PREFACE

The years 1911 to 1915 were among the most turbulent in modern British history. From his seat at the Cabinet table as President of the Board of Education in the Asquith Liberal government, and on the front bench of the House of Commons, Joseph Albert 'Jack' Pease contributed to debate and policy on a cascade of issues of great consequence for the nation.

When we began in the late 1960s to immerse ourselves in Jack Pease's Edwardian and post-Edwardian political world, it was still possible to meet and talk to men and women who had been participants and close observers of the dominating political conflicts and crises of the period in which he flourished: Home Rule, the struggle to limit the power of the House of Lords, Entente diplomacy, financing of the navy and Budget dilemmas, Anglo-German naval rivalry, women's suffrage, Disestablishment, education, land reform, and the course of the war that was to be called 'Great'.

What we learned and began to understand from shared memories and nuanced silences was something of the personal lives and attitudes that lay beneath the official records that were just beginning to emerge. The next generation of men and women who had grown up in the pre-war era also helped us to make better sense of their elders' enmities and friendships, and the evidence of intrigue, anger, prejudice, and ambition, that lay in waiting in long-lost or hidden letters and diaries.

Joe Pease, the third Lord Gainford, had a cornucopia of stories about his grandparents. His mother, the second Lady Gainford, wrote candidly of the personalities of her parents-in-law. Of those who had worked alongside Jack Pease and his colleagues, Sir Horace Hamilton, Principal Private Secretary to successive Chancellors of the Exchequer, explained Lloyd George's nickname, 'the goat', but his twinkling eye hinted at the more salacious popular version. Sir Alan Barlow Bt was more discreet about his association with Pease's Parliamentary Secretary, Christopher Addison. The quiet dignity of Frances, Countess Lloyd George of Dwyfor, illumined her enduring loyalty to the powerful and passionate man she had loved for three decades. Less noticed by historians than her contemporary Frances Stevenson, Sarah Tugander, Lady Melville, Bonar Law's personal secretary, was a fount of information, dipping enthusiastically into her shorthand notebooks as we spoke and corresponded. Lucy Masterman, a widow for four decades, did not hide a resentful sadness about her husband's political disappointments and the alleged ingratitude of his chiefs, especially Lloyd George. The 2nd Lord Rothermere, 16 years old in 1914, shared his father's story of Lloyd George's affair with the actress Julia James and the warning his friends gave him that the press could not be kept silent forever. Sir Harry Verney Bt was the last surviving member of the Liberal government when recalling in 1969 how often he had to remind an unkempt Chief Secretary for Ireland, Augustine Birrell, to do up his fly buttons.

If only we had known enough then to ask better questions of those who were patient and kind to young scholars who were just beginning to search the world that had passed...

Pease's journals and letters record the contest of ideas, the arguments, and the moods of his colleagues, especially the more prominent personalities of the Cabinet—the Prime Minister Herbert Henry Asquith, David Lloyd George as Chancellor of the Exchequer, Winston Churchill as Home Secretary then First Lord of the Admiralty, and Lord Kitchener as Secretary of State for War. Pease was a modest contributor and unassuming witness to the deliberations and rivalries of a unique gathering of political talent, among them Sir Edward Grey, Reginald McKenna, Walter Runciman, Lewis 'Loulou' Harcourt, John Simon, Herbert Samuel, Charles Masterman, John Burns, Lords Morley, Crewe, Haldane, and Buckmaster, and Alick Murray, the Master of Elibank, and many less well-known figures.

Scholarly research on specific themes or policy domains tends to isolate them from the jangling realities and crowded agendas of Cabinet discussions. Following one man's daily record of events in Whitehall, Westminster, and 10 Downing Street, incomplete and subjective as it is, allows us to see the buffetings and diversions and competing demands on time and money that accompany every abstracted sequence of policy argument and decision.

To help explain what Pease records, sometimes in very cryptic notes, our editorial commentaries, footnotes, and brief biographies furnish background information and explanation. No attempt is made to shine a light on every Cabinet decision, or twist and turn of policy. But we have tried to assist readers to understand and place in context the subjects to which Pease refers, including a host of long forgotten domestic and foreign incidents, some of them unpublicised and others that made contemporary headlines. Where we can show what Pease might have known but did not record we have often supplied the detail. Where an issue had broader ramifications than he was likely to have been aware of, selective reference is made to published works and documents that explain the background.

In giving some guidance to the vast (and at times recondite) scholarly literature that throws light on the situations that confronted Pease and his colleagues, we hope to provide the basis of a comprehensive appreciation of Asquith's Liberal government in peace and war.

Knowing that our task would take many years, Joe Pease, the 3rd Lord Gainford, agreed with us that other historians and biographers should be given access to the diaries while our work continued. We have drawn attention to publications in which good use has been made of the Gainford Papers. But it will be obvious that what Pease has said about many topics has not yet been assimilated by scholars. Preoccupation with controversial policies and incidents has left many once salient subjects out of the spotlight. We have tried to illuminate some subjects that were important in their time but have languished in the indifference of posterity. We have drawn attention to what we believe to be mistaken or insufficiently documented contentions or conclusions, but we have not set out to provide compendious reinterpretations or rebuttals of previous studies. We offer a discursive chronicle and guide to reading, not a seamless narrative or an exhaustive bibliographical review.

Sometimes, when we have found revealing unpublished documentation, or a topic has caught our interest, we have taken the liberty of writing rather more than is strictly required to make sense of the text. We therefore have commentary and previously unknown or underutilised sources on the struggle over the Parliament Bill in 1911, the Marconi 'scandal', the withdrawal of the Franchise Bill in 1913, the King's role in the Irish crisis in 1913–14, and the events accompanying the decisions for war in 1914. Editorial passages fill the gaps in the intermittent accounts of Pease's own activities in charge of legislation on education and electoral reform.[1]

[1] Regrettably the journals of Sir Godfrey Baring Bt (1871–1957), JAP's PPS 1911–13, were destroyed by his solicitors on his death. Baring's son, an Eton schoolboy 1911–15, recalled his father affirming that his 'master' was a 'very sound administrator', and always being at pains to refute the charge that he was a political lightweight (Sir Charles Baring Bt–Cameron Hazlehurst, 3 Oct. 1971).

Although he no longer had the intimate daily access to the Prime Minister that he had enjoyed from 1908 to 1910 as Patronage Secretary to the Treasury, the government's Chief Whip, Pease remained a fervent believer in Asquith's political acuity and wisdom. As one of Margot Asquith's oldest friends, he remained a welcome guest for dinner and bridge at 10 Downing Street and occasional visits to Margot's country cottage, The Wharf. Because so much of his focus is on the political leader whom he esteemed, we have referenced and quoted other journals and correspondence where they complement or amplify what Pease has to say about Asquith's political world and social circle.

ACKNOWLEDGEMENTS

Our first and greatest debt is to the late 3rd Lord Gainford, who entrusted us with his grandfather's papers and was a patient supporter of an enterprise that took far too long. Our work on the Gainford Papers began in 1968 and was initially supported by research assistance funded by Nuffield College, Oxford. In 1971 Jack Pease's journals and a large collection of family and official correspondence, government documents, press cuttings, photographs, and ephemera were deposited in the Nuffield College Library. For the welcome acceptance of the Gainford collection, and encouragement to us in embarking on the editorial mission, we gave thanks at the time, and acknowledge now, the indispensable support of the then Warden of Nuffield, Sir Norman Chester, and the Fellow Librarian, Dr Max Hartwell. When the papers came to the library, Christine Kennedy and Eleanor Vallis spared no effort in facilitating our task, as have their successors Elizabeth Martin and Clare Kavanagh.

A succession of research and secretarial assistants, most of whom worked primarily on the diaries for the period 1908–10, also gave us more help on this volume than they might have realised: we thank Derek Abbott, Janice Aldridge, Pauline Barratt, Jan Brazier, Anthea Bundock, Susan Enever, Carol Flanagan, Beverly Gallina, Jan Hicks, Irene Hilleard, Sue Lloyd, Lois Simms, Marion Stell, Mayling Stubbs, and Brenda Unwin.

Sally Whitehead, who played a critical role as co-author of *A Guide to the Papers of British Cabinet Ministers 1900–1964*, gave timely aid, funded by Queensland University of Technology. More recently we were helped in numerous ways by Catherine Dewhirst. Margaret Hammer has kindly made available her Cambridge University doctoral thesis on Pease's friend Sir George Newman and transcripts from the Newman papers.

It will be evident from the notes and commentary that we have benefited greatly from the research of Maurice Kirby on the Pease family and businesses, Martin Pugh on franchise history, Neil Daglish on educational policy and administration, and Thomas Otte on foreign policy. Their work has provided a sure foundation for our treatment of the themes they have made their own. Thomas Otte generously made time as he was correcting the proofs of his major biography of Edward Grey to vet our text. Nicholas Lambert has been our guide on naval policy and strategy, and we are indebted to him for a challenging reading of the entire manuscript. David Dutton has saved us from errors that only someone deeply versed in early twentieth-century political history would have noticed. None of them bears any responsibility for the blemishes that remain.

We have been aided by the editorial notes of Michael and Eleanor Brock on H.H. Asquith's letters to Venetia Stanley and Margot Asquith's diary, documents we had been privileged to see before the Brocks' editions were published.[2] On a broader front, there was inspiration in Elie Halévy's *The Rule of Democracy* and the insights of chapters XII and XIII of R.C.K. Ensor's *England 1870–1914*. Peter Rowland's study of the 'Last Liberal Government' supplied a convenient and reliable narrative framework, graced by the more recent syntheses and interpretations of Geoffrey Searle, Ian Packer, José Harris, Brian Harrison, Zara Steiner and Keith Neilson, Vernon Bogdanor, David Dutton, Trevor Wilson, David Powell, Peter Dewey, Peter Clarke, Philip Waller, Hew Strachan, and Simon Heffer. For the Conservative and Unionist Opposition the works of E.H.H. Green and our greatly missed friend and colleague John Ramsden have been indispensable.

In a project that has stretched over five decades there has been an enormous expansion of scholarly research on early twentieth-century British politics and society, and international relations. As the commentaries, notes, and acknowledgements testify, we have drawn on a wide range of unpublished as well as published sources in clarifying and developing some of Pease's more allusive remarks and observations. A bibliography would add enormously to an already long book; and, as Hew Strachan properly said in his *The Politics of the British Army*, it 'could never do justice to the accumulated reading of years'. We are deeply grateful to those whose published scholarship has made our task so much easier. In Strachan's words, we have conveyed our 'immediate obligations'. And we acknowledge with regret that we might have overlooked or failed to appreciate

[2] A volume of Margot Asquith's diary, in Randolph Churchill's possession when seen in 1967, had reputedly been rescued from a skip. Transcripts of Asquith's letters, kindly made available by Venetia Montagu's daughter Judy Gendel and Robert Jackson, were quoted with the then Hon. Mark Bonham Carter's permission in Cameron Hazlehurst, *Politicians at War July 1914 to May 1915: A prologue to the triumph of Lloyd George*, Jonathan Cape, 1971. Although Michael and Eleanor Brock's footnotes show that they were very familiar with *Politicians at War*, they did not mention it in the appendix on 'Previous Use of the Letters', in *H. H. Asquith Letters to Venetia Stanley*, Oxford UP, 1985, pp.615–17.

important work that bears on the matters considered by Cabinet between 1911 and 1915.

For providing copies of their publications and unpublished research, and for informed guidance that has assisted us to elucidate much of what might otherwise have been opaque or confusing, our debts to other scholars are, as Robert Ensor put it, 'exceedingly numerous'. Sadly many of those who have aided us have not lived to see the culmination of the project. But, believing with Ensor that our colleagues would be content with our private expressions of sincere gratitude, we do not 'display their names here like a row of scalps'.

The Australian National University funded an extended visit to Canberra by Christine Woodland and research trips by Cameron Hazlehurst to the United Kingdom for this and related projects. Two periods as a Visiting Fellow at Trevelyan College in the University of Durham allowed Hazlehurst time for additional research and reflection. Generous and timely support was received from the British Council, the Twenty-Seven Foundation, the Nuffield Foundation, and The Queen's College, Oxford. Queensland University of Technology granted leave, and provided further travel and research assistance.

Research in the United Kingdom in the later stages of the work was greatly aided by the accommodation privileges extended to *quondam* Fellows of Nuffield College and The Queen's College, Oxford, and the companionable hospitality of Deborah Lavin, Robert and Janet Balfour of Burleigh, Anna and Toby Turl, and Wendy Hazlehurst.

Paul Pickering, as Director of the Research School of Humanities and the Arts and Dean of the College of Arts and Social Sciences at the Australian National University, has been a sustaining source of support; the appointment of Hazlehurst as an Adjunct (later Honorary) Professor at the Humanities Research Centre at the ANU gave the project a timely fillip. A term in 2015 as an Archives By-Fellow at Churchill College, Cambridge, made possible some long-postponed sorties to the private papers of some of Pease's contemporaries; and final checks of the Asquith, Harcourt, Simon, and other manuscript collections in Oxford were an unplanned benefit of the award of a Bodleian Libraries Sassoon Research Fellowship in 2016.

Our debts to the many libraries and archives whose staff have gone way beyond the call of duty in responding to our queries is acknowledged in the Archives and Libraries appendix. But we must specially express our gratitude to the Bodleian's Colin Harris, whose indispensable help and friendship spanned the half century since the research began; to Helen Langley, Oliver House, and

Jeremy McIlwaine at the Bodleian; to Allen Packwood and the staff of the Churchill Archives Centre; and the Document Supply Service team at the National Library of Australia, especially Vicki Jovanovski, Deanna Cronk, and Natalie Clough, who were indefatigable in finding and making available books and articles not otherwise accessible to us.

Finally we record our special thanks for their gracious hospitality and the sharing of personal and family memories to Frances, Countess Lloyd George of Dwyfor, Tony Benn, the 24th Earl of Crawford and the Countess Crawford, Lady Lyell, the Hon. Sir Steven Runciman, Henry Illingworth, Jamie and Tania Illingworth, Sir Geoffrey Harmsworth Bt, the Hon. Randolph S. Churchill, Sir Alan Barlow Bt, Sir Horace Hamilton, Sir Harry Verney Bt, Sir Felix Brunner Bt, the 3rd Lord Ponsonby of Shulbrede, the Hon. Laura Ponsonby and the Hon. Kate Russell, Thelma Cazalet-Keir, Douglas Duff, Edward 'Teddy' Goldsmith, Sir Geoffrey Shakespeare Bt, the 2nd Viscount Rothermere, Margaret, Viscountess Stansgate, the Dowager Marchioness of Cholmondeley, Jonathan Peto and the Hon. Selina Peto.

CONTENTS

EDITORIAL PRACTICE AND CONVENTIONS

Except for a few unintelligible passages the text that appears here is a complete transcription of the original handwritten entries now catalogued in the Gainford Papers at Nuffield College Library as 'MS. Gainford 33/1 Diary of Asquith as prime minister by JAP 1908 Mar 30–1911 Jan 25' and 'MS. Gainford 33/2–3 Political diary with key 1911 Feb 6–1915 Jan 7'. Details of the Gainford collection are at https://www.nuffield.ox.ac.uk/the-college/library/special-collections-and-archives/archive/, under Gainford, Lord (1860–1943), accessed 29 Oct. 2022.

Pease's punctuation is slapdash. We have, therefore, inserted or deleted commas, colons, apostrophes, dashes, and underlinings where not to do so might lead to confusion. The day and date provided by Pease at the beginning of most entries have been italicised to make the transition from one entry to the next more perceptible. Unnecessary stops at the end of abbreviated words have been removed. Pease's spelling and capitalisation are also erratic. We have retained enough of his variations to convey the flavour of the original but have sometimes corrected what would otherwise look odd. Thus his occasional 'program' is retained, although he usually, and we in the commentaries, have 'programme'. We have kept his persistent spelling of 'negociation' (it was Loulou Harcourt's form as well) and capitalisations that seem from the context to convey some intended emphasis. Presumed slips of the pen and misspellings have been silently corrected; for example 'Cambrai—Le Cateau' replaces 'Cambrai-le-Chateau'. Attention is drawn to the corrections where the original seems to signify a noteworthy unfamiliarity with a person, place, or institution. On occasions it is evident that Pease has misheard a name or location; whenever possible we have indicated what those closer to the speaker or better informed about the subject might have heard.

The diary is obviously not always written on the day(s) to which the entries refer. When a misdating appears to be accidental (for example, giving consecutive entries the same date), we have checked the calendar and corrected the error. When a misdating is more problematic, we have explained why a different date is more likely. The dating of Cabinet meetings can sometimes be difficult. Comparison with other Cabinet diarists is necessary but not always helpful; Pease's colleagues were at times just as unreliable with dates as he could be. Particular care is necessary with composite accounts of several days. Resort to the Prime Minister's Cabinet letters to the King has usually removed doubts; but there can be pitfalls, especially if it is supposed that the date on which a letter was written and signed was always the date of the meeting(s) that it reports. (We have referred interchangeably to the Prime Minister's letters as they were copied for the Public Record Office from the Royal Archives and to the drafts or fair copies preserved in the Asquith Papers.) A useful check on dates is provided by the announcements in *The Times* that meetings of ministers have occurred.

We follow conventional practice in enclosing doubtful readings and conjectural dates in square brackets with a question mark. Where words clearly have been added to the entry after the original was written this is noted. Pease's style is often so condensed that it would be visually disturbing to insert obviously missing words in parentheses or to make frequent use of *sic*. However, peculiarities or omissions in letters by other writers are recognised and rectified. We have made similar silent changes (corrections of typing errors and trivial blips) to other people's letters and diaries to the ones we have made in Pease's diary and letters.

Almost every individual mentioned in the text has a biographical note. Several who appear frequently in our commentaries, such as C.P. Scott, Sir William Robertson Nicoll, and Venetia Stanley, are also included. Most of these notes are grouped together in a Biographical Gallery at the back of the book. Individuals are listed alphabetically by the surname or title by which they were known at the end of the period covered by this volume. After their birth and death dates, the status or appointment held at the time of first appearance in the diary is given. The exceptions not in the Gallery include (*a*) several people who are mentioned only once or twice and whose relevant details are incorporated in a commentary or a footnote, (*b*) some of those who are initially mentioned by the office they held rather than by name (for example, the Lord Chancellor) and who are identified on the page where they first appear, and (*c*) those of whose identity we are uncertain—probable, possible, or conceivable identifications being given in a footnote or commentary. As in the first volume of *A Liberal Chronicle*, we have a fourth category, those whose identity had eluded us. Happily, we are able to identify almost everyone who is mentioned. Our happiness would have been unqualified had we been able to identify the 'Mr May' whose brother was thought to be married to one of Speaker Lowther's sisters.

Editorial commentaries are italicised. Readers who prefer to read the text alone can therefore readily skip the italicised interpolations.

To save space in the commentaries and notes we have usually referred to Pease as 'JAP', Lloyd George as 'DLG', Asquith as 'HHA', and Churchill as 'WSC'. Titles of books, articles, and theses are abbreviated after the first citation; from the second citation onwards surnames of authors or editors are unaccompanied by forenames except where it is necessary to distinguish between persons with the same surname. Places of publication are London unless otherwise indicated. There are occasions when it can be helpful to acquire information that only publishers can provide; accordingly we normally name publishers, as they present themselves on title pages (Palgrave Macmillan is thus on occasion 'palgrave macmillan'!). We use UP for university press; and if, like Manchester or Cambridge, the press has a territorial name we do not add the place of publication. Most references to universities are in the form 'U. of Melbourne'.

In the companion volume, *A Liberal Chronicle: Journals and Papers of J. A. Pease, 1st Lord Gainford, 1908–1910*, The Historians' Press, London, 1994, pp.1–16, we provided a summary of Pease's family background and his political career until his appointment as Patronage Secretary to the Treasury, the Government Chief Whip, in April 1908. The introduction that follows here stands alone, although it contains some verbatim and paraphrased passages from the first volume; readers will find in the first volume additional detail on Pease's life before he entered the Cabinet. Highlights of the 1908–10 diary and our editorial notes and commentaries are précised and paraphrased in Tim Renton, *Chief Whip: People, Power and Patronage in Westminster*, Politico's Publishing, 2005, pp.206–19, 358–9. We were not aware of Lord Renton of Mount Harry's book until several years after it was published. Unfortunately John William Hancock's account of Pease's work as Chief Whip in his 1992 Cambridge Ph.D. thesis, 'The Anatomy of the British Liberal Party, 1908–1918: A Study of its Character and Disintegration', was not available to us when we were completing our first volume.

Many of the manuscript collections we have cited were first examined when they were in the possession of descendants and, in some cases, before their existence was known outside the families that held them. Some, such as the Runciman and Simon papers and the diaries of Alexander MacCallum Scott and Arthur Ponsonby, were entrusted to us by their owners for extended periods. These exceptionally valuable manuscript troves are now in repositories. Others remain in private hands and are not generally available to scholars. At the time we saw them, most of these collections had not been catalogued or even sorted.

Much of our research in the Gainford papers occurred before they were organised and listed. Where possible we have added details that make it easier for items to be traced in the subsequently catalogued Gainford collection at Nuffield College. Regrettably it has not always been practicable to do this; and there are similar issues with some other collections. Where we have not verified that particular documents have been deposited (for example, some of the items that are likely to be in the Runciman of Doxford papers now in the Newcastle University Library Special Collections & Archives, the Simon papers now in the Bodleian Libraries, the Ewart papers now in the National Records of Scotland, or papers in the Buxton collection in the British Library), we note on the first time they are cited the library or archive in which they are probably to be found and acknowledge the owner who made them available to us when they were uncatalogued; but we do not provide a repository reference on each subsequent occasion.

Scholars familiar with many of the collections of private papers cited might notice that collections are not always described in the same way as in the catalogue of the repository in which they have come to rest. There is no uniformity in the practice of archives and libraries. It is not uncommon for collections to be designated by a family surname, or by the place where the papers were originally held. Sometimes several members of the same family are grouped under one name, even though, for example, the papers of a married couple might have been kept in quite separate files and places.

Our practice is to use the name or title by which people were known at the time of their death. All collections are described as MSS. Thus Jack Pease's papers have always been the Gainford MSS to us but we cite individual files in the Nuffield College format as MS. Gainford xx/xx. Walter Runciman's papers are Runciman of Doxford MSS. Lord Robert Cecil's are Cecil of Chelwood MSS. Lord Curzon was 'Curzon of Kedleston' through successive elevations in the peerage, and that is how he appears throughout. Our own inconsistencies include following the long-established Bodleian Libraries 'MS. Asquith' format rather than the correct but cumbersome Oxford and Asquith MSS, and the Parliamentary Archives short form Lloyd George MSS rather than Lloyd George of Dwyfor. We refer to the papers of Arthur Ponsonby, the first Lord Ponsonby of Shulbrede, as the Ponsonby MSS, the abbreviated title being preferred by the 3rd and 4th Barons, who have made the papers available to us.

Most of our research on collections of private papers now held in the Parliamentary Archives was conducted when the papers were held elsewhere. All of the collections in the Parliamentary Archives (including those previously in the House of Lords Record Office) were recatalogued in the early 1990s. The resulting abbreviated names of collections have been adopted here after the first full citation; thus the Lloyd George papers examined in the Beaverbrook Library become 'LG', the papers of Sir Rowland Whitehead become WHD; and a specific reference previously in the form 'Whitehead MSS 5, HLRO Hist. Coll. 211' becomes Whitehead MSS, WHD/5, PA.

Confusion can be created by changes in the names of other repositories, and by catalogue revisions resulting in revised citation formats. For example, the evolution of Devon Record Office to Devon Archives and Local Studies Service and then to Devon Heritage Centre needs to be borne in mind when reading publications quoting from their holdings. Since 2015 what we would previously have called the Acland MSS have been described as Acland of Killerton MSS; and a specific reference given in 2006 by the editor of Sir Francis and Lady Acland's correspondence as 1148 M/518 has become 1148M add 14/Series II/Correspondence/518!

ABBREVIATIONS

For journals, institutions, document titles, and selected individuals, offices, and appointments referred to more than once in commentaries and footnotes.

Aberdeen U.	University of Aberdeen Special Collections
Albion	*Albion: A Quarterly Journal Concerned with British Studies*
HHA Cabinet letter	Asquith's Cabinet letter to the King
Balliol Col.	Balliol College Archives and Manuscripts
BEF	British Expeditionary Force
BJMilHist	*British Journal for Military History*
BL	British Library
BL: A & AS	British Library: Asian and African Studies (previously Oriental and India Office Library and Oriental and India Office Collection)
Bodl.	Weston Library, Bodleian Libraries
Brotherton Coll., Leeds U.	Brotherton Collection, University of Leeds
Cadbury RL Birmingham U.	Cadbury Research Library, Special Collections, University of Birmingham
CID	Committee of Imperial Defence
CAC	Churchill Archives Centre
CUL	Cambridge University Library
Devon HC	Devon Heritage Centre, South West Heritage Trust (previously Devon Record Office and Devon Archives and Local Studies)
DLG	David Lloyd George
EHR	*The English Historical Review*
Friends Lib.	Religious Society of Friends Library
Glasgow U.	University of Glasgow Library
Glos. Arch.	Gloucestershire Archives

Gov.	Governor
Hants ALS	Hampshire Archives and Local Studies
HHA	Herbert Henry Asquith
Hist. Ed.	*History of Education*
HJ	*The Historical Journal*
Hist.Res.	*Historical Research*
HWJ	*History Workshop Journal*
IHR	*The International History Review*
IWM D	Imperial War Museum Department of Documents
Huddersfield U.	University of Huddersfield, University Archives and Special Collections
I&NS	*Intelligence and National Security*
JAP	Joseph Albert Pease
JBS	*Journal of British Studies*
J.Lib. DH	*Journal of Liberal Democrat History*
J.Lib.H.	*Journal of Liberal History*
JMH	*The Journal of Modern History*
John Rylands Lib. Manchester U.	John Rylands Library, University of Manchester
JSAHR	*Journal of the Society for Army Historical Research*
JSH	*Journal of Social History*
J.Strat.S.	*The Journal of Strategic Studies*
Lambeth PL	Lambeth Palace Library
Liverpool U.	University of Liverpool Library
Newc. U. Spec. Coll.	Newcastle University Library, Special Collections & Archives
NLS	National Library of Scotland
NLW	National Library of Wales
NMM	National Maritime Museum
N. Yorks CRO	North Yorkshire County Record Office
NRAS	National Register of Archives Scotland
NRS	National Records of Scotland
Nuffield Col.	Nuffield College Library
ODNB	*Oxford Dictionary of National Biography*
PA	Parliamentary Archives
Parly Hist.	*Parliamentary History*

PPS	Parliamentary Private Secretary
S&EER	*Slavonic and East European Review*
Soc.H.	*Social History*
TNA	The National Archives (United Kingdom)
UQFL	University of Queensland Fryer Library
West Sussex RO	West Sussex Record Office
W&S	*War & Society*
Wren Lib. TCC	Wren Library, Trinity College, Cambridge
WHR	*The Welsh History Review*
WiH	*War in History*
Women's HR	*Women's History Review*
WSC	Winston Churchill

INTRODUCTION

The Diarist

Joseph Albert 'Jack' Pease (1860–1943) was one of eleven members of his Quaker industrialist family (including cousins and uncles) to sit in the House of Commons in the nineteenth century. Although he was the only one who can properly be regarded as a career politician, there was a dynastic imperative that gave an air of inevitability to Pease's emergence, first in local government as Mayor of Darlington in 1889 at the age of 29, then as MP for Tyneside three years later.

His elder brother, father, grandfather, and great-uncle were among the ten other members of the clan who had preceded him to Westminster. Five years after he entered Parliament, a friendly journalist wrote that the Peases 'must surely form the largest family party in the House... Such a contingent would be well worth securing for any cause or ism if families voted *en bloc*; it is well known, however, that they carefully eschew anything like uniformity of opinion and action.'[1]

The Peases were formidably powerful magnates in the north-east of England in coal, iron, woollens, railways, engineering, and banking. The makers of Darlington and the principal creators of Middlesbrough, they enrolled themselves in a variety of causes and isms. They were champions of movements for peace and disarmament and anti-slavery, and against the opium traffic and the Contagious Diseases Acts. Home Rule divided them. But there was a rich tapestry of Liberal commitment and expectation to shape Jack Pease's political inheritance. He was the one member of the family who seemed from the earliest days to be destined for a political career unhampered by overwhelming business

[1] *The Echo*, 1 Aug. 1897, in Elizabeth Isichei, *Victorian Quakers*, Clarendon P., Oxford, 1970, p.205. On the Pease family background see M.W. Kirby, *Men of Business and Politics: The Rise and Fall of the Quaker Pease Dynasty of North-East England, 1700–1943*, George Allen & Unwin, 1984; Maurice W. Kirby, 'The failure of a Quaker business dynasty: The Peases of Darlington, 1830–1902', in David J. Jeremy ed., *Business and Religion in Britain*, Gower Publishing, Aldershot, 1988, pp.142–63; Marianne V. Pitts, 'Victorian share-pricing: a problem in thin trading', *Accounting, Business and Financial History*, vol.8, no.1, 1998, pp.33–52; Anne Orde, *Religion, Business and Society in North-East England: The Pease Family of Darlington in the Nineteenth Century*, Shaun Tyas, Stamford, 2000. For their paternalist and philanthropic employment practices see Roy Church with the assistance of Alan Hall and John Kanefsky, *The History of the British Coal Industry, Vol. 3, 1830–1913: Victorian Pre-eminence*, Clarendon P., Oxford, 1986, p.283; and on the accumulation and dispersal of the family's fine art collection, Margaretta S. Frederick, 'A Quaker collects: Joseph Whitwell Pease of Darlington', *Journal of the History of Collections*, vol.18, no.1, 2006, pp.59–69.

obligation, quietist tradition, or what Brian Phillips has called 'the creeping hubris' of late Victorian and Edwardian Quaker discourse.[2]

Unfortunately, as M.W. Kirby details in his valuable study of the Pease family's business history, Jack's father, Sir Joseph, made rather a monumental mess of running the family's business and trust responsibilities. In 1902 he and his sons were ruined, barely escaping bankruptcy. But for the timely support of the shipping millionaire Christopher Furness and a consortium of other friends, family, and associates, Jack Pease's career, in politics as well as in business, would have been extinguished before he ever held national office.

His father soon died, a broken man. His older brother, Alfred—forced by his wife's ill-health as well as his own ill-fortune—took government employment in South Africa. Jack alone, sustained by a strong-minded wife, Ethel Havelock-Allan, daughter of the hero of Lucknow, Major-General Sir Henry Havelock-Allan Bt VC, clung to the House of Commons to which he was first elected as MP for Tyneside in 1892. Ethel Pease (better known as Elsie) was a forthright ally in her husband's public life notwithstanding that his politics were notoriously disagreeable to her Liberal Unionist father. 'The General was much annoyed when his daughter, a charming girl, married my old friend, Jack Pease,' George Leveson Gower recalled. 'When she was about to have a baby, it was suggested that it would be convenient if she could have it in her father's house. But it was not to be. He wasn't going to have, he hotly declared, "any damned Home Ruler born in his house".'[3]

Pease had been John Morley's parliamentary private secretary when Morley was Chief Secretary for Ireland in Gladstone's last ministry; and he served as a junior opposition whip from 1899 under Sir Henry Campbell-Bannerman. By the turn of the century he was a seasoned political campaigner. He was knowledgeable from personal experience of the growing strength of Labour in the north-east. He had an unashamedly unobjective view of the kinds of people who voted Tory: 'the stupid, the sullen, the soaker, the sunken, and the society elector,' as he privately described the supporters of one of his opponents.[4] And he was

[2] Brian Phillips, 'Apocalypse without tears: hubris and folly among Late Victorian and Edwardian British Friends', in Pink Dandelion ed., *Towards Tragedy/Reclaiming Hope: Literature, Theology and Sociology in Conversation*, Ashgate, 2004, p.66; John V. Crangle, 'Joseph Whitwell Pease and the Quaker Role in the Campaign to Suppress the Opium Trade in the British Empire', *Quaker History*, vol.68, Autumn 1979, pp.63–74.

[3] George Leveson Gower, *Mixed Grill*, Frederick Muller, 1947, pp.158–9.

[4] JAP–Sir Joseph Pease, 12 Oct. 1900, MS. Gainford 5.

convinced of the need for the Liberals to extirpate the evil of plural voting, which he believed cost him his seat in 1900.

A plain speaker, and no intriguer, Pease was not associated in a spectacular way with any of the great controversies, ambitions, and strategies of the late 1890s and early 1900s. His election addresses were routine endorsements of Liberal Party policy on the House of Lords, Ireland, Rating and Taxation, Pensions, and diminished national expenditure. He carried on the Pease tradition of chairing the Peace Society and was, as his unimpressed imperialist brother, Alfred, commented, 'wobbly' on the Boer War.[5] He voted several times with David Lloyd George and other critics of the government but did not oppose votes of credit; and he denied that he was a Pro-Boer. He uttered the usual rhetoric about 'promoting social legislation for the benefit of the people', but he was no visionary exponent of the 'new Liberalism'. Indeed, working closely with Herbert Gladstone in the Whips' office, he probably imbibed Gladstone's maxim: 'People with advanced opinions do not pay.' Gladstone had told Beatrice Webb this in June 1904, looking at her, she recorded, as much as to say, 'How much have you ever subscribed to party funds, I should like to know?'[6]

Throughout his life Pease loved the outdoors: fox-hunting, shooting, fishing. He was a keen and talented cricketer, captaining the Durham County Cricket Club. (In later years he would extol the game that 'brought out the best in our race'.[7]) He worked hard, without enthusiasm, to surmount educational hurdles. He read History at Trinity College, Cambridge. But Lord Mersey's sketch in the *Dictionary of National Biography*, which mentions that he was captain of the football team, a member of the polo team against Oxford, twelfth man for the University cricket team, and master of the University draghounds, did not refer to the fact that he also took a degree.[8] As a young man Pease had let it be known that he 'disliked being expected to be intellectual'.[9] He had become a practical business man and a competent local government politician and administrator at an early age. He had no illusions about his own abilities. But what he might never

[5] A.E. Pease diary, 28 May 1901, Pease MSS (courtesy of Sir Joseph Gurney Pease Bt).

[6] Beatrice Webb diary, 10 June 1904, in Norman and Jeanne MacKenzie eds, *The Diary of Beatrice Webb, Vol. Two, 1892–1905, 'All the Good Things of Life'*, Virago, 1983, p.326. For Gladstone as Chief Whip see Kenneth D. Brown, *The Unknown Gladstone: The Life of Herbert Gladstone, 1854–1930*, I.B. Tauris, 2018, pp.72–110; and for more glimpses of Pease at work with him, Iain Scott Sharpe, 'Herbert Gladstone and Liberal party revival, 1899–1905', Ph.D. thesis, Institute of Historical Research, U. of London, 2011.

[7] *Sheffield Daily Independent*, 3 Feb. 1911.

[8] Lord Mersey, 'Pease, Joseph Albert, first Baron Gainford (1860–1943)', in L.G. Wickham Legg and E.T. Williams eds, *The Dictionary of National Biography 1941–1950*, Oxford UP, 1959, p.664.

[9] [Sir George Newman], 'Recollections of Lord Gainford', *Friends' Quarterly Examiner*, 1943, pp.110–11.

have quite realised was how little regard Henry Asquith and many other senior political colleagues had for his brain power.

On 26 February 1915, Asquith drew up a class list of members of the government for the pleasure of Venetia Stanley, the most frequent recipient of his confidences. He placed Pease in the bottom group, though ahead of his colleagues T. McKinnon Wood, and Lords Beauchamp, Emmott, and Lucas.[10]

Pamela McKenna, whose husband Reginald had long been a parliamentary colleague, had recorded a private expression of the Prime Minister's condescension in June 1910:

> We dined at Downing Street with Margot and Henry alone—both in very good spirits and he amused us all at dinner by putting his head on one side in a contemplative attitude and saying that he thought it a wonderful achievement for Jack Pease to have got into the Cabinet.[11]

Pease had just been appointed Chancellor of the Duchy of Lancaster after being Chief Whip since Asquith became Prime Minister. It was two years later when Pease, now President of the Board of Education, revealed to Pamela McKenna, whose affection he craved, his sensitivity:

> I don't admire brains so much as many people do. The more I see of life, the more I am impressed with the extent to which cleverness fails, and mediocrity succeeds. There appears to be some compensating arrangement in nature. Just as the cripple exerts an influence on those he meets, far in excess of what could be expected from him, so the brilliant book worm, fails to understand how to put to practical utility, in the service of his fellows, the knowledge acquired, or the talent with which he has been endowed.

In the same letter he would let drop that Margot Asquith was 'a flame of mine in my teens, and there is in her a most extraordinary mixture of goodwill, and a knack of saying the wrong thing, or doing the right thing in the wrong way'.[12]

What Asquith would confide about Pease to his women friends he would also say to a closer colleague. When the terminal illness of Augustine Birrell's wife prompted thinking in March 1915 about a possible replacement for him as Chief Secretary for Ireland, the Prime Minister wrote confidentially to his Cabinet protégé Edwin Montagu:

[10] Roy Jenkins, *Asquith*, Collins, 1964, p.341.

[11] Pamela McKenna diary, 6 June 1910, McKenna MSS, MCKN 12/3, CAC.

[12] JAP–P.McKenna, 15 Sept. 1912, McKenna MSS, MCKN 9/4, CAC.

> There is much truth in your mordant thumbnail sketch of poor J.P. But he has some sterling merits, and is so much pressed by the pinch of poverty that a rise from 2 to 5 thousand a year is to him a matter of great moment. Would it be too much of a scandal to put him in the L.G.B, if Samuel were sent to Ireland? And then who is to do Education? I suppose there is nothing you would loathe more?[13]

Pease remained as President of the Board of Education, the post to which he had been elevated in the autumn of 1911. When he was relegated to the back benches in May 1915, the tributes from officials who had worked with him were more than conventionally warm. Sir Amherst Selby-Bigge, whom he had appointed as Permanent Secretary, recorded that Pease had 'mastered the intricacies and details of our complicated work to a surprising extent...besides taking the responsibility which you have never shirked, you have been a working member as well as Captain of the team'.[14] Likeable as those who worked closely with him found him, there were reservations. His occasional flashes of short temper were not generally known. His relative ineffectiveness in bureaucratic and Cabinet disputes was less easily hidden. Reflecting on a funding battle with the Local Government Board in November 1914, his Parliamentary Under-Secretary Dr Christopher Addison had concluded: 'The plain fact is that Pease is not a match for Samuel in the Cabinet and is rather inclined to put up a case and then run away.'[15] In the wounding judgement of Montagu and Lloyd George: there were ministers who really counted, those who talked and had something to say, and those who didn't count at all but some of whom, like Pease, 'talked a good deal'.[16]

The truth is that Pease was an unexciting, amiable, modest, late Gladstonian Liberal, who entered politics because he thought he should, and stayed when his career choices were reduced by misfortune. Generally, he was prudent enough to back winners. But he was lucky that Campbell-Bannerman bore him no grudge after his ill-advised public rejoicing in 1901 at the supposedly imminent return to the leadership of the Liberal Party of the self-exiled Lord Rosebery. When

[13] Naomi B. Levine, *Politics, Religion and Love: The Story of H.H. Asquith, Venetia Stanley and Edwin Montagu, Based on the Life and Letters of Edwin Samuel Montagu*, New York UP, 1991, p.258.

[14] JAP, *War Reminiscences*, ch.IX, p.132, MS. Gainford 36/2.

[15] Addison diary, 11 Nov. 1914, Bodl. MS. Addison, dep. d. 1. Samuel was a powerful adversary, as Edwin Montagu found when he remonstrated against Local Government Board public works spending on 1 Oct. 1914: 'Surely the unemployment figures now do not justify anything like the expenditure about which you swank.' The next day, firmly rebuffed by Samuel, Montagu told DLG: 'sooner or later...somebody will have to try to persuade Samuel that it is not the most patriotic thing to spend his whole time trying to bag other people's departments' (copies, Montagu MSS, courtesy of Judy Gendel and the Hon. Randolph S. Churchill).

[16] Frances Stevenson diary, 4 Apr. 1915, *Lloyd George: A Diary by Frances Stevenson*, ed. A.J.P. Taylor, Hutchinson of London, 1971, p.40.

the Balfour government collapsed in December 1905, Campbell-Bannerman considered Pease for the Chief Whipship. However the memory of his financial difficulties was too recent. The choice fell, oddly, on George Whiteley, a wealthy cotton manufacturer and convert from the Conservative Party. Whiteley turned out to be a most remarkable fundraiser but left a trail of alienated colleagues and supporters. 'I hear many severe things said', a junior minister's wife wrote in her diary in March 1906, 'chiefly based on the fact that he pokes in the ribs without discrimination and is too much impressed with power of money in party organisation'.[17] A growing number of Liberal backbenchers resented Whiteley's lectures on their alleged transgressions, while many Tories treated him as a renegade. By 1908 he was barely on speaking terms with the Opposition Chief Whip.

When Campbell-Bannerman retired, Pease was the acknowledged second man in the government Whips' office, the obvious successor to Whiteley, whose health had given way. Pease had displayed some pugnacity in comments about the aggressive attitude of the Labour Representation Committee at by-elections, earning himself a rebuke from the normally friendly *Daily News* for breaking the public silence that Whips were expected to observe. However, pointing out the inherent strains in the progressive alliance was not a major sin, and he had not otherwise blotted his copybook. Nor had he been given a chance of showing administrative ability or the debating flair that might have impressed a Prime Minister. He was reluctant to remain a Whip. But Campbell-Bannerman had not responded to his plea in January 1907 for 'any post you could offer me which might be regarded as promotion, a change would not be unwelcome'.[18] And there was already a crowded front bench.

The massive Liberal majority in the 1906 Parliament may well have been elected largely on familiar issues of Free Trade, Liquor Licensing, and Education. But with Winston Churchill and David Lloyd George increasingly disposed to press forward some of the social reform agenda of the more advanced radicals, and the new Prime Minister Asquith not unwilling to move forward with them in tackling problems of old age, infirmity, sickness, and poverty, the political world in which Pease was about to assume a large responsibility was undergoing a transformation.

Nothing Jack Pease himself said or wrote quite captures the essence of the changes in what might now be called 'the policy environment' as well as the

[17] Hilda Runciman diary, 17 [Mar.] 1906, Viscountess Runciman of Doxford MSS, uncatalogued when seen, courtesy of the Hon. Sir Steven Runciman, now in Newc. U. Spec. Coll.

[18] JAP–Sir Henry Campbell-Bannerman, 14 Jan. 1907, copy, MS. Gainford 79/139.

jaundiced perspective embodied in letters written in 1908 by his brother. More in sorrow than in anger, Alfred Pease wrote to his successor as MP for Cleveland, Herbert Samuel, on 19 August 1908:

> Generally there appears to me, a disposition to multiply laws and restrictions on freedom and create artificial conditions, to an extent that is likely to impair our rights and liberties in a very un-English fashion. The idea that the State can take from one class and give to the other classes and take the place of individual enterprise is a very corrupting one—and goes to the root of human relationships.... we are reaching a condition when the bulk of the population are being taught that though those above them in the social scale have learnt they must exercise self-restraint prudence thrift and exert themselves to the utmost in order to marry and in order to provide for the future they may marry when they like have as many children as they like shall have their families provided with food education with work with free this that and the other, the right to have employment the right to have a certain wage the right to have their hours of work state fixed and the right to have pensions from the State.[19]

What Alfred was lamenting was precisely the policy of social and political reform that both his brother and Samuel were most actively promoting. Jack was obliged to say—and may well have genuinely believed—that most of these developments were part of a moral and political duty, a programme of social adjustment grounded in the rights now properly demanded by citizens and mandated by electoral victories.

The Journals

Pease had started a diary several times. There are surviving fragments dealing with a term in Cambridge in 1880, overseas travels, parliamentary events in the later 1890s, and the formation of the Campbell-Bannerman ministry. But it was not until April 1908 when he was 47 that he managed to establish a regular diary-keeping habit that lasted until shortly after he was dropped from the Cabinet in 1915. The journals cover Pease's years as Chancellor of the Duchy of Lancaster and President of the Board of Education as well as his nineteen months as the Government Chief Whip. He resumed diary-keeping in 1917 but, by then on the periphery of Westminster life, his entries were desultory and petered out at the end of the year.

[19] Sir Alfred Pease–Herbert Samuel, 19 Aug. 1908, Samuel MSS, SAM/A155 III 137, PA. Michael Bentley noted that 'Jack Pease's father [*sic*] spat blood over Lloyd George's bastardization of Liberal doctrine after 1909' (*Politics Without Democracy, 1815–1914: Perception and Preoccupation in British Government*, Fontana Paperbacks, 1984, p.345).

Some other colleagues in the Asquith government kept political journals—John Burns, Lord Carrington, Charles Hobhouse,[20] John Morley, John Simon, Alfred Emmott, and Lewis ('Loulou') Harcourt are the best known (though Harcourt's twentieth-century diary notes 'disappeared' until the early twenty-first century).[21] But none was closer to the Prime Minister than Pease, whose diary is more comprehensive than Hobhouse's and rivals Harcourt's as an authoritative source of information on the workings of Westminster and Downing Street during the Asquith premiership. Pease was restored to the ministry, though not the Cabinet, as Postmaster-General in 1916; however he rarely returned to diary-keeping after he became a casualty of the formation of the coalition government in May 1915.

The diary entries vary from a few words to several pages, written in locked volumes until January 1915, on or very close to the date to which they refer. They are frequent during parliamentary sessions; and, from the time Pease joined the Cabinet in March 1910 to May 1915, they include information about almost every meeting he attended as well as others he heard about from colleagues. In total there are about 140,000 words.[22]

Shortly after he joined the Cabinet in 1914 as First Commissioner of Works, the Lancashire textile manufacturer Lord Emmott learned that it was 'considered incorrect to take notes at the Cabinet or record in one's diary what is done there'. Fortunately for historians, after a brief hiatus Emmott resumed acting incorrectly, intermittently.[23] During this period it was well known to Asquith and his colleagues that Harcourt was a habitual note-taker at Cabinet meetings, in spite of being chastised at least once for doing so.[24] Harcourt sat on the Prime Minister's right and would have had difficulty concealing what he was doing, even when

[20] Edward David ed., *Inside Asquith's Cabinet: From the Diaries of Charles Hobhouse*, John Murray, 1977, is a good selection, perceptively introduced.

[21] Cameron Hazlehurst and Sally Whitehead with Christine Woodland, *A Guide to the Papers of British Cabinet Ministers 1900–1964*, Cambridge UP for the Royal Historical Society, 1996, p.176. The diaries were deposited in the Bodleian Library in December 2005. According to the Liberal newspaper editor and official biographer of HHA, J.A. Spender, who had begun to edit them at the request of Harcourt's son, an embargo on publication for many years could be lifted only with 'various consents' (Prime Minister, Foreign Secretary, and Archbishop of Canterbury). Harcourt's son had withdrawn his approval of the editing project 'for publication at some future date', and it was abandoned (Spender–Herbert Samuel, 20 Nov. 1941, Samuel MSS, SAM/A45 f.28, PA). See 'Lewis Harcourt's Journal of the 1914 War Crisis', ed. John W. Young, *IHR*, vol.40, no.2, 2018, pp.436–55.

[22] The first of two proposed volumes, Cameron Hazlehurst and Christine Woodland eds, *A Liberal Chronicle: Journals and Papers of J. A. Pease, 1st Lord Gainford, 1908–1910*, was published by The Historians' P. in 1994.

[23] Emmott diary, 25 Aug. 1914, MS. Emmott, I/2, Nuffield Col., courtesy of Joan Simon.

[24] HHA–Harcourt, 5 Oct. 1916, and Harcourt diary note, 10 Oct. 1916, Bodl. MS.Eng.c.8271.

Asquith was preoccupied in writing a letter to his most intimate correspondent, Venetia Stanley.

It is clear from some of the detail that Pease records that he must also have often been scribbling numbers, names, and fragments of dialogue on loose sheets, some of which have survived. However, no one seems to have called him to account, perhaps because he sat at the end of the table, less visible to the cluster of senior ministers seated next to, and directly across from, the Prime Minister. And because he was known to make pencil sketches and cartoons of people around him.[25]

Pease wrote what was essentially an aide-mémoire. That he, like Emmott and others, should think it useful to do so is hardly surprising. As Asquith reminded the House of Commons in June 1922, before the creation of a Cabinet secretariat at the end of 1916 the practice had been for the Prime Minister to write a letter to the sovereign with an account of each Cabinet meeting. No other record of Cabinet decisions was made or kept. 'The essence of the whole thing', Asquith affirmed, 'was mutual confidence, and not only that, but absolute secrecy'.

> The secrecy was so well maintained, in theory at any rate, and I think in fact also, that I believe in practice no one ever opened the door of the chamber except a Cabinet Minister. There were no messengers. No note was kept of the proceedings by anybody except the Prime Minister. There were occasions when a furtive kind of note was taken, Members taking an independent note of their own, but that was always regarded as a breach of the unwritten law, and the Prime Minister of the time had more than once in my time to exercise the very invidious function of admonishing, privately of course, the peccant Minister for his breach of that unwritten rule.[26]

'At the end of a Cabinet meeting it was the custom for the Prime Minister's private secretaries to enter the Cabinet room and destroy all the odds and ends of paper that were left on the table or the floor.'[27] Pease's diaries, usually it seems written late at night or in the early hours of the morning, display abundant signs of haste and tiredness. There is no evidence of stylistic pretention. And, although

[25] See, e.g., JAP's profile of Lloyd George passed to Lewis Harcourt at a 1912 Cabinet meeting and his drawing of a camouflaged warship with explanatory note annotated by Harcourt 18 Feb. 1915 (http://www.bodleian.ox.ac.uk/weston/our-work/seminars/amm2013/lewisharcourt#gallery-item=149309, accessed 31 Mar. 2016).

[26] HC Deb 13 June 1922 vol 15 cc227–32. 'The observance of secrecy is secured not only by the obligation of an oath but by the existence of an honourable understanding of what is necessary alike in the public interest and in the maintenance of that collective and individual loyalty without which the Cabinet system must inevitably fall into confusion' (Vt Gladstone, Enclosure No. 4, 21 Dec. 1912, in Sth Africa Despatch, Secret, 22/12/12, TNA: CO 551/310).

[27] *Manchester Guardian*, 16 June 1922, in Edward McChesney Sait and David P. Barrows, *British Politics in Transition*, World Book Co., Yonkers-on-Hudson, 1925, p.48.

there are occasional passages that betray pride in achievement, they in no way resemble the 'mirrors in which Burns admired himself'.[28] The diarist's preoccupation is with others, especially the Prime Minister. Family matters rarely intrude; and a separate sporting diary enshrines Pease's prowess with the gun. His journal is primarily a record of things heard, seen, and done in Parliament and 10 Downing Street.

If Pease was introspective, his journal rarely betrays his thoughts. If his private life had passions or peccadilloes, he felt no need to pen obtrusive clues. His wife seems always to have been in his confidence. An Anglican, Elsie respected her husband's Quaker heritage and commitment. He often accompanied her to morning service in the Gainford parish church. But, as he once told a gardener who had offered to give notice because he was unable to give satisfaction to Lady Gainford, 'Is that all?...I have been married to her ladyship for nearly 50 years and still haven't given her satisfaction' (Ld Gainford–CH, 8 Dec. 1994). Did he give satisfaction elsewhere? His daughter-in-law, who came into the family orbit in 1917, admitted he was 'certainly not above a bit of Edwardian slap & tickle—I remember hearing vague rumours at times—but I don't think the affairs were ever very serious & I think that JAP & Elsie were a genuinely devoted couple' (2nd Lady Gainford–CH, 30 Sept. 1975).

Guileless as his writing is, Pease's revelations of self are small and infrequent. His letters to his wife do, however, convey his feelings at moments of political crisis, and add detail complementing the often cryptic diary notes. In retirement he began work on an autobiography and war reminiscences, drawing on the diary. But there was very little documentation there of his own thoughts and deeds; he had not been consumed by self-importance, and does not seem to have been concerned to compile materials for eventual exercises in self-justification. The project remained uncompleted at his death.

In a government of many talents and much ambition, Pease had realistic expectations about his own prospects. He was grateful to be given a vantage point close to the centre of power and responsibilities for matters that were important for the Liberal government and the nation. But his standing was a perpetual disappointment to his ambitious and status-conscious wife. ('I hate the feeling that one is dependent on one's wretched salary & classed with the Winstons & L. Georges & Masterman & c!...I now realize what Lady Grey meant the last time I stayed at Fallodon when she said with great sarcasm & a grim smile

[28] William Kent, *John Burns: Labour's Lost Leader A Biography*, Williams & Norgate, 1950, p.xiii.

"I now consider Edward & Mr Pease professional politicians".'[29]) That said, as Chief Whip he was able to make notable contributions to maintaining the Liberal majority and the momentum of reform. When he lost his Saffron Walden seat in the general election of January 1910, he might have retired from politics and attempted to resurrect his severely diminished family fortunes. But Asquith, who rated him a good second-class man, offered him a place in the Cabinet and told him to find himself a seat. Asquith's private secretary Roderick Meiklejohn told the Prime Minister's daughter, 'some people rather demur at Pease being put in the Cabinet'.[30] Walter Runciman, whom he was eventually to succeed as President of the Board of Education, thought the elevation a scandal.[31] Francis Neilson, a prominent stage and opera director before entering politics as a single-taxer, characterised the Chief Whip he knew as 'a mere plodder'.[32] Yet, for all his colleagues' disdain of his ability, Pease was the only one of Asquith's Chief Whips to attain Cabinet rank.

Perhaps, as some critics thought, Asquith simply did not have the heart to abandon a loyal and agreeable lieutenant whose major faults were being less clever than the cleverest in a clever government, and less adept in his handling of strong men than his exceptionally smooth successor, the Master of Elibank. Being companionable, an old friend of the Premier's wife, and a willing bridge player, brought him into the Downing Street circle.

There are conflicting views about Pease's competence as a political organiser and tactician. But the professional assessment of the Tory Whip Lord Balcarres was unfavourable on Elibank's handling of the Liberal parliamentary party and arrangements for House of Commons business. In these domains, by implication, Pease had the edge. Pease's own diaries provide evidence of Asquith's continuing reliance on his understanding of parliamentary practicalities. The *Manchester Guardian* (19 Jan. 1916) recalled: 'He had the right carriage for a Whip, coming up from his lobby along the floor of the House with a long driving stride, scattering before him the suspense and congestion which always attend the end of a division.' There was a pugnacity about him too—in contrast to 'The Master', the 'consummate diplomatist'.[33] Alfred Emmott observed it as a chairman of

[29] Elsie Pease–JAP, 25 Nov. 1911, MS. Gainford 83/52.

[30] Meiklejohn–Violet Asquith, 17 Feb. 1910, Mark Bonham Carter & Mark Pottle eds, *Lantern Slides: The Diaries and Letters of Violet Bonham Carter 1904–1914*, Weidenfeld and Nicolson, 1966, p.201.

[31] Runciman–Hilda Runciman, 15 Feb. 1910, Viscountess Runciman of Doxford MSS.

[32] Undated annotation on JAP–Neilson, 25 Jan. 1910, Neilson MSS, Box 2/3, John Rylands Lib. Manchester U.

[33] 'Our Parliamentary Correspondent [P.W. Wilson]', *Daily News*, 7 Aug. 1912.

committees: 'On the whole Alec Murray is much gentler & more conciliatory in his methods than Jack Pease.'[34] Where Elibank was also supposedly superior was in invigorating the party in the country, 'generally rehabilitating an organisation which was going to bits under the clumsy handling of Jack Pease'.[35]

It must be conceded too that the 'shrewd, resourceful...pugnacious' Percy Illingworth, had he lived, was certain of promotion had war and coalition not barred his way.[36] War and the Liberal split after 1916 also frustrated the Scottish Free Church social reformer John Gulland; but Gulland was in any case generally considered a failure, being on poor terms with Opposition members.[37] Whiteley, on the other hand, still in his early 50s but evidently suffering from chronic insomnia, was removed to the House of Lords in 1908 as Lord Marchamley and never held another government post. Pease's performance and potential more than matched his predecessor's. He might have lacked Elibank's suave manner. But he was not 'an almighty humbug', as Arthur Ponsonby called Elibank; and he avoided the flaws of judgement that put paid to Elibank's ambition.[38] And when he gave evidence to the Royal Commission on Honours in 1922 he skated dangerously over the truth in asserting: 'In no single case was any honour recommended by me to the Prime Minister directly or indirectly associated with a payment to party funds, and there existed nothing in the system which prevailed to tempt me to traffic in honours with a view to raise party funds.'[39]

[34] Emmott diary, 19 Feb. 1911, MS. Emmott, I/1, Nuffield Col., courtesy of Joan Simon.

[35] Lord Balcarres diary, 17 Nov. 1910, Crawford and Balcarres MSS, John Rylands Lib. Manchester U., seen originally at Balcarres House, courtesy of the late 28th Earl of Crawford; and quoted in John Vincent ed., *The Crawford Papers: The journals of David Lindsay twenty-seventh Earl of Crawford and tenth Earl of Balcarres 1871–1940 during the years 1892 to 1940*, Manchester UP, 1984, p.168.

[36] For HHA's evaluation of Illingworth see Hazlehurst, *Politicians at War*, p.128.

[37] Hazlehurst, *Politicians at War*, pp.132–4; A. Steel-Maitland–J.H. Whitley, 27 June 1914, Steel-Maitland MSS, GD 193/108/2, NLS; John Stewart, '"Christ's Kingdom in Scotland": Scottish Presbyterianism, Social Reform, and the Edwardian Crisis', *Twentieth Century British History*, vol.12, no.1, 2001, pp.1–22. Regrettably a collection of Gulland's papers including 'his diaries (1879–1920), numerous letters...' etc., offered for sale by Sotheby's in their catalogue, 19 Dec. 1981, cannot be traced, Sotheby's being unwilling to assist. The Gulland collection of 60 letters in the National Library of Scotland (Acc. 6868) contains only one item from his period as Chief Whip.

[38] Ponsonby diary, 6 June 1912, Ponsonby of Shulbrede MSS, courtesy of Lord Ponsonby of Shulbrede.

[39] The preceding paragraphs draw substantially, with permission, from Cameron Hazlehurst, 'Whipping Asquith's Liberals: J. A. Pease's Journal as Patronage Secretary to the Treasury 1908–1910', *Archives* (journal of the British Records Association), vol.XXI, no.92, Oct. 1994, pp.183–99. Subsequent paragraphs expand on Cameron Hazlehurst, 'Pease, Joseph Albert, first Baron Gainford (1860–1943)', *ODNB*, Oxford UP, 2004, pp.354–6. Correspondence relating to the Royal Commission on Honours is in MS. Gainford 93/93–8. In his evidence JAP admitted that the list of those from whom he sought money for the Jan. 1910 election 'may possibly have included one or two names of recipients of honours which had previously been recommended by myself or my predecessor' (MS. Gainford 99).

A move to Rotherham gave Pease a constituency that was safe as long as the local miners did not unite behind a Labour candidate. When he entered the Cabinet as Chancellor of the Duchy of Lancaster, colleagues such as Walter Runciman and Edwin Montagu affected to be mystified by the promotion. The Lord Chancellor, Lord Loreburn, dismissed him as a 'nobody'.[40] Pease was, according to Lucy Masterman, 'one of the very few people whom [Lloyd] George thoroughly hates'.[41] Lloyd George blamed him for the Liberals' poor electoral showing in 1910. But the elevation had a considered purpose. Asquith not only appreciated his loyalty but knew that he had a useful working knowledge of electoral law and practice. He was the man to carry forward the government's programme of franchise and electoral reform. His opposition to votes for women assured the Prime Minister that the process would not be diverted. When Pease's Franchise Bill foundered on the rocks of women's suffrage in January 1913, his dismay, like Asquith's, was tempered by relief that votes for women had been thwarted without splitting the government.

A bigger personal disappointment was his failure as President of the Board of Education to enact major educational reforms. Not that he was alone in failing to deliver legislation in this fraught sphere: Birrell, McKenna, and Runciman had all fared badly in what the historian Duncan Tanner would call the 'political graveyard of Education'.[42] Pease's appointment in October 1911 coincided with the departure of the dominating Permanent Secretary, Sir Robert Morant. The new minister reshuffled the senior staff of the department, choosing a team led by L.A. Selby-Bigge that responded well to a competent, considerate, and usually congenial chief. Pease announced his 'great ambition' to work harmoniously to effect administrative reform and coordination. In Selby-Bigge he had a Permanent Secretary who knew that his minister needed him to be alert to

> public opinion, vested interests, the interests of the teaching profession, the susceptibilities of LEA's, the divisions of opinion among educational experts, the rival claims of different branches of the office work for additional Treasury aid and additional staff and all the general considerations of policy which it is not the business of any particular Officer to balance against each other.[43]

[40] Scott 'diary', 6–8 Sept. 1911, Trevor Wilson ed., *The Political Diaries of C. P. Scott 1911–1928*, Collins, 1970, p.53.

[41] Lucy Masterman diary, *'Reminiscences'* [1910], Masterman MSS, B2/2, Cadbury RL Birmingham U.

[42] Duncan Tanner, *Political change and the Labour party 1900–1918*, Cambridge UP, 1990, p.60.

[43] Selby-Bigge–JAP, 14 Apr. 1912, MS. Gainford 83/131, quoted in Geoffrey Sherington, *English education, social change and war 1911–20*, Manchester UP, 1981, p.19. For the Board of Education as Morant shaped and left it, E.J.R. Eaglesham, *The Foundations of Twentieth-Century Education in England*, Routledge and Kegan Paul, 1967, is of enduring value. N.D. Daglish, 'The transfer of power at the Board of

The measures that followed were applauded evidence of a willingness to push forward practical changes when greater reforms were not achievable. Pease strengthened the Board's relations with teachers and Local Education Authorities. He improved professional training. An Elementary School Teachers' Superannuation Act (1912) doubled the normal allowance for teachers; and a War Service Superannuation Act (1913) made war service equivalent to teaching for superannuation entitlement. Using persuasion rather than regulation, Pease also took a lead in promoting evening 'institutes' in London for employed youths to continue their education.

As noted in a valedictory interview in 1915 with the radical MP Percy Alden in *The Friend*, he had served longer than any other minister in the portfolio during the last three parliaments. Over three and a half years he made a range of incremental but significant changes: support for 150 schools for mothers, grants to day nurseries, 50 per cent of the cost of school meals provided by Local Education Authorities, and encouraging classes in domestic economy, 'practical housework', and gardening. With his fellow Quaker and health administrator George Newman, to whom he paid tribute for 'a great diminution of physical defects in our schools', he greatly expanded school medical inspection services. By mid-1915 the state was bearing half the cost of over 1,200 school medical officers. As George Bernstein has said, he 'approached education as an instrument of social reform'. But like his predecessors he was unable to find a formula to appease Nonconformist grievances: 'hardly a day passed without my having to answer some question or other which might easily have provoked bitter feeling.'[44] Through 1912 and 1913 and into 1914 the government trimmed and tacked with a sequence of attempted solutions; but a settlement that satisfied all interests proved beyond them.

Remaining in the Cabinet that made the decisions for war with Germany in 1914 was deeply troubling for Pease. He, like the majority of his colleagues, was

Education, 1911', *Journal of Educational Administration and History*, vol.12, no.2, 2000, pp.1–10, is indispensable. A shrewd Parliamentary Correspondent commented in the aftermath of the Holmes Circular affair: 'The Board of Education and its higher officials will after this little escapade have to keep their absurd prejudices under control' (P.W.W., *Daily News*, 4 Apr. 1911).

[44] The difficulties faced by Pease's predecessors at the Board of Education are charted in D.W. Bebbington, *The Nonconformist Conscience: Chapel and politics, 1870–1914*, George Allen & Unwin, 1982, pp.146–52. See also George L. Bernstein, *Liberalism and Liberal Politics in Edwardian England*, Allen & Unwin, Boston, 1986, pp.141–2; *The Friend*, vol.LV, no.28, 9 July 1915, pp.525–8. For draft bills favourable to Nonconformists in the Board of Education 1914 files see Benjamin Sacks, *The Religious Issue in the State Schools of England & Wales 1902–1914: A Nation's Quest for Human Dignity*, U. of New Mexico P., Albuquerque, 1961, pp.77,242n.37. 'Plans for educational development 1911–14' are discussed and documented in Sherington, *English education*, pp.19–43.

led step by step to assent to what he thought was to be a naval war. When he discovered that the government's senior advisers and Service ministers saw a continental intervention as inevitable, he saw no path back from the fundamental commitment—military and moral—to support France and Belgium. He knew little of the years of confidential planning for economic warfare that would soon be on the Cabinet agenda. But he quickly grasped the strategic issues in August 1914.

At any time the prospect of losing his ministerial salary would have been a stumbling block on the path to a principled resignation. But, although it was no secret that Pease had wavered, as did several others in the Cabinet, he was probably one of those Quakers whom Ruth Fry had in mind when she wrote in 1926 of 'those who found no chasm between their views and those of the majority of their fellow-countrymen, and were able to throw their energies into the prosecution of the war at home and abroad'.[45] John Morley put it less charitably, recalling what he saw of his colleague on 2 August 1914:

> Pease told us he had been lunching with the Prime Minister, who begged him to keep the *conciliabule* to which he was going, 'out of mischief'. Pease also argued that Grey was never quite so stiff as he seemed. His tone convinced me that the Quaker President of the Peace Society would not be over squeamish about having a hand in Armageddon.[46]

Notwithstanding Morley's sour judgement, it is impossible to ignore the evidence of a very real struggle of conscience in the July and August 1914 days, when the issue of war or peace hung in the balance.

Pease tried unavailingly to dissuade his son Joseph from enlisting, and was an early supporter of the Friends' Ambulance Unit, devoting a chapter of a draft memoir to the FAU.[47] But he resigned from the presidency of the Peace Society (to which he had been elected in 1911 and at whose annual meeting in May 1914 he

[45] A. Ruth Fry, *A Quaker Adventure: The Story of Nine Years' Relief and Reconstruction*, Nisbet & Co. 1926, p.xix.

[46] John Viscount Morley, *Memorandum on Resignation August 1914*, Macmillan, 1928, p.16.

[47] The FAU was not endorsed by the Society of Friends. As one Friend wrote: 'It would be deplorable if any of our young Friends should so fall away from their peace principles as to take part in this work' (Edward Milligan, typescript draft biography of Edmund Harvey, 12/10,11, courtesy of Ted Milligan). The rift between the FAU and the Friends' Service Committee crystallised in March 1916 when it was agreed that Friends could join a General Service Section of the FAU to teach, do farm work, and 'other humble and useful occupations'; and the FAU made it a condition of working in the branch that there could be no participation in local peace meetings or peace propaganda (Corder Catchpool, *On Two Fronts: Letters of a Conscientious Objector*, Geo. Allen & Unwin, 1940 [1st edn 1918], p.93).

had said relations with Germany had never in his lifetime been more cordial). Thenceforth he publicly defended the government's position in speeches and pamphlets.[48] The Peace Society placed on record on 22 October 1914 'their cordial appreciation of his desire to relieve the Society from embarrassment arising from the War' (MS. Gainford 85/131–2). He did not resign from the Society of Friends. In an open letter to Harry Gilpin[49] in April 1915 he wrote: 'if the Society intend to disown those who are now actively engaged in the Front, who are fighting for the cause of an enduring peace, they should commence with me.'[50] The support for those young Friends who had enlisted—perhaps between a quarter and a third of those eligible by 1917—was widespread.[51]

Pushed to the margins of high policymaking, Pease undertook relief coordination tasks, the placement of volunteers for temporary assistance in government departments, and the chairmanship of the Professional Classes Sub-Committee of the Committee for the Prevention and Relief of Distress. 'It was essential', he recalled in his 'Reminiscences', 'that all enquiries should be conducted confidentially and tactfully', many people preferring to suffer in secret rather than apply for help (MS. Gainford 35). Mobilising teachers not in uniform, he introduced educational and leisure activities in army training camps, overcoming obtuse resistance from the Secretary of State for War, Lord Kitchener.

As teacher numbers shrank and the demand for child labour in agriculture and elsewhere increased, a Board of Education circular of 12 March 1915 authorised the suspension of compulsory attendance by-laws affecting elementary schools. Although some large towns, including Birmingham, Bradford, and Hull, did not change their policy, the impact of the change was significant. Some 600,000 children under 14, more than double the number previously employed, left

[48] 'Why Did We Go To War?', with 'historical facts which led to the war' for instruction to children, was issued to all headmasters of elementary schools in England and Wales (MS. Gainford 85/139). 'My draft has been approved by the Foreign Office as accurate' (JAP–DLG, 11 Sept. 1914, Lloyd George MSS, LG/C/4/12/7, PA).

[49] Sir (Edmund Henry) Harry Gilpin (1876–1950); Kt 1949; contested (Lib.) Finsbury 1922; chmn, Lib. Party National Executive 1943–6. Gilpin served with the Red Cross and resigned as a Friend because of his support for the war. Some of the dilemmas for young Friends are elucidated in Jessica Meyer, 'Neutral Caregivers or Military Support? The British Red Cross, the Friends' Ambulance Unit, and the Problems of Voluntary Medical Aid in Wartime', *W&S*, vol.34, no.2, 2015, pp.105–20, and Linda Palfreeman, 'The Friends' Ambulance Unit in the First World War', *Religions*, vol.9, no.165, 2018.

[50] JAP–E.H. Gilpin, 30 Apr. 1915, MS. Gainford 86/93.

[51] Margaret E. Hirst, *The Quakers in Peace and War: An Account of their Peace Principles and Practice*, Swarthmore P., 1923, p.538. David Rubinstein, 'Friends and War, 1914–15', *Journal of the Friends' Historical Society*, vol.62, no.1, 2010, pp.67–86, is informed and sympathetic. Joanna Dales, 'John William Graham and the Evolution of Peace: A Quaker View of Conflict before and during the First World War', *Quaker Studies*, vol.21, no.2, 2016, pp.169–92, provides a longer perspective.

school over the next three years.[52] Pease and his advisers had also realised that improved practical training and technical education must be given greater priority. With his new Parliamentary Secretary, Christopher Addison, he pressed for selection and promotion procedures in elementary and secondary schools across the country that would lead to more specialised training. As David Parker concludes: 'The total subordination of the work of the schools to the needs of the war was instant and long-lasting.'[53] From the earliest days of the war Pease understood and acted in concert with Addison on the need to mobilise the nation's scientific and industrial research resources. Weeks before he lost office in 1915, he had signed a seminal Cabinet paper, embodying Addison's case for 'a national scheme of advanced instruction and research in science, technology and commerce'.

On 4 May 1915 Pease became the longest-serving President of the Board of Education. Discarded from the ministry eleven days later when the coalition was constructed—'dear old Pease. He is simply heart-broken,' Addison observed[54]—he served as an unpaid member of the War Claims Commission in France. He was embarrassed by the need to seek a political pension, but by late 1915 he had secured a £2,000 a year consultancy by placing his coal industry expertise and political connections at the disposal of Lord Furness, son and heir of his old friend Christopher Furness. An invitation to rejoin the government as Postmaster-General (outside the Cabinet), following Sir John Simon's resignation and Herbert Samuel's promotion in January 1916, delayed Pease's return to active business life. Egged on by his unquenchably ambitious wife, he submitted an optimistic claim to succeed Augustine Birrell as Irish Secretary after the Easter rebellion.[55] And an

[52] John A. Fairlie, *British War Administration*, Oxford UP, 1919, p.243. Between Sept. 1914 and Jan. 1915 38 local authorities had released 1,413 children aged 11 to 14 for farm work (Alan G.V. Simmonds, *Britain and World War One*, Routledge, 2012, p.200, citing Pamela Horn's pioneering work on rural life). On 13 Oct. 1915, Arthur Henderson told a deputation that 1,538 boys and 53 girls had been granted exemption from school in rural areas, and 540 and 228 respectively in urban areas. Of these 54 were younger than 12, about 930 were between 12 and 13, and the rest between 13 and 14. 1,394 boys and 25 girls were in agricultural work; 121 boys and 14 girls in factory work; and 300 and 179 respectively in other employment (David Swift, 'A "Second State" during the First World War? Labour and the War Emergency: Workers' National Committee', *HWJ* vol.81, no.1, 2016, pp.84–105). For later statistics of exemptions and patterns of juvenile employment see Rosie Kennedy, *The Children's War: Britain, 1914–1918*, palgrave macmillan, 2014, pp.124–8).

[53] David Parker, '"Something a Little Sterner and Stronger": World War I and the enhancement of bias in English elementary education', *Journal of Vocational Education and Training*, vol.52, no.3, 2000, pp.438,442: David H. Parker, '"The Talent at Its Command": The First World War and the Vocational Aspect of Education, 1914–39', *History of Education Quarterly*, vol.35, no.3, 1995, pp.237–59. For a wide-ranging study of the impact of the war and the Board of Education's policy on London's schools see Stefan Goebel, 'Schools', in Jay Winter and Jean-Louis Robert eds, *Capital Cities at War: Paris, London, Berlin 1914–1919, Vol. 2, A Cultural History*, Cambridge UP, 2007, pp.189–234.

[54] Christopher Addison diary, 26 May 1915, Bodl. MS. Addison, dep.c.1.

[55] HHA–Sylvia Henley, 23 May 1916, Sylvia Henley MSS, Bodl. MS.Eng.lett.c.643, ff.661–2.

acid paragraph in his reminiscences conveys the depth of his disappointment when Arthur Henderson left the ministry later in 1916:

> I anticipated on Wednesday, August 9th, after Henderson's retirement, that I might be invited to take up my work at the Board of Education and to secure the passage of the Bill which had been approved by the Cabinet before the War, and which in the following Session was passed by Mr. Fisher[56] as if he had been the author. I was also anxious to carry out my scheme for housing the London University on the Bedford Estate, behind the Museum, which Fisher allowed to be hung up.[57]

Asquith's appointment of Lord Crewe to the Board of Education, adding to his existing responsibilities as Lord President of the Council and Leader of the House of Lords (and occasionally relieving Grey at the Foreign Office), made Pease's continuing exclusion from the Cabinet all the more galling. Residual hopes of further political advancement were extinguished by the formation of the Lloyd George coalition.

Ennobled as Baron Gainford in January 1917 in the Asquith resignation honours, Pease became a leading figure in the post-war industrial world.[58] He spoke for the Mining Association of Great Britain before the coal industry commission in 1919 and was elected president of the Federation of British Industries for 1927–8. As a 'prominent public man unconnected with any of the constituent companies' he was asked to chair the infant British Broadcasting Company in 1922.[59] He became a radio enthusiast, and was deputy chairman and a governor of the British Broadcasting Corporation from 1927 to 1932.[60] A supporter of homeopathy,

[56] Herbert Albert Laurens Fisher (1865–1940); Pres., Bd of Education 1916–22; Lib. MP Sheffield Hallam 1916–18, Combined English Universities 1918–26; historian; member, Royal Commission on the Public Services in India 1912–15; Vice-Chancellor, University of Sheffield 1913–17; Warden, New College, Oxford 1926–40; OM 1937.

[57] JAP, *War Reminiscences*, MS. Gainford 36/2.

[58] Both JAP and his wife had hoped that he would become Lord Pease, but they could not overcome the objections of his older brother to the use of the family name: 'no one will ever know who you were' Elsie lamented on 30 Dec. 1916 (MS. Gainford 87).

[59] Sir William Noble–Gainford, 18 Aug. 1922, MS. Gainford 99.

[60] Asa Briggs, *The Birth of Broadcasting: The History of Broadcasting in the United Kingdom*, Vol. I, Oxford UP, 1961, pp.123–4,127, and *passim*; Philip Elliott and Geoff Matthews, 'Broadcasting culture: innovation, accommodation, and routinization in the early BBC', in James Curran, Anthony Smith and Pauline Wingate eds, *Impacts & Influences: Essays on media power in the twentieth century*, Methuen, 1987, pp.235–57. A lasting impact of JAP's BBC role was prompted by his noticing that whenever his young grandson Joseph (known as "Zef" to distinguish him from the family's other Josephs) was presented to his parents at bath time in London, he would hear the six chimes of Big Ben and gurgle with delight. In Feb.1924, the BBC introduced the six pips to indicate the start of each hour, but JAP insisted on 6pm being announced by the chimes of Big Ben so that babies across the country could enjoy the same experience as Zef. To this day on Radio 4, while the other hours start with the pips, 6pm and midnight are heralded by 'Zef's bongs' (Chris Lloyd, 'Remarkable stories, and pictures, from the Pease memoirs', *Northern Echo*, 2 April 2014). More prosaically, a memo sent on 24 April 1924 by the

he was also a convert to the therapeutic value of music. Lord Gainford encouraged the installation of wireless sets in hospitals. Music, he said, had brought about recovery from shell shock and even insanity; it not only alleviated suffering; it expedited rehabilitation and prolonged life. If each patient in the 16,000 beds in London's 122 hospitals were discharged a day earlier, he said, there would be savings of £300,000 a year and 32,000 other patients could be admitted.[61] It was hardly a surprise when in 1935 he became President of the Radio Manufacturers Association.

As President of the Federation of British Industries in 1927 his themes were also predictable. Industry suffered from growing burdens of rates and taxation. Transport services needed improving and costs lowering; but railways should not compete with road transport. He had to acknowledge that export trades had declined but research and innovation continued. Other industries catering mainly to home markets—wireless apparatus, of course, car manufacturing, artificial silk, electrical engineering, preserved foods—were expanding. By early 1928 there were hopeful signs of a revival of shipbuilding. And, although mobility of labour from trade to trade and area to area was a concern, there was a 'much improved atmosphere in the relations of employers and employed'. Still, there was a way to go before Britain matched American efficiency: 'They have no use for the laggard. Apparently they have no indolent people,' unlike the large number of Britons who were content to live on the 'dole'.[62] The 'new Liberalism' was a fading memory.[63] Nevertheless, as old colleagues like Novar, Runciman, and Simon were easing themselves towards a Conservative lifeline, he told Sir Alfred

Organiser of Programmes to the directors of all stations, notes that children's hour was broadcast on all stations at 6pm. Big Ben would be heard striking the hour every evening except Sundays. Programme organisers were asked to so organise their schedule that the time signal does not interrupt a story or song. 'This is for the benefit and amusement of the children.' (BBC Written Archives Centre, R34/891/1-Time Signals, courtesy of Louise North.) BBC Copyright content reproduced courtesy of the British Broadcasting Corporation. All Rights reserved.

[61] Peter Morrell, 'Aristocratic Social Networks and Homeopathy in Britain', www.homeopathyhistory.com, 5 Apr. 2019, accessed 22 Sept. 2019; *Northern Echo*, 6 Aug. 1927, MS. Gainford 56. The benefits of radio got better with the telling. Within months he was quoting a doctor who believed the average length of stay in hospitals could be reduced from three weeks to two.

[62] *Yorkshire Post Trade Review*, 12 Jan. 1928; *New York Times*, 18 Jan. 1928, MS. Gainford 56. On the origins and development of the Federation of British Industries see Andrew Marrison, *British Business and Protection 1903–1932*, Clarendon P., Oxford, 1996, which unfortunately confuses JAP with his cousin Sir Arthur Pease; Gainford as FBI President is glimpsed in Emanuel Nicolas Bourges Espinosa (2021), 'Managing industrial discontent in Britain, 1927–1930: the industrial cooperation talks and the segregation of the national unemployed workers' movement', *Labor History*, vol.62, issue 5–6, 2021, pp.742–61.

[63] JAP's postwar role as a business spokesman and advocate of industrial reorganisation is a feature of M.W. Kirby's contribution in David J. Jeremy and Christine Shaw eds, *Dictionary of Business Biography: A Biographical Dictionary of Business Leaders Active in Britain in the Period 1860–1980*, Vol. 4, Butterworth, 1985, pp.597–601.

Mond on 28 January 1926: 'I could never be a Tory . . . believing in the innate liberalism of my country' (MS. Gainford 100, when seen).

Well known in his retirement for his concern for water conservation, Pease chaired the Tees Fishery Board and called for the creation of a national authority to deal with river pollution. In November 1938 he was one of five eminent businessmen associated with the Federation of British Industries appointed to advise the government on rearmament programmes. These activities left him much leisure for his favourite pastimes of fishing, hunting, shooting, and embroidery. With his diaries at hand, he made faltering attempts to write his memoirs. He had lived through momentous events and wanted to leave his own considered record of them.

In spite of his chagrin at being cast aside in May 1915, Pease had never wavered in his admiration of his old chief. His tribute in the House of Lords in February 1928 on Asquith's death was lauded as one of the finest speeches of his life. The *Evening Standard*, which thought Haldane was 'too discursive and formless' and Grey 'not particularly striking', said 'the best of them all . . . was Lord Gainford's unstudied but intimate and moving appraisal'.

Pease died at home, Headlam Hall, Gainford, Co. Durham, on 15 February 1943, fifteen years after his old chief. Elsie had died two years earlier. Their son, Joseph, succeeded to the title. Younger daughter Faith had married Michael Wentworth Beaumont, MP for Aylesbury, 1929–38. She died in 1935, leaving a 6-year-old son, Timothy, later Lord Beaumont of Whitley. Miriam, the oldest of the children, made a career as a factory inspector. She became the custodian of the family papers, living on until 1965, when the collection passed to her nephew Joe Pease, who succeeded to the title of Lord Gainford in 1971.

The Pease journals from 1911 to 1915 are an invaluable chronicle of Liberal government in peace and war. They provide an authentic and closely observed record of the Asquithian political world, the Prime Minister's family, and the social circle that revolved around him. By contrast with those of his colleagues who seemed intent on compiling evidence of their own prescience, insight, and political courage, Jack Pease was content to be a witness to 'history'.

Chapter 1
1911

After 22 meetings between 17 June and 10 November 1910 the inter-party conference held to seek a compromise path to constitutional reform was brought to an end. The Liberal Cabinet decided to seek the dissolution of Parliament and a general election. The election was fought largely on the limitation of the Lords' veto, with the rejected Budget a subsidiary issue. The Prime Minister, H.H. Asquith, had been given a secret undertaking by the King in November to create sufficient peers to carry through the government's policy should it prove necessary. The King's pledge would apply if the government had an 'adequate majority'. The Unionist leaders remained in the dark about this contingent guarantee until long after the Parliament Bill was introduced into the House of Commons. Ambiguous and vague as the pledge was, it was enough for the Cabinet to be confident about going forward. These events have been narrated many times but are admirably elucidated in G.H.L. Le May, The Victorian Constitution: Conventions, Usages and Contingencies, *Duckworth, 1979, pp.199–212. A record of the course of negotiations in November 1910 between the King, his private secretaries (Lord Knollys and Sir Arthur Bigge), and HHA and Lord Crewe on behalf of the Cabinet is found in a series of memoranda in Peter Raina,* House of Lords Reform: A History, The Origins to 1937 Proposals Deferred, Book One The Origins to 1911, *Peter Lang, Oxford and Berne, 2011, pp.146–67).*

The December election left the balance in the Commons very much as it had been. In the Treasury sweepstakes, the Chief Whip, the Master of Elibank, had forecast an increase of fifteen Liberal seats, the Prime Minister ten; the First Lord of the Admiralty, Reginald McKenna, still recovering from an urgent appendicitis operation, had predicted ten losses (Pamela McKenna diary, 4 Dec. [1910], McKenna MSS, MCKN 12/3, CAC). In the event, there were 272 Liberals (three fewer than previously); 272 Unionists (one fewer); Labour 42 (up two); Irish Party 84 (two more than before). Although still dependent on Irish and Labour votes, the government clearly had a mandate to pursue its policy of limiting the veto of the House of Lords.

The last few years of struggle had taken their toll on personal relations among ministers. Late in February 1910 HHA had decided: 'no more cabinets for as long as possible ...'. 'I am glad', Reginald McKenna told his wife on 1 March, 'as with my estimates coming on I don't want to be worried by Winston's torrents of eloquence.' (McKenna MSS, MCKN 8/3/1, CAC.)

Leaks about clandestine negotiations aimed at creating a coalition government had damaged the trust between HHA and those of his colleagues who were excluded from the secret parleys. Knowledge that DLG and WSC had been pursuing a separate agenda accentuated the jealousies and enmities. The Prime Minister's mask of imperturbability would slip often enough for those closest to him to detect his feelings. On the Saturday before Cabinet resumed in January 1911, looking well and in good spirits in conversation with McKenna: 'He alluded to Ll.G. once as "that little ruffian". The disillusionment seems to be complete,' Pamela McKenna concluded (Pamela McKenna diary, 14 Jan. 1911, McKenna MSS, MCKN 12/3, CAC).

Not so much disillusioned but concerned, as many colleagues were, about the foreseeable conflict over Ireland once the powers of the House of Lords were curbed, John Burns, President of the Local Government Board, recorded a conversational challenge to the newly elevated Viscount Morley of Blackburn, Lord President of the Council, at dinner: 'Again to JM is this Home Rule of Yours Courage or Folly?' (Burns appointment diary, 8 Jan. 1911, Burns MSS, uncatalogued, accession no. B04/019, London Metropolitan Archives.)

Several hundred people gathered in Downing Street to watch ministers arrive for the first Cabinet meeting of the year. Sir Edward Grey walked across from the Foreign Office. Sydney Buxton, bronzed from a holiday in Switzerland, Reginald McKenna, recovered from a recent operation, and Lord Morley, irritated by press photographers, also walked in. John Burns was noticeable in a black morning suit rather than his usual blue reefer jacket. A knot of suffragettes sprang into action when the Home Secretary came into view. One of them, brandishing a pole topped by a broad silver arrow with a poster inscribed 'Should Winston Churchill go to prison?', tried in vain to dislodge WSC's silk hat with the pole. The King's private secretary Lord Knollys caught the attention of the press when he drove up while the meeting was in progress and spoke for fifteen minutes with the Prime Minister's private secretaries.

'The Chancellor of the Duchy of Lancaster, J.A. Pease, injured in a hunting accident, limped to the door...'.[1]

January 20 1911 Cabinet. 10 Downing St. 11.30. After some handshaking & personal inquiries we resumed our old seats. Crewe explained that the Govmt of India were anxious to get the Delhi coronation over before the January rains & a religious festival, and if the King left on 21 Nov the Durbah would be over by Dec. 15. & the King would return by end of Jany.

The P.M. expressed his surprise that the date of the festival was ignored by the Indian authorities when Jany was fixed for the Durbah.

[1] Details of the arriving ministers are from an unidentified press cutting pasted into the diary next to the opening entry. Diane Atkinson, *Rise Up, Women!: The Remarkable Lives of the Suffragettes*, Bloomsbury, 2018, p.245, places the Downing St incident in context.

Morley chipped out 'you need not be surprised at Indian authorities forgetting anything & speaking from experience, I say you'll find it out by & by'.

The King left England on 11 September aboard the S.S. Medina, *'newest and most splendid' of the P & O line, temporarily commissioned into the Royal Navy for the voyage. He arrived in Bombay on 2 December 1911 and departed 10 January 1912. The religious festival was the Muslim festival of Muharram, celebrated between 23 December and 1 January. Four Councillors of State had been appointed to fulfil the King's duties in his absence: the Duke of Connaught, the Archbishop of Canterbury, the Lord President of the Council, and the Lord Chancellor (Lord Loreburn). The draft Order in Council had the Prime Minister but neither the Duke nor the Archbishop among the councillors (Bodl. MS. Asquith 24, f.59).*

The actual Durbar ceremony was held on 12 December at Delhi in an amphitheatre holding 10,000 people, with 50,000 more on a mound outside the theatre.

The Government of India estimated that the occasion would cost £1 million, plus additional expenditure by the provincial governments. The 1902 Durbar had cost £299,000. H.M. Hyndman protested in a letter to The Times, *14 December 1911, that the Durbar would cost £1,200,000, plus an estimated additional £4 millions for the official buildings in Delhi. These figures almost certainly did not include the cost of arresting and holding in custody hundreds of people 'who might make a disturbance'. Precautions were planned under the direction of Sir Edward Henry of the Metropolitan Police, who had been an Indian civil servant and Inspector-General of Police in Bengal. So nervous were officials for the King's safety that on his first day in Delhi he rode amid a group of officers, with police stationed in every 'native' house along the route. The popular reception turned out to be warm, the safety measures were relaxed, and the monarch drove freely among the throngs thereafter (Niraja Gopal Jayal ed.,* Sidney and Beatrice Webb: Indian Diary, *Oxford UP, Delhi, 1987, pp.184–5 (entry for 3–5 Apr. 1912).*

The Prime Minister said he proposed to nominate (not today) cabinet committees to discuss Navy Estimates, Civil Service estimates, & foreign affairs. The Army Estimates he said, he understood had been agreed to by the Chancellor of the Exchequer, Haldane & George had had 'a deal'. Grey said he wanted help in drafting our reply to Germany.

Germany had been pushing since mid-1909 for a political understanding with Britain to accompany a naval understanding. Recognising that this would not be achieved, the German Chancellor Theobald von Bethmann Hollweg (1856–1921) accepted a proposal for an exchange arrangement. With confirmation from the Cabinet, the Foreign Secretary Sir Edward Grey developed an arrangement involving information on the dimensions of ships laid down; their armour, protection, and speed; and construction and completion schedules. Periodical inspection of private and government shipyards by naval attachés would also be required. The quest for a naval understanding was interrupted and resumed several times over the next year, until it was finally abandoned after a failed mission to Germany by Haldane in February 1912 (T.G. Otte, '"What we desire is confidence": The Search for an Anglo-German Naval Agreement, 1909–1912', in Keith Hamilton and Edward Johnson eds, Arms and Disarmament in Diplomacy, *Valentine Mitchell, 2008, pp.33–52).*

Japanese commercial arrangements were satisfactory. LL. Smith[2] had arranged them with the Japanese Minister & concessions were made wh. would not interfere with Free Trade; but a formula would have to be assented to.[3] The question also of the Declaration of London needed attention.

The Declaration of London in 1909 codified and extended maritime law on blockade, strengthening the rights of neutrals. The House of Lords declined to ratify it; for the role of F. Leverton Harris in coaching 'Balfour, Lansdowne, Desborough and a heap of MPs' see his letter to Bonar Law's secretary Sarah Tugander, 8 July [1912], transcript, Melville MSS, courtesy of Lady Melville (copies now deposited as MEL/1, PA). There was continuing ambivalence and debate in political and naval circles. For 'the bureaucratic decision-making process', the CID and Admiralty discussions leading towards the introduction of a Naval Prize Bill see Christopher Martin, 'The Declaration of London: a matter of operational capability', Hist. Res., *vol.82, issue 218, Nov. 2009, pp.731–5; Isabel V. Hull,* A Scrap of Paper: Breaking and Making International Law during the Great War, *Cornell UP, Ithaca, 2014, pp.141–54; Alan Kramer, 'Blockade and economic warfare' in Jay Winter* et al. *eds,* The Cambridge History of the First World War: Vol. II The State, *Cambridge UP, 2014, pp.462–5; John Ferris, 'Pragmatic hegemony and British economic warfare, 1900–1918: Preparations and practice', in Greg Kennedy ed.,* Britain's War at Sea, 1914–1918: The war they thought and the war they fought, *Routledge, 2016, pp.87–109. For a skilfully constructed but contested thesis about why the British eventually quietly accepted the Declaration see Nicholas A. Lambert,* Planning Armageddon: British Economic Warfare and the First World War, *Harvard UP, Cambridge, MA, 2012.*

[2] Sir Hubert Llewellyn Smith (1864–1945); Perm. Sec., Bd of Trade 1907–19; a Quaker; entered Bd of Trade 1893; member, royal commission on secondary education 1894–5; Sec., Min. Munitions 1915–19; Chief Economic Advisor to Govt 1919–27; KCB 1908; GCB 1919. Sir Robert Chalmers, the Treasury Secretary, said of him on 23 Jan. 1911: 'He had to put his hat on with a shoe-horn' (Sir Henry Bunbury ed., *Lloyd George's Ambulance Wagon: Being the Memoirs of William J. Braithwaite 1911–1912*, Methuen & Co., 1957, p.103).

[3] See 8 Feb. 1911.

Another Committee but one of Experts the Prime Minister suggested should be appointed to ascertain real facts bearing on finance of Home Rule — for finance was a supreme question, having regard to the bankrupt condition of Ireland, & the great financial assistance given her by the land purchase Acts and Old Age Pensions. Birrell said the committee must assume Home rule is accorded or otherwise it could be killed by hostile financial recommendations.

Asquith accentuated his desire for the facts to be ascertained. Morley pointed out how different was the position now to 1886 or 1893 when Mr. Gladstone[4] dwelt so much upon the essential importance of securing social order. This argument was no longer pertinent.

We then discussed programme of business up to Easter. April (Good Friday 14) & The Master of Elibank attended. He indicated 26 days were available for Govmt business 11 days being minimum for essential supply to March 31st—leaving 15 days. I criticised the time he assumed for the address on the King's Speech, his inclusion of the 13th April as a Govmt day, & there being no allowance of contingencies, Private Bills, Motions for adjournment, controversial naval debates &c.—& said we had only 10 days for Parliament Bill & Budget. It was then decided to take private members' time. I thought we could not take all, but the cabinet thought we could if it was made plain it was to force on the veto Bill. The Master of Elibank was invited to bring up another scheme.

Crewe wanted to know how the Lords' work would pan out, & whether the Veto Bill crisis should come before or after the Coronation. Churchill advocated pressing it through before Coronation. The P.M. thought it might come after. It was suggested by Morley the Lords would reform themselves at once, but he pointed out Lord Rosebery had said it would be monstrous except for a responsible Govmt to bring forward a scheme. Crewe interjected 'we needn't mind what Rosebery said'.[5]

It was hoped by Lloyd George he could soon dispose of his 2d edition to the 1910 budget. Churchill said, 'Yes as there will be another so soon again'. Birrell chirped in, 'we shall never catch up that budget, we shall always remain a year behind!'.

[4] William Ewart Gladstone (1809–98); Con. MP Newark 1832–45, Lib. MP Oxford U. 1847–65, Sth Lancs. 1865–8, Greenwich 1868–80, Midlothian 1880–95; Ld of Treasury 1834; U.-Sec. for Colonies 1835; Vice-Pres., Bd of Trade 1841–3; Pres., Bd of Trade 1843–5; Sec. of St., Colonies 1845–6; Chanr of the Exchequer 1852–5, 1859–66, 1873–4, and 1880–82; Leader of House of Commons 1865–6; Prime Minister 1868–74, 1880–5, Jan.–July 1886; Prime Minister and Ld Privy Seal 1892–4.

[5] Crewe's breezy dismissal of Rosebery's opinion was noteworthy because he was Rosebery's son-in-law.

The P.M. talked of postponing Payment of Members but the P.M. was reminded he had promised it 'next year' i.e. 1911. We discussed the amount. Burns advocated £300, Churchill £400, so as to make the educated middle class man available. £500 wh. the newspapers had got hold of was absurd. It was thought we could put up a vote without a bill, Harcourt said, the Tories can then drop it if they come in. Churchill said, 'What a jolly day members would have when they dropped it!'.

Although the payment for MPs ultimately introduced was £400 a year, Burns thought this a 'good Cabinet' (Burns diary, 20 Jan. 1911, Burns MSS, BL Add.MS. 46333, f.35). The financial resolution authorising the payment was approved on 10 August 1911. The background is well told in William B. Gwyn, Democracy and the Cost of Politics in Britain, *Athlone P., 1962, pp.147–226.*

We discussed how to bring in an Invalidity & insurance unemployment bill, in 2 parts. It was thought essential that the measure should be sent to a Select Committee, so that evidence should be public & points disclosed of differences with Friendly Societies & others.

As the Permanent Secretary of the Board of Trade had told his minister, DLG had been 'modifying his [Insurance] scheme very greatly... he is concentrating his mind on the subject, & facing the problem... his present idea is that it would be a good thing to get Unemployment Insurance and Invalidity I[n] read a second time before Easter, & sent to one (or two) Select Committees which could hear actuarial, trade unionist & other evidence, not of course with counsel... I fancy Winston is still hankering after the Unemployment Insurance Bill' (H. Llewellyn Smith–Sydney Buxton, 11 Jan. 1911, Buxton MSS, BL uncat. when seen, courtesy of Elizabeth Clay). JAP's account falls short of saying that the conclusion of a 'considerable discussion' was that the two schemes should 'if practicable' be contained in a single bill (HHA Cabinet letter, 20 Jan. 1911, Bodl. MS. Asquith 6, ff.1–2; report not included in the microfilm of the copies of HHA's reports originally available from the Public Record Office).

We then had up the trouble between the Natural History Museum site required for science exhibition—spirit bottles—& the Education Dept. Morley who represented the British Museum (Nat. History) Trustees had been absent & demurred from the Education & Board of Works point of view. It was decided officials should again meet & be heard.

Because of the large quantity of zoological specimens preserved in spirit, the so-called Spirit Museum was deemed a fire risk and was housed some 50 yards away from the main Natural History Museum buildings. Advocates of the proposed Science Museum argued that there was room elsewhere on the same site for both the Spirit Museum and any expansion of the Natural History Museum: 'After all, there cannot be many undiscovered animals left in the world . . .'. They pointed out that the new Spirit Museum could be housed in a two-storey building, thereby doubling its accommodation. They were particularly anxious that the new Science Museum should be built on this site so that it could be close to the Imperial College and also qualify for a £100,000 grant from the trustees of the 1851 Exhibition (TNA: CAB 37/106/46). For the background see A Liberal Chronicle . . . 1908–1910, *p.211, 8 Nov. 1910. The architect of the Natural History Museum, the Quaker Alfred Waterhouse, had undertaken commissions for the Pease family, including the Darlington market and public offices, and Sir Joseph Pease's Hutton Hall, Guisborough (Mark Girouard,* Alfred Waterhouse and the Natural History Museum, *Yale UP, New Haven, 1981).*

We discussed contribution to be given by Treasury to secure opening of Mall into Trafalgar Square & authorised Beauchamp to give £20,000 & £6,000 reserve & £33,000 in value = £59,000 so as to meet grasping local authorities.

The national memorial to Queen Victoria, the building later known as Admiralty Arch, was to provide additional accommodation for the Admiralty and a ceremonial arch. From 1906 a vexed problem was the widening of the roadway at the Trafalgar Square side of the arch. Two buildings and part of a third had to be removed; this, together with laying a wider road, would cost £146,000. The dispute raged around whose responsibility this was: Westminster City Council, London County Council, or the Office of Works (the latter being responsible for the building itself and the approach along the Mall, as this was in the royal park). The matter had become urgent, since if the roadway was not satisfactory, the coronation procession would have to be rerouted.

The King had been urging action since the previous November. On 14 January 1911 his secretary, Sir Arthur Bigge, wrote to one of the Prime Minister's private secretaries, Vaughan Nash, that 'the King feels that it would be little short of a scandal were the Coronation procession unable to make use of this grand route, which has been in the course of construction for the last nine years' (Bodl. MS. Asquith 2, ff.104–5). The statue of Queen Victoria was to be unveiled in May, leaving the scheme completed except for Admiralty Arch. In his letter to the King reporting this Cabinet meeting, HHA wrote that the Cabinet had agreed to the use of Treasury funds so as to enable the coronation procession to follow its proper route 'with much reluctance, in view of the blackmailing attitude adopted by the local bodies concerned' (HHA *Cabinet letter, 20 Jan. 1911, Bodl. MS. Asquith 6, f.2).*

A committee that had been appointed by King Edward VII in 1901 reported proudly to King George V on 16 May 1911: 'An attempt has been made on a large scale to treat a public memorial in an architectonic spirit, and under the auspices and largely at the initiative of King Edward the Memorial and its surroundings may be said to be the first example in recent times of Town Planning in the Metropolis.' (Esher MSS, ESHR 14/5, CAC.) Despite this apparent conclusion, the dispute dragged on for some years. For the expensive denouement, designed to avoid alterations to Drummond's Bank buildings, see Sir Reginald Blomfield, Memoirs of an Architect, *Macmillan, 1932, p.163.*

In October 2012 the government sold 80,000 square feet of space in the arch on a 250-year leasehold to Prime Investors Capital for £60 million. The sale was conditional on the arch and its interior being restored to its original glory based on the designs of its architect, Sir Aston Webb (Ian Robert Dungavell, 'The Architectural Career of Sir Aston Webb (1849–1930)', Ph.D. thesis, U. of London, 1999, pp.88–117). In August 2013 Westminster Planning Committee approved the new owners' plans for a 100-room hotel, a panoramic restaurant and bar, a private members' club, and up to four serviced residences. As of November 2022 the restoration project, with the Waldorf Astoria as the hotel partner, was still in progress.

We had a word on coinage. Lloyd George asked for Tudor Dragon — as emblem for Wales. Morley said the Welsh might have the Lion on the arms of the Prince of Wales, but The King was not the King of Wales but of the United Kingdom. George said he wanted the dragon to be heard & not the Lion, & suggested Ll. Williams MP shd be heard![6]

The Times *(21 Jan. 1911) reported that the coins being designed for the new reign would differ very little from the old, except for the head facing the opposite direction, as was customary. A royal proclamation giving details of the design, keeping the Latin inscription, was published on 24 January 1911. DLG's request for a Welsh symbol on some coins was not personal whimsy; in March, on a vote for supplementary estimates for the Mint, Hobhouse came under severe criticism because there was no emblem of Wales on the back of the half-crown. DLG's doctor had advised him that morning to rest his inflamed throat for a few weeks. Confessing to his wife that he had talked incessantly that day in Cabinet, he admitted*

[6] William Llewelyn Williams (1867–1922); Lib. MP Carmarthen 1906–18; KC 1912; Recorder of Swansea 1912–15, Cardiff 1915–22; ally of DLG until falling out over conscription in 1916, thereafter a fierce opponent.

that 'I can't help it as long as I am in the melee' (DLG–Margaret Lloyd George, 20 Jan. 1911, in Kenneth O. Morgan ed., Lloyd George, Family Letters 1885–1936, *U. of Wales P. and Oxford UP, 1973, p.155).*

The well-rehearsed coronation of George V was held on 22 June 1911, preceded a few days earlier by a massive women's suffrage procession. 'The marchers were arrayed in a prisoners' pageant, historical pageant, and pageant of empire, followed by contingents from all the different "constitutional" and "militant" leagues and societies' (Ian Christopher Fletcher, '"Some Interesting Survivals of a Historic Past?" Republicanism, Monarchism, and the Militant Edwardian Left', in David Nash & Antony Taylor eds, Republicanism in Victorian Society, *Sutton Publishing, Stroud, 2000, p.100; Lisa Tickner,* The Spectacle of Women: Imagery of the Suffragette Campaign 1907–14, *U. of Chicago P., 1988, pp.122–31). One of the contingents attracting attention was the Church League for Women's Suffrage, whose role in '"A Great and Holy War": Religious Routes to Women's Suffrage, 1909–1914' is Robert Saunders' subject in* EHR, *vol.134, issue 571, 2019, pp.1471–1502.*

Wednesday 25th The Prime Minister commenced by reading a revised program drawn up by The Master of Elibank for the work up to Easter, but was suddenly brought up by the proposal to give only 1 day to the 2d Reading, 1 day to the Comtee stage & 1 day to the report & 3d Reading. I laughed at the allocation of time, Churchill tried to apologise & belittle the error but he had no way out when he looked at the typed document. The P.M. asked me to revise the scheme of work, which I promptly did whilst we considered Departmental bills.

I allotted 7 days to King's Speech address
14" to supply
13" to Parliament (with margin of additional 3 Ap. 11. 12. & 13 to complete bill before Good Friday 14th)
8 days Finance Bill
4 Other bills.[7]

The P.M. appointed Cabinet committees. Foreign Affairs Grey, Morley, Crewe, Ch. Exchequer & Runciman. Spending Comtees Ch. Excheq. Lord-Chellor, Churchill, Crewe Buxton, Burns, Pease, & suggested Tuesday 1 Feb 11.30 & that

[7] The Prime Minister's information for the King was that the government would have 48 days, of which nine would be needed for the Address and procedural motions, sixteen for Supply, leaving 23 for the Finance and Parliament Bills (Bodl. MS. Asquith 6, f.3). The theory and practice of 'Supply and Other Financial Procedures' is expounded by Michael Ryle in S.A. Walkland ed., *The House of Commons in the Twentieth Century: Essays by Members of the Study of Parliament Group*, Clarendon P., Oxford, 1979, pp.346–89.

Haldane, Runciman, & McKenna should appear as witnesses. The H. Rule Comtee Ld Chancellor, Birrell, Ch Exch., Samuel, Churchill, Haldane & Grey.

Runciman's note taken at the Cabinet confirms the committee memberships. 'Winston's face when R read out for foreign affairs a joy to Sydney Buxton!' (Runciman of Doxford MSS).

The Bills urged & agreed to:

Churchill: Shop Hours, Mines, (aliens rejected Burns strongly protested.[8])
Prison Reform
Buxton: Copyright to work in with Colonies
Haldane: official secrets—stealing plans to be an offence, Army Annual
Carrington: Land Banks for agriculturists
Runciman: Children's Boundaries Bill
Pease: Salford Court of Hundred
Burns: Milk
Birrell: Ireland Labourers Cottages
Pentland[9]: Scotchletting—Land Holders to be postponed with H.R. Ireland & Welsh disestab.

A Shops Bill aimed to protect shop assistants from exploitation by limiting their hours of work had received a first reading in August 1909; reintroduced in 1910 by WSC as Home Secretary, it was lost through shortage of time. Introduced again by Charles Masterman on 31 March, the draft legislation limited work to 60 hours per week (excluding meal-times) plus 60 hours overtime p.a., and restricted Sunday openings. The act was passed in much mutilated form in December 1911. An estimated two million workers became eligible for a compulsory weekly half-holiday, but it contained no clauses regulating Sunday trading or hours of work. 'The havoc wreaked on Churchill's Shops Bill' by 'blatantly self interested tradesmen' is tidily traced to its sources in Michael J. Winstanley, The shopkeeper's world 1830–1914, *Manchester UP, 1983, pp.96–104. See also Wilfred B. Whitaker,* Victorian and Edwardian Shopworkers The Struggle to Obtain Better Conditions and a Half-Holiday, *David & Charles, Newton Abbot, 1973, ch.8). For more on the shopkeepers' world see Christopher P. Hosgood,*

[8] See 8 Feb. 1911.

[9] John Sinclair, 1st Baron Pentland (1860–1925), Sec. for Scotland 1905–12. MP Dunbartonshire 1892–5, Forfar 1897–1909; ADC to Ld Aberdeen in Ireland 1886 and sec. to him in Canada 1896–7; Baron Pentland 1909; Gov. Gen., Madras 1912–19; m. Lady Marjorie Gordon, only dau. of the Aberdeens 1904. Studied law and economics at Toynbee Hall from 1887; became a Progressive member of the LCC 1889. He was asst p.s. to Campbell-Bannerman 1892–5, and Campbell-Bannerman's executor (David Torrance, *The Scottish Secretaries*, Birlinn, Edinburgh, 2006, pp.59–69).

'The "Pigmies of Commerce" and the Working-Class Community: Small Shopkeepers in England, 1870–1914', JSH, *vol.22, no.3, 1989, pp.439–60, and 'A "Brave and Daring Folk"? Shopkeepers and Trade Associational Life in Victorian and Edwardian England',* JSH, *vol.26, no.2, 1992, pp.285–308; Geoffrey Crossick, 'Shopkeepers and the state In Britain, 1870–1914', in Geoffrey Crossick and Heinz-Gerhard Haupt eds,* Shopkeepers and Master Artisans in Nineteenth-Century Europe, *Methuen,1984, pp.239–69.*

The Coal Mines Bill had its Second Reading on 17 March 1911 and became law 1 July 1912. Embodying the conclusions of the 1906 royal commission on mine safety, including standards of ventilation, roof support, and fire extinguishers, it was particularly solicitous for the welfare of pit ponies. WSC and others were perhaps spurred on by the fact that accidental deaths in mines reached a peak of 452 in 1910.

In the Commons' debate on the Prisons vote the previous July, WSC had announced his hope to introduce prison reform: substituting fines, with longer periods to pay them, for short prison sentences; minimising the number of children in prisons; and establishing specialised prisons to deal with particular offenders, such as inebriates, prostitutes, the weak-minded, and recidivists. He sent HHA a long memorandum of his ideas on 27 September, and in December reminded him that he hoped to introduce an Abatement of Imprisonment Bill, but lack of time meant no bill was introduced (Randolph S. Churchill, Winston S. Churchill Vol. II Young Statesman 1901–14, *Heinemann, 1967, pp.386–93; Alan S. Baxendale,* Winston Leonard Spencer-Churchill: Penal Reformer, *Peter Lang AG, Oxford, 2011, pp.65–154; and WSC–HHA, 27 Sept. 1910 and Dec. 1910 [*sic*], Bodl. MS. Asquith 12, ff.169,222).*

A committee chaired by Lord Gorell in 1909 had considered the chaotic state of the English copyright laws and how they might be amended to conform with the 1908 Berlin Copyright Convention. Copyright legislation embodying the committee's suggestions, given a first reading in 1910, had lapsed. Negotiations with the Dominions were successful, and Buxton's Copyright Act 1911 came into force on 1 July 1912. Protection was granted to literary, dramatic, musical, and artistic works, including architecture, for the lifetime of the author plus 50 years. Registration requirements were abolished. The National Library of Wales was declared a copyright library, having the right to a free copy of all books published in the United Kingdom. The act covered all the British Empire (each Dominion had the option of adopting it or not), thereby enabling the empire to adhere to the Berlin Convention and gain reciprocal rights wherever the convention was adopted. Australia and Newfoundland were the first to enact complementary laws. The new regime, consolidating elements of more than twenty statutes and numerous common law decisions, was published conveniently in The Government's Record 1906–1913, *Liberal Publication Department, 1913, p.250; Daniel Waley,* A Liberal Life: Sydney, Earl Buxton, 1853–1934, *Newtimber Publications, 1999, pp.224–5;* A Liberal Chronicle . . . 1908–1910 *(13 July 1910), p.193.*

The Official Secrets Act, 'for the better protection of information, the disclosure of which would be contrary to the public interest', was hurriedly introduced in the Lords on 17 July. As Bernard Porter puts it, following the research of David Stafford, the Bill 'was not so much submitted to Parliament as smuggled past it in disguise', passing through all its stages in the Commons in less than an hour on 17 August with only twelve 'Noes'. The act shifted the burden of proof from the State to the accused, wrongful intent being inferred unless the contrary was proved. The intention to do something prejudicial to the safety or interests of the State was sufficient to convict. The Home Secretary's power to declare prohibited places was extended; and powers of search and arrest without leave of the Attorney General were granted, in some cases without warrant (Bernard Porter, Plots and Paranoia: A history of political espionage in Britain 1790–1988, Unwin Hyman, 1989, pp.127–8; David Stafford, Churchill and Secret Service, Abacus, 2001, pp.40–2). For a wide-ranging survey of the nineteenth- and early twentieth-century background and a variety of interpretations of the government's motivation see Christopher Moran, Classified: Secrecy and the State in Modern Britain, Cambridge UP, 2012, pp.23–52.

To assist in making the case for enhanced powers, Haldane, as Secretary of State for War, had obtained advice from the fledgling Special Intelligence Bureau, established in 1909, about 22 cases of suspected espionage that could not be properly investigated because of the defects of the existing 1889 Act. The Security Service 1908–1945: The Official History (Public Record Office, 1999, p.67) concludes: 'The passing of the Act of 1911 made it possible to establish the work of the Special Intelligence Bureau on a satisfactory legal basis and to develop it into an effective counter espionage and security service.' For a convincingly sceptical evaluation of the early evidence about aliens and espionage, and a summary of official claims of successful counter-espionage activities 1912–14, see Christopher Andrew, The Defence of the Realm: The Authorized History of MI5, Allen Lane, 2009, pp.12–52,870–6. More of the historiography is reviewed in the commentary following JAP's diary entry for 15 October 1914.

The Army Act was, until 1955, the legal basis for the existence of the British Army. Renewed routinely every year, the act ensured that Parliament had control over the army. But on 26 July 1911 the Unionist front bencher Andrew Bonar Law would write to The Times pointing out that the House of Lords, even with powers limited by the Parliament Bill, would be able to delay the Expiring Laws Continuation Bill or the Army Annual Bill 'and such action on their part would undoubtedly make the continuance of the Government impossible and compel an election'. In 1914 the Unionists contemplated using their majority in the Lords to amend the Bill, forbidding the use of the army in Ulster. It would take two years under the Parliament Act for the Commons to remove the Lords' amendment, and in the meantime there could be no army. The shadow cabinet discussion of the issue from mid-1913 to March 1914 is elucidated in Corinne C. Weston, 'Lord Selborne, Bonar Law, and the "Tory Revolt"', in R.W. Davis ed., Lords of Parliament: Studies, 1714–1914, Stanford UP, 1995, pp.163–77.

No Land Bank bill appears to have been introduced, though Lord Carrington argued repeatedly against such bills introduced by Conservative peers. For example, Lord Dunmore proposed that county councils should keep a register of land for sale, that no duties should be charged if the acreage sold was small, and that a National Bank should advance capital to would-be purchasers (HL Deb 02 May 1911 vol 8 cc72–114).

Children's Boundaries—probably the Education (Administrative Provisions) Act of 1912. Among other administrative arrangements, it empowered the Board of Education to order a local education authority to pay another for the education of a child living in the first authority's area. The problem arose when it was more economical to educate a child in another area—for example, if the closest school was across a boundary or if the child's parents wanted a secular education that was unavailable in their own area.

The Salford Court of Hundred Bill, of which JAP had the carriage, embodied the reforms of the Salford Court of Hundred proposed by a departmental committee chaired by Lord Mersey. That committee found that, despite some abuses and difficulties, the court continued to serve a useful purpose. If it were to be abolished, an additional county court would have to be appointed. In a minority report, the former Lib.–Lab. MP for Burnley, Fred Maddison, argued that a county court would be cheaper and more convenient. The main problem seems to have been the court's extensive jurisdiction, which caused hardship to those forced to come from a distance; the Bill reduced the area of the jurisdiction. The court was not allowed to consider cases of slander, libel, seduction, or breach of promise (PP, 1911 [Cd. 5530], xl, 873). The Salford Hundred Court of Record Act received the royal assent in December 1911.

Under the Public Health (Milk and Cream) Regulations of 1912, colouring and chemical preservatives were banned (P.J. Atkins, 'Sophistication detected: or, the adulteration of the milk supply, 1850–1914', Soc.H., *vol.16, no.3, 1991, pp.317–39). A Milk and Dairies Bill was not introduced until 1913. Passed in 1914, embodying the report of the royal commission on the relation between human and animal tuberculosis, its enforcement was delayed by the war. (PP, 1911 [*Cd. *5761], xlii, 173). The Bill forbade the sale of milk from infected cows and set up an inspection system to enforce the prohibition (Keir Waddington,* The Bovine Scourge: Meat, Tuberculosis and Public Health, 1850–1914, *Boydell P., 2006, chs 9,10).*

Ireland Labourers' Cottages: the Labourers (Ireland) Bill was introduced on 11 February and received the royal assent on 18 August 1911. It extended the scope of the 1906 act that gave money to Rural District Councils to build labourers' cottages. Under the 1906 act, 11,772 cottages had been built and another 5,172 were under construction. The Bill gave £1 million to provide another 6,000 cottages.

The unique circumstances affecting Scottish land and housing legislation are explored in Ian Packer, 'The Land Issue and the Future of Scottish Liberalism in 1914', Scottish Historical Review, *vol.LXXV, no.199, Apr. 1996, pp.52–71. The Small Landholders (Scotland)*

Act of 1911, introduced as a private member's bill by Liberal MPs Donald Maclean and Arthur Murray, but taken over by the government, codified previous legislation from 1886 onwards, providing for the enlargement of holdings and the creation of new tenancies on privately owned land. An Agriculture (Scotland) Fund of £200,000 p.a. was made available for equipping new holdings, and meeting compensation claims. The Act proved excessively complex and ineffectual in practice (Ewen A. Cameron, Land for the People: The British Government and the Scottish Highlands *c.*1880–1925, *Tuckwell P., East Linton, 1996, pp.138–65). An amendment bill, characterised by a Scottish Unionist backbencher as 'framed to ruin landlords', received a first reading by over 50 votes in March 1914 and went into committee (William Anstruther-Gray diary, 13 Mar., 2 and 30 Apr., 12 May 1914, Kilmany MSS, NRAS 3363/145). The central administrative framework established for Scottish agriculture is described in James Mitchell,* Governing Scotland: the Invention of Administrative Devolution, *palgrave macmillan, 2003, pp.74–83.*

The House Letting and Rating (Scotland) Bill, passed in 1912 (1 & 2 George V, c.53), regulated the letting and leasing of houses below a certain value: notice to quit had to be at least one-third the period of the let; no agreement would be binding if the agreement was made more than two months before the tenant could enter the property. A Royal Commission on Housing in Scotland set up in October 1912 began to take evidence in March 1913. In Glasgow alone by mid-1914 there were 13,000 empty houses; 'the poorest were driven downwards in a spiral which ended in some filthy, ill-lit ticketed house in a backland' (Seán Damer, 'State, Class and Housing: Glasgow 1885–1919', in Joseph Melling ed., Housing, Social Policy and the State, *Croom Helm, 1980, p.90; and Melling's essay in the same volume, pp.139–67: 'Clydeside Housing and the Evolution of State Rent Control, 1900–1939'). It was soon clear that 'private enterprise had failed and that state subsidised housing would be the necessary remedy, probably by the agency of enlarged and strengthened local authorities' (David Whitham, 'State Housing and the Great War', in Richard Rodger ed.,* Scottish Housing in the Twentieth Century, *Leicester UP, 1989, pp.100–3). Mitchell,* Governing Scotland, *pp.83–6.*

Cabinet had decided to defer Home Rule and Welsh Disestablishment, giving priority to the reform of the House of Lords. The nagging issue of how to deal with the consequences of the Osborne judgement remained unresolved. For the earlier history of what JAP described as 'legislation to repeal Osborne decision which prevents the use of trade union funds . . . for political candidatures and objects' see A Liberal Chronicle . . . *1908–1910, pp.169 (11,12,13 Apr. 1910), 192–3 (6 July 1910), 200–204 (Sept.–Oct. 1910). The legal and political background is meticulously surveyed in a series of articles by Michael J. Klarman: 'Osborne: a judgment gone too far',* EHR, *vol.CIII, no.406, Jan. 1988, pp.21–39; 'The Judges versus the Unions: the Development of British Labor Law, 1867–1913',* Virginia Law Review, *vol.75, no.8, Nov. 1989, pp.1487–1602; 'The Trade Union Political Levy, The Osborne Judgement (1909) and the South Wales Miners' Federation',* WHR, *vol.15, no.1, 1990, pp.34–57; 'Parliamentary Reversal of the* Osborne *Judgement',* HJ, *vol.32, no.4, 1989, pp.893–924.*

The idea of paying MPs had gained support as an alternative to reversing the Osborne judgement. DLG announced on 16 May 1911 the government's intention to pay an 'allowance' of £400 a year without travelling expenses or pensions. Relieving the Labour party of its commitment to provide its MPs with £200 a year from its parliamentary fund 'meant that the modest routine costs of Labour's head office could continue to expand despite the Osborne Judgement' (Michael Pinto-Duschinsky, British Political Finance 1830–1980, *American Enterprise Institute for Public Policy Research, Washington, 1981, pp.66–7).*

Payment of Members — but Osborne Judgmt not committed to for this session

Runciman, Samuel & I urged introduction Plural Voting Bill. Churchill tried to make out it was ridiculous to jerrymander electoral roll, we shd defer it to a general electoral bill. I was asked to look into matter & report for next cabinet as to whether a simple bill cd be brought forward, and not a complicated one like Harcourt's, wh. Crewe suggested was one for Lords rejection only!

Harcourt's bill, introduced in 1906, was thrown out by the Lords. It was nearly a year since JAP had reminded the Cabinet that the Liberal Party had a ten-point electoral reform programme, including the abolition of plural voting ('Memorandum in Regard to an Early General Election', 30 Mar. 1910, TNA: CAB 37/102/110). During the December 1910 election campaign HHA promised that, when the veto of the House of Lords had been circumscribed, his government would press forward with electoral reform. But, apart from payment of MPs, the Liberal electoral reform programme found no place in the government's timetable drawn up after the election.

The P.M. read a strong letter from the Editors of the 3 London Lib Dailies, *D. News, D. Chronicle*[10] & *Star* (Parke)[11] & Hirst[12] (*Economist*) urging reduction in naval & military expenditure. The P.M. dwelt on the strength of their view & referred letter to Committee to consider.

[10] The editor of the *Daily News* 1902–19 was Alfred George Gardiner (1865–1946), Pres. Institute of Journalists 1915–16. The editor of the *Daily Chronicle* 1904–18 was Robert Donald (1860–1933), publicity director Gordon Hotels 1899–1904, prospective Lib. candidate West Ham (North) 1903–4; GBE 1923.

[11] Ernest Parke (1860–1944); succeeded T.P. O'Connor as editor of *The Star* 1890–1916; pioneer of the stop-press; when a sub-editor on *The Star* he 'lived on a farm and brought up eggs and butter to sell to his colleagues' (Hamilton Fyfe, *T. P. O'Connor,* George Allen & Unwin, 1934, p.143). Noted for experiments with 'artificial manures' (*Daily Mail Year Book 1907*, p.111). See John Goodbody, '*The Star*: Its role in the rise of popular newspapers, 1888–1914', *Journal of Newspaper and Periodical History*, vol.1, no.2, 1985, pp.20–9.

[12] Francis Wrigley Hirst (1873–1953); editor *The Economist* 1907–16; economist and Liberal writer; second cousin of Asquith; helped Morley with his Gladstone biography; wrote *Early Life and Letters of John Morley* (2 vols, Macmillan, 1927). For his editorship, Cobdenite views, and passionate anti-suffragism see Alexander Zevin, *Liberalism at large: the world according to the Economist*, Verso Books, 2019, pp.141–76.

The 'strong letter' cannot now be found. The Cabinet committee on foreign affairs, set up to consider proposals from the German Chancellor for a naval limitation agreement, had met on 27 February. The Cabinet was sensitive to the views of the government's press allies. Some officials were less impressed. Eyre Crowe at the Foreign Office and Major Grant Duff at the CID listed the Daily Chronicle, Daily News, *and* Nation, *together with the* Graphic, Daily Graphic, Daily Telegraph, and Westminster Gazette *as being 'undoubtedly influenced by the German Embassy' (Adrian Grant Duff diary, 24,30 Jan. 1911, Grant Duff MSS, AGDF 2/1, ff.38–9,43–5, CAC).*

JAP drew the sketch below in February 1911 and then he evidently updated it to reflect later Cabinet changes. On the same page of the diary he included a small sketch of seating arrangements for July 1912 which we have inserted before the first entry for July 1912 The diagrams can be found at the beginning of MS. Gainford 33/2ᵛ. There is a third diagram of seating at 7 August. 1914 (MS. Gainford 33/108ᵛ).

CABINET. Feb. 1911

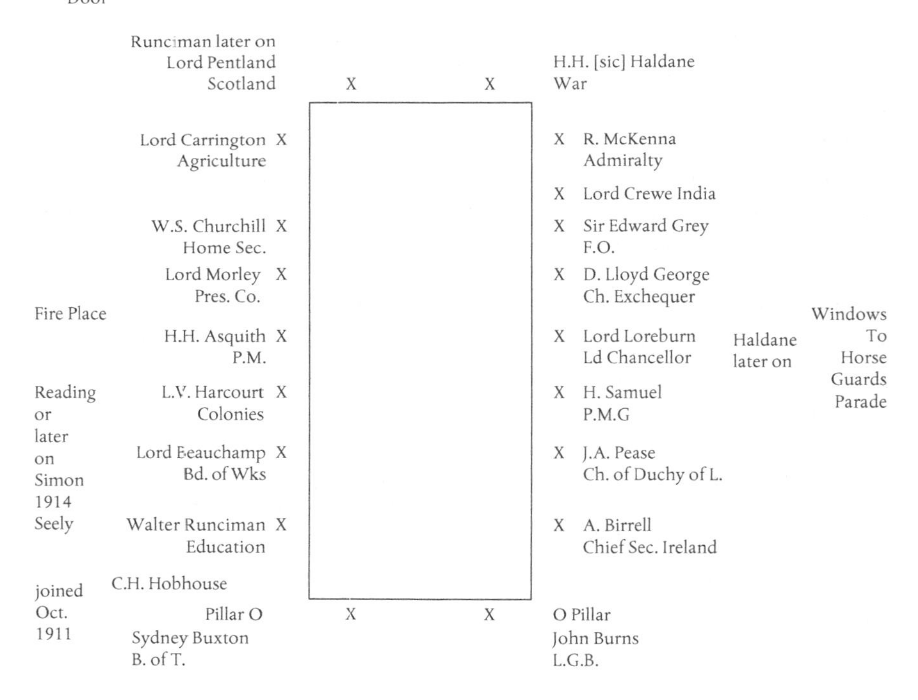

Feb. 1 Considered King's speech. Opening passage framed by P.M. accepted with warm approval, having reference to King Edward's death. I suggested reference to D. of Connaught's[13] visit to S. Africa, but P.M. said all was said that was possible in address at close of session in Dec. & Crewe's passage in regard to Indian coronation was then read. Edward Grey was asked to draw up paragraph relating to Persia, which he did whilst we considered inserting any bills, Churchill strongly urging his & Lloyd George's measures.[14] We all said all or none, and after a talk on the possibilities of securing plural voting, pledges as to Payment of Members, Osborne Judgement modification, it was decided to only refer to those such as Insurance which had not only been promised but money provision had been arranged. Other paragraphs relating to Colonial matters (Imperial Conference) were accepted.

Feb. 4 Ministerial dinner given by P.M. He told me the King insisted on a reference to D. of Connaught, & Nash[15] (his Sec.) had drawn up a colourless paragraph![16] I asked him if the King had made any allusion to the way ministers had observed secrecy in the election. He said 'No, but I have rubbed it in to him'. We had a few sympathetic remarks about poor Edward Grey, who was much crushed by the news of his brother George's death, killed by a lion, in company with my brother. The P.M. said Grey says he can't go [on], & he must give up office. I said, I am not at all surprised he feels like this as his brother was his dearest friend left to him.

Grey received the telegram telling him of his brother's death on the anniversary of his own wife's death. He resigned but came back to work three days later. Over the previous year, George and Edward Grey had made Fallodon their joint home; 'if we grew old we should have done so together. Now all that I counted on is broken up for the second time.' (Sir E. Grey–W. Runciman, 9 Feb. 1911, Runciman of Doxford MSS, uncat. when seen,

[13] Prince Arthur William Patrick Albert, Duke of Connaught and Strathearn (1850–1942); 3rd and favourite son of Queen Victoria; soldier; Field Marshal 1902; High Commissioner and C-in-C Mediterranean 1907–9; Gov. Gen., Canada 1911–16; Duke of Connaught and Strathearn 1874.

[14] WSC was speaking up for DLG, who was in Antibes recuperating from his throat infection.

[15] Vaughan Nash (1861–1932); p.s. to Asquith 1908–12, 1915–16; journalist *Daily Chronicle* 1893–9, *Manchester Guardian* 1900, *Daily News* 1901; author of *The Story of the Dockers' Strike* (1889) and *The Great [Indian] Famine and its Causes* (1900); asst p.s. to Campbell-Bannerman 1905–8; vice-chmn, Development Commission 1912–29; Sec., Min. of Reconstruction 1917–19. Described by Beatrice Webb in 1917 as 'woolly-headed, easily frightened off any decisive step and, like most weak men in responsible positions, suspicious and secretive', quoted in Stewart A. Weaver, *The Hammonds: A Marriage in History*, Stanford, UP, p.133. David W. Gutzke writes of his early social activism in 'Britain, muckraking and transnational exchanges', in Gutzke ed., *British Politics, Society and Empire., 1852–1945: Essays in Honour of Trevor O. Lloyd*, Routledge, 2017, pp.80–1.

[16] Successive drafts and submissions for the King's speech are in Bodl. MS. Asquith 85, ff.73–115.

courtesy of the Hon. Sir Steven Runciman, now in Newc. U. Spec. Coll.) Alfred Pease, who was on safari with George Grey, described his companion's death in a letter to his brother. Alfred had pointed out to Grey and another of their party where a lioness was hiding: 'before I could say a word George was running with only 280 Ross and leaving his gun bearer & big gun & Slatter, & making straight for the bush she was in... he paid no attention to me when I called on him to stop or wait... George threw his life away... racing after the 2 infuriated lions... the lion (the near one) did not take 3 seconds to cover the 80 or 90 yards downhill & all in full view of us at about 250 or 300 yds... You cannot imagine how difficult it is to shoot at a heaving, worrying & bouncing beast on the ground all mixed up with a man...'. It took several shots to kill the lion; the second ran off. When they finally got to Grey, he was fully conscious and said '"Alfred I'm afraid this is a bad business"'. They got him to a doctor but it was too late (A.E. Pease–JAP, 5 Feb. 1911, MS. Gainford 83/68; Joseph Gurney Pease, A Wealth of Happiness and Many Bitter Trials: The Journals of Sir Alfred Edward Pease, A Restless Man, William Sessions Ltd, The Ebor P., York, 1992, pp.296–9; Sir Alfred E. Pease, The Book of the Lion, John Murray, 2nd edn, 1914, pp.43,54,267,279).

Opening the new Parliament on 6 February, King George V alluded to proposals to be submitted without delay for 'settling the relations between the two Houses of Parliament'. The government's intention was to get the Bill into the House of Lords by May in the hope that the constitutional conflict could be resolved before the coronation. A Parliament Bill, identical to the one read for the first time in April 1910, would be introduced on 21 February. Its principal elements were designed to limit the Lords' power to amend or delay money bills; replace the House of Lords' absolute veto over legislation (apart from financial provisions or legislation to extend the duration of a parliament) by a suspensory veto; and reduce the maximum duration of a parliament from seven years to five. It was to be a year before HHA would himself draft the opening sentence: 'The relations between the two Houses of Parliament have been adjusted by the passing of the Parliament Act' (Bodl. MS. Asquith 85, f.120). Various approaches to resolving controversial elements of the Parliament Act are astutely teased out in Joseph Jaconelli, 'The Parliament Bill 1910–1911: the mechanics of constitutional protection', Parly Hist., vol.10, pt 2, 1991, pp.77–96).

Although the House of Lords was the main business of the day, suffragette demonstrations were a persistent distraction. The Metropolitan Police were being instructed on how to deal with 'the probability of further militant action' by members of the various 'Suffrage Societies'. Maintaining order 'in the vicinity of Parliament Square' and when ministers were being picketed and pressed at their residences to give an opinion on the suffrage, was to be effected with 'the utmost moderation'. The Police Commissioner's memorandum emphasised that arrest was to be a last resort: 'in most instances sufficient protection can be given to

Ministers without recourse to this somewhat embarrassing procedure.... But legal advice soon arrived, pointing out that picketing private houses was different from picketing 10 Downing Street, a 'Public Office' surrounded by public offices (Sir Edward Henry–U.-Sec. of State for Home Affairs, 4 Feb. 1911; Herbert G. Mussett, Wontner & Sons, Solicitors–Chief Clerk, Metropolitan Police Office, 15 Feb. 1911, TNA: MEPO 2/1438 x/LO3945). For the memories of the young Special Branch officer assigned to protect DLG see Edwin T. Woodhall,* Detective and Secret Service Days, *Jarrolds, [1930], pp.42–51.*

Quietly pushing on with plural voting, JAP had received three alternative draft bills from Sir Arthur Thring, the Parliamentary Counsel. Thring believed that the imposition of a penalty would be enough to prevent plural voting. 'Plural voters', he argued, 'are usually rather respectable people who would not care to run the risk of the penalty'. Almost casually, Thring pointed out that legislation against plural voting was not necessarily the best solution for the existing electoral problems. It could be argued, he wrote, that they were dealing with a franchise question, which should be treated 'on a par with one man one vote'. Moreover, there was also the argument that 'registration is theoretically the right way of dealing with the matter' (Thring–JAP, 1 Feb 1911, MS. Gainford 133/4).

Thring's bills were sent by JAP to Lewis Harcourt, whose reply was prompt but unenthusiastic. He warned JAP of his fear that 'for the sake of gaining parliamentary time, we are going to sacrifice a large part of the object at which we are aiming'. It would be impossible, Harcourt thought, to replace a hurried and inadequate bill with another 'when you have more leisure'. To attempt such a manoeuvre would expose the government to the charge that, having failed at its first gerrymandering, it was trying again (Harcourt–JAP, 3 Feb. 1911, MS. Gainford 133/5). It was, of course, the standard Tory taunt that Liberal plural voting legislation, unaccompanied by redistribution of seats, amounted to a gerrymander (see, for example, Balfour's remarks in the Parliament Bill debate, HC Deb 2 May 1911 vol 25 c268).

Feb. 7 On the Bench in the House I told the Prime Minister I proposed to consult Sir John Simon in regard to the Plural Voting Bill. I found all opinion strong in regard to the necessity of a measure, but it was difficult to secure the introduction of a measure which would stand possible 3 years of criticism. He said he was glad I was doing this. I asked him if he had heard anything as to what had passed at our Cabinet Committee that morning in reference to naval expenditure. Yes he said there was some temper exhibited, & I explained how Churchill talked of the past, how Crewe had called him to order, & how they both lost their tempers, one asserting he had said nothing disorderly & would not go on, the other explaining he was in the chair, & responsible for relevancy.

Feb. 8 Cabinet. absent Lloyd George & Sir Edward Grey. We discussed Mr. Justice Grantham's[17] extraordinary speech at Liverpool Assizes, when he characterised many M.P.s as liars, and alluded to Sir Henry Campbell Bannerman having 'bought off Mr. Swift McNeill,[18] & the price paid was his character',[19] & the following remark about Canada:

> SURPRISING REMARK ABOUT CANADA.
> At the same sitting of the court Arthur Baker (35), accountant, pleaded guilty to a charge of forgery. He had stolen a cheque book, and then signed a cheque for £50 in the name of a member of a Liverpool firm. He had been sentenced in Toronto to three years, but after serving one year he had been deported to England.
> Mr. Justice Grantham remarked: 'That is the sort of reciprocity that Canada has for England, sending her criminals over here to be punished. In other matters they seek reciprocity with the United States.'
> The prisoner was sentenced to five years' penal servitude.

It was arranged for the P.M. to point out in reply to a question if the House respected Judges there should be reciprocity, that meanwhile the Govmt were considering what steps to take in connection with a unique incident. The P.M. should in fact consult Balfour & Carson if they would concur in a joint Comtee of inquiry into the incident.

Mr Justice Grantham had been appointed to the rota of election judges in 1906. His decisions, particularly regarding Great Yarmouth, were regarded by many as politically partisan. The Irish Nationalist Swift MacNeill organised 345 MPs to demand an inquiry into Grantham's conduct. Sir Henry Campbell-Bannerman declined 'the first step in a course which must lead to nothing less than the removal of the judge from the bench'. Grantham's attitude to MPs may have been embittered by the critical speeches of several Liberal lawyers who had privately written in sympathetic terms (Cornelius O'Leary, The Elimination of Corrupt Practices in British Elections, *Clarendon P., Oxford,1962, pp.218–20).*

Grantham said that he was speaking up, 25 years after he had been made a judge at Liverpool, in order to clear his name and to give Swift MacNeill a chance to reply before

[17] Sir William Grantham (1835–1911); Judge Queen's Bench Division since 1886; Con. MP Surrey (East) 1874–85, Croydon 1885–6; Kt 1886. J.B. Atlay commented: 'among his failings was an inability to refrain from perpetual comment' (Sir Sidney Lee ed., *The Dictionary of National Biography 1901–1911*, Oxford UP, 1912 [henceforth *DNB 1901–1911*], p.152). See also Peter Jordaan, *A Secret Between Gentlemen Vol.I: Lord Battersea's hidden scandal and the lives it changed forever*, Alchemie, Sydney, 2022, pp.235–47.

[18] John Gordon Swift MacNeill (1849–1926); Irish Nationalist MP Donegal (Sth) 1887–1918; Prof. Constitutional and Criminal Law, King's Inns, Dublin 1882–8; Prof. Constitutional Law, Irish National U. 1919–26.

[19] The quotation is from an unidentified press cutting inserted into the text.

either of them died. HHA had been briefed before the Cabinet met by Sir Courtenay Ilbert, Clerk of the House of Commons, on 'the conflict between two rules or principles, one that any imputation on a member as such may be brought up at once as a matter of privilege. The other that a charge against a judge must not be brought except on motion after notice.' Ilbert, who had raised the matter himself after first obtaining the approval of the Speaker, pointed out the 'undesirability of having the question discussed as one of privilege. The House is apt to lose its head when these questions come on suddenly.' While the Cabinet was sitting, Ilbert was summoned and asked whether he saw any objection to the terms of a question that the Prime Minister would be asked and the answer he proposed to give. Although questions about judges were normally disallowed, the Clerk thought that this one would not be. He ventured that he thought the answer was the best way out of the difficulty. 'I wonder', he wrote in a letter to James Bryce on 18 February 1911, 'whether the old ass will resign or will force the adoption of "extreme measures"' (Bodl. MS. Bryce 14, ff.13–14).

The question was asked by the Liberal backbencher Philip Morrell. HHA said that the government was considering whether or not parliamentary privilege was involved. On 1 March he reported to the House that, in view of the universal condemnation that, it was hoped, would prevent any recurrence, no further action would be taken. In a curiously isolated report in The Times *(28 June 1911) Mr Justice Grantham, at Newcastle, declared his readiness to go to prison rather than obey the dictates of ministers. He died of pneumonia shortly afterwards.*

Buxton was authorised to complete Tariff negociations with Japan on lines suggested in his & Grey's memorandum.

Grey and Buxton had circulated a memorandum to the Cabinet on 6 February (TNA: CAB 37/105/9). A commercial treaty between the two countries was signed in April. In exchange for the admission of specified goods into Britain without the imposition of any duty, Japan agreed to decrease duties on cotton and woollen goods, and iron and steel manufactured goods (accounting for 80 per cent of British imports into Japan). The Japanese Naval Attaché had let it be known to the Opposition that his Foreign Minister's concessions were aimed at the renegotiation of the Anglo-Japanese treaty in 1915 (Malcolm Fraser diary, 8 Feb. 1911, Bodl. Sir Malcolm Fraser MSS, MS.Eng.c.4786, f.6). The 1911 revised alliance signed in July is assessed in Ian H. Nish, Alliance in Decline: A Study in Anglo-Japanese Relations 1908–23, *The Athlone P., 1972, pp.60–79; and its economic dimensions are analysed in Christina L. Davis, 'Linkage Diplomacy: Economic and Security Bargaining in the Anglo-Japanese Alliance, 1902–23',* International Security, *vol.33, no.3, 2008, pp.143–79.*

We approved of Army Estimates £150,000 down net. We discussed Churchill's Aliens & Pistols Bill — & when cabinet opposed provision differentiating aliens from Brit. subjects in regard to liability for search, Churchill declined to go on! The P.M. pointed out other [clauses] were alright & after cabinet broke up, talked to this spoilt child! alone.

These aliens said Burns possess the virtues of a slave and the vices of a free man!

Concern had been aroused by the spectacular siege of Sidney Street (3 January 1911). On his return from the scene, WSC wrote to HHA: 'I think I shall have to stiffen the [Adminn?] and the Aliens Act a little, & more effective measures must be taken by the police to supervise the dangerous classes of aliens in our midst...' (Randolph S. Churchill, Winston S. Churchill, Vol. II Companion, Part 2, *p.1033). WSC had circulated a memorandum and a draft bill at the first Cabinet meeting of the year ('Criminal Aliens and draft Bill', 19 Jan. 1911, TNA: CAB 37/105/2). He proposed that aliens would need special permission to carry arms, convicted aliens would be liable to expulsion, and the penalties for harbouring illegal aliens should be increased. The bill, entitled Aliens (Prevention of Crime) Bill, was introduced in April but withdrawn in December.*

Feb. 13 At 10 o'clock I looked in on the Prime Minister & asked him if I might come in. 'Yes' he said 'if you want to' — in I came though obviously he disliked the interruption. The moment however I said I had come to make a suggestion about Grey, & alluded to his late brother George having said he thought in January, Edward's physique & stamina was less than he had ever known it, the Prime Minister became interested. I proceeded to suggest, that as Edward Grey had never got away from his work since Dec. 1905, he should be offered a respite after the coronation, & a fishing holiday during April. The P.M. thought it might make all the difference to him, in his worry & trouble, & agreed if the way opened to suggest a holiday for him during April & to May 8, & after the coronation for 3 months, he undertaking to do cabinet work for Grey.

JAP might well have mentioned a very likely perennial cause of ministerial ill-health: the toll of electioneering in midwinter, a particular strain on the voices of star speakers (Kit Good, '"Quit Ye Like Men", Platform Manliness and Electioneering, 1895–1939', in Matthew McCormack, Public Men: Political Masculinities In Modern Britain, *Palgrave Macmillan, Basingstoke, 2007, pp.143–64). Troubled by a persistent throat ailment, DLG was convalescing in Brighton, attended by a retinue of civil servants and other advisers shaping the national health insurance scheme. DLG told Herbert Samuel the following month that if he had not been ill he would never have prepared the Bill: 'the months of semi-isolation gave him a splendid opportunity to make headway with it' (Samuel–Vt Gladstone, 14 May 1911, Gladstone MSS, BL Add.MS. 45992, f.252).*

In a letter to Lord Crewe on 13 February, the Chancellor of the Exchequer prophesied a backbench revolt over naval estimates. 'Frankly', he added, 'I think our naval expenditure an outrage to Liberal traditions' (Crewe MSS, C/31, CUL). Crewe read 'the substance' of the letter to the Cabinet estimates committee on 14 February, with McKenna, the First Lord of the Admiralty, present. McKenna conceded some reductions, but DLG was unappeased. He returned to London at the Prime Minister's behest, although his throat was, as he told Charles Masterman on 14 February, 'still sensitive & not fit for much blasphemy' (Masterman MSS, A 3/18/1, Cadbury RL Birmingham U.).

On 16 February the Chancellor offered HHA his resignation if further expenditure cuts were not made. Buoyed by the support of C.P. Scott of the Manchester Guardian, *he was briefly taken with the idea of a crusade against the power of the Sea Lords over policy and expenditure. But McKenna outmanoeuvred him with an offer of cuts in the following two years, contingent on contributory reductions in the army vote, and no more expansion by the Germans (Crewe–DLG, 14 Feb. 1911; Hobhouse–DLG, 14 Feb. 1911, Lloyd George MSS, LG/C/4/1/3; LG/C/1/1/2, PA; see also C.P. Scott's contemporary notes, and DLG–Scott, 16 Feb. 1911, Trevor Wilson ed.,* The Political Diaries of C.P. Scott 1911–1928, *Collins, 1970, pp.38–41).*

While fighting the battle over naval expenditure DLG was also looking to the future on constitutional issues. On 14 February he wrote to his Welsh colleague Ellis Griffith:

> You and I have a grave responsibility cast upon us... Shall we insist upon a scheme of Federal Home Rule next year — a scheme which will set up a Welsh assembly empowered to deal inter alia with the Church question — or shall we press for a measure to be carried through the Imperial Parliament?
>
> ...I believe if we are agreed we can get either. Which is the better for the Liberal Party. That is the question.[20]

Feb. 14 I went into Asquith's room with him about 5.0, & explained the lack of method that might be expected if we had to discuss navy votes in cabinet, & made suggestions as to the sort of information that it would be useful to circulate, to promote a business like discussion. The P.M. told me he thought Lloyd George's letter to Crewe was the letter of a maniac. He had already agreed to navy increase had told Murray[21] so at Nice, also McKenna's brother,[22] & now he was going back on his word. Lloyd George must come up on Thursday & have it out.

[20] The last two sentences are translated from the Welsh in DLG's hand (Ellis-Griffith MSS, 448, NLW).

[21] HHA was presumably referring to the Chief Whip, Alick Murray, the Master of Elibank.

[22] McKenna had four brothers. He was most influenced by Ernest McKenna, with whom he had shared a bachelor home. Ernest lived at Cagnes 'with an excellent French chef in a strange mixture of simplicity and Ritz-like luxury in a cottage on the golf-course' (Pamela McKenna–JAP, 18 Feb. 1912, MS. Gainford 83).

I suggested Churchill had influenced him by some letter, but the P.M. said, no I think he does not agree with him, from what he has said to me.

WSC wrote to both DLG and Crewe that day, commenting to the latter about 'our impotent discussion', and proposing a compromise, one element of which—a review of 'the whole question of the British fleets abroad'—was adopted by Cabinet on 1 March (Lloyd George MSS, LG/C/3/15/4, PA; Crewe MSS, C/7, CUL).

Feb. 15 LL. George absent at cabinet. We arranged to bring on Parl. Bill on Tuesday 21st. We discussed taking action on Grantham's speech. Ld Chancellor deprecated action, unless deliberate malice could be shown. The P.M. said he has a hopeless illogical mind, and a lot of Old Adam in him. To bring in a bill for judges to retire at 70, would not meet Grantham's case who before 70 had been equally indiscreet.

Grey alluded to his having told America he would consider 'very sympathetically' any arbitration proposals to cover all causes of dispute between U.S.A. & ourselves. He dwelt on difficulties Taft[23] might have but [*sic*] his earnestness, possible delays owing to Canadian Tariff arrangements. Grey dwelt on moral effect, such an arrangement might produce for European peace. I was much impressed with Grey's seriousness & anxiety to secure this great end. Govmt of U.S.A. cannot commit the Senate.

At a meeting in Washington DC of the Society for Judicial Settlement of International Disputes during December 1910, President Taft had said that he was ready to negotiate with Britain the setting-up of an arbitration tribunal which could resolve any differences which occurred. With international law part of the practice of British foreign policy since the 1830s, there was a 'shared legal framework with the United States'; and British policy from the 1870s had been to settle disputes with the USA by arbitration (for the background see Charles Graham Earles, 'The impact of international law on British foreign policy to the United States, 1836–1846', Ph.D. thesis, U. of Cambridge, 2019). Grey made a friendly reply on 11 March, which, in its turn, was welcomed by Balfour. At a large public meeting, held at the Guildhall on 28 April, HHA and Balfour had moved a resolution supporting the general application of the principle of arbitration. A draft treaty was approved by the Cabinet but rejected by the United States Senate.

[23] William Howard Taft (1857–1930); Republican President of the United States, 1909–13. His father Alphonso Taft had been a US Atty Gen. and Sec. of War. Lawyer; Solr-Gen. 1890–2; judge, Sixth Circuit Court of Appeals 1892–1900; civilian gov., the Philippines 1901–3; Sec. of War 1904–9; prof. of law, Yale, 1913–21; US Chief Justice 1921–30.

The question of Russia's claim to 12 miles for private fishing area round coast — the distance a gun carries — was named. Grey thought it might be referred to Peace conference or arbitration.

A bill to this effect had been introduced in the Duma in January with the avowed object of protecting the Archangel fishing industry. It was greeted with protests by England, Germany, Japan, Denmark, Norway, and Sweden. Negotiations continued throughout the year. Foreign Office papers were circulated to the Cabinet on 22 February and 19 July (TNA: CAB 37/105/14; 37/107/77). Grey declined to answer two questions about it in the Commons, including the suggestion that it be referred to the Hague Court (see 15 March 1911). Twelve miles—about 21,000 yards—was the theoretical maximum range of a 13.5-inch Mk V naval gun as fitted to the latest super dreadnoughts. (We are indebted to Nicholas Lambert for guidance on this point.)

The Cabinet meeting on 15 February was, according to Burns, the 'shortest we ever had'. In the House of Commons lobby that evening Burns, WSC, and the Prime Minister had a 'pleasant talk . . . P.M. quite pleased with the way in which the team had acquitted themselves in first week' (Burns diary, 15 Feb. 1911, Burns MSS, BL Add.MS. 46333, f.49).

Feb. 16 In evening the P.M. told me Lloyd George & McKenna had had a breeze in his room the afternoon before — that it looked very serious, as they could not agree on Navy Estimates, but that LL. George had had another meeting, & had settled the point by McKenna being allowed his estimates, but George got a promise that subj. to no alteration in Navy Law, the estimates should in 2 years be brought down to £40, million 000 [*sic*], (Army & Navy together by 5½ million).

Feb. 17 Elibank at night showed me the agreement made by George.

Feb. 20 George came back to work. He thanked me for my efforts for economy on Estimates Committee of Cabinet & asked me what I thought of his arrangement with McKenna. I said it was the very best that was possible.

The Parliament Bill, identical with the one that received its first reading in March 1910, was introduced into the House of Commons by HHA on 21 February. On 30 November 1909, he said, the House of Lords 'as we have known it' committed suicide. In a supple reply, Balfour highlighted the government's intention to resist compromise on the power and composition of the Lords so that it could pass a Home Rule bill. Two days of debate followed, concluding with the Bill being read a first time with a majority of 124. On the same day, Lord Lansdowne gave notice of a bill to alter the composition of the Lords, and Lord Balfour of Burleigh foreshadowed a bill that would require the submission of certain measures to a referendum. Lansdowne had chaired an Opposition committee established to prepare draft bills on these matters; it reported on 3 February a wide divergence of opinion on the use of the referendum (Wyndham MSS, 11/3, The Grosvenor Estate, courtesy the 6th Duke of Westminster; Derby MSS, 920 DER, 17 4/54, Liverpool Record Office).

Balfour of Burleigh's Reference to the People Bill was introduced the following month but withdrawn when Unionist Tariff Reformers realised that it would be a backdoor way for Free Traders like Balfour of Burleigh himself and Lord Cromer to thwart tariff reform. As Curzon told Wyndham on 26 March after a meeting of the leading Tories: 'we were as nearly as possible landed with a Referendum Bill—a policy which until a day or so ago we had consistently repudiated and the entire principles of our H of L Reform were within an ace of being thrown into the melting pot once more' (Wyndham MSS, 4/1). See Vernon Bogdanor, The People and the Party System: The referendum and electoral reform in British politics, *Cambridge UP, 1981, pp.24–6; Corinne Comstock Weston,* The House of Lords and Ideological Politics: Lord Salisbury's Referendal Theory and the Conservative Party, 1846–1922, *American Philosophical Society, Philadelphia, 1995, pp.157,185. For an insightful review of Edwardian Unionists' support for the referendum see Kevin Manton, 'British Unionism, the constitution and the referendum, c.1907–14',* Hist.Res., *vol.85, no.229, Aug. 2012, pp.505–25.*

Feb. 22nd Cabinet—all present—Carrington told me walking back with Sir Arthur Bigge (King's Sec.) from the Levee, the latter suggested some compromise, in regard to relations between 2 Houses would be come to. NO said Carrington—we intend to proceed with Parliament Bill. We arranged to have a vote on a/c to cover 3 months & a little more, to take us over coronation period.

I explained about Plural voting, the importance attached by agents to our proceeding this session with a Bill. Simon came in & very clearly expounded the various proposals between penalty method, & a register containing names of those only who could vote. We agreed to have the latter proposal printed to see it in black and white. I said failing a short bill we must reintroduce Harcourt's. Churchill said he would see MacDonald at Cabinet Comtee re Osborne case legislation. Burns dissented.

The idea of discouraging plural voting by penalising offenders was set aside in favour of a simple enactment that voters should normally vote in the constituency where they resided. In a draft bill printed on 7 March, provision was made for electors to be registered elsewhere if they had no qualification in the constituency in which they resided. Electors with qualifications in more than one constituency were to disclaim all but one of their qualifications.

Although the draft bill created no new offence or penalty, and did not lend itself to elaborate amendment, it remained open to objection. It did not define the important term 'principal place of abode'. Nor did it, as Simon and Pease admitted, actually abolish the possibility of an elector voting in two constituencies ('Plural Voting', Cabinet papers by J.A. Pease and J.A. Simon, 10 March 1911). It was Simon's second attendance at a Cabinet meeting, the first having been over the Osborne repeal legislation (Simon diary, Bodl. MS. Simon 2, f.4).

Grey said the draft letter to Germany re agreement shipbuilding &c would be shortly circulated.

When the naval estimates' second reading debate began on 13 February, the government was attacked by its own radical supporters. McKenna defended his estimates on the grounds that the navy had to be maintained in ratio to the German navy. Grey promised to do his utmost to make an agreement with the Germans (see Keith Robbins, Sir Edward Grey: A Biography of Lord Grey of Fallodon, *Cassell, 1971, pp.233–4). The Cabinet committee, chaired by HHA and including Grey, Morley, Crewe, DLG, and Walter Runciman, drew up a memorandum to be presented by the British Ambassador in Berlin, in reply to one from Germany (Sir E. Goschen–Grey, 12 Oct. 1910 and enclosed memorandum, G.P. Gooch and Harold Temperley,* British Documents on the Origins of the War 1898–1914, Vol. VI, Arbitration, Neutrality and Security, Anglo-German tension: armaments and negotiation, 1907–12, *HMSO, 1930, (henceforth BD VI), no.400, pp.521–5). A draft British reply was circulated to the Cabinet on March 4, approved March 8, and presented on March 24. The German reply, dated May 9, was not helpful (Grey–Sir E. Goschen, 8 March 1911 and enclosure, BD VI, no. 444, pp.598–600. And see* A Liberal Chronicle…1908–1910, *p.199, 29 July 1910, and below 17 May 1911).*

Feb. 28 On Bench The P.M. in conversation jeered at 200 Tory M.P.s concocting proposals to reform H. of L. — whilst Balfour & Lansdowne were shut up elsewhere doing something that afternoon — & alluded to Tory whine that we would not at present help them.

HHA had introduced the second reading of the Parliament Bill on February 27. A gathering of Conservative MPs was held on February 28 to consider Lords reform. Circulars went to 200 MPs before the meeting seeking their views on the desirability of an elective, nominative, or hereditary second chamber and on any combination of these three types. The Times *(1 March 1911) reported that only about 100 MPs attended; that the results of the circular were not announced and were unlikely to be; and that no resolution had been passed, the MPs being prepared to leave the matter in the hands of their leaders. According to the diary of an anonymous 'parliamentary observer', published the following year, Balfour was 'annoyed at action of young Tories in pushing principle of Second Chamber on an elective basis and trying to force his hands. Revolt nipped in the bud today.' (Diary of 'a parliamentary observer', 28 Feb.1911, Harry Jones,* Liberalism and the House of Lords: The Story of the Veto Battle 1832–1911, *Methuen, 1912, p.248.)*

March 1 Cabinet, all present. The Prime Minister asked for instructions as to how [to] reply to questions in H. of C. asking the Govmt's decision on Judge Grantham—after 25 mins discussion the draft reply of the P.M. was agreed to censuring Grantham but not appointing Comtee, & propose by an address to remove him, necessary in both Houses. The P.M. said he had not consulted Balfour or Carson, but the Lord Chief Justice[24] had condemned Grantham to him. Crewe asked for instructions as to how to reply to question from Selborne dealing with Admiralty notes sent Haldane for speech, & initialled by an Admiralty official & urging their publication as an official quoted document — decided it was not official document.

Haldane had written an introduction to Lt-Gen. Sir Ian Hamilton, Compulsory Service *(John Murray, 1910) that attacked the arguments and figures of the National Service League. Haldane and Hamilton had been briefed by the War Office Finance Director, Charles Harris (Haldane–Harris, 29 Sept. 1910; Hamilton–Harris, 27 Oct. 1910, Harris MSS A314, B7, Balliol Col.). Lord Roberts, aided by L.S. Amery and Professor J.A. Cramb, replied, in* Fallacies and Facts: an Answer to 'Compulsory Service' *(John Murray, 1911), that Haldane had asked Hamilton to write the book and that Hamilton's anti-conscriptionist views were not accepted by all the War Office staff, in particular by Sir William Nicholson, the CIGS (Roger T. Stearn, '"The Last Glorious Campaign": Lord Roberts, the National Service League and Compulsory Military Training 1902–1914',* JSAHR, *vol.87, no.352, Winter 2009, pp.312–30). A second edition of* Compulsory Service, *published in January 1911, included a*

[24] Richard Webster, 1st Baron Alverstone (1842–1915); Lord Chief Justice 1900–13; QC 1878; one of the most successful barristers of his time; Con. M.P. Launceston 1885, Isle of Wight 1885–1900; Atty Gen. and Kt 1885–6, 1886–92, 1895–1900; Master of the Rolls and Bt 1900; Baron Alverstone PC KCMG 1900; Vt Alverstone 1913. 'He was a man of the most unwearying industry, of prodigiously strong physique, with an exuberant geniality of manners, which though not insincere was apt to be a little overdone... neither his speaking nor his examination of witnesses rose much, if at all, above the level of mediocrity' (The Earl of Oxford and Asquith, *Memories and Reflections 1852–1927*, 2 vols, Cassell, 1928, Vol. 1, p.76).

memorandum by Sir Arthur Wilson, the First Sea Lord, supporting the anti-conscription case and urging that any extra money found for defence would best be spent on the navy.

Lord Selborne's question followed this publication. He asked if the views of the First Sea Lord and the former Adjutant-General were the views of the Board of Admiralty and the General Staff. If they were, why had they not been published as such; if they were not, should not the officers concerned be punished for their breach of King's Regulations? Lord Crewe replied that:

> On the opposite side you find that officers of both Services on the active list write, speak, and are freely quoted in support of particular views. No officer on the active list, be he Field-Marshal or anybody else, has any right to criticise the policy of the Government of the day. That is a rule which cannot in all its fullness be adhered to, but if it is going to be broken with the freedom with which it is habitually broken, it is not inadvisable, I think, that opinions of other officers of distinction who for the time being hold office under the Government should be placed before the country.

Sir Arthur Wilson's memorandum had originally been prepared for the use of the War Office to brief ministers for a debate on conscription that was to have taken place the previous November (Dudley Sommer, Haldane of Cloan, His Life and Times 1856–1928, *George Allen & Unwin, 1960, pp.236–7; Stephen E. Koss,* Lord Haldane, Scapegoat for Liberalism, *Columbia UP, New York, 1969, pp.102–04; and HL Deb 1 March 1911 vol 7 c234–9). For Haldane's strong support of the volunteer movement and reluctance to split the Cabinet by voicing his private belief that there might be a time when the voluntary system would fail see* K.W. *Mitchinson,* England's Last Hope: The Territorial Force, 1908–14, *palgrave macmillan, 2008, pp.168–9.*

When the issue of compulsory military service arose again in the House of Lords in March 1914, Jack Seely sent advice to Lord Morley: 'I asked my financial experts here to work out for me what would be the cost of an army of two years training (i.e. an army on the German model) of the strength suggested by the National Service League. At a rough estimate they tell me that such an army would cost an extra £27,000,000 a year, that is to say our present Army Estimates would be almost exactly doubled.' (Seely–Morley, 19 Mar. 1914, Morley of Blackburn MSS, Bodl. MS.Eng.d.3582, f.43.).

Lloyd George said he proposed to set up Deptml Comtee to deal with Local Rates, as promised by Hobhouse. He suggested some clerks of Co Council & Town Clerks in conjunction with Govmt Officials. The personnel of the Home Rule — Ireland finance Comtee was also discussed, Birrell asking for representatives from Ireland, he suggested Lord Pirrie & a Bishop — ridiculed!

Radical pressure had been building up to hasten the land valuation process required to implement the increment value duty and other potential taxation measures under the 1909 Budget. DLG set up a Departmental Committee on Local Taxation chaired by the Controller and Auditor General, Sir John Kempe. 'A Chairman was wanted who knew nothing about Local Taxation, and could therefore bring an unprejudiced mind to bear upon the subject, and I was thought to possess this qualification.' The Committee sat for 122 days from 14 November 1911, reporting in March 1914. Kempe's radical proposal of block grants for specific services taking into account local need and capacity to finance expenditure, was largely accepted by DLG but foundered as part of the failed 1914 budget (Sir John Arrow Kempe, Reminiscences of an Old Civil Servant 1846–1927, *John Murray, 1928, pp.230–40; Christine Bellamy,* Administering Central–local Relations, 1871–1919: The Local Government Board in its fiscal and cultural context, *Manchester UP, 1988, pp.58–60; Martin Daunton,* Trusting Leviathan: The Politics of Taxation in Britain, 1799–1914, *Cambridge UP, 2001, pp.296–301).*

On Irish finance, despite the ridicule, Birrell got his way. The appointment of the committee of experts, to consider the existing financial relations between Ireland and the rest of the United Kingdom, was announced on 7 April. Chaired by Sir Henry Primrose, the former Chairman of the Board of Inland Revenue; its other members were the Most Rev. Denis Kelly (Bishop of Ross), Lord Pirrie, W.G.S. Adams (Gladstone Professor of Political Theory and Institutions in Oxford), the accountant and actuary William Plender, Henry Gladstone (businessman and an older brother of Herbert Gladstone), and the City banker Frederick Huth Jackson, the latter two having served together a few years earlier on a Treasury committee that had rejected the idea of a national guarantee for wartime shipping risks. The secretary was A.V. Symonds, a rising star in the Local Government Board, later to be Secretary, Board of Education (Ivor Thomas, Gladstone of Hawarden: A Memoir of Henry Neville, Lord Gladstone of Hawarden, *John Murray, 1936, pp.187–90;* The Times, *8 Apr. and 5 May 1911). Lord Pirrie, a temporary convert to Home Rule, was in good odour with Birrell for substantially underwriting the cost of refurbishing Dublin Castle's sanitary and drainage system in anticipation of the royal visit in July (James Loughlin, 'The British Monarchy and the Irish Viceroyalty: Politics, Architecture and Place, 1870–1914', in Peter Gray and Olwen Purdue eds,* The Irish Lord Lieutenancy *c.*1541–1922, *U. College Dublin P., 2012, pp.193,198n.69).*

The committee's report, received in autumn 1911 and released in 1912, found fault with Treasury figures and estimated that the 'true' revenue of Ireland amounted to £10,300,000, while expenditure was £11,344,000, a gap that was likely to increase. The deficit occurred, the committee explained, because Ireland, though much poorer than the rest of the kingdom, was expected to keep pace with English standards; old age pensions were a particularly heavy burden because the Irish population had a disproportionately large number of old people. The committee recommended that the Imperial Exchequer meet the cost of old age pensions, that the Irish government have powers to impose and levy taxation in Ireland but not to charge tariffs between Ireland and the rest of the kingdom or foreign powers (HC Deb 11 April 1912 vol 36 cc1414–18; The Times, *20 Apr. 1912; the collection of Sir Henry Primrose's papers in the Rubenstein Library, Duke U., contains 50 items, 1911–12, on the work of the Committee on Irish Finance, OCLC Number: 20120952). The committee's recommendations on what HHA would call 'the very difficult and complicated matter' of finance entailed considerable financial autonomy for Ireland; they did not find favour with the government. Herbert Samuel, who was given the task of framing the financial provisions, had told the leader of the Irish party, John Redmond, on 4 April 1912 that the financial clauses of the Home Rule Bill 'are now water-tight' (Redmond MSS, MS. 15, 224, National Library of Ireland; details of Samuel's scheme are in Patricia Jalland,* The Liberals and Ireland: The Ulster Question in British Politics to 1914, *The Harvester P., Brighton, 1980, pp.44–8).*

The Chief Secretary revealed to the House at the end of March 1913 that 101.6 per cent of those in Ireland of appropriate age were receiving a pension (K. Theodore Hoppen, Governing Hibernia: British Politicians and Ireland 1800–1921, *Oxford UP, 2016, p.217). With greater rigour in assessing claims, the number of pensioners in Ireland fell by 2,000 between 1912 and 1913, while the number for the United Kingdom as a whole increased by 25,000 (Martin Pugh, 'Working-Class experience and state social welfare, 1908–1914: old age pensions reconsidered',* HJ, *vol.45, no.4, 2002, p.787; and for an admirably thorough examination of the data on fraud and misreporting of ages see Cormac Ó Gráda, '"The Greatest Blessing of All": The Old Age Pension in Ireland',* Past & Present, *vol.175, issue 1, May 2002, pp.124–61). For some of the Treasury thinking and calculations on the effect of 'Irish financial autonomy', 'Home Rule Finance', and related matters see memoranda drafted by Ralph Hawtrey in Hawtrey MSS, HTRY 1/4, CAC; and, for Hawtrey's analysis of the dubiously large number of Irish pension claimants, Pauric Travers, 'The Last Years of Dublin Castle: The Administration of Ireland 1890–1921', Ph.D. thesis, Australian National U., 1981, p.306.*

We then discussed result of Estimates Committee work,[25] & George reported that McKenna hoping Haldane would reduce Army Estim £1,400,000 (by reducing troops in South Africa — now over 12000 — & in other ways.) — said he McKenna could reduce Navy by £3 millions in 2 years, the total reductions would reach

[25] See 22 Feb. 1911 for the names of the committee members.

£4,400,000 less than this year's estimate. On this basis a settlement had been arrived at, Haldane stated he could not make army less efficient, or reduce link battalion system, or reduce 'striking' force. Troops 12000 reqd in S. Africa for use Egypt or India reinforcement no barracks at home & economy nil if brought home. We discussed how Colonial Dreadnoughts could be brought home in 1914–15 when we would be weakest at home & whether foreign stations, China, Egypt, Pacific, Mediterranean, could be reduced. It was arranged that the P.M. should fix a committee to look into these matters.

HHA told the King that McKenna's projected reduction in the naval estimates in 1913–14 was £4,250,000, assuming a £3,000,000 saving on 'Home waters expenditure'; and that War Office cooperation would yield a further £1,250,000. However, JAP is correct in recording the proposed total reduction as £4,400,000. McKenna told DLG on 3 March that this sum might be saved on the naval estimates alone provided that German shipbuilding slowed down and British fleets in foreign waters were reduced. The committee appointed to consider the South African garrisons and the fleets outside home waters was: Grey (chairman), Crewe, Haldane, Harcourt, McKenna, DLG, and WSC (HHA Cabinet letter, 1 Mar. 1911, TNA: CAB 41/33/4; Arthur J. Marder, From the Dreadnought to Scapa Flow: The Royal Navy in the Fisher Era, 1904–1919, Vol. I, The Road to War, *Oxford UP, 1961, pp.218–19); Donald C. Gordon,* The Dominion partnership in imperial defense, 1870–1914, *Johns Hopkins P., Baltimore, 1965, pp.27–94).*

On 2 March the second reading of the Parliament Bill was carried in the House of Commons by 368 to 243. Herbert Samuel had concluded the debate 'in a speech of great brilliancy; trenchant, mordant, crushing' (Diary of 'a parliamentary observer', 2 Mar. 1911, Jones, Liberalism and the House of Lords, *p.250).*

Monday Mar. 6 The P.M. called me into his room at the House about 10.30. After telling him of the arrangement made by me & Elibank so as to getting our supplementary votes through without an all night sitting viz. by giving a Friday's sitting, & 3 hours for the report. He said 'I am much troubled over Crewe & the disaster it is a great blow this. Sit down I want to tell you what is in my mind. I must make some changes & I want your advice & opinion'. If Haldane goes to the India Office, & Runciman to the War Office, will you stay where you are or take the Education Office? I said I thought I would accept the administrative post, but would like to think over it a little. He said as the result of Crewe's accident N.B. (at Claridge's on Friday night 3d at the dinner given by Morley for pricking sheriffs, Crewe fainted as he came out, & fell on his forehead. I massaged his heart, undid his collar &c whilst John Burns held his pulse I then went to telephone for his doctor & then to Berkeley Square to see Lord Rosebery. He was dining with the King & so I telephoned there for him & waited to take him on to Claridge's where we found Crewe just conscious in bed).

To most ministers the ritual of nominating sheriffs was a tedious chore, but as Morley had said to his private secretary George Cunningham four months earlier: 'It is very interesting hearing the names of the County families of England'; and, as Beauchamp responded to a suggestion that sheriffs could be abolished: 'It would be most unpopular... as it is the first chance a nouveau riche has of getting into County Society.' (Cunningham diary, Nov. 1910, Miller-Cunningham MSS, courtesy of Juliet Boulting; for 'pricking sheriffs' see A Liberal Chronicle...1908–1910, *pp.158–9.) Crewe had looked overworked and ill during the dinner at Claridge's. He fainted late in the evening and struck his head on the floor, 'fortunately short of the fender at fireplace which would have killed him' (Burns diary, 4 Mar. 1911, Burns MSS, BL Add.MS. 46333, f.60). JAP went to inform Rosebery as he was Crewe's father-in-law. A vivid eye-witness account of the incident was written by George Cunningham:*

> About 10:55 I noticed that Lord Crewe sitting very stiffly upright turned very pale & his eyebrows went with his caricatures by Gould—in an odd shape. I went and told Lord Morley that Lord Crewe was looking very ill—but as he was having a heated discussion with Winston C. he did not rise at once. When he did they all poured into the anteroom Lord Crewe going first. I went in last and just as I went in Lord Crewe shouted a loud 'Oh' and fell with a great bang flat on the floor face downwards. Great consternation ensued, windows thrown open. Doctors sent for. Mr Burns & Mr Pease attended to Lord Crewe who looked as if he was dying. He made a continuous snoring noise & was quite unconscious. Mr Churchill said to me 'What a splendid way to die!' etc.
>
> Lord Morley asked Winston, 'You, Winston have seen lots of people die. What do you think of him' but I did not hear the answer. The Lord Chancellor could not stay in the room but went into the lounge & kept sending us in for information.
>
> FitzRoy[26] tells me that Lord Morley said to him 'We can now only trust in God Almighty, but he so seldom acts when he ought to.'[27]

[26] FitzRoy, Sir Almeric William (1851–1935); Clerk, Privy Council 1898–1923; p.s., Duke of Devonshire 1895–8; KCVO 1909; KCB 1911; wrote *The History of the Privy Council* (J. Murray, 1928). His diary 3–4 Mar. 1911, records Crewe's fall and the aftermath (Sir Almeric FitzRoy, *Memoirs*, 2 vols, Hutchinson, [1925], Vol. II, pp.436–7).

[27] Morley's invocation of the unreliable Almighty epitomises his well-known agnosticism.

After his doctors arrived—Lord Crewe was lifted in a blanket onto a bed—which had been set up in that if it was brown it was a very bad sign.[28]

Lord Morley went to 38 Berkeley Square to see if Lord Rosebery was there: but just missed him as he had gone to Claridge's. Lord Morley returned. Mr Burns said that he would stay on as it would look so bad if anything happened & none of his colleagues was there. Lord M said that it was very unnecessary and somewhat officious as Lord Crewe's servant & doctor were there: also Lord R but JB stayed till 5 am.

When Lord Morley went to his bath next morning he found a note from JB (time 5 am) saying that Ld Crewe was better. I suppose that we shall know some day what was really the matter with him. Next day's bulletins said. 'Concussion of the brain resulting from a fall.' But the fall was caused I think by syncope and a gastric attack.

(Cunningham diary, 4 Mar. 1911, Miller-Cunningham MSS)

DLG told his confidants Sir George Riddell and Sir William Robertson Nicoll on 16 March that he took a serious view of Crewe's illness: 'the real truth is he had a stroke...'. DLG himself had a scare while on holiday in Antibes. 'The mistral got hold of his throat... the chords were red hot wires...'. Until reassured by a doctor in Naples, the Chancellor believed he had cancer ('Visit to Lloyd George Thursday March 16, 1911', Robertson Nicoll MSS, courtesy of Mildred Kirkcaldy, subsequently deposited as MS. 3518 in Aberdeen U.).

Crewe and DLG were not the only Cabinet members showing signs of strain. Alfred Emmott, Chairman of Ways and Means—in effect the Deputy Speaker—grumbled: 'Poor Crewe collapsed on Friday week, Lloyd George still unable to be in the House... McKenna & Harcourt both unable to conduct their election campaigns. On the top of all that the PM promises both Welsh Disest[1] *& Home Rule for next year!' (Emmott diary, 11 Mar. 1911, MS. Emmott, I/1, Nuffield Col., quoted by permission of Joan Simon in Cameron Hazlehurst, 'Herbert Henry Asquith', in John P. Mackintosh ed.,* British Prime Ministers in the Twentieth Century; Vol. I Balfour to Chamberlain, *Weidenfeld and Nicolson, 1977, p.89).*

He the P.M. had talked to Haldane & Grey & asked them to be ready to go to the Lords, Grey at once to help Morley on the front bench, & Haldane to relieve Morley at the India Office within a few weeks. If they go what do you think of Runciman for War Office? I said he would do & I saw no one better in the cabinet. I thought Seely should not be forgotten. He said I'll come later to him. If you go to Education, I can't said he pass over Hobhouse & must put him into the Cabinet at the Duchy. Seely[29]

[28] Crewe's collapse might have been caused by a transient ischaemic attack (a mild stroke); 'brown' vomit, had it been seen, would have been a concerning symptom suggesting a different diagnosis.

[29] HHA had asked for an 'unusual proof of loyalty & good comradeship' in keeping Seely as U.-Sec. for the Colonies in Nov. 1910 to provide 'experienced aid & advice' to the new Sec. of State, Harcourt (MS. Mottistone 1, ff.292–3, Nuffield Col.).

could take his place but Lloyd George wants Masterman. I have told him he can't have this socialist there & to think of the effect on the city. He would take McKinnon Wood, & then Seely could be responsible in the H. of C. for Foreign Affairs — & Robertson J. M.[30] go to Colonial Office. Grey would like Lord Herschell[31] as under sec. colonies. I told him I thought Robertson had prior claim, would assist our debating strength & was an able colleague.

Now about Elibank, he can only be Chief Whip for a few weeks as his Father is moribund.[32] If he goes to the Lords I would like to make him Scotch Sec but I have nothing for Pentland. I suggested chucking Pentland. He thought it was difficult without some governorship & Bombay would not occur for 18 mos![33] Who shall I make Chief Whip? I said Illingworth. He said it is surprising that you & Elibank without collusion agree on the man to succeed you both. Why do you think he would do. I said he has nous. Yes said the P.M. Yorkshire nous is what is wanted.

McKenna came in, & we went over the same ground again, & McKenna agreed with my view, but as we <u>left</u> he said to me we must keep Grey in the Commons as he must succeed Asquith as P.M.

March 8th Cabinet. We discussed terms of German note to be addressed to them in reply to theirs relative to an understanding about future Naval expenditure, & possible limitation.

The Lord Chancellor[34] before we entered upon the words of letter suggested by the cabinet committee asked to be informed as to what was our policy. Grey

[30] John Mackinnon Robertson (1856–1933); Lib. MP Northumberland (Tyneside) 1906–18; journalist for *National Reformer* 1884–93; Parl. Sec., Bd of Trade Oct. 1911–15; PC 1915; wrote two-vol. history of free thought; a leading Shakespearean scholar, literary critic, and friend of Morley, Birrell, and J.B. Bury (Jim Herrick, 'The Politician', in G.A. Wells ed., *J. M. Robertson (1856–1933): Liberal, Rationalist, and Scholar: An Assessment by Several Hands*, Pemberton, 1987, pp.31–57).

[31] Richard Farrer Herschell, 2nd Baron Herschell (1878–1929); Ld-in-Waiting to George V 1910–19 and 1924–9; 2nd Baron 1899; p.s. to Lord Aberdeen, Ld Lt of Ireland 1905–7; Ld-in-waiting to King Edward VII 1907–10; represented Sec. of State for War in Lords July 1912–14; p.a. to Director of the Intelligence Division, ID 25 'Room 40', as Commander RNVR, 1914–18 (Patrick Beesly, *Room 40: British Naval Intelligence 1914–1918*, Oxford UP, 1984 [1st edn Hamish Hamilton, 1982], *passim*). 'Dick' Herschell's accomplishments as a musician, sailor, linguist, and sportsman are admired in Winifred Fortescue, *'There's Rosemary… There's Rue…'*, William Blackwood & Sons, Edinburgh and London, 1940, p.202.

[32] Elibank's father was Montolieu Fox Oliphant Murray, 10th Baron Elibank (1840–1927); Vt Elibank 3 July 1911. He was less moribund than HHA supposed; he did not die until 1927, outliving his eldest son by seven years. Alick Murrray eventually resigned as Chief Whip in Aug. 1911.

[33] Pentland's appointment as Gov. of Madras was announced on 14 Feb. 1912. Lord Willingdon succeeded Lord Sydenham in Bombay a year later. Other men considered for Bombay are discussed in Crewe–Harcourt, 22, 31 Aug. 1912, Bodl. MS. Harcourt 443, ff.18–19,22–3. The accidentally leaked choice of the King's asst p.s. Sir Fritz Ponsonby was spiked when the King let it be known he did not want to lose him (Sir Frederick Ponsonby, first Lord Sysonby, *Recollections of Three Reigns*, Eyre & Spottiswoode, 1951, pp.283–5).

[34] Lord Loreburn *q.v.*

explained his view & to what we had been committed in regard to any private understanding with France. All arrangements with France had been made public, except provision in 1904 by a secret clause, which would enable us to side with France if Morocco had been broken up by German intervention—but this had become nugatory as the hypothetical situation had not occurred, & no announcement of this clause had ever been made. Pichon[35] had by inference intimated the existence (in a recent speech) of an understanding which Germany would interpret as unfriendly towards themselves, & the Lord Chancellor now asked that we should make it clear that we have no military understanding. Churchill asked Grey to at least convey to Germany & also to Cambon (Fr. Minister) our protest so as to clear ourselves from suspicion & that Cambon should be told. Pichon had gone 'too far'. Grey asked him to consider this latter suggestion but deprecated saying anything to Germany, as they had taken no notice of Pichon's speech.

Grey said he had told Metternich in 1906 that if Germany were going to force quarrel with France, arriving out of our settlement of our outstanding differences with France, the feeling would be so strong in this country that we might be compelled to take part. We now recognised that Germany had made up its quarrel with France over Morocco, & this had been privately acknowledged with gratitude. Haldane said, we had *no military understanding*, & he had told General French when he was over at the French manoeuvres last year he was 'on no a/c' to see the French military plans, if they wanted to take him into their confidence. Grey explained — we had no difficulties now in regard to our policy either with Russia or France, & he wanted all European outstanding questions to be settled, as the means to enable all European Powers to work together but not to take any course which might make Russia & France suspicious, lest we lose every friend we possessed in Europe — & that we should lean to the double rather than to the triple alliance. Grey urged settlement of outstanding differences with Germany, Bagdad Railway &c. They had a concession from Turkey which we were bound to respect.

I then urged introduction of words into our letter, to make our friendly and cordial attitude apparent — the letter was too cold and read as if at present our relations were unfriendly. Morley said it was no time for gush or sentiment, we had to reply to the letter of Germany couched in cold terms to us. I urged it was no use holding out 2 fingers to shake hands with a person with whom we

[35] Stephen-Jean-Marie Pichon (1857–1933); French Min. of Foreign Affairs 1906–11, 1913, 1917–20.

wanted a friendly understanding when only 2 fingers were offered—we must put ourselves in a clear position & show an attitude of friendliness, we need not grovel, & in case of future trouble we could then show we were not to blame. Words were introduced which to some extent met my view '*cordial*' friendship, '*assurances*' reciprocated etc. reduction of naval expenditure 'by both powers'.

A concession had been granted to a German company in 1903 to extend the railway line from Konya, in Central Anatolia 162 miles south of Ankara, to Baghdad and Basra. For the development of Grey's policy to 1914, Maybelle Kennedy Chapman, Great Britain and the Bagdad Railway 1888–1914, *Northampton, MA, 1948, and Stuart A. Cohen,* British Policy in Mesopotamia 1903–1914, *Ithaca P., 1976, remain useful guides. A good brief starting point for the vast and recently expanded literature on Anglo-German relations in this period is T.G. Otte, '"The Method in which we were schooled by Experience": British Strategy and a Continental Commitment before 1914', in Keith Neilson and Greg Kennedy eds,* The British Way in Warfare: Power and the International System, 1856–1956: Essays in Honour of David French, *Ashgate, Farnham, 2010, pp.301–23. For a valuable survey of the Cabinet's knowledge of military and naval strategic planning from August 1911 onwards, and the thinking that framed Haldane's piquant 'no military understanding', see Keith Neilson, 'Great Britain', in Richard H. Hamilton and Holger H. Herwig eds,* War Planning 1914, *Cambridge UP, 2010, pp.175–97).*

We then discussed—Council of Trent, also creation of standing estimates Committee of House of Commons on the Churchill plan of 1903 (?) which he had circulated to investigate expenditure—matter deferred, as opportunity would be afforded for increases rather than economies especially in regard to wages. Lloyd George dwelt on powerlessness of Treasury to limit expenditure. Departments never admitted excesses could be returned. Grey was asked to find out from other countries what they did so as to secure care and economy in passing estimates presented to their Governments by departments.

At the Council of Trent in April 1908, the Pope had issued a decree entitled Ne Temere *declaring that marriages between Roman Catholics and persons of different religions were null and void in the eyes of the Roman Catholic Church, even where such religiously mixed marriages conformed to civil law or were made in accordance with Protestant canon law. In the United Kingdom, the decree particularly affected Ireland. One example of its effects was brought before Parliament in February 1911: the Protestant wife of a Roman Catholic had been urged by her husband and by his priest to become a Roman Catholic. When she refused, she was lured out of the house on some pretext while her husband removed all their possessions and children and disappeared (HC Deb 7 February 1911 vol 21 cc150–7).*

In 1901 (not 1903) WSC was one of many MPs expressing concern at the lack of parliamentary control over government expenditure. Their pressure led to the appointment of a Select Committee of which WSC was a member. WSC proposed that the Public Accounts Committee should have only auditing functions; a new committee, the Estimates Committee, would decide whether or not the way policies were being carried out was efficient. WSC's proposals are to be found in a 1902 memorandum (Randolph S. Churchill, Winston S. Churchill, Vol. II, Companion, Part 1, *Heinemann, 1969, pp.126–34). On 22 March Grey circulated a memorandum on how such problems were handled in Italy, Japan, and the USA. William F. Willoughby* et al. *provide an American academic perspective in* The System of Financial Administration of Great Britain: A Report, *D. Appleton and Co. for the Institute for Government Research, New York, 1917. Wan-Hsuan Chiao,* Devolution in Great Britain, *Studies in History, Economics and Public Law, vol.CXXIV, no.1, Columbia U., 1926, pp.86–91,120, is a succinct critique of parliamentary control of expenditure, citing contemporary authorities.*

15 Mar. Cabinet. Morley presided in Asquith's absence in Switzerland, where he had been called by the illness of his daughter Elizabeth[36] (broncho-pneumonia). The question of Russian contention in regard to a 12 mile limit for fishing powers to be reserved to each Nation, instead of the 3 mile limit observed by us, was discussed. It was decided we could not force Russia into our view, after the correspondence, & we must refer the subject to the Hague, & to be settled by arbitration. The cabinet was over in an hour.

JAP's record of the Cabinet's proceedings may be compared with Morley's more expansive letter to the King (TNA: CAB 41/33/6). Learning that Morley was to preside, Lord Rosebery had said to John Simon at dinner the previous evening: 'since I ceased to be Prime Minister, I have never wanted to belong to a Cabinet until now, but I should like to see John preside' (Simon diary, Bodl. MS. Simon 2).

The three-mile limit to territorial waters had been generally adopted at the end of the eighteenth century in recognition of contemporary cannon-range, but other limits were adopted for

[36] Elizabeth Charlotte Lucy Asquith (1897–1945); first child of H.H. and Margot Asquith. She married in 1919 Prince Antoine Bibesco, a Romanian diplomat in London. A friend of Proust, she published short stories, novels, plays, and a book of poetry. She 'is not very attractive and is horrid to Margot and very independent' (P. McKenna diary, 7 Oct. [1910], McKenna MSS, MCKN 12/3, CAC).

different jurisdictions: both Britain and the USA had a twelve-mile customs jurisdiction. The Russians claimed that the extension of their fishing jurisdiction to twelve miles was a recognition of artillery developments. A general extension of the fishing limit to twelve miles would mean the loss to the British fishing industry of about one-third of its trawling area. The Russian bill failed to pass the Duma (William E. Masterman, Jurisdiction in Marginal Seas with Special Reference to Smuggling, *Macmillan, New York, 1929, pp.150–62,286–302; and Sayre A. Swarztrauber,* The Three-Mile Limit of Territorial Seas, *Naval Institute P., Annapolis, MD, 1972, pp.51–78).*

Friday 17 I called on Asquith, who had returned the afternoon before, at No. 12 Downing St., to ask him about who I should appoint to the vacancy Manchester County Court Judgeship. We went through the names & we decided on F. H. Mellor K.C.,[37] the oldest of the barristers on the circuit. He asked me if Atherley-Jones had applied, & suggested it might be a relief to have him disposed of in that way. He told me about Elizabeth's condition & their anxiety, but no crisis imminent. He alluded to Grey's speech in his absence & expressed surprise at its success & the way it had convulsed the world. I praised it, & alluded to the good effect it had had on the party & the good reception it had everywhere been given.

On 13 March, J. Murray Macdonald and Arthur Ponsonby had moved and seconded a motion calling for a reduction in army and navy expenditure. Ponsonby thought Murray Macdonald was 'nervous and dull and not nearly as good as usual. The House was bored.' (Ponsonby diary, 13 March 1911, Ponsonby of Shulbrede MSS.) Reginald McKenna, defending the naval programme, was given an unenthusiastic reception by Liberal backbenchers. But the whips and ministerial colleagues thought well of it, relieved that he had managed to make his case without revealing Cabinet divisions (Martin Farr, Reginald McKenna: Financier among Statesmen, 1863–1916, *Routledge, 2008, pp.203–4).*

Grey, speaking in place of the absent HHA, took up President Taft's recent proposal of arbitration for international disputes. Although 56 MPs supported the motion, it was evident that Grey had impressed many of the radicals. H.W. Massingham, in The Nation *on 18 March, wrote of a new and wider horizon having been opened 'with a prospect of escape from the encircling vision of Dreadnoughts'. But Grey's deprecation of 'this tremendous expenditure on the rivalry of armaments' had the unintended effect of convincing Germany*

[37] Francis Hamilton Mellor (1854–1925); Recorder of Preston 1898–1921; from a prominent legal family; barrister 1880; KC 1903; County Court Judge, Manchester 1911–25; Chmn, Conciliation Boards for Lancs, Cheshire, and N. Staffs under Coal Mining Minimum Wages Act. Played cricket for Cambridge U. and Kent.

that Britain was facing such severe financial strain that it might be forced to moderate its naval expansion (T.G. Otte, '"Chief of All Offices": High Politics, Finance, and Foreign Policy, 1865–1914', in William Mulligan and Brendan Simms eds, The Primacy of Foreign Policy in British History, 1660–2000, *Palgrave Macmillan, Basingstoke, 2010, p.237).*

Monday 20 I explained to the P.M. that I was going to suggest amendments to the Plural Voting Bill, as the result of my conference with the Liberal agents on the 14th inst. & would see Simon (Solicitor General) & Sir Arthur Thring (Govmt Draftsman) tonight.

After the conference with Liberal agents on 14 March, some minor modifications were made and an amended draft bill was considered at the Cabinet on Wednesday 22 March. JAP and Simon explained their views in memoranda printed on 21 March ('Plural Voting,' TNA: CAB 37/105/32). JAP wanted a simple, quick bill, so no mention of the franchise could be made (thereby ensuring that any amendment affecting the franchise would be out of order). Plural voters were to be largely eliminated by only being allowed to vote in the constituency of their principal place of abode. The plan was by no means watertight: a voter who had more than one 'principal residence' could remain on the register unless challenged, but at least a large number of plural voters would be eliminated.

I also told him that I had asked Atherley-Jones whether he would like his claims considering for Manchester, & was awaiting his reply before taking further action.

Atherley-Jones declined the offer of a Lancashire County Court Judgeship, telling JAP on 21 March that he could not accept 'preferment of this character' for reasons that were 'in substance known to you' (MS. Gainford 83/5). He offered no explanation in his memoirs, but his earlier attempts to obtain legal appointments were blocked by the Lord Chancellor, Lord Loreburn, who disliked him (L.A. Atherley-Jones, Looking Back. Reminiscences of a political career, *H.F. & G. Witherby, 1925, pp.192–4). Loreburn had told HHA on 30 September 1910: 'I am sorry for him, but there is no help for a man who is so incurably in error as to his own qualities' (Bodl. MS. Asquith 12, ff.187–8). In 1914 Atherley-Jones resigned the North-West Durham seat he had held since 1885 to become a Judge of the City of London Court.*

I told him Lady Crewe had written me a cheery note about Crewe & he told me he had seen him for 20 mins on Saturday & he chatted about sundry things.

Wednesday 22 March Cabinet. We discussed treaty with Portugal — S. Buxton urging alteration on duties on port to meet Portuguese wishes, & secure favoured nation terms, by reduction on lighter ports to 20 & heavier duties on higher — increase to revenue £17,000. Lloyd George urged only increase, as his duties on poor man's drinks — gauged by alcohol was less on rich man's port. Matter postponed as we could not agree to either proposal.

Buxton had circulated a memorandum, 'Commercial negotiations with Portugal', to the Cabinet on 17 March (TNA: CAB 37/105/29). He circulated another with the same title on 27 March (TNA: CAB 37/106/38). For the background see A Liberal Chronicle...1908–1910 *(13 Oct. 1910), p.203; and, for the complexities caused by DLG's objections, Waley,* A Liberal Life, *pp.225–7.*

Simon came in, & I explained Plural Voting bill provisions—& cabinet agreed to my bill subject to principle being made to apply to Universities. Haldane said bill was ingenious & effective. Samuel urged it on ground we should more easily get rid of University seats later on & that we could not redistribute until we knew how one man one vote would affect the number of voters in electoral areas.

Oxford and Cambridge universities and Trinity College, Dublin, had two seats each. London and two groups of Scottish universities (Edinburgh and St Andrews and Glasgow and Aberdeen) had one each. In December 1910 all of the nine university seats returned Conservatives or Liberal Unionists, six of them unopposed. For an account of their fate in the 1918 Representation of the People Act see J.F.S. Ross, Parliamentary Representation, *Eyre & Spottiswoode, 1943, pp.150–1.*

We discussed Bill to add more Lunacy Commissioners. A most cordial gathering.

The Lunacy Bill was introduced 1 May 1911 and received the Royal Assent 16 December 1911. It was originally intended to incorporate the recommendations of a royal commission that reported in 1908. Pressure of time reduced it to merely authorising the appointment of two additional salaried medical commissioners. The number of commissioners had remained unchanged since 1845 when they supervised 25,000 patients; there were now 120,000 patients. In August 1913 'An Act to make further and better provision for the care of Feeble-minded and other Mentally Defective Persons and to amend the Lunacy Acts' (the Mental Deficiency Act) received Royal Assent. The Board of Control established by the Act had not more than fifteen commissioners, of whom two (one paid, one unpaid) were to be women. The Board's character and early activities are described in Matthew Thomson, The Problem of

Mental Deficiency: Eugenics, Democracy, and Social Policy in Britain, *c.*1870–1959, *Clarendon P., Oxford, 1998, pp.77–93.*

Wednesday 29th The Prime Minister asked our view as to whether the King's Consent[38] should be given to the Opposition to introduce a measure reforming the Lords.

Morley agreed & the P.M. urged this course also, but I urged we must not give the impression by the King's consent being given to the 3rd Reading of the Bill in the Lords, that he concurred in the substance of the bill. The P.M. undertook to make it clear, it was the discussion to which consent was to be given. There were several reflections made on the writers in Liberal Newspapers to the effect they were prize asses.

Grey explained that Japan was considering further naval developments as she doubted our intention to renew the alliance—it would involve us in new naval complications & bigger fleet in far East. He asked for authority to say we were ready to renew the alliance, to say to 1920, & its modification would only be to the effect that it might be suspended simultaneously against any one power with whom we had an arbitration agreement such as we proposed to make with America. This would Grey said avoid any disturbance of status quo with Japan. The authority was given.

The initial move to modify the Anglo-Japanese alliance had come from Britain, which did not want the alliance to conflict with the proposed arbitration treaty with the United States. See Nish, Alliance in Decline, *pp.76–7; Peter Lowe,* Great Britain and Japan 1911–15. A Study of British Far Eastern Policy, *Macmillan 1969, for a detailed description of the negotiations. And, for a broader analysis emphasising concerns about Dominion attitudes, Cornelis Heere, 'Japan and the British World, 1904–14', Ph.D. thesis, Department of International History, London School of Economics, 2016, pp.155–73.*

St. James Park alteration & a site for King Edward VII's statue—it was agreed we should not facilitate any alterations, the twisting path & even the suspension bridge were sentimentally regarded as not open to improvement. I drew a sketch of a stone

[38] The King's consent would be given by a Privy Councillor to a Bill or amendments affecting 'local and personal interests which concern the royal prerogative, the hereditary revenue or personal property or interests of the Crown... The King's Consent cannot be communicated in committee, is generally given at the third reading, and its omission, when it is required, renders the proceedings on the passage of a Bill null and void.' (G.F.M Campion, *An Introduction to the Procedure of the House of Commons, Philip Allan, 1929, p.293*).

bridge which Harcourt took which might have I think been better than the suspension erection. That the King's back should be turned upon all those who crossed the bridge was censured, & the P.M. was instructed to say we gave no consent, that no scheme had even been submitted — our object was to kill proposal. J. Burns waxed eloquent on the monstrosity of St James's Park being turned into a macadamised mausoleum to show up Hankey's mansions & Rockefeller's skyscrapers!

Burns's 'racy description' of the 'macadamised mausoleum... tickled the Cabinet and delighted Prime Minister' (Burns diary, 29 Mar. 1911, Burns MSS, BL Add.MS. 46333, f.121). Queen Anne's Mansions, a hotel and serviced flats, furnished and unfurnished, built for H.A. Hankey 1873–8, and known as 'Hankey's Folly', described by the American novelist Gertrude Atherton as 'gloomy and fortress-like', were demolished in 1971–2 (Gertrude Atherton, Adventures of a Novelist, *Liveright Inc, New York, 1932, p.457;* Webster's Royal Red Book: or Court and Fashionable Register for May, 1917, *140th edn, 1917, p.253). 'Rockefeller's skyscrapers' was presumably a reference to the offices of the Anglo-American Oil Co., designed by Ernest Runtz and built in 1909. Pevsner described them as 'a big Baroque block, undisciplined in its composition, and in character, material, and design, deliberately out of keeping with the rest' (Nikolaus Pevsner, revised by Bridget Cherry,* The Buildings of England, London, Vol. I, The Cities of London and Westminster, *3rd edn, Penguin, 1973, p.637).*

*The path through the park was a short cut from club-land to Parliament. Questions had been asked in the Commons on 27 March, the day on which the scheme for the memorial was approved by the memorial committee. It was proposed to erect a statue to the King on the south side of the Mall. In order to give a view of the statue from the park, a footpath aligned to it was planned, which would be carried over the lake by a low stone bridge (*The Times, *28 Mar. 1911). Sir Edward Poynter Bt, President of the Royal Academy, pointed out that the planned footway recognised only the existing position, that the park was used as a shortcut; that was why the suspension bridge had been erected, and before that, a ferry had existed. MPs were unimpressed by such arguments; they were given assurances that nothing would be done without parliamentary approval, and eventually the St James's Park site had to be abandoned. Similar objections were made to the succeeding proposal, a site in Green Park. King George finally asked the memorial committee to consider a third site, between Pall Mall and the Duke of York Monument, because he had no wish for a memorial to his father to be associated with controversy. The erection of the statue, a bronze equestrian figure by E. Bertram Mackennal, was delayed by the war; it was unveiled on 20 July 1921.*

Churchill explained the Provisions of the Osborne Judgement repeal as amendment Bill, Burns urged its being dropped. Cabinet agreed we could not go back on our previous decision & must carefully consider provisions & ascertain whether Labour would give it support, & further consider its proposals. It went as far towards repeal as we could go—did it go too far? There must be some strain placed on the minority in any case. Sidney Webb[39] & Buckmaster K.C. approved provisions. J. Burns said I would not give two pennorth of gin for Webb's opinion on anything.

We discussed whether the Queen[40] should be called Empress of India & whether she should be crowned at the Durbar—decided to consult Indian Government.

*The Viceroy, Lord Hardinge of Penshurst, had told Sir Arthur Bigge on 26 January 1911 that it seemed to him that for the Queen not to be Queen-Empress, as he had heard was the case, would be especially undesirable in a country 'where women are regarded as being on a lower plane'. Doubts were dispelled in June by the King, who stated categorically that the Queen was Queen-Empress and that she should be described that way in all addresses, programmes, and announcements. The Cabinet discussion on 29 March seems to have been precipitated by a query from Lever Brothers, makers of Sunlight Soap and, by appointment, soap makers to the King. Lord Crewe wrote to Hardinge: 'I suppose the information is needed for purposes of advertisement…'. The company apparently did not get the information in time. Its souvenir leaflet, a photocopy of which is preserved in the Unilever Archives, captions a portrait of the King as 'Emperor of India', leaving the picture of his consort as simply 'H.M. Queen Mary' (*Correspondence and Papers Respecting the Visit of Their Imperial Majesties King George V and Queen Mary to India 1911–12, *Harrison and Sons, 1912, pp.333–4; James Pope-Hennessy,* Lord Crewe 1858–1945, The Likeness of a Liberal, *Constable 1955, p.96; James Pope-Hennessy,* Queen Mary, *Alfred A. Knopf, New York, 1960, p.447).*

Buxton pressed his modified scheme—with a more graduated scale for shop dressing purposes, to secure fairer treatment of Ports from Portugal — assented to. Churchill authorised to bring in bill to enable cost of police & Army to be partly placed on rates, when local disturbance occurred.

In the aftermath of the Tonypandy riots Glamorganshire County Council refused to pay tradesmen who had fed the metropolitan police contingent (and who had received assurances

[39] Sidney James Webb (1859–1947); socialist, economist, reformer, and co-founder of the London School of Economics; m. Beatrice Potter 1892; Lab. MP Durham (Seaham) 1922–9; Pres., Bd of Trade Jan.–Nov. 1924; Sec. of St. for Dominion and Colonial Affairs 1929–30, Colonial Affairs 1930–1; Baron Passfield 1929; OM 1944. Co-wrote with his wife *The History of Trade Unionism* (1894). In 1912 he became Prof. of Public Administration at the LSE.

[40] Queen Mary (1867–1953); only dau. of Francis, Prince (later Duke) of Teck; engaged to marry Duke of Clarence (King Edward VII's eldest son) two months before his death; m. 1893 Duke of York (later King George V).

of payment at the time from a county council official) on the grounds that, if the troops had been called in, the council would not have been asked to pay for their supplies. As the metropolitan policemen were substituted for the troops, the council saw no reason why it should foot the bill. Particular hardship was felt by small shopkeepers, whose interests were vigorously defended by their MP, Keir Hardie. He suggested on 22 March that, since WSC had made the decision to send in the police, without making any financial provision, the outstanding payments should be deducted from WSC's salary as Home Secretary. WSC agreed that this was a proper matter for the House to consider, but it seems to have gone no further, and no bill for regularising the situation was introduced.

In July 1911 Parliament did vote funds to pay for subduing the Tonypandy riots, but other local authorities to whom troops or metropolitan policemen were supplied later that year (Hull, Manchester, Salford, and Cardiff) had to meet the cost themselves. WSC had argued for putting the cost of the troops—two squadrons of the Greys and the South Stafford Regiment had been sent to Salford—as well as of additional policemen on the rates to act as a curb on local demands for outside help (Barbara Weinberger, Keeping the Peace? Policing Strikes in Britain, 1906–1926, *Berg, New York/Oxford, 1991, pp.20–123; Maj.-Gen. Spencer Ewart diary, 7 July 1911, Ewart MSS, NRS RH4/84, kindly lent by Baron (Hector) Monro).*

On 31 March JAP, with Harcourt and Birrell, attended the christening of the McKennas' second son David in the House of Commons crypt. J.A. Spender and Wedgwood Benn were godparents. On 2 April the Census was taken. The omission of female suffrage from the King's Speech on 6 February had prompted a call by suffragette leaders to boycott the Census. For a brilliant analysis of the limited impact of the ensuing campaign see Jill Liddington and Elizabeth Crawford, '"Women do not count, neither shall they be counted": Suffrage, Citizenship and the Battle for the 1911 Census', HWJ, *No. 71 (Spring 2011), pp.98–127, and Jill Liddington,* Vanishing for the Vote: Suffrage, Citizenship and the Battle for the Census, *Manchester UP, 2014).*

April 4[41] At Downing St. conference with P.M. to consider amendments to Parliament Bill—P.M. said he had been detained by the King—that he was anxious we should not fail to give opposition fair opportunity to discuss our Bill. The P.M. said certainly but present tactics might create the crisis about Coronation time, & we proposed to send the Bill to the Lords in May.

Using a favourite informal channel, the King was conveying his own position emphatically. Arthur Bigge wrote 'in confidence' to the sovereign's trusted adviser Sir Francis Hopwood on 7 April: 'The King is insisting that no crisis must take place until after the Coronation &

[41] This entry occurs after the entry for 5 Apr. 1911 in the manuscript.

moreover that if it comes when he is in Ireland Wales or Scotland he will not return to London.' (Southborough MSS, lent by the 2nd Lord Southborough, now Bodl. MS.Eng.c.7362.)

The P.M. said à propos of the tribunal to discuss what was a money bill, that the conference had agreed on a body of 12, with the Speaker giving casting vote, composed of men of both Houses. I suggest 2 advisers all that was necessary & suggested Chairman of Committee & Chairman Public a/cs committee.

April 5 Full Cabinet except for Crewe. We discussed the proposal to take land from Nat. History Museum for Science. S. Kensington & by 9–3 (5 not voting) we carried proposal against Morley Churchill & Grey. This is the only occasion I have seen any matter carried by a direct vote—all other matters are carried by the sense of those present, or by the summing up of the Prime Minister.

The diary of George Cunningham, then private secretary to Lord Morley as Lord President of the Council, provides background to this unique event:

> Lord Morley had to go to see Lord Beauchamp (The First Commissioner of Works) the other day (Wed 14 Dec) about a matter which had been referred to a Cabinet Committee concerning a dispute over a boundary at the South Kensington Natural History Museum on which The British Museum was interested. Lord M told me that...the Brit Museum had been very imperfectly represented to the Committee. I reminded him that Mr Haldane (one of the Committee) proposed settling the matter with a high hand.
>
> 'I know' said Lord M. 'But Haldane is a German. Haldane is a German'.
>
> *(Cunningham diary, 'Dec. 1910', Miller-Cunningham MSS)*

In the Cabinet discussion as reported to the King, the Trustees of the British Museum were represented by Morley and Grey; they were opposed by Haldane, Beauchamp, and Runciman. HHA stated the result of the division, with 'several abstentions', was 'that 5 voted with Lord Morley & 9 or 10 with Lord Haldane' (Bodl. MS. Asquith 6, f.24).

Lloyd George explained his insurance scheme against sickness & invalidity, for upwards of an hour we discussed points. He gave John Burns credit for considerable help. It was left for L. G. to see each member of the cabinet whose department was concerned—Bd of Trade, Post Office, War Office, Admiralty &c—& to then circulate bill.

This was part I of the National Insurance Bill. (Part II was insurance against unemployment; the Cabinet had decided on 20 January to introduce the two schemes as one bill.) An explanatory memorandum had been circulated several days earlier, and, as HHA put it for the King: 'Ministers were therefore prepared to criticise & canvass all its provisions... After a searching examination, the Cabinet expressed warm & unanimous approval of the main & governing principles of the scheme which they believe to be more comprehensive in its scope and more prudent and statesmanlike in its machinery, than anything that has hitherto been attempted or proposed' (Bodl. MS. Asquith 6, ff.24–5). The scheme provided for 10s. sickness benefit per week for thirteen weeks for men (7s. 6d. for women), followed by 5s. per week for a further thirteen weeks (3s. for women), and a disablement benefit of 5s. per week. The Bill also provided a medical benefit to cover the cost of treatment, 30s. maternity benefit (a politically attractive cash bonus for each baby), and the right to sanatorium treatment for tuberculosis. The benefits were raised by a payment of 4d. per week by each employee (3d. by women), 3d. per week by each employer, and 2d. from the state; hence the slogan 'ninepence for fourpence'. For a thorough exposition of the principles and provisions of the legislation see A.I. Ogus, 'Great Britain', in Peter A. Köhler, Hans Friedrich Zacher, and Martin Partington eds, The Evolution of Social Insurance, 1881–1981: Studies of Germany, France, Great Britain, Austria and Switzerland, *Frances Pinter, 1982, pp.166–87. On the contest of ideas and rivalry between the Treasury and the Local Government Board, John M. Eyler,* Sir Arthur Newsholme and State Medicine, 1885–1935, *Cambridge UP, 1997, pp.220–38, builds well on the earlier work he acknowledges.*

The creation of the Medical Research Committee and its role in tuberculosis research is documented by Linda Bryder, 'Tuberculosis and the MRC', in Joan Austoker and Linda Bryder eds, Historical Perspectives on the Role of the MRC: Essays in the history of the Medical Research Council of the United Kingdom and its predecessor, the Medical Research Committee, 1913–1953, *Oxford UP, 1989, pp.1–8. The bacteriologist Sir William Leishman's notes on the early meetings of the committee are at RAMC 563, Box 124, CMAC, Wellcome I. The 'gossip in official circles' about the way in which DLG was persuaded of the critical need for medical research was recalled by Sir Henry Dale ('Autobiography', typescript courtesy of Lady Todd and Wilhelm Feldberg).*

We discussed Sydney Buxton's scheme for insurance against unemployment in specified industries. The cost put at £400,000 thought to be excessive—doubt thrown on the satisfaction which would be given to proposals by labour owing to the small amount contributed by the State. viz. 25 per cent or 1/5 of whole. Cost of working to be further considered by Buxton.

WSC had introduced unemployment insurance to the Cabinet in December 1908, after investigation and planning by Sir Hubert Llewellyn Smith and William Beveridge. It was deferred pending the preparation of an invalidity scheme. Negotiations with unions and employers, the rejection of the 1909 Budget, and the ensuing elections caused further distractions and delay. Following months of interdepartmental disagreement, partly provoked by DLG, the two schemes were again submitted to the Cabinet. The weekly Treasury contribution to unemployment insurance had been fixed at one-quarter of the total collected from the worker and the employer. The figures were 21s./2d., 21s./2d., *and* 11s./4d. *respectively. Thus* 11s./4d. *was one-fifth of the total. Before the Bill was introduced, the government proportion was increased to one-third of the worker's contribution, an average of* 12s./3d. *The industries covered initially were building, construction, shipbuilding, mechanical engineering, iron founding, vehicle construction, and saw milling (José F. Harris,* Unemployment and Politics: A Study in English Social Policy 1886–1914, *Oxford UP, 1972, pp.319–34; Bentley B. Gilbert,* The Evolution of National Insurance in Great Britain. The Origins of the Welfare State, *Michael Joseph, 1966, pp.274–83; for the argument that 'unemployment insurance was a strategy devised by the civil servants of the Board of Trade to weaken workers' demands for wage increases and to improve the competitiveness of British industry' see Tomoari Matsunaga, 'The Origins of Unemployment Insurance in Edwardian Britain',* Journal of Policy History, *vol.29, no.4, 2017, pp.615–39. John Cooper,* The British Welfare Revolution, 1906–14, *Bloomsbury Academic, 2017, pp.165–83, adds detail from the diary of W.H. Dawson, hired by the Board of Trade for his expertise on German social welfare policy. Percy Alden's* Democratic England, *Macmillan, New York, 1912, pp.103–7, is a useful contemporary summary by a Quaker social reformer whose influence on policy might have been underestimated, according to Nicholas A. Loizou, 'Before New Liberalism: The Continuity of Radical Dissent, 1867–1914', Ph.D. thesis, Manchester U., 2019, pp.169–77).*

Morley asked for some help ?£20,000 for study oriental languages. Runciman asked for it to come under education. Morley resisted.

A Special Committee chaired by Lord Cromer had been appointed in 1910 by the Secretary of State for India to 'formulate in detail an organised scheme for the institution in London of a School of Oriental Languages'. The Committee was to make recommendations 'on the lines' of a Treasury Committee on Oriental Studies under Lord Reay, which had reported in 1909. The Unionist MP George Lloyd had questioned the delay in proceeding with the Treasury Committee's 'urgent recommendations'; but the India Office responded that 'it would be impossible to start a school or spend money until further details of staff, syllabus, &c have been decided' (Lloyd of Dolobran MSS, GLLD 16/60, CAC). It was not until February 1917, with a Royal Charter as a College of the University of London, that a School of Oriental Studies was opened by the King Emperor to give 'instruction in the Languages of Eastern and African peoples, Ancient and Modern, and in the Literature, History, Religion and Customs of those peoples' (C.H. Phillips, The School of Oriental & African Studies University of London, 1917–1967, An Introduction, *SOAS Archives, 1967); Ian Brown,* The School of Oriental and African Studies: Imperial Training and the Expansion of Learning, *Cambridge UP, 2016, pp.7–40.*

Winston asked for his bill to enable local charge to be placed on Co. rates when outside Military or Police called in shd be made retrospective to cover Tonypandy riots. Agreed to make it for police only as & from date when County Inspector promised the local financial support. Aliens Bill—Runciman protested against aliens being searched for fire arms.

Japanese Treaty & Swansea appeal case mentioned.

The House of Lords Judicial Committee had dismissed an appeal by the Board of Education over whether the Board had breached its statutory obligations in endorsing the lower rate of salaries that the local education authority was paying to teachers in non-provided or voluntary schools. The dispute had been running since 1908. The judgment and its background are set out in 'The Swansea Schools Case', The Tablet, *15 Apr. 1911, p.35). J.G. Ellis provides a thorough history in 'The Administration of the 1902 Act in Relation to the Church Schools in Swansea', M.Ed. thesis, U. Coll. of Swansea, 1975.*

Tuesday 11th April Cabinet. Discussion on Osborne case. WSC reported Ramsay MacDonald at a private audience had informed him that Labour Party could not support Bill, unless the 2/3rd ballot majority was amended to a bare majority. As it was only put in by Cabinet Committee to give away, resolved to introduce bill without it. Burns demurred but we squashed him.

The government's 1911 Trade Union Bill was carried on its second reading on 30 May, but Labour and the unions were not reconciled to the provision that a special political levy could be raised only as a voluntary payment. Labour opposition was surmounted by the Trade Union Act 1913, which required just a bare majority to set up a political fund and collect a levy from members; 60 of 63 unions approved the proposal (Martin Pugh, Speak for Britain! A New History of the Labour Party, *The Bodley Head, 2010, pp.86–7).*

Smallholdings — Carrington reported he had had an interview with certain Liberal M.P.s. Was amazed at strong feeling against Board of Agriculture & that more was not done — he thought a small committee with Lloyd George should consider whether 8 more commissioners should not be appointed to put pressure on County Councils, as many were not at heart friendly.

On 17 April Carrington wrote to his Permanent Secretary, Sir Thomas Elliott: 'The attitude of the B. of A. at this juncture will be of great service in stopping the unfair attack on the Civil Service which Morant's action and the Archer-Shee case have fanned into a flame... I shall not fail to let the M.P.s know how all the Board threw themselves into the work being determined to spare no effort to make the Small Holdings Act in which they genuinely believe a great & permanent success' (Elliott MSS, courtesy of Sir Hugh Elliott Bt). For the numbers of small holdings created and the 200,000 acres acquired by councils to 1914 see E.J.T. Collins ed., The Agrarian History of England and Wales, Vol. VII 1850–1914, Pt 1, *Cambridge UP, 2001, pp.699–700.*

Unemployed insurance scheme discussed & riddled — & Cabinet committee Churchill Burns Buxton LL. George & self appointed to consider contributions & benefits with experts. Cost estimate £235,000 B of Trade & P.O. £40,000 = £275,000.

Aliens Bill — Churchill reported agreement with Runciman confining bill to pistols & not to firearms!

Churchill's draft bill had distinguished between aliens and British citizens, and authorised the deportation of aliens before they had committed crimes ('naughty principles', as he admitted). The bill lapsed for lack of time (Bernard Porter, 'The British Government and Political Refugees, c.1880–1914', in John Slatter ed., From the Other Shore: Russian Political Emigrants in Britain, 1880–1917, *Frank Cass, 1984, pp.12,42n.56).*

Ap. 19th Cabinet. Absent therefrom — also away McKenna, Crewe, Grey — discussion on Insurance against invalidity scheme — short cabinet.

The meeting might have been short but it heard a heartening announcement from DLG that he thought there would be no need for fresh taxation to cover the apparent prospective deficit. And, after considering the more important amendments to the second clause of the Parliament Bill, it was agreed that the clause as it stood should 'substantially be assented to...reserving of course the consideration of possible concessions at a later stage' (HHA Cabinet letter, 19 Apr. 1911, Bodl. MS. Asquith 6, ff.28–9).

On 20 April debate began on the Parliament Bill's clause 2, which gave the Commons the power to override Lords' rejection of ordinary legislation if a bill had been passed three times in three successive sessions. A forest of amendments from both sides of the House was to be considered. 'The Prime Minister came to the House in a very drunken state. The Tories behaved very honourably. Balfour begged Elibank to take him home' (DLG–Margaret Lloyd George, 21 Apr. 1911, Kenneth O. Morgan ed., Lloyd George Family Letters 1885–1936, *U. of Wales P. & Oxford UP, 1973, p.154, partly translated from Welsh).*

Ap. 26 Cabinet. (Grey & Crewe absent). We discussed future time table. Guillotine time table for report & 3d Reading of Parliament Bill. Date for Insurance Bill, & Budget to be introduced. I proposed Whit holidays from May 31–Ap 13 [*sic*].

Lloyd George explained importance of paying Doctors more than friendly societies, so as to secure better service 4/- p. head to 6/- p. head each 1/- + £700,000!

We raised question of contributing 30/- for maternity cases, and the inclusion of compensation to those suffering from venereal disease, & the age at which contributions & benefits should begin. His proposals met with approval.

Lord Loreburn stayed behind to discuss with P.M. the appointment of magistrates.

May 3 Cabinet. Reform of Lords.

The committee stage of the Parliament Bill ended on 3 May. The government had made concessions but was steadfast in its resolve to remove the absolute veto of the Lords before proceeding with reform of the second chamber. During the committee stage the government had relied on the ordinary closure rule and kept discussion to a minimum by asking their own supporters not to speak. The rule requiring the House to rise at 11.00 p.m. was suspended, and sittings, often acrimonious, regularly lasted until the early hours of the morning (J.H. Whitehouse, 'The Long Parliament', unpublished recollections, p.17, Whitehouse MSS, 210, Isle of Wight County Record Office). JAP was part of a 'harmonious team' with HHA, WSC, Rufus Isaacs, and Herbert Samuel who steered the legislation through: 'with the help of our good friend the kangaroo' (Samuel–Gladstone, 14 May 1911, Gladstone MSS, BL Add. MS. 45992, f.252).

*On 4 May DLG introduced his National Insurance Bill in a speech lasting two and a half hours that was cordially received on both sides of the House. 'The poor man hardly knew if he had promoted a good bill or a bad one, when he found the classes as well as the masses applauding him,' JAP told the Rotherham Liberal Association annual meeting (*Rotherham Advertiser, *[20 June] 1911). The Bill had been in preparation since the autumn of 1908 but was delayed by the clash with the Lords and then by negotiations with friendly societies, insurance companies, and the medical profession. The main principle was a compulsory wage deduction from all whose income was less than £160 a year, and payment of a sickness benefit on an approved scale. A capital sum was set aside to assist local authorities and charities to build sanatoria for 'consumptive' patients, with maintenance to be met from insurance* *contributions and additional State funding. Unemployment benefits initially covered only 2.25 million workers. Timothy T. Hellwig analyses the underlying political forces in 'The Origins of Unemployment Insurance in Britain: A Cross-Class Alliance Approach',* Social Science History, *vol.29, no.1, 2005, pp.107–36. Joseph Melling offers a different perspective in 'Welfare capitalism and the origins of welfare states: British industry, workplace welfare and social reform, c.1870–1914',* Soc.H., *vol.17, no.3, Oct. 1992, pp.468–78.*

For DLG's concern that part 2 of the bill might be postponed in order to get part 1 through see Llewellyn Smith–WSC, 30 July [1911], CHAR 2/52/60, CAC. Initially well received in the Commons, National Health Insurance received the brunt of Tory anger after the passing of the Parliament Act: over 500 amendments were proposed. The most sustained opposition came from the British Medical Association, which demanded an income limit on those covered by the bill (£2 per week), and a payment for doctors of 8s. 6d. plus cost of medicine per patient. Even when Sir William Plender showed in July 1912 that the average cost per patient was 4s. 5d., the association remained adamant. It finally capitulated in January 1913, when 15,000 individual doctors had accepted the government's proposed 9s. per patient (to include cost of treatment).

Virginia Berridge comments: 'The medical elite wanted to stamp out competition; the Fabians wanted state socialism; and Lloyd George saw health insurance as a bulwark against pauperism, not sickness' (F.M.L. Thompson, The Cambridge Social History of Britain, 1750–1950, Vol. 3 Social agencies and institutions, *Cambridge UP, 1990, p.218; see also Sir John Conybeare, 'The Crisis of 1911–13: Lloyd George and the Doctors',* The Lancet, *18 May 1957, pp.1032–35; Bentley B. Gilbert,* The Evolution of National Insurance in Great Britain, *pp.288–303,316–99; Norman R. Eder,* National Health Insurance and the Medical Profession in Britain, 1913–1939, *Garland Publishing, New York, 1982, pp.31–89; Glyn Carpenter, 'National Health Insurance: A Case Study in the Use of Private Non-Profit making Organizations in the Provision of Welfare Benefits',* Public Administration, *vol.62, Spring 1984, pp.71–89; for the ideology of voluntarism underlying the national insurance legislation see Geoffrey Finlayson,* Citizen, State and Social Welfare in Britain 1830–1990, *Clarendon P., Oxford, 1994, pp.184–91); and for a persuasive argument that 'the Edwardian development of national insurance was a move towards an exclusive risk pool, towards contractual entitlement, and towards a self-financing system of intra-personal redistribution', Paul Johnson, 'Risk, redistribution and social welfare in Britain from the poor law to Beveridge', Martin Daunton ed.,* Charity, self-interest and welfare in the English past, *U. College London, 1996, pp.225–48. E.P. Hennock,* British Social Reform and German Precedents: The Case of Social Insurance 1880–1914, *Clarendon P., Oxford, 1987, pp.169–215, is authoritative. Simon Cordery covers the friendly societies' dimension of the story in*

British Friendly Societies, 1750–1914, *Palgrave Macmillan, Basingstoke & New York, 2003, pp.152–74.*

In 1913, after a debate that crossed party lines, the National Insurance Act was amended so that the maternity benefit would be paid directly to insured women or wives of insured men. Only men carrying signed authorisation from their wives could collect the benefit (Susan Pedersen, Family, Dependence, and the Origins of the Welfare State: Britain and France, 1914–1945, *Cambridge UP, 1993, pp.56–7).*

After intense discussion in the Opposition on tactics to adopt in response to the Parliament Bill, on May 8 Lord Lansdowne introduced an elaborate plan to reconstitute the Lords on a largely non-hereditary basis. Lansdowne's biographer, Lord Newton, observed: 'The proposals, which really amounted almost to a sentence of death upon the most ancient Legislative Chamber in the world, were received by a crowded and attentive House in a dignified if frigid silence' (Lord Lansdowne: A Biography, *Macmillan, 1929, pp.414–15).*

May 10 Cabinet. Reform of Lords.

Morley was asked P.M's view on Lansdowne's scheme at first meeting, & asked for his (Morley's) opinion at second meeting.

Morley regarded Lansdowne's scheme a great advance. But it was regarded as impossible for acceptance, & we must make clear that the Parliament Bill must be passed first. 346 an excessive number, & Tory ascendancy would be secured. Royal Prerogative gone, & nothing to safeguard Libs getting their way in such a House. Churchill argued it was a block to chop at.

Tactics were to let differences among Tories find vent.

Grey urged Asquith's 4 conditions must be fulfilled, numbers no solution for deadlocks provided.

Discussed payment of M.Ps £350 agreed to + £50 for travelling. We went through Lloyd George's budget & agreed to dispose of Balance.

45,000 cocoa,
250,000 Payment MP,
50,000 Insurance,
Port of Mombasa to be repaid 250,000,
£2,350,000 to old sinking fund.

2,500,000 Development
1,500,000 Sanitoria,

There was a £5,600,000 surplus from 1910–11. Revenue had exceeded the estimate by more than £4 million. Cocoa duties at that time were slightly protective; readjustment to eliminate this cost £45,000. The £50,000 for Insurance was only for administrative costs.

The quarter of a million pounds for 'Port of Mombasa' was a loan for Ugandan development including the recently completed railway and the Mombasa water supply. HHA's Cabinet notes refer to £2,600,000 allocated to the old sinking fund. No amendments were to be moved to Lansdowne's Reform Bill, and the government would not divide against the second reading (TNA: CAB 41/33/14). Fuller details of the Budget brought in on 16 May are in Bernard Mallet, British Budgets 1887–88 to 1912–13, *Macmillan, 1913, pp.322–31; and for Mallet's assurance to the Chancellor of the Exchequer's PPS that his book was not a covert criticism of Lloyd Georgian finance and that he had been 'in favour of a large development of direct taxation long before these ideas became fashionable' see Mallet–Rowland Whitehead, 28 Jan. 1914, Whitehead MSS, WHD/5, PA).*

The King would have read in his morning newspapers on 13 May of a flying display at Hendon aerodrome organised by the Parliamentary Aerial Defence Committee on 12 May. The event was witnessed by the Prime Minister, DLG, WSC, Haldane, Seely, Samuel, Lord Northcliffe, hundreds of military and naval officers, and a crowd of thousands. Balfour, Seely, McKenna, and the Director of Military Training, Maj.-Gen. Archibald Murray, took to the air with Grahame-White (Hugh Driver, The Birth of Military Aviation: Britain, 1903–1914, *Royal Historical Society, 1997, p.138; R. Dallas Brett,* History of British Aviation 1908–1914, *John Hamilton, [1933], pp.74–5; there is a programme in the McKenna MSS, MCKN 9/4/1, CAC). The Adjutant-General, who spoke to DLG, WSC, and McKenna, had the opportunity to point out the War Office's difficulty in getting sufficient money from the Treasury to make substantial progress with military aviation (Ewart Memoirs, 12 May 1911, Ewart MSS).*

May 14 I wrote a Private letter to P.M. suggesting that we should on third Reading of Parl. Bill make it plain we would treat in no petty party spirit proposals to reform the Lords, but only after Parl. Bill was passed.[42]

1. Help passage of Parl. Bill
2. Keep cabinet united.
3. Induce Tories not withdraw from position Lansdowne had placed them in, & would help them modify proposals to meet Liberal views later on.

On 15 May the government had a majority of 121 on the third reading of the Parliament Bill. It had been thirteen days in committee, and numerous amendments had been resisted during this and the report stage. HHA stated clearly that reform of the Lords was on the government's agenda in the current Parliament. But the Veto Bill had to come first.

May 17 Cabinet — discussed Insurance Bill.

[42] JAP's letter does not survive in either his own or HHA's papers.

JAP did not mention that this Cabinet also discussed the German reply to its memorandum (see 22 Feb. 1911) and the private members' Women's Enfranchisement Bill, which had recently been read a second time. Grey, Runciman, Birrell, and Haldane were in favour of giving the House an opportunity to vote on whether they wanted to go further with this, the second 'Conciliation Bill'. The Lord Chancellor, Chancellor of the Exchequer, and McKenna were opposed, 'as were apparently a majority of the Cabinet' (TNA: CAB 41/33/15).

May 24 Cabinet — discussed Time of House, chance of Plural voting, & how bill could be made operative in 1915 assuming Lords rejected it. I pressed for it this session. Lloyd George pressed for guillotining Insurance Bill. I opposed it. Crewe back.

On 23 May the Imperial Conference convened. HHA told the assembled delegates that it 'was in the highest degree desirable that we should take advantage of your presence here to take stock together of the possible risks and dangers to which we are or may be in common exposed; and to weigh carefully the adequacy, and the reciprocal adaptiveness, of the contributions we are respectively making to provide against them'. Dominion premiers and other leaders were invited to attend three days of meetings of the CID on 26, 29, and 30 May with the Prime Minister in the chair, and the Foreign Secretary, First Lord of the Admiralty, Colonial Secretary, and the Secretaries of State for India and War in attendance, together with the Chief of the Imperial General Staff (Sir William Nicholson), the Director of Military Operations (Brig.-Gen. Henry Wilson), and Lord Esher.

A review of foreign and defence policy by Sir Edward Grey was a franker exposition of the implications of growing German strength than had been presented to the British Cabinet as a whole. But much was held back:

> though I do not think there is any prospect that one can reasonably see at the present moment of our being involved in serious trouble in Europe, it is possible that under such extreme conditions as I have named the question might arise as to whether we ought to take part by force in European affairs, and if we did it would be solely because Sea Power, and the necessity of keeping the command of the sea, was the underlying cause and motive of our action.

It would be six months before JAP and the majority of members of the Cabinet would learn of the military 'conversations' with France on how Britain might 'take part by force in European affairs' (for Grey's remarks and the context see Keith Jeffery, 'The Imperial Conference, the Committee of Imperial Defence and the Continental Commitment', in Peter Dennis & Jeffrey Grey eds, 1911 Preliminary Moves, *The 2011 Chief of Army History Conference, Big Sky Publishing, 2011, pp.20–40).*

After a four-day debate, the Parliament Bill was given an unopposed second reading in the Lords on 29 May. There was a Cabinet meeting on 31 May that JAP appears to have missed. Burns recorded 'Judges etc. Insurance scheme' (Burns diary, 31 May 1911, Burns MSS, BL Add.MS. 46333, f.106). The timetable for the Insurance Bill that was approved on 23 May was endorsed. Grey accepted modifications and additions to a draft reply to Germany on a proposal to exchange naval information. There was no mention of judges in HHA's Cabinet letter (Bodl. MS. Asquith 6, f.41).

Parliament was recessed for Whitsuntide from 31 May to 13 June 1911.

14 June Wed. Business of House, I objected to closuring Insurance Bill but George got his way P.M. taking no part. Several other matters.

There is no report to the King in the Asquith papers of a Cabinet meeting on 14 June. DLG, apparently with the consent of the Cabinet, conveyed to F.E. Smith 'a deal about Insurance Bill... proposed six weeks for all stages... and that no Plural Voting Bill would be introduced' (Balcarres notes, 15 June 1911, Vincent ed., The Crawford Papers, *p.187). DLG might have been surprised to know that one of the Bill's former supporters, Seebohm Rowntree, had just privately advised a Liberal backbencher 'to reject it absolutely'. Rowntree's 'cure for unemployment is to house men far out from cities. Give them allotments on which they can fall back in hard times. Run them into towns to work on cheap railways. Extend light railway system as in Belgium.' Rowntree had seen John Burns the same day and left him in no doubt that he was a 'severe critic' of the Insurance Bill (MacCallum Scott diary, 12 June 1911, MacCallum Scott MSS, lent and quoted by courtesy of John H. MacCallum Scott, now in Glasgow U.; Burns diary, 12 June 1911, Burns MSS, BL Add.MS. 46333, f.113). In the House before dinner JAP joined DLG on the front bench, 'grinning' at an irritated Tory backbencher speaking on agricultural votes (Hon. W.G.A. Orde-Powlett diary, 14 June 1911, Bolton MSS ZBO IX 5, N. Yorks CRO).*

20 June Tuesday We discussed terms of message to be cabled to Bryce (see confidential F.O. dispatch 10713) re the Arbitration Treaty. Also terms Clause 5. renewal of Anglo Japanese Treaty—difficulty in making 2 treaties formed for 2 very different objects consistent. After an hour we solved problem to our satisfaction.

The terms of the draft arbitration treaty, a commentary on it, and subsequent correspondence, can be found in G.P. Gooch and Harold Temperley, British Documents on the Origins of the War 1898–1914, Vol. VIII, Arbitration, Neutrality and Security, HMSO 1932 *(henceforth BD VIII), nos473–514, pp.568–604. For Grey's view that the alliance with Japan was crucial in avoiding the need for a separate fleet in Chinese waters, and a modern historian's conclusion that the alliance was 'less an asset to British strategic policy than a hindrance', see Keith Neilson, 'The Anglo-Japanese Alliance and British strategic foreign policy, 1902–1914', in Phillips Payson O'Brien ed.,* The Anglo-Japanese Alliance, 1902–1922, *Routledge, 2004, pp.58–9).*

Morley & Crewe instructed to resist all amendments to Veto Bill in the Lords.

King George V and Queen Mary were crowned on 22 June. The procession went under the completed Admiralty Arch, emerging at Trafalgar Square, and then swung round through Whitehall and Parliament Street. After speaking to Lord Lansdowne on 23 June, the Archbishop of Canterbury went on to see the King, who made it clear that he had no expectation that the Lords would pass the Parliament Bill 'tamely'. Lord Davidson recorded that day that the King 'realised that there must be a fight, and he encouraged the course of moving amendments, while reserving the question of ultimate adherence to them if the creation of Peers be threatened' (Davidson of Lambeth MSS XII, f.194, Lambeth Palace Library). Davidson despatched a circular to all the bishops seeking to determine who would support Lord Lansdowne. He told Curzon on 27 July: 'I have personally no reason to suppose that any bishop is likely to vote with Lord Halsbury. Presumably the Bishops of Birmingham and Hereford, if in the House, will support the Government.' (Curzon of Kedleston MSS, BL: A & AS, MSS.Eur.F.112 D/3/8 Box 1.) The Archbishop himself voted for the Bill, having, as Lord Carrington noted, switched his vote at the eleventh hour (Carrington Diary, 10 Aug. 1911, Lincolnshire MSS, Bodl. MS. Film 1107). Davidson's thinking on the constitutional crisis is laid out in Michael Hughes, Archbishop Randall Davidson, *Routledge, 2017, pp.38–41.*

June 28 Lords' amendments to Parliament Bill were reported upon by Viscount Morley, who said he was prepared to oppose all at this stage but would speak less vehemently upon the tribunal to determine what was a finance bill, & upon Lord Ancaster's[43] which might enable the instrument itself to be amended under its own provisions. This was assented to. In Harcourt's absence I was authorised to say he thought the time had come when our pledge of secrecy might be removed, & that we should inform the leaders of the Opposition (Lansdowne & Co) that we were in the position to secure the passage of the Bill, if they tried to force amendments on us in the Lords.

[43] Gilbert Heathcote-Drummond-Willoughby, 2nd Earl of Ancaster (1867–1951); Joint Hereditary Lord Great Chamberlain; Con. MP Lincs (Horncastle) 1894–1910; 2nd Earl 1910; Parl. Sec., Min. of Agriculture 1921–4; one of the largest British landholders. With his American heiress wife, Eloise Breese, embarked in 1911 on restoration and modernising of ancestral home, Grimsthorpe Castle. He had proposed an amendment which would prevent any shortening of the suspensory period to less than two years (HL Deb 29 June 1911 vol 8 cc1122–204).

After a protracted discussion, it was suggested that the P.M. should see the King before he left for Ireland and counteract any influence his entourage might have had on him in regard to the possibility of the understanding being made applicable to vital amendments. We decided to await the Lords amendments before calling into conference any Tory leaders, to explain the position. I explained the procedure in regard to amendments, & the importance of not allowing the bill to be dropped by reason of rejection en bloc of all the Lords amendments — This would involve another session & financial complications.

John Burns thought this 'the most critical but most united Cabinet we have had in 5½ years, due in large measure to tact, temper and commanding decisiveness of P.M.' (Burns Diary, 28 June 1911, Burns MSS, BL Add.MS. 46333 in Richard Peter Kezirian, 'David Lloyd George and the Origins of the British Welfare State 1909–1914', Ph.D dissertation, U. California Santa Barbara, 1976, p.149).

WSC explained to his wife on 29 June what had been settled about the Veto Bill:

> As soon as it leaves the Lords we shall tell them through their leaders that we have the guarantees, & that we shall use them at once unless they undertake to pass the bill. We shall not deal with the Lords Amendts in H. of C. until the new Peers are actually made or the others have surrendered, so that if they fight, the Bill will go back not to the present H. of L. but to a new one in which we shall have a majority!!! Secret information points to the fact that the Tory leaders do not mean to fight and are only looking for some means of saving their faces. But it will make no difference to us whatever they do.
>
> *(Mary Soames ed.,* Speaking for Themselves: The Personal Letters of Winston and Clementine Churchill, *Black Swan, 1999, p.50; reproduced with permission of Curtis Brown, London on behalf of The Estate of Winston S. Churchill © The Estate of Winston S. Churchill)*

Restless Liberal and Labour MPs pressed the Prime Minister on 3 July on when the resolution on payment of members was to be taken. Declining even to deny rumours of a postponement to February 1912, HHA insisted that the government's intentions remained the same as they were when the Chancellor of the Exchequer stated them in his Budget speech, 'and subject always to parliamentary exigencies, the Government hope to give effect to them'. Asked if he would explain what parliamentary exigencies were, he replied: 'No, that is beyond the wit of man.' (HC Deb 3 July 1911 vol 27 cc795–6.) An amendment moved by Lord Hugh Cecil excluded any measure for payment of members from the category of money bills (Emily Allyn, Lords versus Commons: A Century of Conflict and Compromise 1830–1930, *Century Co., New York, 1931, p.205).*

July 4 A two hours discussion over situation created in Morocco by France going to Fez — Spain going to [Alcazar][44] & Germany sending ship to Agadir.

We heard Cambon's & Metternich's views, verbal & written conveyed on Saturday. Grey had formally acknowledged them.

The full text of Metternich's aide-mémoire (1 July 1911), the Permanent U.-Sec. Sir Arthur Nicolson's minute (1 July 1911), and Paul Cambon's letter to Grey (1 July 1911) are in G.P. Gooch and Harold Temperley eds, British Documents on the Origins of The War 1898–1914, Vol. VII, The Agadir Crisis, *HMSO 1932 (henceforth* BD VII*), nos338–40, pp.322–4.*

It was obvious that:

1. Spain had been instigated to commit a breach of Algeciras agreement by action of France but more probably instigated by Germany, to enable her to establish herself on the West coast of Africa. McKenna stated that Admiral Wilson thought position of no importance, unless strongly fortified.

Our trade interests were probably 4 to 1 those of Germany but the position was of strategic importance to Britain rather than commercial.

We all agreed we could not announce our policy to the world or Parliament. We must by diplomatic methods make it clear to France that we intended to fulfil our treaty obligations — that we must know their objective, & that we could not recognise any arrangement unless we were party to diplomatic discussion. We could not regard with complacency any attempt for Germany to come in to the Mediterranean — or that any power (but ourselves) should take Tangier. We could not permit a fortified port to be established, and there must be for trade an open door in any partition of Morocco.

To Germany — Grey would make it clear we would not consent to a partition à trois — & we would insist on a voice in any arrangement. We recognised status quo ante was not likely to be restored. That the real motive of German action was establishing herself there (expansion) & not to look after German trade interests wh. were NIL (excuse). We all thought we could not check expansion & it would come & end a bad & barbaric system under the Sultan.

The evils of the Sultan's regime had been publicised in the work of Lawrence Harris, who described Morocco as 'a land of corruption, tyranny, and unscrupulous oppression... Its courts are a veritable sink of chicanery' (With Mulai Hafid at Fez, *Smith Elder, 1909, pp.vi–vii).*

[44] JAP had left a blank where we have inserted Alcazar.

HHA's reaction to Germany's intervention is left in no doubt by his Cabinet letter: 'The sudden discovery of German "subjects" and "threatened interests" in the immediate neighbourhood of the only harbour on the western coast of Morocco, which can be developed into a naval and commercial base, facing the Atlantic, is an interesting illustration of "Real-politik"' (TNA: CAB 41/33/20). The exasperation of the Cabinet over Agadir was intensified by the consequent halt to attempts that had been in progress for months to finalise a technical naval agreement with Germany (Otte, '"What we desire is confidence"...', pp.43–7; T.G. Otte, '"Almost a law of nature"? Sir Edward Grey, the Foreign Office, and the Balance of Power in Europe, 1905–12'; in Erik Goldstein and B.J.C. McKercher eds, Power and Stability British Foreign Policy 1865–1965, *Frank Cass, 2004, pp.101–8).*

JAP does not write about a meeting on Friday 7 July to consider outstanding points on the Anglo-Japanese alliance. Burns noted that several critical matters were discussed, 'all of which went well, (Japan, Morocco etc.). Lords going smoothly' (HHA Cabinet letter, 8 July 1911, Bodl. MS. Asquith 6, f.50; Burns diary, 7 July 1911, Burns MSS, BL Add.MS. 46333, f.128). The Cabinet seems to have been unperturbed by the passing of a referendum amendment in the Lords on 5 July.

July 11 Japanese Treaty Renewal Edward Grey read out paragraph relating to our not going to war with any 3d (U.S.A.) power with whom we had an arbitration agreement. We congratulated him on having so successfully arranged the treaty in this way. He reported: the position in Morocco looked like ending in a friendly way by France giving Germany some privileges in the French Congo, and in regard to this we had no concern. We had made our position clear to the French, as to our objection to Germany having a position in the Mediterranean, or a fortified station on W. coast of Morocco.

Sir Arthur Bigge (Lord ? Sham) [*sic*][45] had written from Dublin to ask what advice he was to give the King as Lord Midleton had conveyed thro' him to the King that the Unionist party were sore, and would like to know what position they were in, in regard to guarantees, & the King wanted to know whether he should respond. We all took a strong view that Midleton could not approach the King, nor could the King take advice as to what communications should pass through his Ministers, & Asquith was directed to write Bigge in this sense. Asquith said it was quite clear that

1. The Bill would pass
2. No real alteration could be made
3. There was no alternative & this held good with or without the creation of Peers.

[45] Sir Arthur Bigge had been created Baron Stamfordham on 23 June 1911.

He cared not for the humiliation of the Tory Lords, but we wanted to avoid bringing the King into the arena. But it was admitted the Tories would force this, so as to minimise their humiliation.

If concession as to Speaker's finance tribunal or on Lord Newton's[46] amendment, it must be in exchange for a quid pro quo, and a settlement. I pointed out Selborne had promised repeal at the earliest moment.

John Burns assessed the Prime Minister on the Veto as 'clear forcible deliberate the rest superfluous in discussion' (Burns diary, 11 July 1911, Burns MSS, BL Add.MS. 46333, f.130). Lord Newton complained that the Parliament Bill would leave the Lords with only the power to delay bills, and even that power was not guaranteed. He wanted the delaying power to be protected by a general election. He proposed that after a bill, which further limited the Lords' power to delay Commons' bills, had been rejected by the Lords three times, it should be postponed until after the next general election and would need to be passed by the new Commons before becoming law. The government saw that the 'loose and vague wording... [could] be applicable to the H.R. bill' (Morley–Simon, 10 July 1911, Simon MSS, uncat. when seen courtesy of the 2nd Vt Simon, now in the Bodleian Libraries). The amendment was withdrawn. For an account that overestimates the influence of Newton's efforts to mobilise Conservative support for the Bill see David Southern, 'Lord Newton, the Conservative Peers and the Parliament Act of 1911', EHR, *vol.xcvi, Oct. 1981, pp.834–40. And for the Master of Elibank's briefing of A.P. Nicholson of* The Times *on the evening of 11 July about the preparation of a list of 500 peers that 'might be required in extreme eventualities' (published the next day as 'Political Notes—the Creation of Peers—the Whip's List') see Renton,* Chief Whip: People, Power and Patronage in Westminster, *pp.230–1.*

Thursday July 13th Caernarvon. Investiture of P. of Wales.[47] I sat with Asquith for an hour, we chatted about Baron de Forest's[48] character; the enthusiasm in Ireland

[46] Thomas Wodehouse Legh, Lord Newton (1857–1942); Con. MP Newton, Lancs. 1886–99; 2nd Baron 1899; Paymaster-Gen. 1915–16; Asst U.-Sec. of St. Foreign Affairs 1916; Controller, Prisoners of War Dept 1916–19.

[47] Prince Edward (known as David to his family), eldest child of George V and Queen Mary (1894–1972); created Prince of Wales on his 16th birthday, seven weeks after his father succeeded as king; King Edward VIII (1936–7); Duke of Windsor 1937–72; m. Wallis Simpson, an American divorcée, 1937. See John S. Ellis, 'The Prince and the Dragon: Welsh National Identity and the Investiture of the Prince of Wales', *WHR*, vol.18, Dec. 1996, pp.272–94. Ellis's *Investiture: Royal Ceremony and National Identity in Wales, 1911–1969*, U. of Wales P., Cardiff, 2008, pp.21–124, is a more wide-ranging study based largely on press coverage and is a major source for Michael D. Kandiah, Judith Rowbotham, and Gillian Staerck, 'The Ultimate Windsor Ceremonials: Coronations and Investitures', in Glencross, Rowbotham, and Kandiah eds, *The Windsor Dynasty 1910 to the Present*, Palgrave Macmillan, 2016, pp.76–9.

[48] Baron (Arnold) Maurice ('Tutti') de Forest (1879–1968); Lib. MP West Ham (N) 1911–18; adopted natural son of Baron Maurice Hirsch (1831–96), Austrian Jewish banker who was richer than the Rothschilds and financial adviser and confidant of the Prince of Wales from 1890 (Philip Magnus, *King*

earlier in the week on the King's visit & its probable effect on the King towards National aspirations. He regarded the omen as a good one & concurred with me Redmond was ill advised to have given the enthusiasm a lead.

The King, the Queen, the Prince of Wales, and Princess Mary made a state visit to Ireland 7–11 July 1911. Redmond 'showed tolerance for the visit, if not enthusiasm' (James Loughlin, 'Crown, spectacle and identity: the British monarchy and Ireland under the Union 1800–1922', in Andrzej Olechnowicz ed., The Monarchy and the British Nation, 1780 to the Present, *Cambridge UP, 2007, p.127). The Dublin Corporation did not offer an official welcome, and there were unfriendly demonstrations by Sinn Fein. But there had been cheering crowds as the party drove from Kingstown to Dublin Castle on the 8th, and an address of welcome from 165,000 women was presented to the Queen on the 10th. A week later there was a warmer reception in Scotland (Hugh Chisholm ed.,* The Britannia Year-Book 1913, *pp.476–7).*

July 19 We discussed what we should do if the Lords tomorrow threw out the Parliament Bill. It was decided to have another cabinet on Friday 21 at 11.0 when the result was known. It was anticipated no Lords would vote against the 3d Reading, in spite of all their bluster.

The P.M. read 2 letters from the Speaker favouring an advisory committee of 2 — Chairman of Comtees in both houses. We all took the view it should be advisory & have no power to override the Speaker — as a vote by a Lord wd be against H. of C. privilege on finance.

Edward the Seventh, John Murray, 1964, pp.218–19); de Forest received the royal licence to use his Austrian title in the United Kingdom in 1900; friend and yachting companion of WSC, active in DLG's land campaign. The flamboyant de Forest had just won a by-election at West Ham (N) having unsuccessfully contested Southport in Jan. 1910. Challenged during the Jan. 1910 election campaign to buy the undeveloped land of Southport at its recent allegedly inflated valuation of £585,000, de Forest called the Tories' bluff by depositing the sum in a local bank pending offers of land that never came (John Liddle, 'Estate management and land reform politics: the Hesketh and Scarisbrick families and the making of Southport, 1842 to 1914', in David Cannadine ed., *Patricians, power and politics in nineteenth-century towns,* Leicester UP, 1982, pp.132–52). There was gossip in March 1910 that his second wife, whom he had allegedly beaten twice, had left him for a time (Pamela Horn, *High Society,* p.99). His marriage having broken down as a result of his wife's affair with a young guardsman, in April 1911 he had laid 'bare in vain his family skeleton' in imprudently suing his wife's uncle and sister for slander (*New York Times,* 16 Apr. 1911). The King had told HHA that, if he had to create peers to ensure Lords reform, de Forest's was the only name he would decline to accept (Derby's Memorandum, 20 Aug. 1911, Randolph S. Churchill, *Winston S. Churchill, Vol. II, Young Statesman,* p.343). Cited to the Public Prosecutor as pro-German in 1914, de Forest (an RNVR lt-cdr) pointed to his generous contributions to the war effort, and the offers of his houses to the War Office and Red Cross and his yacht as a hospital ship. He became a citizen of Lichtenstein 1932, where he was a Counsellor of State and created Count de Bendern. Attempts to locate his papers have been unsuccessful.

We decided to go on with motion for payment of M.P.s & have no exceptions except ministers speaker & 2 chairmen. Winston spoke up for men in army & navy, & Harry Chaplin[49] on civil list getting their £400.

Eventually it was agreed that all members of the government, officers of the House, and officers of the Household should not receive payments. MPs on political pensions were to receive the MP's salary, but their pension was to be reduced commensurately (HC Deb 30 October 1911 vol 30 c521). The only MP then on a pension was the 70-year-old former Conservative Cabinet Minister Henry Chaplin, who had received £1,200 p.a. since 1900 (PP, 1912–13 [169], xlix, 1). Payment of salaries to MPs was authorised by a Commons resolution and funded by a supplementary estimate, thereby preventing the Lords from interfering (HC Deb 14 August 1911 vol 29 c1603). After protracted interdepartmental correspondence—involving the Treasury, the Audit Department, the Inland Revenue, the Solicitor-General's Office, and the Paymaster General's Office—it was decided that £100 of the £400 to be paid to MPs was an allowance for expenses, and therefore was not assessable for income tax. Henry Chaplin sought to avoid reduction of his tax-free pension by declining to accept payment as an MP. But the Solicitor-General's office contended that whether a person received a salary or not was irrelevant; the very fact of entitlement entailed a corresponding reduction in pension (TNA: T 1/11481/22787/1912).

An enquiry from the government Whips' Office to the Paymaster General on 27 February 1912 elicited a confidential list of fourteen MPs who had signified their intention not to draw, or had not drawn, any salary. The list included the Earl of Ronaldshay, who had drawn two quarterly payments before deciding to take no more; he had not repaid the amounts received. Only two, Cecil Harmsworth and Percy Molteno, were Liberals, both very wealthy. 'One of the leading Members of the Irish Party' wanted to put a question on the subject, but the matter had been raised in November 1911, and the Financial Secretary to the Treasury, T. McKinnon Wood, had declined to give the particulars. The Speaker also preferred that the information not be made public (Wedgwood Benn–Ashby St Legers and reply, 5 Mar. 1912, Stansgate MSS, ST/14, PA). The Irish Parliamentary Party had at first decided to decline to take payments, intending thereby to maintain their independence from the British state, but changed the decision by August 1911 (Fergus Campbell, The Irish Establishment 1879–1914, *Oxford UP, 2009, pp.139–40).*

[49] Henry Chaplin (1840–1923); Con. MP Surrey (Wimbledon) 1907–16, Mid-Lincs 1868–85, and Lincs (Kesteven) 1885–1906; popularly known as 'the Squire'; Chanr, Duchy of Lancr 1885–6; PC 1885; Pres., Bd of Agriculture 1889–92; Pres., Local Govt Bd 1895–1900; Vt Chaplin 1916. Chaplin figured in one of the greatest scandals of his age. A few days before their wedding date in 1864 his fiancée Lady Florence Paget eloped with the Marquess of Hastings. His story can be followed in Anne de Courcy's biography of his daughter: *Society's Queen: The Life of Edith, Marchioness of Londonderry*, Sinclair-Stevenson, 1992.

Harmsworth had noted when payment of members was carried by a Commons resolution: 'I did not vote although in favour of the principle—my view that the measure should not be carried by resolution but by a Bill and that it should not apply to Members of this Parliament' (Harmsworth diary, 10 Aug. 1911, Andrew Thorpe and Richard Toye eds, Parliament and Politics in the Age of Asquith and Lloyd George: The Diaries of Cecil Harmsworth, MP, 1909–1922, *Cambridge UP for the Royal Historical Society, 2016, p.95).*

A canvas of backbench Unionist MPs organised by Arthur Lee in November 1912 revealed that 270 were in favour of discontinuing payment of members when the Unionist Party returned to power; seven favoured continuing; 30 were open minded or doubtful. Of the 270, about 24 were in favour of making an exception 'in favour of poor men, who should be enabled to claim a salary on making a proper declaration' (Arnold Ward–Bull, 22 Nov. 1912, Bull MSS, Bull 4/6, CAC). About 180 Unionists returned their first and subsequent cheques, but as the years passed they silently melted away until in the Parliament of 1918 'only one stalwart remained' (Viscount Lee of Fareham, A Good Innings and a Great Partnership, being the Life Story of Arthur and Ruth Lee, Vol. I (1868–1914), *privately printed, 1939, p.454. On the Liberal side, some members found the payments 'no unmixed blessing', as Sir Richard Winfrey recalled: 'I had taught my constituents not to expect me to subscribe to a hundred and one cricket and football clubs, bazaars, etc. After receiving the £400 I could not well refuse, so they got most of it.'* (Leaves from my Life; Memories of Bygone Days, *West Norfolk and King's Lynn Newspaper Co Ltd, King's Lynn, [1936], pp.196-7.) In* The Government of England, *2 vols, The Macmillan Company, New York, 1912 [1st edn 1908], Vol. I, p.234, A. Lawrence Lowell estimated the cost of 'nursing a constituency' at 'a number of hundred pounds a year'. Michael Dawson has case studies in 'Money and the Real Impact of the Fourth Reform Act',* HJ, *vol.35, no.2, 1992, pp.369–81; and see J.R. Howe, 'Liberal Party Organisation in Gloucestershire before 1914',* Southern History, *vol.9, 1987, pp.114–40.*

The position of Germany claiming all French Congo abutting on sea & S. of Cameroons was considered. We determined to find out from France her attitude — not to tell Germany at once we shd take steps, but if she & France could not agree we shd press for a conference & that we could not support France in going to war, if she excluded Germany from some partition of Morocco. Our interests must be safeguarded, & to tell France she must produce counter proposals to Germany.

We talked of military strength of various powers to the indignation of Lord Loreburn who was provocative in tone towards Grey who has a most difficult part to play, as France wants us to pull all the chestnuts out for her.

The Parliament Bill, as rewritten by the Lords, was given its third reading without a division on 20 July. The Bill now provided that any measure establishing home rule for any part of the United Kingdom, affecting the Protestant succession, or which, in the view of a joint committee, 'raises an issue of great gravity upon which the judgement of the country has not been sufficiently ascertained', would not receive royal assent until approved by the electors. It also amended the provisions for determining what constituted a money bill. After dinner, the Conservative whip, Robert Sanders, observed that HHA came into the House 'in such a state he could hardly speak two words' (Sanders diary, 27 Apr. 1911, in John Ramsden ed., Real Old Tory Politics: The Political Diaries of Sir Robert Sanders, Lord Bayford, 1910–35, *The Historians' P., 1984, p.27). At the next morning's Cabinet, John Burns found the Prime Minister 'short simple clear decisive as all through this issue with the Lords. From beginning to end he has been wise and courageous.' (Burns diary, 21 July 1911, Burns MSS, BL Add.MS. 46333, f.135.) The 21 July Cabinet was reported to the King on 22 July (TNA: CAB 41/38/3).*

July 21 1911 House of Lords crisis. Full cabinet except for Pentland (Sinclair). P.M. asked us to decide, what we should do now the Lords had passed the bill. Churchill stated Northcliffe had told him the backwoodsmen 100 strong & more would force a creation of 300 peers before giving way, & they could not be restrained by Lansdowne. Morley, Crewe agreed that many meant to force us.

Asquith reported he had written to Balfour, & sent a note to Lansdowne with a copy wh. he had acknowledged to say, he thought it courteous to let him know that if the Lords' amendments were insisted upon the King would on advice of Ministers create peers to enable Bill to pass without the amendments. We decided that on Monday, the P.M. should say that we were not prepared to accept any of them, though alterations not against substance of measure which could be shown to be of advantage we had been always ready to meet. But these were not ones upon which our differences were determined, & those proposed went to root of the Bill — & we would resist them & we would not send back the Bill until we knew they would not be insisted upon, or until we had so altered the House of Lords that the Bill approved by the Commons would be accepted. The procedure I urged was a debate on motion the Lords be now considered & an adjournment of the debate, & the order kept on the notice paper, I asked Asquith what about the King. He said the King pressed that he should make known his intention to create peers to our opponents, & Asquith said *NO*, he would do it.

The understanding of the autumn should not be even referred to until memoirs were written.

At Question Time on 19 July, the wily Liberal backbencher Handel Booth had asked the Prime Minister whether, 'in any prospective creation of Peers, he will consider the suggestion of recommending for that honour some representative working men and trade unionist officials?' HHA had responded: 'This appears to be a purely hypothetical question.'

In fact, the 'understanding of the autumn'—no longer hypothetical—was formally disclosed by HHA during a vote of censure on 7 August (see 3 Aug. 1911). Balfour had learned from Lord Esher on 6 July about the pledge to create peers; but many of his shadow cabinet did not believe it when told the next day. The King's private secretary, Lord Knollys, and his confidant Esher, had known and kept the secret from Balfour since before the December 1910 election (Knollys–HHA, 3 July 1911, Bodl. MS. Asquith 2, ff.233–4). HHA had written to Balfour on 20 July. But DLG had already told Balfour and Lansdowne at a meeting on 18 July, canvassing with them the government's intentions and expressing their reluctance to create peers. Knollys had informed Balfour on 19 July. A meeting of about 170 Conservative peers at Lansdowne House was told on 21 July ('Note of Conversation with Mr Lloyd George in Mr Balfour's room, July 18th, 1911', Balfour MSS, BL Add.MS. 49730, ff.243–5; Harold Nicolson, King George the Fifth: His Life and Reign, *Constable, 1952, p.152). Lansdowne had apparently told Knollys that 'a mere intimation if it were not in writing would not be of much use' (Knollys–Balfour, 20 July 1911, Bodl. Sandars MSS, MS.Eng.hist.c.763, f.109).*

The Duke of Devonshire, Lansdowne's son-in-law, had assessed the stance of those present at the shadow cabinet meeting at Lansdowne House on 21 July:

> L^d L read the letter & advised not pressing amendments. Considerable debate. St Aldwyn, Curzon, Harris [the former England cricket captain and Governor of Bombay], Galway & myself for moderation. Selborne, Salisbury, Halsbury, Somerset for extreme steps. Norfolk, Bedford moderate.
>
> Meeting at George Curzon's afterwards. Strong lot. Curzon, Midleton, Donoughmore, Clinton, Hindlip, Revelstoke, Churchill [Viscount Churchill, a distant cousin of WSC], Goschen, Dalhousie, Newton, Harris & self & one or two others. Sent circular to several to support Ld L. Cannot quite see how issue will work out.
>
> *(Victor Cavendish, 9th Duke of Devonshire diary, 21 July 1911, Devonshire MSS, DF7/1/17, courtesy of the 11th Duke of Devonshire, The Devonshire Collections, Chatsworth)*

Lack of clarity about the future reflected a lack of leadership. Balfour, enraged by Knollys's deception, was unclear about the strategy he preferred—limited resistance, sufficient to provoke the creation of 50 to 100 peers. As he told Lady Elcho on 23 July: 'I personally don't much care what they do, provided they do not compel the creation of a number so great as more or less permanently to destroy such power as the House still possesses' (Jane Ridley and Clayre Percy eds, The Letters of Arthur Balfour and Lady Elcho 1885–1917, *Hamish Hamilton, 1992, pp.262,266–7). Balfour's public and private equivocation left the field open for unconstrained wrangling between 'hedgers' and 'ditchers'.*

Halsbury, Selborne, Salisbury, Balcarres, Chamberlain, Smith, Carson, Lord Willoughby de Broke, Wyndham, and others were leaving no doubt of their intention to resist the government. In a formal division at the shadow cabinet they voted 'For Resistance' and, to Balfour's bitter dismay, ignored the convention of Cabinet solidarity and 'went out into the world proclaiming their differences' (J.S. Sandars, Note on Balfour's Resignation, Balfour MSS, BL Add.MS. 49767, ff.301–17, quoted by Jane Ridley, 'Leadership and Management in the Conservative Party in Parliament 1906–1914', D.Phil. thesis, U. of Oxford, 1985, pp.204–5). Lansdowne's position continued to baffle Balcarres, now Conservative Chief Whip in the Commons. Why, if his only fear was 'swamping', did Lansdowne not say so? (Balcarres diary, 24 July 1911, Vincent ed., The Crawford Papers, *p.199).*

The Duke of Norfolk wrote expressing his disappointment that Lansdowne seemed disposed to yield to the threat of the creation of peers. Lansdowne responded, explaining his position:

> I have never thought that we ought to yield to a mere threat on the part of H M's Govt, but in my view further resistance becomes useless, & worse, when once it is established beyond question that they have secured the King's full support, & that the Bill must therefore become law in its House of Commons shape. The Prime Minister's letter leaves no room for doubt upon these points.
>
> I told you that I should not be sorry to see a certain number of 'token' Peers created, so as to afford an absolute demonstration that we were not free agents but I do not think the supporters of H.M.G. will permit them to take this course, the disadvantages of which, from their point of view, are obvious.
>
> There is another considn which weighs with me: a dissolution is not within our reach, but I am also convinced that our party do not desire one & probably would not face one...
>
> *(Lansdowne–Norfolk, 23 July 1911, Norfolk MSS, Arundel Castle Archives; the version of this letter quoted in Kerry,* Lansdowne, *p.216, is a fair copy in the Lansdowne papers)*

Morocco. Grey explained the telegrams he had sent to France, & the line of his proposed message to the German ambassador this afternoon viz:—no threats but if France & Germany could not agree as to the terms upon which Germans should leave Agadir, that we should have to consider our position, as our interests were threatened by Germany remaining.

Grey had telegraphed the Ambassador in Paris, Sir Frank Bertie, on 19 July to ask for the French government's views on possible proposals regarding German demands in Morocco and the Belgian Congo to be made by Britain to Germany. Grey described the conversation with the Ambassador, Count Metternich, which followed this Cabinet in a letter to Goschen (BD VII, Grey–Bertie, 19 July 1911, no.397, p.376; Grey–Goschen, 21 July 1911, no.411, pp.390–1).

France to be told. The cause of France, in having all Morocco, was not one in itself wh. we could go to war about with them, although we insisted on being consulted à trois. It was thought these messages would give a fillip to the 2 powers coming to an agreement, & avoid our asking for a conference.

The state of the labour world was discussed & the increased cost of living & production, which was unsettling as wages had not risen. Buxton sanguine — Churchill anxious for future.

On 22 July WSC circulated a Home Office memorandum, 'The industrial situation'. Warning his colleagues that 'those conversant of labour matters in practice anticipate grave upheaval', he urged that the Prime Minister should hold a private meeting with 'the biggest employers of industry to ask their advice' or immediately appoint a committee of carefully chosen employers, union leaders, and Labour MPs to enquire into the causes of the present unrest and disturbances especially in the shipping and coal industries. The next day, George Askwith, Controller General of the Commercial, Labour, and Statistical Department of the Board of Trade, produced a detailed scheme for the creation of a Conciliation Commission. A Board of Trade Cabinet paper on 'The present unrest in the labour world', prepared by Askwith, was disseminated by Sydney Buxton on 25 July. It warned that the cheap press and better means of communication made workmen 'more inclined to act in masses, and more conscious of their numbers and strength' (TNA: CAB 37/107/70). The outcome of Askwith's recommendations was the establishment in October of an Industrial Council of thirteen representatives each of employers and labour, with Askwith himself as chairman. Relying on moral suasion, it proved ineffectual (Waley, A Liberal Life, *pp.211–17; Rosemary Aris,* Trade Unions and the Management of Industrial Conflict, *Macmillan, 1998, pp.75–86).*

Tuesday July 25[50] Cabinet at 5.30 H. of C. No allusion was made to the scene of the day before when Lord Hugh Cecil,[51] Goulding[52] Remnant[53] & 2 or 3 more 3d rate Tories howled down the Prime Minister.

The House of Commons was to consider the Lords' amendments to the Parliament Bill on 24 July. As HHA rose, there were shouts of 'Traitor' led by Lord Hugh Cecil and F.E. Smith; HHA could not be heard above the din. George Lloyd, MP for West Staffs, jumped up and was heard by JAP's PPS, Sir Godfrey Baring Bt, across the chamber to say: 'if I had a revolver I would shoot you…'. The young Liberal whip Dudley Ward, who had stroked the Cambridge crew when Lloyd had been cox, subdued Lloyd by calling imperiously: 'Sit down, George. You are making a fool of yourself.' (George W. Keeton, A Liberal Attorney-General: Being the Life of Lord Robson of Jesmond (1852–1918) with an account of the Office of Attorney-General, *James Nisbet & Co., 1949, p.194.) The Speaker adjourned the House in view of the 'grave disorder'. The Prime Minister's speech was printed in full in the following day's press. The House was again in uproar on 25 July when government backbenchers gave Cecil and Smith a taste of their own medicine. For the Unionist Chief Whip's attempt to dissuade the 30 or so Tory malcontents from their 'organised outcry' see Balcarres diary, 24 July 1911, Vincent ed.,* The Crawford Papers, *pp.198–9.*

He proceeded to tell us all he knew about the position. The King saw him on Sat. & also on Monday. He asked leave to see Lansdowne & Balfour, & the P.M. consented so long as it was a private & unofficial call. They had nothing to say but promised him they would do their best to induce the Tories to avoid the necessity for the creation. They were gloomy about their party prospects, the King thought. The King had hoped that the Lords would have had the Bill back

[50] There appears to be no copy in HHA's papers of the letter to the King for the Cabinet of 25 July 1911.

[51] Lord Hugh Cecil (1869–1956); Con. MP Oxford U. 1910–37 and Greenwich 1895–1906; asst p.s. to Sec. of St. for Foreign Affairs (his father, Lord Salisbury) 1891–2; PC 1918; Baron Quickswood 1941; Provost of Eton 1936–44; known as 'Linky', he was Churchill's best friend until the latter became a Liberal, and was best man at WSC's wedding.

[52] Edward Alfred 'Paddy' Goulding (1862–1936); Con. MP Worcester 1908–22, Wilts (Devizes) 1895–1906; barrister 1887; Chmn, Tariff Reform League Organisation Dept 1904–12; director, Rolls Royce 1912–21; chmn, Rolls Royce 1921–36; Bt 1915; PC 1918; Baron Wargrave 1922. An ardent imperialist and keen social reformer with a particular interest in old age pensions, shorter shop hours, and extending workmen's compensation to agricultural labourers.

[53] James Farquharson Remnant (1862–1933); Con. MP Finsbury (Holborn) 1900–28; barrister 1886; member for Holborn, LCC 1892–1900; Bt 1917; Baron Remnant 1928. Specially interested in metropolitan police welfare; backed Bonar Law for the Unionist leadership in Nov. 1911.

from the H. of C. before the question of creation arose. Asquith explained the bill might be thereby killed, & a new session should be avoided. The King saw the reason of this. We discussed for half an hour the possibilities — but deferred the question of numbers of peers to be created until we knew the Bill was not safe. Asquith thought Lansdowne could himself support the motion that the Lords' amendment be not insisted upon. Many members thought he could not vote against his own amendment to the Bill.

HHA's reading of Lansdowne's position was optimistic. In a circular to Unionist peers on 24 July Lansdowne had stated what had to be decided:

> whether, by desisting from further opposition, we shall render it possible for His Majesty's Government to carry the Bill in the House of Lords as at present constituted, or whether, by insisting on our amendments, we shall bring about a creation of Peers in numbers which may overwhelm the present House, and paralyse its action in the future without in any way retarding the passage of the Parliament Bill.

Lansdowne concluded that 'the former alternative is preferable in the interests of the House, the Unionist Party, and the Country' (Balfour of Burleigh MSS, 56, courtesy of Lord Balfour of Burleigh). Five days later he wrote to Arthur Balfour: 'I have told any number of people that I was not asking any one to vote with the Govt, & that I should not do so myself. And I have stalled off several attempts to involve me in a conspiracy to put a number of Peers in the Govt lobby.' Alfred Rothschild, the flamboyant younger brother of Lord Rothschild, had passed on the substance of a conversation in which HHA had told him that he would be glad if the Tory leadership would give an undertaking to help get some men to vote with the government and thus avoid the creation of peers. Lansdowne 'refused to give Alfred any encouragement'. He expected that some peers would have to be made; 'but it would not at all vex me if the Govt peers aided by a dozen bishops & perhaps as many lay Unionists were to outvote the ditchers whose strength is, I fancy, less than they would have us believe' (Lansdowne–Balfour, 29 July 1911, Bodl. Sandars MSS, MS.Eng.hist.763, ff.122–5). Lansdowne wrote the same day to Curzon saying that he hoped too many peers would not go so far as to vote for the Bill. 'There is an extraordinary amount of bitterness about, and we must not let it sink in too far.' (Curzon of Kedleston MSS, BL: A & AS, MSS.Eur.F.112 D/3/8.)

In a letter in The Times *on 28 July Lord Camperdown had declared that he would vote with the government. Responding in* The Times *four days later, Lansdowne proclaimed under prompting from Balfour that in no circumstances would he do that. He had already emphatically told his son-in-law, the Unionist Whip in the Lords, that 'no organisation shall be started to get Unionist peers to vote with the Govt' (Devonshire diary, 27 July 1911, Devonshire MSS, DF7/1/17).*

We agreed to amend the Speaker's tribunal & my original suggestion of Chairman of public a/cs comtee & the chairman of ways & means should be an advisory committee. We agreed not to amend Lansdowne's amendment even in regard to accepting the proposal to exempt the Protestant succession, as there was no likelihood of that being required (admitted by Lansdowne) & because the Lords by eliminating all in it except Home Rule might put us in a worse position.

Grey said he had nothing to report about Morocco, except that the French had made a substantial offer of territory in Congo. Cambon was strongly in favour of resisting Germans in Morocco as the French would not stand them there at any price. See papers relating to Grey's interviews with Metternich & Cambon.

The Cabinet had before it printed copies of Grey's descriptions of his interviews with Metternich in letters to Sir E. Goschen, dated 24 and 25 July, and of his interview with Cambon in a letter dated 25 July to L.D. Carnegie, chargé d'affaires *in Paris (Gooch and Temperley, BD VII, nos417,419,420, pp.394–401; HHA Cabinet letter, 26 July 1911 (re 25 July meeting), TNA: CAB 41/38/4). Grey does not appear to have reported his encouragement to the Chief Whip to provide* The Times *with information to show that the Cabinet was not divided and that the old Boer War divisions were no longer salient in Liberal Party ranks (Keith M. Wilson,* Empire and Continent: Studies in British Foreign Policy from the 1880s to the First World War, *Mansell Publishing, 1987, pp.46–7). HHA spoke in the House on 27 July on the gravity of the situation. He was followed by Balfour, who pledged support for the government, saying that anyone who thought that domestic differences presented an opportunity did not understand the temper of the British people.*

July 31 P.M's room. H. of C. 5.30. Absent Haldane. Grey reported progress of negociations bet. Fr. & Germany. Evidently strained as result of conversations on 28 & 29 & France willing to give up both Islands & adjust boundaries Congo & Cameroons, including port but not harbour. Germans not able to reduce their previous demands. We agreed that if negociations broke off we should ask Germans to consent to conference to discuss the breach of the Algeciras Act & what was required. Easier for French to give way to European arrangement than a German ultimatum. We expected Germans would continue conversations for some time. Morley & Loreburn asking what we could go to war for, & urging they would be no party to it in regard to Morocco. Most of us held our tongues. George attacked for his Mansion house speech; position defended by Grey & George, as calculated to avert war.

In his speech on 21 July DLG had warned that Britain would not stand by while matters affecting its interests were decided. His speech had been submitted for Grey's approval and was in line with the Cabinet's discussion of 21 July (see Keith Wilson, 'The Agadir Crisis, the Mansion House Speech, and the Double-Edgedness of Agreements', HJ, *vol.xv, no.3, 1972, pp.513–32, and more recent studies in Christopher Clark,* The Sleepwalkers: How Europe Went to War in 1914, *Allen Lane, 2012, pp.209–13).*

We then discussed Parl. situation & agreed that we should look to Monday 7th & 8th for Lords amendments to be considered in Commons & Lords respectively. That we should secure support if no creation made. Asquith put figures

Liberals	70.
Lib. Unionists	30. including Knollys & Bigge
	100

Tories loyal to Lansdowne 330 out of 400. Morley said 420 all Lords could muster — that 90 would be total of Halsbury Selborne & backwoodsmen. Privately Forster H.W. told me we could not yet be told their strength, as they did not yet know — but the Tory party were anxious not to have to support us. I repeated conversation to Morley & P.M. Granard at night told me Heneage[54] said he could rely on 80 Liberal Unionist peers to outvote Selborne in the Division lobby. I wrote this to Morley & Asquith & told them I asked Granard to get Heneage to put it on paper.

JAP added later: 'This proved an error. Heneage wrote he would support us but looked to Liberal vote of 80!' Granard had said that Heneage and other Liberal Unionists would support the government because they 'hated Selborne & Halsbury & Austen trying to kick out Balfour & Lansdowne' (JAP–EP, 1 Aug. 1911, MS. Gainford 189/102–3). HHA was wrong to include Knollys and Bigge in the government column; they did not vote. 'Halsbury, Salisbury, Selborne and others, whose numbers multiply daily—they were thirty last week and are ninety now—by "fighting to the end" mean that they will insist on Lansdowne's amendment, whatever may happen, until they are beaten by an adverse vote in the House of Lords' (George Wyndham, circular, n.d. Wyndham MSS). Perhaps unbeknown to JAP, HHA was floating

[54] Edward Heneage, 1st Baron Heneage (1840–1922); Lib. MP Lincoln 1865–8, Lib. MP Grimsby 1880–6, Lib. Unionist 1886–92, 1893–6; Chanr, Duchy of Lancr Feb.–Apr. 1886; Baron Heneage 1896. Hainton Hall, 14 miles NE of Lincoln, was the family seat for 600 years. For Heneage's activities after the 1886 Liberal split see Ian Cawood, *The Liberal Unionist Party: A History*, I.B. Tauris, 2012, *passim*.

compromise proposals to the divided Opposition leaders. He sent Crewe to sound out Lord Cromer, who was seeking to corral Unionist peers who could be persuaded not to join the Diehards.

On 2 August Cromer reported to Lansdowne and to Curzon, the most senior of the peers urging that the Parliament Bill be passed when it returned from the Commons with Lords' amendments removed. Crewe had shown Cromer a draft of a proposal that was 'liable to modification, there being manifestly much difference of opinion in the Cabinet':

> Briefly it amounts to this—if we guarantee X peers there will be no new creations. What is X? I cannot at present say, but I think I shall get 50 which is to include any bishops I can mop up—of the three normal Radicals—Birmingham, Hereford, and Chester.
>
> But what is more important is this—he said that it was an entire delusion to suppose that in any case a small number of peers would be made . . . I asked how many. He replied 'about 300'—and yet Lansdowne tells me, Selborne is going about pledging his word of honour that in [any] case the numbers of creations will be small.
>
> *(Curzon of Kedleston MSS, BL: A & AS, MSS.Eur.F.112 D/3/8)*

Balfour's consigliere Jack Sandars told Lansdowne that the government was bluffing. After their 'purely informal conversation', Cromer sought definite assurances from Crewe on 2 August that he could take to a meeting at the house of his father-in-law, the Marquess of Bath, in two days time:

> how many Unionist peers would be required to vote with the Government against insisting on the Unionist amendments, in order to obviate any fresh creations of peers?
>
> . . . can you give me a distinct assurance that if the number which you will name in answer to my first question vote with the Government, no peers will be created?
>
> . . . can you tell me how many peers will be created?
>
> *(Peter Fraser,* Lord Esher: A Political Biography, *Hart-Davis, MacGibbon, 1973, p.224; Peter Fraser, 'The Unionist Debacle of 1911 and Balfour's retirement',* JMH, *vol.35, no.4, 1963, p.359; Cromer–Crewe, 2 Aug. 1911, copy, Galway MSS, Ga C 9/42, Nottingham U. Bath's 'studious moderation' was conveyed in detail on 20 July to the Clerk of the Privy Council [*FitzRoy, Memoirs, *Vol. II, pp.454–5])*

Crewe met Cromer on the afternoon of 3 August and emphasised that the government did not propose to send any formal answer to the questions posed. 'There is nothing therefore in the nature of a bargain between the Government and any section of Unionist peers,' Cromer noted. There were two things that Lord Crewe was 'willing to inform Lord Cromer':

> the Government will return the bill to the Lords after they have considered the amendments, without advising the creation of any peers.
>
> ...in the event of any motion to insist on a Lords' Amendment being carried against the Government, the Government will be compelled forthwith to advise a creation of Peers sufficient definitely to safeguard the Bill against any opposition it could possibly encounter in the House of Lords.

Cromer sent this information to Crewe's cousin, Lord Galway, and told Curzon that Crewe had read over the notes several times and 'concurred in their correctness'. In light of the information that the government had given up the proposal to advise the immediate creation of peers, Cromer and St Aldwyn had decided that they should abstain from voting. This would avoid a great deal of friction in the Unionist Party and remove any excuse for the 'Norfolk section' to go over to the 'ditchers'. In what appears to have been a calculatedly vague understatement, Crewe 'admitted' that the number of peers to be created if the amendments were lost 'was between 300 and 400' (Cromer–Curzon, 3 Aug. 1911, Curzon of Kedleston MSS, BL: A & AS, MSS.Eur.F.112 D/3/8).

A list of 249 'men of Liberal conviction' whom HHA 'proposed to ennoble should the need arise', found in the Asquith papers, was published in J.A. Spender and Cyril Asquith, Life of Herbert Henry Asquith, Lord Oxford and Asquith, *2 vols, Hutchinson, 1932, Vol. I, pp.329–31, and again in Jenkins,* Asquith, *pp.539–42. Members of the government were under the impression that there was a much larger number. Harold Spender, who was close to many sources of Westminster gossip, wrote in 1915: 'Some four hundred British families trembled on the brink of ennoblement'* (Herbert Henry Asquith, *G. Newnes, [1915], p.128). At Doxford over the weekend 25–8 August Alfred Emmott picked up from Runciman and Grey*

> enough to make me think that the Whips had an excellent list of 500 men suitable in the circumstances to be made Peers; but I do not believe that a great majority of these had been asked or consented. E.g. Ed. Grey was asked to sound a certain individual. He did not speak to him because (1) he thought that he could make a much more effective appeal if & when the necessity arose & (2) he found it so difficult to say 'Will you be a Peer if necessary & not a Peer if unnecessary'.
>
> *(Emmott diary, 1 Sept. 1911, MS. Emmott, I/2, Nuffield Col.)*

Aug. 3 Cabinet. 2 hours discussion on situation. P.M's voice had quite gone. We discussed business for last half hour & adjournment to Nov. — & autumn session arranged. Morley gave us his figures, which I estimated would with 10 independents & 3 Bps give us 96 out, 'diehards' 68, & we agreed to risk situation.

Every word HHA said 'had to be interpreted by Harcourt who sat next to him, as though the P.M. could only speak some guttural language and Harcourt was the only man who knew it and English as well'. HHA did not look ill. But Crewe, thin and sallow, did not seem to have recovered from his breakdown. DLG, turning grey, was 'as tireless as ever' (Samuel–Gladstone, 15 Sept. 1911, Gladstone MSS, BL Add.MS. 45992, f.259).

Edwin Montagu, Morley's Parliamentary Under-Secretary at the India Office, told Venetia Stanley on 5 August: 'Lord Morley has a list of 76 supporters and there will be four or five others' (Montagu MSS, II B1/17, Wren Lib. TCC). JAP's calculations do not concur with Walter Runciman's contemporary note of estimated Liberal support: '4 King's men, 46 certain, 7 Cabs, 1 Under, 2 Whips 3 Bps certainly', total 59 [sic]; '5 Bps possibly, 20 Likely Libs', total 84; '? Cromer, St Aldwyn & Co.'. Runciman added: 'The Prime Minister was so hoarse today that we could not hear what he said. He whispered to Harcourt who repeated what had been said like an interpreter' (Runciman's Cabinet note, 3 Aug. 1911, Runciman of Doxford MSS). As the matters discussed at this meeting were exclusively related to political intelligence and tactics, it is not surprising that no report to the King seems to have been made.

The uncertainty in the government camp was understandable given that the balance of the fragmented forces in the Opposition was shifting hour by hour. And the ditchers, alarmed by the possibility of more defectors like Camperdown, were encouraging reports that underestimated their strength (Miles Stephen Campisano, 'The Unionists and the Constitution, 1906–1911', B.Litt. essay, Nuffield Col., Oxford, 1977, p.145). HHA was relying on Elibank to communicate to the Unionist leadership through the Opposition Chief Whip, Lord Balcarres. Balcarres, whose diary and contemporary notes are an invaluable record of events as they were seen and understood within Balfour's entourage in the Commons, had concluded on 31 July that 'it seems to become a contest between Selborne and Curzon'. Overconfident about his own sources of intelligence, Balcarres mistakenly believed that Crewe, 'though Leader of the Lords is probably not kept completely informed'.

In fact, recognising Lord Cromer's pivotal position with those Unionists whose goal was to avoid the creation of an army of new peers, Crewe was tasked by HHA to convey to him the government's intentions. Cromer was at the heart of what came to be called the 'Judas group', whose other prime movers were thought to be Lords St Aldwyn and Heneage, and included Lords Cobham, Lichfield, Blythswood, Galway, and Lytton (Corinne Comstock Weston and Patricia Kelvin, 'The "Judas Group" and the Parliament Bill of 1911', EHR, *vol.99, no.392, 1984, pp.551–63). As the correspondence of Cromer, Galway, Curzon, and others shows, the Judas Group's shared concern to avoid a catastrophic creation of peers was beset by serious divisions over tactics and changes of heart, notably the surprise abstention of St Aldwyn, upon whom Cromer had relied to give a lead (Cromer–Edmund Gosse, 12 Aug. 1911, Gosse MSS, MS. 19c Gosse D, Brotherton Coll., Leeds U.).*

On 4 August Cromer sent copies of his correspondence and notes of his meeting with Crewe to Galway with this warning: 'The Halsbury group and others are under a profound delusion ... so far as the advice that the government would tender to the King is concerned, there never was any question of creating a small number of peers; it was either none or such a number as would absolutely swamp the House of Lords, some 300 or perhaps more.' Cromer sent a similar message on 5 August to Lord Ridley, Chairman of the Tariff Reform League, who had been denying rumours that he intended to vote for the Parliament Bill (Ridley MSS, ZRI/97/25/109, Northumberland Archives). At the meeting at Lord Bath's house on 4 August it had been unanimously concluded that no attempt ought to be made to organise a Unionist vote in favour of the government. 'Individual peers must, of course, exercise their discretion, though personally I hope few of them will vote with the Government, as if they do so it will give an excuse for the Norfolk group to secede from their pledges given to Lansdowne and vote with the "no-surrender" men. The situation has been enormously eased by the abandonment of the idea to make peers immediately.' (Galway MSS, Ga C 9/41–3, Nottingham U.) Nevertheless, Balcarres reportedly threatened the Bishop of London that 'if the Bishops voted for the Parliament Bill they need not expect Conservative support on Disestablishment question' (Sanders diary, 5 Aug. 1911, Ramsden ed., Real Old Tory Politics, *p.32).*

By 4 August Cromer could tell Curzon: 'if there is a vestige of commonsense left amongst the "ditchers" and the Norfolk group we ought to get out of the creation altogether ...'. Yet it remained a worry that even Lansdowne still seemed to think that only a small number of peers would be created. In fact, as he had told Galway, Cromer was certain that the alternatives were no peers at all or 'such a large number as absolutely to swamp the House of Lords'. Crewe had pointed out that the government was making a large concession for which it would be much criticised by its own party. Cromer had naturally responded that the Liberals stood to get out of serious difficulty with the King, who might have been pressed to make 300 peers

> and must infallibly have yielded ... Reading between the lines, I have very little doubt that the very hazardous statements made by Selborne, Salisbury and others is that they have been listening to Court gossip and know that the King is very reluctant to make peers. That, however, would be a very weak reed on which to lean.
>
> *(Cromer–Curzon, 4 Aug. 1911, Curzon of Kedleston MSS, BL: A & AS, MSS.Eur.F.112, D/3/8)*

Lansdowne wrote to Balfour's aide, Jack Sandars, on 6 August of the 'St Aldwyn Peers': 'a few men whom Cromer calls the "uncontrollables" (of the Galway type) will no doubt go into the Government lobby...'. Two days earlier he had told Norfolk that it would be 'deplorable if a large number of Peers, who had deliberately decided that abstention was the proper policy, were to be driven off their course owing to the action of half-a-dozen men whom Cromer aptly describes as uncontrollable' (Bodl. Sandars MSS, MS.Eng.hist.c.763, f.161; Lansdowne–Norfolk, 4 Aug. 1911, quoted in B.H. Holland, typescript biography of 15th Duke of Norfolk, Norfolk MSS, Arundel Castle Archives). In the end Cromer was prevented by gout from coming to the House to speak, but he let it be known that to prevent the creation of hereditary peers he would have voted for the bill, entrusting Heneage with explaining his position in the debate (Cromer–E. Gosse, 12 Aug. 1911, Gosse MSS, MS. 19c Gosse D, Brotherton Coll., Leeds U.; Roger Owen, Lord Cromer: Victorian Imperialist, Edwardian Proconsul, *Oxford UP, 2004, p.373). David Gilmour's* Curzon, *John Murray, 1994, overlooks Cromer's important role in concert with Curzon. But Cromer's concurrent organising role with Curzon in the anti-suffragist campaign is narrated in Brian Harrison,* Separate Spheres: The Opposition to Women's Suffrage in Britain, *Croom Helm, 1978, pp.126–46.*

The Lords amendments were briefly referred to — cabinet counsel comtee day before had gone through them.

Grey reported position re Morocco & that Cambon had reported France was ready to make concessions to let Germans have access on to Congo, & French onto Niger.

With King's leave & wish we decided to announce the Nov 15. communication to House on Monday.[55]

Aug. 7 Great speech from P.M. in reply to vote of censure. Opposition made little case against us, & his statement of facts convincing & unanswerable. Tories depressed at result.

HHA's was not the only lauded speech. Arnold Rowntree, the Quaker businessman and Liberal MP for York, left the chamber enthusing to his wife about the 'brilliant satirical reply'

[55] The King had been told on 15 Nov. 1910 that ministers 'cannot take the responsibility for advising a dissolution unless they may understand that in the event of the policy of the Government being approved by an adequate majority in the new House of Commons his Majesty will be ready to exercise his Constitutional powers, which may involve the prerogative of creating Peers, if needed... His Majesty will doubtless agree that it would be inadvisable in the interests of the State that any communication of the intentions of the Crown should be made public unless and until the actual occasion should arise' (Nicolson, *King George the Fifth*, p.136). B.S. Markesinis has a good discussion of the precedents in *The Theory and Practice of Dissolution of Parliament: A comparative study with special reference to the United Kingdom and Greek Experience*, Cambridge UP, 1992, pp.54–105.

to F.E. Smith, Lord Robert Cecil, and other Tories by Ellis Griffith, the U.-Sec. for Home Affairs and leader of the Welsh Parliamentary Party: 'Balfour was hesitating and feeble and F.E. foolish when dealing with the Lords, clever when criticising Irish policy, but HHA's reply to Balfour was admirable and to my thinking complete...'. DLG and Walter Runciman were in unison with Rowntree's praise for HHA and Griffith (Ian Packer ed., The Letters of Arnold Stephenson Rowntree to Mary Katherine Rowntree 1910–1918, *Camden Fifth Series, Vol. 20, Cambridge UP, 2002, p.60; DLG–Margaret Lloyd George, 7 Aug. 1911,* Lloyd George Family Letters, *p.157; Runciman–Hilda Runciman, 7 Aug. 1911, Viscountess Runciman of Doxford MSS).*

On 9 August Morley moved that the Lords consider the Commons' reasons for disagreeing with the Lords' amendments that would have excluded from the Bill's ambit legislation to create national parliaments for Ireland, Scotland, Wales, or England and also excluded any legislation deemed by a Joint Committee to be of great gravity and on which the judgement of the people had not been sufficiently ascertained. The plain purpose of the amendments was to block Home Rule and to require a referendum on measures to which an overwhelming majority of peers were opposed. Parliamentary procedure entailed that a bill was automatically lost if either of the Houses inserted an amendment for the second time after it had been rejected by the other chamber.

The following day Morley stated that if the Bill were defeated that night the King had agreed to assent to the creation of as many peers as would be necessary to ensure that it would not be defeated again. This was now no secret, but its solemn iteration left no doubt that the moment of decision had arrived. Lords Rosebery and Curzon, in whose house the 'forces which ultimately enabled Lord Lansdowne to prevail' had met every day for a fortnight, urged that the peers should desist from their course of rejection. Curzon recalled when assembling a file years afterwards that the 'more active spirits' in his group were the Duke of Devonshire and Lords Midleton, Dunmore, and Hindlip (Curzon of Kedleston MSS, BL: A & AS, MSS.Eur.F.112 D/3/8). Lords Halsbury and Milner remained immovably opposed to the government.

*Corinne Comstock Weston's instinct that Selborne, not the ancient Halsbury, was the real leader of the Diehards was well founded. Comstock Weston (*The House of Lords, *pp.176–202) tells the history of the rift between Curzon and Selborne. For Selborne's report to his wife on 9 August of Balcarres doing all that he could 'to defeat the blacklegs & to get abstainers to leave Lansdowne to help us, but Lansdowne and Curzon won't give him the least assistance', see George Boyce ed.,* The Crisis of British Unionism: Lord Selborne's Domestic Political Papers, 1885–1922, *The Historians' P., 1987, p.62. The result was in doubt till the end.*

Aug. 10 Passage of Parliament [Bill] through the Lords, without the creation of Peers—a memorable scene at night when Bill carried without the Lansdowne amendment by 131–114. George Wyndham bet me on steps of the throne £4 to £5, the die hards would win. Churchill laid £50 to £40. We did not credit their strength above 100, & we thought we should get over so many of the Bishops, Cadogan,[56] & other Unionists were unexpected adherents!

Devonshire, who 'said a few words' in the debate, felt: 'General impression was that the Ditchers would win. Tremendous excitement & some rather foolish speeches... Much bigger division than I expected' (Diary, 10 Aug. 1911, Devonshire MSS). On the other side, Wyndham, who had been working closely with Lords Willoughby de Broke and Milner, was actually losing confidence that day. He was expecting ten bishops and 21 Unionist 'RATS' to vote with the government. This, he told his wife, Sibell, Countess Grosvenor, would produce a dead heat. If Norfolk spoke and voted, he might carry 'a few' with him. But Curzon and Midleton were working so passionately for the government they might 'detach more abstainers and turn them into RATS'.

Summarising the arithmetic, Wyndham concluded 'if Norfolk carries three with him and frightens three into the Government lobby we shall win by 1. If he frightens five we shall be beat by 1' (Max Egremont, The Cousins: The friendship, opinions and activities of Wilfrid Scawen Blunt and George Wyndham, *Collins, 1977, pp.277–8). Haldane, alluding in passing to having '30,000 men under arms', wrote to his friend Edmund Gosse on 11 August that 'until the division was two thirds over I was very doubtful of the outcome' (Gosse MSS, MS. 19c Gosse D, Brotherton Coll., U. of Leeds). The same day Wyndham invoked the Old Testament for his wife: 'Well—we are beaten. But I call the 114 Peers who voted like Gentlemen the "Beaten" Gold' (Wyndham MSS). The 112 peers and two bishops who voted against the Parliament Bill are conveniently listed and characterised in Gregory D. Phillips, 'The "Diehards" and the Myth of the "Backwoodsmen"', JBS, vol.XVI, no.2, 1977, pp.106–20.*

The Prime Minister called cabinet on 9th & 10th but postponed them.

The postponement of Cabinet meetings was a relief for ministers, who were undergoing a summer of extreme heat—London's temperature on 9 August was a record 97°F in the shade. HHA himself had slipped away to the village of Ewell in Surrey, and thence to Bad Gastein. Over the week since the Cabinet had decided to 'risk the situation' by proceeding with the

[56] George Henry Cadogan, 5th Earl Cadogan (1840–1915); Vt Chelsea 1874–3; Con. MP Bath 1973; U.-Sec. of St. War 1875–8; U.-Sec. of St. Colonies 1878–80; Ld Privy Seal 1886–92; Ld Lt Ireland (with a Cabinet seat) 1895–1902; KG 1891; friend of Edward VII and adviser to Queen Victoria. In 1880 he owned about 800 acres in London, much of it in Chelsea, where he was lord of the manor, first Mayor, and builder of working-class housing.

Parliament Bill without creating peers, the lobbying and counting of pledges had been unremitting. Officials responsible for putting into effect the creation of peers could not assume that the government would win. When the newly ennobled Vt Elibank (the Chief Whip's father) took his seat in the Lords on 1 August, Harcourt and HHA had been noticed timing the proceedings with 'great nicety'. Sir Courtenay Ilbert set to work to calculate the time it would take to introduce the expected new peers (the Master of Elibank later showed him the box allegedly containing a list of 550 names): 'at least ten minutes must be allowed for each peer. Six peers an hour, how many sittings of (say) 5 hours each would be required!' (Balcarres diary, 2 Aug. 1911, Vincent ed., The Crawford Papers, *p.209; Ilbert–Bryce, 15 Aug. 1911 [addition to letter begun on 12 Aug.], Bodl. MS. Bryce 14, ff.32–5).*

Until the last moment, according to Harcourt, the Cabinet had believed there were likely to be 109 Halsburyites; and they had 'no intimation' of the support of the 37 Unionist peers who voted with them (Guy Desvaux de Marigny, 'The Public Career Of Lewis Harcourt (first Viscount) 1905–1916', MA thesis, U. of the Witwatersrand, Johannesburg, 1987, p.228). George Wyndham with Willoughby de Broke believed there were 115 promises of resistance. But Wyndham hoped for a late rally from undeclared independent peers. In the event, the majority of peers abstained. According to Wyndham, 37 Unionist peers voted with the government, plus both Archbishops and eleven bishops (Wyndham–Lady S. Wyndham, 10 Aug. 1911, J.W. Mackail and Guy Wyndham eds, Life and Letters of George Wyndham, *2 vols, Hutchinson [1925], Vol. II, p.699; Wyndham–Wilfrid Ward, 13 Aug. 1911, Guy Wyndham comp.,* Letters of George Wyndham, *2 vols, T. & A. Constable, Edinburgh, 1915, Vol. II, p.471). 'I was disgusted at the number of so-called Unionists who voted with the Gov[t]', Lord Portsmouth wrote, foreshadowing a struggle of the 'stalwarts' with Central Office for control of the party organisations (Portsmouth diary, 10–11 Aug. 1911, 6th Earl of Portsmouth MSS, 15 M84/5/9/1, Hants ALS). When the dust had settled, Wyndham explained to Wilfrid Scawen Blunt that he 'did not count on so many traitors being found to vote their own destruction...' (Blunt diary, 22 Aug. 1911,* My Diary, *p.775).*

Jack Sandars listed 29 Unionist peers who had voted in the government lobby ('A Diary of the Events and Transactions in connection with the passage of the Parliament Bill of 1911 through the House of Lords' [12 Aug. 1911], Bodl. Sandars MSS, MS.Eng.hist.763, f.214). On 11 August he had advised Balfour: 'Feeling runs very high against the 35 [sic]... Only one dared to show his nose in the Carlton after the division and he... had to leave shortly' (Alan Sykes, Tariff Reform in British Politics 1903–1913, *Clarendon P., Oxford, 1979, p.245).*

For Austen Chamberlain's private denial that he, Selborne, and others who urged resistance were 'actuated by the desire & have the intention of creating a revolt against the leadership of Balfour & Lansdowne' see Chamberlain–H.A. Gwynne, 25 July 1911, Gwynne MSS, courtesy of Vice Admiral Sir Ian Hogg, Documents 6465, IWM). And, for the belief that this was precisely what Chamberlain and F.E. Smith, 'an unscrupulous advocate on the make', were seeking, see J.St.Loe Strachey–Curzon, 1 Aug. 1911 (Curzon of Kedleston MSS, BL: A & AS, MSS.Eur.F.112 D/3/8). Comprehensive background is provided in David Dutton, 'His Majesty's Loyal Opposition': The Unionist Party in Opposition 1905–1915, *Liverpool UP, 1992, and Gregory D. Phillips,* The Diehards: Aristocratic Society and Politics in Edwardian England, *Harvard UP, Cambridge, MA, 1979, pp.128–40. Jason Tomes's thematic essay at http://www.oxforddnb.com/view/theme/95282, accessed 1 July 2014 (*ODNB*) is a brief discussion and listing of some Diehards. Still valuable is Ronan Fanning, '"Rats" versus "ditchers": the die-hard revolt and the Parliament Bill of 1911', in Art Cosgrove and J.I. Maguire eds,* Parliament & Community, Historical Studies, XIV, *Appletree P., Belfast, 1981, pp.191–210. Ben Sayle reassesses the ditchers in '"Populist Constitutionalism" and the Unionist Party during the 1911 House of Lords' Crisis',* Parly Hist., *vol.40, pt 3, 2021, pp.521–42.*

JAP and several of his colleagues celebrated their victory with supper at the Automobile Club lasting until 1.00 a.m. (JAP–Elsie Pease, 11 Aug. 1911, MS. Gainford 188/104). Two days later Margot Asquith reached out to her old friend George Curzon, telling him that 'Henry was so absolutely free from fear that he even went away & wired daily to know how the children & I were, adding "there won't be one peer made"' (Curzon of Kedleston MSS, BL: A & AS, MSS.Eur.F.112 D/3/8). Very soon a seething Marquess of Salisbury was telling Lord Robert Cecil of intelligence from F.E. Smith, via the junior whip Lord Edmund Talbot:[57]

> after one division, F. E. asked Lloyd George in a friendly way, what in fact the Govt would have done if we had beaten them. Lloyd George replied that they would have gone to Lansdowne and asked what his friends would do, then upon his answer (which he had no doubt would have been given) that most of his friends would continue to abstain the Govt would have asked the King for 150 peers but that he did not think they would have got more than 100...
>
> ...There was to be no swamping. Bluff backed by our Front Bench (unknowingly no doubt by Lansdowne) and put into the King's mouth, and the King was made to tell a lie.
>
> *(Salisbury–Cecil, 22 Aug.1911, Cecil of Chelwood MSS, CHE 52/46–7, Hatfield House Library and Archives)*

[57] Lord Edmund Bernard Talbot (1855–1947); Con. MP Sussex (Chichester) 1894–1921; 3rd son of 14th Duke of Norfolk; assumed name of Talbot in place of Fitzalan-Howard 1876; resumed latter name 1921; soldier; p.s. to Sec. of St. War 1896–8 and to U.-Sec. of St. Foreign Affairs 1898–9; asst sec. to St John Brodrick 1900–5; Junior Ld of Treasury 1905; Unionist Ch. Whip 1913–21; Joint Parl. Sec. Treasury 1915–21; Dep. Earl Marshal of England 1917–29; PC 1918; Ld Lt, Ireland 1921–2; Vt FitzAlan of Derwent 1921; his family were the leading lay Roman Catholics in England.

After the division, many of the Diehards, from both Houses, repaired to the 1900 Club in Pickering Place, St James's Street. The recently elected Basil Peto, who had been closely involved with Salisbury and Willoughby de Broke, was among the throng: 'The club was far too crowded for everyone to bother about seats. F.E. Smith was standing, with his back to the wall, close to the fireplace in the principal room and there was a general shout to him for a speech... he made a most wonderful impromptu speech... I never heard him better' ('Recollections and Reflections 1862–1941', typescript memoirs, Peto MSS, courtesy of Jonathan Peto). For the opening of an additional room at the club earlier in the year and a list of 31 members who had recently visited it see an unidentified press cutting, 9 Apr. 1911, Queenborough MSS 14, courtesy of the 7th Marquess of Anglesey.

August 11th The P.M. had lost his voice again after his great speech on the 7th—but was audible at the cabinet held this day at 12.0 in Downing St. He had called that morning on the King, who was much relieved, & attributed the victory to Rosebery's lead & influence.

During the debate on the Bill Rosebery had said that he was against it but would abstain from voting. On 10 August he entered a ten-point protest against the Bill in the House of Lords' Journal, then dramatically announced that he would vote for it. After the vote he never entered the Lords again (Robert Rhodes James, Rosebery: A Biography of Archibald Philip, Fifth Earl of Rosebery, *Weidenfeld and Nicolson, 1963, pp.465–70). JAP wrote to Elsie on 11 August that the 114 Diehards were 30 or 40 more than the press had calculated: 'Rosebery's action brought about 20 Unionists over. Men... who weren't going to allow their rebels to force the creation of 400 peers' (MS. Gainford 188/104). JAP would not have known that a promise from Rosebery to 'render the King any service in his power' had been called in, or that Rosebery had to be 'unearthed' in his club by Walter Long and carried off to the Lords to fulfil his pledge (Esher journal, 14 Oct. 1911, James Lees-Milne,* The Enigmatic Edwardian: The Life of Reginald, 2nd Viscount Esher, *Sidgwick & Jackson, 1986, pp.232–3).*

Lord Stamfordham wrote of the King to the Prime Minister's private secretary, Vaughan Nash, on 11 August: 'He has gone off happy.' (Michael Bentley, 'Power and authority in the late Victorian and Edwardian court', in Andrzej Olechnowicz ed., The Monarchy and the British Nation, *p.186.) The King may have been happy, but the Opposition leadership now had a new worry, as Jack Sandars explained for Lord Northcliffe. Even if the government did not have to create peers to pass the Parliament Bill, they would create a large batch of peers, possibly up to 50, about Christmas or the New Year, thus not disappointing those whose hopes had been excited over the summer. The incidental benefit for the Liberals would be that they would 'fill up their Exchequer' (J.L. Sandars–Northcliffe, 31 Aug. 1911, Northcliffe MSS,*

BL Add.MS. 62153, ff.123–4). No large batch was created. A relieved Herbert Samuel told an erstwhile front-bench colleague of the risk that 'no small proportion of our gallant three or four hundred would have regarded it as the task of their lives to prove to their wives and families that they were not *party hacks after all' (Samuel–Gladstone, 15 Sept. 1911, Gladstone MSS, BL Add.MS. 45992, f.263). By the time the next normal list of peers was being created, Charles Lyell told his father: 'I don't think I need to say to you that I think it would be a mistake to pay anything more than a modest sum to A[lick]. M[urray]. for the position!' (n.d. [1911], Lyell MSS, courtesy of the late Lady Lyell, Kinnordy House).*

Morley explained that the message he read out from the King on the Thursday afternoon, were words he himself put down, & submitted them for King's approval to Bigge the same morning. Morley described Milner's speech as 'silly & bad'. Churchill reported Lord Galway[58] had been hissed out of the Carlton the previous evening for his vote! Botha[59] told Harcourt, that Lyttelton[60] had approached him to try & heal the deep & bitter feeling which had arisen in the Unionist party & asked him to see Selborne! Botha of course declined to be mixed up in these internecine quarrels.

Asquith reported the King was much perturbed at the extension to which the strike moving was extending — London docks & food for London especially. We agreed we must protect food supplies coming in, so as to prevent starvation. Churchill had 20,000 police Haldane 50,000 troops — convoys of provisions when landed should be taken to distributing areas. Horses & forage were to be also protected.

There were more strikes in 1911, especially in July–August, than in any year since 1889. A successful seamen's strike in several ports in June encouraged the various waterside workers' unions to demand recognition, increased pay, and improved conditions. A joint conference of London employers and union officials, chaired by Lord Devonport of the Port of London

[58] George Edmund Milnes Monckton-Arundell, Vt Galway (1844–1931); 7th Vt (an Irish peerage) 1876; Con. MP Notts (N) 1872–85; ADC to Queen Victoria 1897–1901, to King Edward VII 1901–10, and to George V 1910–20; Baron Monckton (in UK peerage) 1887; a great huntsman, he was MFH, Vt Galway's hunt 1876–1907. Galway had not been deterred by advice that his son's prospects of Central Office support for parliamentary candidature would be injured if he voted with the government (Balcarres diary, 9 Aug. 1911, Vincent ed., *The Crawford Papers*, p.215).

[59] Botha, Prime Minister of South Africa, was in London for the Imperial Conference and King George's coronation; he sailed for South Africa on 12 Aug.

[60] Hon. Alfred Lyttelton (1857–1913); Lib. U. MP St George's Hanover Sq. 1906–13, Warwick and Leamington 1895–1905; barrister 1881; Sec. of St. for Colonial Affairs 1903–5; PC 1903; a nephew of W.E. Gladstone by marriage, his first wife Laura Tennant (d. 1886) was Margot Asquith's favourite sister. On his second marriage to Edith Sophy Balfour he acquired Arthur and Gerald Balfour as brothers-in-law. A great sportsman, his wicket-keeping and batting were described by W.G. Grace as 'the champagne of cricket' (*DNB* 1912–21).

Authority (PLA), led to the Devonport Agreement on 27 July. However the union officials had misjudged the mood of their members: the agreement was rejected and a strike began on 3 August. Sir Arthur Rollit (steamship owner, ex-MP, commercial and civic leader), called in to arbitrate, awarded the men some of their pay demands, but the strike continued and was extended. Meetings at the Board of Trade under George Askwith were held 8–11 August, when an agreement was reached at midnight.

Sydney Buxton had meanwhile circulated on 9 August a memorandum on 'Conciliation and the Board of Trade' outlining ideas for new machinery for preventing or settling disputes (Bodl. MS. Asquith 14, ff.41–6). Most of the men returned to work on 14 August, but there was more disruption when the PLA refused to take back some 3,000 men. Sixteen years later Harry Gosling, President of the National Transport Workers' Federation, remembered being asked to see WSC at the Home Office. 'Closing the door by which I had entered, Winston crossed to another in the far corner, opened it, looked out, shut it, and walked to the opposite corner where he did the same again.' Inviting Gosling to sit at his desk, he asked, in a low voice: 'Tell me, is there any German gold in this?' (Harry Gosling, Up and Down Stream, *Methuen, 1927, p.152; for Sir Guy Granet as the source of German gold stories see Paul Addison, 'Winston Churchill and the Working Class, 1900–14', in Jay Winter ed.,* The Working Class in Modern British History: Essays in Honour of Henry Pelling, *Cambridge UP, 1983, p.61).*

Grey reported progress N. Sea fisheries & difficulties in arranging with Russia the Limit—conference agreed to with possibility of arbitration later on if necessary so as to avoid 12 miles international agreement. English Channel no protection if this secured—we were ready to see some extension from the 3 mile limit.

Wed. Aug. 16 In reference to the strikes McKenna asked whether he was to land naval men if called upon. Asquith said yes, there is no difference between the 2 services in respect to rendering assistance to the civil power. Philipson[61] had reported as sec. to dock authorities that he could not arrange matters with the few hundred men still outside St Katherine's Gate — upon wh. the settlement of the dispute really depended.

Burns & Runciman thought the trouble was all due to the secret methods of Laws,[62] who had been bested by other ship owners & was creating trouble by bringing in free labour to unload the *Highland Laddie*, & the *Lady Jocelyn* (contain-

[61] Robert Philipson (1860–1916); gen. mgr, Port of London Authority 1909–13; sometime asst sec., Tyne Improvement Commission; Sec., Thames Conservancy 1900–9.

[62] Cuthbert Laws (?1864–1933); succ. father as gen. mgr, Shipping Federation 1901–33; Sec., 1890–1901; renowned as strike-breaker and orator with 'a genius for organisation' (L.H. Powell, *The Shipping Federation: A History of the First Sixty Years, 1890–1950*, Commercial Print and Stationery Co., 1950).

ing provisions) on Thursday & had asked for police protection. Churchill anxious to send for 10,000 troops from Aldershot to support free labour. Cabinet opposed to this and in favour of stopping the ships from unloading at a moment when such action would promote conflagration. Grey wisely said, with other ships unloading by local labour (80 per cent asserted) it was absurd to pull chestnuts out of fire for the Atlantic Transport Co. & to unload in an aggressive way should be resisted unless cause could be shown why these vessels can't be unloaded in the same way as others.

The Highland Laddie, *built by Cammell Laird at Birkenhead in 1910, was a first-class passenger/cargo ship for Nelson Steam Navigation Co. Ltd's London–River Plate frozen meat service.* Lady Jocelyn, *a much older clipper, built in 1852 for the General Screw Steamship Co., had been a New Zealand immigrant ship but was now the Shipping Federation's black-leg depot ship. The Federation, led by Cuthbert Laws, was supporting the Port of London Authority in resisting the newly formed National Transport Workers' Federation's demands for union recognition, a wage increase of* 8d. *an hour, and improved working conditions. It was also backing Cardiff shipowners in refusing to grant similar demands by the seamen's union. Alessandro Saluppo tells the story from the Shipping Federation Archives: 'Strikebreaking and Anti-Unionism on the Waterfront: The Shipping Federation, 1890–1914',* European History Quarterly, *vol.49, no.4, 2019, pp.14–18. For Cardiff in July see Campbell Balfour, 'Captain Tupper and the 1911 seamen's strike in Cardiff',* Morgannwg: Transactions of the Glamorgan Local History Society, *vol.14, 1970, pp.62–80. The dispute in the London docks was settled on 18 August, when the PLA agreed to have their calling-on stands outside the dock gates and therefore subject to union control (J.R. Lovell,* Stevedores and Dockers. A Study of Trade Unionism in the Port of London, 1870–1914, *Macmillan, 1969, pp.150–79). Gordon Phillips and Noel Whiteside,* Casual Labour: The Unemployment Question in the Port Transport Industry 1880–1970, *Clarendon P., Oxford, 1985, pp.85–106, discuss government initiatives towards decasualisation of dock labour.*

Grey's words about the absurdity of pulling chestnuts out of the fire for the Atlantic Transport Company would have resonated with his Cabinet colleagues. The American Atlantic Transport Line was part of a shipping combine financed by J.P. Morgan that included the White Star Line, whose ships were registered in the United Kingdom. The creation of the American combine early in the century had caused consternation in Britain. Cunard was given a large loan by the British government to construct the turbine-powered Lusitania *and the* Mauritania. *To meet the challenge for North Atlantic dominance, Morgan's International Mercantile Marine Co. ordered the White Star Line's* Titanic, *launched on 31 May 1911, and her sisters,* Olympic *and*

Britannic *(Jonathan Kinghorn,* The Atlantic Transport Line, 1881–1931: A History with Details on All Ships, *Macfarland, Jefferson, N. Carolina, 2012). Financial support for building (and arming) the Cunard ships was justified by the soon discarded argument that they would be an effective counter to German trans-Atlantic raiders (Matthew S. Seligmann, 'Germany's Ocean Greyhounds and the Royal Navy's First Battle Cruisers: An Historiographical Problem',* Diplomacy & Statecraft, *vol.27, no.1, 2016, pp.162–82).*

Buxton was not hopeful of effecting a settlement on R'ways, & Managers could not undertake to meet railway men's leaders. Burns said only 116,000 out of 700,000 men in union. It was admitted we only had at the moment 500 guardsmen in London — no other soldiers!

The railway strike was one of a complex series of strikes originating in Liverpool. As in the London dock strikes, the Liverpool strikes had begun with a seamen's strike, which was remarkable for the support from other workers. The seamen's success encouraged the dockers to demand union recognition, and improved pay and conditions. A strike was averted on 29 June when the shipping companies recognised the unions and agreed to negotiate on wages and conditions.

The railway workers were dissatisfied with the conciliation boards set up in 1907. The railway companies had refused to recognise the trades unions by this agreement, refusing even to sign the same copy of the agreement as the union officials. In exchange for the establishment of the boards, the union officials had agreed not to strike until 1914. This freed the companies from any compulsion to settle grievances, and the conciliation process was taking up to eighteen months to reach a simple decision. The result was a growing alienation between the men and their union officials. On 5 August porters working for the Lancashire and Yorkshire Railway went on unofficial strike. They were disowned by their unions and put on the owners' blacklist. The company tried to bring in other porters, but this only spread the strike. 'Liverpool is in a state of revolution' George Askwith wrote to his wife on 30 June (Askwith MSS, courtesy of Betty Askwith, the Hon. Betty Miller Jones). By 8 August all the dock railways were stopped (they handled 75 per cent of the goods passing through the port). The men called for the support of all railway men in Liverpool and the help of all Liverpool transport workers; the strike spread to Manchester and Preston.

Despite the orderliness of the various marches and meetings (the Liverpool Head Constable reported to the Home Office on 8 August that there had been no disturbances of the peace), the Liverpool magistrates had called for additional police and troops. There was resentment at their presence and a rapid increase in violence. At the same time, the railway and shipping companies were making their stand. Instead of trying to negotiate the passage of vital supplies, the railway companies tried to force through lorry-loads of goods (including beer and oysters). The unions had organised a system of permits whereby milk, bread, hospital supplies, and even overseas mail passed through the picket lines, but the companies refused to negotiate for other essential supplies. The shipping companies claimed that the agreement on 29 June was not being kept and locked out their workers. As a result a mass meeting was called for Sunday, 13 August. There was much violence at the meeting (one researcher claims that the police attacked the orderly crowd) and in the days that followed, culminating on 15 August in two men being shot by the troops. A politically connected Unionist businessman told his Swedish mistress 'last week London was nearly starved, whilst on Sunday 200 people were wounded in Liverpool' (F. Leverton Harris–Ella Strom, 15 Aug. [1911], Ella Strom Grainger MSS, Grainger Museum). Comforted by advice from the law officers, Rufus Isaacs and John Simon, the government suspended the Army Regulation that required the requisition of troops from a civil authority (Nigel Morgans, 'The Military Response of the Authorities to the Industrial and Civil Unrest in South Wales c.1910–11', MA thesis, U. of Wales, Newport, 2013, p.18). P.J. Waller, Democracy and Sectarianism: A political and social history of Liverpool 1868–1939, *Liverpool UP, 1981, pp.249–69, is an amply documented but succinct and witty account of the labour disputes that 'paralysed Liverpool in the summer of 1911'.*

Neither JAP, nor HHA in his Cabinet letter to the King, mentioned the violent mass meeting nor the killing of the two men. On 16 August hundreds of troops and police were deployed to escort a convoy of food from the docks to the city. The next day, with planned 'military preparations' reported in detail, the railway union officials realised that unless they supported their members they would lose all their influence, so they declared the strike official and called for a national stoppage. The government's handling of the strikes in 1911 is covered from the President of the Board of Trade's perspective in Waley, A Liberal Life, *pp.211–19. Hugh Armstrong Clegg,* A History of British Trade Unions since 1989, Vol. II 1911–1933, *Clarendon P., Oxford, 1985, pp.24–74, is a judicious survey of industrial unrest 1911–14. Joe White argues for an interpretation of 'two concurrent labour unrests…the upsurge of the hitherto unorganised and unrecognised…[and] the upsurge of old trade unionists' ('1910–1914 Reconsidered', in James E. Cronin and Jonathan Schneer eds,* Social Conflict and the Political Order in Modern Britain, *Croom Helm, 1982, pp.73–95).*

We discussed then Home Rule a topic Asquith described as a matter of less temperature in the parliamentary political ocean.

We agreed Irish M.P.s should be in Imp. Parl., Birrell protesting against Irish H.R. being included in a devolution Federal scheme for Wales & Scotland which the country had never discussed. Asquith protested against the mark of servitude by leaving Irish Bills on the table of H. of C. —& urged that some less marked way should be secured to meet nonconformists' view of a subordinate Parl., which could not pass Catholic laws to oppress Protestants. H.R. was, said George, regarded as unpopular & with suspicion unless subordinate Parl. was manifest. We agreed an address to throne to repeal was certainly to be provided for but words left over for consideration.

17th Aug. Thursday at 11.30. Grey explained position of negociations between Cambon & K–Waechter[63] at Berlin — that there were 3 courses open to us if Germans landed in Morocco.

to land also, to summon conference of powers, to await until occasion arose — latter determined upon, it being understood no ship should be even sent without cabinet being summoned during recess.

Buxton informed us of negociations with R'way men — & Lloyd George suggested the Prime Minister should accompany Buxton & urge importance of an inquiry by a rapid & small Royal Commission.

HHA and Sydney Buxton met the trades union leaders at the Board of Trade on 17 August. HHA offered a royal commission to investigate the failings of the conciliation boards but he was unconciliatory; his offer was refused and the strike began. DLG then intervened, and an agreement was reached on 19 August, prompting next day HHA's effusive thanks for the Chancellor's 'indomitable purpose, his untiring energy, and the matchless skill' he had brought to settling 'one of the most formidable problems we have had, as a Government, to confront' (Lloyd George MSS, LG/C/6/11/13, PA). By this agreement, a royal commission was set up. It reported 18 October 1911, but the trades unions rejected the report. The companies refused to meet union officials until they were threatened with a renewed strike and the Commons had passed a resolution that the two sides should meet. The result was a new conciliation agreement (11 December 1911), but it was not much more satisfactory than the 1907 agreement.

The companies continued to refuse to recognise the trade unions but conceded that the workers might be represented on the boards by anyone they chose (the earlier agreement had insisted that the workers' representatives be railway company employees, thereby excluding trades union officials). Union dissatisfaction was such that the unions handed in a year's notice to end the agreement in November 1913, the earliest possible date, and it seems probable that there would have been a serious dispute in the winter of 1914 but for the outbreak

[63] Alfred von Kiderlen-Wächter (1852–1912); German Foreign Secretary 1910–12; diplomat in Copenhagen, St Petersburg, Paris, Constantinople, and Bucharest.

of war (H.R. Hikins, 'The Liverpool General Transport Strike, 1911', Transactions of the Historic Society of Lancashire and Cheshire, *vol.113, 1961, pp.169–95; Bob Holton, 'Syndicalism and Labour on Merseyside, 1906–14', in Harold R. Hikins ed.,* Building the Union: studies on the growth of the workers' movement, Merseyside, 1756–1967, *Toulouse P. for Liverpool Trades Council, Liverpool, 1973, pp.121–49; Frank McKenna, 'Victorian Railway Workers',* History Workshop, *no.1, 1976, pp.61–5). Sam Davies and Ron Noon, 'The rank-and-file in the 1911 Liverpool General Transport Strike',* Labour History Review, *vol. 79, issue 1, Apr. 2014, pp.55–81, is a comprehensive analysis of the Liverpudlians caught up in the strike and civil disturbance.*

We discussed whether men in navy should become blackleg stokers at Liverpool to prevent city being plunged into total darkness! I urged no troops should be used for more than protecting property life & men willing to work. I urged it should be open by terms of reference to enable the right of official recognition of leaders by employers to be included.

I got leave to prepare a franchise bill in lieu of mere plural voting one.

With a new provision to include the university constituencies, the Registration (Plural Qualifications) Bill had been printed again on 8 August. At this last Cabinet before the summer recess, however, the Cabinet decided to drop the bill. The form of JAP's sentence suggests that he himself had been in favour of a changed approach. But the phrasing is not conclusive; nor is there any direct evidence that JAP advocated a wider bill.

Certainly, until the end of May, and presumably until the beginning of August, both JAP and Simon were acting on the assumption that their bill would be the government's first legislative proposal of 1912. This priority was necessary if new registers were to be operating in time for a general election in January 1915. Indeed, Simon seems to have taken the lead in suggesting that the bill should be introduced in 1911 and taken to a second reading 'in order to draw the fire of the other side and run the racket of criticism from our own' (Simon–JAP, 30 May 1911, MS. Gainford 133/23). JAP actually prepared a draft speech with which to move the first reading; and the Cabinet discussed on 24 May how the bill could be made operative in 1915, assuming that the Lords rejected it.

JAP's planned speech had included a declaration that the government intended, 'if opportunity permits, to introduce an Electoral Reform and Redistribution Bill towards the end of this Parliament'. What persuaded HHA and his colleagues to change their minds about the simple plural voting bill? A letter from JAP to his wife on 1 August indicates that the Chief Whip, the Master of Elibank, had opposed the introduction of the bill; but the basis of Elibank's objections—apart from personal hostility to JAP—is not clear (JAP–EP,

1 Aug. 1911, MS. Gainford 189/102–3). At any rate, the Cabinet decided that the Liberal Whips' office should collect information in preparation for the possible introduction of a franchise bill in the next session.

The origins of the new course are partly illuminated in a letter to Elibank, written in the following month by DLG: 'As you know, I proposed to the Cabinet, having first of all obtained your assent to the proposition, to drop the idea of introducing a mere Plural Voting Bill and to immediately press forward a measure for the simplification and extension of the Franchise. To this they agreed' (DLG–Master of Elibank, 5 Sept. 1911, Murray of Elibank MSS, MS. 8802, f.308, NLS). At Elibank's suggestion, the task of gathering and summarising information from Liberal Federation agents, and preparing a report upon which a bill might be framed, was entrusted to the chief organiser at Liberal Party headquarters, William Allard (JAP–Master of Elibank, 17 Aug. 1911, MS. Gainford 141/2).

It had been JAP's hope to have a draft Bill ready for Cabinet consideration by the end of October. In a gentle remonstrance on 30 August Elibank made it clear that he felt Allard's time was being wasted in seeking information that, according to John Simon, was already available in government departments (Master of Elibank–JAP, 30 Aug. 1911, MS. Gainford 141/3). Allard produced an interim report in less than a month. He had consulted Liberal agents, talked to Joseph King, Liberal MP for Somerset North (whose book Electoral Reform *he described as 'an admirable manual'), and studied colonial electoral systems with the help of W.A. Robinson of the Colonial Office. 'Whatever is attempted', he concluded, 'ought to be on broad and generous lines and aim at Manhood Suffrage'. Plural voting should be abolished and a single qualification should replace the surviving ancient franchises.*

Allard sought to keep to essentials: defining the classes of person entitled to a Parliamentary vote (including Peers), revising the residential qualification, and eliminating the privilege of multiple votes. He dismissed as a side issue the question of whether to abolish the disqualification of voters who had received 'temporary or non-personal parochial relief or other disqualifying alms'. This was one of the points raised by the Society of Certificated and Associated Liberal Agents in a memorandum submitted to HHA in 1909 ('Amendments of Laws Relating to the Franchise and to the Registration of Electors', very confidential, enclosed by Allard with his letter and interim report on 13 Sept.1911, MS. Gainford 141/4). The activities and opinions of Liberal agents are best studied in Kathryn Rix, Parties, Agents and Electoral Culture in England, 1880–1910, *Boydell P. for the Royal Historical Society, Woodbridge, 2016.*

One provision was notably absent from Allard's report; there was no mention of female suffrage. A few days before Allard had communicated with JAP, DLG had expressed anxiety on this subject to the Chief Whip. Elibank acted at once on DLG's suggestions; and the answers to the questions posed to Liberal agents were tabulated by Renwick Seager, the head of the Registration Department at Liberal headquarters, and put at the disposal of a Cabinet committee, which met in late October and November. The agents were 'strongly and unanimously in favour of a simple Residential franchise'. They were also agreed that the Conciliation Bill introduced by the Liberal MP Sir George Kemp on 5 May 1911—proposing that every woman householder would have a vote in the division in which she resided but if married could not vote in the same constituency as her husband—would mainly enfranchise upper- and middle-class women who were most likely to vote Tory ('Mr Seager's Report', 8 Nov .1911, in Chief Whip's Cabinet Memorandum, 16 Nov. 1911, MS. Gainford 141/7; TNA: CAB 37/108/148). Proponents of the Bill cited some survey evidence and calculations based on selected municipal rolls suggesting that over 80 per cent of the new voters were likely to be working-class women (Mitzi Auchterlonie, Conservative Suffragists: The Women's Vote and the Tory Party, *I.B. Tauris, 2007, p.160). DLG had promised time for a third reading, and the Bill was defeated on 28 March 1912. HHA had promised a government bill in the next session that would be open to a women's suffrage amendment, but it was mid-December before concrete proposals reached the Cabinet.*

August 1911 was a particularly trying month for HHA. A ferocious squabble broke out between Runciman and DLG over control of university grants. After two days of 'bluster & threats & wild statements' by DLG, and threatened resignations, a peace formula averting a Cabinet row was mediated by Elibank 'in order to ease Asquith's burden which is heavy and his voice which is feeble' (Runciman–Hilda Runciman, 14,15,16 Aug. 1911, Viscountess Runciman of Doxford MSS). It is not clear whether HHA was aware of the quarrel that had erupted a few weeks earlier between JAP and Alick Murray. Elibank had established a very close relationship with the Prime Minister, so much so that Lord Knollys had complained of his visits to the Palace with HHA, unprecedented for a Chief Whip. In this government, Knollys told Jack Sandars, Balfour's principal aide, 'the Whips had a power which had never been exerted in such fashion before' (Sandars–Balfour, 8 June 1911, Bodl. Sandars MSS, MS.Eng.hist.c.763, f.91). Elibank may well have been irritated by the Prime Minister's penchant for seeking advice from JAP, his predecessor, on matters that were within the remit of the Chief Whip. JAP was certainly unhappy at Elibank's opposition to the introduction of a Plural Voting Bill. Whatever the cause, JAP said he would never enter the Whips' Office again (JAP–EP, 1 Aug. 1911, MS. Gainford 189/102–03).

Haldane reported to his sister that the premier 'looks over-tired and ill' (Elizabeth Haldane diary, 18 Aug. 1911, Elizabeth Haldane MSS, MS. 20240, f.11, NLS). Not only did the Prime Minister have to deal with the Agadir Crisis and a crescendo of industrial unrest on the docks and among transport workers, but on his way back to London on 21 August his car collided with a woman bicyclist. She was very badly injured and at first there was little hope of her recovery. HHA sent down a specialist, who was able to save her life. The Cabinet met on 22 August to discuss the troubles on the railways (HHA Cabinet letter, 23 Aug. 1911, TNA: CAB 41/38/5).

JAP, like most members of the Cabinet, was not privy to much that was being contemplated on foreign, naval, and military matters through the late summer and early autumn. He knew nothing of the secret meeting of a 'sub-committee' of the CID on 23 August 1911 at which naval and military war plans were dissected. As M.L. Dockrill writes in his 'British policy during the Agadir Crisis of 1911' in F.H. Hinsley ed., British Foreign Policy under Sir Edward Grey, *Cambridge UP, 1977, p.281: 'it appeared that foreign and military policy… had fallen into the hands of a small clique consisting of Asquith, Grey, Haldane, Lloyd George and WSC, with Henry Wilson, the Director of Military Operations at the War office, acting as their military adviser…'. For those on the fringe of the decision-making group there was increasing disquiet. Confiding in Harcourt, Runciman wrote on 21 August that they could no longer rely on the 'stability of balance in the Cabinet':*

> Nor can peacefully inclined persons be much reassured by the addition yesterday of Winston to the Defence Committee…
>
> The one thing to keep these rampageous strategists in check would be a definite decision of Cabinet that under no circumstances conceivable in the present Morocco controversy would we be prepared to land a single British soldier on the Continent. I draw a sharp distinction between action by sea and the certain destruction of British troops in Belgium or France and I believe that if we emphatically forbid the latter we shall check the mad desire for war which has overtaken some unreliable politicians.
>
> *(Runciman of Doxford MSS)*

Harcourt, a permanent member of the CID, was incensed at being excluded along with Esher and Morley from the 23 August meeting: 'the feeling that these things are going on behind one's back is very disturbing.' (Harcourt–Runciman, 26 Aug. 1911, Runciman of Doxford MSS.) On 4 September Runciman elaborated on WSC's development of 'great schemes—on paper… happily there is no risk whatever of our being involved in any commitments without a Cabinet decision'. Runciman was appalled at the respect being given to 'expert' opinion on the landing of British troops on the Continent—'and Winston is now numbered among the experts! It is a point of policy and I would never allow any expert to decide it for me' (Runciman of Doxford MSS). By 10 September the Prime Minister was telling Harcourt: 'I begin to hope that the Morocco affair has become a question of haggling' (Bodl. MS. Harcourt 421, ff.176–7). But a week later 'Admirals & Captains summoned onboard Hercules. Admiral Callaghan told us the situation was very serious & that 1st Lord of Admty had told him we might expect to be attacked on Sunday p.m' (Capt. Dudley de Chair diary, 16 Sept. 1911, de Chair MSS, Documents 7865, IWM).

The national railway strike from 17 to 19 August continued until 23 August in the north-east, where the North Eastern Railway Company had threatened to withhold recognition of the Amalgamated Society of Railway Servants (see R.J. Irving, The North Eastern Railway Company 1870–1914: an economic history, *Leicester UP, 1976, pp, 69–70; and Geoffrey Alderman,* The Railway Interest, *Leicester UP, 1976, pp.208–09,219). An alarmed King George had telegraphed the Home Secretary on 17 August seeking reassurance that order could be preserved. Maintaining order was not a problem, WSC replied. The difficulty was maintaining order without loss of life. His anxieties unallayed, the King had his private secretary write to the Prime Minister expressing his fear that renewed disturbances might lead to 'political elements being introduced into the conflict which might perhaps affect... the position of the Crown' (Catherine Bailey,* Black Diamonds: The Rise and Fall of an English Dynasty, *Viking, 2007, pp.115–16).*

For the deployment of troops as seen by Maj.-Gen. Ewart, who was at WSC's side at the Home Office from 10.00 p.m. on 17 August until the early hours of the next morning, and again at an evening gathering on the 19th with Haldane, the Prime Minister, Lord Ashby St Legers, and Maj.-Gen. Nevil Macready, who was commanding the troops in the Rhondda Valley, see the Ewart Memoirs (pp.1012–14, Ewart MSS), closely paraphrasing his contemporary diary. In the following month, George Askwith, at Balmoral to be knighted, found the King 'bent on repression' (Askwith–E. Askwith, 17 Sept. 1911, Askwith MSS). For DLG's story of how he deployed the German menace to bring about the settlement see Robertson Nicoll's memorandum of a lunch at the Savoy with DLG and Riddell on 12 October 1911, Robertson Nicoll MSS.

At this time WSC's gaze was also turning to the threat of violence in Ulster. 'I hear from more than one quarter', he told Augustine Birrell on 23 August, that there was 'a grt deal of arming going on in Ulster'. It occurred to the Home Secretary that the Chief Secretary for Ireland might want to set up some Secret Service work. He did not know if there was an Irish secret service fund or an adequate one, but his own machinery was available if it would be of use. Birrell replied complacently on 26 August from his 'comparatively peaceful and police ridden island' that he had been assured that there had been no 'considerable importation' of arms into Ulster as yet, although there had been some orders, many bogus, placed abroad. Amongst his police officers there was considerable difference of opinion on the momentous question, 'Will Ulster fight?' (Verney MSS, courtesy of the late Sir Harry Verney Bt).

On 8 September HHA wrote to his old colleague James Bryce in Washington that 'the new unrest in the industrial world' presented 'some very ugly symptoms'. If the railway strike had lasted a few days longer 'the strain upon the whole social & political machine would have been unprecedently severe' (Bodl. MS. Bryce, UB1, quoted in R.E. Ellins, 'Aspects of the New Liberalism 1895–1914', Ph.D. thesis, U. of Sheffield, 1980, p.63). The same day the premier circulated a memorandum to the Cabinet embodying the communication from the King about strikes (TNA: CAB 37/107/107). The King was urging the government to draw up legislation preventing strikes, particularly 'sympathetic' strikes, and prohibiting 'peaceful picketing'. HHA had replied that, although his government had been considering the problem for some time, he could foresee no helpful legislation. He thought the legislation governing picketing was strong enough: the difficulty, which would remain even if the law was strengthened, was to obtain evidence that intimidation had occurred.

In the hope of minimising the costly reliance of local authorities on emergency military support, WSC communicated with all police authorities proposing that they compile registers of men who could form a reserve to act as special constables (Weinberger, Keeping the Peace?, *p.63). For the official responses to industrial unrest in 1911–12, an outstanding short guide is Jane Morgan,* Conflict and Order: The Police and Labour Disputes in England and Wales, 1900–1939, *Clarendon P., Oxford, 1987, pp.49–65. In response to the Prime Minister, Herbert Samuel sent a discursive letter on 23 September suggesting that an independently compiled analysis of the cost of living would be helpful. JAP had sent in his thoughts a fortnight earlier:*

Confidential

Headlam Hall
Gainford
Darlington

Sept 12. 1911

My dear Asquith,

In reply to your circular to the cabinet of Sept. 8th I may say I concur in your view that the law if properly enforced is strong enough to deal with the intimidation which has accompanied picketing, or has *un*accompanied it, during the recent strikes.

An alteration of the law to prevent peaceful suasion is not to be entertained, and it is no argument for its abolition by picketing, that intimidation has occurred.

I do not think intimidation has been encouraged by the Trades Disputes Act, and when feeling is running high as the result of a strike, I believe the same amount of intimidation would occur if all picketing could be stopped.

Let me give an illustration:—

On Aug 21st a North Eastern Railway rolley, distributing goods to Darlington tradesmen was overturned, & rain only prevented it being burnt up, subsequently police protection was given to another set of rolleys, and before goods were delivered, the drivers were induced by threats & appeals from the crowd to hand the reins over to the police, & the tradesmen were informed that if they accepted delivery of the goods, their windows would be broken and their premises destroyed, — more than half the goods had consequently to be taken back to the N.E.R. goods office & were not delivered until the strike was over. No one will come forward and give evidence.

I submit no alteration of the law will prevent such intimidation, and the question is merely this:— Can evidence be procured to convict? I am not surprised at the King feeling much disturbed at the unrest in the labour world, but I do not share his apprehensions in regard to the position of the Crown, and I do not think, it possible to devise any scheme which would be acceptable to employers and trades unionists at the present time.

I presume the miners are the most powerful and best organised trades unionists in this country. They are now asking their employers to grant them a minimum wage. A conference of the North of England coal owners met at Newcastle on Saturday, and appointed Sir Hugh Bell,[64] Sir Lindsay Wood,[65] and the mining engineer of Pease & Partners (Mr T. Y. Greener[66]) to go to London to confer with other coal owners. Yesterday I had a long chat with Mr Greener and other mining engineers, and they informed me, the miners are now wanting a strike, in every generation a large number like the excitement, the holiday and to get back in strike pay their contributions which they have paid out of their wages over a series of years; and that whether the miners are reasonably met or not, they will find a reason for coming out during the next few weeks.

The owners I trust will make it as impossible as they can to give the men any justification for throwing down their tools, and paralysing the whole of the industries of the country dependent upon fuel, but in their present frame of mind to suggest any legislation would be useless. See how, the Trades Union congress at Newcastle rejected the provisions of the bill introduced by Will Crooks,[67] & how they censured him, Enoch Edwards,[68] Henderson & Fenwick[69] who backed it! We must in the immediate future rely on conferences, conciliation, compromise and common sense, and the mass of the working classes are not devoid of the last named quality.

[64] Sir (Thomas) Hugh Bell, Bt (1844–1931); iron master and colliery owner; director (sometime chmn), London North Eastn Railway 1903–31; father of Gertrude Bell; chmn, Tees Valley Water Bd; 2nd Bt 1904; member, coal owners' committee during 1912 strike; Lib., later Lib. Unionist.

[65] Sir Lindsay Wood, Bt (1834–1920); mine owner; man. dir., Helton collieries 1866–1911; Pres., Institute of Mining Engineers 1875–8; member, royal commission on accidents in mines 1879–86 and royal commission on coal supplies 1903–5; Bt 1897; Unionist.

[66] Thomas Young Greener (1855–1934), gen. mgr, Pease & Partners collieries; gen. mgr and agent, Holmside and South Moor Collieries 1913–32; leading negotiator between Durham Coal Owners' Association and the 'Workmen's Associations' (Durham Mining Museum Who's Who, http://www.dmm.org.uk/whoswho/g902.htm, accessed 21 Dec. 2015).

[67] William ('Will') Crooks (1852–1921); Lab. MP Woolwich 1903–Jan. 1910, Dec. 1910–1921; cooper; member for Poplar, LCC 1892–1910; chmn, Poplar Bd of Guardians 1897–1906; Mayor of Poplar 1901; PC 1916. Crooks had introduced the Labour Disputes Bill on 17 Aug. (PP, 1911 [360], ii, 871), proposing imposition of a 'cooling off' period after notification that a strike was to be called (Paul Tyler, *Labour's lost leader: the life and politics of Will Crooks*, Tauris Academic Studies, 2007).

[68] Enoch Edwards (1852–1912); Lab. (Lib. 1906–9) MP Hanley 1906–12; miner; Gen. Sec., North Staffs Miners' Assoc. 1881–1912; Pres., Miners' Federation of Great Britain 1904.

[69] Charles Fenwick (1850–1918); Lab. (Lib. until 1910) MP Northumberland (Wansbeck) 1885–1918; miner 1860–85; Sec., Parly Committee, TUC 1890; PC 1911.

We must not mistake the hooliganism and intimidation outside the law, to which strikes give rise, with the genuine demand of labour to improve their conditions, reduce their hours, and raise their wages under the existing law.

Believe me

Yours ever
Joseph A. Pease
(Bodl. MS. Asquith 24, ff.46–7)

There was a ministerial reshuffle on 23 October. Parliament reassembled on 24 October. His Majesty in Council appointed JAP as President of the Board of Education that day. Hobhouse replaced JAP at the Duchy and was succeeded as Financial Secretary to the Treasury by McKinnon Wood, who was replaced as Under-Secretary of State for Foreign Affairs by Francis Acland. Acland was replaced as Financial Secretary to the War Office by HHA's brother-in-law H.J. Tennant. Tennant had spent 5–9 October at Glen with JAP (Visitors Book, Glen House, Glenconner MSS, seen in situ 1980, courtesy of the 3rd Baron Glenconner); he was replaced as Parliamentary Secretary to the Board of Trade by J.M. Robertson. Lord Lucas followed Sir Edward Strachey Bt as Parliamentary Secretary to the Board of Agriculture and Fisheries. Strachey was dropped from office and made a peer. Lucas was replaced as Under-Secretary of State for Colonial Affairs by Alfred Emmott, who was also elevated to the Lords.

The Prime Minister's PPS, Charles Lyell, explained the minor shuffles to his father: the 'move was really to find room for Robertson who certainly ought to be in the Government but could not very well go anywhere but at the Board of Trade, so a vacancy had to be found for Jack Tennant' (C. Lyell–Sir L. Lyell, 31 Oct. 1911, Lyell MSS). Lyell might have been right. But HHA explained other elements of the scheme to Loulou Harcourt on 15 October. It began, he said, with Lord Carrington giving up the Board of Agriculture and taking the sinecure of Lord Privy Seal. Lord Lucas, who was knowledgeable and keen about the subject, was to go to Agriculture as Under-Secretary. The Prime Minister thought Lucas, Harcourt's Under-Secretary since March, would not mind 'the slight ostensible loss of status'. To replace 'Bron' Lucas, HHA sought Harcourt's assent to the appointment (with a peerage) of Alfred Emmott—'with his limitations…an excellent man, a name of power in Lancashire'. The well-regarded Halifax cotton spinner and Congregationalist J.H. Whitley would not be advanced into the ministry because of his crucial value as Deputy Speaker: 'it is highly important that we should have Whitley in the Chair during Insurance, Home Rule &c' (Bodl. MS. Harcourt 421, ff.180–1).

Among those happiest at the changes was Thomas McKinnon Wood. DLG and the Permanent Secretary of the Treasury, Sir Robert Chalmers, were both strongly in favour of the appointment. As Wood told his aunt, the Chancellor is a genius — a wayward genius — a casual genius. He does marvellously the work upon which he is concentrating his attention, but he won't read reports or give his mind to the general work of the Department so that I shall have a big and varied responsibility and I will have to decide very important matters without expecting his assistance in arriving at a decision... I shall have more real power than three fourths of the Cabinet, because, to a certain extent, I shall hold the national purse strings.

(T. McKinnon Wood–'Aunt Ann', 26 Oct. 1911, McKinnon Wood MSS, courtesy of Gwendolen McKinnon Wood)

Others were less pleased, not least Francis Acland, son of the wealthy and influential educationist Sir Arthur Dyke Acland Bt. 'Things go to the pushers not to the waiters, and though I know I could run Education or Agriculture or the F. Sec ship to the Treasury well I suppose I really haven't done enough work that anyone knows about to have a real claim to any of these' (Francis Acland–Eleanor Acland, Oct. 1911, Acland of Killerton MSS, 1148M add 14/Series II/Correspondence/518, DHC; Gary Tregidga ed., Killerton, Camborne and Westminster: The Political Correspondence of Sir Francis and Lady Acland, 1910–29, *Devon and Cornwall Record Society, New Series, vol.48, Exeter, 2006, p.57). Francis Acland had been assistant director of education for the West Riding before being adopted as Liberal candidate for Richmond (Anne Acland,* A Devon Family: The Story of the Aclands, *Phillimore, 1981, p.141). His father had been President of the National Liberal Federation 1906–7, and was on the list of men to be ennobled if the Lords rejected the Parliament Bill.*

HHA had hoped to 'wire confidentially', but JAP had neglected to take his cipher with him. The Prime Minister wrote to JAP from his brother-in-law Frank Tennant's Archerfield House near North Berwick on 18 October:

I am doing a certain amount of re-shuffling & re-arrangement. Carrington goes from Agricre & takes the Privy Seal, Runciman succeeding him.

I wish to propose to you that you should go to the Board of Education, where you will find a larger & more fruitful field for your energies. I hope you will see your way to comply with my request.

As matters are rather pressing, I should be glad if possible to have a telegraphic reply...

(MS. Gainford 39/30)

JAP telegraphed back: 'If you wish but he tells me he is quite happy...'. His copy is annotated:

The telegram was worded thus to avoid confidential offer and acceptance of new office leaking out prematurely through Post Office operators — & to also give Asquith impression I was contented to remain where I was.

(MS. Gainford 83/63)

JAP's succession to the Board of Education was, according to The Annual Register... 1911 *(p.231), 'to the general surprise'. Aware that he lacked the depth of knowledge, fluency, or flair of many of his colleagues, JAP told his wife on 18 October that without her 'propelling influence I should long ago have chucked public life' (Harrison,* Separate Spheres, *p.92). He admitted to Elsie the next day: 'Education is not my strong point, but I can help with I hope tact & organising ability & common sense.' (MS. Gainford 133/105.) 'I cannot understand Jack Pease being given the Education Office—as he is a "Friend" perhaps it may ease the Nonconformist restlessness...', Earl Spencer surmised (Spencer–Lord Fitzmaurice, 31 Oct. 1911, Fitzmaurice MSS, courtesy of the 8th Marquess of Lansdowne). Arthur Acland, who did not keep his low regard for JAP to himself, later told Lord Haldane: 'if you saw and heard as much as I do of secondary and elementary education you would groan aloud as I do at the presence of Jack Pease at the head of state control of education' (Sir A.H.D. Acland–Haldane, 21 Oct. 1912, Haldane of Cloan MSS, MS. 5909, f.270, NLS, quoted in Daglish, 'The transfer of power at the Board of Education', p.3).*

Walter Runciman was disappointed by his move from Education to Agriculture, but he had been damaged by the Holmes Circular imbroglio (see commentary 28 Nov. 1911) and what a remorseful Sir Robert Morant called 'a most deplorable obloquy', press criticism even in friendly newspapers (Morant–Runciman, [22 Mar. 1911]; J.A. Spender–Runciman, 22,23 Mar. 1911; Charles Geake–Runciman, 30 Mar. 1911; H.W. Massingham–Runciman, 21 Apr. 1911, Runciman of Doxford MSS). Samuel could not be persuaded to go to Agriculture, and took the Post Office instead. The new Postmaster General enjoyed telling his wife on 24 October: 'everyone is chaffing Runciman in the lobby about turnips & the price of bacon' (Samuel MSS, SAM/A571/582, PA). Wilson ed., Political Diaries of C. P. Scott 1911–1928, *p.52, has Samuel as Postmaster General six weeks early and JAP at Agriculture, for which he was never considered.*

The most notable of the changes were the transfer of a disbelieving and reluctant McKenna to the Home Office and an overjoyed WSC to the Admiralty (McKenna–Runciman, 2 Oct. 1911, secret, Runciman of Doxford MSS). Elizabeth Haldane wrote that her brother had suggested McKenna's move so that he could be First Lord: 'Most anxious for Navy to be brought in touch with Army...'. On 17 October she wrote:

> The rearrangement of the Ministry is going on, but R. is not to get the Admiralty as he wished. He and Winston met at Archerfield and the PM listened while they argued it out. The PM cannot face up to a step like this though he must know R. would be the best person to put in.
>
> *(E. Haldane diary, 18 Sept., 17 Oct. 1911, Elizabeth Haldane MSS, MS. 20240, f.13, NLS)*

At Archerfield on 16 October Lady Battersea (née Constance de Rothschild) joined the Asquiths for lunch. It was 'very rough, untidy, uncomfortable', Connie Battersea told her sister, Annie Yorke, the next day. 'The P.M. kind and extremely cordial—but how he has changed...! Quite different from what he used to be. He gave me a shock' (Lucy Cohen, Lady de Rothschild and her Daughters 1821–1931, *John Murray, 1935, p.297).*

Oct. 25[70] Full cabinet. Carrington now at Privy Purse, Runciman at Agriculture, I placed at Education (see correspondence with Asquith. I had no strong desire to go there, & sorry to leave the Duchy), Churchill Admiralty and McKenna at Home Office.

Why the latter exchange was made no one knew, except members of Defence Committee.

Grey reported situation abroad much as in telegrams.

Home Rule, Disestablishment & Electoral Reform Committees set up.

McKenna I found 2 days later shut up with Lord Loreburn & Harcourt. Harcourt then conveyed to me later the facts re McKenna's leaving the Admiralty. He declined on Aug 23 — & in Sept. to arrange for fleet to convoy our troops to aid the French, without cabinet sanction. Asquith was weak & thought no cabinet was necessary but later on he saw he had backed the wrong horse & on Nov 15 we won a great victory for a principle. Haldane had to climb down to agree to our terms. Asquith, Grey Haldane, Lloyd George, Churchill, thought they could boss the rest, but were mistaken.

Nov. 1 We discussed at length the situation which caused McKenna's exchange — when we thought we had come to the conclusion that in future.

> No communications should take place between the general staff with the staff of another country for concerted action against a 3d power either directly or indirectly without the previous approval of the cabinet.

Grey said he could not conduct negociations with France, if he was [not] to be able to assume our landing forces to help France, if Germany invaded her. This further discussion was deferred. Asquith laid down the constitutional doctrine as to cabinet control in very effective words but majority of us felt he had been a

[70] JAP misdated this entry 24 Oct. *The Times* and HHA's Cabinet letter (Bodl. MS. Asquith 6, ff.73–4) referred to a meeting on 25 Oct. Most ministers were sworn or affirmed into their new offices on 24 Oct. JAP 'did not turn up', but his seal was retrieved from the Duchy office for bestowal on Hobhouse, and he affirmed on the 25th (FitzRoy, *Memoirs*, Vol. II, pp.466–7).

party to a defence Comtee arrangement on Aug. 23 which included Lloyd George & Churchill — but excluded Harcourt, Morley & Esher — & they had rigged an arrangement to go to war if necessity arose. I protested against a policy wh. would tend to naval exhaustion & rival shipbuilding & wh. prejudiced friendly diplomacy, & made a power determined to ignore diplomatic relations when they knew military consultations for concerted action were taking place.

HHA's colourless report to the King spoke of Morley having raised 'the inexpediency of communications' being held or allowed between the British General Staff and those of other states 'such as France' without 'the previous knowledge and direction of the Cabinet'. Haldane, HHA, and Grey assured fractious colleagues that the French understood that questions of policy were reserved for the Cabinet (Bodl. MS. Asquith 6, ff.76–7). The events of November 1911 leading to the 'great victory for a principle' have been recounted many times. Subsequent accounts of the Cabinet 'crisis' over foreign policy have added little to the reconstruction in Keith M. Wilson, Empire and Continent, *pp.110–25. Much of the detail of the Cabinet confrontation was divulged more than once by Loreburn, who told the story to C.P. Scott on 23 October 1914:*

> Morley as the senior member of the Cabinet was chosen to lead off which he did, L. said, very well. Practically there was no defence, though every effort was made to divert the discussion to the merits of the action taken & away from the fact of the concealment...
>
> *(Wilson ed.,* The Political Diaries of C. P. Scott 1911–1928, *p.63)*

Loreburn, who sat on Grey's left at the Cabinet table, would recall a few years later that after the second meeting 'Grey got up to go he muttered to himself; but loud enough for Loreburn to hear: "I always said we ought to have told the Cabinet."' (Percy Molteno diary, [4 Jan. 1915], quoted in Francis Hirst, 'A Man of Principle—The Life of Percy Alport Molteno, M.P.', unpublished, corrected, and annotated galley proof, p.449, http://www.moltenofamily.net/wp-content/uploads/2013/12/Hirst-1-page-a-screen-p.-201-END.pdf, accessed 23 Apr. 2016.) Grey would express similar sentiments in his own autobiography (Twenty-Five Years 1892–1916, *2 vols, Hodder & Stoughton, 1925, Vol. II, p.99). The untroubled CIGS, Sir William Nicholson, told the Adjutant-General 'now that the German peril is less menacing, certain of the Government are inclined to rend us for our military intimacy with the French... Just like them. But we are well covered by "instructions" in the D.M.O's safe' (Ewart diary, re 31 Oct. 1911, Ewart MSS).*

JAP later added a note at the top of this entry about the latest episode in the relentless campaign by the Free Church Council (and Nonconformist MPs) to get the government to commit to legislation on education:

Nov. meeting non con Ministers in Asquith's room. I gave him statistics, which he used effectively, Dr Clifford[71] &c. He only promised his intention legislate within life time of pres. Parl.

On 6 November JAP attended a dinner at Brooks's for his predecessor at Education, Runciman, and was seated opposite the guest of honour. There, and over the next few days, he had several conversations with his friend Sir George Newman, chief medical officer to the Board of Education (with responsibility for the school medical service), advising him not to accept an offer from DLG to become vice-chairman of the National Insurance Commission. DLG wanted Newman to help launch the new Commission and then move on to the Local Government Board as Chief Medical Officer. McKenna joined JAP in successfully urging Newman to resist DLG's blandishment (Newman diary, 5–23 Nov. 1911, TNA: Newman MSS, MH 139, transcript courtesy of Dr Margaret Hammer).

Nov. 8 all quiet & ordinary day to day questions.

JAP passes over in silence HHA's surprise public intimation on 7 November of the government's intention to introduce a manhood suffrage bill with a simple residential qualification, and Arthur Balfour's announcement on the 8th that he would resign from the leadership of the Unionist Party. JAP also makes no mention of the coalition feelers being made in late October and early November by DLG and the Master of Elibank to Ramsay MacDonald. Being low in DLG's estimation, and no friend of Elibank, he was unlikely to be consulted about relations with the Labour Party (David Marquand, Ramsay MacDonald, *Jonathan Cape, 1977, p.142).*

A memorandum dictated in late November by the proprietor of the News of the World, *Sir George Riddell, reveals the background to HHA's announcement about manhood suffrage. According to the Chief Whip, the Prime Minister had not made up his mind until hearing the arguments of the leading Nonconformist MP, Silvester Horne. DLG had confirmed the Master of Elibank's story. He said that 'the whole of the Prime Minister's training made it difficult for him to take such a step and that while he was heartily in sympathy with the people yet he had the lawyer's fears of the uneducated . . . up to the last moment Lloyd George and Alec Murray were very doubtful whether he would take the plunge'. DLG had said that 'this will be one of the greatest changes that has taken place for many years'. Yet, as Riddell pointed out, the press was far more interested in Balfour's*

[71] Dr John Clifford (1836–1923); first Pres. of the Baptist World Alliance 1905–11, pastor, Praed Street Baptist Church 1858–1923, evangelist and social reformer especially interested in education, member of the Fabian Society.

resignation, announced that day, 'a mere event of temporary importance' (Riddell MSS, BL Add.MS. 62956, ff.47–8).

Murray and DLG had themselves been sending discreet messages to female suffrage supporters about the implications of a Reform Bill for their cause. DLG's conditions for not standing in the way of a female suffrage amendment or a revived Conciliation Bill, and keeping WSC neutral, were conveyed to the Conciliation Committee hon. sec., H.N. Brailsford, initially via C.P. Scott and then directly: 'they think they can get John Redmond's support to include women in the Reform Bill by leaving them provisionally out of the Home Rule Bill—a vile dodge' (Brailsford–Ld Lytton, 7 Nov. [1911], 27 Oct. [1911], Lytton MSS). On 17 November HHA and DLG received a deputation representing nine suffrage societies and confirmed that the proposed Reform Bill would be drafted so as to be capable of amendment, and that facilities would be granted for any bill that met the same qualification. The WSPU portrayed the government's hedged position as evidence of hostility and DLG as a betrayer of their cause. In a speech at Bath on 24 November DLG said the militants' attitude had 'torpedoed' the Conciliation Bill and 'the way is clear for a broad and democratic amendment of the suffrage for women'. For the Chairman of the Conciliation Committee's repudiation of the disingenuous torpedo charge see Lytton–DLG, 25 Nov. 1911, draft, Lytton MSS. The events of May to December 1911 are well described in Andrew Rosen, Rise Up, Women!: The Militant Campaign of the Women's Social and Political Union 1903–1914, *Routledge & Kegan Paul, 1974, pp.146–55.*

Nov. 15 resumed Discussion of Nov. 1. Resolution passed. But Grey was helpful — Churchill warlike. Asquith said it was an unwritten rule that Cabinet members kept no record of F. Office debate! This was a hit at Harcourt, Churchill being promoter!

The warlike WSC was just back from a day at sea on HMS Neptune, *the flag ship of the Home Fleet: 'sea sick but much impressed,' noted Capt. A.L. Duff (diary, 13,14 Nov. 1911, Duff MSS, courtesy of Lady Duff, now deposited in the National Maritime Museum).*

The last sentence of the 15 November entry was added in red ink. Hobhouse, in his diary entry of 30 October, had recorded: 'Loulou Harcourt took copious notes of the proceedings' (Edward David ed., Inside Asquith's Cabinet, *1977, p.106). JAP's diary entries for 8, 15, and 22 November were written at the same time and subsequently revised. HHA's account for the King of the 15 November meeting (of which there is no copy in the CAB 41/33 series in TNA) is the much quoted formal summary of the constraining agreement imposed on Grey (Bodl. MS. Asquith 6, ff.79–80).*

Nov. 22 all smooth, sundry topics, questions to ministers. I reported result of my meeting with nonconformist M.Ps.

JAP had met a delegation of Nonconformist MPs on 21 November. The delegation was led by Sir Albert Spicer, Sir William Howell Davies, C. Silvester Horne, and G. Hay Morgan, the secretary of the parliamentary committee of Nonconformists. They urged the desirability of an education bill in the next parliamentary session. The fear expressed to JAP was that support for Home Rule would be eroded if education legislation languished; and, if Home Rule did proceed ahead of education, Irish MPs might be less committed to the removal of religious grievances in England. JAP, though sympathetic, pointed out the length of the government's programme. The following weekend he enjoyed shooting, bridge, and billiards at the Jack Tennants' 'big new Lutyens house' in Kent. The party included the wealthy MP for South Derbyshire, 'a fat rather jolly old Jew' Sir Herbert Raphael and his wife, Charles Lyell, Sir Thomas Esmonde Bt (Irish Nationalist MP for North Wexford), 'and a rather flashy lady secretary' of Mrs Tennant (C. Lyell–Sir L. Lyell, 28 Nov. 1911, Lyell MSS).

Nov. 28 Asquith sent for me to talk over Morant's departure. I told him that McLure Master of Mill Hill school had a great record, I thought a man outside Education Office might be found, but I had formed no definite view.[72] There was jealousy inside, & no man really head & shoulders above his colleagues. We discussed Blair,[73] of London Co Council, Struthers of Scotch Office.[74]

The appointment of Sir Robert Morant, Permanent Secretary of the Board of Education since 1903, as Chairman, National Health Insurance Commission, had been announced that morning. Morant was captivated by the vision of creating a Ministry of Public Health. DLG 'pledged himself to me to help it forward howsoever and whensoever possible' (Morant–Masterman, [26 Nov.] 1911, Masterman MSS, CFGM A3/4/16, Cadbury RL Birmingham U.). But disillusion soon set in: 'L-G has been utterly elusive & failed me in all his pledges & in all whole five weeks' (Morant–Runciman, 3 Jan. 1912, Runciman of Doxford MSS 68, transcript courtesy Neil Daglish).

There was unfinished business on JAP's desk. Morant had been attacked by The Schoolmaster *and other journals for circulating an injudicious confidential memorandum*

[72] John David McClure (1860–1922); Head Master of Mill Hill School 1891–1922; Prof. of Astronomy, Queen's College London 1889–94; barrister 1890; Joint Hon. Sec., Incorporated Association of Head Masters 1904–12, Pres. 1914–15, Treas. 1920–2; Kt 1913; compiled Congregational hymnal 1909–16; Chmn, Congregational Union of England and Wales 1919–20. (M.L. Jacks, 'McClure, Sir John David (1860–1922)', rev. M.C. Curthoys, http://www.oxforddnb.com/view/article/34685, accessed 22 May 2016).

[73] Robert Blair (1859–1935); Education Officer, LCC 1904–24; teacher 1882–93; schools inspector 1894–1900; Chief Inspector of Technical Ed. in Ireland 1900–1; Kt 1914.

[74] Sir John Struthers (1857–1925); Sec., Scottish Ed. Dept 1904–22; Inspector of Schools, Scotland 1886–98; Asst Sec., Scottish Ed. Dept 1898–1904; KCB 1910. Ian Russell Findlay, 'Sir John Struthers KCB—Secretary of the Scotch/Scottish Education Department, 1904–1922—a study of his influence upon Scottish educational development', Ph.D. thesis, U. of Dundee, 1979.

by the Chief Inspector of Elementary Schools, the Buddhist poet Edmond Holmes, on elementary school inspectors, insultingly contrasting the ex-schoolteachers ('uncultured and imperfectly educated') with the 'Varsity type' ('of real culture and enlightenment'). Morant's departure, and that of the President of the Board of Education, was accelerated by the political controversy over what had become known as the 'Holmes–Morant circular' (M.J. Wilkinson, 'The Holmes Circular Affair', Journal of Educational Administration and History, vol.XII, no.2, July 1980, pp.29–38; and an able summary in Asher Tropp, The School Teachers: The Growth of the Teaching Profession in England and Wales from 1800 to the Present Day, William Heinemann, 1957, pp.199–203). Incensed by the campaign against him by the National Union of Teachers, Morant wrote to JAP of his 'fair name being dragged in the mire'. He had hoped that JAP would not receive a deputation from the NUT, scheduled for 12 December. The meeting went ahead (Neil Daglish, Education Policy-Making in England and Wales: The Crucible Years, 1895–1911, The Woburn P., 1996, pp.436–70).

As Education Officer for the London County Council, Robert Blair had frequently been in conflict with the Board of Education, most recently in a clash over the excessive size of classes in London schools. Blair was a formidable if somewhat over-zealous administrator who was reputed to have spotted 'a full-stop printed upside down' in a report prepared for the LCC education committee (D.W. Thoms, Policy-Making in Education: Robert Blair and the London County Council 1904–1924, Museum of the History of Education, U. of Leeds, 1980, p.16; Andrew Saint, 'Technical Education and the Early LCC', in Andrew Saint ed., Politics and the People of London: The London County Council 1889–1965, Hambledon P., 1989, pp.89–91).

Sir John Struthers, head of the Scottish Education Department, had been instrumental with John Sinclair, Secretary for Scotland, in initiating the 1908 Education (Scotland) Act that enforced medical inspection, free meals, and grants for clothing, free books, travel, and bursaries; and created a consolidated Education (Scotland) Fund, which had grown fifteen fold to £27,404 by 1911 (Lindsay Paterson, Scottish Education in the Twentieth Century, Edinburgh UP, 2003, p.43). The high regard in which Struthers was held was demonstrated in his appointments to the committees on physical deterioration for England and Wales (1904) and local and imperial taxation (1912); and to the joint board of insurance commissioners (1912). DLG had appointed him to the Departmental Committee on Local Taxation in March 1911. A.H.D. Acland liked Struthers: 'first rate capacity, real knowledge & width of view and very sympathetic' (MS. Gainford 83/101). But there were reservations. After talking to the Scottish whip Jack Gulland, Trevelyan concluded on 30 November that the best men in the department would have the advantage of 'knowledge of English conditions, controversies, and religions… He apparently is tactful with Roman Catholics. But they are a mild problem in

Scotland compared to our warring sects.' (MS. Gainford 83/102.) JAP would reflect five years later that Struthers

> had no refinement, and would never get on with English University men at the Board of Education. Scotch Education runs itself, people in Scotland believe in it, but this side of the border they don't take to it gladly, or realise its necessity, and Struthers would never have made them do so, or understood Englishmen himself.
>
> *(JAP–EP, 11 Aug. 1916, MS. Gainford 190 and* War Reminiscences, *ch.IX, p.219, MS. Gainford 36/2)*

A plethora of other names had been touted: Sir Michael Sadler, Vice Chancellor of the University of Leeds, perhaps the best-known educationist of his generation, thought correctly 'the govt will feel I am not a sufficiently colourless candidate' (Michael Sadleir, Michael Ernest Sadler (Sir Michael Sadler, KCSI), 1861–1943: a memoir by his son, *Constable, 1949, p.216). Others brought to the minister's attention were Sydney Olivier, 'Governor of Jamaica for 4 years and is a very able man', by Loulou Harcourt; Graham Wallas, 'real vigour and originality... though might not be regarded as having administrative experience enough', and Pember Reeves, though probably earning too much as Principal of the London School of Economics, by Charles Trevelyan. Fabian Ware, former editor of the* Morning Post, *put himself forward. Acland thought E.K. Chambers, the Board's adult and continuing education expert, would be disastrous, and W.N. Bruce was 'getting too old' (he was 53). The most likely candidate, Lewis Amherst Selby-Bigge, principal assistant secretary of the elementary branch, would be 'a weak appointment'. But, unmoved by representations from Liberal MPs to find an outsider like Sir James Yoxall, in touch with Liberal and Nonconformist opinion, JAP opted for the man he knew best (Compendium of letters in MS. Gainford 83/97–126). The radical journalist Harold Spender was unimpressed: 'You give Parliamentary control to a man like Pease, and Pease of course selects as the chief of his Department the man with the biggest eyeglass and the most impressive name' (Harold Spender–F.S. Marvin, 14 Dec. 1911, Marvin MSS, Bodl. MS.Eng.lett.0260, transcript courtesy of Neil Daglish).*

Selby-Bigge was the safe if uninspiring choice to lead the Board after Morant's departure. The 51-year-old barrister had worked closely with Morant and was a skilled administrator and negotiator. JAP would find him a staunch ally (N.D. Daglish, 'Bigge, Sir Lewis Amherst Selby-, first baronet (1860–1951)', ODNB, *Oxford UP, 2004; online edn, Jan. 2008, http://www.oxforddnb.com/view/article/63835, accessed 20 Feb. 2016).*

Nov. 29 Cabinet. Foreign affairs. &c.

Dec. 6 Persia—Grey explained situation. Business of the House. Considered what bills to drop—sugar convention attitude.

*Grey had made an important speech on Persia in the Commons a week earlier (HC Deb 27 November 1911 vol 22 cc43–65). HHA's Cabinet letter to the King on 8 December outlines 'recent Russian proceedings' in Persia, and a statement by Morley in the Lords on 7 December presented the position the Cabinet had taken. Firuz Kazemzadeh clarifies the issues between Russia and Britain over the threatened restoration of the former Shah (*Russia and Britain in Persia, 1864–1914: A Study in Imperialism, *Yale UP, New Haven, 1968, pp.598–661). For Persia in British politics see Mansour Bonakdarian,* Britain and the Iranian Constitutional Revolution of 1906–1911: Foreign Policy, Imperialism, and Dissent, *Syracuse UP in assoc. with the Iran Heritage Foundation, 2006, pp.224–352; and David McLean,* Britain and her Buffer State: The collapse of the Persian empire, 1890–1914, *Royal Historical Society, 1979; and, for Grey's Liberal critics, D. McLean, 'English Radicals, Russia, and the fate of Persia, 1907–1913',* EHR, *vol.XCIII, no.367, Apr. 1978, pp.338–52. For Foreign Office thinking about a proposed Trans-Persia railway 'through-line' from Russia to India see Grey–Lord Ronaldshay and reply, 8, 9 Nov. 1911, Zetland MSS, ZNK X 10, NYCRO.*

There had been a large increase in the price of sugar. Under the terms of the Brussels Sugar Convention of 1902 a Russian surplus of some 500,000 tons could not be imported into convention countries. The Cabinet decided to notify its fellow members that, unless the Russian sugar was made available, Britain would renounce the convention (TNA: CAB 41/33/32). The operations of the International Sugar Union and Britain's withdrawal from the Sugar Convention as from 1 September 1913 are explained in Michael Fakhri, Sugar and the Making of International Trade Law, *Cambridge UP, 2014, Part II.*

Dec.7 cabinet to discuss Home Rule Bill, I was not present, had to go to Cockermouth to speak.[75]

JAP had spoken on 1 December to the Monmouthshire Education Committee on agricultural education. Cockermouth, lost previously because of Labour intervention, had been won back for the Liberals by the radical Sir Wilfrid Lawson in December 1910 when Labour withdrew. JAP's main speech on 7 December focused on 'the Education Problem', the Insurance Bill, and Home Rule. He was now about to be confronted with a bureaucratic boundary dispute with Runciman, who was still smarting from being shifted to Agriculture and denied the chairmanship of the Development Commission, which he believed HHA had promised him (Runciman–HHA, 18, 21, 23 Oct. 1911, copies, telegrams 14, 19, 21 Oct. 1911, HHA–Runciman, 23 Oct. 1911, Runciman of Doxford MSS; Jonathan Wallace, 'The

[75] Hobhouse notes a discussion of opening communications with the Irish with agreement to show Redmond and John Dillon a financial memo. prepared by Samuel but not the draft Bill (Diary, 9 Dec.1911, referring to meeting on Thurs. 7 Dec., David ed., *Inside Asquith's Cabinet*, pp.108–9). An unpublished paragraph of the 9 Dec. entry says JAP, supported by Beauchamp and Haldane, sought approval for an Education Bill for 1913.

Political Career of Walter Runciman, 1st Viscount Runciman of Doxford (1870–1949)', Ph.D. thesis, U of Newcastle-upon-Tyne, 1995, pp.92–3,117).

7 Dec 1911
8, BARTON STREET, WESTMINSTER.
Strictly Private

My dear Hopwood,

Pease tells me that Dick Cavendish[76] saw him last week and that he (Cavendish) agreed with Pease's views about the proper authority to undertake and develop Agricultural Education.

I can scarcely believe that he told Pease anything of that kind.

Yours sincerely,
Walter Runciman
(Southborough MSS, Bodl. MS.Eng.c.7346)

7 Dec 1911
8, BARTON STREET, WESTMINSTER
Confidential

My Dear Hopwood,

The controversy between ourselves and the Board of Education is in no way diminished by the moving of Morant, for Pease himself is taking up a pronounced attitude antagonistic to the Board of Agriculture.

He writes me that in his view, all Agricultural Education should be under the control of his Board. This is a view which, I understand, the Development Commissioners would not tolerate for a moment, indeed the thing has once more reached a deadlock, for the modus vivendi between the two Boards had broken down.

This weekend Pease and I are writing two memoranda from our respective points of view, and the Prime Minister is to arbitrate between us. I am quite hopeful, although anxious, and I am sure that you will agree that we must make Agricultural Education practical rather than Academic. The Board of Agriculture can make it practical; the Board of Education can only make it academic.

[76] Lord Richard Cavendish (1871–1946); g'son of 7th Duke of Devonshire, elevated in 1908 to rank of a Duke's son on accession of elder brother as 9th Duke; chmn Development Commission 1910–46; Lib. Unionist (Lib. from 1904) MP Lonsdale (Lancs. N) 1895–1906; Chmn Royal Commission on Systems of Election 1908–10; PC 1912: on HHA's 1911 list of prospective peers possibly needed to pass the Parliament Bill. For his Territorial Army service: Tom Williams, 'The Death of a Battalion: The 5th King's Own Royal Lancaster Regiment at the Second Battle of Ypres', Spencer Jones ed., *Courage Without Glory: The British Army on the Western Front 1915*, Helion & Co., 2015, pp.228–57.

If the Prime Minister could receive any hint that you of the Development Commission would prefer Agricultural Education to be under the Board of Agriculture, I have not the least doubt that he would decide in our favour, which would gladden the hearts of agriculturalists and relieve their apprehensions.

Do you think that you could drop him this hint sometime before this weekend?

Am I right in assuming that, if the Prime Minister decides in favour of the Board of Agriculture administering the Farm Institutes Grant as well as the Agricultural Colleges, that you of the Development Commission would agree to that money being transferred from the supervision of the Board of Education to that of the Board of Agriculture?

Yours sincerely,
Walter Runciman
(Southborough MSS, Bodl. MS.Eng.c.7346, f.130)

The dispute with Runciman had a history going back to the 1909 Budget and the Development and Road Improvement Funds Act (José Harris, Unemployment and Politics, *pp.340–47). Edwin Montagu had suggested to HHA that the development activities foreshadowed by DLG should be under the wing of the Board of Agriculture. Instead a Development Commission was created to advise the Treasury, with Lord Richard Cavendish as chairman and Francis Hopwood as paid vice-chairman. JAP lost the battle with Runciman, who announced in January 1912 that the Development Commission would be responsible for a significant share of the capital and running costs of the agricultural colleges. Congratulating Runciman, JAP said: 'I admit I thought I had the best of the argument, but I have great faith in Asquith's power of summing up pros. & cons. and we shall of course... certainly consult the B. of A's wishes in all we did with the Development grant.' There would be 'a real disposition' to work with the Board of Agriculture on technical classes (JAP–Runciman, 6 Jan. 1912, Runciman of Doxford MSS, R/1/16, Newc. U. Spec. Coll). For developments in agricultural education see Collins ed.,* The Agrarian History of England and Wales, *Vol. VII 1850–1914, Pt 1, pp.622ff.*

JAP's Parliamentary Under-Secretary, Charles Trevelyan, suggested that the purpose of the Prime Minister's decision to transfer the Farm Institutes to the Board of Agriculture was 'to give Runciman a chance of helping the party fortunes by creating a popular Liberal policy for agriculture' (Trevelyan–JAP, 15 Jan. 1912, MS. Gainford 83/4). Selby-Bigge's Boxing Day letter to his minister about his holiday reading into 'this agricultural & Development Fund stuff' concludes that Education would have to make a working arrangement with Agriculture and exercise a large influence on the Farm Institute work (MS. Gainford 83/130). The origins and early work of the Commission are best told in Alan Rogers, The most revolutionary measure: A history of the Rural Development Commission 1909–1999, *Rural Development Commission, Salisbury, 1999, pp.6–27,130.*

Dec. 13 I reported having seen Thring — & suggested I should issue a memorandum on Franchise bill as Simon was too ill. Sugar convention attitude. Business of House discussed. King's Speech—short sitting.

As Christmas approached, JAP received a letter from HHA that was disturbing on a number of levels. Ostensibly seeking advice on 22 December from an old whip on how to lessen the number and weight of the government's commitments, HHA conveyed concern that the 'best men will be driven out of the House'. But the real message was the question: what could be done to 'lighten the ship and shorten its voyages? It is to be remembered that this Parliament can legally exist until Dec 1915' (MS. Gainford 89). If it wasn't obvious at first, it was a week later when JAP wrote a confidential postscript to his 6 January letter to Walter Runciman:

> Asquith wrote me the other day, about the heavy work in front of us in the coming session. He obviously wanted me to throw over the Franchise & abolition of plural voting bill, until 1913 — in the hope we could secure its passage, by means of the Parliament Bill in 1915 — our last possible session. I wrote back, that the risk of postponement & increasing the possibility of the return of another govmt pledged to protective tariffs, through our neglect in passing the bill in 1912 ought not to be run & after his & the Master of Elibank's pledges, I thought we could not defer the measure, but must work it in in a time table & after Easter take the whole time of the House.
>
> I am hoping to limit the points in it, so as to make it as short & concise as possible. I hope your view coincides with my own.
>
> J. A. P.
>
> *(copy, MS. Gainford 83/64)*

Elsie Pease was still wondering in late November whether her husband would retain responsibility for the suffrage bill (EP–JAP, 25 Nov. 1911, MS. Gainford 83/52). He did. But there was a fight ahead to push through the kind of comprehensive bill he championed. At his elbow he would have the enthusiastic aid of his Permanent Secretary who took time on Christmas Day to assure him that 'I have fallen into most of the pitfalls of our work & have learnt some caution, but I shall never feel aggrieved or be discouraged if you tell me to be more cautious'. It was a great comfort, Selby-Bigge said, 'to know that one's Chief is keeping a wary eye on one's doings from a wider point of view than is possible for the absorbed official to take' (MS. Gainford 83/127–32).

Chapter 2
1912

From the end of October 1911, electoral reform ranked with Home Rule and Disestablishment of the Welsh Church as one of the three principal measures in the future Liberal programme. A Cabinet committee on franchise legislation was appointed on 24 October. JAP, though he had now been transferred to the Board of Education, continued as the minister mainly responsible for the preparation of franchise reform plans. William Allard had prepared a memorandum for him on 'The Franchise' on 13 September 1911, urging: 'Reform in this sphere must aim at simplification, and should not stop short of manhood suffrage' and that redistribution should follow (MS. Gainford 141/5). Over the Christmas and New Year break several of JAP's colleagues favoured him with their thoughts.

Harcourt was convinced that a definition of 'residence' was needed. He agreed that, if possible, there should be a redistribution before an election on the new franchise, but he would not postpone application of the Franchise Act until redistribution had been effected. He supported the idea of equal electoral districts, with 'electorate' rather than 'population' as the basis of redistribution, but admitted that it would probably be impossible. One likely outcome of the recommended residential qualifications was that the City of London would become a constituency of 'caretakers and charwomen only' (Harcourt–JAP, 15 Dec. 1911, MS. Gainford 141/10).

Herbert Samuel wrote on 18 December that it was 'a matter for consideration whether the great advantage of the simplicity of the residential qualification outweighs the disadvantage of preventing people from exercising any voice in the levying of rates which they have to pay'. The habitually cautious Samuel's view was that simultaneously with any large franchise extension the voting age should be raised to 25. 'There is all the more reason for this if women are to be enfranchised.' (MS. Gainford 141/11.)

Edwin Montagu's 'cursory criticisms' spread over five typed pages. 'Great parliamentary difficulty will be overcome if the Government's intention to proceed with redistribution is statutorily manifest.' He hoped for consideration of a system of automatic redistribution based on population as determined by the census; a House of Commons of two to three hundred members, and limits on election expenditure. If they were to be included in a comprehensive Reform Bill, which they weren't, Montagu was keen for urgent reform of the

Corrupt Practices Act, and favoured alternative voting but not minority representation (Montagu–JAP, 2 Jan. 1912, MS. Gainford 141/9).

While JAP was entrusted with guiding the progress of franchise legislation, he also remained, to some of his colleagues' disquiet, in charge of education. Elizabeth Haldane recorded her brother's thinking:

> He is sad about Education. Pease put into the Office for which Hobhouse was said not to be fit. No money for it just now. R. would like what is impossible—to be Chancellor of the Exchequer and survey the finances of the country, allocating the money as circumstances demand. L. G. quite keen about education, but no big survey and really only a peasant's point of view...
>
> *(E. Haldane diary, 8 Jan. 1912, Elizabeth Haldane MSS, MS. 20240, f.17, NLS)*

25 Jan. Cabinet discussed Home Rule, & Redmond's & John Dillon's[1] criticisms, especially on proposal for devolution (i.e. bills to Scotch Irish & English grand committees) to other portions of U.K.

The Conservative leadership had noticed in the previous autumn that 'many of the members of the Government connect their Home Rule policy with a scheme of Home Rule all round'. Lansdowne asked Curzon if he had seen the announcement of the Liberal candidate for Kilmarnock Burghs, Sir J.D. Rees, that he was in favour of Home rule for Scotland but not for Ireland (Lansdowne–Curzon, 25 Sept. 1911, Curzon of Kedleston MSS, BL: A & AS, MSS. Eur.F.112 D/2/10). Rees, a former Indian civil servant and author of Modern India *(1910), was unsuccessful at Kilmarnock, switched parties, and was Unionist MP for Nottingham E. 1912–22.*

Thinking about ideas of 'Home Rule All Round' was focused by plans from WSC and DLG. WSC, influenced by the Round Table group, would speak in his Dundee constituency on 12 September 1912 advocating a federation of the British Isles with a further prospect of Imperial Federation. He had not dealt with Ulster, but the debate on federation schemes had been ignited, becoming inextricably linked with Home Rule. WSC now proposed dividing the United Kingdom into ten areas, with regional legislatures balancing those from Ireland, Scotland, and Wales. DLG, recognising the urgency of meeting Irish Nationalist demands, proposed Home Rule in stages, with English, Scottish, and Welsh MPs sitting in regional parliamentary grand committees (Andrea Bosco, The Round Table Movement and the Fall of the 'Second'

[1] John Dillon (1851–1927); Irish Parliamentary Party, later Irish National Federation MP Co. Tipperary 1880–3, East Mayo 1885–1918. Leading land reformer, member of the original committee of the Irish Land League, spearheading policy of 'boycotting'. Joined Irish National Federation after Charles Stuart Parnell's divorce case split the Irish Nationalists. Imprisoned six times; critical though constitutional opponent of Britain's Irish policy 1914–18. Defeated by de Valera's Sinn Féin party 1918.

British Empire (1909–1919), Cambridge Scholars, Newcastle upon Tyne, 2017, pp.24–9; Alan J. Ward, The Irish Constitutional Tradition: Responsible Government and Modern Ireland, 1782–1992, *Catholic U. of America P, Washington D.C., 1994, pp.93–4). Speaking for the government at the King's Theatre, Edinburgh, on 8 November 1913, McKinnon Wood promised that a Home Rule bill for Scotland would be drafted (David C. Elliot, 'The Liberal Party in Scotland from the Midlothian Election to the First World War', Ph.D. thesis, Harvard U., 1950, p.161).*

H.J. Hanham writes of the support for devolution among Scottish Liberals and the Conservative opposition in Scottish Nationalism, *Faber & Faber, 1969, pp.91–107. James Kennedy,* Liberal Nationalisms: Empire, State, and Civil Society in Scotland and Quebec, *McGill-Queen's UP, Montreal, 2015, is a comparative analysis with an excellent chapter on 'Scotland and the Search for Federation'. For Scottish back-bench stirrings see MacCallum Scott diary, Mar.–Apr. 1911, MacCallum Scott MSS. For Wales see J. Graham Jones, 'E. T. John and Welsh Home Rule, 1910–14',* WHR, *vol.13, Dec. 1987, pp.453–67.*

Feb. 2 We received through Cassel, an invitation for a minister to go over to Berlin & stay with the German Emperor to discuss international affairs, Grey being suggested. We agreed to send Haldane over unofficially.

There is no report by HHA of a Cabinet meeting on 25 January. In his letter to the King on 3 February HHA describes the meeting the previous day as 'the first meeting of the Cabinet in the present year' (Bodl. MS. Asquith 6, f.91). JAP appears to have telescoped two meetings here. Cabinet had met on 2 February to discuss the new German naval programme. The Admiralty had predictably flagged a corresponding increase in the navy estimates. Thinking that there might be a possibility of negotiating a better outcome, the Cabinet mooted sending Grey to Berlin, but this was deemed premature. A less formal approach through Haldane was suggested, and adopted at the next Cabinet meeting on 6 February (Bodl. MS. Asquith 6, f.95; Michael G. Fry, Lloyd George and Foreign Policy, Vol. One, The Education of a Statesman: 1890–1916, *McGill-Queen's UP, Montreal, 1977, p.157).*

The merchant banker, international financier, and philanthropist Sir Ernest Cassel (1852–1921), intimate and highly honoured friend of King Edward VII, financial adviser to the Churchills and Asquiths, was closely connected with the German shipowner Albert Ballin. Through Ballin he was a conduit for secret conversations with the German government. Cassel's life and work are discursively narrated in Anthony Allfrey, Edward VII and his Jewish Court, *Weidenfeld & Nicolson, 1991, admirably reconstructed by Pat Thane in*

'Financiers and the British state: the case of Sir Ernest Cassel', Business History, *vol.28, 1986, pp.80–99, and compressed in Thane's essay 'Cassel, Sir Ernest Joseph (1852–1921)',* ODNB, *http://www.oxforddnb.com/view/article/32323, accessed 22 June 2014. Haldane's diary of his Berlin visit 8–10 February 1912 was printed and circulated as a Cabinet memorandum (*BD VI*, no.506, pp.676–85).*

Lady Galway, who saw Haldane on his return, noted criticism by Wickham Steed, then The Times *correspondent in Vienna, that Haldane was not fluent in German: 'He is supposed to have said in Berlin that England was in "a queer place". I imagine he wished to say* eine Sonder-Stellung, *"a unique position", and used* sonderliche, *the German for "queer", instead' (Marie Carola Galway,* The Past Revisited: People and Happenings Recalled, *The Harvill P., 1953, p.114;* sonderliche *might now be translated as 'special' or even 'strange'). Four years later Haldane told Sir Charles Harris at the War Office, who might well have known better, that 'down to 1914 there was little fear of a breach with Germany'. The Expeditionary Force, he said, had a double purpose from the first. 'It was intended as a possible help to France if we made an agreement with Russia. But this was a State Secret. The Cabinet hardly knew it' (Haldane–Harris, 20 Nov. 1916, Harris MSS A31 8, Balliol Col.).*

Feb. 7 King's Speech decided.

JAP is confused here. There was no Cabinet meeting on 7 February. He had a long conversation from noon in his room at the Board of Education with Newman and DLG, and Burns also arriving in the early evening (DLG appointment diary 1912, J.T. Davies MSS, NLW; Newman diary, Feb. 1912, TNA: Newman MSS, MH 139). There was a meeting on 6 February at which there was an extended discussion of the Government of Ireland Bill, ending in a compromise agreement to give ministers power to alter or drop the bill should it seem expedient to do so—a formula that unlocked the door to the exclusion of Ulster. 'In the meantime careful and confidential inquiry is to be made as to the real extent and character of the Ulster resistance' (TNA: CAB 41/33/35; Cornelius O'Leary and Patrick Maume, Controversial Issues in Anglo-Irish relations, 1910–1921, *Four Courts P., Dublin, 2004, pp.16–18). DLG had proposed that every county should have the option of 'contracting out' of Home Rule. In the advice to the King, the idea that ministers would be sensitive to public opinion and 'ready to recognise the necessity' of special treatment 'for the Ulster counties' was attributed to Crewe. Hobhouse noted that he had supported Crewe and HHA together with WSC and Haldane, and that Birrell vowed he would have nothing to do with any Bill different from those of 1886 and 1893 (Hobhouse diary, 11 Feb. 1912, David ed.,* Inside Asquith's Cabinet, *p.111).*

JAP overlooks a meeting on 8 February at which the King's speech was dealt with. WSC passed a note to DLG telling him he had been lunching with the independent Irish nationalist MP Tim Healy. DLG: 'Did you suggest anything about Ulster?' According to WSC, Healy was 'vy friendly. Still hopes to stand on same platform as Redmond over this. Means to support the Bill however rotten' (BL, RP3353). The Asquith MSS contain no Cabinet letter for meetings on 8 or 12 February. There was a meeting on 10 February at which there was discussion of seizure of 'ships and cargoes with enemy destination, ownership or origin; the closing of museums and Belgian economic situation' (TNA: CAB 41/36/4).

Feb. 12 Haldane's Report see his printed circular, recording visit. We discussed situation, especially their new increase in Navy law, which was inopportune if we came to a friendly arrangement. With German new law might provide in new construction in Dreadnoughts.

before seeing Haldane			our answer		
1912.	3.	we pressed	2	5	4
1913	2	better than	3	4	5
1914	2	the modification	2	5	4
1915	2	suggested to	2	4	4
1916	3	Haldane	3	5	5
1917	2		2	4	3

Cabinet sat late on the 12th listening to Haldane on his Berlin visit: 'a most important, & on the whole a successful mission admirably done', Runciman told his wife, adding the next day 'Winston got a wigging from Morley & Asquith in the Cabinet, & took it humbly enough' (Runciman of Doxford MSS). Negotiations with Germany over the next few weeks revealed irreconcilable understandings of the status of Haldane's mission and the possible territorial outcomes that the British government might consider, including the cession of Pemba and the British Protectorate of Zanzibar (R.T.B. Langhorne, 'Great Britain and Germany, 1911–1914', in F.H. Hinsley ed., British Foreign Policy Under Sir Edward Grey*, Cambridge UP, 1977, pp.288–305). Grey's thinking at this time is best conveyed in T.G. Otte's tour de force,* Statesman of Europe: A Life of Sir Edward Grey*, Allen Lane, 2020, pp.430–44.*

A report to the King on 14 February incorporated advice from Sir David Harrel, a former Dublin Metropolitan Police Commissioner and Under-Secretary for Ireland, on likely resistance to Home Rule (TNA: CAB 37/169/23).

Feb. 15 Naval requirements discussed. Churchill asked to further look into position.

Feb. 20 We discussed at length 2 hours position & situation. Decided Grey with Haldane should see Metternich & explain if new construction in Germany was announced it would make us look ridiculous at same time to say our friendship was secured, & pass pious formulas of our intention not to attack one another. If Germany expanded her Navy law we would have to respond by further increasing our fleet by some 14 millions in 6 years, and building 2 keels to one.[2]

Pemba & Zanzibar arrangements could not be entered into except as a separate deal, with some quid pro quo.

Grey was to dwell on advantage already gained, but point out how difficult all the German increases by additional men & squadrons were in helping negociations.

We pressed for no new construction, & limit efforts to establish 3d Squadron. We could not take exception to Germany making existing fleet effective, but to increase it was not to show spirit of amity.

The first business on 20 February had been considering a letter from Sir George Askwith and resolving that the time had come for government intervention to prevent, 'if possible', the threatened national strike in the coal industry. The strike was made possible by a change in the rules of the Miners' Federation in October 1911. Following the passage of the Eight Hours Act in 1908, there had been increasing discontent among miners with their revised scales of pay, particularly for the harder seams of coal. On 18 January the Federation announced that a ballot of its members showed 445,801 out of 561,522 in favour of strike action beginning on 1 March, should the union's demands not be met. There were different pay scales at almost every pithead. The miners were prepared to negotiate new rates by districts but they insisted on a national minimum of 5s. for men and 2s. for boys. They met the Miners' Association on 7 February. Most of the owners were prepared to concede to the minimum wage, but the South Wales owners refused to consider it and withdrew from negotiations. The wider policy and intellectual background of minimum wage arguments and the Liberal government's Trade Boards legislation are surveyed in Sheila Blackburn, 'Must Low Pay Always Be with US? The Origins of Britain's Minimum Wage Legislation', Historical Studies in Industrial Relations, *vol.23/24, Spring/Autumn 2007, pp.61–101, and James Thompson, 'Political economy, the labour movement and the minimum wage, 1880–1914, in E.H.H. Green and D.M. Tanner eds,* The Strange Survival of Liberal England: Political Leaders, Moral

[2] Pencilled notes of remarks at this meeting by DLG and Asquith are at Bodl. MS. Harcourt 442, f.2. Harcourt's 'diary' has no entry for this date.

Values and the Reception of Economic Debate, *Cambridge UP, pb 2011 [1st edn 2007], pp.62–88.*

Cabinet decided to intervene to break the deadlocked negotiations. HHA, DLG, Buxton, Grey, Askwith, and Board of Trade officials arranged to meet both sides separately on February 26 (HHA Cabinet letter, 21 Feb. 1912, TNA: CAB 41/33/37). DLG summarised the situation for Robertson Nicoll on 24 February: 'The South Wales owners are thoroughly unreasonable, but so are the new leaders of the South Wales men. The colliers have thrown over their own leaders and are being guided... by rather featherbrained Socialist organisers.' If the Government were prepared to take a strong line, DLG thought the 'older and saner leaders would regain their prestige' (Robertson Nicoll MSS).

There is no Cabinet letter for the meeting of 29 February. But Harcourt's notes that day list Morley, Crewe, Hobhouse, McKinnon Wood, and JAP 'at Council' (Bodl. MS. Harcourt 442, f.2). The Secretary of State for War had already instructed the Adjutant General Sir Spencer Ewart on 19 February 1912 to make preparations with 'the maximum of secrecy' for troops to be moved at 'the last moment—say on the 28th' and added on the 27th: 'No decision is possible before midday tomorrow. We must just keep our troops back' (Ewart Memoirs, Ewart MSS). Given his continuing business interests, JAP's omission of the decision to intervene is curious.

As the diary is mostly confined to Cabinet and Parliamentary matters, it is less surprising that JAP does not mention the wrangle he had been drawn into over medical treatment of children in DLG's Insurance Bill. Supporting George Newman, he had pressed the Chancellor, his new Parliamentary Under-Secretary, Masterman, and Treasury Permanent Secretary, Sir Robert Chalmers, for a substantial allocation of funds. Newman noted in his diary on 15 February that they had fought for £100,000 but would probably get £60,000 (TNA: Newman MSS, MH 139). Commenting on Chalmers to his minister on 22 December, Selby-Bigge had admitted: 'I don't the least know if I can trust him. I am sure it is good policy on my part to appear to trust him, but I must look to you to warn me if I am too confiding. Morant would of course say that I could not and ought not to trust him a yard, but he can hardly express an impartial opinion just now.' (MS. Gainford 83/127.) Morant's seething resentment of Chalmers' 'swaggering ignorance' was poured out to Masterman on 24 April 1912 (Masterman MSS A 3/4/16, Cadbury RL Birmingham U.). Out of favour with DLG, Chalmers was appointed Governor of Ceylon in June 1913. Observing his farewell dinner, Runciman mused to his wife on 30 July 1913 on 'the tragedy of Chalmers' triumphant entry and his disheartened almost broken-hearted departure' (Viscountess Runciman of Doxford MSS).

On the background to the introduction of a medical treatment grant see the corrective to Bentley B. Gilbert's account in The Evolution of National Insurance *(pp.131–43) in J. D. Hirst, 'A failure "without parallel": The School Medical Service and the London County*

Council 1907–12', Medical History, *vol.25, issue3, 1981, pp.281–300 and Hirst's 'The Growth of Treatment through the School Medical Service, 1908–18',* Medical History, *vol.33, issue3, 1989, pp.318–42; Bernard Harris,* The health of the schoolchild: A history of the school medical service in England and Wales, *Open UP, Buckingham, 1995, pp.64–9; and Cooper,* The British Welfare Revolution, *pp.214–24; and, for previous support for medical inspection and treatment by McKenna as President of the Board of Education, Walter Rea (Lib. MP for Scarborough), and Jack Tennant (then a backbencher), see Neil Daglish, 'Robert Morant's hidden agenda? The origins of the medical treatment of schoolchildren',* Hist. Ed., *vol.19, no.2, 1990, pp.139–48.*

Feb. 29[3] We discussed the Navy Estimates again, the Coal Strike, & authorised Churchill to bring in estimates under assumption that the Navy law would not increase the building programme of Germany, & we authorised the P.M. to enter into negociations with the Masters & men to bring about a settlement.

HHA and DLG led the ministers who met the miners' representatives at the Foreign Office on 29 February. The Prime Minister informed the union leaders that the Cabinet unanimously agreed 'a case has been made out for ensuring to the underground workers in the coal industry... a reasonable minimum wage'. He affirmed that, if a reasonable minimum wage could not be secured by agreement, the government would secure it. But his appeal to allow 'a reasonable latitude of discussion' was not persuasive. For the transcript of the speeches in which red lines were put through the Prime Minister's incautious rhetorical riffs and his undertaking that 'effective attainment' would be secured 'by every step and by every means' see Bodl. MS. Asquith 93, ff.6–21.

Among the steps and means that had been considered were coercing the miners (no one could think of a way of doing this) and coercing 'recalcitrant coal owners'. Pencilling on 10 Downing Street notepaper, Runciman wrote of some talk of 'a Bill laying down proposals for the putting in of a receiver to work the mines. Churchill and I were opposed to any onesided action, & it was surprising to find that we were the only two who protested—although the P.M. asseverated his intention of even handedness' (Runciman Cabinet note, 29 Feb. 1912, Runciman of Doxford MSS). DLG had been impressed with the idea of a Receiver 'on the analogy of the Court of Chancery when a dispute between partners threatens to stop a colliery... but you cannot compel a million of men to go down a pit and hew coal' (DLG–Robertson Nicoll, 24 Feb. 1912, Robertson Nicoll MSS). HHA reported to the group

[3] HHA apparently did not report this meeting to the King; but *The Times*, 1 Mar. 1912, recorded a Cabinet 'yesterday', and Harcourt also kept rough notes dated 29 Feb. (Bodl. MS. Harcourt 442, ff.190–1).

'at Council' that 60 per cent of owners agreed to the government's proposals; but the men were 'very unreasonable' and 'must realise we mean business on minimum wage'. DLG said a fortnight's strike would lead to more drink, but a month to less. JAP and Burns disagreed: the wives would get the strike money, so it would be 'a temperate strike' (Bodl. MS. Harcourt 442, f.190). Arguing that, as agreement was blocked by only a few of the owners, the strike should be postponed and negotiations reopened, it was suggested that negotiations should be by district, with a government representative to arbitrate if necessary. However, the men would begin such discussions only if their national minimum was accepted; the South Wales owners continued to refuse to consider the minimum wage, and the strike began on 1 March. Talks were resumed on 7 March but without making any progress.

At DLG's instigation, Sir George Riddell and Vernon Hartshorn drew up a bill to establish a minimum wage varying by district, to be settled by district boards; this was introduced on 19 March. The miners continued to insist that a national minimum of 5s. and 2s. be included in the bill. The government, mindful that a 'parliamentary minimum wage' would be a dangerous precedent, continued to refuse (Cooper, The British Welfare Revolution, *pp.273–5). The bill became law on 29 March. The miners' representatives decided to consult their members; a second ballot was held. The results were announced on 3 April: only 244,011 out of 445,024 supported the confirmation of the strike, less than the two-thirds majority needed. The largest drop in support for the strike came in South Wales. The district's strike funds had been very low at the beginning of the strike because of strikes there in 1910–11 and were by then exhausted, and there was little alternative employment in the area. The result was a gradual but embittered return to work. See Peter Rowland,* The Last Liberal Governments. Unfinished Business 1911–1914, *Barrie & Jenkins 1971, pp.148–54; R. Page Arnot,* The Miners: Years of Struggle. A History of the Miners' Federation of Great Britain (from 1910 onwards), *George Allen & Unwin 1953, pp.90–110; M.W. Kirby,* The British Coalmining Industry, 1870–1946: A Political and Economic History, *Macmillan, 1977, pp.18–23; and for a deeper understanding of the strike see Roy Church, 'Edwardian Labour Unrest and Coalfield Militancy, 1890–1914',* HJ, *vol.30, no.4, 1987, pp.841–57.*

Churchill proposed that we should not introduce any Navy Estimates but have a mere vote on a/c, until Germany had disclosed her intentions — it seemed to me his main idea was to avoid having to defend his estimates twice over! Asquith & Morley, & Harcourt were horrified at this suggestion.

Runciman noted tersely: 'Army estimates have been issued without any discussion in or permission from the Cabinet. Navy Estimates discussed but contested by no one…'. Sitting outside the Cabinet room during this meeting, Charles Lyell heard 'every now & again a voice raised even through the closed doors! Generally Winston's!' (C. Lyell–Sir L. Lyell, 29 Feb. 1912, Lyell MSS). WSC had produced navy estimates of £44,085,000 compared with £44,392,000 the previous year. DLG expressed disappointment, McKenna having promised a reduction of £1,500,000 in 1912, and the same the next year. But, as Harcourt somewhat waspishly recorded, 'Ll. Geo cannot criticise them in detail'. WSC's raised voice might well have been a response to the fact that the whole Cabinet was against his proposal to defer the estimates until May '& laughing' (Bodl. MS. Harcourt 442, f.190). Yet voices did not need to be greatly raised to be overheard. As Frederick Leith Ross noted, on one of his last days as one of the Prime Minister's private secretaries (he was replaced by Gerald Pinsent), McKenna and Birrell were concerned about his proximity to the Cabinet room. It was very dangerous for private secretaries to hear what was said in the Cabinet. 'My dear McKenna', Birrell assured his colleague, 'You know one can trust a cart load of P. Secs rather than Cabinet Ministers' (Leith Ross diary, [?15 Nov. 1913], TNA: T 188/263). See Andrew Blick and George Jones, At Power's Elbow: Aides to the Prime Minister from Robert Walpole to David Cameron, *Biteback Publishing, 2013, Ch. 3.*

March 6 Full cabinet. The Prime Minister wanted to know our view as to whether the King should go around early in May for 3 weeks paying his respects to the Monarchs of Europe—he wanted to go to Austria & Germany. We agreed he could not pass through France without paying his respects to our friendly republican neighbours, & he could not omit the Russian Czar[4] & that Grey should go with him, this would do good. Having regard to the unsettled affairs at home, & to the King's absence in India for 3 months so recently we decided to postpone the visits for another year. The P.M. said Italy & Spain might be further deferred, but it would be expected some time. Grey said he would go round himself in the autumn. The P.M. spoke in a very depressed sense of the defeat in So. Manchester & regarded the election very seriously, & that if public opinion was against us, there was no prospect of passing through into law Home Rule, Disestablishment. He also said Sir George Kemp[5] cd not be prevented fr. retiring immediately for N.W. Manchester.

At luncheon with the Prime Minister at 10 Downing Street before the Cabinet DLG and Haldane had a jolly time, Violet Asquith, Edmund Gosse, and the 86-year-old Lady Dorothy

[4] Nicholas II (1868–1917); succ. father 1894; a nephew of Queen Alexandra.

[5] Sir George Kemp (1866–1945); Lib. MP Manchester (NW) 1910–12; Lib. Unionist MP Lancashire (Heywood) 1895–1906; flannel manufacturer; served in the S. African War (Lt-Col. 32nd Imperial Yeomanry), at Gallipoli, and was Brig.-Gen. 42nd Div.; Kt 1909; Baron Rochdale 1913.

Nevill among the party (Gosse–Nellie Gosse, 6 Mar. 1912, Ann Thwaite, Edmund Gosse: A Literary Landscape, *Tempus, Stroud, 2007, p.458). In the Cabinet room HHA had set a sombre tone, talking of losing moral authority and facing accusations of clinging to office after seven years in power. Morley asked: what would the Irish say if the government resigned? DLG seized the moment to insist that they discuss future political strategy. His Insurance Bill was going to be popular. They must go on with Home Rule and Disestablishment. Haldane, although he would have liked to go out, agreed that they must stay for the sake of the Irish and the Welsh. Birrell also said they were bound to the Irish and to the Nonconformists on education. WSC was eager to see £100,000 spent on a campaign promoting Insurance and Home Rule, and raised again the idea of separate treatment for Ulster. Grey's view was that before they could do anything else the coal strike had to be settled (Harcourt Cabinet note, 6 Mar. 1912, Bodl. MS. Harcourt 442, ff.192–3).*

Kemp, who had reservations about Liberal policy on Irish Home Rule, Welsh Disestablishment, and 'Lloyd Georgian finance', was retiring for business reasons, in spite of emphatic requests from HHA and Alick Murray, who hoped he might be able to support the Home Rule Bill (Kemp–[C.P.] Scott, 20 Sept. 1911; Kemp–Murray, 26 Jan. 1912, Murray–Kemp, 7 Feb. 1912, copy, CHAR 2/53/29–31; CHAR 2/56/13–15,30–32,38–43, CAC). Kemp spoke against the Home Rule Bill. He did not vote; nevertheless HHA deferred a promised peerage because of the 'speculation and possible misunderstanding' that it might provoke (P.F. Clarke, Lancashire and the New Liberalism, *CUP, 1971, p.304). Kemp reached out to the Tories seeking an assurance that his claims on them would be recognised; they were not (Balcarres diary, 7,9 May 1912, Vincent ed.,* The Crawford Papers, *pp.274–5). He had beaten Bonar Law handsomely in December 1910; but when the by-election was held (9 Aug. 1912), the Liberals' Gordon Hewart lost the seat by a large majority. The Manchester rubber and cotton manufacturer and banker Frederick Smith had earned himself a baronetcy by offering to pay Kemp's expenses, and £1,000 a year to the Liberal Party 'as long as I live', plus additional subventions for elections and emergencies. A baronetcy was 'much better than the House of Lords,' he said (William Jones MSS 5452, NLW). He became Baron Colwyn in the 1917 Birthday Honours. Kemp was elevated as Baron Rochdale in 1913.*

Morley pointed out we were under a pledge to the Irish Nationalists, & bound to pursue the policy, as we did in 1893 with a smaller majority to work with. L. George was strongly inclined to our going on & said he knew all along Insurance bill wd react on us. The position in regard to negociations in the coal Trade was reported to us by the P.M. We could only ask him to go on meeting & bringing parties together. I said the men might find some other alternative to their own schedule of minimum rates for the various districts. They must save their face by alleging that equal rates to those asked for had been secured. Burns agreed & said other trade unionists were pressing Colliers to come in, as their own funds were being exhausted in a strike in which they took a slight interest.

I told Asquith after Cabinet not to be disheartened at Sir Arthur Haworth's loss of Manchester, that in 1909 seats were going wrong in the same way, & we recovered them in 1910. I thought we could run Agar Robartes[6] in safely for Cornwall to take the place of Haworth. It seemed to please him to have these points made.[7] A dinner was to have been given to P.M. on 8th to mark our appreciation of his leadership through the Parliament Bill fight. As a court was fixed a luncheon was arranged & a good deal of emotion was apparent in both the P.M. & his audience.

Following his appointment as a junior whip, Haworth was compelled to seek re-election. He was unexpectedly defeated by Philip Glazebrook on 5 March, partly as a result of the activities of the medical staff at Manchester University, who opposed the Insurance Act, and the lack of enthusiasm in the constituency for a national insurance scheme that was less generous than many local employees, warehousemen and clerks, already enjoyed. For Haworth as a leading Manchester radical and an analysis of the two Manchester by-elections see Samantha Wolstencroft, The Progressive Alliance and the Rise of Labour: Political Change in Industrial Britain, 1903–1922, *Palgrave Macmillan, 2018, pp.63–87; and the classic work of Peter Clarke,* Lancashire and the New Liberalism, passim. *DLG also told his brother on 6 March: 'Strike—suffragettes, undoubtedly prejudicially affected result, probably lost us the seat' (J. Graham Jones, 'Lloyd George and the Suffragettes at Llanystumdwy',* J.Lib.DH, *vol. 34/35, 2002, p.6; and reprinted without the dash in J. Graham Jones,* David Lloyd George and Welsh Liberalism, *Welsh Political Archive, NLW, 2010, p.147).*

Haworth had been returned unopposed in December 1910, Glazebrook having arrived at Manchester Town Hall six minutes after nominations had closed. He had been overseas

[6] Hon. Thomas Charles Reginald Agar-Robartes (1880–1915); Lib. MP Cornwall (St Austell) 1908–15; eldest son of 6th Vt Clifden. Close friend of Rosebery's sons, Lord Dalmeny and Neil Primrose; best known for his amendment to the Home Rule Bill (11 June 1912) to exclude Antrim, Armagh, Down, and Londonderry. Recommended for the VC in 1915 for his part in rescuing a severely wounded sergeant; he died from wounds received in this exploit. Agar-Robartes, who had been elected for Cornwall (Bodmin) in 1906 but then unseated on petition, had been returned unopposed for Cornwall (St Austell) in Dec. 1910, having first won the seat at a by-election in Feb. 1908. See Paul Holden, '"A Very English Gentleman" The Honourable Thomas Charles Reginald Agar-Robartes MP (1880–1915)', *J.Lib.H.*, issue 66, 2010, pp.8–17. Martin J. Gibson leaves little doubt that there was an intimate relationship between Agar-Robartes and Neil Primrose (*A Primrose Path: The Gilded Life of Lord Rosebery's Favourite Son*, Arum P., 2020).

[7] Sir Arthur Adlington Haworth Bt (1865–1944); Lib. MP Manchester (S) 1906–12; cotton merchant; leading Congregationalist layman; Lib. Junior Whip Feb.–Apr. 1912; Bt 1911. For Haworth's wartime chairmanship of the Congregational Union, and opposition to conscription see Clyde Binfield, *So Down to Prayers: Studies in English Nonconformity 1780–1920*, Dent, 1977, pp.239–44.

*when the by-election was called, but the Liberals sportingly delayed the poll for three days (*The Times, *3 Dec. 1910, 26 Feb. 1912; and see T.G. Otte and Paul Readman eds,* By-elections in British Politics, 1832–1914, *Boydell P., Woodbridge, 2013, p.14). For the Manchester electorate see James R. Moore,* The Transformation of Urban Liberalism: Party Politics and Urban Governance in Late Nineteenth-Century England, *Ashgate, Aldershot, 2006,* passim; *Tony Adams, 'Labour Vanguard, Tory Bastion, or the Triumph of New Liberalism? Manchester Politics 1900–1914 in Comparative Perspective',* Manchester Region History Review, *XIV, 2000, pp.25–38; Steve Fielding, 'Irish Politics in Manchester 1890–1914',* International Review of Social History, *vol.XXXIII, 1988, pp.261–84, and Mervyn Busteed,* The Irish in Manchester *c.*1750–1921: Resistance, Adaptation And Identity, *Manchester UP, 2018, pp.172–205; and for other views on the March by-election see Paul Readman and Luke Blaxill, 'Edwardian By-elections', in Otte and Readman eds,* By-elections in British Politics, 1832–1914, *pp.232,238. HHA's* cri de coeur *on 6 March—there 'must be a seat somewhere safe!'—was saved by Harcourt for posterity (Bodl. MS. Harcourt 442, f.192). On suffragette support for Labour at by-elections 1912–14 see Susan Pedersen,* Eleanor Rathbone and the Politics of Conscience, *Yale UP., New Haven, 2004, pp.130–5.*

The luncheon to HHA was given at the Covent Garden Theatre. Among about 600 guests were 46 Ministers, 36 Liberal Peers, 200 Liberal MPs, and 300–400 representative Liberals. Sir Charles Rose, MP for Newmarket, presided. DLG spoke of his appreciation and loyalty to HHA. The list of those present, published in The Times *on 9 March 1912, does not include JAP. 'He does it so well,' Arthur Ponsonby reflected on the Prime Minister's performance, 'speaks excellently is quite admirable in the House and I cannot understand why he seldom if ever rouses one to enthusiasm' (Ponsonby diary, 8 Mar. 1912, Ponsonby of Shulbrede MSS). Morley, who had carried much of the burden of the Parliament Bill in the Lords, was 'deeply hurt' that 'no one, not even the Cabinet had thanked him' (Cunningham diary, 25 Mar. 1912, Miller-Cunningham MSS).*

I told the P.M. at the Court I was so sorry not to be present but I had to take charge of Croydon Marks' Bill on single school areas. The P.M. said he knew why I was away and that it was a most touching occasion.

Sir G. Croydon Marks had introduced a bill amending the Education Act where it affected schools that were the only ones in their areas. His bill would force such schools to be transferred to the local education authority, under varying conditions. The schools would then be supported by the rates; and religious education would be in accordance with the Cowper–Temple compromise. Denominational teaching would be allowed two mornings a week, if the parents desired it, and would be carried out by someone other than the regular teachers. In this way, Croydon Marks hoped to meet the grievances both of Nonconformist parents and of teachers who could often not be considered for headteacher positions because of their religion. JAP, who sought the advice of his colleagues on 14 March (Harcourt's Cabinet note, 14 Mar. 1912, Bodl. MS. Harcourt 442, f.225.), spoke kindly about the bill, but The Annual Register 1912 *(p.42) describes it as being 'smothered by systematic obstruction'.*

The Party was pleased with his speech but he was obviously worried with the strike negociations still hanging fire.

HHA spent the weekend with a small, mostly family, party at 'a nice little villa in the New Forest which has been lent me for a few weeks by an almost unknown cousin'. He wrote from there to Viola Tree[8] *on 10 March that he had '(like St Paul at Ephesus) been after the manner of men fighting with beasts—Gorgons & Hydras & Chimaeras dire—as Milton says somewhere. The struggle is not over, but there is a Sunday pause' (BL Add.MS. 59,895, ff.17–18; Viola Tree,* Castles in the Air: The Story of My Singing Days, *Leonard & Virginia Woolf at the Hogarth P., 1926, p.239). The Pauline allusion would be dusted off again on other Sunday pauses with young women.*

In preparation for the next meeting Askwith brought the Prime Minister and the miners' leader Robert Smillie together at a small dinner party on 10 March (Dinner Book 1912, Askwith MSS). On Sunday 12 March the Prime Minister took the chair at a conference at the Foreign Office of coal owners and the Miners' Federation executive. HHA, Grey, and Buxton were supported by Board of Trade Officials, Llewellyn Smith, Askwith, Askwith's deputy, (Isaac) Haig Mitchell, and H.J. Wilson, and the Prime Minister's private secretary, Maurice Bonham Carter. The conference of the 'Consultative Committee' reconvened at 11.30 on the 13th, its confidential proceedings having been leaked to the Daily Telegraph *and* The Morning Post, *possibly by Bonar Law's PPS Johnny Baird, who was in close touch with the mine owners*

[8] Viola Tree (1884–1938); dau. Sir Herbert Beerbohm Tree; actress and journalist; m. 11 July 1912 Alan Parsons (1887–1933) with Anthony Asquith as page, Elizabeth Asquith a bridesmaid, and gifts of a silk crepe flowered shawl from Raymond and Katharine Asquith, a silver sugar caster from Herbert and Cynthia Asquith, and 10 vols of Shakespeare from HHA (Uncatalogued Tree Family Archive, Accession no. RA/420, U. of Bristol Theatre Collection). Parsons, civil servant then drama critic; p.s. to McKenna from May 1915; chronic asthmatic (Christabel Aberconway, *A Wiser Woman? A Book of Memories*, Hutchinson, 1966, p.95). 'Alan was completely a-moral—he had the make-up of a Greek faun' (Sir Alan 'Tommy' Lascelles–John Gore, 24 Feb. 1965, Duff Hart-Davis ed., *King's Counsellor: Abdication and War: The Diaries of Sir Alan Lascelles*, Weidenfeld & Nicolson, 2006, p.412). In Nov. 1912 Viola's scheduled operatic debut in *Salomé* in Genoa had been thwarted by a serious throat illness (Madeleine Bingham, *'The Great Lover': The Life and Art of Herbert Beerbohm Tree*, Hamish Hamilton, 1978, pp.213–14). HHA said in 1914 that she would be one of the very few people who would feel his loss when he died. She did (Jenkins, *Asquith*, pp.332–3; Viola Parsons, *Alan Parsons' Book: A Story in Anthology*, William Heinemann, 1937, pp.89–90).

(Sykes, Tariff Reform in British Politics 1903–1913, *pp.260–61,328). With agreement still not reached, the meeting was adjourned until 3.00 p.m. the next day to allow for 'a very important Cabinet' that had been postponed from the regular Wednesday.*

March 14 Cabinet. Asquith reported position and situation in connection with the coal strike, but there was no understanding arrived at in cabinet, if the men & masters failed to arrive at a solution. It was quite evident that the Welsh & Scotch coal owners would not concede the minimum wage & equally clear the men's leaders were having an internal difference but neither party were not [*sic*] intending to accept compulsory arbitration. They were to meet again at 3.0. We then discussed the terms of a telegram Metternich wanted to send to Germany to strengthen Bethmann Hollweg against Tirpitz[9] in their struggle for the Chancellorship. We were told that a generous formula of friendship would enable the new Navy to be almost withdrawn. We agreed to the following words.

(Prefix as to both countries desiring an understanding)

> 'England will neither make nor join any[10] unprovoked attack upon Germany and pursue no aggressive policy towards her. Aggression upon Germany is not the subject and forms no part of any treaty, understanding or combination to which England is now a party nor will she become a party to anything that has such an object.'

I asked Sydney Buxton the 2 following questions:—

1. Do the more reasonable section of the men propose to remain out until after each district arrives at a settlement?

His answer was: Yes at present: they may alter this.

2. Assuming Wales & Scotland are coerced is there machinery to which these men assent which must end in local settlements (i.e. arbitration failing arrangement) if so may we presume the men would at once go back to work?

Answer: Not yet: but we are working towards it and may make progress today (though doubtful) but they shy much about 'arbitration'.

[9] Alfred von Tirpitz (1849–1930), Sec. of St., Imperial Navy Department 1897–1916; chief builder of German Navy in the 17 years preceding World War I and a dominant personality of Emperor William II's reign. Ennobled in 1900; adm. 1903; grand adm. 1911; rtd 1916.

[10] According to a marginal note by JAP, the underlined words were added in red ink on 16 March. The original amended draft as noted by Harcourt was: 'England will [not] make [any] no unprovoked attack...' (Bodl. MS. Harcourt 442, f.245). The background is elaborated, with extensive quotations from Harcourt's diary memoranda and official documents, in David Owen, *The Hidden Perspective: The Military Conversations 1906–1914*, Haus, 2014, pp.140–78.

I saw A.F. Pease[11] late Thursday night at Brown's Hotel. He complained that Asquith had kept the masters in the room at the F.O. debating what the Schedule prices should be, although it was obvious no agreement was possible, & Asquith knew the owners' position was they would only discuss these prices in their various districts. A.F.P. thought it was the only mistake he had made. It had irritated the coal owners. The men & masters met again next day, & broke up Asquith telling them legislation must be introduced, & both sides agreed to appoint men to meet the Govmt draftsman on Saturday. Sydney Buxton explained to me at Lord Brassey's[12] party at night, if Asquith had not kept the owners sitting late on Thursday, the conference would have ended abruptly & he was determined to stop this, & showed his sagacity; the result was that both sides had separated realising the importance of the step the Govmt proposed. Buxton asked leave to buy 100,000 tons of coal fr. U.S.A. Runciman & McKenna opposed this successfully.

Buxton, concerned about gas, water, electricity, and sanitary services, had already been exploring the availability of American coal. Runciman, supported by McKenna, objected to 'speculating', and coal purchasing was abandoned (Bodl. MS. Harcourt 442, f.224). JAP does not mention, and might not have known of, the negotiations with Vernon Hartshorn being carried on behind the scenes by Sir George Riddell. HHA told his PPS that Hartshorn 'who is so extreme to the men outside was one of the most moderate & conciliatory in the conference' (C. Lyell–Lady Lyell, 31 Mar. 1912, Lyell MSS). Four weeks of Cabinet tension and back-room negotiations in February and March are told from Riddell's informed perspective and participation in J.M. McEwen ed., The Riddell Diaries 1908–1923, *Athlone P., 1986, pp.33–40.*

After lunching at 10 Downing Street on 15 March with the Prime Minister, Margot Asquith, Lady Frances Balfour, and Augustine Birrell, Marie Belloc Lowndes recorded: 'All the talk was of the strike. Mrs Asquith is strongly on the side of the men, Birrell evidently terribly irritated at the whole thing. I thought Asquith looked very ill and preoccupied. He came

[11] Arthur Francis Pease (1866–1927); director (with JAP) of Pease & Partners Ltd; JAP's cousin; represented Durham coal owners in 1912 negotiations; 2nd Civil Ld of Adm. 1918–19; Bt 1920; High Sheriff of Durham 1920.

[12] Thomas Brassey, 1st Earl Brassey (1836–1918); son of millionaire contractor; Lib. MP Devonport 1865 and Hastings 1868–86; a great yachtsman, he wrote a five-volume encyclopaedia of the British navy and (with others) edited *The Naval Annual* (*Brassey's Naval Annual* from 1914) 1886–1918; Civil Ld of Adm. 1880–4; KCB 1881; Parl. Sec. to Adm. 1884–5; Baron Brassey 1886 (after being defeated in two elections); Ld-in-waiting 1893–5; Gov. Victoria 1895–1901; Ld Warden of the Cinque Ports 1908–13; Earl Brassey 1911; described by V.W. Baddeley, *DNB 1912–1921* (p. 63) as 'a rich man, of no outstanding ability but with great powers of industry, and of kindly, genial, and equable temperament'. For sympathetic glimpses of Brassey as an old man, 'his sententious periods quavering between the querulous and the urbane', see Rupert Hart-Davis ed., *Siegfried Sassoon Diaries 1915–1918*, faber & faber, 1983, pp.163–71 (15–18 May 1917).

in only for about a quarter of an hour and the day before had spent fourteen hours practically on end, talking either to the men or the masters' (Susan Lowndes ed., Diaries and Letters of Marie Belloc Lowndes 1911–1947, *Chatto & Windus, 1971, p.29).*

For the fourth day of the conference the previously indisposed DLG cut through to the heart of the matter, telling the miners that the government agreed with them that there should be a national settlement on the principle of a minimum wage. But a principle alone was nothing, a 'pure myth ... a delusion'. A way had to be found to translate the principle into cash by what HHA called 'effective and promptly working machinery'. The conference was brought to a close with agreement that the government would draft and enact minimum wage legislation in the next few days. The miners would resume work when an Act had been passed, with a time limit of a month to resolve details, and the new rates to be retrospective to the date when work resumed. (Transcript of the conference proceedings, Fife and Kinross Miners' Association Papers, Dep.304/4, NLS.)

Sat. Mar. 16 10.45 Cabinet. I was stopped going North Friday evening, & we were all present. Asquith explained that he could not call us together before the conference broke up the evening before, but he & his 3 colleagues Grey, George & Buxton all concurred in his taking responsibility on themselves to introduce legislation to settle the schedules & bring in 35 per cent of the coal owners who had declined to recognise the minimum wage.

Morley then very courteously but firmly expressed his regret that the P.M. had committed the cabinet to a procedure he could not support, & that the course taken was never sanctioned. To fix wages by law, & introduce compulsory arbitration could alone be justified on grounds of expediency & he could not see there were any facts to justify this course. Morley argued his point well. George equally well pointed out that as factories were regulated by law, so could coal mines, & if arrangements were not accepted, he would justify the state stepping in & acquiring the mines, & working them. He made a very clever speech in support of the course to which the P.M. had committed the Gov. Edward Grey then summed up the situation & pointed out with irresistible logic that there was no other course open, unless chaos, riots, bloodshed, national loss, disaster & misery were to be allowed to have their way & no Gov. could stand to one side & see such occurrences, & ignore their own responsibilities. Churchill took a great exception to the proposals and said he could not accept legislation, it was a surrender to menace, it gave the victory to the men when they were in the wrong, & at the very moment when they were breaking up all over the Kingdom & quarrelling among themselves, & many ready to go back to work & end the strike.

Buxton then replied, the Govmt proposals would not prejudice the men, & show bias to the miners. The owners would be safeguarded, settle the minimum wage locally to suit them just as much as the men. I pointed out that the expediency had been justified by Grey's logic, but I did not like the idea of a settlement by legislation, it was an encouragement to strike, & if a min. wage could be secured by legislation in one industry, it would be asked for in other, quarrying for instance. I hoped the bill would set up a machinery for mines for all time, but an ad hoc settlement, for a limited period, owing to the National welfare being at stake. Burns & George & Morley supported the experimental view, Morley not definitely committing himself until we had discussed the bill on Monday but making it clear, he reserved power to dissent. Churchill's attitude was similar. He & George had evidently differed before they came into the cabinet, & their eyes & teeth were flashing & set respectively, but nothing was said to justify the loss of temper by either.

Germany

We then discussed how our formula to Germany might be amended to further suit Metternich. He wanted us to meet the critical situation at Berlin and to introduce the words to show our neutrality if other powers were at war. Grey said he thought we might add words as inserted in red ink and meet Metternich's criticism of the first sentence, as being too 'abrupt' by putting in the words Haldane used at Berlin to the effect that both powers being desirous &c to arrive at a cordial & mutual friendly understanding.[13]

At 1.0 p.m. Grey & Churchill were to see Metternich.

Harcourt, Grey, and Haldane had met late on 14 March to discuss a note from Metternich, who was pressing for 'the neutrality clause. E.G. very stiff: evidently afraid of losing French Entente'. Harcourt argued: 'we cd not sacrifice Bethmann Hollweg to Tirpitz' (Harcourt diary, Bodl. MS.Eng.c.8267). Full reports of Grey's interviews with Metternich are to be found in Grey–Goschen, 15 Mar. 1912, in BD VI, no.539, pp.714–15; Grey–Goschen, 16 Mar. 1912, no. 544, pp.718–19; and Grey–Goschen, 19 Mar. 1912, no. 545, pp.719–21. In the end, the German Chancellor rejected the formula as 'so elastic as to be valueless…'. Sir Arthur Nicolson commented in a letter to Sir Edward Goschen (no. 534, pp.711–12) on 13 March 1912: 'Grey, unfortunately, is entirely absorbed in these coal conferences and has no time to attend to foreign affairs except intermittently…'. On 18 March WSC announced a

[13] See 14 Mar. 1912, and note.

programme of naval construction designed to counter German naval expansion. Any retardation or reduction in German shipbuilding would be followed by 'fully proportionate reductions'—this 'naval holiday' was rejected by the Kaiser. Eager to placate radical critics, WSC renewed the idea in March 1913 and again in a speech on 18 October 1913, but it met predictably strong opposition from Germany.

Some colleagues including Crewe were appalled: 'whoever heard of Navy Estimates being talked of in public beforehand!' (Margot Asquith diary, referring to 19 Nov. 1913, Bodl. MS.Eng.d.3210, f.142). HHA mused at the Cabinet that France was opposed to a naval holiday 'as she knows that any money saved on Navy by Germany wd be spent on her Army' (Harcourt diary, 8 Dec. 1913, Bodl. MS.Eng.c.8268). WSC hoped to raise the subject again on a proposed visit to Germany in the spring of 1914; but Grey vetoed the discussion of arms control negotiations (John H. Maurer, 'Churchill's Naval Holiday: Arms Control and the Anglo-German Naval Race, 1912–1914', J.Strat.S., *vol.15, no.1, Mar. 1992, pp.102–27, and 'Averting the Great War? Churchill's Naval Holiday',* Naval War College Review, *vol.67, no.3, 2014, pp.25–42. For the Kaiser's pre-emptive repudiation of the idea of a naval holiday see Matthew S. Seligmann,* Spies in Uniform: British Military and Naval Intelligence on the Eve of the First World War, *Oxford UP, 2006, pp.48–9).*

Monday March 18 Cabinet summoned again. Ministers cheerier, & hoping that their proposals would be accepted by the House. 4 drafts of bill distributed among 20 ministers gave little opportunity to discuss clauses clearly. We adhered to lines of 4 resolutions agreed to omit all penalties—a business like discussion considering the absence of time given to consider proposals of far reaching character. Agreed to meet again following day.

We then discussed procedure & time of House. I was authorised to see our Whips & ascertain Conservative view by Asquith. I saw—& Gulland—afterwards at House saw Balcarres & the P.M. to whom I reported, the Tories would refrain from hostile action, if the bill was one ad hoc to the emergency, & not one to establish a principle applicable to other disputes. If the latter Balcarres said we must expect opposition to the Bill & to supply, & closure both by guillotine motion. I dissented & said in a National Emergency, we must be united.

March 19 Tuesday we reconsidered draft bill, struck out clauses giving elasticity to the minimum wage during the 3 year period of bill. This subject occupied our attention most of the time. Morley quiet. No dissension anywhere in cabinet or varying views to proposals P.M. would make in House that afternoon.

The P.M.'s speech was impressive logical and appealed to M.P.s Bonar Law poor, & opposition without alternative policy.

Following Law's poor showing—'He is still not firmly in the saddle', the Unionist backbencher Lord Winterton concluded (Winterton diary, 19 Mar. [1912], Bodl. MS. Winterton 10)—the lobbies were rife with rumours of a deal between the Conservatives and Labour. A motion of rejection then appeared on the order paper in the name of A.J. Balfour, prompting wild speculation that the former Unionist leader might be contemplating a return as the man of destiny, 'prepared to govern with bayonets if need be' (C. Lyell–Sir L. Lyell, 20 Mar. 1912, Lyell MSS).

On 20 March the Peases entertained Haldane, Grey, Newman, May Tennant, and Louise Creighton (historian, reluctant suffragist, and social reformer, widow of JAP's private tutor Mandell Creighton), at dinner. Earlier in the day JAP had spoken on educational progress at Watford Grammar School. Newman recorded that Haldane discussed medical education at the dinner, saying the time was 'one of hope... very fertile in ideas... new life bursting old bonds' (TNA: Newman diary, 20 Mar. 1912, Newman MSS, MH 139).

March 21 Another cabinet to discuss the situation, caused by Opposition having given notice to oppose the minimum wage Bill, & the Labour Party & the coal miners insisting on the schedule being inserted. We decided to neither alter nor add to the Bill any clause giving a minimum wage of even 5/- for men & 2/- for boys, which was an alternative proposal. Haldane dwelt upon the Govmt's double policy one: to pass Bill, and two: to give opposition opportunity to come in, if Liberals were defeated by Tory & Labour uniting forces. Morley McKenna & I were demurred to this view. Churchill was for forcing men with soldiers, & advocated a strong course to induce men to come back to work by gov. protection & higher pay guaranteed. We all listened to such twaddle with impatience. McKenna told us the Govmt could arrange to work 300,000 tons p. week, near sea board Whitehaven & other similar isolated areas. Haldane had some 45,000 troops ready & could recall our 17,000 reserves if necessary.[14] Lloyd George absent, but had telephoned urging Churchill to advocate for him a settlement by putting into Bill a 5/- minimum wage.

Balfour moved rejection of Bill. The P.M. followed, not effective. Grey was at close of debate. 2d Reading carried by 123.

[14] Eight months later, in a 'Note on possibilities of economy in Army Expenditure', Charles Harris wrote: 'We are employing about 40,000 National Reservists in various capacities to guard bridges, railways, & vulnerable points, &c—mostly middle aged men with families who, with their separation allowance are probably costing us 4 millions a year' (Note sent to P.M. [reconstructed], 10 Nov. 1912, Harris MSS B4, Balliol Col.).

March 22 Friday. We were called for 4th time in the week—met in P.M's room at House of Commons. George said in absence of any definite promise that the men would return to work on Monday. He could not ask us to put into bill 5/-s minimum, we all argued against it, on ground of principle & expediency & the P.M. summarised views & firmly resisted the idea. Grey thought masters & men might be invited to confer. This course was about 9 o'clock at night adopted. After 14 hours sitting we got bill through committee. P.M. went in working clothes to big Liberal party at the Cravens.

HHA and his wife, with other prominent Liberals, including the Peases, were dinner guests of the Earl and Countess of Craven in Mayfair. The 4th Earl of Craven (1868–1921), Captain of the Yeomen of the Guard (deputy chief whip in the House of Lords), was married to Cornelia Martin (1877–1961), daughter of the multi-millionaire expatriate American banker Bradley Martin. A reception to meet the Prime Minister was held after the dinner; Lady Craven's mother's house, next door at 4 Chesterfield Gardens, was needed for the overflow.

There had been rumours in February that Craven might succeed Earl Spencer as Lord Chamberlain. But the American wives of both Craven and another putative candidate, Lord Granard, were thought to count against them. Pamela McKenna had noted in her diary on 17 June 1910 that Lady Granard was 'delicious to look at but very self-willed and uncontrollable' (McKenna MSS, MCKN 12/3, CAC). The American press made much of her wealth, lavish entertainment, and ambition for her husband (Maureen E. Montgomery, 'Gilded Prostitution': Status, money, and transatlantic marriages, 1870–1914, *Routledge, 1989, pp.77,79,222). The* New York Times *(15 Feb. 1912) reported the belief that the American women 'might exercise undue pressure' on their husbands in relation to invitations to royal functions. In Craven's case: 'Persons conversant with Court affairs' had pronounced that he had 'no claim whatever to the post'. For Cornelia Martin, married at 16 to the 4th Earl of Craven, see Gail MacColl and Carol McD. Wallace,* To Marry an English Lord: The Victorian and Edwardian Experience, *Sidgwick & Jackson, 1989, p.341 and* passim; *and for her parents, the hyphenated Bradley-Martins, see Anne de Courcy,* The Husband Hunters: Social Climbing in London and New York, *Weidenfeld & Nicolson, 2017, pp.214–26,265–70,279; and Richard W. Davis '"We Are All Americans Now!" Anglo-American Marriages in the Later Nineteenth Century',* Proceedings of the American Philosophical Society, *vol.135, no.2, 1991, p.158. The Cravens' family history, a saga of personal tragedies and crippling death duties, is distilled and illustrated in Penelope Stokes,* Craven Country: the story of Hamstead Marshall, *1996. Spencer's brother in-law, Lord Sandhurst, succeeded him.*

At 12.0 I had to go for the P.M. on his return to 10 Downing St. & pull him back to Grey's room—I found him in Mrs Asquith's bedroom. She was in bed, Violet standing by the fire. He came quite willingly. He had had as hard a 3 weeks as any Minister ever had, but did not look much the worse for it. He is a constitutional wonder!

March 26 Tuesday morning at 11.0. Another cabinet. The Prime Minister explained that Monday masters wouldn't entertain any idea of agreeing to a 5/- min. for men & 2/- for boys—& asked the Cabinet for views. Haldane advocated passing bill, preparing for military protection to those willing to work. McKenna urged negociations with 2 classes of men exempt, those recently employed, & the infirm & the old & settling this question by a National umpire to be appointed & called on to report in 3 days. Sir Edward Grey advocated the loss for one year to coal owners should be made good to them by £250,000 distributed among them & a National Board to be created to settle disputes when local bodies failed to meet grievances. I pointed out objection to doles the Colly owners wd not accept a bribe in exchange for loss of principle, it meant little in dividends say 1/3rd on share cap. and insignificant as compared with loss of capital in closing mines on margin of profit. Ultimately McKenna's suggestion was approved as one to be tried on Masters & men.

P.M. told me in the evening that neither side would look at it. The P.M. was much moved by having to tell House his 3 weeks effort to settle & obtain agreement had failed, but the Gov. had decided to go on with Bill.

We got it through after a 12 hours sitting—the P.M. being warmly cheered as he left the House at 3.0 in the morning.

A dramatic ending owing to Labour Party refusing to accept the 3rd reading of the Bill, & speeches from Lloyd George & John Ward[15] castigating labour leaders for rejecting a bill conceding principle for which the strikers had struck.

Mine Owners & Miners alike in conversation paid high tribute to Asquith's untiring efforts, & having done all that was possible.

On March 27 Margot Asquith recorded in her diary: 'Last night our emergency coal bill—the Minimum Wage Bill—was carried at 3 o'clock (this morning 27th) by 213 votes to 48. I sd say this is perhaps the most dangerous & unhappy moment of our or indeed any-one's political

[15] John Ward (1866–1934); Lib. MP Stoke-on-Trent 1906–29; self-educated politician and soldier; joined Social Democratic Federation 1886; founded Navvies' Union 1889; against independent political activity by the Labour Party, he joined the Libs; recruited five labour battalions 1914.

xperience' (Bodl. MS.Eng.d.3210, f.17; quoted with minor variations in transcription in Bailey, Black Diamonds, *p.117). Cabinet members (and probably the Prime Minister's wife) were not apprised of the way in which fears about civil unrest had been linked with the apprehension that 'evilly disposed persons' could cause damage to colliery powerhouses in time of war. The diary of the Chief Inspector of Mines records a conference at the Home Office with the Permanent Under-Secretary, Sir Edward Troup, Maj.-Gen. Nevil Macready (Director of Personal Services at the War Office), and the Inspector of Constabulary, Leonard Dunning, 'to consider means to be taken for protecting the collieries in the event of rioting' (Sir Richard A.S. Redmayne,* Men, Mines, and Memories, *Eyre & Spottiswood, 1942, pp.170–1).*

To the displeasure of the Home Secretary, who had not been consulted, a battalion was moved from Aldershot to Chirk collieries near Wrexham; and another from Lichfield to Huntington collieries, Cannock, to prevent intimidation of men returning to work. A permanent detective force was established in the Welsh coalfields. WSC as Home Secretary and later at the Admiralty was aware of widespread German espionage in the South Wales strike area, and the activity of a German agent subsidising the Liverpool dock strike the previous August (Ewart Memoirs, p.1031, re 27 Mar. 1912, Ewart MSS; Thomas Boghardt, Spies of the Kaiser: German Covert Operations in Great Britain during the First World War Era, *Palgrave in assoc. with St Antony's College, Oxford, 2004, pp.118–19).*

While ministers were focused on these exhausting matters, JAP's ally in the anti-suffragist cause, Loulou Harcourt, had been leading a 'desperate fight to beat the suffragists in the House of Commons' on 28 March. 'For the last two months,' he told Lord Esher the next day, 'I have been taking a personal canvas of the House of Commons, but I kept the results secret until the last moment. I only told the Prime Minister five minutes before the Division what was going to happen.' (Esher MSS, ESHR 19/5, f.152, CAC.) Harcourt corralled 220 votes, including JAP, HHA, DLG, and WSC. A majority of 12 ensured the deferment of the second reading of the Parliamentary Franchise (Women) Bill for six months.

Friday 29 March Half an hour's wrangle between Haldane & McKenna. McKenna pressed for Home Office to control moving of troops to strike areas, this assented to, & Haldane had to take back seat! After a short discussion on possibilities of coal strike ending, & men's ballot & the form of words to be submitted to them, we switched on to Grey's recent interviews with Metternich. Lloyd George & I pressed Grey to alter our words & introduce neutrality to please the Germans, & play up to Hollweg. It was agreed that we should invite the Germans to criticise & make suggestions. Grey & Churchill wanted no further weakening of our words. The Germans would be obviously at an advantage over us in a neutrality basis, subject to existing treaties, as they had a triple alliance. We had nothing (except old one with Portugal).

Lloyd George then explained very badly his budget he had not got it up at all—but changes were to be almost NIL.

Wednesday April 10th[16] Cabinet. Asquith looked tired—he had his Home Rule speech very much on his mind, & we spent half an hour to an hour in details for his speech—on matters which could have been much better discussed with H.R. cabinet committee. Grey explained recent position with Berlin. I pressed for more favourable alteration of words, & introduction of neutrality to meet Germany, but the feeling was Germany were placing us thereby in worse position than themselves, & we had gone as far as reasonable men should go.

After Cabinet I saw Margot Asquith who told me Henry was very brain fagged. She wanted to get him away for a fortnight after the 1st Reading of Home Rule. I lunched with the Asquiths, & told him that I knew the Tennants would be at Lympne & he could go there.[17] He seemed pleased. He talked about the coal strike, it still being also on his mind. I saw the Master of Elibank. I told him of Mrs Asquith's anxiety & he said it would be easy to spare the P.M. I said bring him up for 1st and 2d Reading Division of Disestablishment to show he was alright & stop rumours. John Morley told me on the 12th when I saw him that Asquith had admitted on the 10th to him before cabinet that he felt overdone & physically unfit.

*The Master of Elibank had himself just returned 'with his health thoroughly re-established after a refreshing rest in the exhilarating air of his native Scotland' to be greeted by a proposal from WSC for spending £50,000 to £60,000 each on propaganda on Home Rule and Insurance by the end of the year (*Daily Chronicle*, 11 Apr. 1912; WSC–'Alick', 9 Apr. 1912,*

[16] HHA introduced the Home Rule Bill on 11 April. The last sentence of this entry appears to have been written on or after 12 April. There is a perfunctory one-paragraph report to the King on the 10 April meeting in Maurice Bonham Carter's hand (Bodl. MS. Asquith 6, f.130).

[17] The derelict Lympne Castle on the Kent coast near Hythe, bought by Margot Asquith's brother Frank Tennant in 1906, was restored and enlarged by Robert Lorimer. The Great Hall was furnished with mid-seventeenth-century furniture and two fifteenth-century Burgundian tapestries. Lorimer was commissioned to add new pieces of furniture, of which the most praised was a grand piano decorated by Phoebe Traquair. Frank Tennant collected paintings by Rossetti. He was later described by his sister Margot as 'the artist among the boys… he was born with a perfect ear for music and eye for colour and could distinguish what was beautiful in everything he saw…'. Lympne was occupied by the RFC during the war and sold to Harry Beecham in 1917, the Tennants' son Mark having been killed in 1916 (Gavin Stamp and André Goulancourt, *The English House 1860–1914: The Flowering of English Domestic Architecture*, Faber & Faber, 1986, pp.106–7; *Country Life*, 12 Nov. 1910, pp.682–9; and for Lorimer's commissions see http://www.achome.co.uk/antiques/antiques_withhistories.htm, accessed 13 Sept. 2015).

Murray of Elibank MSS, 8803, ff.41–2, NLS). He was well aware of the toll that public crises and private indulgences were exacting on the Prime Minister's health. HHA's critical self-appraisal and the 'brain fog' noted by his wife also coincided with a surging intensification of his feelings for his young friend Venetia Stanley. As her prescription 'to get him away' attests, Margot Asquith was alert to the shift in her husband's affections (Michael and Eleanor Brock eds, H. H. Asquith Letters to Venetia Stanley, *Oxford UP, 1985, pp.2,19,431,532).*

Writing about a more serious collapse of the Premier's health in October 1915, Margot recalled that HHA had suffered from high blood pressure in the 'coal strike week' (Michael and Eleanor Brock eds, Margot Asquith's Great War Diary 1914–1916: The View From Downing Street, *Oxford UP, 2014, p.202). In fact, her diary on 9 April 1912 showed that her concern then was much more profound than she allowed others to see. He had come into her bedroom and said 'quite gently' that he did not feel well. 'This from him was like my saying I felt dying... he told me he had felt giddy for the last 3 weeks... he was on the edge of a very great collapse...'. Their doctor dispelled fears that he might have had a stroke. Margot does not mention a conversation with JAP, but she apparently went down to the House after lunch where she saw McKenna and Burns and was not greatly comforted by McKenna's 'Oh I've seen him much worse—just before he went yachting when the King died' or Burns's 'Oh but not like today. Why didn't you see him at the Cabinet he held on to the table & chairs he's never done that before' (Bodl. MS.Eng.d.3210, ff.22–3). Unaware of HHA's condition, Henry Chaplin on the Opposition front bench thought the Prime Minister presented the Home Rule Bill 'without conviction and with little force' (Chaplin–Lady Londonderry, 10 [sic] Apr. 1912, Londonderry MSS, D2846/1/6/6, PRONI).*

Since February JAP had begun to spend more time in the company of Pamela McKenna. It was little more than an innocuous flirtation with the vivacious wife of his Cabinet colleague. Mother of two small boys, and some 30 years JAP's junior, Pamela seems to have enjoyed the attention of a mature political figure who was neither predatory nor promiscuous. For JAP, a surge of feeling is detectable in apologies that he had missed a luncheon invitation, could not make plans for a half-holiday, 'much less a day's golf', and had to keep a promise and go home to have dinner with Elsie ('she hates being alone'). He 'answers to & is known by the name of "Jack",' he would scribble on a card; but was cautious enough usually to sign letters with his usual 'Joseph A. Pease'.

A cache of letters sent over the next few months, and kept in a special box by JAP, charts a deepening yet always restrained relationship. But evidently it was not restrained enough for Pamela's husband, himself only three years younger than JAP. Reginald McKenna reportedly expelled JAP from his country home in early 1915, having seen him holding Pamela's hands. 'Apparently McKenna is a monster of jealousy as well as of most other things,' the Prime Minister's daughter-in-law concluded on 5 June 1915 (McKenna MSS, MCKN 9/4/2,

CAC; Lady Cynthia Asquith Diaries 1915–1918, *Hutchinson, 1968, p.38;* A Liberal Chronicle…1908–1910, *p.30).*

April 16 Cabinet. We discussed Welsh Bill & at end I urged claims of franchise bill, & Prime Minister asked me to bring it up at next meeting of cabinet.

JAP did not mention that at this meeting it was decided to set up a small Cabinet committee (Haldane, McKinnon Wood, Buxton, and Beauchamp chaired by DLG) to initiate talks with 'employers and employed', seek ways of averting stoppages of work, and take 'precautionary measures' with 'the possibility of serious trouble in the transport and distributive trades' in mind (Chris Wrigley, David Lloyd George and the British Labour Movement: Peace and War, *Harvester P., Hassocks, 1976, p.73). The committee was assembled with invited outsiders on 30 April (DLG–Sir Guy Granet, 24 Apr. 1912, Granet [family] MSS). Buxton had written an analysis of 'Industrial Unrest' on 13 April and attached a memorandum on 'Labour Unrest' by Sir George Askwith. But the papers were not printed for the Cabinet until 30 April (Bodl. MS. Asquith 93, ff.30–8).*

April 25[18] Cabinet. Morley explained his attitude at F.O. (Grey being away) towards U.S.A.

*It had been announced on 16 April that Grey 'needed rest after close application to work' and that he was to take a short holiday (*The Times, *16 Apr. 1912). He had been at Fallodon for five days at the beginning of April, returned briefly to the Foreign Office, and then left for a fortnight of fishing. He was back in London on 30 April. Grey had written to his confidante, Katherine Lyttelton, on 8 April that he had 'a mental and spiritual yearning for freedom from work, which all but renders me incapable of doing work'. He had gone on to reflect that the coal strike was the beginning of a revolution in which power was passing to the trade unions: 'labour is now organized and conscious of its power…There are unpleasant years before us; we shall work through to something better, though we who have been used to more than 500 pounds a year may not think it better.' (Jeff Lipkes ed.,* Dear Katherine Courageous: The Letters of Sir Edward Grey to Katherine Lyttelton, *The Brabant P., 2014, pp.188–9.)*

Inquiry into *Titanic* disaster the holding up of witnesses &c. Bryce reported, the inquiry would only go on so long as the Commission occupied chief head lines in Newspaper.

[18] JAP dated this entry 23 April but the Cabinet met on 25 April (HHA Cabinet letter, 25 Apr. 1912, Bodl. MS. Asquith 6, f.133; *The Times*, 26 Apr. 1912). JAP advised Thring and Simon on the 25th: 'The Cabinet this morning considered the terms of the Franchise and Registration Bill.' (MS. Gainford 141/27.)

The Titanic *sank on 14 April on its maiden voyage from Southampton to New York. Five days later, when the RMS* Carpathia *docked with survivors, the US Senate Commerce Committee had launched a Committee of Inquiry into the loss of some 1,500 lives (more than 700 were saved) and was detaining all witnesses in Washington until its investigations were completed. An attempt by the Foreign Office to have President Taft put pressure on Senator W.A. Smith, chairman of the Commerce subcommittee, to vindicate the Board of Trade was rebuffed. Taft said he could not control Smith, who would continue his investigation 'as long as it would keep his name in the papers' (Victoria Fletcher, 'Foreign Office tried to sway US inquiry into Titanic sinking,'* The Times, *9 Apr. 1998, p.5, The Times Digital Archive). The inquiry finished on 28 May with a report of more than 1,200 pages. Senator Smith made the headlines he wanted with the conclusion in relation to the British authorities: 'We shall leave to the honest judgment of England its painstaking chastisement of the British Board of Trade, to whose laxity of regulation and hasty inspection the world is largely indebted for this awful fatality' (http://www.titanicinquiry.org/USInq/USReport/AmInqRepSmith01.php, accessed 26 Nov. 2022).*

The British special commission of inquiry had been announced on 23 April. Presided over by Lord Mersey (a leading commercial silk before elevation to the bench; Wreck Commissioner 1912–14), with Rufus Isaacs as counsel, it reported on 30 July that the ship had not heeded the iceberg warnings it had received either by altering course or by slowing down. The commission recommended that all ships above a certain size be equipped with wireless and sufficient trained officers to maintain a continuous service. The Board of Trade safety regulations were to be altered to ensure that there would be sufficient lifeboat accommodation for all aboard ship (PP, 1912–13, Cd. 6352, lxxvi, 541). When the Board published draft lifeboat rules early in September, they were criticised by shipowners as making ships top-heavy, cluttering up the deck, and reducing the number of passengers.

I explained views of cabinet committee on franchise & registration reform. It was decided against my advice & to eliminate women suffrage troubles, to omit L. Gov. Electors.

Following the Municipal Franchise Act of 1869, unmarried women with the requisite property qualifications were able to register as local government electors. By admitting local government electors to the parliamentary franchise, the Liberal government would have favoured wealthier women without securing the presumed electoral advantage of the working-class female vote. JAP had that day urged the 'Necessity for a Bill this Session' (MS. Gainford 140/9–19). A report on the Cabinet committee's agreed position and JAP's notes on the conclusions of the Cabinet are bound immediately before a new draft bill dated 2 May 1912

(MS. Gainford 141/26, 141/29). JAP's arguments and the Cabinet's decisions are summarised in Martin Pugh's monograph, Electoral Reform in War and Peace, 1906–1918, *Routledge, 1978, pp.3–8. JAP advised Thring and Simon on 25 April 1912 (MS. Gainford 141/27).*

May 1[19] Cabinet. Had liver attack & in great pain, & could not dress, so remained in bed until 3.0. Cabinet discussed business of house & arranged for 2d Rdg of Disestablishment before Whitsuntide & alteration of standing orders to facilitate passage of Comtee stage of Home Rule.

That afternoon Pamela McKenna had sent JAP Cabinet gossip and a posy of roses. His thank you to 'My dear Pamela' was discreetly signed 'Yours ever Joseph A. Pease' (McKenna MSS, MCKN 9/4/2, CAC). The next day, with Selby-Bigge and E.K. Chambers in attendance, JAP received a deputation from the Boy Scouts Association led by Sir Robert Baden-Powell and Earl Grey. The Scouts were not seeking financial assistance but the help of the Board of Education in establishing closer relations with education authorities. JAP's extempore reply could have given Baden-Powell and his delegation no comfort. The physical drill being taught in schools, he said, was the best in the world and is 'practically a compulsory subject'; there was a system of gardening, natural history lessons, 'less book work and more real interest and of a real educational character, which is stimulating the initiative of a boy and doing exactly similar work to which you are devoted'. The role of the 'bookish system' had been changed. Examinations had been discarded 'and we are sometimes taunted that we are making the boy's life too pleasant and that his life is entirely a primrose path'.

JAP turned finally to 'one or two practical questions', leaving his visitors politely in no doubt what he thought of their movement: 'We are very anxious here that no militarism should be associated with our elementary education ...'. Popular opinion was not in favour of it, and some parents were afraid that the Boy Scout movement would be associated with a military movement, 'to secure compulsory service all over the country'. If there had been any thought in Baden-Powell's mind that the Board of Education might direct education authorities to cooperate with him, JAP's conclusion was unambiguous: 'Suggestions are not resented, but anything like dictation often is' (MS. Gainford 126/16). Allen Warren provides evidence of the Scout movement's shift in 1913–14 to a declared 'non-militaristic' stance ('Sir Robert Baden-Powell, the Scout movement and citizen training in Great Britain, 1900–1920', EHR, *vol.101, no.399, Apr. 1986, pp.376–98). For the policy, ideological, and bureaucratic arenas in which the movement was seeking a foothold see Harry Hendrick,* Images of Youth: Age, Class, and the Male Youth Problem, 1880–1920,

[19] JAP dated this entry 30 April, but the Cabinet met on 1 May (HHA Cabinet letter, 1 May 1912, Bodl. MS. Asquith 6, ff.135–6; *The Times*, 2 May 1912).

Clarendon P., Oxford, 1990; John Springhall, Youth, Empire and Society: British Youth Movements, 1883–1940, *Croom Helm, 1977, provides context on the activities of Scouts and other organisations for youth. For 'Muscular Quakerism? The Society of Friends and Youth Organisations in Britain, c.1900–1950' see Mark Freeman's comprehensive essay in* EHR, *vol.125, no.514, May 2010, pp.642–69.*

Friday May 10[20] Cabinet. We discussed Tom Mann's conviction[21] & agreed it was unfortunate to prosecute & advertise him but he had forced his sentence by admissions in Court. McKenna was asked to ascertain view of Judge.

On 14 March, Mann had associated himself with an Industrial Syndicalist *article urging soldiers in the British army not to shoot fellow workers. The editor and printers of the journal had already been arrested under the 1797* Mutiny Act. *Mann was also arrested, convicted, and sentenced to six months' imprisonment. He served seven weeks. McKenna told the Cabinet on 10 May that he was in communication with the judge, Mr Justice John Eldon Bankes (Bodl. MS. Asquith 6, f.137). The best account of the Cabinet's concerns, and thinking about the implications of prosecuting syndicalists for dealing with suffragette law-breaking, and the arguably seditious rhetoric of Sir Edward Carson, is Ian Christopher Fletcher, '"Prosecutions... are Always Risky Business": Labor, Liberals, and the 1912 "Don't Shoot" Prosecutions',* Albion, *vol.28, no.2, 1996, pp.251–78.*

We talked for an hour over Defence Comtee meeting in Whitsuntide recess. Evidently Churchill (who was absent from cabinet) had manoeuvred P.M. into arrangement to go there [Malta] on *Enchantress* & have a meeting to bring on himself limelight. Whole cabinet objected to formal sittings & at most Kitchener should come to see P.M. though we thought even that would excite criticism in Europe which it would be well to avoid.

At this Cabinet, disquiet over the implications of WSC's developing Mediterranean naval strategy led Morley, Haldane, Grey, and some other ministers to oppose even a 'preliminary' meeting of the CID in Malta. HHA told WSC in a letter that day, 'I feel bound (tho' I do not altogether share their apprehensions) to give effect to their considered views... This will not

[20] JAP dated this entry 'Friday May 11'; 11 May 1912 was a Saturday. HHA's Cabinet letter to the King records a meeting taking place on 10 May (TNA: CAB 41/33/49).

[21] Tom Mann (1856–1941); trade unionist; revolutionary syndicalist; friend of Engels and Eleanor Marx; joined Social Democratic Federation 1885; first Pres., Dockers' Union 1893; member, Royal Commission on Labour 1891–4; Sec., Independent Labour Party 1894; in Australia, New Zealand, and South Africa 1901–10; joined British Socialist Party 1916; founder member, British Communist Party 1920.

prevent our taking Malta in on the cruise, and meeting Kitchener there, for an informal discussion of the problems' (Randolph S. Churchill, Winston S. Churchill, Vol. II, Young Statesman 1901–1914, *p.570, and Gilbert ed.,* Companion, Part 3, *Heinemann, 1969, p.1552; see also Samuel R. Williamson Jr,* The Politics of Grand Strategy, Britain and France Prepare for War, 1904–1914, *Harvard UP, Cambridge, MA, 1969, pp.267–70).*

£20,000 was promised reluctantly to Buxton for Ghent international exhibition as Belgians had voted £300,000! & other countries were voting money.

The Ghent International and Universal Exhibition was opened by the King of the Belgians in April 1913. It had been hampered in general by strikes, and the British Exhibition in particular by British prosperity: two exhibits had to be withdrawn at the last minute because they were wanted for sale. The British Exhibition included an Arts and Crafts Room, a Hall of Machinery, a Post Office exhibition, and exhibits provided by the Board of Agriculture and Fisheries, and the prison service. The latter included the last set of gibbet irons used, the plan of a model prison, and prisoners' art. According to Buxton's memorandum on the exhibition (TNA: CAB 37/110/69, 9 May 1912), the Board of Trade originally had not been very interested because it was too soon after the Brussels exhibition. But British manufacturers, especially makers of pottery and textile machinery, were anxious to participate fearing that a strong German showing might weaken their dominance of the Belgian market. Eleven million visitors were attracted before the Exhibition closed early in December 1913. There is a brief online history and extensive photographic record: http://aps.org.au/wp/wp-content/uploads/2015/04/Ghent-1913.pdf, accessed 28 Nov. 2022.

He reported Mann's sentence had upset transport workers who might strike.

Franchise Bill—alternative bill having been circulated postponed.

May 15 Touching & great speech by P.M on 2d Reading of Welsh Disestablishmt.

JAP had written that day to Pamela McKenna:

> The delicate scent from my Aloysia Citriodora [lemon verbena or lemon beebrush] pervades my room and reminds me of you and your kind thought in pandering to my weakness. No I won't call it a weakness to love plant life, it is an instinct which is natural and ennobling. The path of love is strewn with vicissitudes, leaves fall, others become besmirched, twigs die, stems canker but in spite of storms & clouds which shatter & cool, the germ of life remains and nourished below by mother earth & above by glorious sunshine plants & love blossom forth to enjoy life & add to the world's happiness.
>
> *(JAP–P. McKenna, 15 May 1912, McKenna MSS, MCKN 9/4, CAC)*

May 16 Edward Grey reported that in the case of Miss Malecka who was sentenced as British subject to 4 years in Siberian mines hard labour & exile there for life, for having transmitted revolutionary letters—contents possibly unknown to her. He had asked for mercy & clemency of Czar but full report of trial not yet received.

Kate or Katie Malecka (1872–?), the daughter of an English mother and a naturalised Russian Pole, had gone to Warsaw, where she earned a living as a music teacher and was arrested for political offences in the summer of 1911. On 10 May 1912 a Russian Court found her guilty of belonging to a revolutionary organisation that demanded Polish independence from Russia. According to Russian law, she was a Russian citizen and she was sentenced to four years' penal servitude and deportation to Siberia for life. There was a public outcry in England, led by the Daily Chronicle, *and much criticism of Grey. A petition to the Foreign Secretary gathered over 60,000 signatures. Malecka, a British subject, born in Britain, 'was guilty of nothing that would be accounted a crime by her countrymen and women'* (Glasgow Herald, *15 May 1912). On 11 June 1912, after much unpublicised diplomatic intervention, the Russians agreed to release her and to expel her from Russia for life (Katie Malecka,* Saved from Siberia: the true story of my treatment at the hands of the Russian police, *Everest & Co., London, 1914; Nicholas Griffin ed.,* The Selected Letters of Bertrand Russell: Vol. 1 The Private Years, 1884–1914, *Allen Lane The Penguin P., 1992, p.396, and, for a close examination of the Foreign Office records, Keith Neilson, '"Incidents" and Foreign Policy: A Case Study',* Diplomacy & Statecraft, *vol.9, no.1, Mar. 1998, pp.67–76).*

Churchill wanted leave to arrange disposition of fleet with France in case we helped each other in war with Germany. Loreburn expressed himself strongly opposed to policy—agreed on tactful intervention by P.M. to postpone matter until Whitsuntide recess. Grey pressed for early reply, obviously anxious to carry out policy of an agreement with France toward which we had been moving for 6 yrs. Loreburn protested such arrangements were behind our backs, & he would opposed anything of sort. We discussed Franchise points & agreed to leave women's franchise untouched but to allow L. Gov Elector to come under same machinery for sake of simplicity as Parliamentary elector.

An accident while playing tennis had JAP hobbling with a ligament injury. From Darlington he wrote at length to Pamela McKenna, provoked by a booklet by H.G. Wells she had sent him. The booklet was a compilation of a series of articles on 'The Labour

Unrest' in the Daily Mail, *13–20 May 1912 (David C. Smith ed.,* The Correspondence of H. G. Wells, Vol. 2 1904–1918, *Pickering & Chatto, 1998, p.319):*

I read Wells' articles this morning from 4.30 to 5.30 in bed. I have a nasty feeling about him from his books & his views on your sex, but I read all he says very carefully & my first impression was, a wonderfully brilliant diagnosis of the cause & reason of unrest. But I was woefully disappointed at his conclusions & his remedies.

He claims to be a socialist, yet he realises men must have a self interest in their own work for themselves, he even asks for royalties to be given them for further specialization by improvement in labour saving machinery.

The problem of how to nationalize the resources & instruments of production he absolutely leaves untouched.

He speaks of co-partnership & here we & many other employers have been for years doing our best to induce the men to come in. We offer them in this business better interest for their savings than the shareholders get—& yet we have never got more than 5% of our pitmen to put in any of their savings. They as a body prefer to be independent and free from responsibility or the accumulation of wealth.

He appeals to the schools for a 'studied & elaborated project of conciliation & social co-operation' but he fails to make a new practical suggestion.

We now teach domestic economy, cleanliness, hygiene & how to make homes pure, sweet & clean for the million.

Housing by garden cities only of course touches a fringe, & he admits it, though he makes this a suggestion.

He jibes at the Govt for occupying time over Disestablishment instead of over social unrest — he ignores Wales, & the feelings of the 100,000 present at Swansea yesterday. There were only 10,000 to hear [Harry] Gosling[22] at Tower Hill.

His great suggestion is proportional representation. He faces no difficulties, as to how a govt is to be carried on if parties vanish, or how you elect at bye elections under such a scheme.

However, I must cease scrawling & stop. But thank you for sending me the booklet.

(JAP–P. McKenna, 30 May 1912, McKenna MSS, MCKN 9/4, CAC; Richard Toye, '"The Great Educator of Unlikely People": H. G. Wells and the origins of the Welfare State', in Roger Backhouse and Tamotsu Nishizawa eds, No Wealth But Life: Welfare Economics and the Welfare State in Britain, 1880–1945, *Cambridge UP, 2010, pp.161–87; Richard Toye, 'H.G. Wells and the New Liberalism',* Twentieth Century British History, *vol.19, no.2, 2008, pp.156–85)*

[22] Harry Gosling (1861–1930); Lab. Party politician and trade union leader. Waterman; member, Amalgamated Society of Watermen, Lightermen and Bargemen, gen. sec. 1892; involved in London dock strikes 1911–12; Pres., TGWU 1922–30; member, London County Council 1904–25; member, Port of London Authority 1908–30; unsuccessful Lib. Party candidate Dec. 1910; Lab. MP Stepney, Whitechapel and St George's 1923–30; Min of Transport Jan.–Nov. 1924; Paymaster-Gen. May–Nov. 1924. CH 1917.

June 4 Crewe summoned a cabinet at H of C. in absence of Asquith & Churchill in the *Enchantress* at Malta. Morley raised danger of our sending a dark skinned representative of Indian Govmt to Lassa; to try & secure safe convoy for some 500 Chinese troops who were besieged & would otherwise be massacred.

Morley was referring to Laden La, a Superintendent of Police in Darjeeling. A Sikkimese Buddhist with special knowledge of Tibet, he had acted as liaison officer between the Government of India and the Dalai Lama during the latter's exile. The problem in Lhasa was that the Chinese garrison had mutinied, partly in reaction to the revolution in China, and partly because of the resulting lack of their own supplies and pay. In response to Chinese plundering, the Tibetans had taken up arms and were besieging the garrison. The Chinese had asked for British help in negotiating their retreat from Tibet, which led to the 1914 Simla Conference. An India Office 'Secret' briefing paper was circulated by Lord Crewe to his colleagues on 18 Oct. 1913 'explaining our present position in relation to Tibet, as it is not easy to construct a coherent picture from the telegrams which have been printed during the course of negotiations with China' (Bodl. MS. Asquith 93, ff.234–6).

The problem was complicated by the 1907 Anglo-Russian treaty, which forbade the presence of anyone who might be seen as British Resident in Lhasa. Although the Dalai Lama knew of this agreement, he had asked for a British official to accompany him on his journey back from exile. The Government of India hoped to meet his request but not alarm the Russians by sending Laden La: not being white, his presence, it was felt, would be regarded by the Russians as being less significant. Lord Hardinge had proposed the mission to Crewe on 31 May 1912, but Laden La was already on his way. After the Imperial Government had refused to accept Hardinge's proposal, he was stopped only some 50 miles from Lhasa. In the hope of mitigating this transgression of the 1907 agreement, London told Russia and Japan of Laden La's presence in Tibet.

Laden La's next mission was to escort four Tibetan boys sent by the Dalai Lama to England for their education. See Alastair Lamb, The McMahon Line. A Study in the Relations between India, China, and Tibet, 1904–1914, Vol. II: Hardinge, McMahon and the Simla Conference, *Routledge and Kegan Paul, and U. of Toronto P., 1966, pp.371–85; B.J. Gould,* The Jewel in the Lotus. Recollections of an Indian Political, *Chatto & Windus, 1970, pp.23–4,27–32.*

The best account of Anglo-Russian relations, Persia, and Tibet 1911–12 is Jennifer Siegel, Endgame: Britain, Russia and the Final Struggle for Central Asia, *I.B. Tauris, 2002, chs 5,6.*

We discussed our position in regard to Dock Strike, & agreed to support by force convoy of food from port to markets but not to provoke outrage & breach of peace by safeguarding in advance, blacklegs on ships working—but if breaches of peace occurred must act to maintain peace. Our action not to be provocative but directed to maintenance of peace.

Wed. June 5 Summoned again but position not much altered. Men reasonable, & offering to place securities to test good faith in keeping agreements if masters would federate & be equally bound.

Matter left to Lloyd George & McKenna.

I explained position of Local Gov. proposal in franchise bill, matter deferred until P.M. returned & to be settled at next cabinet.

Still lame from his ligament injury, JAP spoke on his education estimates on 6 June in what he described to Pamela McKenna the next day as 'my humble contribution to a momentary educational peace' (McKenna MSS, MCKN 9/4/2, CAC). On 7 June Pamela professed herself especially glad about the increase in the number of women inspectors and the new system of teachers' pensions. 'When I remember the state of feeling roused by Reggie's vigorous and uncompromising policy, and stimulated by Runcy's absence of any policy at all, it seems to me no less than a miracle that in eight short months you should have so transformed the temper and feeling of all the people concerned with education both in theory and practice.' (MS. Gainford 83/143.) Selby-Bigge hoped he would not be suspected of flattery when he wrote after the debate: 'I have heard all the Estimates Debates for the last 8 or 9 years & I have never seen the House so well disposed towards the Minister... I knew you would get on to good terms with the Board's old enemies before very long, but I never thought you would be able to clear up the mess so soon or so completely.' (MS. Gainford 83/132.)

June 11 Prime Minister back, discussed strike & came to no conclusion.

Harcourt suggested some further alterations with regard to Germany & exchanges of land in Africa.

The Colonial Secretary, with Grey's agreement, had been revising the Anglo-German convention of 1898 concerning Portuguese colonies in Africa with the German Colonial Minister, Wilhelm Solf. The two powers had agreed on a division of the territory, should Portuguese rule collapse. This seemed very likely in 1912, following the Portuguese revolution. As well as revising the partition, Harcourt agreed that Britain would recognise Germany's right to intervene to protect its interests or citizens. In exchange, Grey insisted that the new agreement be published, with the 1898 agreement and the 1899 Treaty of Windsor, in which Britain promised to defend Portugal. Grey argued that the publication of all three agreements would make it clear that Britain stood by her commitments to Portugal. The two sides failed to agree on this point, and in March 1914 the negotiations were discontinued. See P.H.S. Hatton, 'Harcourt and Solf: the Search for an Anglo-German Understanding through Africa, 1912–14', European Studies Review, *vol.1, no.2, 1971, pp.123–45; C.J. Lowe and M.L. Dockrill,* The Mirage of Power, Vol. One, British Foreign Policy 1902–14, *Routledge and Kegan Paul, 1972, pp.51–2,124–7. Arthur Nicolson described the agreement as 'one of the most cynical diplomatic acts in my memory' (Lowe and Dockrill,* The Mirage of Power, *Vol. One, p.124).*

June 13 Crewe reported position in Thibet.

I was then unexpectedly called on by P.M. to explain what alterations I was proposing to Franchise Bill.

I explained nature of Local Govmt proposals, & after talk of over an hour, cabinet agreed not to alter ownership vote for L.G. register.

Churchill asked for military not to be given votes, & argued it from 1.30 to 2.15. At last only himself & P.M. left, we one by one went out, a comic proceeding!

Loulou Harcourt, who had been collaborating with JAP, explained to his anti-suffragist ally Violet Markham on 14 June that 'it is impossible in our Parliamentary Franchise Bill to touch the qualifications of the Local Government Franchise. The two have never been dealt with together in a single Bill and if we were to do so on this occasion it would lengthen the measure so much as to make its passage this Session impossible' (Helen Jones ed., Duty and Citizenship: The Correspondence and Political Papers of Violet Markham, 1896–1953, *The Historians' P., 1994, p.53). The Franchise and Registration Bill, ordered to be printed on 12 June, was on sale for 3d. The Act was to come into force on the first day of June 1914 'or on such earlier day as may be fixed by Order of His Majesty in Council'.*

JAP himself, wanting 'to mollify the Opposition by not attempting to place at too high a figure the advantages which abolition of the Plural Vote may secure to our Party', had enlisted the aid of party officials in making the case that the number of seats that the Liberals might be expected to win had been 'considerably exaggerated'. JAP produced a list of 35 constituencies which would lose 1,000 votes if plural voting was abolished; nine of them would likely be Liberal wins (MS. Gainford 141/1). He also sought 'one or two extravagant instances which show the absurdity and the ridiculous character of the eleven different Parliamentary Franchises which now exist, together with their variations' (JAP–Sir Jesse Herbert, 10 June 1912, MS. Gainford 141[47]). HHA told JAP on 17 June that in the first instance 'I do not think you need say anything about the soldiers' (MS. Gainford 83/67). For estimates of the number of plural voters and the Edwardian franchise more generally see H.C.G. Matthew, R.I. McKibbin, and J.A. Kay, 'The franchise factor in the rise of the Labour Party', EHR, *vol.XCI, issue CCCLXI, Oct. 1976, pp.723–52, and the note on critical literature in Ross McKibbin,* The Ideologies of Class: Social Relations in Britain 1880–1950, *Clarendon P., Oxford, 1990, pp.66–7. JAP introduced the Franchise Bill on 17 June, making what Lord Winterton called with some exaggeration 'an extraordinarily feeble speech' (Winterton diary, 17 June 1912, Bodl. MS. Winterton 11).*

June 19[23] Cabinet. We had a most interesting discussion on the Navy policy, & whether we should withdraw from the Mediterranean.

Grey reported interview with von Marschall.[24] new German ambassador. He was quite uncommittal & studying situation.[25]

In the absence of McKenna, we agreed not to come to any decision. Churchill amused us by referring to his last memorandum attacking McKenna's earlier memorandum, as his 'appreciation' of McKenna's. After a good long time had been spent on giving names of vessels, cruisers, recent dreadnoughts, built & building by various Powers, it was agreed we should discuss policy before construction. Morley & Harcourt put forward the view that we should have no alliance with France. Haldane, Churchill advocating it, but Grey checked them by saying no one knew what would be the position between ourselves & France in 2 years time. I took advantage of this to urge that whilst we might send attaché to France, & reciprocate information our attitude ought to be uniform & on the principle we had no quarrel with anyone, & were prepared to treat all our neighbours alike & in a friendly spirit. It might be my Quaker blood, but I thought our construction programme would be influenced by such a policy, & show other countries Germany especially that we were not aggressive. My views were received sympathetically, but Seely the new cabinet minister said he thought we must have special friends, & could not afford to be independent.

Seely had been promoted to Secretary of State (from Under-Secretary) for War on 12 June 1912, when Haldane was appointed Lord Chancellor. For a whimsical story about WSC's recommendation of Seely for the post see John Colville, Footprints in Time, *Collins, 1976,*

[23] JAP dated this entry 21 June, but the Cabinet met on 19 June (HHA Cabinet letter, 20 June 1912, Bodl. MS. Asquith 6, ff.147–8; *The Times*, 20 June 1912). The discussion in the absence of McKenna occurred at a meeting on 27 June, which JAP does not record (HHA Cabinet letter, 28 June 1912, Bodl. MS. Asquith 6, f.149; Hobhouse diary, 27 June 1912, dated 28 June in David ed., *Inside Asquith's Cabinet*, p.116).

[24] Baron Adolf Marschall von Bieberstein (1842–1912); German Amb. London May–Sept. 1912; German Foreign Secretary 1890–7; Amb. Constantinople 1897–1912. His arrival in London distressed the French, who feared that Germany was about to renew overtures to Britain. HHA is reported to have said that, had Marschall lived, there would have been no war (Lady [Norah] Lindsay–Madeline Whitbread, Apr. 1918, Lindsay MSS, courtesy of Allyson Hayward).

[25] These sentences were added later in a note at the top of the page.

p.83. The promotion of Seely to a Secretaryship of State over the heads of several Cabinet ministers entailed 'a tough fight' (Haldane–Seely, 7 Mar. 1912, MS. Mottistone 2, f.102, Nuffield Col.). Haldane had at last achieved the Woolsack after Loreburn, who was out of sympathy with his colleagues, resigned following a heart attack in May. Seely's Under-Secretary was H.J. Tennant, who was succeeded as Financial Secretary to the War Office by Harold Baker, an intimate of the Asquiths and Pamela McKenna.

Churchill asked me what I would advocate in the Med. I said the status quo, retaining ships to watch our interest & maintaining prestige, & we could await the development of friendly communications with Germany. Von Marschall's presence might change for the better, international feeling, & promote understandings with Germany which would help reduction in armaments.

The Prime Minister asked Churchill to prepare figures showing strength of Italian & Austrian fleets for next cabinet.

HHA, WSC, Kitchener (Agent and Consul General, Egypt), and Prince Louis of Battenberg (First Sea Lord), had met in Malta 29 May–1 June 1912. WSC's feuding with Kitchener had ended, and the First Lord agreed to concentrate the British fleet in the North Sea and English Channel. Paul G. Halpern, The Mediterranean Naval Situation 1908–1914, *Harvard UP, Cambridge, MA, 1971, pp.13–46, is the classic treatment of the Malta meeting and the 'basis of the Anglo-French Entente in the Mediterranean'; there is additional documentation in Nicholas A. Lambert,* Sir John Fisher's Naval Revolution, *U. of South Carolina P., Columbia, SC, 1999, pp.255–9, and Geoffrey Miller,* The Millstone: British Naval Policy in the Mediterranean, 1900–1914, the Commitment to France and British Intervention in the War, *U. of Hull P., 1999, pp.256–83.*

The British Ambassador to Spain, Sir Maurice de Bunsen, thought he had impressed HHA and WSC with the danger of driving Spain into the arms of Germany (Edgar T.S. Drysdale, Maurice de Bunsen: Diplomat and Friend, *John Murray, 1934, p.267; T.G. Otte, '"The Pick of Ambassadors": Sir Maurice de Bunsen, Edwardian Diplomatist', in T.G. Otte ed.,* Diplomacy and Power: Studies in Diplomatic Practice: Essays in Honour of Keith Hamilton, *Dordrecht, 2012, pp.72–4).*

Writing from Downing Street on 22 June to one of his young female friends, Dorothy Beresford, HHA described a 'rather variegated week—what with the Home Rule Bill, deputations on all manner of subjects, the strike, and a huge political dinner, which we gave here last night to about 50 of our rank & file in the House of Commons, I have hardly been out of doors'. The remedy: escape with his son Arthur to Ewelme and thence to golf at Huntercombe (Dorothy Kidd MSS, courtesy of Dr Tony Stokes). The Prime Minister was back in London for the Glenconners' 'squash' on 27 June and was attacked by two suffragettes, and two men (C. Lyell–Lady Lyell, 28 June 1912, Lyell MSS).

This sketch of the Cabinet seating arrangement in July 1912 was inserted in the diary underneath JAP's sketch for February 1911.

CABINET. JULY 1912

	Runciman Hobhouse	
McKinnon Wood		R. McKenna
Churchill		Crewe
Morley		Lloyd George
Prime Minister		Grey
Harcourt		Haldane
Rufus Isaacs		Samuel
Col Seely		Pease
		Birrell
O Buxton		Burns O

Friday 5th July Cabinet. We discussed memorandum I had circulated on the advisability of withdrawing 'occupation' as one of the qualifications for the Parliamentary register, & Harcourt was instructed to drop it in a delicate way on Monday.

JAP's memorandum 'Franchise and Registration Bill' (TNA: CAB 37/111/88, 4 July 1912), coupled with a note by Simon, pointed out that the bill had set no lower limit on the value of the property that would qualify its owner to vote (as was currently the case). The retention of a value test was opposed by those who objected to the link between the ballot and wealth, and by Liberal agents who had fought many cases in the electoral courts to test property values. But if no value was set, Liberal agents feared a rush of 'faggot votes'—election agents in marginal seats could buy a piece of land and sell parcels to their party's supporters. Simon urged that the property qualification be dropped altogether, but that a redistribution of seats would then become necessary to equalise the value of votes in different constituencies.

We discussed business, & agreed to take Budget, & rise on Aug. 2nd & postpone Home Rule Bill, Welsh Disestablishment & Franchise Committee stages until Oct 1, when we would guillotine the lot!

Mediterranean Fleet. Asquith reported that with Fisher & Wilson present the Defence Committee on previous day had considered the strategic position of the Navy & had agreed that we should possess a Med. fleet equal to any one Power other than France in the Medit. & have a reserve of force as against Germany in the North Sea. Churchill was to look into the question carefully & see what this policy involved. We sat under an hour, & what was anticipated a stormy sitting with McKenna & Churchill both present in regard to our alliance with France, thus passed over without a ripple to disturb the surface.

Wed. 10 July After arrangements in regard to business, & dates upon which remaining votes & subjects in supply should be taken, the P.M. called upon Churchill who slowly developed the following figures relative to our Mediterranean policy.

In 1915.	Italy would have under naval attaché view	6 Dreadnoughts
		6 Pre " "
		—
		12
	but more likely 4 & 6. under Admiralty view	10.
	Austria would have.	4 Dreadnoughts
		3 pre " "
		3 cruisers.
	say	10

Churchill proposed to send to the Med. at once 2 cruisers of the Invincible class:—

	British.				Germany		
	Dread	Battle Cruisers	Nelson class	Total	Dread	Battle Cruisers	Total
Dec. 1912	14	6	2	22	10	3	13
June 1913	17	8	2	27	13	3	16
Dec. "	18	8	2	28	13	4	17
June 1914	22	9	2	33	16	5	21
Dec. 1914	24	9	2	35	16	5	21
June 1915	25	10	2	37	17	6	23

By 1920. we shall have scrapped our pre dreadnoughts & they are not counted in the above.

	Dr.	B.C.	Nelson	
1912	14	4	2	
1913	17	4	2	Position in
"	18	4	2	North Sea
1914	22	5	2	if we do not
"	24	5	2	increase
1915	21	8	0	program
"	24	8	0	
	32			

(we shall have 32 to 23)

Churchill wanted margin 60 per cent North sea, Churchill asked for the 3 more D. to be ordered now. We all declined except Haldane to commit ourselves, but we agreed we should have to have 6 Battle & 4 BC for Med.

We all thought we should send Battle ships to Med. & await events. Canada helping us might alter position. C. threatened to resign if his claims not acceded to — we simply ignored the threat.

WSC's proposals and the CID deliberations that preceded the Cabinet discussions of Mediterranean strategy are usefully summarised from Cabinet, Foreign Office, and Admiralty records in Jon K. Hendrickson, Crisis in the Mediterranean: Naval Competition and Great Power Politics, 1904–1914, *Naval Institute P., Annapolis, MD, 2014, pp.114–31.*

On Sunday 14 July, JAP played golf at Huntercombe in the Chilterns, 'the game of my life— round in 76 & 78'. 'Hot weather suits my golf!' he told Pamela McKenna the next day in a letter written during the Cabinet meeting. Pamela had sent him Edward Carpenter's new book The Drama of Love and Death: a Study of Human Evolution and Transfiguration. *He hastened to assure her that 'my Quakerism is very broad & honestly I am interested!' He had 'read myself asleep... in appreciative reading of the Chapter:— "Love as an art"'. 'The subject is a most mysterious one, & is most ably discussed. I would have preferred the title "The Drama of Love & Life" rather than "Death"' (McKenna MSS, MCKN 9/4, CAC).*

15 July Discussed addition to Judicial Bench to enable work to be dealt with arrears occurring. Haldane urged one additional judge assented to.

The appointment of the Recorder of Windsor, Sidney Rowlatt, as a Justice of the King's Bench Division was announced on 9 August. The recent history of accumulating backlogs and insufficient judges was set out by the Attorney General in moving for the appointment of another additional judge in October 1912 (HC Deb 25 October 1912 vol 42 cc2559–635).

Prime Minister urged Churchill to renew discussion on Med. He hesitated, but Lloyd George & I asked him what he was going to say on Monday & not commit us to building 3 more Dreadnoughts & adding some 7 millions next year on to estimates. I urged we should not admit any change of Med. policy, as we had never agreed as a cabinet to clear out. P.M. summed up the policy during past 6 years in Med. & then discussion turned by P.M. on to answer we should give Cambon to his question, would we allow their naval attaché to now discuss what we would do under altered circumstances & proceed on same footing as a year ago.

Grey tried to frame words to effect. Yes we would resume and naval or military experts might consider joint operations of 2 powers on a non committal basis that we were not bound to support one another in event of outbreak of war.

Harcourt asked that words should be inserted to express the view this action should not lead to the expectation of help to one another. Grey urged this was tantamount to telling France we might contemplate a war with France. McKenna urged we must not let us be driven into position by France, she expected protection on Northern coast line from us, now undefended from German attack, & that only sending battle cruisers to Mediterranean looked like our relying on France to help us in Med.

Discussion adjourned — a hot day!

Grey had first raised Cambon's request at the 16 May Cabinet meeting. The discussion dragged on (see, e.g., 21 Nov. 1912) in the Cabinet and in the CID. Assent to the discussions was given on 10 February 1913.

July 16 The P.M. announced that he had seen some of his colleagues and he had placed on papers the reasons why some of them (McKenna Runciman &c) thought we ought to retain a battle squadron in the Mediterranean rather than 4 battle cruisers.

A copy of HHA's paper was attached to his Cabinet letter to the King (TNA: CAB 41/33/59). It listed the following arguments against the Mediterranean cruiser squadron:

(1) in case of war with Germany, the cruisers would be needed in Home Waters, leaving the Mediterranean inadequately defended;

(2) if the Mediterranean were a theatre of war (e.g. if Austria was a belligerent), the cruiser squadron would not be strong enough;

(3) a battle squadron based on Gibraltar was no alternative, as it would be vital in the defence of Home Waters against Germany, with the same result as (1);

(4) a One-Power Standard in the Mediterranean could only be maintained by keeping a battle squadron there.

He had sent this statement to Churchill, & he asked Churchill to reply to the arguments. Churchill read out views, recorded in 1782 and today as to policy in strategy & naval tactics—the 2 deckers with speed (sail) being the battle cruisers of today. The guns strength was summarised as follows.

	England.	Austria.
1914–5	4 Battle Cruisers	32. 12" guns
	32. 12" guns	4 Dreadnoughts
	16. 9" "	24. 9" guns
	14. 7.5" "	
	25. 5 superior speed mobility	superior armour speed 20–21

It would leave us in the North sea weak during 2d & 3d quarters 1914.

England.	Battle.	B. Cruisers.	Germany	
	24	5	Battle	16
			B.C.	5

We have of course predreadnought superiority.

An Admiralty memorandum on 'Standards of Strength', printed on 8 February 1913, conveyed the understanding that the 'present approved standards' were:

> *Sixty per cent above Germany in new construction of Dreadnought battleships and battle cruisers.*
> *Fifty per cent above Germany to be maintained in home waters.*
> *Equality with Austria in Dreadnoughts in the Mediterranean.*
> *All ships provided by the Colonies to be additional.*
> *(TNA: ADM 116/1677 in Matthew S. Seligmann, Frank Nägler, and Michael Epkenhans eds,* The Naval Route to the Abyss: The Anglo-German Naval Race 1895–1914, *Ashgate for the Navy Records Society, Farnham, 2015, p.461.)*

David G. Morgan-Owen continues the historiographical debate about battle cruisers in 'Continuity and Change: Strategy and Technology in the Royal Navy, 1890–1918', EHR, *vol.135, issue 575, Aug. 2020, pp.892–930).*

Churchill said Borden had undertaken to help us with dreadnoughts but could not announce decision until his return to his Canadian colleagues.

Churchill urged our commencing 1914 programme in 1913, so as to start the Canadian vessels next March, & spend perhaps £150,000 over them this year, and thus place us in strong position for 1915 — when he would want 3 more dreadnoughts in order to maintain 3 to 2 strength in home waters. It was agreed we should not announce this policy until after Borden had spoken & speak in general terms as to next year's estimates. They will apparently in any case reach 48 million, 1 million supplementary being due to new German Navy Law.

Naval defence was fiercely controversial in Canada. Borden's negotiations with WSC on an 'emergency' contribution of three dreadnoughts for the Royal Navy, the Canadian wish for a voice in imperial foreign policy, and the French Canadian opposition to Borden's naval policy are recounted in Robert Craig Brown, Robert Laird Borden: A Biography, Vol. I: 1854–1914, *Macmillan of Canada, Toronto, 1975, pp.235–47, and also by Marc Milner,* Canada's Navy: the First Century, *Toronto UP, 1999, pp.19–37, and Michael Hadley and Roger Sarty,* Tin-Pots and Pirate Ships: Canadian Naval Forces and German Sea Raiders 1880–1918, *McGill-Queen's UP, 1991, pp.53–75. The Liberal leader, Sir Wilfrid Laurier, urged the construction of a separate Canadian navy. The fundamental disagreement resulted in the absence of any Canadian naval contribution in 1914.*

For WSC's intention to control the Canadian ships, and his doomed proposal in March 1913 to create an 'imperial squadron' see Richard Toye, Churchill's Empire: The World that Made Him and the World He Made, *Macmillan, 2010, pp.126–31; and on the relationship of the 'three Canadian ships' to the broader shipbuilding programme and Mediterranean and Pacific strategy see Nicholas Lambert, 'Economy or Empire: the fleet unit concept and the quest for collective security in the Pacific, 1909–14', in Greg Kennedy and Keith Neilson eds,* Far-flung Lines: Essays on Imperial Defence in Honour of Donald Mackenzie Schurman, *Frank Cass, 1997, pp.55–83; and a contrary view in Christopher M. Bell, 'Sentiment vs Strategy: British Naval Policy, Imperial Defence, and the Development of Dominion Navies, 1911–1914',* IHR, *vol.37, no.2, 2015, pp.262-81. For WSC's approach to Botha on 30 July, 'a private letter from one friend to another', asking that South Africa consider providing for the Imperial Service a squadron of small fast cruisers to be laid down over the next three years see Bodl. MS. Harcourt 462, ff.238–9.*

George urged that next year there should be no increase in taxation. I said I should want 1 or 2 million to settle education. George admitted the possibility but the money would not be wanted before 1914–15.

We then turned to wording reply the French Govmt, who want to know if Navy attaché might now resume position with the New Admiralty Board.

Our reply was agreed to (after 20 minutes twisting words to suit all views) as follows.

> 'Yes — but it is clearly understood that anything that passes between the experts naval or military must not be taken as prejudicing the freedom of decision of either Government so as to commit either government to come to the assistance of the other in time of war.'

Words underlined inserted by P.M. to meet Harcourt's & my view, Grey objecting in case they gave rise to suspicion as to why they were inserted at all. Asquith amused us all, by asserting that: 'The Liberal press was written by boobies for Boobies' this was apropos of denunciation of our naval policy, which was based on the utmost economy in construction based upon national safety.

July 24[26] Absent from cabinet. Discussed possible days for autumn session & debate raised on Lloyd George's land policy, & what he was after. He seemed vague, but insisted on talking on the land during recess but told cabinet he was not a single tax man.

Since the December 1910 election there had been over 170 Liberal and Labour MPs in the parliamentary Land Values Group. Land taxation had been forced on to the government's agenda after by-elections in North West Norfolk and Hanley were won by prominent single taxers, E.G. Hemmerde and R.L. Outhwaite. DLG's messages of support to each candidate had signalled, mostly by implication, his sympathy for a renewed attempt to introduce taxation of land values. The official endorsement of Outhwaite to run in a miners' stronghold precipitated a rift with the Labour Party that was to have serious electoral consequences (Roy Douglas, Land, People & Politics: A History of the Land Question in the United Kingdom 1878–1952, *Allison & Busby, 1976, pp.156–8; Ian Packer,* Lloyd George, Liberalism and the Land: The Land Issue and Party Politics in England, 1906–1914, *Royal Historical Society/Boydell P., 2001, pp.81–2; Michael Charles Griffin, 'The British Electorate in the Age of Imperialism and Reform, 1885–1914', Ph.D. thesis, U. of South Carolina, 1980, pp.299–300).*

[26] JAP dated this entry 23 July, but the Cabinet met on 24 July (HHA Cabinet letter, 25 July 1912, Bodl. MS. Asquith 5, f.159; *The Times*, 25 July 1912).

The Liberal Chief Whip, the Master of Elibank, himself a 'moderate', was alarmed at the gathering momentum and divisiveness of the 'extreme land policy' being advocated by the single taxers (Paul Michael Mulvey, 'Land, Liberty and Empire: Josiah C. Wedgwood and Radical Politics, 1905–1924', Ph.D. thesis, London School of Economic and Political Science, 2003, pp.64–71; also Paul Mulvey, The Political Life of Josiah C. Wedgwood: Land, Liberty and Empire, 1872–1943, *Boydell P. for the Royal Historical Society, Woodbridge, 2010, p.28). On Hanley see also Martin Petter, 'The Progressive Alliance',* History, *vol.58, no.192, Feb.1973, pp.52–4; and on Norfolk, Alun Howkins, 'Edwardian Liberalism and Industrial Unrest: a class view of the decline of Liberalism',* HWJ, *vol.4, no.1, 1977, pp.143–61.*

July 31[27] We discussed situation with Portugal, and the anomaly of our anxiety to end our treaty with her, on the ground that her conduct in her own colonies was reprehensible & retrograde, whilst at the same time we were carrying on negociations with Germany (commenced by Tories before 1906) to parcel out parts of Portuguese territory, if & when the time came to annex them. To give notice to terminate the first would never be accepted as the real reason, the coincidence being what it was a motive to grab would be alleged if we tried to free ourselves from the treaty engagement. I advocated a silent completion of German negociations to promote friendship & understanding, but not a 10 years notice (asked for by Grey) to Portugal, but a freedom to do so after an interval of 3 years by notice, if we were not satisfied the steps being taken were satisfactory, from the standard of European civilisation. There was no decision arrived at as to publicity being given in regard to our negociations with Germany.

We discussed Churchill's visit to Canada, & all objected unless Laurier[28] was prepared to join in cordiality of invitation. Otherwise we thought a party aspect would be given. It was decided to ask Borden (who was then in London) whether the Govmt could take his part in the Canadian naval policy without charges being brought against us of interference, & troubling Laurier to express a view unfairly.

Aug. 6 p.m. told us that he had seen Borden, & that he was quite reasonable and appeared to see our point of view. The matter was left until the way was clear.

[27] JAP dated this entry 30 July, but the Cabinet met on 31 July (HHA Cabinet letter, 1 Aug. 1912, Bodl. MS. Asquith 6, ff.160–1; TNA: CAB 41/33; *The Times*, 1 Aug. 1912).

[28] Sir Wilfrid Laurier (1841–1919); leader, Canadian Lib. Party 1887–1917; Lib. MP Drummond-Arthabaska 1874–7, Quebec E. 1877–1919; Prime Minister of Canada 1896–1911; GCMG and PC 1897; after he had refused to join a wartime coalition government in 1917, his party suffered great electoral losses.

Borden had invited both WSC and HHA to visit Canada in a letter dated 27 July 1912 (Randolph S. Churchill ed., Winston S. Churchill, Vol. II, Companion, Part 3, *pp.1616–17). The Canadian Prime Minister enjoyed a convivial lunch with DLG, Haldane, Grey, WSC, Birrell, Isaacs, and Simon on 2 August (Simon diary, Bodl. MS. Simon 2, f.10). All seemed well until Borden insisted on rewording a memorandum prepared to assist him to make a case for 'emergency action' to the Canadian Cabinet, Parliament, and public. WSC spelled out to HHA the difficulties: there would need to be continued reference to German preparation, 'which will not be well viewed by our supporters'; he could not admit on behalf of the Admiralty that 'we are not doing our duty in making our country safe'; and*

> I cannot say in a public document that 'we are safe at present but unless you come forward and help us we shall have to make further provision next year above all that is now in contemplation' because the Cabinet have not at present agreed to that.

Over the next few days WSC produced a statement for publication that had to be 'very bald and guarded, and will not in consequence, I fear, be very convincing' (WSC–HHA, 30 Aug. 1912, Bodl. MS. Asquith 24, ff.166–70; Martin Thornton, Churchill, Borden and Anglo-Canadian Naval Relations, 1911–14, *Palgrave Macmillan, 2013, is a detailed account). By 15 September HHA was telling Harcourt that he thought WSC 'has quite abandoned the idea of going to Canada' (Bodl. MS. Harcourt 421, f.183).*

We discussed guillotine motion for all 3 bills on & after we resumed.

Time allotted to bills slightly revised. We discussed how to get bills to H of Lords. We thought all by Feb 3. & Crewe thought Lords cd. not then delay after March 3d or so.

JAP had presented the conclusions of a Cabinet committee, which he chaired, on the allocation of time during the rest of the Session between the three important government measures: the 'Irish Government Bill', the Welsh Church Bill, and his own Franchise Bill. A final decision was deferred until Cabinet reassembled after the recess. HHA took the occasion to remind his colleagues that they should be thinking about 'considering and formulating' proposals for a reconstituted second chamber foreshadowed in the preamble to the Parliament Act (HHA Cabinet letter, 7 Aug. 1912, Bodl. MS. Asquith 6, f.162).

P.M. in touching terms announced resignation of The Master of Elibank in his presence—the latter broke down & could not effectively acknowledge the tribute, except to say he had done his best.

Grey read out private document from an authority not named — a friend of Kiderlen-Waechter's — which showed that the German Emperor stipulated when the German Battle ship went to Agadir, that there should be no war — & that the move was only made to ascertain how far the entente between ourselves & France was understanding to support each other mutually against Germany.

The unnamed authority was the Roumanian Finance Minister, Také Jonescu. He had spent three days with Alfred von Kiderlen-Waechter, sometime Ambassador in Bucharest, in November 1911. Their talks were reported to Grey by H.A. Gwynne, editor of the Morning Post, *in a memorandum dated 25 July 1912 (BD VII, p. 795, editorial note to no.767). A meeting of the CID on 23 August endorsed the War Office strategy of despatching an expeditionary force to the continent if general war should break out. But it did not entail a commitment to come to the support of France.*

Throughout the recess between Aug. 8 and Oct. 7 I had no communication with the Prime Minister.

Embarrassed by revelations of what appeared to be insider trading in Marconi shares, the Master of Elibank had resigned as Chief Whip, and took up a partnership in Lord Cowdray's construction, oil, and power business, S. Pearson & Sons. He was replaced as expected by Percy Illingworth. JAP dined with Elibank tête à tête *at the Savoy the night before Elibank resigned. Admitting to Pamela McKenna on 11 August that he didn't know everything that influenced Elibank's decision, JAP nevertheless thought 'in my own quiet way I expect I know more than my colleagues, but I don't trust any pen on paper, not even my own!' He did trust his pen to tell of a Liberal Social Council gathering of 2,500 hosted by his parents-in-law at which Neil Primrose spoke for twenty minutes and probably did not quite rise to expectations. Primrose had spoken so well at an indoor meeting in Newcastle that 'a reputation was made which it will be difficult to maintain'. Pamela was as usual less inhibited: 'I think it is utterly squalid of the Master of E to leave us, all for the sake of filthy lucre. I always thought he had a mean spirit,' she wrote on 9 August. Nor could she resist a joking allusion to the Mental Deficiency Bill, which her husband was shepherding: 'We are all being deliberately feeble-minded.'*[29]

[29] An envelope of letters from Pamela McKenna to JAP in Aug. and Sept. 1912 was preserved in a despatch box with a label addressed by JAP to his executors, noting that the box contained 'private papers relating to affairs which should be carefully considered before they are destroyed'. Doubtless sensitive about warm letters ending 'Love', 'Ever loving', and 'Always your devoted', JAP's daughter Miriam affixed a statement to the box in Oct. 1966 just before the papers were entrusted to us: 'I do

As he had in 1908, 1909, and 1911, JAP next spent several summer days in a shooting party at Glen House, Innerleithen, Peeblesshire, home of HHA's brother-in-law, Lord Glenconner. From 12 to 16 August, with his wife and daughter also at Glen, he shot with Eddy Glenconner, Edward Grey, Jack Tennant, General Sir J. Wolfe Murray, his son, Major Evelyn Wolfe Murray, and Glenconner's son, Edward. On 13 August, the party 'had 428 brace of grouse; on the 14th four drives, 170 brace; and on the 15th, 304 brace' (Visitors Book, Glen House, Glenconner MSS). JAP went on to Tennant's Edinglassie estate, Strathdon, where there was excellent fishing. All the while Selby-Bigge kept him supplied with files (McKenna MSS, MCKN 9/4/2, CAC). Back in London he dined at the Savoy on 23 August with DLG, Isaacs, and Masterman, who had survived a close contest at Bethnal Green the previous month (Eric Hopkins, Charles Masterman (1873–1927), Politician and Journalist: The Splendid Failure, *Edwin Mellen P., Lewiston, NY, 1999, p.118). Other Liberal candidates had suffered misfortune in a series of autumn by-elections (Petter, 'The Progressive Alliance', pp.45–59).*

Bye Elections went against us at Crewe, Oldham & Midlothian owing to labour candidates splitting forces who would in Parliament support the Govmt. The general feeling of resentment existed against the Master of Elibank retiring for or with a Peerage and unwisely trying to intervene in selection of candidates in Midlothian after he retired. Lloyd George came in for a good deal of abuse owing to his attitude on having a private land system inquiry, & running a land question campaign through satellites at the bye elections.

The loss of Crewe, where the Liberal candidate was Sir John Simon's 30-year-old secretary, was readily explained by Labour intervention. But there was more to the loss of Oldham in the previous year (Clarke, Lancashire and the New Liberalism, *pp.316–17,386; W.H. Chaloner,* The Social and Economic Development of Crewe 1780–1923, *Manchester UP, 1950, p.171). Alfred Emmott, whose elevation to the Lords had caused the vacancy, recorded local beliefs that the Insurance Bill had cost 'a few hundred' votes and 'many*

not like to alter or destroy a note of Father's but I think I should explain that Pamela McKenna had "soul friendships" and was one of the "soul set". She was always a friend of mother's and mine. Moreover if any lady made advances to father mother gave him hell promptly and the lady disappeared from the scene!' In a letter to Cameron Hazlehurst, 3 July 1995, Lord Gainford recalled his Aunt Miriam rendering a brilliant impression of his 'grandmother's shrill voice on any occasion when she thought that a lady was making unsuitable advances: "Jack! That woman's poison!"' Pamela was of course too young to have been a 'soul'. But she had moved among them from her childhood. As she told JAP on 19 Sept., 'Margot's mania for autobiography is growing on her and though I have known every detail of her love affairs since I was ten years old it comes to me as a fresh shock each time that she should feel no reticence about trusts that ought to be safe and secrets in her keeping ... she always speaks of you with real affection'. Pamela McKenna's letters are now in MS. Gainford 83/139–43, 84/33–41.

hundreds' voted Labour because the Liberal candidate, Arthur Stanley (Venetia Stanley's brother), was the son of a peer[30] *(Emmott diary, 16 Dec. 1911, MS. Emmott, I/2, Nuffield Col.). Caroline Bedale's research reveals the potential electoral importance of increasing numbers of food retailers, owners of small manufacturing enterprises, and professionals in the town ('Property Relations and Housing Policy: Oldham in the late Nineteenth and early Twentieth Centuries' in Melling ed.,* Housing, Social Policy and the State, *pp.49–52). On the day of the by-election Ramsay MacDonald spoke to the Liberal Chief Whip wanting to know 'if coalition were possible at next election. We should like it, he said but it is question for those who would come in' (MacDonald diary, 13 Nov. 1911, MacDonald MSS, 8/2, TNA: PRO 30/69, transcript courtesy of Lord Morgan).*

Convinced that DLG's 'vague land policy... vote catching' would actually lose votes, Margot Asquith had secretly implored Percy Illingworth on 15 August to warn Alexander Shaw, the unsuccessful candidate at Midlothian, '<u>*not*</u>* to talk about the land except in the vaguest way... I tremble at Outhwaite's schemes & ideas & feel sure our best chance is to skate very very lightly on the land ice'. The new Chief Whip was assured that his letters to the Prime Minister's wife would be 'absolutely private. I shall never show them to my husband unless you wish me to. In the holidays I talk little to him about politics.' (Margot Asquith–Sir J. Simon, 18 Aug. 1912, Simon MSS; Illingworth MSS, courtesy of Jamie Illingworth.)*

The Liberal cause had been hurt by the recently retired Chief Whip, Alick Murray, whose praise for the Labour candidate, Robert Brown, in a letter to the chairman of the Midlothian Liberals, had appeared in the Glasgow Herald *before it reached its intended recipient. Elibank explained to Alex Shaw's father that he and his predecessors in the constituency, Lord Dalmeny and Sir Thomas Gibson-Carmichael, owed their positions to Brown and the miners. He would have left the field clear for Brown, the secretary of the Scottish Miners' Federation, in 1910 if he had wished to come forward. Elibank had sent £1,000 to the Scottish Whip for the campaign, and had also made an unsuccessful private appeal to Brown to withdraw his candidacy. But the damage had been done. Brown polled 2,413 votes; Shaw lost to the Conservative John Hope by 33 votes (Murray of Elibank–Lord Shaw, 14 Aug. 1912, Craigmyle MSS, courtesy of the 3rd Lord Craigmyle).*

As the by-election contest unfolded, Shaw had made it known that he had invited Outhwaite to speak and that they were fighting together because they were 'full believers in taking the taxes off houses & putting them on the value of land which was the creation of the community'.

[30] Hon. Arthur Lyulph Stanley (1875–1931); eldest son of 4th Lord Sheffield; barrister 1902; Lib. MP Cheshire (Eddisbury) 1906–10; PPS to Postmaster-Gen. (S. Buxton) 1906–10; Gov. of Victoria 1914–19; KCMG 1914; 5th Baron Stanley of Alderley and 5th Baron Sheffield (known by former title) 1925. 'His marvellous knowledge, swift comprehension and decision, and defiance of difficulties would have been still more effective [in London education politics] had it not been for his impetuosity and impatience' (J. Scott Lidgett, *My Guided Life*, Methuen, 1936, p.174).

Consequently HHA was under pressure to make a statement that the government's land policy would not be announced until it was fully considered and approved by the Cabinet. But Illingworth advised the Prime Minister to say nothing lest it be interpreted as a total repudiation of the gestating land policy (Illingworth–HHA (draft), [c.29 Aug. 1912], Illingworth MSS). In a long survey of political prospects, WSC, on the Admiralty Yacht at Sheerness, had warned DLG on 21 August 1912 that the land movement 'must either be disavowed or guided'. Liberal unity could be ensured 'if we don't quarrel among ourselves, if we don't play the fool over the women, & if we don't come to bloodshed in Ulster' (Sotheby's Catalogue, Hotspur, *18 Dec. 1986, item 248). The Scottish Liberal Party Organising Committee (9* Apr. *1914) attributed the by-election losses in Leith and Midlothian to poor organisation (Gordon Brown, 'The Labour Party and Political Change in Scotland 1918–1929: The Politics of Five Elections', Ph.D. thesis, U. of Edinburgh, 1981, p.34).*

The Prime Minister followed me to Edinglassie, and to Dornoch and I heard of him from my daughter Miriam who played golf with him at Aboyne, & from Mrs McKenna our hostess at Dornoch. He seemed well enjoying his holiday & happy, but irritated by suffragettes pursuing him on golf courses, & at Lloyd George running a land campaign on his own.

The holiday lasted five weeks and included a week with the McKennas at Oversteps in Dornoch early in September. Reginald McKenna was indisposed for several days and some awkwardness ensued. Molly Harcourt had noticed late in July that Pamela McKenna was 'very restless & excitable' and thought that the holiday 'where in the splendid air she will play golf & be quiet' would do her a great deal of good (M. Harcourt–L. Harcourt, 26 July 1912, Bodl. MS. Harcourt dep. adds. 271, unfoliated). Something happened that prompted JAP to write: 'There are many occasions when words are difficult to find, & I am afraid my adieu at Oversteps left a lot to be assumed & understood, but please be under no illusion, as to my having had a most enjoyable visit, & my great gratitude to you & Reggie for all your charming kindness' (JAP–P. McKenna, 8 Sept.1912, McKenna MSS, MCKN 9/4, CAC).

The Aboyne golf club, adjoining the Loch of Aboyne in Royal Deeside, 30 miles west of Aberdeen, had a convenient village railway station. At the Royal Dornoch course, 45 miles north of Inverness, as Pamela McKenna told JAP after he left, suffragettes 'infested the links and painted votes for women all over a gloomy granite fountain which serves as a hazard at one of the holes. Here he [the Prime Minister] has only been molested once but stalwart detectives follow him round the links and are wonderfully useful at finding lost balls…'. Her own husband had been attacked, but only with strong language. 'As you know,' she went on about HHA, 'he does not readily discuss politics but I gather there is a great slump in Lloyd George and he is very much annoyed about his land indiscretions' (P. McKenna–JAP, 11 Sept. 1912, 13 Aug. 1912, MS. Gainford 84/40 and 38).

At an overnight stop at Inverness Station Hotel JAP had a long conversation with Lord Charles Beresford, retired Admiral and now a Unionist MP:

> Winston's conduct in talking to seamen about their work & the insurance bill, he said was resented by officers & men alike. He said Winston asked one man how he liked his work. He said 'not at all'. 'What is wrong with it', asked Winston. The man replied, 'What I want to know from you sir is, what is right with it.'! To this poser, Winston had no response.

'Charlie B.' went on:

> Bonar Law's social achievements were far from what the Party expected. I suppose he eats his peas with his knife—and he admitted they have no one for a prime minister. Long has gone back in their estimation & they can't see Austen there though he admittedly does well in debate.
>
> He thinks we may stay on until just before the Parliament Act would bring the 3 bills into Acts of Parl. over the Lords' heads—i.e. 2 years ahead. This is an indication that the Lords will throw out all 3 bills at the end of this session.
>
> *(JAP–P. McKenna, 8 Sept. 1912, McKenna MSS, MCKN 9/4, CAC)*

As JAP moved around Scotland, stalking, fishing, and 'studying nature', the correspondence with Pamela McKenna continued. 'We are all rather depressed at the loss of Midlothian,' Pamela told him on 11 September, 'though a majority of thirty-one on a split vote is slender ground for Tory jubilation'. The good news for the McKenna camp was that the result might 'serve to chasten these land maniacs':

> Owing to a telegraphic inaccuracy or a postmastery pun our telegram arrived from Perky Illingworth which added irony to the bitter blow. I had a terrible time with Margot who quite lost her self-control, cursed Ll.G and the Marquis of Elybank in language quite unknown to me and ended by saying she would give her soul to murder them both. The P.M. told me he had heard that feeling was so strong in the constituency that if Elibank had shown his face there he would have been hooted and stoned.
>
> *(P. McKenna–JAP, 11 Sept. 1912, MS. Gainford 84/40)*

From Glenquoich, Invergarry, on 15 September, JAP wrote at length about the character and behaviour of several colleagues including Elibank, and essayed a transparent appreciation of his own virtues:

It is so easy to criticise but I am really sorry that the Master, for whose appointment as Chief Whip I am largely responsible, should have left office under the shadow of motives prejudicial to the interest of the party he served, and of injudicious efforts to influence the choice of his successor. If only the Prime had ruled him with a firmer hand, and been less pliant, his whipship would not have ended in this way.

The Master had ways of his own, which both made me recommend him, as well as hesitate in doing so. His methods were veiled & he loved a sort of harmless subtlety, which deceived no one, but got round men.

(JAP–P. McKenna, 15 Sept. 1912, McKenna MSS, MCKN 9/4, CAC)

Reporting on 19 September on holiday golfing with the Prime Minister, Pamela said 'he seemed in such splendid health and spirits. Margot implored me not to give him any champagne and he appeared to be perfectly happy with claret. His hand didn't shake like it used to and his eyes looked much clearer...'. The links air had stiffened HHA's political resolve: 'I don't think he means to stand any nonsense from Ll.G about the land and he is certainly not going to pursue his usual policy of drift' (MS. Gainford 84/41).

JAP would spend the last week of September partridge shooting with Loulou Harcourt before giving a few speeches in his constituency. With nothing fresh to say on the 'worn out topics on which we are legislating', he sought 'Reggie's speeches to help me, as soon as they are reported'. He does not record that he escorted George Newman to a meeting at 10 Downing St on 22 September with DLG, Haldane, McKenna, Crewe, Runciman, Harcourt, Burns, and Christopher Addison, and a gathering of Local Government Board and Board of Education officials (Newman diary, 22 Sept. 1912, TNA: Newman MSS, MH 139). In rude health as a result, he said, of all the walking, exercise, and good air he had enjoyed in Scotland, JAP enjoyed the shoot at Stanton Harcourt, 14 miles from Nuneham, more than ever before. JAP eulogised his 'model hostess' but was a touch smug in telling Pamela that 'Loulou is growing in figure & countenance more like his father every day' (JAP–P. McKenna, 27 Sept. 1912, McKenna MSS, MCKN 9/4, CAC).

HHA left for Venice with Margot and Elizabeth on 20 September. They returned to London on 3 October. While the Prime Minister was away, James Craig had organised an enormous anti-Home Rule demonstration, and some 218,000 men had signed Ulster's 'Solemn League and Covenant', pledging no surrender. Even more women had signed a similar document (Patrick Buckland, Irish Unionism Two: Ulster Unionism and the Origins of Northern Ireland 1886–1922, *Gill and Macmillan, Dublin, 1973, pp.55–9). Edward Carson, along with several other well-known figures, were filmed as they signed the Covenant, a publicity initiative devised by Craig to reach English audiences as well as Irish rural communities (Alvin Jackson, 'Unionist Myths 1912–1985',* Past & Present, *no.136, Aug. 1992, p.171; Michael Foy, 'Ulster Unionist Propaganda against Home Rule 1912–14',* History

Ireland, *vol.4, no.1, 1996, pp.49–53; Daniel M. Jackson,* Popular Opposition to Irish Home Rule in Edwardian Britain, *Liverpool UP, 2009). As David Thackeray points out, the extremist members of the British League for the Support of Ulster and the Union, founded in 1912 by Willoughby de Broke, but before long effectively run by Lord Milner, would soon be openly acknowledging that they were ready to act illegally to resist Home Rule (*Conservatism for the democratic age: Conservative cultures and the challenge of mass politics in early twentieth-century England, *Manchester UP, 2013, pp.75–6; and compare Gregory D. Phillips, 'Lord Willoughby de Broke and the Politics of Radical Toryism, 1909–1914',* JBS, *vol.XX, no.1, Fall 1980, pp.218–24, and Jeremy Smith,* The Tories and Ireland 1910–1914: Conservative Party Politics and the Home Rule Crisis, *Irish Academic P., Dublin, 2000, pp.172–7).*

Bonar Law had proclaimed on 27 July that his party would take 'whatever means seem to us most effective' to deprive the Liberal government of the 'despotic power which they have usurped'. On 1 August, at dinner with Sir Arthur Paget (C-in-C. Ireland), HHA was heard by Maj.-Gen. John Cowans (Quartermaster-General) 'laughing at the idea of any resistance in Ulster and seemed to think it all bluff. He (the P.M.) said that Carson was looking very seedy and would be glad to recall some of his speeches' (Ewart diary, 3 Aug. 1912, Ewart MSS). Seven weeks later, on 13 September, Lansdowne quietly assured Curzon: 'I do not think I should myself have used the language which Bonar Law used in his Blenheim speech, but as he has promised uncompromising opposition to Home Rule "under present conditions" I am entirely with him; and although I do not mean to shoulder a musket I certainly should not think of snubbing the Ulstermen or of dissociating myself from Bonar Law' (Curzon of Kedleston MSS, BL: A & AS, MSS.Eur.F.112 D/2/11).

For a speculation that Law 'was perhaps just play-acting' see Daniel Ziblatt, Conservative Parties and the Birth of Democracy, *Cambridge UP, 2017, pp.152–3, and compare Paul Bew's highlighting of Jim Garvin's observation of 'the note of restraint, even of magnanimity' that Carson was 'impressing upon the Ulster controversy' (*Ideology and the Irish Question: Ulster Unionism and Irish Nationalism 1912–1916, *Clarendon P., Oxford, 1994, p.70). For Walter Long, the Dukes of Westminster, Devonshire, Bedford, and Norfolk, and the Marquesses of Salisbury and Londonderry, 'perhaps like Lansdowne' finding it 'prudent or seemly' not to sign the Covenant, see David Spring, 'Land and Politics in Edwardian England',* Agricultural History, *vol.58, no.1, 1984, p.40. And for secret contributions to Ulster resistance by Bedford (£10,000), along with Waldorf Astor (£30,000 'subject to certain conditions'), Lords Rothschild and Iveagh (£10,000 each, the latter already giving £1,000 a month), the Duke of Portland (£5,000), and Sir Ernest Cassel (£4,500) see Pamela Horn,* High Society: The English Social Elite, 1880–1914,

Alan Sutton, Stroud, 1992, pp.179,212. Walter Long's role as fund raiser and designated successor to Carson is documented by David Spring, 'Willoughby de Broke and Walter Long: English Landed Society and Political Extremism, 1912–14', in Negley Harte and Roland Quinault eds, Land and Society in Britain, 1700–1914: Essays in Honour of F.M.L. Thompson, *Manchester UP, 1996, pp.177–90.*

In a move that can only have bemused JAP, female suffrage had been included in a draft constitution for the Ulster provisional government; but, as Ian Christopher Fletcher puts it, 'the romance between daring suffragettes and chivalrous Orangemen was probably doomed from the start... Carson declined to confirm the commitment in March 1914' ('"Women of the Nations Unite!": transnational suffragism in the United Kingdom, 1912–1914', in Ian Christopher Fletcher, Laura E. Nym Mayhall, and Philippa Levine eds, Women's Suffrage in the British Empire: Citizenship, nation, and race, *Routledge, 2000, p.109). The falling-out between the WSPU and the Irish Nationalist Party in 1912, the conflict between Irish and English suffragists over Home Rule, and the renewal of suffragette militancy from March 1914 is sketched in Senia Pašeta,* Suffrage and citizenship in Ireland, 1912–18, *The Kehoe Lecture in Irish History 2018, Institute of Historical Research, 2019, http://www.humanities-digital-library.org, accessed 9 Apr. 2020.*

He went to Italy travelled all the way home, went on through the night again to Scotland, and back the next night Oct 6th to London.

Through the autumn, rifts were growing in the Liberal Party. A gloomy Edward Grey told Haldane's sister that the government was breaking up. He feared an election before Home Rule was granted. If the Unionists came in with a small majority, moderate Liberals would have to support them against the Irish and Labour. DLG would lead 'the other party'. Lord Esher learned that Haldane forecast 'serious cleavages' in the party if the government went out; DLG would 'go off on Land Reform etc. and fight for his own hand' (Esher–Harcourt, 29 Sept. 1912, Bodl. MS. Harcourt dep. adds 72, ff.110r–v). Haldane himself, his sister believed, thought the government might not last long (E. Haldane diary, 23 Sept., 1 Oct. 1912, Elizabeth Haldane MSS, MS. 20240, ff.24–5, NLS).

In trying to decipher DLG's intentions, Lord Selborne, whose wife had been asked to 'pump' Grey, had concluded 'either Ll.G. is prepared to quarrel with his party... of course deliberately & for his own purposes or he is manoeuvring by speeches of extreme violence to draw us to commit ourselves to opposing the government policy in advance whatever it is' (Selborne–Lady Selborne, 14,16 Sept. 1912, Bodl. MS. Selborne 102/64–7,70–1). Divisions over land reform were intensifying. In what the Western Mail *(2 Oct.1912) called 'his latest flamboyant piece of indiscretion', the recently re-elected Edward Hemmerde had asserted that DLG was at one with him and the other extreme land taxers (David Dutton tells 'The strange case of Edward Hemmerde', in* JLibH, *issue 69, 2010–11, pp.6–16; there is an unflattering character sketch in MacCallum Scott's diary, 12 Jan. 1927, MacCallum Scott MSS).*

HHA knew that eventually he had to repudiate any suggestion that Hemmerde's views were those of the government. And DLG himself was scrupulous about observing proprieties, telling the secretary of the Land Enquiry Committee to ensure that no papers prepared by the Enquiry 'should be communicated to anybody until the Prime Minister has first seen them... I lay great stress on all reports and papers being placed before him by me in the first instance. Afterwards, of course, I propose that Runciman and Grey and Haldane and other Cabinet Ministers should have full access to all the information we possess' (DLG–Roden Buxton, 7 Oct. 1912, copy, Lloyd George MSS, LG/C/2/1/50, PA).

He denounced a single land tax in his speech to his constituents & this cleared the air. All this travelling apparently helped to upset him, & when we met at the Cabinet on Oct. 7th at noon he looked bloodless and seedy. Next day he had a carbuncle cut out of his back, & the operation was renewed on Oct. 14, and he had a further discharge Oct. 15 — but he came to cabinet on Oct. 16 & 17, looking much better.[31]

His only appearance & effort in the House was on Thursday the 10th when he got through his task with amazing success in justifying the guillotine resolution on the Home Rule Bill.

No one tried to meet his points — & the debate developed into a general attack & defence of Liberal policy.

The government, with an overcrowded legislative agenda when Parliament re-assembled on October 4, extended the session into March 1913. HHA's closure resolution was condemned by Bonar Law as 'the first fruits of your Parliament Act... the clearest evidence that the Act can never work unless the majority are willing to make this House cease altogether to be a legislative assembly and to become instead a machine for registering the decrees of the Government'. The Unionists did everything they could to slow down and disrupt proceedings, refusing to grant pairs, and bringing on snap divisions (Jeremy Smith, The Tories and Ireland 1910–1914, *pp.61–2). Percy Illingworth in response organised a system of 'espionage' with*

[31] According to Margot Asquith, her husband had a cyst 'unattended to' for twelve years (E. Haldane diary, 12 Nov. 1912, Elizabeth Haldane MSS, MS. 20240, f.27, NLS). Morley, who had spent the weekend with the Asquiths after the surgery (on HHA's right shoulder), said the doctors had been handicapped because their patient dreaded anaesthetics, refused chloroform, and would not have a nurse (Cunningham diary, 21 Oct. 1912, Miller-Cunningham MSS).

a check board at the entrance of the Whips' Office carrying information about the current whereabouts and contact details of government members, the movements of Unionist MPs and the numbers in the Chamber, monitored by a vigilance committee. No Liberal member could be absent from the House without leaving an address at which he could be reached by telegram or telephone (British Weekly, *7 Jan. 1915).*

Oct. 7 Cabinet. Grey explained European position. We talked over King's visit to Colonies & Foreign Powers & vetoed it. Business arranged. Franchise postponed to after Xmas.

JAP took the opportunity to have his private secretary send, for Harcourt's information, a letter he had written to Sir Robert Chalmers on 13 August to alert the Treasury to the extra expense likely to be incurred by local authorities in preparing continuous registers of electors (H.S. Fass–L. Earle, 8 Oct. 1912, Bodl. Harcourt MSS dep.443, ff.50–4). Cabinet agreed to allocate 25 more days to the committee stage of the Irish Government Bill, seven days to the report, and three to the third reading. In total, this would give the Bill more than twelve full weeks of parliamentary time.

The King had been invited informally by Botha to open the new parliamentary buildings in South Africa. The Cabinet decided that acceptance would inevitably lead to similar invitations from Australia, Canada, and New Zealand, and to the King's prolonged absence from the United Kingdom, which some believed would tend to confirm the dangerous idea that the country could get along without a King (Harcourt memo. to Prime Minister, 30 Sept. 1912, Bodl. MS. Harcourt 464, f.19). The matter is not mentioned in HHA's Cabinet letter for this meeting but in the letter describing the meetings of 30 October and 1 November (TNA: CAB 41/33/66). The decision had been taken at the Cabinet on 16 October. The Governor-General of South Africa, Lord Gladstone, who was about to leave London, had been authorised to tell Botha privately that the visit would not happen unless he heard otherwise when he reached South Africa. Harcourt therefore did not send a despatch. All this had to be explained to the King's Private Secretary without confessing that the King had not been informed of a decision taken two weeks earlier. Harcourt told Knollys on 31 October that he had 'discovered, after informal consultation with my colleagues, what was likely to be their decision on the matter' (Bodl. MS. Harcourt 464, ff.18,28).

JAP, oblivious as were most of his Cabinet colleagues, to the damaging disclosures that were in store, did not mention that on 7 October Cabinet's attention was drawn to 'statements and suggestions' circulating over the recess about 'supposed private profits' allegedly made by certain ministers in connection with the contract between the Post Office and the Marconi Wireless Telegraph Company. The Postmaster General was instructed to move as soon as possible for reference of the contract and the preceding negotiations to a Commons Select Committee. The Committee was set up on 11 October to inquire into the Marconi Agreement with the government (HHA Cabinet letter, 8 Oct. 1912, Bodl. MS. Asquith 6, f.164).

On 7 January 1912 the government had accepted a 'tender' from the English Marconi company to construct and maintain a chain of wireless stations across the empire at a cost of £60,000 each. There had been a year of negotiations between the Marconi managing director, Godfrey Isaacs (brother of the Attorney General, Sir Rufus Isaacs), and a Post Office committee led by the Postmaster General, Herbert Samuel. Lack of transparency about the process, rumours of speculation by ministers, allegations of market rigging in both English and American Marconi shares, and innuendo about corruption, excessively generous terms in the agreement, and swirling gossip about a 'scandal', left the government with little choice but to facilitate a debate on the appointment of a Select Committee. The debate itself brought DLG to his feet to demand that there be no shrinking in the committee from investigating the 'sinister rumours ... passed from one foul lip to another behind the backs of the House'.

The amiable, modest, unambitious, and slightly deaf Sir Albert Spicer Bt (1847–1934), a paper manufacturer and stationer, and Liberal MP for Hackney Central, was chosen to chair the committee. According to the very ambitious MacCallum Scott, Spicer's appointment resulted from a casual suggestion to Illingworth from a fellow MP who knew that Spicer was talking of retirement and thought it would be a good idea to put him on a committee. 'He had never even been member of a committee before & knew nothing of procedure' (MacCallum Scott diary, 4 June 1913, MacCallum Scott MSS). Spicer's son, Sir Stewart Spicer Bt, thought: 'The selection was a high compliment to his integrity, but it revealed his limitations. His first step on receiving the invitation was to ask the Chief Whip to answer two questions: (1) Did the Cabinet feel that he was strong enough for the position? (2) Would he be personally acceptable to the Committee as a whole?' In the event, as Stewart Spicer admitted, 'he failed to dominate the Committee as a stronger chairman might have done' ([Captain Sir Stewart Spicer Bt RN], Albert Spicer, 1874–1934. A man of his time, by one of his family, Simpkin & Marshall, 1938, pp.39–49, courtesy of Mrs G.E.D. Wood who identified her brother as the author). The minutes of evidence of the Select Committee are at BT Archives, TCB 272/9.

The standard work on the Marconi contract, Frances Donaldson, The Marconi Scandal, Rupert Hart-Davis, 1962, is usefully complemented by Hugh Barty-King, Girdle Round the Earth: the story of Cable and Wireless and its predecessors..., Heinemann, 1979, pp.160–1. A file prepared on 6 Aug. 1913 by Captain Maurice Hankey for the Prime Minister's guidance contains extracts from CID papers in 1911, Admiralty advice on the 'strategic urgency of the erection of an Imperial chain of Wireless Stations', the Agreement between the Marconi Wireless Telegraph Company and the Postmaster General, with an extensive background Treasury Minute of 30 July 1913 (Bodl. MS. Asquith 93, ff.150–232).

Oct. 16 Grey announced Peace had been arranged the night before between Turkey & Italy.

Italy had taken the opportunity during the Agadir crisis to seize the Tripoli coast from Turkey and had issued an ultimatum on 28 September 1911 demanding an Italian occupation of the area to restore order. The Ottoman government's refusal had led to a declaration of war. The Italians were sufficiently successful by 5 November 1911 to proclaim their possession and to name their colony 'Libya'; but the Turks withdrew to the interior, waged a guerrilla war, and stalemate resulted. The Italian navy had then attacked (unsuccessfully) the Dardanelles forts and seized thirteen of the Dodecanese Islands. Fearful that the war might spread to the Balkans and the rest of the Aegean, Italy and Turkey began negotiations in July 1912 (Ryan Gingeras, Fall of the Sultanate: The Great War and the End of the Ottoman Empire 1908–1922, *Oxford UP, 2016, pp.70–9).*

Negotiations were sped up by the mobilisation of the Balkan League, and on 18 October 1912 the Treaty of Ouchy ended the war. By its terms, Turkey renounced its sovereignty over Libya, but the Italians agreed to maintain the Sultan's religious authority. Italy was to evacuate the Dodecanese as soon as Turkey evacuated Libya, but the Turks gave guarantees of the islands' autonomy. The Italians also gave Turkey an indemnity. As a result, the great powers recognised Italy's sovereignty over Libya; the Libyans were less amenable, and guerrilla fighting continued (Christopher Seton-Watson, Italy from Liberalism to Fascism, 1870–1925, *Methuen, 1967, pp.366–81; more recent literature and relevant archives underpin John Gooch's account of 'The Libyan War, 1911–12' in his* The Italian Army and the First World War, *Cambridge UP, 2014, pp.38–50); the Turkish perspective is documented in Eugene Rogan,* The Fall of the Ottomans: The Great War in the Middle East, *Basic Books, New York, 2015, pp.14–18. The course of British diplomacy is charted in Joseph Heller,* British Policy Towards the Ottoman Empire 1908–1914, *Frank Cass, 1983.*

The appointment of Lichnowsky as German ambassador.

We discussed whether Home Rule Bill should be altered to exclude Post Office. The general sense was for stamps & rates to be retained by Imp. Parl. but Irish administration handed over. Churchill & George advocated total reservation of whole service — Morley Harcourt Birrell & I the other course. It was arranged for Birrell to see Redmond, & that we should meet again.

I asked for £200,000 from Exchequer to meet Expense of Franchise Act. Matter referred to Estimates Committee. I asked for Parl. time for bill to abolish ½ timers — deferred.

Oct. 17 Birrell gave P.M. letter Redmond had written protesting against retransfer of P.O. to Imperial Parl., but readiness to concede stamps, rates of postage and mobilisation &c for defence. Cabinet agreed & thought internal postage rates might be altered by Irish Parliament but not external.

We agreed upon words expressing pleasure at terms of Peace bet. Italy & Turkey.

Samuel & I agreed for an indication of our friendliness to Italy, as our protection of Turk in Greece at Turkish request might be interpreted as hostile to Balkan States. It was suggested we should protect Montenegrins in Turkey as a set off.

Oct. 22 French arrangement words given Cambon.[32] Eastern question.

The possible closing of the Dardanelles was the subject of 'anxious consideration' because of the large quantities of grain lying ready for shipment in the Black Sea ports. Injury to trade and price rises were feared; but, if the Straits could be kept open for a fortnight, the bulk of the produce for export could be cleared (HHA Cabinet letter, 23 Oct. 1912, Bodl. MS. Asquith 6, f.168). The Russian situation is narrated in D.W. Spring, 'Russian Foreign Policy, Economic Interests and the Straits Question, 1905–14', in Robert B. McKean ed., New Perspectives in Modern Russian History, *Macmillan, Basingstoke, 1992, pp.203–21.*

JAP had used the recess to prepare and circulate a paper on education, presenting 'some reasons for thinking that we should not again make a direct attack upon the existing dual system'. HHA meanwhile was flirting with the 20-year-old Lady Diana Manners, 'a heartless little beast... haunting the London shops, and enjoying life, and devastating the world, and you never give a moment's thought to your friend & companion in so many delightful hours' (HHA–Lady Diana Manners, 25 Oct. 1912, Lady Diana Cooper MSS, BL Add.MS. 70,704).

Oct. 30 Cabinets—all going very smoothly. Eastern question.

HHA reported a long discussion on the French Ambassador's vague and ambiguous 'proposed formula' to express the character and purpose of the Anglo-French entente. A letter drafted by Grey, 'criticised and to some extent remoulded by the Cabinet', and shown to Cambon, was transmitted to the King (HHA Cabinet letter, 1 Nov. 1912, Bodl. MS. Asquith 6, ff.170–1).

Nov. 1 Time table settled — holidays — guillotining — women's suffrage. Churchill's demand for navy pay increase of 330 thousand instead of £530,000 he sulky — usual threat! Eastern question.

[32] This entry and those for 30 Oct. and 1 Nov. were probably written at the same time. The 'words given Cambon' were discussed on 30 Oct. not 23 Oct.

The Cabinet had before it an unsigned memorandum proposing the establishment of a Second Chamber of 180 members. A third of the members would be nominated by the Crown; the others would be elected by 'large constituencies' for nine year terms, 40 of them subject to re-election every three years. Conflict between the two Houses would be settled by joint sittings. Unsurprisingly no agreement was reached, and a committee to be chaired by the Prime Minister was set up (Peter Rowland, The Last Liberal Governments, *p.187). Discussion of rival reform schemes proposed by Haldane and Samuel exposed a wide divergence of solutions. Chris Ballinger concludes: 'more pressing political issues prevented the Cabinet from devoting to Lords reform the energy which would have been needed to reach agreement, if agreement was possible at all' (*The House of Lords 1911–2011: A Century of Non-Reform, *Hart Publishing, Oxford, 2012, p.31).*

Sulky as he might have been in the morning, at dinner in the evening WSC was buoyantly discussing the prospects of the Turco-Bulgarian war and the collapse of the Turks, agreeing with the idea of encouraging a Balkan confederation (Bulgaria, Servia, Montenegro, and Greece), but allowing the Turks to save face by retaining possession of Constantinople. He concurred with Maj.-Gen. Ewart that it would be foolish to antagonise Turkey, a possible ally of Germany in the event of war (Ewart Memoirs, p.1047, Ewart MSS).

Venetia Stanley, who had spent the week at 10 Downing Street, told Edwin Montagu on 6 November that the Prime Minister seemed much better, his shoulder wasn't hurting and he was playing golf, but that he seemed 'horribly bored by my constant presence at breakfasts, lunch and dinner' (Montagu MSS, I I A1/65, Wren Lib. TCC).

Nov. 6 Stuart Samuel's position.[33] Reduction troops fr. S. Africa. Asquith fully recovered in health & always on the spot in debate & on the bench a good deal up to dinner hour. [Eastern question].

As a director of Samuel Montagu & Co, which had a government contract to buy silver for the Indian mints, Sir Stuart Samuel might be thought to be breaking the law of 22 Geo. III, c.45 (1782) which forbade MPs to make or be involved in contracts with the government. An MP breaking this law was regarded as having vacated his seat and being under a £500 penalty for every time he voted. Sir Frederick Banbury had demanded that Sir Stuart leave the House. HHA assured the King on 7 November that Edwin Montagu (Under-Secretary for India) had no knowledge of the transaction nor any connection with his brother's firm (Bodl. MS. Asquith 6, f.173). The eternally depressive Montagu nevertheless believed he was under a cloud. He was 'bad stock' he told Walter Runciman on 4 December 1912. By 23 December he

[33] Sir Stuart Montagu Samuel (1856–1926); Lib. MP Tower Hamlets (Whitechapel) 1900–16; elder brother of Herbert Samuel; banker; director, Samuel Montagu & Co., Bt 1912.

had heard nothing from any of his friends in the Prime Minister's circle: HHA himself ('well he wouldn't'), Margot, 'Bongie' Bonham Carter, Roderick 'Mikky' Meiklejohn,[34] *Harold 'Bluie' Baker, and Geoffrey Howard. Violet Asquith sent a short note, and promised a letter that had not come. Montagu wrote yet again to Runciman on 31 January 1913: 'if I really want to serve the Liberal party unselfishly I ought to clear out as the third and most easily spared Jew' (Runciman of Doxford MSS).*

On the question of whether Samuel had vacated his seat, the advice of the government's principal law officers, Isaacs and Simon, was guarded. Their joint opinion signed on 9 November was that it was one of 'great difficulty and considerable doubt'. In additional informal advice accompanying the opinion on 11 November, the Attorney General explained that, as the matter might find its way into the courts in an action for penalties, they had 'refrained from expressing any opinion except as to the course to be pursued' (Bodl. MS. Asquith 24, ff.220–2).

In the Commons HHA argued that the position, in view of modern financial developments, was no longer clear; he asked for a Select Committee to inquire into the matter, but its members failed to agree. In April 1913 the courts decided that he had indeed disqualified himself from sitting. Sir Stuart then dissociated himself from the firm and stood for re-election; he was returned, but the Conservatives increased their vote by 23 per cent. In May 1913 a suit to extract from him the financial penalty failed, and an indemnity bill introduced into the Commons was dropped (4 Feb. 1913, note).

Nov. 8 Cabinet called hurriedly at H of C. to consider position Grey anxious to have Cabinet support. Austria & Germany united to support with arms Italy's & Austria's private agreement to prevent Servia having outlet into Adriatic — Servia now insisting on dividing Albania up & getting access — Russia backing the allies against the triple Alliance — Grey urged that we should attempt to secure a settlement when war was concluded, & not look at an isolated point wh. might produce friction. Prime Minister asked what he was to say at Mansion House on the following night, jocosely referred to his 4 years previously having backed the Young Turks! I said warn Powers not to do anything until war ended on lines of Grey's policy, this was concurred in.

[34] Roderick Sinclair Meiklejohn (1876–1962); civil service p.s. to HHA 1905–11, assigned to draft Old Age Pensions legislation; entered War Office 1899; transferred to Treasury 1902; p.s. to Sir E. Hamilton and Duke of Devonshire; principal clerk, Treasury 1911–20; Dep. Controller of Establishments, Treasury 1921–4; Dep. Controller of Supply Services, Treasury 1925–8; First Civil Service Commissioner 1928–39; CB 1911, KBE 1931. A homosexual, described by his friend Siegfried Sassoon to Dame Felicitas Corrigan as 'a dear, kind soul, but a bleak unbeliever—sustained by food and wine and Bridge and the classics—revering Dante, Shakespeare, Virgil & Milton etc but only as great literature—a sad stoic' (extract courtesy of Max Egremont; Egremont's *Siegfried Sassoon: A Life*, Farrar, Straus and Giroux, NY, 2005, p.85).

In his speech on 9 November, HHA said that the Eastern position had been entirely changed by the actions of the Balkan Confederacy. He said that the victors were not to be robbed of the fruits of their victories and warned against trying to settle particular questions in isolation. Four years earlier, on 9 November 1909, he had congratulated the Turkish Ambassador on the success of the Young Turks and had described their revolution as amazing and beneficent. His 1912 speech was warmly received at home and abroad.

During the 8 November Cabinet meeting Grey read out his cable to Bertie, sent the previous day (printed for Cabinet 12 Nov.1912), quoting Cambon as informing Grey that Raymond Poincaré, the French Premier and Foreign Minister, was ready to accept Grey's draft letter of 30 October but would like added: 'si ces mesures comportaient une action les ententes de nos Etats majors produissent leur effet...'. Harcourt and JAP exchanged notes:

> [LH] 'If these measures involved taking action, effect will be given to the conversations of our general staffs'
> [JAP, pencilled] On merit. I don't like committing ourselves in advance—obviously regard should be had to them.
> In my hurry, reading I thought 'nos Etats majors' had reference to ourselves the great powers!!
> 'General Staff' was not in my French vocabulary at school.
> *(Harcourt–JAP, JAP–Harcourt, notes, [8?] Nov. 1912, Bodl. MS. Harcourt 443, f.156)*

The background to Grey's negotiations with the French since March 1912 is documented from the French archives in John Keiger, 'Sir Edward Grey, France, and the Entente: How to Catch the Perfect Angler?', IHR, vol.38, no.2, 2016, pp.285–300. Drawing attention to documents published by a German spy in the Russian embassy in London, Samuel R. Williamson Jr concludes that 'the so-called secret conversations were chiefly secret from Parliament and the British public' ('German Perceptions of the Triple Entente after 1911: Their Mounting Apprehensions Reconsidered', Foreign Policy Analysis, vol.7, no.2, 2011, p.208).

Nov. 11[35] Asquith amused us all by reading Balfour's speech of July 1905—4 mos before he resigned & we all roared with laughter at A.J.B.'s speech. It was so appropriate but Churchill pointed out the obvious differences in situation. Diminished strength in parties—old Parliament &c. &c.

[35] JAP dated this meeting 11 Nov. but it was 12 Nov. on which HHA reported that the 'accidental adverse division in the House of Commons yesterday afforded no reason for resignation' (Bodl. MS. Asquith 6, f.177).

On 20 July 1905, during the debate on the vote for the Irish Land Commission, Balfour's government had been defeated when an amendment by John Redmond to decrease the vote was passed by 200 to 196. The Irish MPs were angry at not being consulted over the workings of the 1903 Land Act. On 24 July Balfour announced that he would not resign in view of past precedents. The Annual Register 1905 *(p.197) commented '(as to which [past precedents] few impartial persons could doubt that he made out an excellent case)'.*

We agreed to rescind Banbury's amendment to the Irish Resolution.

On 11 November during the debate on the Report Stage of the Home Rule Bill, the government had been defeated in a surprise vote favouring an amendment by Sir Frederick Banbury that limited the amount the Exchequer would be allowed to pay to the Irish Exchequer. Banbury's amendment was based on the argument that the British taxpayers should not subsidise a government over which they had no control. The vote, a pre-arranged manoeuvre, found the government unready: only two Cabinet ministers were in the House. While in court representing the Post Office John Simon received a note from HHA asking him to 'take a hand in the finance debates'. Simon arrived 'just in time to vote in the fatal division—228 to 202' (HHA–Simon, and note by Simon, 11 Nov. 1912, Simon MSS; Cameron Hazlehurst, 'Herbert Henry Asquith', in John P. Mackintosh ed., British Prime Ministers in the Twentieth Century, Vol. I, Balfour to Chamberlain, *Weidenfeld and Nicolson, 1977, pp.97–8).*

*The government had been let down by the whips, who had ignored warnings from the Irish whip Patrick O'Brien and Labour's John Ward, who had 'overheard Tories talking about it in groups' (Violet Asquith–Venetia Stanley, 17 Nov. 1912, Bodl. MS. Bonham Carter 155, f.55). Sir George Robertson and Sir William Priestley had been allowed to attend a Liberal demonstration in Bradford even though they could not get pairs (*Manchester Guardian, *12 Nov. 1912). JAP, Grey, and Runciman were also among those not present (Maurice Bonham Carter–Violet Asquith, 11 Nov. 1912, Mark Bonham Carter & Mark Pottle eds,* Lantern Slides: The Diaries and Letters of Violet Bonham Carter 1904–1914, *Weidenfeld & Nicolson, 1996, p.340).*

For Margot Asquith, the snap defeat demonstrated not only the inferiority of Illingworth and Gulland in the Whips' Office, but that 'Bongy' Bonham Carter, though an 'excellent fellow', was 'in no ways equal to Nash', whom he had replaced as HHA's principal private secretary; and Charles Lyell, the PM's Parliamentary PS, was 'useless & probably not in the House'. Taking it upon herself to call the King's private secretary, the Prime Minister's wife learned from Lord Knollys that 'the King was dreadfully upset at the idea of us resigning... I told Knollys there cd be no question of this. It was an old joke & a very bad one that had been played by us on A.J.B. & he took no sort of notice of it tho his majority was dwindling hourly in 1904–5.' What the King was really upset about—he wrote in his own hand to say so on 16 November—was the fact that HHA did not tell him directly about the snap defeat or the proposed action to reverse it or of the subsequent disorder in the House (Bodl. MS. Asquith 3, ff.136–7). The evening ended with a rollicking dinner for six: the Asquiths, DLG, WSC, Isaacs, and Harcourt, joined later by Grey, who had dined with 'a lady' (Grey's intimate friend, Margot's sister-in-law, Pamela Glenconner). Margot wrote 'Henry in tearing form. I never heard him better in my life... L. George... is much the best company—he & Henry romped over the others' (Margot Asquith diary, 11 Nov. 1912, Bodl. MS.Eng.d.3210, ff.57–63).

Meanwhile a dejected Illingworth had written a letter of resignation but was persuaded by Simon not to send it (Illingworth–Simon, 12 Nov. 1912, Bodl. MS. Simon 49, ff.20,50–1). Charles Lyell, feeling no guilt himself, told his mother on 21 November: 'the division of course was the snappiest snap that could be imagined, all carefully planned, & very cleverly arranged to take place on the one occasion which was almost irreparable...'. The Liberals had numbers of businessmen, bankers, merchants, shippers, and 'others who have to earn a living... in Manchester or Liverpool or Newcastle, & who try to do it by working very hard all Saturday, & coming up on Monday evening'. Lyell stated the obvious truth that Illingworth and the other whips ought to have known that and arranged speakers to defeat snap motions (Lyell MSS).

Nov. 13 We discussed merits of Banbury's motion & I suggested how the P.M. might show in his speech in moving motion to rescind Banbury's amendment, the difference from an electoral point of view between position in July 1905 when we defeated Balfour & clamoured for a general election & now, & how then the Elections had gone against us, & how those that had taken place in 2 years had shown 250,000 Home Rulers to 209,999 against.

HHA proposed a motion that would negate the events of 11 November. Sir Frederick Banbury moved an amendment, declaring that such a suggestion was 'an affront to this House' (HC Deb 13 November 1912 vol 42 c2031). Explaining the debacle to Montagu, who was in India, Crewe wrote on 15 November that 'without malice on the Speaker's part... no inkling was given to us that the motion to rescind Banbury's amendment ought to be regarded as an abuse of the majority's powers' (Crewe MSS, I/5 (10), CUL). The debate on the amendment led to hysterical scenes. Sir William Bull was invited to withdraw for the rest of the day after confessing that he had been crying out the unparliamentary expression 'Traitor! Traitor'. The Sitting was suspended for an hour under standing order no. 21; then, because of the continuing 'grave disorder', the House was adjourned. Debate had been brought to a standstill by repeated chanting of 'Divide' and 'Adjourn'. These were not unparliamentary expressions;

therefore the Speaker, James Lowther, believed that individual members could not be suspended. Lowther was probably wrong, but he thwarted an attempt by the Liberal backbencher Leo Chiozza Money, citing Erskine May, to challenge the ruling (draft autobiographical notes, p.277, Chiozza Money MSS, Add. 9259/1 [2], CUL). The well-informed Daily News *correspondent Philip Whitwell Wilson revealed on 15 November that after the scenes of disorder Lord Knollys had a conference at the Speaker's House with HHA and Mrs Lowther, which 'no doubt' had an influence on the Speaker's suggestion that the House be adjourned to enable the government to consider their course of action.*

More interesting to headline writers than arcane arguments about procedure and precedent was the six foot six inch Ronald McNeill's throwing of the Speaker's copy of the standing orders at WSC. McNeill apologised the next day, and the House resumed its business on 18 November when cooler tempers prevailed. An implied threat of resignation by the Speaker was instrumental in persuading HHA and the Tories to compromise (T.M. Healy, Letters and Leaders of My Day, *2 vols, Thornton Butterworth [1928], Vol. II, p.509). Most of the Unionist press condemned the events. Michael Shelden points out that few accounts of the assault on WSC 'note how serious the impact would have been from a large book thrown by a "giant"' (*Young Titan: The Making of Winston Churchill, *Simon & Schuster, 2013, pp.283–4,350). In fact, as WSC's friend and DLG's PPS Eliot Crawshay-Williams observed, the book 'drew a spot of blood' (*Simple Story: An Accidental Autobiography, *John Long, 1935, p.122).*

We discussed Panama & letter to be sent to Bryce.

The US Congress had passed the Canal Act (1912), which exempted American coastal shipping from tolls for passage through the Panama Canal. This was a violation of the Hay–Paunceforte treaty, which stated that the canal should be operated on terms of equality. Theodore Roosevelt argued that, as the canal had been paid for by the US, Americans should get the benefits. The matter became a major campaign issue in the 1912 presidential election. Bryce prolonged his term as ambassador in his efforts to achieve satisfaction and he was able to persuade the new president (Woodrow Wilson) that Britain had reasonable grounds for complaint. The Act was eventually repealed in June 1914 (see E.S.A. Ions, James Bryce and American Diplomacy, *Macmillan, 1968, pp.237–41).*

The Persian position & how to raise money with Russia to secure a Govmt on security of Crown jewels.

The Persians had sought a loan in December 1909, but the Russian terms were unacceptable (see JAP's records of 29 June and 8 Nov. 1910, A Liberal Chronicle…1908–1910, *pp.191,208–9, and 6 Dec. 1911 and n.). They then tried to raise a loan on the crown jewels (valued by a French jeweller at £750,000) from Seligmans of London. Cabinet agreed to sound Russia about a possible £1 million loan, half guaranteed by Russia, half by Britain and India, but the loan was not secured (Bodl. MS. Asquith 6, ff.179–80; Peter Avery,* Modern Iran, *Ernest Benn, 1965, pp.149–78; David Kynaston,* The City of London, Vol. II, Golden Years 1890–1914, *Pimlico, 1996, pp.510–11; and a wide-ranging interpretation of British interests in 'The Ottoman Empire and Persia, 1838–1914', in P.J. Cain and A.G. Hopkins,* British Imperialism, 1688–2000, *Longman, 2002, pp.340–59).*

Thursday Nov. 14 I dined with the Prime Minister & 'Margot' at No. 10. Rufus Isaacs, Sir John Simon & my wife were there, & Beb (Herbert)[36] Asquith. We discussed the situation and had a pleasant cheery dinner. The P.M. seemed well. The following day he played Illingworth at golf and in the evening at the Glenconners' party told him how he had been beaten, by Illingworth doing two holes in two strokes each — but they had a close game.

After dinner I explained to Mrs Asquith & Simon my view that if we passed our 3 bills through the Commons — & the Dissolution came before they became law under the Parliament Act, then we would unite the friends of the bills & unionist free traders against the Tariff Reform food taxing party & should do well. The P.M. played Bridge with Beb against Isaacs & my wife. The latter won 37/- but the P.M. took his loss at the game in a cheerier spirit than usual. He loves to be a winner!

HHA's cheerier spirit may have been fostered by the expected receipt of a cheque for £1,000 from his host. Lord Glenconner had inherited from his father, Sir Charles Tennant, a commitment to pay his brother-in-law £1,000 on 15 May and 15 November each year as long as HHA remained in office (Sir C. Tennant–HHA, 17 Dec. 1905, copy; HHA–Sir E. Tennant, 14 June 1906, 8 May 1911, Glenconner MSS).

John Simon's diary note on the dinner throws light on the conversation:

> Mrs Asquith told me endless stories, amongst others she recounted Winston's apt observation when the Archbishop of Canterbury made his speech in the House of

[36] JAP omitted the brackets which should surround 'Herbert'. Herbert Asquith (1881–1947), the Prime Minister's second son, known as 'Beb'; m. 1910 Cynthia Charteris (Lady Cynthia Asquith on her father's succession as 7th Earl of Wemyss in 1914); lawyer and poet; commissioned into the Royal Marine Artillery. Soon in ill-health and drinking heavily, Beb had extended leave. Transferring to the Royal Field Artillery and later to a staff appointment, he served until 1919, resolving never to go back to the Bar. The impecunious couple perched in different homes, often separately, throughout the war, from which Beb emerged with shell shock. The couple are recognisable as the Chatterleys in D.H. Lawrence's *Lady Chatterley's Lover* (1928).

Lords defending Chinese Labour as a regrettable necessity: 'I was always afraid he would prefer the Man in the Street to the Man on the Cross.'

She told me that Edward [*sic*] Montagu once plucked up courage and walked back from the House with Arthur Balfour. Montagu asked Balfour why it was that the Tories disliked McKenna. Balfour replied that personally he liked McKenna, but that many Tories did not trust him; they did not think he told the truth.

'Much as our side feels about Bonar Law,' said Montagu. 'Yes,' said Balfour, 'but there you are right'.

(Bodl. MS. Simon 2, f.11)

Monday Nov. 18 The P.M. explained to the House the proposals of the Gov. to meet the situation & after his speech, moving the discharge of the order, no one rose and the House accepted the alternative, in tribute to the P.M.

Nov. 20 Cabinet. I was absent in North. Discussion on time table. It was decided to take Welsh Disest. & cut down Franchise Bill to least dimensions.

The course of Welsh Disestablishment through Cabinet and Parliament is documented in G.I.T. Machin, Politics and the Churches in Great Britain 1869 to 1921, *Clarendon P., Oxford, 1987, pp.305–10. As Matthew, McKibbin, and Kay comment, 'a cabinet which in November 1912 put Welsh Disestablishment far ahead of the fourth Reform bill hardly seemed seized of any particular need to advance the constitutional pale, particularly if they believed the franchise extensions would have benefited them . . . there was constant dragging of feet' (McKibbin,* Ideologies of Class, *pp.92–3).*

Nov. 21 I pointed out at cabinet, we could not cut down our bill on Franchise & Registration to plural voting — everything depended on what was done about women voting — if excluded there would be time enough to get bill in to Lords by Feb. 10. Of all our bills this Bill had the most backing in the party & we cd. not now introduce a new bill, or prevent title covering all the bill, & too much evisceration would be out of order.

A long chat & discussion at times warm over pay to sailors. Churchill asked for 376,000 increase. George willing only to give £300,000 — eventually Churchill asked to defer pay for another year & bring his scheme down to £340,000 — 4*d* p day after 7 yrs. service.

WSC had submitted a Cabinet paper on the pay of officers on 17 October and another on improving the pay of ratings on 11 November. After the 'warm' discussion, he circulated a 38-page Admiralty brief on 23 November (TNA: CAB 37/112/114,124; CAB 37/113/127). Increases were announced in that month, and WSC said in a statement on the Navy Estimates:

'I am satisfied that these increases of pay—although perhaps they were not in many cases all that I should have liked to see given—and the methods in which the funds available have been distributed, have produced a very good impression throughout the naval service' (HC Deb 26 March 1913 vol 50 c1778).

We agreed to offer to French Cambon's added words to our proposals plus the following words

> 'plans of the General staff would at once be taken into consideration & the Govmts would then decide what effect should be given them.'

We agreed to prevent Irish Parl. being able to reduce duties on customs below our own, on ground to avoid search on vessels irritating, & the platform point that we had to pay more for necessaries of life than Irish & had to contribute also to their deficit!

Summing up the recent Commons debacle for his mother, Charles Lyell could conclude 'we have rounded the corner now with the loss of a fortnight of Parliamentary time, but we have had a serious knock & won't be able to stand another of the same kind' (C. Lyell–Lady Lyell, 21 Nov. 1912, Lyell MSS). Shaken by the snap defeat, the Whips' Office laid down fresh conditions for giving notice of unavoidable absence, leaving the House by the main door only, never without a pair, unless one was unobtainable and the whips were notified, and informing the whips if a private pair was arranged. 'It is only by paying close attention to these suggestions that a misadventure such as recently occurred can be frustrated' (Whips' Notice, 22 Nov. 1912, Illingworth MSS). 'The usual customs of the House with regard to pairs' had been set out by the Chief Whip in a guidance note for new Members in February 1911. The practice when a Member was responding to an urgent call was to inform the Whip on duty, 'and not to pass out of the House by any exit other than the door to the Members' Cloak Room' (MS. Gainford 89).

Nov. 27 Full Cabinet. George raised the question of Sheffield's appeal for Univ. building grant. I explained that other appeals would follow if case granted but I supported the appeal on general grounds. On ground that Sheffield could afford her own Univ. better than some others decided Ministers to respond to appeal.

JAP's account is confusing. Sheffield University's request for a grant of £9,000 was refused (Bodl. MS. Asquith 6, f.186). DLG's motive seems to have been to open the door to subventions to Welsh university colleges, Cardiff having already received a similar sum (Hobhouse diary, 27 Nov. 1912, unpublished). Earlier in the year, prolonged wrangling between the Board of Education and the Treasury over control of university grants had resulted in the Treasury formally retaining the 'Vote' but JAP's department having effective control. The interdepartmental struggle, DLG's determination to avoid the political embarrassment of admitting publicly that Treasury had lost its authority, and Haldane's mediation, are documented in Eric Ashby and Mary Anderson, Portrait of Haldane at Work on Education, *Macmillan, 1974, pp.95–101.*

Sheffield University's accommodation for arts, science, and medicine had opened in 1905; an applied science building, 'in a confident neo-Baroque style in red brick with stone dressings', was completed in 1912. But as a result of expanding numbers of departments, staff, and students, the university needed additional space. The leading local Liberal, Sir William Clegg, overcame opposition from the public and councillors who thought the university had been well supported, and secured a City Council grant of £10,000 (Ruth Harman and Roger Harper, 'The Architecture of Sheffield', in Clyde Binfield et al. *eds,* The History of the City of Sheffield 1843–1993, Vol. II: Society, *Sheffield Academic P., 1993, p.50; Helen Mathers,* Steel City Scholars: The Centenary History of the University of Sheffield, *James & James, 2005, p.71. We are grateful to Dr David Vessey for providing the latter reference). The Prime Minister's attitude to Sheffield University could well have been influenced by his belief that the Vice-Chancellor, Sir Charles Eliot, a former East African colonial official, had been badly treated by the previous government. HHA believed that Eliot's talents (he was a Balliol man, gifted linguist, and orientalist) were wasted in the Sheffield post. But the support that he and his wife gave for Eliot to be appointed Governor of Trinidad in 1909 had proved fruitless. Eliot was appointed to the Vice Chancellorship of the new university in Hong Kong in 1912. After the war he served as High Commissioner in Siberia, and then as Ambassador in Japan (Esther Simon Shkolnik,* Leading Ladies: A Study of Eight Late Victorian and Edwardian Political Wives, *Garland, New York, 1987, pp.500–3; Oliver Elton and Bernard Pares, 'Sir Charles Eliot',* S&EER, *vol.10, no.28, 1931, pp.172–4).*

I raised new site for R. Col. of Art buildings, & matter was referred to expenses Comtee.

JAP's request for £150,000, 'in the long run' (an extraordinary ambit claim), for the Royal College of Art at South Kensington was referred to the Cabinet Estimates Committee. (Bodl. MS. Asquith 6, f.186.) The College had been formally separated from the Victoria and Albert Museum complex since 1910. On 5 November 1912 a departmental committee had recommended that the Office of Works erect a new building for the college on a triangular 'island site' opposite the Museum. The cost of replacing the College's existing scattered and overcrowded accommodation was estimated at £65,000 with a further £7,500 to adapt buildings behind the V. & A. for the Museum's future needs. Although the Cabinet committee thought the costs 'rather excessive', £65,000 was allocated in the 1913 Public Buildings Bill and plans were approved by the Board of Education. The coming of war halted progress on the site and it was another 40 years before the proposed relocation plan was revived (Christopher Frayling, The Royal College of Art: one hundred and fifty years of art and design, *Barrie and Jenkins, 1987, pp.83–4; Hilary Cunliffe-Charlesworth, 'The Royal College of Art Its Influence on Education, Art And Design 1900–1950', Ph.D. thesis, Council for National Academic Awards, 1991, pp.157–63, provides more detail on JAP's role).*

Churchill urged more pay for sailors agreed to his scheme No. 4 giving 3*d* p day for men after 6 years, & 4*d*. for Petty Officers = £350,000. He made an impetuous protest, & warned Govmt of inadequacy of increase & difficulties when estimates came on.

Grey reported a pleasant interview & understanding between Russian Czar & Austrian Ambassador[37] which heralded complete understanding, & of settlement of Balkan situation. Servia would have to accept right of access to international Albanian ports. Islands with Grecian population to be given Greece. What about Cyprus, general feeling it was no use to our Empire & we could give it up, if we had a quid pro quo. Hobhouse protesting against this course as unpopular. Grey favoured it.

The possibility of Cyprus being ceded to Greece had been discussed as long ago as 1878. With Grey in support of the idea, WSC and DLG would canvass it in unofficial conversation late in the year with the Greek premier Eleuthérios Venizélos. They had considered, but stopped short of proposing, the cession of Cyprus in exchange for a naval base at Argostoli (C.M. Woodhouse, 'The Offer of Cyprus, October 1915', P. Calvocoressi et al., Greece and Britain During World War I, *pp.77–8, Institute for Balkan Studies, Thessaloniki, 1985).*

I alluded to time table for Franchise, urged 5 days for guillotine & to end suffrage debate after 2 days.

P.M. seemed not at all sanguine we could carry the bill in time left us. I thought we could, & said so. Colleagues all quiet, but I think with me.

At a meeting on November 28 with the Deputy Speaker (Whitley) and the First Parliamentary Counsel (Thring), JAP settled the vital question of procedure for the Franchise Bill:

> The (4) woman suffrage amendments (to be named) shall have precedence over all other amendments; and until they have been disposed of the bill shall not on any day appear as first order of the day.

[37] Duglas Graf von Thurn und Valsássina-Como-Vercelli (1864–1939); Austrian Amb. St Petersburg Mar. 1911–Oct. 1913.

The debates shall be taken on all the amendments together.

At the end of the debate the Chairman shall forthwith put each amendment until one is carried or all are rejected.

(MS. Gainford 135/54)

Visit to Sutton Courtney[38]

Dec. 2

Went down on Nov 30. with Mrs Asquith (Margot) from Paddington to Didcot. She chatted freely about 'Henry' and her own troubles. Her inability with Violet about to talk freely to her own spouse. She could always ask her own children Elizabeth & Puffin to withdraw but step children were in a peculiar position towards their father. She agreed that Violet ought to tell Hugh Godley[39] that he was to be no more than a friend or marry him. She Margot had to do this for six months when she had to make up her own mind about Henry, & she stopped Peter Flower[40] Ernest Crawley,[41] Alfred Milner & others writing to her. She alluded

[38] The village known now as Sutton Courtenay was frequently spelled Sutton Courteney by contemporaries, including the Asquiths as their address for telegrams on the letterhead of 'The Wharf, Abingdon'. JAP's 'Sutton Courtney' was a variant also used by Viola Parsons, whose mother (Lady Tree) had bought the barn and cottage; Helen Langley, 'Political Houses 1880–1914', Malcolm Airs ed., *The Edwardian Great House*, Oxford U. Dept of Continuing Educ., 2000, pp.99–103). Until 1974, when it was transferred to Oxfordshire, the village was in Berkshire.

[39] Hon. Hugh Godley (1877–1950); barrister 1902; member, Central Control Bd (Liquor Traffic) 1917–21; Asst Parliamentary Counsel to Treasury 1917–23; Counsel to Ld Chmn of Committees 1923–44; 2nd Baron Kilbracken 1932. His prolonged and ultimately unsuccessful attachment to Violet Asquith led to the coining of the phrase to 'be Hugh-ed', meaning 'to be kept dangling indefinitely and then rejected' (*Asquith Letters*, p.530). His first marriage in 1919, to Helen Usborne, a widow, was dissolved in 1936. He then married Leonora Taylor.

[40] Lewis ('Peter') Flower (?1856–1902); inherited share of extensive property in Battersea managed by his brother Cyril (later Lord Battersea, 1843–1907); despite chronic ill-health was a prominent sportsman, 'one of the boldest riders in the hunting field' (Lady Battersea, *Reminiscences*, Macmillan, 1922, p.170). Margot Asquith's eyebrow-raising published account of her love for Flower, and of his improvidence and indifference to politics and religion, concluded that 'matrimony had not been the austere purpose of either of our lives' (*The Autobiography of Margot Asquith*, Vol. I, Thornton Butterworth, 1920, pp.253,262). In a note on the copy dedicated to 'the man I love and whose praise has rewarded me' she wrote that the account of her 'love affair' with Flower was 'understated, not quite accurate' (Bertram Rota Catalogue 275, 1995, p.2). In her diary 6 Aug. 1913, she said she had written to him every day for eight years, and he twice a day to her; but he had 'the wiles of a woman, the temper of the devil' and she did not have 'goodness for two'. She had made a confidante of 'Asquith', as he was called then, and she thought it was seeing her passion for Flower that made him fall in love with her (Bodl. MS.Eng.d.3210, ff.90–1). The 'eroticised friendship' is documented in Nancy W. Ellenberger, *Balfour's World: Aristocracy and Political Culture at the Fin de Siècle*, Boydell P., Woodbridge, 2015, pp.258–61; and with more embellishment from Margot's diary in Anne de Courcy, *Margot at War: Love and Betrayal in Downing Street 1912–16*,Weidenfeld & Nicolson, 2014, pp.19–20,78–81.

[41] (Henry) Ernest Crawley (1865–1931); sportsman and insurance underwriter; member, Lloyd's; played tennis and rackets for Cambridge; p.s. to Lord George Hamilton as First Lord 1885–92; Silver Racket for real tennis 1892, 1898, 1905 (his friend Sir Edward Grey won 1889–91, 1893–5, 1897, 1899–1904); defeated Grey for the Amateur Tennis Championship 1892–4; lost to Grey 1895–8;

to times when Henry was not in a mood to be approached, & she had only once beseeched him strongly to put his foot down, & that was on the Land policy of Lloyd George's, but he would not respond to dictation, but a kiss, often ended interviews. I told her in 30 seconds Asquith always had responded to me, & heard me fairly out no matter his mood. After luncheon I went motoring alone with the Prime Minister from Margot's House, the Wharf, Sutton Courtney[42] to Huntercombe.[43] The ground was frozen over. I gave him a stroke a hole played 12 holes in the cold, & beaten him 3 & 2.

We discussed the women's suffrage question and franchise bill, & I told him what I proposed to do, and the only way in which the issues might be fairly presented to the Committee by selection of amendments under the guillotine with Kangaroo but not necessarily with allotted days. I undertook to ascertain if it was possible to stick to plural voting penalty clause & drop others, if pressure of time compelled this course. I explained that the title of the bill might be regarded to be so wide as not to have proper relationship to contents, and it might be more difficult to get a fresh bill through than the whole of the bill which had secured a 2d Reading. He twice repeated the question is full of complications. The whole position is attributable to the P.M. having committed himself to go on with the Bill, as a Govmt under Parl. Act under a belief his Ministers & party were against him — whereas a majority of the cabinet are prepared to stand by the bill only if women are excluded.

He worked in his room from 5 to 8 and we played a long game of Bridge (Lady Horner[44] & I against Asquith & Margot) from 9.45 to 12.0.

captain, Suffolk Yeomanry 1899–1902. Described by Margot (diary, 12 Apr. 1913) as her 'oldest schoolboy friend . . . He has been passionately fond of me all his life . . . I made him marry . . . I love him he has a beautiful character' (Bodl. MS.Eng.d.3209, ff.247–8). Not to be confused with the anthropologist, sexologist, and tennis player (Alfred) Ernest Crawley (d. 1924).

[42] The Asquiths had first occupied The Wharf in July 1912. Margot bought the riverside property from Lady (Maud) Tree, who had disregarded Margot's advice to buy up 'the adjoining land, the public house in front, the private house next door, the cottages on the other side. Pull down that hideous hut, flood the garden, knock down the wall and dam the river' (Daphne Fielding, *The Rainbow Picnic: A Portrait of Iris Tree*, Eyre Methuen, 1974, p.46).

[43] Huntercombe golf club was regarded as one of the finest inland courses in the country. Sylvia Henley found it a challenge when taken there by HHA in Sept. 1915: 'You lose balls right and left' (Bodl. MS.Eng.lett.*c*.642, ff.145–6). James Bond told Goldfinger that he played off nine there (http://www.huntercombegolfclub.co.uk/history, accessed 23 Nov. 2022).

[44] Lady Horner (1858–1940); Frances Graham, m. John Horner 1883; he was knighted 1907 and d. 1927. Patron of the arts and great friend of HHA. Her dau. Katherine married HHA's son Raymond. Margot Asquith described her as comprising 'all that is best in my sex' (*Autobiography*, Vol. I, p.191). Cynthia Asquith described her as 'beautiful as well as scholarly—"Did she not know Greek"—she was the most accomplished needlewoman of her day' (Lady Cynthia Asquith, *Diaries 1915–1918*, Hutchinson, 1968, p.508).

All Asquith took for dinner in the way of liquor was a whisky & soda & a glass of mild port from the wood. At 12.0. a tumbler of Perrier water and I am told except when dining out he rarely takes more but his opponents still libel him by the nick name 'Perrier Jouet'.[45]

Before going to bed, I expressed my views as to the importance of dropping all but the tithe in regard to disendowment & spoke of the feeling of many Liberals in the country in a desire not to deprive theology of money & to direct it to secular use. He said I entirely agree with you, & we must see what more can be done, & then went on to describe the change which had come on the scene since he introduced his bill in 1895 when nonconformists took a much stronger line on disendowment.

A major difficulty in dealing with the Disestablishment of the Anglican Church in Wales was the disposal of its assets. The 1912 bill was very similar to the first bill, introduced in 1894, but its disendowment proposals were less severe. The 1895 bill, introduced by HHA, lapsed with the fall of Rosebery's government. It left to the Welsh church only its cathedrals, churches, moveable property, parsonages, closed burial grounds, and private benefactions made since 1662 (the date of the Act of Uniformity). The property taken from the church was to be administered by commissioners, who would pass it to the county councils. The 1912 bill left to the church income from Queen Anne's Bounty from Welsh sources, the Welsh share of parliamentary grants, and a share of the income from English sources of the Ecclesiastical Commissioners and Queen Anne's Bounty. This left the church with £102,000 p.a. out of property estimated to be worth £260,000 p.a. The remaining property was to be handed over to local councils to use for public works such as hospitals, libraries, village halls, and schools. The National Library of Wales and the University of Wales were also to benefit.

For a detailed history of Welsh Disestablishment see P.M.H. Bell, Disestablishment in Ireland and Wales, *SPCK, 1969, pp.226–329; Paul O'Leary, 'Religion, Nationality and Politics: Disestablishment in Ireland and Wales, 1868–1914', in John R. Guy and W.G. Neely,* Contrasts and Comparisons: Studies in Irish and Welsh Church History, *Ceredigion Welsh Historical Society and The Church of Ireland Historical Society, Cardiff, 1999, pp.89–113; and Kenneth O. Morgan's classic account,* Wales in British Politics 1868–1922, *U. of Wales P., Cardiff, 1963, pp.259–74.*

Sunday Dec 3 p.m. breakfasted with us at 10.0 — read his F.O. papers through — & retired to his room until luncheon.

[45] Perrier-Jouët, the brand of champagne to which HHA was supposedly partial.

In the afternoon he motored to Huntercombe & won easily a game against Mrs Parsons (Viola Tree that was). We discussed at dinner, biographies, & he said his would never be written.[46] He had covered up his tracks, but he admitted he thought Margot had kept his letters but he knew how to write to people in accordance with the prospect of letters being retained or destroyed & he wrote accordingly.

Margot said she would write his life for him, if he predeceased her & I said I wanted to pen one chapter.

We discussed Ministers' salaries & Asquith said, the P.M. ought to have as much as the Lord Chancellor £10,000 a year, & all other Ministers £5,000. The Ministry with exception of Burns & Buxton were the only M.P.s who had not benefited by our being in office, since we came in! We had one short game of bridge & solved a chess problem together. He then talked to me with ill concealed pride about his sons, & Cis[47] & Raymond's rival Oxford successes & about Raymond standing for Derby.

Both Cyril 'Cys' and Raymond (and HHA himself) had won the First Balliol Scholarship. They both got firsts in Moderations and Greats (classical languages, literature, history, and philosophy), and both won the Ireland and Craven Scholarships. Raymond had also won the Derby Scholarship; Cys the Hertford. HHA himself had got a first in Mods and Greats, won the Craven Scholarship, and been proxime accessit *to the Hertford and Ireland Scholarships. HHA's pride in his third son Arthur Melland 'Oc' Asquith (1883–1939) evidently was better concealed. 'Oc' left Oxford without a degree, joined the Egyptian civil service, and in 1911 found employment in Buenos Aires with an Argentine firm, Franklin and Herrera (Christopher Page,* Command in the Royal Naval Division: A Military Biography of Brigadier General A. M. Asquith DSO, *Spellmount, Staplehurst,1999, pp.4–21). On 3 December, Raymond Asquith had been invited to address the general council of the Derby Liberal Association with a view to his being asked to stand for the constituency at the next election.*

[46] Two biographies of HHA had already been published: J.P. Alderson, *Mr Asquith*, Methuen, 1905, and Frank Elias, *The Right Hon. H. H. Asquith, M.P.; a biography and appreciation*, J. Clarke, 1909. HHA admitted at the end of Oct. 1914 he had destroyed 'the greater part' of the letters he had received 'sometimes not without a malicious complacency at the disservice I am doing to any biographer who may be foolish enough hereafter to take me in hand' (*Asquith Letters*, p.299).

[47] Cyril Asquith (1890–1954); H.H. and Helen Asquith's 4th son; fellow, Magdalen Coll. Oxford 1913; Queen's Westminster Rifles 1914; medically unfit, employed in Min. of Munitions 1916–18; barrister 1920; undistinguished legal career culminating as a Law Lord, Baron Asquith of Bishopstone. Co-author of his father's official biography.

The sitting member, Sir Thomas Roe, was not going to seek re-election. On 6 December Raymond spoke and was asked to stand.

Dec. 4 Cabinet. Grey explained the situation in the East, which he & the Prime Minister both referred to as 'serious'.

(1) The speech of the German Chancellor promising support by arms to Austria if she thought her interests were at stake.
(2) The collection of 200,000 soldiers by Austria on the frontier of Roumania.
(3) The absence of any reply from Austria to our invitation to attend a conference of ambassadors to discuss the situation.
(4) The agreement attempted behind the other Powers' backs to come to an arrangement by Austria with Servia.

All were somewhat ominous. Haldane thought Hollweg was thought weak, & might be trying to show he was firm.

Grey reported Greek ambassador[48] explained Bulgaria's settlement left Turks in position to reassert their power & rearm, & recover their position & this was reason why they dissented from signing terms of peace.

On Grey's ominous warning on 4 December to Prince Lichnowsky about the possible consequences of a European war arising from an Austrian attack on Serbia leading to Russian intervention, then German, and then French, 'and no-one could foretell what further developments might follow', see the recent comments and allusions to other literature in Sir Christopher Clark, 'Sir Edward Grey and the July Crisis', IHR, *vol.38, no.2, 2016, pp.329–31. For Bulgaria and the Balkan Wars, a good starting point amid a vast literature is still Richard J. Crampton,* Bulgaria 1878–1918: A History, *East European Monographs, Boulder, distributed by Columbia UP, NY, 1983, Part III. A wider perspective is provided by Margaret MacMillan,* The War that Ended Peace: The Road to 1914, *Random House, New York, 2013, pp.466–500.*

Fearing that the Balkan War might escalate into a broader European war, Grey had invited a 'Reunion of the Ambassadors of the Six Great Powers, signatories of the Treaty of Berlin'. The conference began on 17 December. The complex issues that were to be faced are expounded

[48] Joannes Gennadius (1844–1932); Greek Amb. London and accredited as Amb. to the Netherlands 1910–18; diplomatic service from 1873 in Constantinople, Washington, Vienna, The Hague, London; bibliophile, donated library and archives (the Gennadeion) to the American School of Classical Studies in Athens.

in Richard C. Hall, The Balkan Wars 1912–1913: Prelude to the First World War, *Routledge, 2000, esp. pp.72–9. Hall's essay on 'Bulgaria and the Origins of the Balkan Wars, 1912–1913', in M. Hakan Yavuz and Isa Blumi eds,* War and Nationalism: The Balkan Wars, 1912–1913, and Their Sociopolitical Implications, *U. of Utah P., Salt Lake City, 2013, pp.85–99, is also helpful, as are Ronald Bobroff, 'Behind the Balkan Wars: Russian Policy Toward Bulgaria and the Turkish Straits 1912–13',* Russian Review, *vol.59, no.1, 2000, pp.76–95, and Gul Tokay, 'Ottoman diplomacy, the Balkan Wars and the Great Powers', in Dominick Geppert, William Mulligan, and Andreas Rose eds,* The Wars before the Great War: Conflict and International Politics before the Outbreak of the First World War, *Cambridge UP, 2016, pp.58–75. T.G. Otte's contribution on 'Entente diplomacy* v. *détente, 1911–1914' to the Geppert* et al. *volume is characteristically perceptive; and on Grey's policy should be read in conjunction with Rose's essay 'From "illusion" and 'Angellism' to détente—British radicals and the Balkan Wars', pp.320–42. There are useful summary articles and bibliographies in Richard C. Hall ed.,* War in the Balkans: An Encyclopedic History from the Fall of the Ottoman Empire to the Breakup of Yugoslavia, *ABC-CLIO, Santa Barbara, Denver, and Oxford, 2014, and an analysis of the 'four Balkan crises... which could have resulted in war' in Jared Morgan McKinney, 'Nothing fails like success: The London Ambassadors' Conference and the coming of the First World War,* Journal of Strategic Studies, *vol.41, no.7, 2018, pp.947–1000.*

By March 1913 Grey was supposedly telling Lord Esher 'he had no fear of a European war this year'. Never one to be modest about his inside knowledge, Esher told Lord Newton that Edward VII was not responsible for the promise to send the army to support France. 'Thinks it chiefly a matter of honour that has gradually evolved & agrees that War Office people think of little else. Says we ought never to have promised them more than naval assistance. Admiralty will be afraid to guarantee transport of force' (Newton diary, 7 Mar. [1913], Newton MSS).

Asquith called upon me to explain my views on Education Bill. I reflected on my colleagues for the absence of help given—and made a short sincere speech which I think pointed out difficulties, & the line of the only possible course. George tried to criticise my proposals, but had not read them & I pulled him up abruptly 2 or 3 times. Crewe & Haldane sided with him but in vague terms. Runciman pointed out difficulties. I made a general reply but expressed myself willing to consider whole question with a new Committee to which fresh thought from outside might be added.

Given the views they expressed, the nomination of DLG, Haldane, Crewe, and Runciman to join JAP on the committee would not have been his choice. But their remit indicated that significant hurdles were foreseen: to call into consultation 'a few of the leading outside experts and endeavour to arrive at a basis of agreement which could be defended both on educational and political grounds' (HHA Cabinet letter, 5 Dec. 1912, Bodl. MS. Asquith 6, f.188).

Seely asked for instructions in respect to Lord Roberts[49] & conscription, & he was unanimously urged on all sides to denounce compulsory military service.

The King was told something different on 5 December: 'The effect of recent speeches by Lord Roberts & others in checking recruiting for the Territorial army was seriously considered, and adjourned for further discussion.' (Bodl. MS. Asquith 6, f.188.) While compulsory service competed with education, foreign affairs, Home Rule, and Disestablishment on the Cabinet agenda, the Opposition leadership was avoiding declarations on policy, instead taking a broad view of political strategy. A meeting of about 22 ex-Cabinet ministers, other frontbenchers, the party's chief whip in the Commons, Lord Balcarres, and the party chairman, Arthur Steel-Maitland, was held at Lansdowne House on 5 December. Lord Curzon listed House of Lords reform, the referendum, land, land purchase, the Army and Navy, compulsory service, and Tariff Reform as matters on which definite lines were needed before the next general election. Lord Robert Cecil added national insurance. Bonar Law shrewdly then elicited the thoughts of Arthur Balfour, the previous leader in the House of Commons. Balfour's views were noted by Lord Ashbourne, former Lord Chancellor of Ireland: 'A.J.B. sd he did not think it was for an Opposition to formulate a programme, no more than general views—leaving details for any future Cabinet ... B. Law agreed with general views of A.J.B. Platform shd deal with general principles and not details' (Ashbourne diary, [5 Dec. 1912], Ashbourne MSS, Ash/A, PA). '"What you have to fight", stammered old Joe [Chamberlain] last Sunday night, "is public indifference. You have to interest the country",' J.L. Garvin told Lord Burnham on 27 December (Burnham MSS, courtesy of the 5th Lord Burnham).

JAP might have missed, or just not written up, the Cabinet meeting of 10 December at which there was considerable discussion on Army and Navy estimates and the financial situation generally. DLG 'protested strongly' against any expenditure increase that would lead to increased taxation. Crewe, 'and others', supported him against the assertions of Haldane, WSC, and Seely that their claims were the lowest compatible with security (HHA Cabinet letter, 11 Dec. 1912, Bodl. MS. Asquith 6, f.190).

[49] Field Marshal Frederick Sleigh Roberts, 1st Earl Roberts (1832–1914); last C-in-C of the Forces before the post was abolished in 1904. Known as 'Bobs'; pre-war champion of conscription as Pres., National Service League from 1905. VC, KG, KP, GCB, OM, GCSI, GCIE, KStJ, VD, PC.

17 Dec. Cabinet. We discussed endowments in Wales & what concession should be given. It became apparent that[50]

The Eccl. Comsns gave the Church for repairs	£ 40,000 p.a.
The Income for endowments	£260,000
Total income	£300,000

[Cathedrals[51]

Churches	values *say*	£1,000,000
Manses	=	£35,000 p.a.

Annual Expend by
Eccl Comns in repair = £40,000]

[Endowments removed

Ancient Glebe	£17,000
Stocks shares invested	
£16,000	£158,000
from Glebe & Tithe	
Tithe	£125,000

but from this £66,000 should be deducted being commuted life interest 12 yrs purchase 3½% (nett reduction £92,000) average expectation of incumbent 15½ yrs]

Endowments left by Bill	
Private sources since 1662	18,600
Payment from English Sources [(including savings by Eccl. Comsn)]	68,400
Parl. grants 1801 & onwards	6,000
Qu. Anne's Bounty [saved by accumulations for benefit of Church]	9,000
	102,000
Eccl. Coms will pass £28,000 (now annually invested) each year to accumulate to meet stipends, — which will be met by life interests reserved under bill (value 66,000) and £3,000 fr. Qu. Anne's Bounty [can be found & handed over (many benefices Church would not fill again if bill passes)]	31,000
	£133,000

[50] See Bell, *Disestablishment in Ireland and Wales,* for a discussion of these figures.
[51] The square brackets in these figures are in the original manuscript.

Dec. 31[52] Discussed Foreign Affairs. Home Rule & Welsh Amendments Ulster Question being predominant & Carson's letter to the P.M. was read.

Possibly this was the letter to HHA signed by nineteen Unionist MPs, urging him to accept their amendment to the Home Rule Bill, which excluded Ulster from its scope. They urged that this was the only way to preserve peace. The amendment was moved by Carson the next day and repudiated by HHA as meaning 'the wrecking of the whole Bill' (Ian Colvin, The Life of Lord Carson, *Vol. II, Victor Gollancz, 1934, pp.165–8; Geoffrey Lewis,* Carson: The Man Who Divided Ireland, *Hambledon and London, 2005, pp.116–17). On the Cabinet discussion of 31 December see Jalland,* The Liberals and Ireland, *pp.109–10.*

We decided to stick to policy of no concession now to those who admittedly pursued a hostile attitude to bill even if concessions could be given—but it was recognised that any now would be fatal to the financial & other proposals of this Bill, & we must proceed with it. Churchill & George blew off steam.

DLG, Edward Grey, and Rufus Isaacs dined with the Prime Minister (Margot Asquith diary, 31 Dec. 1912, Bodl. MS.Eng.d.3209, f.219). WSC blew off more steam at Percy Illingworth's New Year's Eve supper at the Hotel Cecil with 45 Liberal and Labour MPs for Scottish constituencies, including HHA.

Following JAP's presentation to the Cabinet early in December, his 'Memorandum on the policy and main features of an Education Bill for 1913', a condensed version, dated 2 December 1912, of his paper of 24 October 1912 (TNA: CAB 37/112/117), was circulated to Cabinet on 13 December. He pointed out that HHA had committed the government to an education bill in the next session in a letter (1 Mar. 1912) to the Rev. F.B. Meyer, Secretary of the National Council of Evangelical Free Churches (Bodl. MS. Asquith 13, ff.63–4; letter is dated 29 Feb. in the copy on file in MS. Gainford 109). Deputations had convinced JAP that Nonconformists had modified their views on areas with only an Anglican school (single-school areas): they accepted that any attempt to close voluntary schools would be vetoed by the Lords and would open the government to charges of violation of trusts, confiscation of property, and, not least, vast expenditure, up to £18 million. Moreover, Irish MPs would not tolerate the suppression of Roman Catholic schools.

JAP argued that these factors ruled out any wide-ranging bill. Nevertheless, in what was colourful language for him, he suggested 'in effect, the evisceration of the Act of 1902

[52] Harcourt's notes on this meeting at 11.30 (Bodl. MS.Eng.c.8267) are headed 'H of C men only'. He paraphrases HHA as saying: 'this not a meeting of the Cab.—concerns H of C men only—letter from Irish Unionists as to exclusion of Ulster . . .'.

so far as it establishes in a privileged position Voluntary Schools and their Managers, as against Council Schools and Local Education Authorities, and deprives the Local Education Authorities of effective control of secular instruction'. He proposed early but modest changes to increase local education authority (LEA) control over voluntary schools and to improve council schools. The most important of these changes were increased grants to the LEAs and LEA control of the appointment of headteachers of voluntary schools. JAP proposed a grant of 55s. per child, less the product of a 6d. rate. This would cost an extra £1,656,000. But, with an additional grant of one-third of any expenditure above 55s. per child, it would encourage the employment of qualified teachers, help repay high loan charges where site values were high, and offset increased local costs in poorer areas with many children.

The Cabinet committee of JAP, Crewe, Haldane, DLG, and Runciman began work on 19 December. Haldane was in the chair, and the Cabinet ministers were supported by Selby-Bigge, Struthers, Arthur Acland, and A.E. Hutton, chairman of the Northern Counties Education League and a proponent of building new council schools rather than taking over existing denominational schools (HHA Cabinet letter, 5 Dec. 1912, TNA: CAB 41/33/78). Before the committee met, Haldane had conferred with DLG; both of them were determined to push for a big scheme, but it was soon apparent that their priorities were different. The Board of Education laboured at compromise drafts, but progress was slow and tortuous.

Chapter 3
1913

Late in 1912 Bonar Law and Lord Lansdowne had announced that they were abandoning the pledge made before the November 1910 election by Balfour, then the Unionist leader in the House of Commons, to hold a referendum before introducing 'taxes on food'. As Willie Bridgeman told Wilfred Ashley on 6 January, 'it is a ticklish business for our leaders to go backwards over the tight-rope on which they crossed the stream' (Mount Temple MSS, BR 73, courtesy of Philip Williamson). The resulting disarray in Opposition ranks, and a threat of resignation by Bonar Law, were quickly resolved with the aid of Sir Edward Carson, James Craig, and Bonar Law's friend, Sir Max Aitken. With the agreement of all Unionists in the House of Commons, a face-saving compromise Tariff Reform policy, in words crafted by Bonar Law, was endorsed. All but a handful of Unionist MPs signed a letter to the party leaders asking them, 'as a compromise, to pass the manufactured goods duty, part of T.R., immediately after the next election, but defer Food Taxes until after the Dominions had been consulted and there had been another general election' (Winterton Diary, 9 Jan. [1913], Bodl. MS. Winterton 11).

The memorial presented to Bonar Law urging him not to resign, the draft of his own response, and his guidance for the press on the terms of the policy that was adopted are in a file preserved by his press adviser Malcolm Fraser (Bodl. MS.Eng.c.4789, ff.20–49). The contemporary notes and analysis of party sentiment by the Tory Chief Whip, Lord Balcarres, are an indispensable source (Vincent ed., The Crawford Papers, *pp.288–305); and there is percipient commentary in Andrew S. Thompson, 'Tariff Reform: an Imperial Strategy, 1903–1913',* HJ, *vol.40, no.4, 1997, pp.1033–54.*

Tariff Reform would once again recede in salience. But divisions now intensified over the attitude the Unionists should take to the impending Home Rule legislation. The formation of the Ulster Volunteer Force in January 1913, sanctioned by the Conservative Party leadership, lit a long and potentially revolutionary fuse (Michael Thomas Foy, 'The Ulster Volunteer Force: Its Domestic Development and Political Importance in the Period 1913 to 1920', Ph.D. thesis, The Queen's U. of Belfast, 1986, pp.32–140). Gun-running in 'relatively large numbers' had been known to police since December 1911. There was sufficient uncertainty about the legality of drilling and the right to carry arms to make prosecution unlikely (Timothy Bowman, Carson's Army: The Ulster Volunteer Force, 1910–22, *Manchester UP, 2007, pp.34–7,138–42). Carson's proposal on New Year's Day 1913 of an amendment to exclude all nine Ulster counties gave 'implicit consent to Home Rule for the rest of Ireland'* (*Hoppen,* Governing Hibernia, *p.307*). *For thoughtful accounts of subsequent Unionist discussions and action see Hoppen, pp.307–12, and Robert Saunders, 'Tory Rebels and Tory Democracy: The Ulster Crisis, 1900–14', in Bradley W. Hart and Richard Carr eds,* The Foundations of the British Conservative Party: essays on Conservatism from Lord Salisbury to David Cameron, *Bloomsbury Academic, New York, 2013, pp.65–83.*

For JAP, having lost control of education policy to Haldane, the most pressing concern was the fate of his Franchise Bill, and the perennial distraction of how to deal with proposals to extend the vote to women, an issue that cut across party lines but nevertheless held potential for embarrassment for the minister with carriage of the Bill.

Private

Queens Hall Meeting

My dear Curzon,

I am as vehemently opposed to the Parliamentary vote being extended to women as you are, & would like to cooperate with you, in openly resisting the effort about to be made to include women on the Parliamentary register.
As minister in charge of the Bill I think however it prudent at this juncture not to take a prominent public part. You may however rely upon my doing all I can quietly to prevent any amendment being accepted.

You will therefore understand why I am not accepting your invitation to be present at the Queen's Hall on the 20th, & why I am not writing a letter for publication to explain my absence.

Yours sincerely,
[sgd] Joseph A. Pease
(JAP–Curzon, 3 Jan. 1913, Curzon of Kedleston MSS,
BL: A & AS, MSS.Eur.F.112 D/1/8)

Jan. 8 Cabinet. Grey told us of the position & how the Ambassadors of the Powers proposed to force Turkey to concede Adrianople by a Naval demonstration.

He suggested we should be satisfied by sending ships to Besika Bay, it might be more friendly, & if trouble occurred at Constantinople we should be ready to help the British population — & again send in a gun to the Embassy in a coffin.[1]

[1] We have been unable to find any other references to the gun in a coffin.

Two months earlier, following a night of terror for the European population of Constantinople on 5 November 1912, the cruisers Hampshire *and* Weymouth *were sent to Constantinople.*

We talked over the Islands, & destroying & levelling their fortifications, including Rhodes, & our objection to Italy's retention of this Island. It was agreed to try & secure this kind of settlement & if Greece occupied Islands, her sea power would not give rise to jealousies.

JAP's summary here is amplified by Hobhouse's note that Cabinet 'talked of the Aegean Islands, which Russia had proposed should go to Greece on condition that there should be no fortifications thereon, and no cession of sovereignty subsequently' (David ed., Inside Asquith's Cabinet, *p.129). HHA explained to the King that Italy, supported by the other two powers of the Triple Alliance, proposed that, in consideration of the cession of Adrianople, Turkey should be allowed to retain four islands in the mouth of the Dardanelles, and Mytilene and Chios on the Adriatic coast. Grey objected that force would be needed in putting the Turks back and in subduing subsequent agitation. Cabinet resolved that all six islands should go to Greece subject to stringent conditions preventing their use for naval or military purposes or cession to any other Power (HHA Cabinet letter, 9 Jan. 1913, Bodl. MS. Asquith 7, f.1).*

The Prime Minister in a felicitous sentence alluded to the great part Edward Grey had played in preventing war between the Powers, and in solving these difficulties by friendly arrangements & to the solution of the Balkan & Turkish differences by bringing the parties to consider terms of peace — & commended his action amid the applause of his colleagues. Grey was visibly affected. We then discussed my proposed alterations to Franchise Bill — I explained that cabinet committee agreed:

1. occupation qualification to go
2. Registration Rules to be hereafter discussed by H of C & done by order in Council.
3. Grant from the State to cost of registration to be sum of 3*d* p. name.

Prime Minister dwelt on difficulty of justifying our alteration of first, after we had put it in the bill, & alluded to Harcourt's Gladstonian phraseology in throwing it over in his 2 Reading speeches, & told Burns to defend it now in the House of Commons. The question of altering age to 25 was deferred for a week.

Harcourt reported secret treaty with Germany had been arranged in connection with Germany & ourselves in event of redivision of Portuguese colonies in Africa.

Harcourt reported telegrams passed between Smutz [*sic*][2] Gladstone & him in regard to their proposals to remove preference duties, and provide a similar revenue to assist Naval defences of the Empire. We urged a revision of the first proposal.

An anxiety was obviously hanging over our heads — in connection with the thoughtless investments of the Attorney & Chancellor in American Marconis — but nothing was said.

HHA had told Harcourt on 6 January that he had just heard from Illingworth that, after the English Marconi contract had been signed, DLG, Isaacs, and the Master of Elibank had 'a big gamble' in American Marconis and made 'large profits'. They were not the only ones believed to have profited from the launch of American Marconis, which the stockbroker Lord Victor Paget advised his brother, the Marquess of Anglesey, on 16 April 1912, 'should be good for a quick rise' (6th Marquess of Anglesey MSS, 20). Admitting there was nothing corrupt, Harcourt wrote that it was 'inconceivable' that a Chancellor of the Exchequer should have done this and 'monstrous' that, when the question of whether anyone had an interest in the Marconi companies came before the Cabinet, they did not tell the Prime Minister (Harcourt diary, 6 Jan. 1913, Bodl. MS.Eng.c.8268). The anxiety was hanging over ministerial heads (not hearts, as transcribed in Bentley Brinkerhoff Gilbert, 'David Lloyd George and the Great Marconi Scandal', Hist.Res., *V, LXII, no.149, 1989, p.305).*

Jany. 14 P.M. with a headcold, & dined with him at Downing Street.

Jan. 15 Home Rule Debate. (I was away). The Prime Minister's speech on 3rd Reading was everywhere highly commended. John Dillon said, 'the man was inspired' — all agreed it was delivered brilliantly, & affected the whole House who appeared to be under a spell, & quietly listening to every word.

Jan. 16 Cabinet. We discussed Franchise points: City of London — reduced to caretakers, Tommy Atkins being given a vote for barracks, Sailors not. Age to be 21.

P.M. took little part left me to do the talking.

We discussed guillotine Resolution.

We discussed other topics.[3] Grey told us the position of Powers & his difficulties. Crewe alluded to Persia briefly.

[2] Jan Christian Smuts (1870–1950); Min. of Interior, Defence and Mines in the first Union of South Africa Cabinet; founder Sth African Defence Force; Prime Minister, South Africa 1919–24, 1939–48; Min. without Portfolio and member of UK War Cabinet 1917–19.

[3] Samuel read a letter just received from the Marconi company asking to be released from their Post Office contract on the ground of delay. Before any decision was taken, the letter was to be submitted to the Select Committee of the House of Commons for their 'observations' (HHA Cabinet letter, 9 Jan. 1913, Bodl. MS. Asquith 7, ff.1–2).

P.M. asked me to luncheon. Arthur Acland there & we discussed Education proposals. P.M. admitting to my view we could not close transform or duplicate denominational schools.

Since June 1909 Arthur Acland (1847–1926), Vice-President of the Council of Education with a seat in the Cabinet under Gladstone and Rosebery 1892–5, had been chairing a Consultative Committee on Practical Work in Secondary Schools. Among its members were Michael Sadler, previously Director of the Office of Special Inquiries and Reports in the Board of Education and Professor of History and Administration of Education at the University of Manchester, now Vice Chancellor of the University of Leeds. Sadler had been a close colleague of Robert Morant until his resignation after a falling-out with Morant and the then minister, Sir William Anson, in 1903. He would write of Morant's 'eager untiring interest in his job and a craving for opportunities to exercise his talent for negotiation and leadership... At critical moments in his career he was not scrupulous' (Roy Lowe, 'Personalities and Policy: Sadler, Morant and the Structure of Education in England', in Richard Aldrich ed., History and Education: essays presented to Peter Gordon, *The Woburn P., 1996, pp.98–115).*

A week after his lunch with HHA and JAP, Acland took Sadler into his confidence on a broader plan. The next day Sadler told the Archbishop of Canterbury, 'very secretly', what he had learned. Taking care not to name his source (whom Randall Davidson had no difficulty in identifying), Sadler had concluded 'the Government does mean business as regards a great Education policy'. He indicated that Haldane, knowing little of the details of English education and advised by Struthers and the ubiquitous Sir William McCormick (Secretary of the Carnegie Trust and chairman of the advisory committee on 'grants in aid of colleges furnishing education of a university standard'), was inclined to a system of grants similar to those in Scotland. That was the substance. But the purpose, Sadler explained, was another matter.

As the Archbishop recorded in a memorandum of a breakfast with Sadler at Lambeth on Friday 24 January, 'the whole scheme is intended to divert the public mind from the Land Question, about which the Government is in difficulties'. DLG having been converted, it had been taken up 'in order to make a popular cry'. Sadler himself did not approve the motive, nor was he under any illusion about why he had been drawn into the conversations. The interview with Acland (whom he did not name but the Archbishop identified in a pencilled note on his typed memorandum) was, he surmised, 'intended to hang before him the tempting bribe of very large funds for Higher Education provided the religious difficulty could be got over'. 'Radicals of the Clifford type' would have to be squared; and 'the denominational interests, especially in elementary schools would be ruthlessly sacrificed to this end'. Sadler's view was that if the single school area religious difficulty was to be tackled it should be in a separate bill—a proposal almost certain to be resisted by 'Dr Clifford and Co', who would want a victory in country schools as the price of support for a larger reform. Sadler expected to be asked to see DLG and would make plain his reservations (Davidson of Lambeth MSS, 6/103, Lambeth PL).

Jany 22[4] Cabinet. I explained alterations to bill in regard to making continuous register up to 4 months to meet urban areas, & alteration to meet common councilmen on city municipality.

Grey — & then Churchill's Naval estimates met out of surplus!

The Budget presented on 22 April 1913 showed a surplus of £185,000 after noting that a sum of £1,000,000 was to be taken from Exchequer Balances for shipbuilding arrears of 1911–12 and 1912–13 (Mallet, British Budgets, *pp.406–7). Cabinet had accepted the week before that the previous year's surplus of £1,500,000 would wipe out an estimate deficit of £800,000 (HHA Cabinet letter, 16 Apr. 1913, TNA: CAB 41/34/14).*

The government had no fear of defeat over the Franchise Bill but was expecting strong opposition. The abolition of the occupation qualification—'an astounding volte face' as the Daily Telegraph *had called it on 20 February—would allegedly disfranchise between 150,000 and 200,000, mainly Unionist voters, 'destroy the political status of the City of London and materially reduce the electorate in other great commercial centres'. Even querulous Liberal voices could be heard. The coal magnate Sir Arthur Markham Bt observed that some three million men were being enfranchised who had never asked to be enfranchised and who were 'by no means the most intelligent part of the community'. But this would be the consequence of conferring the vote on 'every male person'.*

As for the other persons who were clamouring to be enfranchised, the Cabinet's discussion of the implications of 'the possible acceptance or rejection of the various woman suffrage amendments' is a notable omission from JAP's account. The government was bound by HHA's pledge, given during the January 1910 election campaign, to allow a free vote on a women's suffrage amendment to a reform bill. Hobhouse speaks of a disturbed atmosphere in Cabinet. WSC said that Cabinet ought not to be bound to the Parliament Bill if female suffrage was added: 'Grey burst in that much had been whispered in the lobby as to the possible embarrassment and resignation of the P.M. if suffrage was carried' (David ed., Inside Asquith's Cabinet, *p.130). 'It was agreed', the Prime Minister told the King, 'that whatever*

[4] JAP misdated this meeting, which occurred on 21 Jan. (TNA: CAB 34/3).

might be the decision of the House of Commons, the members of the Government holding diverse views would not regard the result of such division this year as calling for their resignation of office' (22 Jan 1913, Bodl. MS. Asquith 7, f.5). The next day, at a meeting with a suffragette deputation, DLG insisted that there was not 'a scrap of truth' in rumours that anti-suffrage ministers would resign if women's suffrage amendments were carried (Diane Atkinson, RISE UP. WOMEN!, *pp.364–5).*

Jan. 24 Mr Speaker's ruling in regard to women's suffrage amendments.[5]

Cabinet called suddenly Jan. 24 — after an allnight sitting guillotine motion for franchise. P.M. had a cold. He very quietly explained the situation that the Speaker had told Illingworth that he had come to the conclusion on the Wednesday night that women could not be included in a male reform bill, & that he consequently had told the House in advance the day before that the bill might if amended be withdrawn. Churchill said the Speaker had alluded in conversation to his 'bomb shell'. The P.M. said it was clear the vote on women's suffrage could not be regarded as a vote on the merits, & whilst he claimed he had fulfilled his compact, yet he thought if the Speaker adhered to his view by Monday we could not go on with a bill, which could not have attached to it the amendments which he had promised opportunity would be given to move. We agreed to say nothing to the House that evening, but to put a question to the Speaker on Monday.

JAP was ambivalent about the extraordinary fate of his Franchise Bill. Until the last, as Pugh has put it, 'the Cabinet were not attempting to sabotage the women by means of technicalities but, rather, smoothing the way for them' (Pugh, Electoral Reform, *p.41). Sir Edward Grey had given notice of an amendment to omit the word 'male' so that as the Bill progressed there could be an opportunity to consider the eligibility of women for the franchise. Alerted by Bonar Law to the likelihood that such an amendment would fundamentally alter the character and intent of the Bill, Speaker Lowther contentiously ruled that any prospective female suffrage amendment would amount to a new bill. The London Liberal MP Willoughby Dickinson, a leading backbench advocate of women's suffrage who had spurned preferment rather than abandon his work in the women's cause, expressed a widespread view in his diary on 24 January:*

> Last night the Speaker stated that in his opinion if the Bill came up from Committee with material alterations it would be a new bill and have to be sent back for second

[5] This entry was written entirely in red ink.

> reading. This was aimed at the Women's Suffrage and since then he has said that he means this. The opinion is clearly wrong as everyone admits and I am sure he has acted as usual by prejudice against the Bill...Anyhow this announcement has made it impossible for us to have the fair field promised by Asquith and so after consultation with Lloyd George and Grey they decided to ask for a Cabinet meeting this afternoon and to suggest the withdrawal of the Bill in order to give a fresh opportunity next session. However up to now it seems the House of Commons have not agreed and all is uncertain.
>
> *(Hope Costley White,* Willoughby Hyett Dickinson 1859–1943: A Memoir, *privately printed, John Bellows Ltd, Gloucester, 1956, pp.127–8).*

'The Speaker's astonishing indication of opinion on the Franchise Bill . . . was quite unforeseen and is generally regarded as being wrong,' Herbert Samuel told his mother on 26 January (Samuel MSS, SAM/A156/427, f.983, PA). John Simon too, writing to his father on 27 January, said the ruling was 'very surprising to most of us' (David Dutton, 'Private Papers: the Case of Sir John Simon', Archives, *vol.xxxi, no.112, 2005, p.78). A sceptical Maud Selborne wrote: 'It is an extraordinary oversight on the part of such acute lawyers as Asquith, Isaacs, and Simon, and though people might have doubts about the Prime Minister, Simon is absolutely above suspicion. Of course the poor militants think it was a carefully arranged trap' (Lady Selborne–Patrick Duncan, 28 Jan. [1913], Deborah Lavin ed.,* Friendship and Union: The South African Letters of Patrick Duncan and Maud Selborne 1907–1943, *Van Riebeck Society for the Publication of Southern African Historical Documents, Cape Town, 2016, p.143). On 25 January the acute HHA had pointed the Speaker forward:*

> I understand that you have privately intimated to some of my colleagues that the adoption of any of the woman suffrage amendments to the Franchise Bill would involve such a fundamental alteration as to bring it within the practice as to withdrawal.
>
> The belief or apprehension that some such ruling may be expected tends to make the discussion that has now begun unreal. Nor is it desirable that at this stage of the Session there should be any avoidable waste of Parliamentary time.
>
> In the circumstances, although the time for a direct ruling has not in strictness arrived, I propose to ask you on Monday whether you will at once favour the House with your view.
>
> *(HHA–Lowther, 25 Jan. 1913, Ullswater MSS, HA47/B3/347, Suffolk Archives)*

HHA's withdrawal of the Bill was accompanied by an undertaking to give facilities in the next session for a private member's bill. Harcourt wrote of 'acrimonious discussion', HHA having told Cabinet that his pledge was 'absolutely fulfilled' and the 'slate was now wiped clean' (Harcourt diary, 24 Jan. 1913, Bodl. MS.Eng.c.8268). Elizabeth Haldane had heard from her brother of 'fearful tension... on part of Asquith, Grey, and Harcourt. A. proposed a joint game of bridge'. Grey and Haldane were resolved to resign if pledges were not honoured (Diary, 24 Jan. 1913, Elizabeth Haldane MSS, MS. 20240, f.28v, NLS). Given the deep divisions in Cabinet on the subject, the Speaker's ruling was probably more welcome, and less surprising, to the Prime Minister than he allowed it to appear. The Speaker would be 'consulted every day in private as to his view on a point of order' (J.G. Swift MacNeill, 'The Completion of the Speakership', Fortnightly Review, *vol.115, 1921, pp.302–13); and it would have been possible to raise the matter in sufficient time to adopt a different course. In advising the King, HHA asserted that the government was 'for the moment disabled by the Speaker's ruling which was wholly unexpected, & for which they are in no way responsible.' (Bodl. MS. Asquith 7, f.7.) He had calculated with Harcourt that they might have beaten Grey's amendment by nineteen or twenty votes; but 'the others', as Margot Asquith's diary records, thought they 'might have just won' (Bodl. MS.Eng.d.3210, f.80).*

For an interpretation emphasising the unexpectedness of the Speaker's ruling see Pugh, Electoral Reform in War and Peace, 1906–1918, *pp.41–2. Pugh notes that JAP's anti-suffragist Cabinet colleagues Crewe and Harcourt quietly gave financial support to the anti-female suffrage campaign and acted as go-betweens for HHA and the leading Tory Anti, Lord Curzon. JAP's stance in opposition to women's suffrage was no secret. Within the Society of Friends his views were in harmony with the main body of opinion, and he could decline with impunity to meet a deputation from the Friends' League for Women's Suffrage (JAP–T.E. Harvey, 17 Oct. 1912, MS. Gainford 135/83); Thomas C. Kennedy,* British Quakerism 1860–1920: The Transformation of a Religious Community, *Oxford UP, 2001, p.233; Pam Lunn, 'You Have Lost Your Opportunity' British Quakers and the Militant Phase of the Women's Suffrage Campaign: 1906–1914',* Quaker Studies, *vol.2, no.1, 1997, pp.30–56. But, unashamedly sympathetic as he was to the anti-suffragist cause, JAP did not court public controversy. Whether it was his own constituents, Sylvia Pankhurst for the WSPU, an ILP branch, or Walter Rea for the Women's Suffrage Campaign chaired by Arthur Henderson, the response was the same. He had heard all the arguments and no useful purpose would be served by a meeting. For the minister charged with carrying forward franchise legislation it was the prudent course (Martin Pugh,* The March of the Women: A Revisionist Analysis of the Campaign for Women's Suffrage, 1866–1914, *Oxford UP, 2000, p.159).*

Unlike those of his colleagues who were physically assaulted, JAP appears to have escaped with property damage. Helen Crawfurd spent a month in Holloway for hurling stones that broke two windows of his London home. Crawfurd was given two stones with messages attached demanding women's enfranchisement; she taxied early in the morning to Piccadilly and made her way quietly to Hertford Street. In her autobiography she expressed pride that her aim had been true (Our Red Aunt. Exhibition by Fiona Black, Glasgow Women's Library, 6 Feb. 2018, https://advisor.museumsandheritage.com/features/red-aunt-glasgow-womens-library, accessed 26 Dec. 2018).

On Sunday 26 January the Peases went to Windsor. There JAP had a long conversation with the Archbishop of Canterbury, who made a record of the assurance he was given on education that the government 'means business & wants (or he wants) to legislate on large lines, supposing he can obtain from the Treasury the necessary funds'. JAP wished to secure a secondary and higher education for every child worthy of it, 'passing children on freely from elementary schools'. Davidson commented that these ideas were 'a little windy & ill-defined, showing no real grip of the necessary details'. What JAP did make clear was that the 'denominational system must retain its place as an element' in the educational 'fabric'. Moreover, he saw no insuperable difficulty 'once it be admitted that [Lord] Halifax, [Dr Henry] Wace [Dean of Canterbury] & Clifford must respectively be thrown overboard. He wished however to guard himself about the single-school areas. He'. There the memorandum in the Davidson of Lambeth MSS, 12/105, Lambeth PL, frustratingly ends.

Monday. Jany 27 I & my wife spent Sunday at Windsor. I told the King that we should probably withdraw the bill, & give the women another chance next session.

The P.M. read out 2 letters, one he had written to the Speaker, asking him to give his reply as to whether any women's suffrage amendment would be in order to save an unreal debate & waste of time. The Speaker replied he would do so, whilst reserving his right to only do so after amendments had been added to a bill.

We assumed the Speaker adhered to his view.

I thereupon explained to my colleagues the effect of a simple Plural voting Bill, & how it could be at once introduced — the alternative of Harold Baker's[6] bill which was cumbersome, complicated in machinery. The P.M. at once said, I will be no party to guillotining anything else through *this* session, & we agreed to postpone a plural voting bill until early next session.

We then quickly agreed to withdraw the Franchise Bill though I made one appeal, that if time were given next session to a woman's suffrage bill, we were not justified within 7 days of the passage of our abolition of plural voting, &

[6] A bound volume, 'Plural Voting Bill, 1913' (MS. Gainford 142/1–51), contains Cabinet memos, notes, and draft bills, annotated by JAP, plus correspondence and amendments. Harold Baker's bill was the Registration (Plural Qualifications) Bill, introduced on 17 Feb. 1912 (PP, 1912–13 [1], v, 69). It allowed electors to register to vote only in the constituency in which they lived. If they lived in more than one constituency, their name could be removed from a register if it could be shown that it appeared on another.

giving easy registration to electors to withdraw the bill if the P.M's honour was satisfied & pledges fulfilled by time given later on to a woman's bill.

The view held was, that it might prejudice women's suffrage, if in advance 2 million male voters were added to the roll of electors, & we must allow bill to be introduced pari passu next session, & provide time for both a private bill for women's suffrage, & for a Gov. plural voting abolition bill.

The discussion only took an hour, & we had no thoughts for other subjects.

The P.M. in the afternoon, climbed down as well as it could be done and without criticising the Speaker made it quite clear his ruling in our view was not according to precedent. The Party were depressed but admitted no one could have done it better. The loss of abolition of plural voting was the factor which weighed with all the supporters in the House, & no one felt it more acutely than I did, but I tried to appear cheery under the opinion I expressed we could still pass a measure before 1915 spring.

I told George he had not played cricket in supporting my bill. He told me he ignored such a remark as it only came from me! I however withdrew and he did the same. He however knew & admitted he had never cared about the bill — he was not getting Kudos for it I suppose!

Harcourt's diary for January 27 (Bodl. MS.Eng.c.8268) gives a clue to JAP's feelings. DLG had said: 'We shd give a banquet to Bonar Law & the Speaker.'

Feb. 4 Cab — met in House. Tories tried another snap, reduced us to 28, but the P.M. took no notice of the figure when the last member of the cabinet returned to our meeting in his room & announced the numbers. We discussed the date of proroguing and meeting again for the new session — postponing until Feb. 12, the preparation of The King's Speech.

The P.M. showed concern as to the Indian balances being lent to Banks in city, connected with individuals who were on the Indian Finance committee, & fixed rates of interest.

I & others protested against our continuing such a system. The P.M. Haldane & Crewe advocated a joint Select Comtee to inquire & advise — but most of us demurred; & a cab. comtee was asked to see Schuster[7] & look into the matter.

[7] Sir Felix Otto Schuster, 1st Bt (1854–1936); banker; Lib. Imperialist and free trader; German born, naturalised in 1875; Director, National Provincial Bank; Gov., Union Bank of London 1895–1918; Lib. candidate City of London 1906; Bt 1906; member, Sec. of St. for India Committee 1906–16.

The Cabinet committee consisted of DLG, Morley, Crewe, McKenna, Runciman, and HHA himself (a rare occurrence reflecting the sensitivity of the issue). Silver for coining had been purchased for the Government of India by Samuel Montagu and Co. Herbert Samuel's brother, Sir Stuart Samuel, was a director and Edwin Montagu's brother, Louis Samuel Montagu, 2nd Baron Swaythling, was head of the firm. The balances had been deposited mainly in London with Glyn Mills Currie, and Smith's Bank, of which Sir Felix Schuster was chairman; Schuster was also a member of the Secretary of State's Committee. These activities were defended on the grounds that the respective company and bank had offered the best terms. But another question had already been raised: whether Sir Stuart Samuel had vacated his seat by reason of Messrs Samuel Montagu & Co. having purchased silver for and on behalf of the Secretary of State for India. (See 6 Nov. 1912). The position was obviously unsatisfactory; the government appointed a royal commission chaired by Austen Chamberlain that recommended various procedural reforms (Cd. 7236, Apr. 1914). David Sunderland, Financing the Raj: The City of London and Colonial India, 1858–1940, *Boydell P., Woodbridge, 2013, pp.86–98, is a concise, well-documented account of the silver-purchasing controversy.*

Samuel asked to reduce postage to Germany, France Belgium & Holland to 1d or 1½d cost £250,000 — but made good in 14 years. George refused & it was postponed.

Samuel had argued that Post Office profits were up by £1,000,000 and that the Office made a profit of 1½d (181 per cent) on every letter posted to the continent. If he were allowed to reduce the postage to 1½d, the office would still make a profit, and the resultant increases in traffic would reduce the size of the cut in profits ('Postage rates with the Continent', 1 Jan. 1913, TNA: CAB 37/114/1). The Cabinet was not persuaded: 'In the present state of the finances, the consideration of the matter was indefinitely postponed' (HHA Cabinet letter, 5 Feb. 1913, TNA: CAB 41/34/6).

Late on 5 February the House passed the third reading of the Welsh Disestablishment Bill: 'great enthusiasm an unexpectedly high majority of 107. Welshmen sang "The Land of our Fathers" in Welsh in the inner lobby in a dense crowd. DLG's speech in the afternoon was a masterpiece of freshness and vivacity on a subject that has become threadbare from debate' (Ponsonby diary, 5 Feb. 1913, Ponsonby of Shulbrede MSS).

Also fresh and vivacious was DLG's handwritten letter to Runciman on 10 February headed 'Land': 'I have seen the P.M. and he has "unleashed" me. I told him you & I wanted to see him together this week on the subject. He agreed. You will get the papers either today or tomorrow' (Runciman of Doxford MSS). The potential unleashing of Runciman's recently appointed Permanent Secretary, the Fabian Socialist Sir Sydney Olivier, had already sent ripples through Unionist ranks. The MP for Chelmsford and former junior minister, E.G. Pretyman, had written to Olivier's predecessor at the Board of Agriculture: 'Many believe it to be a part of the scheme for overthrowing the present system of land tenure & ownership & that he will be a facile tool in L. G. & the land taxers hands' (Pretyman–Sir Thomas Elliott, 9 Jan 1913, Elliott MSS).

Feb. 11 I opened proceedings by asking the cabinet what I should do at the V. & A. Museum, as suffragettes were intending to break Raffael [*sic*] cartoons, library books & ceramics. It was agreed that the valuable portions ceramics, loan collections, Jones[8] & The Salting[9] collections should be closed, & the vulnerable portions watched more carefully, & if anything occurred to close at once.

The threatened attack on the Victoria and Albert Museum did not occur, perhaps because of the imposition of more stringent admission procedures, some of them temporary. Suggestions that no women be admitted, or that they be admitted only by ticket, were rejected. But 'sticks, umbrellas, bags and parcels were left at the entrance (ladies' muffs were subject to "discreet" examination); several galleries, including the Jones galleries, the Ceramics and Salting collections and the Loan Court were closed to the public; the number of warders was increased, bolstered further by cleaners and attendants, and plain clothes detectives mingled with visitors.' In 1914, the Museum's admission charges were abolished, in part because of the Board of Education's reasoning that increased visitor numbers would provide additional security against militant suffragette incursions. The worst of the recorded 'outrages' had been the scratching of a handrail with a hatpin (http://www.vam.ac.uk/__data/assets/pdf_file/0008/259919/Suffragettes-in-the-V-and-A-Archive.pdf, accessed 22 Feb. 2016).

We discussed prison treatment and prosecution. The Attorney was instructed to prosecute whenever cases of inciting to breaches of peace occurred.[10]

[8] John Jones (*c.*1800–82), an army clothier, bequeathed a collection of French furniture of the Louis XIV to XVI periods; Sèvres, Dresden, Chelsea, and oriental porcelain; French gilt bronze work (ormolu); paintings; miniatures, snuff-boxes, etc. The collection is still displayed together.

[9] George Salting (1835–1909), an Australian with sugar and sheep interests, was left £30,000 a year in 1865 and devoted himself to art collection, specialising in oriental porcelain and English miniatures. He bequeathed his collection to the National Gallery, the British Museum, and the Victoria and Albert Museum. His bequest to the V&A was opened to the public 22 Mar. 1911 and displayed together until the Second World War (Isabelle Gadoin, 'George Salting [1835–1909] and the discovery of Islamic ceramics in 19th-century England', http://miranda.revues.org/4468, accessed 16 May 2014).

[10] The Atty Gen. was, HHA's letter to the King notes, 'instructed to take proceedings against Mrs Pankhurst for the speech, reported yesterday, in which she took responsibility of inciting others to the recent acts of violence & pillage' (12 Feb. 1913, Bodl. MS. Asquith 7, f.13). WSC had wanted to deport the miscreant suffragettes. 'Where to & under what conditions?', Harcourt asked (Harcourt diary, 11 Feb. 1913, Bodl. MS.Eng.c.8268).

McKenna wanted to release before death, except when ticket of leave was possible owing to long sentence convictions, & then they could be brought back at will to complete sentence.

We drafted King's Speeches — & followed precedent of 1893. We agreed to insert plural voting & Education — but not to proceed with latter — but pass it through in a subsequent session with as George said a swim in butter.

*HHA wrote in his Cabinet letter 'The year 1894 [*sic*] affords an almost exact precedent in the matter of dates...' (TNA: CAB 41/34/7). Following that precedent, the prorogation speech was to be short and formal; and the speech for reopening Parliament was to include references to foreign, colonial, and Indian affairs.*

In concert with Haldane and Crewe, JAP had worked from late 1912 on developing proposals for educational reform. With nonconformist grievances mainly in his mind, DLG had consistently urged wide-ranging changes. However, to DLG's annoyance, Haldane announced in a speech at the Manchester Reform Club on 10 January that education was 'the next and most urgent of the great social problems to be taken up'. It wasn't. As Morley said, Haldane spoke without Cabinet authority (Harcourt diary, 27 Jan. 1913, Bodl. MS.Eng.c.8268).

According to DLG, Haldane had 'consulted himself and Pease and the Prime Minister, but had spoken quite vaguely to each, representing to each in turn that he had fully consulted the other two and had their sanction for his proposals thus obtaining an easy assent from the third'. In fact all three had been given vague and perfunctory explanations, and there had been no Cabinet consultation. Haldane's disingenuous letter to JAP on 9 January bears this out (MS. Gainford 84/12). DLG told C.P. Scott that he had not intended to begin his campaign for land reform until 'rather later', but his hand had been forced by Haldane's 'magniloquent speech'. Land reform was to be the next great social problem to be taken up by the government (Scott 'diary', 16 Jan. 1913, Wilson ed., The Political Diaries of C. P. Scott 1911–1928, *pp.68–9). Nevertheless, JAP annotated a Cabinet memorandum with the colourful phrase DLG had used in Cabinet: 'Chancellor Exchequer intimated Feb. 11.1913 he would find money for a big scheme & it would swim through on butter' ('Education Bill, 1913—Cabinet Committee. The Single School Area', printed 24 Jan. 1913, MS. Gainford 124/32).*

Haldane would not surrender. There was contention over the wording of a reference to education in the King's Speech on 10 March. Elizabeth Haldane claimed that the sentence in the speech about education was inserted at her brother's insistence:

> by some intrigue (Education Office?) it had been modified to indicate merely certain changes in the administration of education and R. was much concerned. However what appeared was a good compromise. Of course nothing can be

passed this session but it is good to have it in. Mundella sent petition to P.M. and Massingham good in Nation.

(E. Haldane diary, 12 Mar. 1913, Elizabeth Haldane MSS, MS. 20240, f.45, NLS)

HHA had pencilled a draft: 'proposals will be submitted for laying the foundations of reform of the National System of Education', adding that 'Lloyd George and Pease approve of this'. As the speech was being readied to send to the King, HHA struck out the words his colleagues had approved and substituted proposals 'dealing with certain fundamental aspects of National Education in England and Wales'. Alert and disingenuous, the King asked: 'what generally speaking', the 'fundamental aspects' were, and why was Scotland excluded? In transmitting the King's question to Bonham Carter on 4 March, Stamfordham ventured: 'Education in Scotland is on a different footing to that in England and Wales—certainly there are no sectarian bothers over the border'. The compromise, inserted by hand on a printed copy, read: 'Proposals will be submitted to you for the development of a national system of education' (Bodl. MS. Asquith 85, ff.156,164–5,181,205,209; HL Deb 10 March 1913 vol 14 c4). And, in spite of the prompt work of the department in producing comprehensive draft legislation by April, it was soon apparent that only a very limited bill would proceed (Ashby and Anderson, Portrait of Haldane, *pp.114–20; Neil Daglish, '"Over by Christmas": the First World War, education reform and the economy. The case of Christopher Addison and the origins of the DSIR',* Hist. Ed., *vol.27, no.3, 1998, p.318).*

Reference made to Persian situation & policy of small branch lines, rather than a through railway route to India.

Cabinet considered and approved a draft despatch from Grey to the Ambassador in Russia (Sir George Buchanan) defining the British attitude to railway construction in Persia (Bodl. MS. Asquith 7, f.13).

JAP missed the next Cabinet meeting on 18 February and 'business…of a routine and unimportant character' as well as the decision to authorise Admiralty negotiation to acquire for 'about £2,000,000' a controlling interest in the Anglo-Persian Oil Co. (Bodl. MS. Asquith 7, f.15).

— after a fortnight's holiday —

Thursday 6 March Cabinet. Birrell Runciman, Seely & Churchill absentees. We discussed amendment of H of Lords to our bills, Temperance Scotland Trades Union Bill &c. King's speeches terms of both.

We then discussed McKenna's cat & mouse bill to take up suffragettes again after let out for hunger strike — no decision arrived at.

P.M. looked well, he said he had played golf at Huntercombe most days. He gave me instructions relating to Plural Voting Bill & simplicity. We Ministers all dined with the P.M. on March 9 at 10 Downing St — wonderful harmony & all in good trim & spirits.

JAP's two words 'Temperance Scotland' give no clue to the controversy over the Temperance (Scotland) Bill over which McKinnon Wood was encountering strong resistance. The 'local option' provisions of the Bill had been diluted so that there could be no referendum before 1917 and no public house would be closed before 1918. But it took the threat to use the Parliament Act before the Lords finally capitulated. The story is told entertainingly in David Torrance, The Scottish Secretaries, *pp.75–6, briefly by John Greenaway,* Drink and British Politics Since 1830: A Study In Policy Making, *Palgrave Macmillan, 2003, pp.85–6, and in more detail in Greenaway's 'The Local Option Question and British Politics, 1864–1914', Ph.D. thesis, U. of Leeds, 1974, pp.386–91.*

Angered at the fate of the Franchise Bill, yet another setback to their cause, militant suffragettes intensified an arson campaign against private property. On the night of 12/13 February 1913 bombs were placed in cupboards in a house being built by Sir George Riddell for DLG near the Walton Heath Golf Club. The first bomb exploded and blew out the candle attached to the second bomb. The culprits were not caught, but Emmeline Pankhurst proclaimed herself responsible; she was arrested, tried, and sentenced on 3 April to three years in prison. She immediately went on hunger strike, but no attempt was made to forcibly feed her. She threatened unavailingly to walk about her cell unclothed (McKenna–P. McKenna, 'Wednesday' [11 Apr. 1913?], McKenna MSS, MCKN 8/3/2, CAC). The Cabinet had decided a month earlier that when she was convicted Mrs Pankhurst could not be forcibly fed because of her 'weak heart' (Harcourt diary, 12 Feb. 1913, Bodl. MS.Eng.c.8268).

Apprehensive that Mrs Pankhurst might die in prison, the government hurriedly brought on the Prisoners' (Temporary Discharge for Ill Health) Bill, allowing hunger-striking prisoners to be released and recover their health before being returned to prison. The policy had prevailed over 'a strong protest by Mr Burns who thinks', the King was told after the Cabinet meeting on 6 March, 'that no steps (beyond the provision of facilities for food & drink) should be taken to prevent prisoners who are so minded from starving themselves' (Bodl. MS. Asquith 7, f.17). The Bill received Royal Assent on 25 April. Thereafter its provisions were used repeatedly to license Mrs Pankhurst's temporary release and return to prison, often after a period as a fugitive. At a Garter service at Windsor on 13 June 1914 the King told Lord Selborne that Simon, Haldane, and Buckmaster agreed with McKenna that the one thing to avoid was 'the death of one of them in prison or on a voyage of transportation'. The King was receiving threatening letters every day. The new fear was that the militants would take 'life for life, a Minister's or the King's'. Selborne said 'grimly' that it would be better if it came to that as then they would be hung. He thought the King agreed with him, but 'the Ministers were all the other way' (Selborne–Lady Selborne, 14 June 1914, Bodl. MS. Selborne 102/120–3). On 10 August 1914 the Home Secretary announced that all suffrage prisoners would be unconditionally released.

Especially good among a vast literature are Elizabeth Crawford, 'Police, Prisons and Prisoners: the view from the Home Office', Women's HR, *vol.14, nos3–4, 2005, pp.487–506; J.F. Geddes, 'Culpable Complicity: the medical profession and the forcible feeding of suffragettes, 1909–1914',* Women's HR, *vol.17, no.1, 2008, pp.79–94; June Purvis,* Emmeline Pankhurst: A biography, *Routledge, 2002, pp.217–31; Martin Pugh,* The Pankhursts, *Penguin, 2001, pp.261–97, and Pugh,* March of the Women, *pp.208–10; John Mercer, 'Buying votes: purchasable propaganda in the 20th-century women's suffrage movement', Ph.D. thesis, U. of Portsmouth, 2005; David Vessey, 'Words as well as Deeds: The Popular Press and Suffragette Hunger Strikes in Edwardian Britain',* Twentieth Century British History, *vol.32, issue 1, 2021, pp.68–92, and 'Votes for Women and Public Discourse: Elite Newspapers, Correspondence Columns and Informed Debate in Edwardian Britain',* Media History, *vol.27, issue 4, 2021, pp.476–90. For a comparative perspective on 'hunger as political critique' see James Vernon,* Hunger: A Modern History, *Belknap P. of Harvard UP, Cambridge, MA, 2007, pp.41–80; for the experience of Irish suffragettes see William Murphy,* Political Imprisonment and the Irish, 1912–1921, *Oxford UP, 2014, pp.11–33; and on 'British Suffragettes and the Russian Method of Hunger Strike' see Kevin Grant's article in* Comparative Studies in Society and History, *vol.53, no.1, 2011, pp.113–43.*

On 13 March Cabinet agreed to proceed with a single clause Plural Voting Bill (TNA: CAB 41/34/9). The Bill passed the Commons twice before it was stalled by the outbreak of war in 1914.

March 19 Cabinet. We discussed position of bills.

Plural voting — to be introduced by me, early day.
Soudan loan } by Lloyd George
Revenue Bill }

The King's speech had said that authorisation would be sought for 'the Imperial Exchequer' to guarantee a loan by the Government of the Soudan ensuring the territory's prosperity and the development of its cotton growing industry (Bodl. MS. Asquith 85, ff.182,187,193).

Prime Minister said he had correspondence with Bowles,[11] & had torn up his letter in which he had told him he was neither a Hampden or a Cromwell for preventing collection of Income Tax prior to Budget, but he thought with Bolingbroke who when asked 'why he had not replied to a critic' said 'I never wrestle with a chimney sweep'.

In June 1912, the magazine proprietor and former Conservative MP Thomas Gibson Bowles—briefly a Liberal MP in 1910 but now once again a Conservative—had successfully sought an injunction restraining the Bank of England from deducting income tax from dividend warrants on the authority of a Ways and Means resolution. Bowles subsequently wrestled with HHA over the taxation of the costs of the action, concluding: 'When I remember that the decision of identically the same question cost Hampden his life and the country a civil war, I think my judgment cheaply won' (see Leonard E. Naylor, The Irrepressible Victorian: The Story of Thomas Gibson Bowles, Journalist, Parliamentarian and Founder Editor of the original 'Vanity Fair', *Macdonald, 1965, ch.14, and Jonathan Guinness with Catherine Guinness,* The House of Mitford, *Hutchinson, 1984, pp.204–10).*

On 17 March 1913, DLG said that legislation would be introduced to legalise the custom that the decision in Bowles v. Bank of England had prevented. The Provisional Collection of Taxes Act was passed on 16 April 1913, thereby ensuring that customs and excise duties and increased income tax could be collected as soon as they had been announced, subject to being refunded if the proposals were not enacted within a limited time. For a modern analysis see Joseph Jaconelli, 'The "Bowles Act"—Cornerstone of the Fiscal Constitution', Cambridge Law Journal, *vol.69, no.3, Nov. 2010, pp.582–608.*

Imprisonment of suffragettes bill
Defective & Mentally Deficient Bill
Children Employment
Education Bill — I reported progress in cabinet comtee —
P.M. commented favourably on my 'judicious' speech at Sheffield on 15th.

JAP had addressed a meeting of the West Yorkshire County Teachers Association on the government's education policy. He said that there was to be no destruction of the established system

[11] Thomas Gibson Bowles (1841?–1922); founder *Vanity Fair* and *The Lady*. Con. MP King's Lynn 1892–1906; became Lib. in 1906; Lib. MP King's Lynn Jan.–Dec. 1910; rejoined Con. Party 1911; son of radical MP Thomas Milner Gibson; educ. in France; Inland Revenue official; master mariner; journalist. Joseph Chamberlain once said: 'Bowles combines the 2 most objectionable things in the world: he is a Bastard & he is a dwarf; moreover he has been editor of a society journal.' (Balcarres diary, 8 July 1910, vol.xxi, f.56, Crawford and Balcarres MSS.)

but its development by increasing the powers of the local education authorities and by increased government grants. The difficulties of dealing with the denominational schools were 'insoluable'. Secondary education would be surveyed before any proposals were made. The government's proposals would be introduced into the Commons, but no action that session could be promised. JAP concluded that the key to the problems was money and that large quantities of money spent on the military would be far better spent on education. The speech had been submitted to HHA for approval on 12 March. Amendments were made by both HHA and Haldane. (JAP–HHA, 12 Mar. 1913, copy, MS. Gainford 126/no.12.) The new line of advance was spelled out in two Cabinet papers on 17 March with the recommendations of the committee that JAP chaired.[12]

Appellate Jurisdiction Bill — grant to new Judges £5000 + clerks allowance of £600 to be put in at first.

Discussion on how to work Parl Act. & give Tories power to 'suggest' amendments to be put in by Lords. Cab. comtee appointed to consider procedure. Discussion re Arch at end of Mall — ask for £30,000 for widening approach postponed. Seely asked for Latin inscription to be corrected. Asquith said 'gratissima' was approved by best scholars.

Churchill said, — 'I am glad it will be put right. It has rather jarred on me'.

W.C. knowledge of Latin proverbially short — his serious acting caused much laughter.

The inscription reads: 'ANNO DECIMO EDWARDI SEPTIMI REGIS VICTORIAE REGINAE CIVES GRATISSIMI MDCCCCX'. Harcourt's papers include a file of correspondence and notes of suggestions and comments for the inscription, but they do not seem to include the final version (Bodl. MS. Harcourt 458, ff.101–40). None of the proposed inscriptions uses 'gratissima'; in the sense of good things bestowed by the Queen, 'gratissima' would imply that the erection of the arch was an act of monstrous flattery.

Lever's[13] — offer. £60,000 in value of site Stafford House considered & postponed. Harcourt asked to alter his conditions.

[12] Education Bill—Cabinet Committee, 'Heads of Education Bill, 1913 Draft 2' and 'Further Proposals for the Organisation and Extension of the Power and Duties of Local Education Authorities', bound with other papers relating to the Education Bill in MS. Gainford 124/39,38 (neither included in the PRO *List of Cabinet Papers 1880–1914*).

[13] Sir William Hesketh Lever Bt (1851–1925); soap manufacturer; founder of Lever Brothers (Unilever); philanthropist and art collector; founded Port Sunlight 1888; Lib. MP Cheshire (Wirral) 1906–9; advocate of old age pensions and a graduated income tax. Bt 1911; Baron Leverhulme 1917; Vt Leverhulme 1922. It was rumoured in 1915 that he had exchanged his soap works in Germany for German chocolate works in Switzerland or France, and the soap factory was manufacturing nitro-glycerine (Crawford diary, 15, 22 Jan. 1915, Crawford and Balcarres MSS).

In November 1912, Sir William Lever, a regular and substantial donor to Liberal Party funds, offered to give the magnificent Stafford House, newly purchased from the Duke of Sutherland, to the nation. Lever then went on a tour of the Congo (where he had extensive palm-oil interests) for four months. He had been trying to persuade the Colonial Office to grant him landholding concessions in Nigeria similar to those he had in the Congo, but the government refused to allow any land to be alienated from the native population (Sir Rex Niven, Nigeria, *Ernest Benn, 1967, pp.137–8; see also Marjorie Perham,* Lugard. The Years of Authority, 1898–1945, *Collins, 1960, pp.665–6, for a sympathetic view of the use Lever made of his powers in the Congo, which he wished to apply to Nigeria).*

The Cabinet was at first divided on the merits of Stafford House, with Harcourt and Beauchamp 'very touchy'. 'As a Guest House for Receptions very good. As a London Museum site not good. Building unsuited, congests still further Museum objects in West End' (Burns diary, 17 Dec. 1912, Burns MSS, BL Add.MS. 46,334, f.224). Burns was especially unhappy: 'Pointed out unsuitability of Stafford House for museum incapable of extension, not large enough inaccessible for Londoners and environment not suitable for large crowds. suggested near County Hall or Bethnal Green or some other site L.G obdurate, he regards it more as a monument than a museum' (Burns diary, 19 Mar. 1913, Burns MSS, BL Add.MS. 46,335, f.69[v]*). On 31 December 1912, William Moore (Irish Unionist MP for North Armagh) suggested that Lever had made the offer of Stafford House in the hope of more favourable consideration of his application for concessions (HC Deb 31 December 1912 vol 46 c204; see also 13 November 1912 vol 43 cc1967–9, when Alfred Lyttelton questioned the extent of the concessions Lever was said to be seeking).*

Before Cabinet eventually agreed to sanction a government contribution to 'Mall improvement', provided that the County Council and Westminster Council came up with 'a reasonable proposal', 'considerable divergence of opinion was expressed'. Some ministers, including Grey and Runciman, felt strongly that 'the money of the general taxpayer ought not to be expended on purely London purposes'. Turning to Stafford House, the offer to purchase the freehold for £120,000 was declined. Harcourt was told to 'enter into communication' with Lever over the conditions attached to his offer of a 28-year lease (HHA Cabinet letter, 20 Mar. 1913, Bodl. MS. Asquith 7, ff.21–2).

Lever had withdrawn his offer but was persuaded to renew it again by the end of April, when it was accepted. The ground rent was to be £758.15s.0d. per annum. Stafford House became the home of the London Museum; Beauchamp was a director and Burns became a Trustee (BL Add.MS. 46,302, ff.238–41). Lever changed the name of the building to Lancaster House to symbolise the ownership of the King (Duke of Lancaster) and to commemorate his own origins.

26 March. Ap. 2.[14] *9. 16. 23* Cabinets. Without incidents of great importance, 1 or 2 very short ones. — absent on 23 — ministers discussed Eastern position — blockade &c Prime Minister impressive. Grey absent fishing in Scotland.

HHA wrote a long report to the King on 3 April about Eastern Europe, a proposed naval demonstration on the coast of Montenegro, the Bulgarian advance towards Constantinople, and the British attitude in the event that Constantinople should fall. He did not tell the King of Grey's revelation that Noel Buxton (Lib. MP, North Norfolk, and leading light of the Balkan Committee) had offered Asia Minor to Germany and said he had 80 MPs with him: 'This is sort of thing one has to deal with' (Harcourt diary, 3 Apr. 1913, Bodl. MS.Eng.c.8268). Grey, away fishing with his brother, said 'I escaped when foreign things seemed to be in a fair way to settlement: they seem to be progressing favourably'. He planned to stay away until the end of April, unless 'fetched back by some unfavourable turn'. The Ambassadors' Meeting a few days earlier had discussed whether the Powers should jointly guarantee a loan to Montenegro, each contributing £200,000. 'After six months of crisis,' he told Runciman on 20 April, 'this seems small beer' (Runciman of Doxford MSS).

DLG's imminent financial statement was considered by Cabinet on 16 April. After detailed consideration of expenditure, revenue, debt reduction, etc., HHA enjoined DLG to 'make some perfunctory remarks on desirability of economy'. More than perfunctory, Harcourt hoped. 'Mr Gladstone always did this,' said HHA. Yes, Sydney Buxton agreed: 'But then he believed in it' (Bodl. MS.Eng.c.8268). The Cabinet does not seem to have been told that HHA had agreed on 9 April to a request by Runciman for the establishment of a Cabinet committee 'to help <u>*me*</u> *with wages, rents, and housing, the latter being the only thing I wished to touch . . . I selected my men: Jack Pease, Beauchamp, Ll.G., & Edwin'. Runciman appears to have thought that HHA had told him that DLG was '*<u>*not*</u> *to have his Land Campaign' (Runciman–Hilda Runciman, 9 Apr. 1913, Viscountess Runciman of Doxford MSS). For Runciman's proposed cottage-building programme see Mark Swenarton,* Homes Fit For Heroes: The Politics and Architecture of Early State Housing in Britain, *Heinemann Educational Books, 1981, pp.40–4. Beauchamp's gratitude for 'valuable' memoranda circulated by DLG, his emphatic endorsement of a minimum wage for agricultural workers, and advocacy of a land*

[14] The Cabinet met on 3 Apr. not 2 Apr. (HHA Cabinet letter, 3 Apr. 1913, Bodl. MS. Asquith 7, ff.25–6; *The Times*, 4 Apr. 1913). On the way to the meeting Seely's driver was caught speeding (15 mph) in Birdcage Walk; Seely pleaded with his responsible Cabinet colleague for the driver's licence not to be endorsed (Seely–Beauchamp, 3 Apr. 1913, Beauchamp MSS). That evening JAP presided over a dinner at the Hotel Cecil given by the government for the International Congress of Historical Students.

court 'with every possible latitude', came on 15 April with an offer of help in 'your campaign' (Peter Raina, The Seventh Earl Beauchamp: A Victim of His Times, *Peter Lang, Bern, 2016, pp.219–20).*

24 April (not 23 April as JAP thought) was largely taken up with a discussion of the fall of Scutari and what should be done if Montenegro refused to surrender to the 'Powers'. The champion of the Albanians in the Commons, Aubrey Herbert, was attuned to the strains of Balkan diplomacy. 'There has been a row at the F.O.,' he told his wife late in April, 'Grey and Tyrrell on one side against Sir A [Nicolson] on the other. Sir A. appealed to the Prime, who took his side. Grey then said, "Damned if I will have anything more to do with this business. We have promised Austria and I won't go back." He was pressed to say that he was ill but insisted on telling the truth that he was "going to catch big and little fishes"' (Bejtullah Destani and Jason Tomes eds, Albania's Greatest Friend: Aubrey Herbert and the Making of Modern Albania, Diaries and Papers 1904–1923, *I.B. Tauris, 2011, p.87).*

The Cabinet then found itself divided over the possibility of state assistance to the proposed National Theatre: Haldane and DLG in favour, 'in principle'; HHA, Morley, and Birrell against (Bodl. MS. Asquith 7, ff.25–33).

There is no clue in JAP's narrative about what some observers felt was the dangerous situation the government was in. The Opposition was constantly watching for opportunities to catch the Liberals unawares. On 28 and 30 March DLG—whose erstwhile colleague Lord Loreburn thought him 'a simpleton in such things & that it was really all Isaacs' fault'[15]*—was being interviewed by the Marconi Select Committee. Sir Courtenay Ilbert, Clerk of the House of Commons, reported privately to James Bryce late in March:*

> The Opposition are in a nasty mood, & we shall have very difficult times next month, especially when it becomes necessary...to propose special procedure for dealing under the Parliament Act with the Home Rule Bill and the Welsh Church Bill after their re-introduction. The Government will have to sit very tight, and it will need all Asquith's prestige, sagacity & imperturbability to keep them in their place.

Ilbert noted that on 13 March Herbert Samuel had announced in the House that the government's proposal for a new second chamber would not contain a vestige of the hereditary principle; and under no circumstances would the absolute veto be restored (Sir C.P. Ilbert–James Bryce, 28 Mar. 1913, Bodl. MS. Bryce 14, ff.80–1).

[15] Newton diary, 22 Apr. [1913], Newton MSS, courtesy of the 4th Lord Newton.

JAP passed silently over his annual statement on 11 April, which did not draw back the veil over the government's intentions on education; but, in the meantime, as Philip Whitwell Wilson put it: 'we have an excellent record of vigilant administration. Mr Pease is establishing a kind of reputation at the Board of Education that Lord Gladstone—also promoted from the Whips' Office to Cabinet—made for himself at the Home Office, a reputation based upon sound work behind the scenes rather than controversy in the House' (Daily News, *11 Apr. 1913).*

30 April Grey impressed cabinet with serious position created by fall of Scutari to Montenegrins, their unwillingness to evacuate at request of Powers, Austria's intention to take hostile action — involving reply from Russia with Germany France Italy drawn in. Austria's pressure on us to join in using force — we resolved to decline unless all Powers united. I suggested that a deputation might be sent to King Nicholas & argue point with him. Asquith reply, yes we could get him to see in interest of his own country he should not force Austria to an attack, but his dynasty, & his throne and his people won't allow him to deprive his soldiers of their one fruit of victory.

Grey had explained his policy to Bonar Law who agreed: 'will help us to avoid European war, but if Montenegro is bullied & strong feeling here, Opposition may become much more critical' (Harcourt diary, 30 Apr. 1913, Bodl. MS.Eng.c.8268). The Scutari crisis was, in R.J. Crampton's words, 'the most dramatic and dangerous of the problems created by the Balkan wars' (The Hollow Détente: Anglo-German Relations in the Balkans 1911–1914, *George Prior [1980], p.93). Scutari, held by the Turks, had been besieged by Montenegrin forces, aided by Serbia, and fell on 23 April. For the Great Power deadlock in 1912–13, Britain's tough stand with Russia, warnings to Austria, cooperation with Germany, and the six-million-franc loan to Montenegro that followed the agreement of King Nicholas (Nikita) (1841–1921) to withdraw from Scutari early in May see C.J. Lowe and M.L. Dockrill,* The Mirage of Power, Vol. One, British Foreign Policy 1902–14, *pp.112–16; Crampton,* The Hollow Détente, *pp.79–86; F.R. Bridge, 'Sir Edward Grey and Austria-Hungary',* IHR, *vol.38, no.2, 2016, pp.264–74.*

A disgruntled Arthur Acland, frustrated about the slow progress of educational reform wrote to Crewe, 6 May 1913:

> As regards Government Education Bill I am not very sanguine. But I am afraid I cannot help much. It's (between ourselves) a grave misfortune that you have in the Commons such a weak man as Pease for Minister. His mind never gets to root of things & never will. You or Haldane who could grapple with objectors & doubters Non conformists & others are elsewhere! Then George is too occupied at present

at any rate. I have a good deal of influence with him but I don't see how to use it at present.

If ever you think I can be of any particular service with George or in any other way you will I daresay tell me.

Crewe replied, 10 May 1913, saying nothing about Pease:

Later on, I hope you will have a talk to Lloyd George on the Bill question: he seems now to be in favour of confining present energies to a simple single-school-area Bill, rather on the lines of McKenna's effort. There are arguments for this, purely political of course; and the question is whether such action might not burke the larger scheme altogether.

(Crewe MSS, C/1, CUL)

May 7 Grey told us position now settled by withdrawal of Montenegrins from Scutari — that we had arranged to send in troops from the international squadron. That the International relations were all happy, & we could press upon Italy she had no more right to keep Islands, than any other great power had to get any territory as the result of the Balkan States war.

We discussed Education for half an hour, and expressed our views. I was asked to draw up a mem. to include certain figures showing progress of school transfer in rural & urban areas, & to place bill in draft before colleagues. Money involved.[16]

In a Cabinet memorandum by JAP of 23 May 1913 ('Education Bill', TNA: CAB 37/115/32), the abolition of half-timer attendance—affecting some 34,000 children—and the raising of the school-leaving age to 14 were two of three main points brought up for Cabinet decision. JAP pointed out that this would be very unpopular with the textile manufacturers in Lancashire and the West Riding, as well as raising the cost of education. The major strategic questions were whether or not to try in the current parliamentary session to meet the wishes of Nonconformists; and whether provision could be made for £2 million in 1914–15 and up to £7 million by 1920 for a national scheme of education. The Board had drafted a comprehensive bill, but Cabinet was in no mind to pursue it immediately. JAP would have to come back again (Neil Daglish, 'Education policy and the question of child labour: the Lancashire cotton industry and R.D. Denman's Bill of 1914', Hist. Ed, *vol.30, no.3, 2001, pp.291–308; Sherington,* English education, social change and war 1911–20, *pp.28–31; and, for a longer perspective, Michael J. Childs, 'Boy Labour in Late Victorian and Edwardian England and the Remaking of the Working Class',* JSH, *vol.23, no.4, 1990, pp.783–802).*

[16] JAP's memorandum and draft bill are in TNA: CAB 37/115/32–3, 23 May 1913.

HHA and WSC, 'on holiday' in Greece early in May, had talks with Greek leaders about disputed territories of Epirus and southern Albania. On 17 May, a peace treaty was signed in London between the Balkan League (Bulgaria, Serbia, Greece, and Montenegro) and the Ottoman Empire.

June 4 Asquith back from cruise in Mediterranean looking well. Grey explained position Foreign affairs & negociations between Powers & Balkan powers in regard to terms of settlement. Business of House discussed. I asked to raise Education, but postponed.

In the previous fortnight, JAP had circulated two memoranda on education (TNA: CAB 37/115/32,33). His mind now set on getting his education proposals through Cabinet, JAP made no mention of WSC's declaration that he would not stay at the Admiralty unless there were three Dreadnoughts for every two Germans in Home waters. WSC's acceleration proposals 'generally commended themselves to the Cabinet' (Harcourt diary, 4 June 1913, Bodl. MS.Eng.c.8268).

June 6[17] H. of C. Friday 12.0. After 1 or 2 small points The P.M. called upon me to open the matter, & I alluded to the general principles of the proposals which had been circulated. The necessity of more money, the continuance of dual system under condition. The single school area proposals, alteration of Grant system, Trust in L.E.As, the control by B. of E., the obligation placed on L.E.As to meet requirements in all branches of Ed. for exceptional & normal child or student.

George argued in favour of a bill sometime to satisfy Noncons. All present appeared to accept more money as a necessity which should be met — but some wanted to defer it LL.G. especially whilst admitting case for it.

On whole pleased with progress, though most of criticism was on policy & not on proposals themselves. Further discussion deferred at 1.30. to another cabinet.

June 10 I was unhappy about disclosure of loss of £30,000 of Party funds by Master of Elibank — made in Marconi H of C. committee day before & Illingworth's evidence that he had no knowledge of this & the investment of £9000 in Marconi American shares for the Party. That so little confidence was shown by The Master in the P.M. or Illingworth — that he should conceal the matter from them from Aug. 1912 until a witness at the committee exposed it,

[17] JAP dated this entry 5 June and HHA signed his letter to the King on the 7th, but the Cabinet met on Friday 6 June (HHA Cabinet letter, 7 June 1913, Bodl. MS. Asquith 7, f.41; *The Times*, 7 June 1913).

was to me deplorable. The investment showed lack of discretion — but conduct shook confidence in him.

As WSC had told Lord Northcliffe in a private and personal letter on 5 June, the newly revealed transaction of the Master of Elibank was 'a complete surprise to us all. Neither the Chancellor of the Exchequer nor the Attorney General nor anyone else in the Government had the slightest knowledge of it.' While the investment itself was unobjectionable, WSC said, the 'concealment of it from colleagues and friends, & from the Prime Minister is deplorable' (Northcliffe MSS, BL Add.MS. 621565, f.53). So incensed had Illingworth been at Tory imputations he overheard on the previous Monday, he had to be forcibly restrained by the Attorney General, Rufus Isaacs. 'One shudders at the thought of what might have happened…he is one of the best amateur boxers in the country.' (Daily Citizen, *11 June 1913.) Illingworth's anger was doubtless intensified by his knowledge that HHA was aware of what had happened earlier than he admitted (Denis Judd,* Lord Reading: Rufus Isaacs, First Marquess of Reading, Lord Chief Justice and Viceroy of India, 1860–1935, *Weidenfeld & Nicolson, 1982, p.99, summarises the evidence of what HHA knew and when; and for Guglielmo Marconi disclosing that HHA advised Isaacs and DLG to remain silent after he learned that they had bought American shares see Marc Raboy,* Marconi: The Man Who Networked the World, *Oxford UP, 2016, p.373).*

I therefore told the P.M. I thought that the practice I had adopted of only altering investments with knowledge of my Co. trustees when I was a whip was sound & that possibly it should be re-established, & no unlimited power given to overdraw on banks by transferring securities, should be permissible. He expressed his ignorance of all the Master had done, & seemed relieved as I was at the opportunity of a quiet talk. He stalked up & down the room for 10 or 15 minutes & it was like old times listening to his clear cut concise expression & summing up of an unpleasant situation but he took the worry of it all very philosophically.

June 11 —Discussed business—The Highlands & Islands of Scotland & Tubercular work — whether L.G.B. Scotland or new Authority should be set up — agreed to set up new authority but to be reviewed in 2 years time with possibility of a transfer of work to the L.G.B.

The Prime Minister's report to the King (Bodl. MS. Asquith 7, f.43) reveals that responsibility for administering the new £42,000 grant for medical relief was unsuccessfully claimed by those whose departments stood to lose. The Secretary for Scotland, Burns, and Runciman all contended that the duty could be better performed by the Local Government Board. In what Harcourt described as 'a long wrangle' with McKinnon Wood, Haldane and DLG supported the position of the committee that had recommended a new authority (Harcourt diary, 11 June 1913, Bodl. MS.Eng.c.8268).

Bag of flour hurled at P.M. when speaking in H. of C. by man in gallery.

The flour was hurled by Lawrence Marvin, a member of the Men's Political Union for Women's Suffrage. He shouted 'Remember Miss Davison' as he threw the flour (the suffragette, Emily Wilding Davison, had stepped on to the track into the path of the King's horse during the Derby race on June 4 and died four days later).[18] The Times *commended HHA on his courage for remaining in position, for it was not immediately known whether or not a bomb had been thrown.*

That evening in the House, Arthur Ponsonby was surprised to find 'what a large number of members were in favour of Ll. George resigning and of course Isaacs too. I think myself this would be a mistake though I found Massingham and many others at the Nation luncheon today hotly in favour of it. We are in a very tottering state and I think George going would be the last straw.' (Ponsonby diary, 12 June 1913, Ponsonby of Shulbrede MSS.) Margot Asquith wrote to DLG on June 13 conveying a message:

> I dined alone with my husband last night—he was in Derby form—he said he wanted to see you and Rufus to have a careful talk over the speeches 'if Lloyd George & Rufus play their cards well, show the proper spirit, I will let the opposition have it! They shall sweat under what I've got to say!' I told him you said you wd give them Hell. He didn't mind xcept he said you must choose a good moment (quite between ourselves you might ask him when you are absolutely alone, so that no one will ever know, what sort of day he advises) ... The 3 speeches sd cover like a miniature mosaic all the ground.
>
> *(Lloyd George MSS, LG/C/6/12/2, PA, some punctuation added!)*

June 17 Cabinet suddenly called for noon to discuss Marconi debate. P.M. asked George & Isaacs to let us know what they proposed to say, so that we should then decide how the govmt should proceed having regard to the terms of Cave's motion, censuring Ministers for concealment and speculating in Marconi shares. George had a spark of fire in his eye, & pointed out the way in which he had suffered from a sense of unjust attacks & suspicion of corruption. Isaacs

[18] For suggestions that Davison's death was a 'horrendous miscalculation' see Daryl Worthington, 'The Mystery Behind Emily Davison's Death', *New Historian*, 4 July 2016, http://www.newhistorian.com/mystery-behind-emily-davisons-death/6760/, accessed 4 July 2016.

less bellicose. After a desultory debate in which Churchill kept on expressing himself, Burns pointed out that the House wanted Ministers to appear in a whitish sheet. Morley took the same line & I piped in, the less said the better so long as the 2 ministers, stated the transactions were such as they thought ought to have been avoided.

Grey kept the discussion well to the point; & it was hoped that after admissions Tories might withdraw their motion & the P.M. should speak early.

The King was advised that the Attorney General and the Chancellor of the Exchequer had 'explained in outline' their proposed statements, 'which, while disclaiming anything in the nature of impropriety will admit error of judgement' (Bodl. MS. Asquith 7, f.45). Lord Morley told his private secretary the next day that when he was in 10 Downing Street for the Cabinet meeting he met Sir Charles Matthews, the Director of Public Prosecutions, coming out of the Prime Minister's room. 'Hullo! You here!' Morley said 'Looking for criminals!!' Morley said that he ought not to have said it as there were messengers looking on (Cunningham diary, 18 June 1913, Miller-Cunningham MSS).

Shortly after he became First Lord of the Admiralty WSC had appointed a committee under the Fourth Sea Lord to investigate problems of oil fuel. A decision in April 1912 to lay down four fast oil-fired battleships accelerated the need to better understand the use of oil fuel. WSC now urged the establishment of what became the Royal Commission on Fuel and Engines. Encouraging Lord Fisher, who was to chair the inquiry, he wrote on 11 June: 'You have got to find the oil; to show how it can be stored cheaply: how it can be purchased regularly and cheaply in peace, and with absolute certainty in war. Then by all means develop its application in the best possible way to existing and prospective ships.' In a memorandum to the Cabinet on 16 June WSC reported the Admiralty view that a six-month war reserve was essential. To meet the requirements he proposed the immediate purchase of sufficient oil to double the amount provided for in the existing estimates, and forward contracts that would guarantee supply at favourable prices.

Negotiations had been in train with Shell to develop the oil industry in Trinidad: 'It is a delicate matter to make a monopoly which is not a monopoly' (G. Grindle–L. Earle, 2 Mar. 1912, Bodl. MS. Harcourt 463, ff.302–4). But the quest for reliable supplies needed to be much wider. At Cabinet on 18 June, a proposed contract with Pearson's Mexican oil company provoked McKenna into accusing WSC of laying down 'oil ships... without provision for the oil'. HHA had to quell WSC's angry response: 'this is not the way to conduct Cabinet discussion' (Harcourt diary, 18 June 1913, Bodl. MS.Eng.c.8268). The intense ensuing interdepartmental and Cabinet discussions culminated in an agreement with the Anglo-Persian Oil Company (Marian Kent, Moguls and Mandarins: Oil, Imperialism and the Middle

East in British Foreign Policy 1900–1940, *Frank Cass, 1993, pp.42–67; a useful summary is Martin Gibson, '"Oil fuel Will Absolutely Revolutionize Naval Strategy": The Royal Navy's Adoption of Oil before the First World War', in Ross Mahoney, Stuart Mitchell, and Michael LoCicero eds,* A Military Transformed? Adaption and Innovation in the British Military, 1792–1945, *Helion and Co., Solihull, 2014, pp.110–23, and see Joost Jonker and Jan Luiten van Zanden,* From Challenger to Joint Industry Leader, 1890–1939: A History of Royal Dutch Shell [Vol. 1], *Oxford UP, New York, 2007, pp.130–2).*

June 18 We discussed the purchase of oil for the Navy. Treaty with Portugal about port — & the exclusion of other wines under that name. Grey reported position in negotiations [?] Greece & Albania. I asked for education, but discussion was adjourned. After Cave & Lord Helmsley's[19] speeches H. of C. Isaacs opened & George followed — they then withdrew. Isaacs' apology was too conditional 'had he known &c' George attacked his critics for rumours circulated & on no evidence & then admitted indiscretions, carelessness, unwise if you like, but honour of House, & no desire to conceal could or had been shown.

George Cave KC, Unionist MP for Kingston, had moved the resolution that the House regretted the transactions of certain of His Majesty's Ministers and their 'want of frankness' in addressing the House a week earlier. His speech was described by Tim Healy as 'an icy analysis of Lloyd George's position, which was wonderful in power and balance, and a passionless summary of the facts. It seemed as if he were at the Day of Judgment summing up as counsel against a sinner, but presenting everything that could be said in his favour.' (Letters and Leaders of My Day, *Vol. 1, p.525.) Morley, who had been present when the Cabinet discussed what Isaacs and DLG should say, told his private secretary on 23 June that 'the Marconi speech delivered by Rufus Isaacs last week in the H of Commons was* not *the speech that he showed to the P.M.' (Cunningham diary, 18 June 1913, Miller-Cunningham MSS). A photograph of the first page of a heavily amended draft of Isaacs's statement appears in Judd,* Lord Reading, *p.301, where it is confused with the draft amendment to Cave's motion approved by DLG and moved by Sir Ryland Adkins.*

[19] Charles William Reginald Duncombe, Vt Helmsley (1879–1916); Con. MP North Riding of Yorkshire (Thirsk and Malton) 1906–15; styled Vt Helmsley 1881–1915; m. Lady Marjorie Greville, dau. 5th Earl of Warwick and Daisy, Countess of Warwick, 1904. Succ. g'father as 2nd Earl of Feversham 1915. Killed leading his battalion during the Battle of the Somme on a Sept. 1916 day on which three of JAP's cousins were also killed. According to one of his subalterns, Anthony Eden, he was 'a popular commanding officer with the riflemen, not least because he was essentially a countryman… happiest on a horse' (Gerald Gliddon, *The Aristocracy and the Great War*, Gliddon Books, Norwich, 2002, p.435).

Margot Asquith's attempt on 5 June 1913 to get Isaacs to wear a white sheet, the agony she saw in his face, and her husband's confirmation that the sketch of the speech Isaacs had shown him in no way resembled what he said in the House, is described at length in her October 1913 diary (Bodl. MS.Eng.d.3210, ff.131–3).

June 19 P.M. was to follow A. Lyttelton.

Alfred Lyttelton died on 5 July, three weeks after speaking in the Marconi Debate. The government won by 78 votes; three Liberals voted with the Opposition including Ronald Munro-Ferguson, who told JAP on 16 February 1914 'you have always been my best friend on our side' (MS. Gainford 97 when seen). Bentley Brinkerhoff Gilbert attributes the defeat of the Cave resolution and the saving of the careers of Isaacs and DLG to HHA's tactical decision that the 'culprits...would speak and withdraw. He would take charge of the battle after they had gone.' However, a whipped vote along party lines was inevitable after failed negotiations towards a compromise motion in which the House would not express regret at the actions of the ministers but would accept their expressions of regret. Gilbert discounts stories that WSC attempted to broker a deal between Bonar Law and DLG about a form of words *('David Lloyd George and the Great Marconi Scandal',* Hist.Res., *V, LXII, no.149, 1989, p.315).*

But the crucial evidence about the drafting of the resolution to be put to the House rests in the papers of Percy Illingworth. It is clear that Gilbert overrates HHA's magnanimity in publicly defending Rufus Isaacs and DLG. And HHA's conditional assurance to Isaacs delivered by Margot ('I'm going to stand by both of them') was demonstrably disingenuous (Colin Clifford, The Asquiths, *John Murray, 2002, p.211). Two documents kept by the Chief Whip show that the Prime Minister had been prepared to go further towards allowing the House of Commons to express its regret at his colleagues' actions than has hitherto been supposed. There were frequent suggestions in late 1916 and afterward that DLG had ill repaid his chief's loyalty to him over Marconi. Yet it had taken an emphatic refusal by DLG to prevent a form of words being agreed between the Prime Minister and the Leader of the Opposition that would have been tantamount to a parliamentary censure on the besieged ministers.*

The resolution crafted by HHA and Illingworth in the Prime Minister's room in the House of Commons on 19 June was more damning of their colleagues than the first typed draft over which the two men had laboured the day before. The new version contained the phrase that the House 'concurs with them in regretting that such purchases [of shares in the American Marconi company] were made & that they were not mentioned in the debate of Oct. 11th last'. DLG rejected this formula, insisting on the words 'accepts their expressions of regret'. Illingworth, who seems to have kept very few papers, took pains to preserve this pencilled draft with the annotation: 'It was the substitution of these words which found favour with the Chancellor. Otherwise!' (Illingworth MSS, courtesy of Henry Illingworth; Cameron Hazlehurst, review of Bentley Brinkerhoff Gilbert, David Lloyd George: A Political Life. Volume 2: Organizer of Victory, 1912–1916, *Ohio State UP, Columbus, 1992, in* JMH, *vol.67, no.4, 1995, p.931; Roy Hattersley,* David Lloyd George: The Great Outsider, *Abacus, 2012 [1st edn Little Brown, 2010], pp.325–6), draws on Illingworth's file, which he said was 'previously unexamined', but overlooks the key passage on which DLG had insisted and Illingworth's emphatic annotation.*

Judd, in an otherwise reliable account, errs in suggesting that DLG and Isaacs 'obediently followed' guidelines furnished by HHA on 16 June. But he draws attention to the scatty recollection of Margot Asquith to Lord Reading, as Isaacs had become. Why had her husband saved DLG over Marconi? Because 'Ll.G was young and he loved you. Had it not been for you he would have let Ll.G go.' (Lord Reading, *pp.100–1.) Margot Asquith's diary 18 May 1913 provides evidence that HHA at one point had been convinced, and seemingly unconcerned, that 'it has done for Lloyd George... he will never get off' (Bodl. MS.Eng.d.3210, f.110). As the dust settled on 20 June, Edward Grey wrote sympathetically to DLG:*

> There was a very true sentence in your speech about mistakes being often more heavily censured than misdeeds... I have often thought in public affairs that one is always being over praised or over blamed. But there is one great abiding cause of satisfaction in having been in this Cabinet—we have been in it 7½ years and I believe it can be said with truth that the personal relations of all of us have not only stood the long strain but have gained in attachment to an extent that must be very rare if not unprecedented in the history of Cabinets.
>
> *(Lloyd George MSS, LG/C/4/14/9, PA)*

As a former Chief Whip, JAP was less concerned about the reputations of DLG and Isaacs than with the consequences for the government's contractual negotiations with Marconi of Alick Murray's purchase of shares on behalf of the Liberal Party. 'We all want to bury the Marconi affair but Simon (with whom I have been discussing the situation) & I feel strongly that the matter will be constantly raked up as long as any A Marconi shares are held by any of our colleagues or the Party... possesses any interest in them...'. The solution, proposed in a heavily corrected undated draft typescript letter to the Prime Minister on Simon's Fritwell Manor, Banbury, stationery, was that ministers should part with their shares and 'the Chief Whip should cut his losses, leaving to Murray to take on himself the responsibility of these investments made by him... & make such restitution later on to the Party as he can afford'. The letter was unfinished, presumably never sent, evidently torn up many years later, but kept (MS. Gainford 84/106).

June 24 Cabinet called at 10.30 to consider terms of Insurance Bill. We objected to length & controversy it might arouse — & talked over provisions which might remain.

There is no hint of dissension in HHA's report to the King on 26 June of 'small but real points of grievance' and 'inconsiderable' additional costs. Nor is there a trace of DLG's disturbing pronouncement, captured by Harcourt, that every friendly society in the country was insolvent (Bodl. MS.Eng.c.8268). JAP was probably unaware that, after a meeting on 20 June with DLG, Birrell, the Law Officers, Malcolm Ramsay (Treasury principal clerk), and Customs & Excise officials, HHA had decided that 'foreign arms carried coastwise to Ireland were to be forfeited in every case except where they were duly entered in a cargo book as foreign goods' (W.M.G.H., untitled memo., 24 June 1913, Bodl. MS. Asquith 41, f.1).

June 25[20] Cabt at House — after dealing with East African Uganda finance we discussed Education Bill & after desultory discussion Cabinet agreed to my indicating policy except on Nonconformist proposals and on 2dary school (inspection & registration) = Large brush & money. Was satisfied to get now. Money to be given to help L.E.As. at once. Bill to be considered again in autumn for next session.

In a memorandum circulated to the Cabinet on 23 June 1913 ('Education Bill', [867], printed 24/6/13) JAP argued for a new grant system, to replace eight previous grants that were full of anomalies. The bid was for £1,890,000, £3,000,000 in year 2, rising to £5,500,000 by 1920. As a minimum at least £50,000 for School Medical Service and £100,000 in aid of new loan charges incurred by LEAs 1913–14 for higher and elementary education would be needed (MS. Gainford 124/55). HHA's summary for the King on 26 June was that any proposals in the current session would be confined to 'a modest grant of pecuniary aid to the local authorities'(Bodl. MS. Asquith 7, ff.49–50).

Discussed Aeroplanes & dirigibles. P.M. thought we were bound to spend money on 2 large & 4 small although their life & use was very problematical ?£490,000! With sheds — spares &c.

[20] Hobhouse dates this meeting at the Commons 26 June. JAP dated his entry 26 June, but the Cabinet met on 24 and 25 June (HHA Cabinet letter, 26 June 1913, Bodl. MS. Asquith 7, ff.49–50; *The Times*, 26 June 1913). Notes exchanged between Morley and Harcourt on 25 June confirm the date (Bodl. MS. Harcourt 427, f.253), as does Harcourt's diary note of a meeting at the Commons at 4.15 p.m. on 25 June (Bodl. MS.Eng.c.8268). Harcourt, pleased with getting his own way on the 'East Africa Loans Bill', learned that Morley had 'a slightly grim irony in his gizzard, seeing rag after rag of old decent political clothing vanishing down the wind'. Under the East African Protectorates (Loans) Bill, a loan of £3,000,000 sterling to the Protectorate of Nyasaland, the East African Protectorate, and the Protectorate of Uganda was authorised early in Aug. 1914.

JAP was tripping over the arithmetic. WSC had circulated a memorandum by Seely on 'Aerial Navigation' on 10 June (MS. Mottistone 15/235–41, Nuffield Col.). In Germany and France the use of airships as adjuncts for naval warfare had gone from experiment to fact. Germany's new programme was two squadrons of four airships and one reserve plus sheds, gas plants etc. with replacements to be made every four years. The Admiralty had purchased two small airships for training and scouting and was asking for £420,000 for ships plus sheds etc., £160,000 in the current year, and £350,000 for aeroplanes. They were planning to begin building Zeppelins. Seely followed on 16 June with information about dirigibles in Germany, France, Austria–Hungary, and Italy, compared with the War Office's three small dirigibles and one under construction. More papers from WSC and Seely would follow within weeks (MS. Mottistone 15/264–70; 'Development of the German Airship fleet' [956], printed 16/7/13 [sic], report from Lt Col. Alick Russell, Military Attaché, Berlin: MS. Mottistone 15/323–5, circulated to Cabinet by WSC 14 July 1913, Nuffield Col.).

Naval intelligence had reported on German airships and their 'possible utility in Naval warfare' since 1908. Progress in airship construction was watched, the delivery of the first 'Zeppelin' for the German Navy was noted on 18 October 1912, and more detailed memoranda on 'Dirigible Airships in Time of War' and 'German Naval Airships and other Aerial Matters' were despatched on 7 December 1912 and 24 April 1913 (Matthew S. Seligmann ed., Naval Intelligence from Germany: The Reports of the British Naval Attachés in Berlin, 1906–1914, Ashgate for the Navy Records Society, 2007, pp.460,466–8,492–5). Seligmann shows that the naval and military attachés in Berlin 'barraged their superiors with warnings about the substantial prowess of German lighter-than-air travel' (Spies in Uniform, pp.250–3). Navy records and relevant papers of the CID are in Capt. S.W. Roskill ed., Documents Relating to the Naval Air Service, Vol. 1 1908–1918, Navy Records Society, 1969. The beginnings of 'the aircraft revolution' are outlined from British and German documents in Norman Friedman, Fighting the Great War at Sea: Strategy, Tactics and Technology, Seaforth Publishing, Barnsley, 2014, pp.97–9. For the interest of The Times in the 'aerial problem' see Charles à Court Repington–Geoffrey Robinson, 2 Apr. 1913, in A.J.A. Morris ed., The Letters of Lieutenant-Colonel Charles à Court Repington CMG: Military Correspondent of The Times 1903–1918, Sutton Publishing for the Army Records Society, Stroud, 1999, pp.206–7.

On 'The Air Panic of 1913' and sustained criticism of the government, especially the Secretary of State for War, Jack Seely, on the inadequacy of British air defence preparation see Alfred Gollin, The Impact of Air Power on the British People and their Government, 1909–14, Macmillan in assoc. with King's College, London, 1989; Brett Holman, 'The Phantom Airship Panic of 1913: Imagining Aerial Warfare in Britain Before the Great War', JBS, vol.55, no.1, 2016, pp.99–119. Recent studies of airship and aircraft developments in both

Germany and Britain 1912–14 are reflected in James Goldrick, Before Jutland: The Naval War in Northern European Waters August 1914–February 1915, *Naval Institute P., Annapolis, 2015, pp.56–7. During a debate on Seely's salary, in which it emerged that only 44 of 80 aeroplanes were fit to fly, the government got wind of a planned snap division and won 280 to 247 (W. Anstruther-Gray diary, 30 July 1913, Kilmany MSS, NRAS 3363/144). For the developing divergence between the naval and military wings of the Royal Flying Corps in 1913 see Eric Grove, 'Seamen or Airmen?: The Early Days of British Naval Flying', in Tim Benbow ed.,* British Naval Aviation: The First 100 Years, *Ashgate, 2011, pp.17–25.*

JAP introduced the Mental Deficiency Bill on 27 June. He had help the previous day from George Newman in preparing his speech (Newman diary, 26 June 1913, Newman MSS, TNA: MH 139). He now turned to action in response to the final report of the Royal Commission on the University of London, chaired by Haldane (Cd. 6717, HMSO, 1913, repr. 1914). The report attracted criticism after its publication in April for not recommending the creation of a medical faculty for the new university (Thomas Neville Bonner, Iconoclast: Abraham Flexner and a Life in Learning, *Johns Hopkins UP, Baltimore, 2002, pp.90–6), JAP's proposals were submitted to Cabinet on 2 July (TNA: CAB 37/116/44).*

July 2 I raised the question as to whether I might appoint a committee with Sir George Murray[21] in the chair, to consider, how best to carry out the practical proposals of the Royal Commission, & that legislation would of course be required; & if steps were to be taken at all the cabinet must realise what they would be committed to as suggested in the terms of my memorandum. P.M. appealed to Haldane, who accepted the obligation, & urged the course I suggested.

I then told the Cabinet, the £100,000 authorised at last cabinet would need legislation to regularise it, unless we raised the money through appropriation bill, & pointed out the irregularity & the emergency.

Grey reported on F.O. Affairs — Balkans. Samuel on Marconi &c.

Although Grey seems to have thought otherwise, the Marconi affair had soured relationships in the Cabinet. DLG defended himself in a speech at the National Liberal Club on 1 July. Morley, who had arrived early for the 2 July Cabinet meeting (at which Samuel was due to

[21] Sir George Herbert Murray (1849–1936). His appointment as an Armstrong Whitworth director Feb. 1912 'sent a shock through all ranks of the Civil Service'; he had chaired a committee that reported in 1907 in favour of increasing reliance on private armaments firms (Philip Noel-Baker, *The Private Manufacture of Armaments*, Vol. I, Victor Gollancz, 1937, pp.58–9,172,180); Perm. Sec. Treasury 1903–11 (jointly to 1907); civil servant 1872–1911; p.s. to W.E. Gladstone 1892–4, Ld Rosebery 1894–5; KCB 1899; GCB 1908; PC 1910; GCVO 1920. There is no mention in HHA's Cabinet letter or Harcourt's diary of a Royal Commission or of JAP's request for a committee.

report progress on negotiations with Marconi over a new contract), found DLG, whom he had hoped to avoid, alone. 'They then came to words,' Morley's private secretary recorded: 'Lord M. told him that his speech was bad for Asquith who had stood nobly by him, bad for the Party. Lloyd George dissented. Lord M. told him that he knew far more about the Party than he did. Etc. etc.' (Cunningham diary, 2 July 1913, Miller-Cunningham MSS). Reflecting six months later on the Cabinet tensions at this time, WSC was heard telling a dinner party including Illingworth and the McKennas that 'if the Marconi affair had been properly managed it would have broken the Government' (Duff Cooper diary, 15 Jan. 1914 [referring to 13 Jan.], Norwich MSS, DUFC 15/1/4, CAC). At the National Liberal Club on 1 July he had vehemently repudiated the 'campaign of calumny and slander unequalled in recent annals' (Wedgwood Benn's notes, Stansgate MSS, ST/15 f. 237, PA).

July 9 Edward Grey reported that in spite of Bulgaria being worsted by Montenegrins, Greeks & Servians, he did not expect Turks to intervene.

European Powers were true to policy of non-intervention, & Russia France & Germany & ourselves were agreed as to policy of localising war. Austria's and Italy's representatives referred questions to their own govmt & were non-committal. Russia & Austria were still not likely to work together. We discussed oil fields & Persian contract, P.M. against a fixed 20 years contract & I backed him up.

A Cabinet committee over the next few days concluded that the best way to meet the Admiralty desire for a fixed price from an independent British oil company (German interests were involved in Shell) providing oil from a location on the navy's route that could be defended easily was to take a controlling interest in Anglo-Persian. The Cabinet agreed on 11 July, and WSC announced the planned new arrangements in his speech on the naval estimates on 16 July. There would be protracted negotiations to follow on the precise terms of the contract and the financial support to be given to the Company (Agreement with the Anglo-Persian Oil Co. Ltd, with an Explanatory Memorandum, and the Report of the Commission of Experts on their local investigation', PP, 1914, Cd. 7419, liv, 50). Kent's Moguls and Mandarins *is a well-documented exposition of these events, which are placed in a wider context by Siegel,* Endgame, *chs 7,8. There is more background on company structures and German links in the official history of Shell: Jonker and van Zanden,* A History of Royal Dutch Shell, *Vol. 1.*

July 11 We had special meeting about oil fields contract following, Cabinet committee meeting on the Thursday. I left to take charge of Plural Voting bill, & left my views with Grey in writing opposed to fixed 20 years contract behind back of H of C.

On an urgent warning from the Whips' Office that government numbers were very short for an impending division, the rest of the Cabinet walked over to the House of Commons and resumed their meeting in the Prime Minister's room (Harcourt diary, 11 July 1913, Bodl. MS. Eng.c.8268). The Tories attempted another snap division on the Army Vote later in the month (Harmsworth diary, 30 July 1913, Thorpe and Toye eds, Parliament and Politics in the Age of Asquith and Lloyd George: The Diaries of Cecil Harmsworth, *p.146).*

July 14 Sat with P.M. on bench for 2 hours 3d Rdg of Plural Voting — told him about allegations against Young[22] a Secondary inspector he was satisfied an enquiry was right course.

The Plural Voting Bill was read a third time after three Parliamentary days (10, 11, and 14 July), the compiler of the Annual Register 1913 *saying it did not 'require extended notice' after earlier describing JAP's use of the kangaroo closure to deal with Unionist amendments (pp.153,159).*

July 16 — Cabinet discussed oil again — left early to attend to plural voting.[23]

July 22 I introduced Education proposals. P.M. heard me out & complimented me.

Ambitious education plans outlined publicly by Haldane in January (without Cabinet endorsement) had gradually been scaled back, not least because of DLG's determination to make land reform the central plank of Liberal policy. Five months later JAP circulated two memoranda and a draft bill to the Cabinet (23 May 1913, MS. Gainford 124/42,55,57). He continued to argue that big changes would be blocked by the Lords and would take three years to pass under the Parliament Act. Moreover, there was no parliamentary time that session. In the meantime, smaller reforms were urgent. To the contrary, DLG said that a sweeping bill should be presented that session, withdrawing aid from voluntary schools and enabling LEAs to take them over. JAP responded that tampering with bricks and mortar would arouse overwhelming opposition. Considerable improvement could be obtained by making LEAs responsible for the appointment of head teachers. The LEAs could remove religious tests for these appointments and make teaching in rural (usually poor) schools a

[22] This appears to refer to the case of a secondary school inspector who was removed from office in 1911 because of his alleged inability to discharge efficiently the duties of his office. After a legal challenge and an inquiry ordered by JAP in 1913, a confidential settlement was reached and the allegations were withdrawn (HC Deb 20 July 1914 vol 65 cc27–8).

[23] JAP missed Birrell's presentation of his Irish Land Purchase Act with what Hobhouse called 'that wonderful mixture of sentiment, irony, sarcasm, and cynicism which makes his expression of opinion different from all other men's' (David ed., *Inside Asquith's Cabinet*, p.143).

prerequisite for promotion. In return for this extension of their powers the LEAs could finance improvements to voluntary school buildings and playgrounds, and specialised teaching, domestic and technical education (MS. Gainford 124/32).

In a confronting 'secret' memorandum of 23 June 1913 (TNA: CAB 37/115/41) JAP asked 'DOES the Cabinet approve' his proposals? The Cabinet was asked to decide which policy to adopt, bearing in mind that a reformed, national school system would cost £2 million in 1914–15. Ministers were also asked to rule on whether to raise the school-leaving age to 14 and to consider JAP's memorandum on single school areas. The government's deliberations in the latter part of 1912 are summarised in the concluding commentary after the diary entry of 31 December 1912. In a confidential letter to the Government Chief Whip on 9 May 1913, J. Scott Lidgett had exposed the differences between the Free Church leaders on single school areas. There was enthusiasm for a bill if it would make the Single School a Council School 'carrying therefore no right of rating, & that the means of purchasing the school or building another in its place, was entirely supplied from the Exchequer'. But if the government were forced to make concessions on denominational teaching it would 'destroy any warmth of welcome' (Illingworth MSS). When WSC commented at the Cabinet that JAP's proposals ought to be brought forward after the election, HHA said 'this is cynicism supported by sophistry' (Harcourt diary, 25 June 1913, Bodl. MS.Eng.c.8268).

JAP finally introduced the Education (No. 2) Bill on 22 July 1913. It simply authorised a grant to LEAs of £100,000 for loan charges and £50,000 for school medical services. Even this modest bill was dropped in August for lack of parliamentary time. The Bill would have amended the 1870 Act so as to permit parliamentary grants for building, enlarging, or improving elementary schools: the Board of Education could thence give immediate financial relief to local education authorities. Only 'preliminary recognition of the necessities' was provided, and the government, JAP said, would do its best to bring in a more comprehensive measure the following year.

In his speech on 22 July 1913 JAP optimistically outlined wider-ranging proposals to be introduced in 1914, first identifying the two defects of the present system of national education: it was not national; and it was not a system (HC Deb 22 July 1913 vol 55 cc1907–24). The Board of Education continued to marshal arguments for and against the Chancellor of the Exchequer's 'clean sweep' policy. (See 7 May, 6 June, 22 and 30 July 1913, and 30 April 1914.)

July 23 Cabinet. Harcourt dwelt on situation in S. Africa — removal of ½ Imperial troops not approved owing to disturbed labour situation.

New Insurance Bill. George authorised if Comtee could agree (Buxton he & ?) to help men to attend local Insurance Meetings by payments when loss of work involved —

Grey explained Foreign situation & unity of Austria & Russia in resisting Turks remaining at Adrianople & violating Treaty made in London.

P.M. gave garden party.

War had erupted again in the Balkans on 29–30 June with Bulgaria attacking Greek and Serbian forces in Macedonia. On 12 July the Ottoman Empire declared war on Bulgaria, which asked for peace the next day. An armistice on 31 July was followed on 10 August by the Treaty of Bucharest ending the war. The King's Speech was left open to the last moment to mention the 'cessation of hostilities, which I hope will be permanent' (Bodl. MS. Asquith 85, ff.219–21,224).

July 30 Cabinet. Grey explained situation in Balkans, & why he thought it best to postpone placing pressure on Turkey to observe Treaty of London & retire from Adrianople until other states had settled their differences. The difficulty was the obvious danger of allowing Russia to use armed force in favour of Bulgaria without upsetting concert.

The Treaty of London had been signed on 30 May 1913, at the end of the London Conference of 1912–1913. It dealt with territorial adjustments arising from the end of the First Balkan War. T.G. Otte explains Grey's policy and how Adrianople came to remain in Turkish hands in Statesman of Europe, *pp.461–6.*

I asked P.M. to let me raise question of the Opposition to my little 1 clause bill, but he suggested we should wait & see how it developed. The cabinet only lasted an hour.

Aug. 4 Saw P.M. asked that my bill should be pressed making Defective Act compulsory. He demurred obviously he did not intend to allow any work to prevent the session ending on 16[24] — but he said I might try — he looked very flushed but tired.

N.B. Bill was dropped. Sir Fredk. Banbury blocked the bill, & insisted on its being controversial.

The Elementary Education (Defective and Epileptic Children) Bill was attacked on its second reading by many MPs for setting up a dual control over the 'mentally defective'. The Mental Deficiency Bill, establishing a board of control over all the 'feeble-minded' over 16 years

[24] JAP missed the next two Cabinets before the summer recess. On 6 Aug., referring to the King and Stamfordham 'talking very badly about possible insistence on dissolution by the King', WSC reportedly said 'Stamfordham has become a public danger' and HHA added: 'He will have to have his wings clipped before this business is over' (Harcourt diary, 6 Aug. 1913, Bodl. MS.Eng.c.8268).

old, was then in committee. The government had encountered considerable resistance to a bill introduced in 1912 that prohibited marriage with a 'defective' and provided for the segregation of the 'feeble-minded' so as to prevent them procreating. Amended legislation was passed in July 1913 after a valiant but futile attempt at obstruction by Josiah Wedgwood and Handel Booth (Mulvey, Political Life of Josiah C. Wedgwood, pp.38–40). The class and gender implications of the Act to which Wedgwood objected are developed in Mark Jackson, '"A Menace to the Good of Society": Class, Fertility, and the Feeble-Minded in Edwardian England', in Jonathan Andrews and Anne Digby eds, Sex and Seclusion, Class and Custody Perspectives on Gender and Class in the History of British and Irish Psychiatry, Editions Rodopi B. V., Amsterdam, New York, 2004, pp.271–94.

JAP's bill would have given control of those under sixteen to the Board of Education, entailing expenditure of £115,000 for residential schools, mainly in country areas. After compulsory school attendance was attacked as depriving parents of the presence of their children, parents were given the right to refuse to have their children sent away to residential schools. The background is explained in G.R. Searle, Eugenics and Politics in Britain 1901–1914, Noorhoff International Publishing, Leyden, 1976, ch.9, and Mark Jackson, The Borderland of Imbecility: Medicine, Society and the Fabrication of the Feeble Mind in Late Victorian and Edwardian England, Manchester UP, 2000, pp.203ff. There is analysis from a different perspective in Nikolas Rose, The psychological complex: Psychology, politics and society in England, 1869–1939, Routledge & Kegan Paul, 1985, pp.103–11. Harvey G. Simmons: 'Explaining Social Policy: The English Mental Deficiency Act of 1913', JSH, vol.11, no.3, 1978, pp.387–403; and 'Mental Handicap and Education', Oxford Review of Education, vol.9, no.3, 1983, special issue, are superseded by Thomson, The Problem of Mental Deficiency, pp.36–50.

JAP does not mention the spirited bid made by Reginald McKenna in the summer of 1913 to entice Dr George Newman, JAP's key aide and adviser, to leave the Board of Education and take up the chairmanship of the Board of Control for Lunacy & Mental Deficiency established under the Mental Deficiency Act. McKenna promised a 'larger screw' of £1,800 a year and an independent position answering only to the Secretary of State. Haldane, he said, agreed that the move was the right one for Newman. But Newman was unpersuaded, and JAP was gratified by his conclusion that the Board of Education was more 'fundamental, constructive and enduring'. Robert Morant was 'unspeakably delighted' that 'the one & only man in the world now, to whom I talk at all freely' had opted to stay at Education (Morant–Newman, 17 Aug. 1913, TNA: Newman MSS, MH 139).

As JAP told Newman, HHA had been supportive of Newman retaining his post at the Board of Education. After a Cabinet meeting on 13 August (which JAP missed), Newman learned that JAP had been to the Prime Minister, who said: 'I shd not think of requiring a Civil servant to leave the work he liked & cd. do best, particularly if his devotion to his work was at *the sacrifice of salary. Pease was v. pleased & so am I.'* (*Newman diary, 24, 26 June; 4, 8, 12–13 Aug. 1913, Newman MSS, TNA: MH 139.*)

With their eyes on the general election due in 1915, through July and August, ministers had been circulating memoranda and corresponding on land issues. After the Cabinet meeting on 23 July a relieved Minister for Agriculture recorded that the meeting was 'mainly useful for a clearing of the air on land on which nobody is to be committed to anything until after the Cabinet has further discussions + decisions' (Walter Runciman–Hilda Runciman, 24 July 1913, Runciman of Doxford MSS, 303, quoted in Wallace, The Political Career of Walter Runciman, *p.135). This had not inhibited Runciman from telling a Liberal supporter the next day that the Cabinet was committed and anxious to make an announcement on land policy and that it was safe to advocate a national rural housing scheme. Cabinet had arrived at 'no definite conclusions' on tenure, rent courts, and a minimum wage; but nothing was to be said about this (Runciman–E.D. Morel, 25 July 1913, copy, Runciman of Doxford MSS). At HHA's garden party after the 23 July Cabinet meeting Haldane's sister found DLG 'Full of Land policy. R's scheme of land reform etc. In great spirits' (Elizabeth Haldane diary, 28 July 1913, Elizabeth Haldane MSS, MS. 20240, f.49, NLS).*

At the 13 August Cabinet meeting, not recorded by JAP, HHA had indicated that the land campaign being developed by DLG would be discussed when Cabinet met next on 14 October. Runciman and DLG met to clear the ground the day after the Cabinet (Runciman–HHA, 18 Aug. 1913, Runciman of Doxford MSS). With Grey, Haldane, and the previously reluctant McKenna, the Chancellor produced compromise proposals on 21 August. At a meeting six weeks later with the Prime Minister, Runciman, and Chief Whip Illingworth, DLG secured consent in principle to a suite of measures. But, as Charles Trevelyan told Runciman on 10 September, the Chancellor was 'still feeling his way as to policy . . . making up his mind I think that he has got to go in for rating of land values. He can't possibly get driving force without it. His main appeal for <u>*power*</u> *must be to the towns . . . The connecting link between town and country is emancipation of improvements from taxation and the full tax burden on unused or half-used land' (Runciman of Doxford MSS).*

The rural land campaign was launched in a speech by DLG at the Bedford skating rink on 11 October. He had met the target date he had nominated in the summer in a conversation on strategy when dining with Riddell, Masterman, and the editor of the influential Nonconformist journal, the British Weekly, *Sir William Robertson Nicoll (Robertson Nicoll memorandum, 9 July 1913, Robertson Nicoll MSS). On 13 October, delegates at a land taxation conference at Cardiff were cheered by a message from the Chancellor wishing them God speed in the mission to end the land monopoly. Much detail remained to be settled. Measures were approved to protect urban leaseholders and business tenants, and facilitate land acquisition by local authorities. But broader urban land policies were still to be worked out and endorsed. A sceptical private secretary to the head of the Foreign Office put it to a friend:*

> The idea is for a flood of irresponsible orators who will propound all sorts of ideas. If one catches on it will be adopted—if it fails it will be described as unauthorised. The beginning of this business was inaugurated by our egregious Under Secretary [Francis Acland] who employs the leisure it is necessary in the public interest to ensure him from F.O. work to ramp up and down the country seeking whom he may devour. He started the ball by making a violent and intemperate attack on landlords who Lloyd George had been at pains to describe as public spirited individuals labouring under difficulties.
>
> *(Lord Onslow–Dougal Malcolm, 20 Oct. 1913, MS. 393, All Souls Col.)*

Two admirable accounts of these events are Ian Packer, Lloyd George, Liberalism and the Land, *especially pp.77–148, and Avner Offer,* Property and Politics, 1870–1914: Landownership, Law, Ideology and Urban Development in England, *Cambridge UP, 1981, pp.363–400. Paul Readman,* Land and Nation in England: Patriotism, National Identity and the Politics of Land, 1880–1914, *Royal Historical Society/ Boydell P., Woodbridge, 2008, pp.68–160, demonstrates from the language of DLG and his associates that 'Liberal land reform involved patriotic concern for race'. For the Opposition response: E.H.H. Green,* The Crisis of Conservatism: The politics, economics and ideology of the British Conservative party, 1880–1914, *Routledge, 1995, pp.289–94; Thackeray,* Conservatism for the democratic age, *pp.61–2.*

Neither the Cabinet nor the Opposition had been idle during the recess. As the Unionist leader in the Lords pointed out to the party's press liaison officer, these were 'days of high pressure, when the programme of a single year comprises materials which, in more easy-going days, would have sufficed for half a dozen Sessions' (Lord Lansdowne–M. Fraser, 23 Sept. 1913, Sir Malcolm Fraser MSS, Bodl. MS.Eng.c.4788, f.24). The King's perplexity and anxiety over Home Rule intensified through the autumn. He could see no way forward other than a conference of the parties. His assistant private secretary Fritz Ponsonby wrote to his brother Arthur from Balmoral on 28 August that the King had seen HHA

> and asked him whether in his opinion there was any possibility of his refusing assent to the Home Rule Bill being seriously considered constitutionally practicable by the people of this country…the impression seemed to have gained ground that now that the Veto of the Lords had been abolished, the Royal Assent had become a real thing, and that it was up to him to consider whether he should give it or not. Asquith stoutly denied that this was the case…It was merely a nominal Veto and nowadays there was no question of a constitutional monarch using it. The King quite agreed that this was the case but pointed out that this was not properly

understood by the man in the street, who would accuse him of betraying Ulster and having caused civil war.

...

The King then asked him whether he thought Ulster's opposition was serious and what would be the outcome of the passing of the Bill. The P.M. regarded the whole situation with almost frivolous optimism. He admitted there would be trouble in Ulster but he hoped it would soon evaporate. He thought it would have died away long ago had it not been for Carson.

The King however stuck to his point—that he was to give Royal Assent to a Bill which inevitably entailed civil war and that the army would look to him to prevent their being placed in the unenviable position of having to shoot down their fellow countrymen. Asquith was very nice and took the point. He said he would be quite willing to accept a compromise.

The compromise HHA had in mind was a scheme by which Ulster could contract out for say five years. He thought there was nothing to be gained by a conference but had no objection to the King's declared intention to put the idea to Lansdowne. He promised to send the King a memorandum on the subject. Crewe, who had also been to Balmoral, had no suggestions to offer, and thought there would probably be a civil war (Ponsonby of Shulbrede MSS).

Within days a memorandum by the former Unionist minister, Lord Balfour of Burleigh, handwritten on 1 September 1913, revealed the King's unhappiness with the way he was being treated by the government. The Prime Minister, he said, did not keep him informed. He had promised to provide a statement of his views on the constitutional question but had not yet done so. When he did, Lord Rosebery had counselled that the King must act on ministerial advice; but that HHA's paper must be answered point by point with future publication in mind. When the Chief Secretary for Ireland had said there would be trouble, the King had asked: if 'my troops' were to be used 'to shoot down those whose only offence is loyalty to me? Am I to give my consent to an Act which will bring that about without being sure the people wish it?' Birrell had, it seems, told the King that he was not himself averse to 'taking Ulster out for 5 or 7 years followed by a referendum'. But it was for the Unionists, not the government, to propose a compromise. 'The King then said—Mr Birrell had said he has a complete system of espionage & knew all that was said in Ireland as completely as the Russian Government did in Russia'. (Bowman, Carson's Army, *p.34, documents Birrell's complacency at this time, 'happily disregarding the warnings of impending militant action' in Royal Irish Constabulary reports.)*

Balfour of Burleigh recorded that he had advised the King to avoid any action that would enable the government to change the issue from the merits of their own legislation and administration, 'whether Insurance Act, Home Rule or Marconi', to one involving the constitutional position of the monarchy. The King spoke of having received a great deal of correspondence suggesting that he had the power to act. If he did not have the power 'he was no use and they had better have a republic' (Balfour of Burleigh MSS, 199).

Lord Lansdowne heard from the King 'in strict confidence' that Birrell was now convinced that 'Ulster was not merely bluffing, that he recognised that H.M.G. would have to reckon with serious resistance' ('Ld Ld Conversation with the King, Sept 6' [and 9 Sept.] 1913, Lansdowne MSS, uncat. when seen, BL). HHA sent the memorandum 'for royal consumption on the Constitutional position of the sovereign', expecting it to reach Balmoral while the Attorney General was in attendance. He wrote to Simon on 9 September that he had 'every reason to believe that H.M. is getting—or has got—into a sound frame of mind... But he is a good deal perturbed as to his moral obligations to seek peace & ensure it, by bringing about Conferences, consultations, confabulations, compromises & all the other C's (except civil war)' (Simon MSS). Speaking in confidence to his daughter on 13 September, HHA said that the King realised that Home rule was inevitable: 'He is just in a blue funk. Poor little man he isn't up to his position' (Bonham Carter & Pottle eds, Lantern Slides, p.391).

The King's frame of mind, made plain to Lansdowne and Bonar Law, was recorded in detail on 16 September 1913 by Lord Curzon after a conversation at Balmoral. The monarch's views had changed little since he had spoken to Balfour of Burleigh a fortnight earlier. The government was holding the sovereign to 'passive acquiescence in their declared policy of (a) refusing a referendum or a Gen. Election on Home Rule (b) demanding his assent to the Bill next June (c) postponing the coming into operation of the Act for 6 months or a year and taking a General Election in the interim'. Although his suggestion of a conference had been 'received with scorn', he was prepared to renew it now that the idea had been advanced by the former Liberal Lord Chancellor, Lord Loreburn, in a letter published in The Times on 11 September. He was still waiting for the memorandum HHA had promised on his constitutional duty, the possibility of separate treatment for Ulster, and the position of Ulster in relation to civil war (Curzon of Kedleston MSS, BL: A & AS, MSS.Eur.F.112 D/2/1).

By 6 October Fritz Ponsonby disclosed again to his brother Arthur that the Prime Minister had written 'several able memoranda but they don't help matters much'. Lansdowne was 'most uncompromising. He wouldn't hear of any conference and refused to give an inch. Bonar Law was much more inclined to listen to reason... Ever since Loreburn's letter however the whole of the Conservative Party smelt a trap and they fear they may be had.' (Ponsonby of Shulbrede MSS.) There is an important reminder by Nicholas Mansergh of the tactical differences between Lansdowne and Bonar Law: 'should the Unionists refuse to negotiate or should they concentrate their resistance on Ulster? Bonar Law favoured the first, Lansdowne the second... Bonar Law consistently emphasised Lansdowne's co-leadership status and paid deference to his opinions, *even when he did not share them'* (The Unresolved Question: The Anglo-Irish Settlement and its Undoing 1912–72, *Yale UP, New Haven and London, 1991, p.49).*

For the King's discomfort at the destruction of 'the very foundation of those precedents to which he would naturally look for guidance at the present time' see Vernon Bogdanor, The Monarchy and the Constitution, *Clarendon P., Oxford, 1995, pp.124–5, the exchange of correspondence with HHA in August, September, and October 1913 printed and analysed by Iain McLean in* What's Wrong with the British Constitution, *Oxford UP, 2010, pp.273–83,346–7, and Jane Ridley,* George V: Never a Dull Moment, *Harper, New York, 2021, pp.196–200.*

Oct. 14[25] Cabinet. Reassembled ministers all tanned except Haldane Runciman & Wood. Churchill took his seat without a nod to anyone, all others greeted one another. A cheery cabinet & no dissension but usual inability to complete points owing to interruption of others and great difficulty in those slow of speech or commencement getting an innings in the discussion.

Asquith gave a good a/c of Mrs Asquith who was staying at Cloan.[26] John Burns had been hiding in Spain, & much enjoyed his trip. P.M. asked Grey what he had 'to tell us'. Grey — the relations between Turkey & Greece had been very warlike, but at the moment there appeared a prospect that war might be temporarily averted. Turkey threatened Salonika if Aegean Islands are not restored. At Scutari — & in regard to the Albanian frontier, Austria had been an obstructive — her Admiral had withdrawn from Admiral Burney's[27] committee. The new commission was about to take over control & our Admiral would then be withdrawn.

The P.M. said this cabinet had been called to discuss land policy, but he thought he ought to inform his colleagues especially having regard to Lord Loreburn's letter to *The Times*, of the contents of 2 memoranda he had prepared for the King

1. Concerning the constitutional Power of the King to exercise his veto on legislation
2. The situation in Ireland created by the Home Rule Bill.

[25] In addition to the diary text for this date, there are six pages of notes that apparently form the latter part of JAP's original record from which the diary entry was compiled. Although there is a heading for 15 Oct., it is followed by a blank page. The following page is undated, but clearly refers to 14 Oct. and links the diary text for 14 Oct. with the loose notes.

[26] Cloan, in Perthshire, the Scots baronial seat of Richard Haldane and his sister Elizabeth.

[27] Admiral Sir Cecil Burney (1858–1929); head of special international naval force off Montenegro; Sub-Lt 1877; Cdr 1893; Cdr, Plymouth, Home Fleet 1911; Cdr 3rd Battle Squadron 1913; KCB 1913; 2 i-c, Grand Fleet 1914–16; Admiral 1916; 2nd Sea Lord 1916–17; Bt 1921. From Apr. to May 1913 Burney blockaded the Montenegrin coast; he then occupied Scutari May–Nov. 1913 until the council of peace was held. He received a special Foreign Office and Admiralty citation for his work.

Loreburn had said that passage of the Home Rule Bill was very likely, but that it would almost certainly lead to serious rioting. He therefore urged a conference of party leaders. A copy of the letter was circulated to the Cabinet by HHA on 20 September. HHA's two memoranda for the King are printed in J.A. Spender and Cyril Asquith, Life of Herbert Henry Asquith Lord Oxford and Asquith, *Hutchinson, 1932, Vol. II, pp.29–34. The King's reply is in Nicolson,* King George the Fifth, *pp.225–9. The Cabinet's reaction to intervention by Loreburn, 'an always disgruntled ex-colleague', as the Chief Secretary for Ireland called him, is crisply summarised in Ronan Fanning,* Fatal Path: British Government and Irish Revolution 1910–1922, *faber and faber, 2013, pp.79–81.*

The King asked for the 2 documents, & Asquith asked the King they should be treated by him as confidential, & Asquith thought there was no reason to believe he had shown them to anyone. The first memorandum appeared to have some effect on the King. In regard to the 2d all he knew was that the King was angry with Carson. In the 1st mem. he referred to the Power of the Sovereign to the Tudor days, & to the recognition of the Tudor monarchs that there was a reasonable limitation of the Powers to act over the head of Parliament. The Stuarts had pushed their powers beyond these limits with the result that Charles I lost his head & James II lost his throne, & disappeared into exile. This naive statement of history for the King's benefit produced much laughter. Since Qu. Anne the veto had never been exercised (no matter how the Monarch differed in his private view). It was Ministers who accepted the responsibility for the advice they gave, & for securing on their advice the assent of the King to the passage of bills. The King possessed the power to make suggestions or to advocate alterations or alternative courses, these had always been carefully considered, & possessed no less force than if they came from any other source no matter how great. The Sovereign had not exercised a veto for 200 years therefore & the last occasion on which on his own initiative he had changed his Ministers was 1834. When Wm IV one 'of the least wise of our monarchs' (laughter) dismissed Melbourne, who in a few months was recalled & remained in power 6 years.

The Parl. Act. did not deal with the constitution of the Crown but with the occasion when a difference occurred between the 2 Houses. The throne was at present free from responsibility for legislation but if the King intervened now, the people no longer would regard him as outside Party politics, & he would enter the arena of party and become in turn 'the football of contending factions'. This mem. ended by a reference to an opportunity being offered to the next Parliament, to deal with a situation before the Irish Parliament could itself meet, & obviously any resolution which occurred prior to such a date would be premature.

The P.M. then said in summing up to us 'The mem. after all only contains to us rudimentary truths, but sometimes it is as well to record them in plain language, & place them before the King'. He had obviously done this & we all laughed.

Mem. No. 2. Informed the King that the Importation of arms into Ulster had been comparatively small — some tens of thousands of inferior antiquated Italian weapons, but so far as the Police knew no ammunition had been provided, & Seely said he was advised none was now made, & it would cost £100,000 before plant could be erected to make one cartridge. If the Bill passed there would be resistance in places, with tumult probably in Belfast & possibly riot. If the bill was vetoed & wrecked Ireland would become ungovernable, strong feeling aroused outside in overseas dominions, coercion would ensue & an intolerable situation would be created.

The memoranda stated that subject to the passage of the bill, & its principles, if any proposals to meet Ulster were submitted they would be considered. But it was idle to regard a General Election as decisive on the question, as Marconi, Insurance, & other matters of interest would be bound to enter. Moreover a General Election would be opposed to the object for which the Parliament Bill was passed, & render it impotent.

The P.M. then looked at L.G. to begin & open a discussion on the Land Question but as there was obviously on his part a lack of preparation to open this discussion Crewe chipped in & asked Birrell to let us know how he regarded the situation in Ireland.

Irish situation

Birrell said the policy of giving rope to the Ulstermen up to the time of Loreburn's letter had been a success & Orange effort was proving itself to be more & more futile. The executive action had been wise prudent & produced good results. The publicity the theatrical display was regarded as signs of an organisation which if civil war occurred would be hopelessly smashed, but then came Loreburn's letter which was in Ireland interpreted as a White flag move prompted by a communication from his old colleagues — the flood of talk & press effort had had a bad effect. Carson's attitude was altered for the worse, 'the result of any civilian taking a salute always turns a man's head' (laughter).

The R.C. Clergy & Carsonians had so far restrained their followers, but an outbreak might anytime occur, & bloodshed to some extent was almost inevitable.

Morley urged, that the Irish Nationalist Leaders should be approached & that we should not attempt to find a means to conciliate Orangeism, unless the Nationalists would support the 3rd Reading of a bill. The question would not be settled if the Nationalist party abstained — owing to concessions which we might make to Ulster.

Birrell said he had had a talk with Lansdowne, who said he could not support Home Rule for Kerry,[28] & that it was equally impossible for Devlin[29] to except Belfast & his constituents from such a measure.

Churchill asked the cabinet not to close the door to a temporary exclusion of the homogenous anti national part of Ulster, & thought if we could avert a crisis by exempting Ulster for 5 years we ought to do it but only 'if Carson & the Tory party would accept the compromise' & agree not to repeal it'.[30]

Grey said we ought to find out whether we could pass the bill by consent — but to reject the measure meant prolonged coercion passive resistance, & the creation of hopeless position for the Liberal Party if they were in power.

We then discussed the land. I elicited from L.G. that the unsigned memorandum[31] which had been circulated was the work of Thring on instructions from a committee of which McKenna Grey Haldane & himself were self constituted members. L.G. began to roam a bit, & the P.M. then said the subject divided itself into several parts:

1. Labourer — remuneration, conditions, housing
2. Occupier — relations to owner, security, game damage, compensation for disturbance &c.
3. Owner — His powers & rent — & sale price of land

[28] Lansdowne had been the second largest landholder in Ireland in 1880. His favourite house, Derreen, was in Kerry. He was known as Ld Kerry from 1863 until he succeeded his father as 5th Marquess in 1866.

[29] Joseph 'Joe' Devlin (1871–1934); MP Belfast W 1906–22, Kilkenny N 1902–6; journalist (*Irish News* 1891–3 and *Freeman's Journal* 1895); leading Irish Nationalist party and National Volunteers organiser; argued that Ulster Unionist campaign was a 'gigantic bluff'. Sympathetically portrayed in A.C. Hepburn, *Catholic Belfast and Nationalist Ireland in the era of Joe Devlin, 1871–1934*, Oxford UP, 2008.

[30] JAP appears either to have omitted half of a pair of quotation marks or to have put in an extra half. As this portion of the text is highlighted by a manicule in the margin thus ☞, and as it is not clear where the missing quotation marks (if they *are* missing) should be placed, we print the text as it stands.

[31] The nine-page 'secret' memorandum, 'Land', 'which embodies the suggestions of some members of the Cabinet', had been circulated on 21 Aug. (TNA: CAB 37/116/56).

Runciman — urged the labourer's question was the most urgent — but the solution was very difficult as variations were so great. If we raised wages, the farmer could recoup at expense of labourer, in 3 ways

1. by raising rent of cottage
2. by diminishing or charging higher for allowances
3. by reducing labour employed turning plough into grass.

L.G. advocated creation of a Commission of Experts, with full power to deal with all these matters — so as to make labourer independent. He should be guaranteed a min. living wage, & all allowances abolished, an alternative house if sacked with an acre of land.

Hobhouse asked whether he advocated a method of farming to employ most labour, or that it should be farmed in the best way from an economic stand point.

Grey urged when land was bought, terms of purchase shd. be true value.

The P.M. said, if state credit were given for houses for labourers, it was difficult to prevent urban population absorbing them & that other interests mining &c wd want similar state help for new housing.

I referred to farmers displacing worst class of labour, by paying for piece work in lieu of time & a class of unemployed created, especially if we got the farmers' backs up.

Crewe put forward other difficulties, the incessant & unwieldy numbers of appeals.

Churchill advocated expropriation of landlord & eviction of tenants where land was not used to the best interest of the State.

Discussion adjourned to Wed. Oct 15.

Under Part III of the Housing of the Working Classes Act 1890 local authorities had built some 20,000 houses by 1914. The Housing and Town Planning Act 1909 had given the Local Government Board power to require local authorities to adopt Part III of the 1890 Act but requests for Exchequer grants to assist with the provision of subsidised housing had been rebuffed: 'in 1911 effective demand by well over a million households was too low in relation to costs for them to have a separate house' (A.E. Holmans, Housing Policy in Britain, A History, *Croom Helm, 1987, pp.32–49). The course of parliamentary debate on 'the housing and land problem' was abridged for students by Carlton Hayes in* British Social Politics: Materials Illustrating Contemporary State Action for the Solution of Social Problems, *Ginn, Boston, 1913, pp.263–346.*

DLG's Land Enquiry Committee, chaired by Arthur Acland, would recommend in 1914 that local authorities be required to provide 'adequate and sanitary housing accommodation' for the working-class population living or working in their areas. The Local Government Board was gathering information early in 1914 on housing across the country to determine the number of houses unfit for human habitation, or seriously defective in structure and convenience. Plans were in train for the 1915 budget to include an Exchequer grant of £4 million a year for urban authorities making satisfactory progress in providing local housing (Herbert Samuel, 'Urban Land & Housing Reform', Speech at Sheffield, 14 May 1914, Samuel MSS, SAM/A44/6, ff.13–21, PA; Paul Wilding, 'Towards Exchequer subsidies for housing 1906–14', Social and Economic Administration, *vol.6, no.1, 1972, pp.3–18; and Robert Millward and Sally Sheard, 'The urban fiscal problem, 1870–1914: government expenditure and finance in England and Wales',* Economic History Review, *XLVIII, no.3, 1995, pp.501–35).*

The anxious King's intention to follow the advice of his ministers had been conveyed to the Unionist leadership after HHA had made clear to the sovereign that, no matter what the outcome of an appeal to the electorate, the Unionists would continue to resist Home Rule (Loughlin, The British Monarchy and Ireland, *p.292, citing Stamfordham–Lansdowne, 9 Oct. 1913, Bonar Law MSS, BL/30/3/17, PA). HHA appears to have kept to himself the fact that he had arranged to have 'an informal conversation of a strictly confidential character' with Bonar Law at Sir Max Aitken's house, Cherkley Court, on the morning of 14 October. This was the first of several unpublicised meetings at which the party leaders sought to find common ground. Jack Sandars's notes on these meetings in October, November, and December are in Bodl. MS.Eng.hist.c.765, ff.195–203.*

As late as 19 November HHA declined to tell Margot who had arranged the meetings or where they were held (Margot Asquith diary, re 19 Nov. 1913, MS.Eng.d.3210, f.145). A valuable summary is R.J.Q. Adams, Bonar Law, *John Murray, 1999, pp.132–41. For the broader context of the tensions besetting Bonar Law see Thomas C. Kennedy, 'Troubled Tories: Dissent and Confusion concerning the Party's Ulster Policy, 1910–1914',* JBS, *vol.46, no.3, 2007, pp.570–93; John Ramsden,* The Age of Balfour and Baldwin 1902–1940, *Longman, 1978, pp.65–105, and an incisive article by Richard Murphy, 'Faction in the Conservative Party and the Home Rule Crisis, 1912–14',* History, *vol.71, no.232, 1986, pp.222–34.*

October 15 & 16[32]

[32] Possibly JAP has run together a description of three Cabinet meetings on 14, 15, and 16 Oct. In the text he wrote 'October 15 & 16' and left a blank page. HHA described the three meetings in one Cabinet letter on 18 Oct. (Bodl. MS. Asquith 7, ff.67–8). Harcourt has separate accounts of each of the three meetings (Bodl. MS.Eng.c.8268). Hobhouse's 17 Oct. entry covers '3 very long Cabinets' (David ed., *Inside Asquith's Cabinet,* pp.146–8). J.A. Cross, 'The Ministry of Land—1914 Version', *Public Administration,* Summer 1965, pp.215–20, the first scholarly study of these events, remains useful.

Oct. 18

At this point in the diary JAP attached a copy of a typescript memorandum with the following annotation:

> At the suggestion of Harcourt Ll. George on Oct 18. 1913 sent round the notes of the points upon which Cabinet decision was taken on the Land Question on Oct. 15. 1913.

Formation of Ministry of Lands and Forests.

To have cognisance and supervision of all questions affecting the user of land in town and country. [Scotland and Ireland outside: Scotch and Irish Secretaries to have corresponding powers.]

Powers

a. Powers now being discharged by Board of Agriculture, including Ordnance Survey.
b. Land transfer and whole existing machinery for registration of title.
c. Powers under settled Land Act and under Lord Chancellor's new Bill to enable trustees and life tenants to deal with the land.
d. Land valuation.
e. New powers for dealing with waste land and under–cultivated land, reclamation, afforestation, land purchase, conditions of the agricultural labourer (wages and hours) differences between landlord and tenant that interfere with the effective development and cultivation of the soil.

Operating through Commissioners failing conciliation.

Towns

Improvements tenant wishes to effect in town tenancies of business premises.
Conditions of renewal of leases.
Alterations in conditions of lease.
Prohibitions and restrictions.

Acquisition of Land

Extension of powers of municipalities to acquire land in town and country for present or prospective uses.

Value of Land

Present moment capricious and extravagant.

Price to be fixed by Commissioners.

Municipalities — Admiralty,[33] housing, small holdings.

To deal with cases where landlord cannot afford to improve or reclaim, especially owing to family charges or mortgage.

a. Power to authorise scheme.
b. To authorise loans.
c. To make it first charge where mortgagee agrees.
d. To abate family charges.

Game

Disputes between landlord and tenant.

Additional protection to tenant.

Cases of Undercultivation

Power to acquire and develop land where uncultivated or undercultivated either through:

a. Game.
b. Lack of capital or enterprise.
c. Grazing — wilson wilderness.[34]

Waste Land

Powers of reclamation and afforestation.

Wages and Hours of Labour

Powers to deal with this either by wages board, or order of the Land Ministry acting through Commissioners.

[33] Admiralty concern about the housing of men to be employed in the new naval base at Rosyth prompted consideration of a co-partnership scheme 'on garden city lines' and the need for a 'general housing policy' (Swenarton, *Homes Fit for Heroes*, pp.44–7).

[34] 'Runciman told me about the Wilson Wilderness in Berkshire and Wiltshire. Run like a ranch' (MacCallum Scott diary, 30 June 1913, MacCallum Scott MSS). There are copies of the memo, with slight variations in the covering note, in the Illingworth MSS and Harcourt MSS with DLG's covering letter to 'my colleagues' referring to 'the points upon which the Cabinet decision was taken during our discussion this week on the Land Question' (Bodl. MS. Harcourt 443, ff.201–5).

Capricious Evictions

Conciliation — Failing that then through Commissioners:

a. Award compensation, or,
b. Keep cultivator on ground.

Sale of estates not to be sufficient ground for giving notice to quit.

Rent

No interference with landlord's power to exact present rent or to increase; but appeal to land ministry where:

a. Contributions towards minimum wage.
b. Increase of rent.
c. Great change in agricultural conditions.
d. In all cases of small farms for existing as well as future rents.

Conciliation to come first.

Conditions of Tenancy

Where they interfere with the best use of land.

Cottages (tied)

Some extension of length of notice.

Housing

In rural areas to be undertaken by Central authority.
To be let as far as possible at economic rent.

What the Cabinet appears to have agreed on 15 October echoes some of the arguments in a memorandum by Haldane's brother Sir William Haldane advocating a powerful land commission. A copy of the 'Note on Land Reform' written in September was with the Prime Minister (Bodl. MS. Asquith 25, ff.56–62). Runciman had given it to DLG, who passed on a copy to Harcourt after the 14 October meeting, describing 'Willie's scheme' as 'a singularly able document' (E. Haldane diary, [Oct.–Nov. 1913], Elizabeth Haldane MSS, MS. 20240, f.56, NLS; Bodl. MS. Harcourt 443, ff.192–200). On 17 October Sir George Riddell prepared the ground for the next edition of the British Weekly, *whose last leader was, according to DLG, 'the only one in which the true inwardness of the situation had been indicated'. The Chancellor's next 'great speech' would be at Swindon the following Wednesday, 'when he will explain in detail the plan which has been determined by the Government. This was settled at the Cabinet yesterday.' (Robertson Nicoll MSS.)*

At Bedford, as Runciman's PPS Cecil Harmsworth reported to his chief on 19 October, 'Ll-G was received with unabated fervour in spite of Marconi' (Runciman of Doxford MSS). With the Cabinet now committed, DLG announced at Swindon on 22 October a programme encompassing an agricultural minimum wage, the proposed new ministry, and State land purchase. And, as his former colleague and veteran land reform campaigner, the Marquess of Lincolnshire, rejoiced to his wife the next day, 'a Land Court: to which farmers can appeal' (Lincolnshire MSS, Bodl. MS. Film 1140 [7]). Site value rating was not mentioned. A rare handwritten letter by DLG to Clementine Churchill on 24 October shows the Chancellor's commitment to harnessing his colleagues to the reform agenda: 'Winston's Manchester speech was first rate. How well he put the labourers' case. I want him so much to help in this great struggle. No living man can present an issue as brilliantly as he can' (Lady Spencer-Churchill MSS, CSCT 3/15, CAC). In a note on 27 October to Pamela McKenna, who had written to congratulate him, DLG said: 'The Home Secretary has helped me so much over the Land Question that I feel he has a large share in the success of the Government Scheme.' (McKenna MSS, MCKN 9/5, CAC.) On the dismal failure of minimum wage advocacy see Alun Howkins and Nicola Verdon, 'The state and the farm worker: the evolution of the minimum wage in agriculture in England and Wales, 1909–24', Agricultural History Review, vol.57, no.2, 2009, pp.257–74. It was not until a speech at Middlesbrough in the second week of November that DLG allayed the fears of those in the party who thought that 'some influence must be at work to keep him quiet on the Rating question' (C. Trevelyan–DLG, 2 Nov. 1913, Lloyd George MSS, LG/C/12/4/3, PA; Trevelyan–Runciman, 3 Nov. 1913, Runciman of Doxford MSS; P.W. Raffan–C. Trevelyan, 7 Nov. 1913, Trevelyan MSS, Newc. U. Spec. Coll.). DLG's land tax scheme, announced in the 1909 budget, entailed differentiating between gross value (including improvements) and site value without improvements. Valuation of all the land was expected to take until 1915 and require some 5,000 Inland Revenue staff (Offer, Property and Politics, 1870–1914, pp.363–9, is the best guide to the land taxation proposals). On the operational and legal difficulties encountered in the administration of the undeveloped land duty, increment value duty, and reversion duty see John H.N. Pearce, 'Lloyd George's Land Values Duties', in Peter Harris and Dominic de Cogan eds, Studies in the History of Tax Law, Vol. 9, Bloomsbury Publishing, 2019, pp.279–306.

Although JAP makes no reference to it in his jottings on Cabinet proceedings and other conversations, the government could not have been unaware of the political strategy now being pursued by their opponents. In mid-1913 Conservative Central Office was encouraging a national campaign against 'Home Rule, Socialism, and Radical Land Robbery' (H.V. Emy, 'The Land Campaign: Lloyd George as a Social Reformer, 1909–14', in A.J.P. Taylor ed., Lloyd George: Twelve Essays, Hamish Hamilton, 1971, p.54). But the emphasis shifted at the end of October. The Opposition Chief Whip and Party Chairman had sent out a 'strictly *confidential' letter to Unionist members urging that every opportunity should be taken of 'voicing your own horror that civil war should be thrust upon us'. And they were not to be 'led away into attacking Mr. George's Land Policy, but to dismiss it either in silence or quite shortly with ridicule and contempt'. DLG's advocacy was 'only a blind to obscure the real issue'; devoting attention to his proposals was 'only to play his own game' (Lord Edmund Talbot and Arthur Steel-Maitland, 30 Oct. 1913, Sir Malcolm Fraser MSS, Bodl. MS.Eng.c.4788, f.30: Ian Packer, 'The Conservatives and the Ideology of Landownership, 1910–1914', in Martin Francis and Ina Zweiniger-Bargielowska eds,* The Conservatives and British Society 1880–1990, *U. of Wales P., 1996, p.45). For an acute appreciation of Bonar Law's thinking see Andrew Taylor, 'Conservative Electoral Strategy, Creating Political Stability and the Advent of Mass Democracy, 1914–18', in Keith Dockray and Keith Laybourn eds,* The Representation and Reality of War: The British Experience; Essays in Honour of David Wright, *Sutton Publishing, Stroud, 1999, pp.127–51.*

Bonar Law's objective of forcing the government to a general election over Home Rule is set out persuasively in Jeremy Smith, 'Bluff, Bluster and Brinkmanship: Andrew Bonar Law and the Third Home Rule Bill', HJ, *vol.36, no.1, 1993, pp.161–78, which should be read with his valuable essay 'Conservative Ideology and Representations of the Union with Ireland, 1885–1914', in Francis and Zweiniger-Bargielowska eds,* The Conservatives and British Society 1880–1990, *pp.18–38. Daniel Ziblatt offers an argument that the Conservative Party was becoming 'increasingly nimble and self-confident' at this time (*Conservative Parties and the Birth of Democracy, *pp.159–53). Mansergh's chapter on 'The Unionist Dimension 1912–14: One Nation or Two?' is as insightful as it is elegant (*The Unresolved Question, *pp.43–78).*

JAP missed the last two Cabinet meetings in October: 'we talked nothing but land and housing' Harcourt told him on 24 October. 'The typed memo. of Ll.G as to our decisions was circulated at my request in order to avoid misunderstanding, and I think the Swindon speech fairly represents our conclusions though not stated exactly in our language' (MS. Gainford 84/20). The Ministry of Lands and Forests document had already found its way into the Board of Agriculture; and before the Cabinet DLG had expounded the policy embodied in it at lunch with Lord Lucas, Runciman's Parliamentary Secretary (Arthur Gaye–Runciman, 23 Oct. 1913, Runciman of Doxford MSS). For an interpretation of the Swindon speech as making land reform 'consonant with a radical tradition of social reformist patriotism' see Readman, Land and Nation in England, *pp.72–7.*

November 11 All present except McKinnon Wood.

The P.M. alluded to the bye elections at Reading & Linlithgow. He admitted Reading loss was a foregone conclusion — but there had been a dropped [vote] of 1000 & an increased vote of 1300 to the Tory & apparently largely due to

Ulsteria — & Ulster canvassers work. George said he thought Larkin's[35] imprisonment in Dublin had much to do with labour dissent.

I said it was not so much Larkin's imprisonment but the contrast between the Govmt prosecution of Larkin for sedition, & neglecting to prosecute a man in Carson's position who preached sedition if H.R. passed & armed & drilled forces to resist law, which rankled in the minds of the electors, & I had found at Rotherham it was hard to justify.[36] Ll. George alluded to the acrimony & method of prosecution. Crewe & Morley [said] it was in Carson's best style in days of yore. Birrell said, tradition died down slowly in Ireland; but that if there had been no prosecution, the mob would have got the upper hand, & the soldiery would have been introduced with fatal results. It was decided to liberate Larkin early but the occasion was left to Birrell.

James Larkin had been found guilty of sedition and sentenced to seven months' imprisonment on 27 October. The charge arose from riots in Dublin in August, when Larkin had asked for support of his striking tram-men by a general withholding of rent (David Dickson, Dublin: The Making of a Capital City, *Profile Books, 2014, pp.425–34, is a perceptive analysis of the social and industrial context; and see Anastasia Dukova,* A History of the Dublin Metropolitan Police and its Colonial Legacy, *palgrave macmillan, 2016, pp.112–14). A meeting, in the Albert Hall on 1 November, demanding his release, was chaired by George Lansbury; the speakers included George Bernard Shaw. Reporting to the King about a Cabinet meeting on 11 November, HHA revealed that the Chancellor of the Exchequer and the Attorney General 'commented severely' on the packing of the jury and the tone of the prosecution by the Irish Law Officers. 'A large majority of the Cabinet was of opinion that the prosecution was impolitic & unnecessary & calculated to do more harm than good' (Bodl. MS. Asquith 7, f.69, misdated 12 Nov. by the writer).* The Times *reported on 12 November that 'three of the most prominent men in the Ministry' supported Larkin's release. The newspaper went on: 'the outcome of the deliberations of the Cabinet appears to be that the circumstances*

[35] James Larkin (1876–1947); organiser, Irish Transport and General Workers' Union 1906–14; in USA 1914–22, he was deported for 'anarchistic activities' (he had denounced conscription); expelled Ireland 1924 (he was born in Liverpool); represented Ireland at Third International and claimed to be one of 25 men whom the Soviet government had chosen to rule the world; elected to Dail 1927, but election declared invalid because of his bankruptcy; elected to Dail 1937.

[36] In his diary for 11 Nov., Hobhouse wrote: 'Pease added that he had been severely heckled by his constituents over Larkin and Carson' (David ed., *Inside Asquith's Cabinet*, p.149). Seven months later the *Sheffield Telegraph* London correspondent wrote of seeing JAP 'wandering about the smoke-room of the House of Commons, a lonely and solitary figure, trying vainly to get on terms of good fellowship with Labour members' (*Rotherham Express*, 25 July 1914).

of Larkin's trial will be considered afresh and that occasion will shortly be found for his discharge from prison . . .'. The Cabinet (reported The Times*) feared that Larkin's release would be seen as a sop for Labour votes just before by-elections. Larkin was released on 13 November. By contrast to the Cabinet, 'the majority of Nationalist MPs were hostile to, threatened by and unprepared for the radicalization of Irish labour under Larkin' (James McConnel,* The Irish Parliamentary Party and the Third Home Rule Crisis, *Four Courts P., Dublin, 2013, p.181). There is an abundance of source material and interpretive essays in Donal Nevin ed.,* James Larkin: Lion of the Fold, *Gill & MacMillan, 2006, and Conor McNamara and Pádraig Yeates eds,* The Dublin Lockout, 1913: New Perspectives on Class War & its Legacy, *Irish Academic P., Newbridge, 2017.*

Rufus Isaacs had narrowly held Reading in December 1910. On his appointment as Lord Chief Justice, the Liberals nominated the respected European historian G.P. Gooch. Gooch had won Bath for the Liberals on 1906 but could not hold it in 1910. Major Leslie Wilson, the previously defeated Unionist who had been 'sitting on the doorstep for three years', had a comfortable victory in Reading. Wilson recalled in his unpublished memoirs: 'F.E. Smith at a crowded meeting at the Town Hall said: "I advise you to set Mr Gooch free to devote his talents to History. He might write The Decline & Fall of the Liberal Party & two other volumes How I lost Bath & the second How I lost Reading."' (Sir Leslie Orme Wilson MSS, UQFL36, Box 1A, courtesy of Peter Wilson.) Gooch's well-known temperance advocacy and doubts about his soundness on defence had not helped him. Nor had patchy unpopularity of national insurance, which had also been a factor in earlier by-election defeats at Somerset South (Sept. 1911), Ayrshire North (Dec. 1911), Midlothian (Sept. 1912), and Newmarket (May 1913). The campaigning of the anti-Semitic League for Clean Government was a negligible factor, but the intervention of a British Socialist Party candidate who won over 1,000 votes, more than 10 per cent of the total, was critical (Kenneth Lunn, 'Political Anti-Semitism Before 1914: Fascism's Heritage', in Kenneth Lunn and Richard C. Thurlow eds, British Fascism: Essays on the Radical Right in Inter-War Britain, *Croom Helm, [1980], pp.20–40; Bill Moran, '1913 Jim Larkin and the British Labour Movement',* https://www.irishlabourhistorysociety.com/labour-history/1913-lockout/, accessed 1 Dec. 2022, Irish Labour History Society; *G.P. Gooch,* Under Six Reigns, *Longmans, Green, 1958, p.159; Frank Eyck,* G. P. Gooch: A Study in History and Politics, *Macmillan, 1982, pp.177–84). Stephen Yeo,* Religion and Voluntary Organisation in Crisis, *Croom Helm, 1976, is informative on welfare, Labour, and politics in Reading; and, for A.L. Bowley's research in 1912 showing that 19 per cent of the town's population, and 47 per cent of children not earning, were living in primary poverty, see David J. Jeremy,* Capitalists and Christians: Business Leaders and the Churches in Britain, 1900–1960, *Clarendon P., Oxford, 1990, pp.153–5.*

Although J.W. Pratt held Linlithgow for the Liberals, the majority of his admired predecessor, Alexander Ure, shrank by 75 per cent. Observers noted the large number of Irish in *the Scottish constituency and the presence of 'emissaries' of the Irish Labour Party at both Reading and Linlithgow (*The Spectator*, 15 Nov. 1913, p.18). There had been no Labour candidate at Linlithgow, and there was press speculation that the Tories benefited from working-class voters protesting against the treatment of Larkin and his supporters (Griffin,* The British Electorate*, p.312).*

Potentially significant speeches were to be given by the Prime Minister and the Opposition leader. The Palace was closely monitoring developments. Stamfordham agreed with Hopwood that 'Asquith went as far as he could' on Ireland. He wrote to Bonar Law to 'beg him to meet the P.M. half way & say nothing which may tend to close the door against the suggested frank interchange of views' (Stamfordham–Hopwood, 27 Oct. 1913, Southborough MSS, Bodl. MS.Eng.c.7362).

Asquith then told us that, after his speech at Ladybank & Bonar Law's at Newcastle, he had had a private interview with B.L. at a place not far from London. No one knew of it, & they had freely discussed the position. Any proposal for Home Rule within Home Rule, or separate Parliament for Ulster was out of the question. He & Carson favoured one settlement by consent between the 2 parties, namely, that there should be a group of counties in Ulster left out of the Bill. The Prime Minister suggested 'temporarily' only. Bonar Law said no permanently but with power after a period to come in when they wished by a plebiscite of all the counties, but not separately. They discussed Post Office & the P.M. said we had transferred so little that that might be arranged, & kept in Imperial hands. Police was a reserved service. Apportionment of money might be arranged. Education was difficult & required consideration as we could not take it on at Whitehall. Home Office might be left where it was in factory & mines.

He had not in any way committed himself or his colleagues. B.L. said that he would have no less difficulty than the P.M. might have but the Diehard group would resent any giving H.R. to any part of Ireland — & Lansdowne & Balfour took this view but the H of L. would accept such a settlement.

The P.M. asked us to consider the proposal before meeting again on Thursday.

The meeting, at Sir Max Aitken's Cherkley on 6 November, is described from a contemporary memorandum and letter by Law, in Adams, Bonar Law*, pp.136–9. Ronan Fanning (*Fatal Path*, p.99) explains the genuine misunderstanding about the conclusion of the meeting: Law believing that HHA would himself propose to Cabinet what the two men had tentatively agreed rather than merely report it.*

I told George in preparing estimates we would want at B. of E. 2 millions.

JAP was not to know that DLG would dine with HHA, Crewe, Grey, and Haldane that night to discuss naval estimates and the budget, the Irish question, and electoral strategy (Note of Points discussed at dinner at 11 Downing St, November 12th 1913, typescript, Lloyd George MSS, LG/C/14/1/10, PA). Bentley Gilbert thought this meeting 'something of a mystery', as the ministers invited were 'all cronies of Asquith not of Lloyd George' ('David Lloyd George: the Reform of British Land-Holding and the Budget of 1914', HJ, *vol.21, no.1, 1978, p.127). These were nobody's cronies but the most senior members of the Cabinet, who were there to talk about the political future of the government. The absence of WSC might have been a clue. The deliberations of the group and the ensuing treatment of plans for educational expenditure are well described in Bruce K. Murray, 'Lloyd George, the Navy Estimates, and the Inclusion of Rating Relief in the 1914 Budget',* WHR, *vol.15, no.1, 1990, pp.58–78.*

Nov. 13 All present — we discussed fully the Ulster situation, & eventually the P.M. summed up the situation that he should see Redmond & explain to him the position.

1. Ulster would fight — was arming — could arm — & had plans (Birrell, George).
2. Soldiery could be relied on to overcome opposition (Seely).
3. The shedding of blood might set back Home Rule (as Morley said).
4. To pass H.R. with Ulster excluded would be impossible. Liberals would have none of it (Harcourt & Burns).
5. To pass H.R. with Ulster temporarily excluded might mean loss of consent Carson could not accept it (Asquith).
6. To pass HR. with Ulster temporarily excluded, would arouse permanent Ulster opposition (Crewe).
7. To pass H.R. by consent would make opposition of Ulster very half hearted as years went on (Churchill & Pease) & worth much.
8. 7 could not be adopted if Irish would not have H.R. at the price.

*HHA saw Redmond on 17 November and gave him an account of the meeting and the proposal, attributed to DLG, to exclude the Protestant counties of the North for five years. In what Fanning (*Fatal Path*, p.91) calls 'a languid display of economy with the truth', the Prime Minister conveyed the impression that neither he nor the Cabinet had come to a conclusion on this suggestion. In fact, if the report to the King is to be believed, DLG's suggestion 'met with a good deal of support' (Bodl. MS. Asquith 7, f.72). HHA also told Redmond the results of his talks with Bonar Law. He asked Redmond to consider these and to let him know his comments (Memorandum by HHA, 17 Nov. 1913, Bodl. MS. Asquith 39, ff.23–6). Redmond replied with a long letter on 24 November (Bodl. MS. Asquith 39,* *ff.29–35). Extracts from the letter are included in Denis Gwynn,* The Life of John Redmond, *George C. Harrap, 1932, pp.234–7.*

DLG met John Dillon on the same day. Dillon was prepared to contemplate temporary exclusion but not before the Home Rule Bill had passed. Redmond was 'much more hostile' and preferred 'local autonomy to Ulster'. Neither man wanted proposals or offers to be made to the Unionists at this stage. HHA let it be known that rumours of Cabinet divisions were unfounded. The Prime Minister and Nationalist leader publicly affirmed their loyalty to each other (Joseph P. Finnan, John Redmond and Irish Unity, 1912–1918, *Syracuse UP, 2004, pp.63–4). The announced formation of the Irish Volunteers in Dublin on 25 November 1913 was a harbinger of conflict that the government could not ignore. The Volunteers were an independent force outside the control of Redmond's Nationalist Party although Redmond was soon to sanction the Volunteers as 'a home rule army' (McConnel,* The Irish Parliamentary Party and the Third Home Rule Crisis, *p.270).*

After Cabinet I asked Asquith if I could have the Sec. & Medl. Officer salaries raised at the B. of Education. I thought the status should be raised. He very kindly replied, it ought to be done all round B. of E. & B. of A., & he would talk to the Chancellor but I knew the difficulties.

The Permanent Secretaries at the Boards of Education and Agriculture were paid £1,800 p.a., the Chief Medical Officer £1,500. The Permanent Secretaries (or their equivalent) at the Local Government Board, the Home Office, and the Treasury, were paid £2,000 p.a. The Treasury Secretary would soon join his counterpart at Foreign Affairs on £2,500. All of them were entitled to a non-contributory pension of one-sixtieth of salary per year of service (J.D. Rimington, 'Some Observations on the Salaries of Permanent Secretaries', Public Administration, *vol.60, winter 1982, p.473).*

A few weeks later Sir George Newman, still the Chief Medical Officer at the Board of Education, wrote to tell JAP that Lord Moulton had offered him the post of Secretary to the newly formed Medical Research Council at a salary of £2,000 p.a. After discussing the offer with Sidney and Beatrice Webb, Waldorf Astor, his long-term ally Sir Robert Morant, and Christopher Addison, Newman said that he preferred to stay where he was, but could not afford to continue at the same salary. He pointed out that when he had come to the Board in 1907 he had been earning £1,500 in private practice, but had accepted a salary of £1,200; his salary was raised to £1,500 in 1910. HHA agreed with JAP that Newman 'ought to be retained for Education' and undertook to do what he could to have his salary raised to 'an adequate figure'. To retain the differential between the Chief Medical Officer and the Permanent Secretary, Sir Amherst Selby-Bigge, Newman's salary was augmented by a personal allowance of £300 p.a.

from February 1914 (Newman diary 18, 20 Dec. 1913, 6, 15 Jan. 1914, Newman MSS, TNA: MH 139; Newman–JAP, 29 Dec. 1913, 1 Jan. 1914; HHA–JAP, 3 Jan.1914, and Selby-Bigge–JAP, 16 Jan. 1914, MS. Gainford 85/2–9).

He told me Margot was better, & Elizabeth now acquiring some new language — Spanish?

Nov. 17 Asquith took very serious view of announcement in *Times* that showed cabinet leakage. Such leakage may mean the loss of H.R. — & disaster. Morley Crewe & Buxton admitted meeting The Editor at Country House from Sat to Mon — but all assured the points named had been ignored in their conversations.

McKenna told Hobhouse that WSC was the offender. Hobhouse thought that the culprit, 'though unintentional', was Morley (Hobhouse diary, 18 Nov. 1913, David ed., Inside Asquith's Cabinet, *p.150). McKenna had his own reasons for pointing to his successor as First Lord, having suspected that WSC had leaked against his navy estimates. Two days later HHA was denouncing both DLG and WSC in a long conversation during a drive to Windsor. DLG, he said, was disloyal only by temperament but WSC was mentally disloyal and 'a cad': 'a more unteachable creature or one more hopelessly without judgment I haven't got in the whole Government…'. The condemnation continued with an unflattering assessment of WSC's senior naval advisers. The more he saw of the navy's best men, 'the more disappointed I am in their brains' (Margot Asquith diary, referring to 19 Nov. 1913, and note added re information from DLG in Mar. 1914, Bodl. MS.Eng.d.3210, ff.138–41).*

We discussed estimates. George was for no increase of taxation but Churchill wants 6 M. & I wanted 2! P.O. servants also discussed.

Runciman's notes on '1914–5 Finance' (Runciman of Doxford MSS) show that, in addition to the funds required for the Navy and Education, the Army needed an extra £800,000 and the Civil Service £1,250,000. 'The above figures', Runciman wrote on 17 November, 'were recited with the object of warning the spending depts of the calamities their extravagance brings on us!' The Prime Minister's three-page summary of the deliberations on the prospective financial situation gave prominence to JAP:

> Mr Pease urgently pressed the needs of the Education Department. The proportion of the burden falling on the local rates, as compared with that borne by the Exchequer, has enormously increased—in a vastly swollen total—since Mr Balfour's act of 1902. The local authorities are clamouring for the relief, which has long

been promised them but, so far, not granted. He estimates £3,800,000 is the smallest additional sum which the Exchequer can be called upon to pay, but would be reluctantly content during the coming year with £2,000,000.

HHA and DLG had seen JAP coming. 'They assented entirely to the reasonableness of his claim, which both thought ought to be put eventually at not less than £5,000,000 ...'. But the local authorities had an 'equally neglected grievance'. They needed £5,000,000 for roads, housing, sanitation, asylums, and other services of a national character. Without economies elsewhere in the Budget, more than 3d. would have to be added to the income tax. Over the next two days Cabinet also heard Samuel's representations about unrest in the Postal Service and the need for over £500,000 for immediate wage increases and another £200,000 for 'inevitable' future increases. On 18 November he was authorised to make some 'small additional concessions' to the worst-paid classes (Bodl. MS. Asquith 7, ff.74–5). He had already secured approval to offer the 'suave and assured meritocrat' railway manager and industrial conciliator Sir Guy Granet £3,000 a year to assist 'in the management of this vast department'. Granet declined the appointment (Samuel–Granet correspondence, 13, 25, 28 Nov. 1913, Granet MSS, MSS 191, MRC; David Howell 'Railway Safety and Labour Unrest: The Aisgill Disaster of 1913', in Chris Wrigley and John Shepherd eds, On the Move: Essays in Labour and Transport History Presented to Philip Bagwell, *Hambledon P., 1991, p.132).*

Although JAP's account does not mention them, naval estimates were again discussed on 18 November. Leith Ross, about to return to the Treasury after two years as one of the Prime Minister's private secretaries, squeezed key points into his appointment diary: 'Churchill wants 52 millions. Rather a rumpus. Chanc^r^ thinks he can provide 6 mills without further taxation' (TNA: T 188/263).

Nov. 18[37] We discussed Samuel's estimates — & Ll. George tried to reduce his demands.

We discussed situation in Natal & Harcourt undertook to wire to Gladstone to find out position of Indian Coolies & their treatment. Decided to assert ourselves as to suitable treatment as subjects under Crown but not to intervene in regard to admission or exclusion from dominions.

In June 1913 the South African Government had amended its laws governing Indian immigration, giving itself the power to exclude anyone deemed 'undesirable' on the grounds of race, class, occupation, or character. It imposed an education test on would-be immigrants.

[37] JAP misdated this entry 19 Nov. (HHA Cabinet letter, 18 Nov. 1913, Bodl. MS. Asquith 7, ff.74–5; *The Times*, 19 Nov. 1913).

In addition, the Orange Free State had debarred Asians from trading, farming, or owning land. It also imposed a £3 poll tax on Indians remaining after their indentures had expired. The various measures had been questioned by the Government of India without any result, and in September 1913 a passive resistance movement (led by M.K. Gandhi) began. The arrest of Gandhi and other leaders led to a wave of strikes by the Indians that seriously affected the Natal coal mines and sugar plantations. By 19 November 19 this had become a general strike among the Indians, who demanded that the Imperial Government intervene.

A speech by the Viceroy of India condemning the 'unjust and invidious' South African laws infuriated Harcourt. Lord Hardinge escaped serious rebuke for the embarrassment he caused the Colonial Office, and the South African government appointed a committee of inquiry whose recommendations were put into law in July 1914. The poll tax was abandoned and immigration rules forbidding the entry of Indian wives were relaxed. Gandhi left South Africa for India in the same month, describing the settlement as 'generous'. The Cabinet's position was doubly complicated, for at the same time the Government of India was protesting against Canada's total exclusion of Indians (Gandhi's activity at this time is illuminated by Ramachandra Guha, Gandhi Before India, *Allen Lane, 2013, pp.455–529, and, from a different viewpoint, Ashwin Desai and Goolem Vahed,* The South African Gandhi: Stretcher-Bearer of Empire, *Stanford UP, 2015; for Harcourt's perturbation and the cool response of Crewe as Secretary of State for India see Guy Desvaux de Marigny, 'The Public Career of Lewis Harcourt (first Viscount) 1905–1916', MA thesis, U. of the Witwatersrand, Johannesburg, 1987, pp.199–200).*

I urged my claim to 2 million for education on its merits but got little support.

Before Cabinet saw George & Asquith. Both admitted my case for money, but afraid of new taxation. Asquith argued it but thought on line of help for loan charges an arrangement could be come to.

19.XI.13.[38]
Board of Education,
Whitehall,
London, S.W.

Private

My dear Walter,

Haldane's utterance at the Eighty Club on Monday has given me a good deal of correspondence. He has never altered, & never seems to have fully grasped our

[38] Perhaps written in Dec. and wrongly dated.

view — he talked the same way in 1902, & was the only Liberal who supported that bill, he never realised its blemishes, only its coordinating merits. He has been consistent & explained that in stating 'one party was just as sectarian as the other' [*sic*] he was only stating his own view. It is as you know *not* the view of his colleagues & you had better tell your correspondent this. I told this to the deputation, Drs Clifford, Shakespeare, Meyer, Lidgett[39] &c who saw the Prime Minister & me on Wednesday, & satisfied them I think.

My own words, which your correspondent asks about, had reference to a resolution which the leaders of the Nonconformists have passed, in which they ask for a rent to be paid for schools belonging to other denominations in single school areas. These proposals seem to me to go beyond what we ought to do, & by endowing the church, will queer the pitch if later on we can get rid of the dual system in other than single school areas. I referred to their proposal as one which did not 'champion confiscation' & which our opponents always say, is part of our programme.

Yours ever,
Joseph A. Pease
(Runciman of Doxford MSS)

This seems to refer to a letter a few days earlier from the Batley textile manufacturer and Liberal councillor Hamilton Crothers, known to JAP as an active figure in the movement for the suppression of the opium trade. Crothers spoke of fears caused by Haldane's remarks, 'which it took yourself, Mr Percy Illingworth & others some trouble to allay'. Haldane's words have been 'seized on by Tories everywhere'.

[39] *Dr John Howard Shakespeare* (1857–1928); Sec. of Baptist Union of Great Britain and Ireland 1898–1924, European Sec. of Baptist World Alliance, Pres., National Council of Evangelical Free Churches 1916, Moderator of Federal Council of Evangelical Free Churches of England 1919–21, trusted adviser to DLG when Prime Minister (Peter Shepherd, 'John Howard Shakespeare and the English Baptists, 1898–1924', Ph.D. thesis, U. of Durham, 1999). *Dr Frederick Brotherton Meyer* (1847–1929); leading Baptist pastor and evangelist; minister, Regent's Park Church; Pres., Baptist Union 1906–7; 'Quaker ancestry…not by nature a controversialist' (Jane T. Stoddart, *My Harvest of the Years*, Hodder and Stoughton, 1938, p.141; Ian Randall, 'Mere Denominationalism: F. B. Meyer and Baptist Life', *Baptist Quarterly*, vol.35, no.1, 1993, pp.19–34). *Dr John Scott Lidgett* (1854–1953); Wesleyan Methodist, founder of the Bermondsey Settlement, foremost Methodist theologian and spokesman of his generation; LCC Progressive alderman 1905–28 (Alan Turberfield, *John Scott Lidgett: Archbishop of British Methodism?*, Epworth P., Peterborough, 2003). See also Anthony R. Cross, *Baptism and the Baptists: theology and practice in twentieth-century Britain*, Wipf & Stock, Eugene, Oregon, 2017, pp.43–52.

Nov. 24[40] We discussed Ulster. P.M. told us he had seen a deputation come in a Nicodemian fashion of protestants from Ulster who favoured unity & no exclusion under a Home Rule Bill.

The sympathetic Pharisee, Nicodemus, 'came to Jesus by night' (John 3:1). HHA met the Irish deputation secretly. Its members, differing widely in religion and politics, claimed that only a very small number of workers wanted revolution. Nevertheless pressure was exerted on the workers to join the Volunteers, and they estimated that 20 per cent of all Protestants belonged to the Volunteers, of whom some 10,000–20,000 would resort to violence.

He read a letter from Redmond asking Gov. not to initiate any proposal to settle Ulster question or exclude it. We decided that we should not commit ourselves, but to be ready to close with any reasonable proposal which meant H.R. by Consent whenever it came — that to float H.R. in blood was not the right way to promote Home Rule as a settlement, but we must adhere to a H.R. Parl. & Exec. at Dublin.

On 29 October the London correspondent of the Glasgow Herald *had revealed Redmond's growing sensitivity about the reporting of his speeches: 'Mr Redmond seems to have been at unusual pains to obtain fair and accurate reports of the speech he made today. Of late he has written most of his speeches, but I do not know that he has ever before supplied the press with advance copies.'*

JAP does not mention the meeting of 1 December at which the Attorney General briefed on the Common and Statutory law penalising illegal drilling, and Cabinet decided to do nothing until there had been 'overt acts of violence'. A previous conclusion was confirmed that with three 'so-called "armies" being organised it was expedient to take advantage of the provisions of the Customs Act for the temporary prohibition by Order-in-Council of the importation and transit of arms and ammunition' (Bodl. MS. Asquith 7, ff.80–1; TNA: CAB 37/117/82, for Simon's paper on 'Illegalities in Ulster').

Dec. 8[41] Cabinet met. Hot discussion Naval Estimates.

[40] JAP has here reported on successive meetings on Mon. and Tues., 24 and 25 Nov. HHA's letter to the King on 26 Nov. covers both meetings (Bodl. MS. Asquith 7, ff.77–9). Harcourt records the two meetings separately. Fanning, *Fatal Path*, p.93, dates this discussion to a meeting on 25 Nov., citing RA PS/PSO/GVK/2553/2/94.

[41] The Prime Minister's two reports on the Cabinet meetings of 8, 11, 15, 16, 17, and 18 Dec. are in Bodl. MS. Asquith 7, ff.82–9. MS. Asquith 7, ff.82–3, is dated 11 Dec.; the outside cover refers to 8 and 11 Dec. Hobhouse (David ed., *Inside Asquith's Cabinet*, p.153) says in an entry dated 20 Dec. (a Saturday) that there had been a succession of Cabinets dealing mainly with Navy estimates; and David interpolates '[8,15,16 December]'. Bodl. MS. Asquith 7, ff.84–9, dated 20 Dec. & RA Geo V R.137 refers to meetings 'in the last week' i.e. 15–18 Dec., Mon. to Thurs. The draft in MS. Asquith is annotated

P.M. had another meeting with Bonar Law. Margot told me the result discouraging under secrecy pledge at dinner. I played Bridge with P.M: against Lady Sheffield[42] & Arthur Stanley after dinner.

Margot Asquith's disclosure to JAP of the Prime Minister's second meeting with Bonar Law is remarkable, given that initially HHA would not tell her who had arranged the meeting, or where and how they would meet. He had also refused to tell his closest Cabinet colleagues, Crewe and Grey, thinking it 'fairer on Bonar Law & easier for them if they were ever asked'. Margot had no details of the talks but knew that she should keep silent about the fact that they were occurring at all. 'I can't help thinking the secret will get out. Winston will talk.' Realising that the secret had also been divulged to Violet Asquith, she wrote: 'Thank God I've never let out a Cabinet secret... (tho I live in a hot-bed of gossip of every kind)' (Margot Asquith diary, ? Dec. 1913, Bodl. MS.Eng.d.3210, ff.144–6).

Urged by the Chief Whip, from late November onwards constituencies were mobilising in support of the government's land policy. The Midland Liberal Federation alone had organised 52 meetings and 66 lectures by early March 1914 (Gavin Freeman, 'Beyond Westminster: Grass-roots Liberalism in England, 1910–1929', Ph.D. thesis, U. of Leicester, 2013, p.38). Briefed by DLG on 'the position of the land movement', HHA launched the Central Land and Housing Council on 9 December to inaugurate 'an organised movement... to inform and stimulate public opinion' about the urgency of the land problem and the necessity of land reform. Although his private mutterings and grumbles were not completely extinguished, the Prime Minister was now fully and openly committed to the cause. It would not escape notice that his greatest tribute was not to the Chancellor of the Exchequer, but to 'my old friend and colleague Mr Arthur Acland', who had led the Land Enquiry: 'a statesman of great experience, keen popular sympathies, and ripe equitable judgment' (Bodl. MS. Asquith 25, ff.63–76a).

There was a Cabinet meeting on 11 December at which DLG led a discussion of Estimates, projecting a deficit of £1 million if Navy and Army Estimates stayed at their present level. WSC said that if the 50 per cent superiority over Germany in the North Sea were reduced, he would resign (Harcourt diary, 11 Dec. 1913, Bodl. MS.Eng.c.8268). Now was the time for JAP to fight his corner. On 13 December he circulated a 'Note on the Necessity for Increased Financial Aid to Local Education Authorities in 1914–15' (TNA: CAB 37/117/90). He reminded his colleagues

'Cabinets Dec 15th 16th & 17th 1913'. But inside it also says the final meeting was held on the Thurs. afternoon, 18 Dec., only to consider a paper by Samuel on Lords reform; discussion of naval estimates was adjourned until after Christmas.

[42] Mary Katherine Stanley, Lady Sheffield (1848–1929); dau. Sir Lowthian Bell, 1st Bt; m. 1873 Hon. Edward Lyulph Stanley (1839–1925). He succ. brother as 4th Baron Stanley 1903 and his kinsman as 4th Baron Sheffield 1909; Lib. MP Oldham 1880–5; PC 1910; much interested in social, especially educational, problems. HHA's intimate friend Venetia Stanley was their youngest daughter.

that he had made a pledge when introducing his Education Bill in July, in words approved by the Prime Minister, of 'a large and substantial additional sum of money, which will rise progressively in the second and third years'. It was, he said, 'obviously impossible for me to continue to administer the work of the Board unless I am able to fulfil the pledge'. DLG, unmoved by the thinly veiled threat of resignation, was quick to challenge the underlying arithmetic.

Board of Education, Whitehall, London. S.W.,
16.12.1913.

My dear Prime Minister,

Yesterday, in discussing with me my proposal that £1,250,000 should be provided in relief of Education Rates, the Chancellor of the Exchequer said that this sum would only relieve Local Authorities to the extent of a ¾*d*. rate over the whole country and that such small relief would satisfy nobody. As a matter of fact, the produce of a penny Education Rate over England and Wales is about £823,000; and £1,250,000, if spread evenly over the whole country, would therefore relieve rates to the extent of nearly 1½*d*.

He may, however, have been referring especially to the proposed Grant of £1,000,000 in aid of Elementary Education only — the remaining £250,000 being given to Higher Education. The £1,000,000, if spread evenly, would represent nearly a 1¼*d*. rate.

As a matter of fact, I do not propose that the relief should be spread evenly. There are some 50 Authorities who have no claim at all to relief of rates and who, even if the complete reform to the Grant System which I advocate were carried out, would get no additional State money. If these Authorities are disregarded and £1,000,000 is distributed among the remaining Authorities on a graduated system giving most relief to those who need it most, the relief to the rates would range in different areas from a very little up to 1/–s.[?] in the pound. The net effect would be to bring all Elementary Education Rates down to a figure between 10*d*. and 21d. (the present range is from 6*d*. to 3/-). There can be no doubt whatever that the most heavily burdened Authorities (who, of course, are those whose pressure on me for more money is most severe) would hail such a relief of the rates as a very substantial relief, and as going a very long way to redeem our pledges.

Yours very faithfully,
Joseph A. Pease
(Bodl. MS. Asquith 13, f.171)

At an afternoon Cabinet meeting on Monday 15 December (which JAP did not record) Harcourt discerned a 'climb down' on Navy Estimates. A figure of £49,966,200 was produced, which DLG and HHA with Treasury concurrence had concluded on Saturday must be accepted. Army Additional Estimates would have to be reduced; and £3½ million of the sinking fund would have to be suspended. DLG had explained to the House of Commons in March 1910 when the delay in passing the Finance Bill resulted in a revenue shortfall: 'the whole of the interest in respect of borrowing upon Treasury Bills is paid in advance in the form of discount. The suspension of the new Sinking Fund… as proposed in the Treasury (Temporary Borrowing) Bill will have the effect of reducing the amount which would otherwise have had to be borrowed…'. The suspension procedure was expounded by the Treasury's Henry Higgs in A Primer of National Finance, *Methuen, 1919, pp.81–2.*

DLG made it clear that, even putting aside JAP's 'urgent demand' for an additional £2,000,000, taxation would have to be raised. JAP then spoke up for the extra £1¼ million he 'must' have (Harcourt diary, 15 Dec. 1913, Bodl. MS.Eng.c.8268). The following day the Estimates deliberations were reopened with 'Samuel fighting well for economy' and HHA evidently leaning towards the position of the 'economists'. WSC was, in Harcourt's words, 'most violent & theatrical—threatens immediate resignation and accuses Ll.G. of having betrayed him' (Harcourt diary, 16 Dec. 1913, Bodl. MS.Eng.c.8268). 'This was', according to Hobhouse, 'the third important occasion on which the so-called minor members of the Cabinet have beaten the more prominent ones since I have been there' (Hobhouse diary, 20 Dec. 1913, David ed., Inside Asquith's Cabinet, *p.154).*

Dec. 17 P.M. said he would talk to Carson to see if he could advance matter.

HHA had told Bonar Law at their last meeting that the Cabinet 'might be brought to agree either to the temporary exclusion of Ulster with an understanding that it was to come in automatically at the end of a fixed period; or to Home Rule within Home Rule'. Law responded that neither could possibly be accepted. The only possibility for a settlement was the exclusion of Ulster with the right to come in if they chose to; and, for the rest of Ireland, modification of the Bill's provision for Customs, Post Office, and judicial appointments by the Imperial Parliament. HHA said he would consider the Unionist proposals, but Law's impression, as he told Curzon on 13 December, was that 'the chance of a settlement is very small. My belief is he simply means to drift' (Curzon of Kedleston MSS, BL: A & AS, MSS.Eur.F.112 D/2/1).

Over the next nine months possibilities for the partition of Ireland as a solution to the Home Rule crisis would be a recurrent subject of Cabinet reporting and consideration. Law, and the Unionist political tacticians, realised that refusing HHA's offer they would improve the government's position and worsen their own (Lord E. Talbot–J. Sandars,13 Dec. 1913,

Balfour MSS, BL Add.MS. 49,863, ff.44–5). Compact summaries of the course of events to August 1914 are in M.C. Rast, Shaping Ireland's Independence: Nationalist, Unionist, and British Solutions to the Irish Question, 1909–1925, *palgrave macmillan, Basingstoke, 2019, pp.119–61; Thomas Hennessey,* Dividing Ireland: World War One and Partition, *Routledge, 1998, pp.43–7, and Fanning,* Fatal Path, *pp.76–133.*

On 17 December HHA received a deputation of about 40 Liberal MPs on armaments. There was a Cabinet meeting on 18 December mainly on House of Lords reform, at the end of which there was unanimous support for indirect election (Harcourt diary, 18 Dec. 1913, Bodl. MS.Eng.c.8268). WSC had come to Cabinet with Estimates in excess of £50 million. 'Winston was quite chastened on Thursday & the subject was not mentioned,' JAP told the absent Runciman on 20 December (Runciman of Doxford MSS). Faced with strong resistance, WSC came back with a reduced figure; but no agreement had been reached when ministers dispersed for Christmas.

On the 23rd HHA succinctly put the position in simple terms for the sympathetic Liberal backbencher Leo Chiozza Money:

> The Navy Estimates for the next financial year are not yet finally settled. Such increase as they will show (and it must be substantial) is due, with insignificant exceptions, to the completion of work and equipment of services already sanctioned by the House of Commons.
>
> I asked my friends, who came the other day, whether they proposed that we should repudiate or postpone the meeting of these obligations. They failed to make any articulate answer.
>
> The large increase of expenditure in the last 3 years is owing (as you know) to three main causes: (1) rise in prices of almost all materials, and in wages: (2) new services, such as air-craft: (3) increased average annual cost of maintenance in full commission of the big ships of the new types, as compared with their forerunners.
>
> I need not say that we do not contemplate any extension of the programme of construction already publicly foreshadowed.
>
> *(Sir Leo Chiozza Money,* On the Brink of War *[draft autobiography], 1939, pp.105–6, Chiozza Money MSS, MS. Add. 9259/I [1], CUL)*

The friends 'who came the other day' were told much the same thing. But, as Percy Molteno, who led the deputation, told fellow radical MP Annan Bryce on 19 December: 'I have heard a good deal as to the struggle going on in the Cabinet, but I can't repeat it; and the Prime Minister placed us under a seal of confidence as to his statement.' (Hirst, A Man of Principle, *p.416.)*

Chapter 4
1914

Dissension over naval estimates had escalated following the publication on New Year's Day of an interview with DLG in the Daily Chronicle *in which he said the time was opportune to 'overhaul our expenditure on armaments'. Most of the Liberal press cheered the calls of radicals and the chairman of the National Liberal Federation, Sir John Brunner, to reduce naval expenditure. Division in the Cabinet ran deep, and discussion was not helped by uncertainty about what had been decided. WSC had written to his private secretary, James Masterton Smith, on 3 January: 'That there is a row everyone will know after the Chancellor's interview, but whether it is about 2 ships or 6 ships or 7 ships should remain, for the present, in security' (Churchill MSS, uncat. when seen, courtesy the Hon. Randolph Churchill).*

Charles Hobhouse, in weekend conversation with Sydney Buxton on 11 January, discovered that Buxton 'regarded the Navy estimates apart from the question of 2 or 4 new big ships, for 1914–15 as accepted. I did not so understand the attitude of the Cabinet. I thought the whole question remained open... the friends of economy have procured delay, we have brought the Ch. of Ex out of his tent, and we had, though perhaps it is not now, procured the hesitation of the P.M.' (Hobhouse—Harcourt, 15 Jan. 1914, Bodl. MS. Harcourt 444, ff.3–5; James Edwin Lindsay, 'The Failure of Liberal Opposition to British Entry into World War I', Ph.D. thesis, Columbia U., 1969, p.30). WSC's position was set out in a nineteen-page secret memorandum, 'Naval Estimates, 1914–15', signed on 10 January and printed on 12 January. There were, he concluded, 'five distinct questions on which the Cabinet must give a decision' (Bodl. MS. Asquith 25, ff.30–9). The course of the arguments in Cabinet in 1913–14 is laid out in G.C. Peden, The Treasury and British Public Policy, 1906–1959*, Oxford UP, 2000, pp.52–5.*

22 Jany Cabinet. Navy Estimates discussion. W.C. left in disappointed and dissatisfied mood. All urged 60 per cent but not big balance of expend. beyond.

JAP met DLG on the morning of 23 January. The Chancellor of the Exchequer said he would be ready in the next few days to discuss the increased expenditure needed for education and other proposals to be included in JAP's bill in that session. Thinking that DLG 'really means business', JAP cancelled a planned journey abroad so as to be able to attend the following week's Cabinet meeting (JAP—EP, 23 Jan. 1914, MS. Gainford 189/1).

23rd Jany Cabinet. Somaliland — discussion & Expenditure of £17,000 to occupy Burrow [*sic*].

In August 1913, Muhammad Abdallah Hasan, known by the British as the Mad Mullah, had intensified his campaign against the British and tribes friendly to them. His major success had been to defeat the Somaliland Camel Corps at the battle of Dul Madoba. British policy was to administer the coast and leave the interior to the 'friendlies', but this defeat had forced the abandonment of Burao (not 'Burrow'), the Camel Corps' base. The colonial administrators felt that some show of force was necessary to maintain their control. Burao was reoccupied by the end of 1913. For the background see A Liberal Chronicle...1908–1910 *(9 and 30 Mar. 1910), pp.160–1,166.*

The 1914 Estimates included £25,000 for Somaliland, which enabled the Camel Corps to be increased from 150 to 500. But the Colonial Office's policy was to try merely to contain the Mullah's activities and to wait for his death (he was reputed to be old and dropsied). For the 'Somaliland disaster' and bibliography see Thomas Paul Ofcansky's brief life of the Camel Corps commander, Richard Conyngham Corfield, http://www.oxforddnb.com/view/article/75560, accessed 27 Jan. 2016; and I.M. Lewis, A Modern History of the Somali: Nation and State in the Horn of Africa, *James Currey, Oxford, Btec Books, Hargeisa, Ohio UP, Athens, 4th edn, 2002, pp.74–7.*

The P.M. reported meetings with Bonar Law on 16th[1] — he took 'a gloomy view'. He then saw Carson — wrote to him as result of more encouraging interview, in which he on own responsibility offered to chuck P.O., — customs, — & so get onto Federal & Imperial lines & he offered to give Ulster (as defined) members power to appeal to Imp. Parl. against any legislation passed; to withdraw patronage, Education, religion, & industrial matters from control of majority in regard to Ulster.

JAP added a marginal note in red ink: 'See my private cabinet white paper circulated by P.M. to colleagues in Jany...'. We can find no Cabinet memorandum about Ireland signed by JAP and circulated by HHA. It is possible that JAP was referring to an unattributed memorandum, 'Suggestions in regard to Irish Government Bill', printed 29 Jan. 1914 (TNA: CAB

[1] Hobhouse's diary says HHA met Law on 10 and 16 Dec. (David ed., *Inside Asquith's Cabinet*, p.156).

37/119/20), which discussed the points raised in this paragraph. For HHA's correspondence with Carson, including a memorandum written to open up discussions, see Ian Colvin, Life of Lord Carson, *Vol. 2, Victor Gollancz, 1934, pp.262–71. Hobhouse's account of the January parleying with the Irish leaders has more detail (David ed.,* Inside Asquith's Cabinet, *pp.155–7). On Carson's 'delicate, if not impossible, political high wire act' from late 1913 see Jeremy Smith, 'Federalism, Devolution and Partition: Sir Edward Carson and the Search for a Compromise on the Third Home Rule Bill, 1913–14',* Irish Historical Studies, *vol.35, no.140, 2007, pp.496–518.*

Carson wrote to decline it, & Bonar Law assented. On being pressed after another interview on Jany 8 for alternative, nothing but total exclusion of all Ulster M.P.s would satisfy. If they got this, effort made to make bill success.

Note admission of principle — throwing over Irish protestants in S. & W. of Ireland. P.M. promised to write again after cabinet. We considered it, & thought some statement must be made of concessions suggested in H. of C. without publishing anything wh. had passed at interviews & in confidential correspondence.

As HHA reported to the King on 23 January, 'the general opinion of the Cabinet' was that the plan he had offered on his own responsibility on 23 December, which the Unionist leaders refused to discuss, 'went to the extreme limits (some, like Lord Morley, were tempted to think that it exceeded the limits) of generosity in its concessions to the fears & the sentiment of "Ulster"'. DLG, Churchill, and some other unnamed ministers felt strongly that, if the Cabinet were to endorse the Prime Minister's suggestions, Parliament and the country should be informed of the proposed concessions at the earliest practicable opportunity (Bodl. MS. Asquith 7, ff.90–1).

The overtures and rebuffs on Ireland continued daily. The King, doing all that he could to avert civil war, urged moderation on both sides. He was, as he told HHA, 'in a most difficult position, such as no sovereign of this country has experienced for centuries' (George V–HHA, 26 Jan. 1914, RA: GVK/2553 [3] 76, in Bogdanor, The Monarchy and the Constitution, *p.127). He had earlier opened his heart to the Archbishop of Canterbury, who found him on the evening of 22 January 'more upset and vehement than I had ever seen him'. The King 'drew graphic pictures of what history would say about him if he had been coward enough to shelter behind the responsibility of Ministers, and allow the Nation to drift into Civil War' (Davidson Memo, 22 Jan. 1914, Davidson of Lambeth MSS, XII, f.361, Lambeth PL). Behind the scenes, royal advisers wrestled with ideas and language that the King might take up. 'I agree with you', Stamfordham told Francis Hopwood secretly on 26 January, 'that the King should make clear to the Opposition leaders that he will not allow Civil War & that he will support any terms not "extravagantly unreasonable" proposed by the Government'. But the question was 'what would H.M. consider as not "extravagantly unreasonable"'? (Southborough MSS, Bodl. MS.Eng.c.7362). For Bonar Law telling Stamfordham on 26 January that there were only two courses open to the government: either submit their Bill to the will of the people or 'prepare for the consequences of civil war', see Mansergh,* The Unresolved Question, *p.67.*

Whatever the King might say about not 'allowing' civil war, the Opposition leaders were no longer in control. The Duke of Northumberland's soldier son and heir, Earl Percy, outlined the evolving situation to his father on 24 January after a talk with Lord Roberts:

> it is quite probable that isolated outbreaks may occur in Ireland which will give the Government a pretext for sending troops to restore order, that these outbreaks may very well be the fault of the Ulstermen...the Government will represent such outbreaks as aggressive acts of lawlessness on Ulster's part, this will be passionately resented by Unionists and the net result will be chaos because the Government's supporters will be urging them to deal summarily with the insurgents while Unionists will be trying to persuade the troops not to go. Officers will be resigning their commissions or refusing to obey orders, also large numbers of the rank and file.

There was a wider concern. A large section of labour might take the view that if troops could be used to suppress a strike they could equally be used to suppress a rebellion in Ireland. Civil war might not be confined to Ireland.

> Milner therefore wants to ask as many leading men as possible to pledge themselves to use every means in their power to prevent the troops being employed. He suggests that one most effective way is to induce the King to revive 'constitutional powers which have long lain dormant'. If HM contemplated doing so it would strengthen his hands considerably if, say a million signatures were obtained to a petition direct to him to exercise his veto...
>
> The situation as regards the army is much more serious than many people imagine. Regiments in India have been getting up subscriptions for Ulster! At a recent staff conference, at which representatives of the various staffs of commands all over the British Isles met, many officers reported that they could not only not depend on the forces in case of their being sent against Ulster, but that there were certain battalions which would go over in a body to help the Ulstermen!
>
> I believe Roberts will, if the Bill passes go over to Ulster himself and will advise officers to refuse to obey orders, in his capacity as senior Marshal. But this is very confidential so don't say anything about it.
>
> *(Northumberland MSS, DP/D7/I/245, Alnwick Castle Archives, courtesy of Vanessa Bell and Christopher Hunwick)*

Jan. 28[2] Cabinet. King's view in regard to Ulster considered. Harcourt policy in Somaliland agreed to. Camel corps increased to protect friendlies.

Over the last days of January several of JAP's colleagues—McKenna, Simon, Samuel, Beauchamp, Masterman, Hobhouse—had collogued with a view to strengthening DLG in his resistance to Churchill's naval estimates. Simon warned the Chancellor on 26 January that he could not hold himself 'bound to join you in acquiescing in Winston's figure of £54 millions'. Their recent close association began because of DLG's sympathy with the criticism directed against a figure so large as £50 millions: 'the upshot of the crusade for economy is, so far, an increase of £4 millions: a conclusion at once tragical and laughable' (Lloyd George MSS, LG/C/8/3/6, PA). Churchill's active Cabinet adversaries did not fully appreciate the extent to which DLG's thinking was focused on 1915, the 'much more critical' parliamentary and electioneering year, with a majority prospectively down to 50 or 60, of whom 40 would be Labour men.

Impelled by the need to resolve the current impasse, DLG prepared notes for the Cabinet meeting on 28 January. 'My Plan' to 'Settle in two years', in the hand of his secretary and mistress Frances Stevenson, admitted: 'No genuine economies can reduce this year's total to level where taxation can be avoided' (Lloyd George MSS, uncat. when seen in Beaverbrook Library). He had told the Cabinet the previous day that he could 'now find £2,500,000 surplus this yr to meet supplementary estimates—this will cover all monies properly payable during this year' (Harcourt diary, 27 Jan. 1914, Bodl. MS.Eng.c.8269). The intense review and calculations over the last week of January by DLG with senior Treasury, Inland Revenue, and Customs and Excise officials of the effect of various changes to income tax on earned as well as unearned income, super tax, land value duties, and death duties is recorded in a series of memoranda by the Chairman of the Board of Inland Revenue, Sir Matthew Nathan (TNA: IR 63/46). The Chancellor had advice from Sir George Paish confirming forecasts from various sources of smaller profits than the previous year and an expected 'falling off in trade' reaching 'serious proportions in the late autumn'.

The premier brought naval estimates matters to a head by threatening a dissolution if agreement could not be reached. In pencilled notes clarifying his own thinking, he sketched a stark picture. The probability of losing a general election was great. Defeat would mean the Parliament Act 'utterly destroyed'; House of Lords reconstructed on Tory lines, 'which only a revolution can alter'; Home Rule and Welsh Disestablishment lost. The resignation of

[2] JAP dated this entry 29 Jan., but the Cabinet met on 27, 28, and 29 Jan., not 29 and 30 Jan. (HHA Cabinet letter, 29 Jan. 1914, Bodl. MS. Asquith 7, ff.93–4; *The Times*, 28, 29, and 30 Jan. 1914). Hobhouse's diary makes clear that the discussion about Ulster was on the 28th (David ed., *Inside Asquith's Cabinet*, p.159).

Churchill would not mean splitting the party: 'large Admiralty estimates may be capable of being carried only because W.C. has gone...'. And 'the feeling that the Cabinet fights for economy but pursues Home Rule unflinchingly is just what is wanted'. The majority of the Cabinet 'certainly take this view' (undated notes [Jan.–Feb. 1914], Bodl. MS. Asquith 25, ff.148–9). What HHA did not say was that, if the badly strained friendship of DLG and WSC could not be repaired, it was DLG whose continuing presence in the government was vital.

The 29 January meeting appeared to end inconclusively. Hobhouse recorded that both Churchill and DLG 'endeavoured to get the Cabinet to assume that £54½ millions were the estimates agreed to. We separated having come neither to this nor any other agreement' (David ed., Inside Asquith's Cabinet, *p.160). In fact, unknown to the rest of the Cabinet, HHA and DLG had a secret pledge from Churchill to reduce his estimates the following year. The major change in naval policy, which would permit substituting cheaper submarine construction for battleships, is convincingly documented in Nicholas A. Lambert, 'British Naval Policy, 1913–1914: Financial Limitation and Strategic Revolution',* JMH, *vol.67, no.3, 1995, pp.595–626.*

Jan. 29 Cabinet. Discussed ways and means. George propounded policy providing for total liabilities out of new taxation this year, & to increase education & Highway relief later 1915–16, out of such taxation — but reduction on Navy sine qua non. Churchill's bombshell — not agree to future reductions. Appeal made by P.M. for unity in face of peril of great interests H.R. &c.

As Bruce K. Murray explains: 'Lloyd George had not planned on a "taxing" Budget for 1914; it was only after Churchill's demands at the Admiralty rendered new taxation inevitable, that he decided to impose substantial new taxes to provide not only the finances for the Navy but also for a new system of Exchequer grants in relief of rates on improvements.' ('"Battered and Shattered": Lloyd George and the 1914 Budget Fiasco', Albion, *vol.23, no.3, 1991, p.484; and also Murray's 'Lloyd George, the Navy Estimates, and the Inclusion of Rating Relief in the 1914 Budget',* WHR, *vol.15, no.1, 1990, pp.58–78.) For DLG's intention that 'the taxation of site values shall henceforth form an integral part of the system of local taxation', and the valuation process that had been set in train in 1910, there is an expert study by Brian Short,* Land and Society in Edwardian Britain, *Cambridge UP, 1997.*

Treasury thinking on land values, rating, and local taxation is embedded in memoranda by principal clerk R.G. Hawtrey, Oct. 1913 and Jan. 1914 (Hawtrey MSS, HTRY 1/8, CAC). David Spring's essay 'Land and Politics in Edwardian England', Agricultural History, *vol.58, no.1, 1984, pp.17–42, is an incomparably luminous analysis of the resistance to Liberal land policy. And, in a penetrating discussion of relations between central and local government, P.J. Waller observes that DLG's land tax proposals 'alienated former friends by annexing revenues which they claimed for local authorities'* (Town, City, and Nation: England 1850–1914, *Oxford UP, 1983, p.261).*

Hawtrey also attempted valiantly to dissipate some of the confusion around navy estimates, pointing out that 'there is no vote for shipbuilding as such at all... In order to show the estimated expenditure on new construction separately it is necessary to transform the entire Vote [8] on to another basis altogether (see pp.180/1 of Estimates for 1914/15). The Vote so re-arranged is called "The programme".' It had been ruled that excesses on items of 'The Programme' as such did not require Treasury sanction. The consequence of this was that 'the Admiralty can divert enormous sums from shipbuilding to repairs &c vice versa, without knowledge of the Treasury' ('Navy Votes & Surrender of Unspent Balances', Apr. 1914; untitled analysis of a series of estimates for 1913/14 to 1916/17 that 'Mr Churchill declares himself willing to accept', 23 Jan. 1914 (Hawtrey MSS, HTRY 1/9, CAC). On Treasury's resistance to the 'object based' system of military accounting advocated by Haldane and Charles Harris see Warwick Funnell, 'Social reform, military accounting and the pursuit of economy during the Liberal apotheosis, 1906–1912', Accounting History Review, *vol.21, no.1, 2011, pp.69–93. DLG had discussed Hawtrey's analysis with C.P. Scott on the afternoon of 25 January. Writing from the train on the way back to Manchester, Scott drew attention to*

> Hawtrey's strong opinion that the whole 4 or 5 millions of the delayed construction cannot be made good this year even if the money for it be voted is surely a strong reason for not voting it. I don't know if you noticed Hawtrey's extremely ingenious proposal for dealing with the arrears. Churchill's proposal is for estimates of just under 50 millions apart from arrears and, under pressure from you, he is now engaged in cutting that figure down by a million or two. Hawtrey, as I understand him, would apply these retrenched millions and nothing more to making good arrears.
> *(Scott–DLG, 25 Jan. 1914, Scott MSS, BL Add.MS. 50,901, ff.104–5)*

Hawtrey's solution could deliver 'the virtual certainty of substantial economies this year and much larger ones next year... the beauty of it is that it violates no undertaking... and is not open to effective public attack' (Scott–DLG, 25 Jan. 1914, Wilson ed., The Political Diaries of C. P. Scott 1911–1928, *p.79).*

Sunday Feb. 1 Received letter from Samuel enclosing copy of letter signed by Runciman McKenna Beauchamp Simon Hobhouse (McWood?) expressing loyalty to Asquith but urging reduction in votes on ground that expansion was dangerous, irritating to Germany, & party opposition. Samuel wrote to the P.M. associating himself with it. I wrote to P.M. whilst generally doing so I objected to signing letters with colleagues on principle, that I viewed any hesitation to meet full liabilities as a worse blow to free trade, than if we failed to meet liabilities as they occurred & became due.

Hobhouse writes in his diary for 29 January of the letter from Runciman and others as having been signed by McKinnon Wood. But the letter, in Simon's hand, does not have McKinnon Wood's signature (David ed., Inside Asquith's Cabinet, *pp.160,273–4; Bodl. MS. Asquith 25, ff.170–7). The signatories affirmed at the end that their 'single desire' was to promote absolute unity under HHA's leadership, to give Home Rule the best possible chance under his guidance. Neither JAP's nor Samuel's letter has survived in HHA's papers. There is no mention of a letter by Samuel in his* Memoirs, *Cresset P., 1945, or John Bowle,* Viscount Samuel, *Victor Gollancz, 1957, or Bernard Wasserstein,* Herbert Samuel A Political Life, *Clarendon P., Oxford,1992. However, there is a handwritten memorandum in the Asquith papers written eleven days earlier in which Samuel criticised WSC's statistics (Bodl. MS. Asquith 25, ff.150–4; Wasserstein,* Herbert Samuel, *p.159).*

That I thought the Admiralty had been rather 'mild' in their expenditure as illustrated by sinking of a battle ship wh. could admittedly have been sold for £50,000 & thought — except for unforeseen & very exceptional circumstances we must publicly state we should reduce Navy estimates for 1915–6 to pay £48,000,000 from the £52½M.

On 4 November 1913 the decommissioned Royal Sovereign class battleship Empress of India *was used as a target to test the effect of shells on heavy armour plating and provide realistic marksmanship practice. When launched in 1891 it cost over £900,000; two of its class had been sold recently for £40,000–42,000. Lord Charles Beresford protested in a letter to* The Times *(11 Nov. 1913) against the waste of public money and the loss of valuable information by siting and sinking it in deep water (David K. Brown,* Warrior to Dreadnought: Warship Development 1860–1905, *Chatham, 1997, pp.176–7).*

Tuesday Feby 3[3]

Full cabinet (except Runciman). The Prime Minister informed his colleagues that he had with Birrell seen John Redmond the day before at No. 10.

The view of the King, that he was 'no automaton', had a constitutional right to change his ministers — & would exercise it, if he thought it would stop civil war, even though it might bring the Crown into the cockpit of political party strife, was a consideration which was new to Redmond, & which he pressed Asquith to assert more definitely.

[3] JAP mistakenly dated this entry 'Tuesday Jany 3'. A few days earlier HHA's masseur had overheard John Burns telling the Prime Minister as a Cabinet meeting broke up: 'Well Redmond won't like it...'. HHA responded: 'No but it is better than civil war' (Shane Leslie diary, 31 Jan.1914, Leslie MSS 56/1, Georgetown U. Library, Special Collections Division).

The King surrounded as he was, yet was, Asquith told him Not opposed to Home Rule, he recognised at the General Election it was expected Home Rule would follow the passage of the Parl. Act. If the King did not force an election by change of ministers, the responsibility was all the more placed upon the Cabinet to do all in their power to stop civil war, the danger of which was not so evident when the last election took place. Asquith suggested the administrative changes he was prepared to offer as the price of Home Rule by consent. Redmond admitted they were offensive to Nationalism, but the P.M. formed the view he would accept them later on, with protest.

Feb. 3 King's Speech.

Although the Cabinet was opposed to the exclusion of Ulster, in whole or part, even temporarily, they felt that something had to be offered to the implacable Opposition. Carson still pressed for exclusion. If it were not granted, he would, 'regardless of personal consequences, go on with the people to the end with their policy of resistance'. Bonar Law, less belligerent, questioned the government's moral authority in the absence of endorsement of its policy at a general election. Stamfordham had been determined 'to guard against the possibility of the P.M's saying he had been living in a fool's paradise & had no idea of the King's views & intended attitude'.

In daily communication with Hopwood, Stamfordham advised that the King must be told what the government intended if 'the conversations' proved fruitless. As for the King, he was advised to say that his time would come when the Bill came up for assent. If it had not been settled by consent, he should say something to the effect of: 'I must with every care consider the political situation and decide what in my judgment would be my best line of action' (Stamfordham–Hopwood, 2, 4, 5 Feb. 1914, Southborough MSS, Bodl. MS.Eng.c.7362). The King asserted himself, telling Asquith that it was his duty as King to do what in his own judgement was best for the people. The Prime Minister responded that refusing assent to a bill passed by Parliament had not been done since Queen Anne's reign and 'would undoubtedly prove disastrous for the Monarchy'.

At the King's side, his private secretary had been saying since the summer that 'the total exclusion of Ulster with the right to "come in" to be decided by a referendum of the people of Ulster was the only chance of a peaceful settlement'. But, as Stamfordham told Lord Rothschild on 9 February, the Opposition and The Times *preferred a general election, which they would not get 'unless the government is beaten on some side issue' (John Cooper,* The Unexpected Story of Nathaniel Rothschild, *Bloomsbury, 2015, p.325). Even with the aid of Stamfordham and Hopwood, the King was no match for HHA's dialectical subtlety.*

In his speech opening Parliament on 10 February the sovereign spoke the words provided by the government, calling for 'foresight, judgment and in the spirit of mutual concession' to 'heal dissension and lay the foundations of a lasting settlement' (Finnan, John Redmond, *p.66; Nicolson,* King George the Fifth, *pp.233–5). At dinner that night with Lansdowne, Lords Salisbury, Selborne, Midleton, Curzon, and the Duke of Devonshire exhibited 'Considerable difference of opinion as to what the paragraph about Ireland means' (Devonshire diary, [10 Feb. 1914], Devonshire MSS, DF7/1/17).*

Feb. 5 More Navy. Somaliland.

Having reviewed the figures, WSC presented a fresh set of estimates totalling just under £52 million. His argument for acceleration of two ships 'in default of the Canadians', though acceptable to HHA, foundered on the rebuttal that it would constitute a new standard above 60 per cent. As McKenna told the absent Runciman on 6 February:

> Ll.G. by this time was aware which way the cat would jump, and although quite silent in the fight now made the suggestion that Winston should say in the House that Borden was being invited over to discuss the naval situation, and in the meanwhile nothing would be done with regard to the Canadian ships. The P.M. approved this proposal & the economists were satisfied. Winston raged & talked about not going on, but as it was 1.30 the company quietly dwindled away.
>
> *(Runciman of Doxford MSS)*

Feb. 9 Navy.

Feb. 11 Navy vote agreed to Churchill undertaking 'to do my utmost to bring estimates down to £49,500,000 & not to build ships instead of Canadian ones merely to accelerate this year' & 'to get out of building the 3 additional ships if Canada fails us' & that it will not be necessary to exceed our programme.

HHA's version for the King of what WSC had agreed has different figures: 'The total of the Navy Estimates for 1914–15 were fixed at £51,580,000, and Mr WSC was willing that the Government should announce that the total for the following year should show substantial reductions: he thinks he can practically guarantee a saving of £2,000,000' (Bodl. MS. Asquith 7, ff.97–8). A minute to the Joint Permanent Secretary of the Treasury Sir John Bradbury on 13 Feb. 1913, initialled by DLG, stated that the Cabinet on Wednesday approved the following totals for Navy Estimates: 1913/14 (supplementary) £2,500,000 1914/15 £51,550,000 (Lloyd George MSS, LG/C/24/3/34, PA).

McKinnon Wood confided to the radical backbencher Percy Molteno that Cabinet had settled not to agree to WSC's wish that three ships should be built to take the place of the three that Canada had failed to build. And, as Molteno put it in his diary on 12 February, 'the idea of a fleet for world requirements stationed at Gibraltar has been knocked on the head... the ratio of sixty per cent superiority to Germany is to be over all, and is not to be exceeded for special requirements such as the Mediterranean' (Hirst, A Man of Principle, *p.419).*

JAP did not mention Cabinet changes that took effect on this date: Herbert Gladstone had retired as Governor-General of South Africa and was replaced by Sydney Buxton. John Burns moved from Local Government to replace Buxton at the Board of Trade. Samuel turned down an offer of the Board of Trade and happily replaced Burns expecting to find 'a wide field of activity opening' at the Local Government Board (Samuel–Clara Samuel, 11 Jan. 1914, Samuel MSS, SAM/A/156/452, PA; Wasserstein, Herbert Samuel, *p.153). Hobhouse replaced Samuel at the Post Office, and Masterman replaced Hobhouse at the Duchy.*

JAP himself had laboured on 5 February over a plea to the Prime Minister to speak to DLG, as he had said he would, about raising the position of the Board of Education to that of other departments of state. And, if this could not be done, to consider his qualifications ('knowledge of some of our great national industries, and experience in labour disputes') for the rumoured vacancy at the Board of Trade. He unashamedly emphasised how much the additional emoluments would mean, given that all his capital had gone to his father's creditors, and he had served as an opposition whip for eight years without remuneration. HHA wanted him where he was, and there was to be no enhancement of status in a time of budget stringency (MS. Gainford 85/61).

Having accepted an office of profit under the Crown, Masterman was obliged to vacate his seat and face the electors of Bethnal Green again. He was narrowly beaten—'poor Charlie! It is maddening to think a turnover of 13 votes did it', DLG lamented to Pamela McKenna on 20 February (McKenna MSS, MCKN 9/5, CAC). Masterman tried again at Ipswich in May but was defeated by the 32-year-old barrister John Ganzoni (later Lord Belstead), 'a rich young Tory doing it for fun' (T.E. Harvey MP–W. Harvey, 21 May 1914, Harvey MSS, Friends Lib., courtesy of Ted Milligan).

JAP recorded little of the divisions in the Cabinet on Ireland in early February. The diary of one of DLG's Welsh parliamentary colleagues throws light on the growing tensions. In a long conversation on 14 February, W. Llewelyn Williams was told:

> several times that matters were very critical, that the 'Old Man'—as Asquith is called—is very nervy, and if he is discouraged, is quite capable of chucking up the sponge. T.P. [O'Connor] said that the Old Man had offered terms to Bonar Law without consulting anyone, and that George did not even know till sometime afterwards that he had done so. George himself told me that last Monday he had had his first and only 'stand up fight' with the Prime Minister in the Cabinet. Asquith wanted to publish the whole of the terms he was prepared to offer on Tuesday. He was supported by the whole of the Cabinet except George, McKenna and Samuel. George insisted, and

he shook Winston and Grey. The Prime Minister then said that as the Cabinet was not united he would not persist. George told McKenna, whom we met in the golf house…that the Prime Minister was not convinced that the right tactics had been adopted, and was very pleased he had given way. So were all the rest, except Harcourt. The more one hears of what is going on behind the scenes the more hopeless the situation seems to become. Plot and counter-plot, intrigue and manoeuvring for position, are the daily tasks of Ministers…

(Llewelyn Williams diary, 15 Feb. 1914, in J. Graham Jones, 'A Proved and Loyal Friendship: the Diary of W. Llewelyn Williams M.P., 1906–1915', The National Library of Wales Journal, vol.34, no.3, 2008, p.356)

As concern grew about the deteriorating situation in Ireland, Elsie Pease reported on gossip she had picked up via her brother's wife Edie, Lady Havelock-Allan, from Edie Havelock-Allan's sister-in-law Lady Mabel Sowerby about 'Ld Annesley's efforts in mobilization apparently the district is preparing for war—and all houses commandeered as hospitals… She has a tale I know not from whom that the King sent for Walter Long & Bonar Law to consult them — & they said he must consult his ministers — this is supposed to be very fine!!' 'The Annesley gang' were supposedly 'obsessed by the idea of Catholic domination, Catholic rate collectors etc.…'. It was doubtful if the Tories 'could control their hotheads who are longing for an excuse to fight. Edie says they write her—a match will set fire to the whole thing at any moment. I tell her to work at the other side & consider what wd happen if Home Rule now were denied. She says "Oh! but they are not organized". I tell her that wd be much worse as they wd be under no control at all & the result wd be too appalling.' (EP–JAP, 17 Feb. 1914, MS. Gainford 85/74.) The 6th Earl Annesley, a week short of his 30th birthday, would be dead eight months later after serving in an armoured car at Antwerp and as an aviator in the Royal Naval Air Service. His Bristol biplane disappeared over the Channel.

In the spring of 1914 the Ulster Volunteers were certainly organised. Basil Peto, then MP for Devizes, was using his car to convey 'mysterious packing cases (very heavy) wh. had to be put on the London & North Western rail at various stations, such as Wembley, Harrow, & the like, to avoid suspicion. They came from a warehouse William Bull had taken in his constituency at Hammersmith, & their destination was Belfast… the Duke of Bedford was the most munificent supporter of our 1900 Club Ulster Volunteer Organisation & wd always let us have £1,000 when we wanted it' (Peto, Recollections and Reflections 1862–1941, *Peto MSS). For the 'front' business of antiques and second-hand artefacts set up by Bull's brother-in-law Captain Budden, and other gun-running operations, see A.T.Q. Stewart,* The Ulster Crisis, *Faber and Faber, 1967, pp.122,128,132–3.*

Feb. 18 Discussed Parliamentary work — & how to deal with Irish situation & how to meet Army Annual Bill rejection, Lords, Marconi Committee &c.

In uncharacteristically colloquial language HHA informed the King on 26 February about the committee that the Lords had resolved to appoint 'to dive further into the Marconi business'. As all the Law Lords had declined to serve, it seemed doubtful if it would be possible to form a committee 'whose composition would be such as to give it any authority' (Bodl. MS. Asquith 7, f.99).

It was no secret that the Unionist leaders were considering, in the words of Felix Cassel KC MP, 'consonant with constitutional principle and usage', refusing to the Executive a Standing Army for more than a short period with a view to 'making the Executive conform to the wishes of the nation' ('Memorandum as to Annual Army Act', n.d., Sir Malcolm Fraser MSS, Bodl. MS.Eng.c.4790, f.130; Cassel was the nephew of Sir Ernest Cassel, who aligned himself with the Diehards in 1911). Cassel's advice, received by Bonar Law on 2 February, was consistent with that of the last Conservative Attorney General, Sir Robert Finlay, and supported by 'the three Cecils, Selborne, Austen Chamberlain and Carson' (Law–Lansdowne, 2 Feb. 1914, Lansdowne MSS, BL, uncat. when seen; Lewis, Carson, *pp.133–4). Lansdowne and Bonar Law advised their senior colleagues on 12 March 1914 that they had reluctantly decided on amending the Army Annual Bill. But they were opposed by leading party figures including Lords Derby, Curzon, the Duke of Devonshire, and now Selborne, and the plan was dropped on 20 March.*

Henry Wilson, from inside the War Office, had told Law that any attempt to coerce Ulster would trigger wholesale defections (Jack Beatty, The Lost History of 1914: How the Great War Was Not Inevitable, *Bloomsbury, 2012, pp.107–9). Iain McLean and Tom Lubbock offer a tidy narrative linking the consideration of the Army Annual Bill with the Curragh 'mutiny' and the subsequent Larne gun-running in their argument that 'Ulster Protestants and their allies, who included the king and the leader of His Majesty's Loyal Opposition, mounted a successful coup d'état against the elected government' ('The Curious Incident in the Night Time', in Iain McLean,* What's Wrong with the British Constitution?, *pp.100–21). A thorough and more conventional account is supplied by Jeremy Smith, '"Paralysing the Arm": The Unionists and the Army Annual Act, 1911–1914',* Parly Hist., *vol.15, issue 2, June 1996, pp.191–207; and for a cogent narrative of the government's failure to deal effectively with the 'grave and treasonous threat' posed by the UVF see Benjamin Grob-Fitzgibbon,* Turning Points of the Irish Revolution: The British Government, Intelligence, and the Cost of Indifference, 1912–1921, *palgrave macmillan, New York, 2007, pp.13–71.*

Grey reported on Mexican situation.

The Diaz dictatorship in Mexico had finally been overthrown in November 1910. In June 1911 Francisco Madero, a believer in the innate goodness of man, was elected President; he rapidly lost popularity, failing to grapple with Mexico's economic and political problems.

Mexico descended into anarchy, culminating in the 'Tragic Ten Days' of February 1913 when General Huerta, 'a villain on an Elizabethan scale', had Madero killed and, by a technical device and brute force, claimed to succeed as President (Henry Bamford Parkes, A History of Mexico, *Houghton Mifflin, Boston, 1950, p.332). Rebellion against Huerta quickly arose led by Emiliano Zapata and Pancho Villa. In February 1914 the USA lifted its embargo on arms shipments to Mexico to favour the rebels and in July 1914 Huerta fled the country. Misleading information about President Wilson's attitude towards Mexico conveyed to Grey by Wilson's emissary Edward House in the summer and autumn of 1913 is detailed in Joyce Grigsby* Williams, Colonel House and Sir Edward Grey: A Study in Anglo-American Diplomacy, *U. of America P., Lanham, MD, 1984, pp.22–7. Anglo-American relations over Mexico can be followed in G.R. Conyne,* Woodrow Wilson British Perspectives, 1912–21, *St Martin's P., New York, 1992, pp.16–43, and Lloyd C. Gardner,* Safe for Democracy: The Anglo-American Response to Revolution, 1913–1923, *Oxford UP, 1984, pp.45–61; and see Jonathan C. Brown,* Oil and Revolution in Mexico, *U. of California P., Berkeley, 1993, ch. 3.*

A more specific reason for the Cabinet's consideration of Mexico was about to arise: on 20 February W.A. Benton, an Englishman resident in Mexico for 25 years, was shot by Villa. Benton's friends claimed that there was no justification for his death. The nearest British consul (in Galveston, Texas) was instructed to investigate, but he was unable to cross the border because of the prevailing anarchy. As the Permanent Secretary at the Foreign Office explained: 'there is an alternative course... to furnish Huerta with arms and money and to ask him to obtain reparation from Villa. This... would undoubtedly raise a storm of protest in America and also it is open to doubt as to whether Huerta would be able, even if willing, to bring Villa to book' (Sir A. Nicolson–Sir Louis Mallet, 2 Mar. 1914, Mallet MSS IV 1 1, Balliol Col.). For an earlier dispute arising from Benton's fencing off his land and denying villagers access see Alan Knight, The Mexican Revolution, Vol. 1, Porfirians, Liberals and Peasants, *Cambridge UP, 1986, pp.119–20,126; and for his alleged insult or threat to Villa see Knight,* Mexican Revolution, Vol. 2, Counter-revolution and reconstruction, *pp.109–10. Foreign Office advice on 'The Benton Affair' was provided on 5 March 1914 (TNA: CAB 37/119/37). Beatty,* The Lost History of 1914, *pp.128–74, distils the modern literature on 'The United States and Mexico' in 1914.*

Spent Sat. & Sunday with P.M. & Margot at Wharf Raymond & wife, Mastermans. Cold & wet.

On Monday HHA dined at Grillion's with the usual gathering of courtiers, literary men, retired diplomats, soldiers, civil servants, and political friends. The diners included Haldane,

Harcourt, Devonshire, Stamfordham, Sir John Fortescue (Royal Librarian and military historian, just two months before marrying Winifred Beech, an actress 28 years his junior), Sir Frank Lascelles (former Ambassador to Germany), Field Marshal Lord Nicholson, Lord Welby (former head of the Treasury), the Conservatives Sir Herbert Maxwell Bt and George Cave, the whimsical judge Sir Charles Darling, and Edmund Gosse, Librarian of the House of Lords. This was HHA's other world.

Feb. 25 Short cabinet rose at 12.50 discussed.[4]

Board of Education,
Whitehall,
London, S.W.
3. 3. 14

Dear Bonham Carter,

Selby Bigge thinks the words Educational proposals, in the paragraph agreed to this morning in the King's Speech, might be thought to refer to my small bill which was introduced & not proceeded with & suggests an alternative which kindly submit to the P.M.

Yours sincerely,
Joseph A. Pease

P.T.O.
Words approved at cabinet.
(from memory)
J.A.P.
A measure will be submitted to carry out the educational proposals announced last session.

((Words now suggested as an improvement:—

A measure will be submitted to give effect to the proposals for the developement [*sic*] of a National system of Education which were announced last session.))[5]

(Bodl. MS. Asquith 85, ff.243–4)[6]

[4] JAP's sentence was unfinished.

[5] The sentences in the double brackets were written in red ink.

[6] We can find no other record of a Cabinet meeting on 3 March. The meeting referred to in JAP's letter to Bonham Carter could have been an unrecorded meeting of ministers on that day.

see Mar 10 King's Speech last session & also my speech July 22, 1913.[7]

JAP had been told by Illingworth of a call by the chairman of the Parliamentary Labour Party, Ramsay MacDonald, on 4 February 'to discuss the whole situation' but does not mention DLG's overture to MacDonald, on 3 March, about 'the relations of Liberalism and Labour' and the broad-ranging discussion that evening between DLG and Illingworth for the government, and party secretary Arthur Henderson with MacDonald for the Labour Party. Speaking with 'the full consent of Mr. Asquith' in the expectation that resistance to Home Rule would not be overcome and an election must follow, DLG canvassed a deal over parliamentary candidatures, agreement on a programme to be pursued after the election, and Cabinet representation for Labour if they wanted it (Illingworth–JAP, 3 Feb. 1914, MS. Gainford 85/37; Marquand, Ramsay MacDonald, *pp.159–61). In a review of contemporary and academic thinking about 'The Liberal Party and the General Election of 1915', Ian Garrett concludes: 'Progressivism in 1915 still had the capacity, if only just, to build an election-winning coalition of voters' (*J.Lib.H.*, issue 95, 2017, pp.4–11). Assessing the balance of opinion in the Liberal Party, Eugenio Biagini concludes that 'Home Rule was the cause neither of the elderly and old-fashioned, nor primarily of the front-benchers who were most immediately interested in the survival of the government, but of the young, the up-and-coming generation of radicals, who carried the flame of "New Liberalism", social reform and democracy' ('The Third Home Rule Bill in British history', in Gabriel Doherty ed.,* The Home Rule Crisis, 1912–14, *Cork UP, 2014, pp.412–42).*

Mar. 4 We seriously discussed plan of Ireland. George reported result of interview with Dillon Devlin & Redmond. They were prepared to allow Ireland to be polled by Counties for temporary exclusion until after a General Election — foregone conclusion Tories will reject it but reasonableness seems convincing. Churchill remarked that if it was rejected, & rebellion occurred, we could then please ourselves as to shooting them down.

It was admitted that if the Tories really objected, they could find plenty of excuses for a wrecking malevolent policy, but if accepted — there were points upon which accommodation might be found — grouping counties, period 3 to 6 years to elapse, P.O., Finance, & Customs.

The three Irish leaders and T.P. O'Connor had been joined in a meeting with HHA, DLG, and Birrell on 2 March (Erica S. Doherty, 'Ulster "will not fight": T.P. O'Connor and the third

[7] JAP was referring to the sentence on education in the 3 March 1913 King's speech and his own speech on 22 July 1913 introducing his proposals. The sentence in the 1913 King's speech was 'Proposals will be submitted to you for the development of a national system of education.' See 11 Feb. 1913.

Home Rule bill crisis, 1912–14', in Gabriel Doherty ed., The Home Rule Crisis 1912–14, *Mercier P., Cork, 2014, pp.136–66). The terms of the compromise settlement that the Prime Minister was to present to the House of Commons on the following Monday, and the reasoning underlying it, were articulated in his report to the King (Bodl. MS. Asquith 7, ff.103–4). Leaks in the* Daily Chronicle *(4 March) and* Daily News *(5 March) prompted a minute from HHA to the Cabinet and denials of responsibility by possible culprits (Simon–HHA, 5 Mar. 1914, copy, Simon MSS). As late as Saturday morning 7 March, when Stamfordham saw HHA, the Prime Minister did not know whether Redmond would accept the six-year exclusion (Stamfordham–Hopwood, 13 Mar. 1914, Southborough MSS, Bodl. MS.Eng.c.7362). Redmond's actions from late January to mid-March can be followed in Dermot Meleady,* John Redmond: The National Leader, *Merrion, Sallins, Co. Kildare, 2014, pp.258–66. Alvin Jackson summarised the government's evolving 'last words' on the exclusion of Ulster between 2 and 6 March: 'Within four days… Redmond and the Nationalists were compelled to accept the principle of temporary exclusion, and then to acquiesce in two redefinitions of what "temporary" meant' (*Home Rule: An Irish History, 1800–2000, *Weidenfeld and Nicolson, 2003, p.127).*

HHA opened the Home Rule Bill second reading debate on 9 March. On 12 March the government proposed that, after the passage of the Bill, but before a Dublin parliament opened, the nine Ulster counties would be given the opportunity to vote on whether they wished to be excluded for six years. The implication was that there would be two general elections before the choice had to be made. Redmond had acquiesced, relying on the government to enforce Home Rule when it was passed. Bonar Law thought that Nationalist agreement signified that they expected the Unionists to reject it. Redmond spoke of force being met with force; and Churchill affirmed on 19 March that if Crown forces were attacked the response would be firm. Bonar Law had rejected the time limit but on 19 March offered to accept the government's plan if it was first submitted to a referendum. Taken by surprise, HHA replied lamely, in effect rejecting the proposal. Amid rumours of imminent arrests Carson rose and announced to an excited Opposition that he was leaving for Ulster.

*A day later the government was engulfed in the maelstrom of threatened officer resignations and dismissals at the Curragh. Fearing armed Ulster Volunteer resistance, the Army and Navy had been instructed to initiate precautionary measures to protect ammunition depots. A cataract of misunderstandings, incompetence, bluff, and panicky reactions ensued. There is a large literature on these frantic days, including a privately circulated essay (Cameron Hazlehurst, 'Winston's Coup'), an early draft of which is referred to in Jalland's excellent account (*The Liberals and Ireland, *pp.207–47). Ian Beckett's compilation of documents,* The Army and the Curragh Incident, 1914, *Bodley Head for the Army Records Society, 1986, is indispensable. Subsequent work by Beckett and Keith Jeffery is discussed in*

M.L. Connelly, 'The army, the press and the "Curragh incident", March 1914', Hist.Res., *vol.84, no.225, Aug. 2011, pp.535–57. Beckett adds 'More Curragh Correspondence, March–April 1914',* JSAHR, *vol.98, 2020, pp.168–74. A deeper understanding of the Irish military establishment in 1914 is provided in Loughlin Sweeney,* Irish Military Elites, Nation and Empire, 1870–1925: Identity and Authority, *palgrave macmillan, 2019, pp.141–72. For an interpretation emphasising WSC's role in ratcheting up tension see Paul Bew,* Churchill and Ireland, *Oxford UP, 2016, pp.63–82.*

From March 7th to Tuesday 17th I was abroad visiting schools at Munich Berlin & Paris & missed cabinet on March 11th & March 17th. The discussion on the last was explained to me as a cabinet which George described as the bloody Assize, as the cabinet decided to move troops in Ireland to protect Government stores, & made provision as precautionary steps for their support in the event of the Ulster volunteers opposing the movement. It was decided to send a fleet from Gibraltar to Lamlash, so as to be ready, to have a division at Aldershot ready, & to summon Sir Arthur Paget[8] & give him instructions to take all necessary steps to secure the proper protection of Govmt arms & ammunition.

March 23 On Monday the 23rd another cabinet was suddenly called — owing to refusal of officers in Ireland to obey orders — I only received summons at 8 o'clock at Headlam, & arrived as cabinet was breaking up.

This historical cabinet was apparently concerned with the Irish difficulty owing to rebellious spirit disclosed. Seely explained Gough[9] & other Colonels[10]

[8] General Sir Arthur Henry Fitzroy Paget (1851–1928): C-in-C Ireland 1912–14; served in Ashanti War, Sudan, Burma, Second Boer War; C-in-C Eastn Command 1908–12, Sthern Army 1916–18; KCVO 1906, PC Ireland and GCB 1913; m. Mary (Minnie) Paran Stevens (1853–1919), a wealthy American society hostess and intimate of Edward VII (de Courcy, *The Husband Hunters*, pp.209–13). When she was a charming and beautiful debutante, guests at receptions reportedly stood on chairs to get glimpses of her (Alice Hughes, *My Father and I*, Thornton Butterworth, 1923, pp.92–3).

[9] Brig.-Gen. Hubert de la Poer Gough (1870–1963); GOC Curragh 1911–14, resigned after the Curragh 'Mutiny'; served India 1890–8, S. Africa 1899–1902; Maj.-Gen., GOC 3rd Cavalry Bde 1914–15, 2nd and 7th Cavalry Divs 1915; Lt-Gen. 1Corps 1915; GOC Fifth Army 1916–18; rtd as General 1922; KCB 1916, KCVO 1917, KCMG 1919, GCB 1937.

[10] The other colonels were Lt-Col. M.L. MacEwen (1869–1943), 16th Lancers, hit by shrapnel and shot in leg 26 Aug. 1914, CB 1915, tmpy Brig.-Gen. July 1916, rtd July 1918 as Hon. Brig.-Gen. on grounds of ill health contracted on active service; Lt-Col. (later Brig.-Gen.) Arthur Parker (1867–1941), 5th Lancers, served S. Africa 1899–1902, European War 1914–18 (Ciaran Byrne, *The Harp and Crown, the History of the 5th (Royal Irish) Lancers, 1902–1922*, Lulu Books, 2007, ch. 3; Barry Keane, 'The Curragh Mutineers 1914: Who were they?', https://www.academia.edu/43417902/, accessed 16 July 2022); and Col. (later Brig.-Gen.) Felix Frederic Hill (1860–1940), commanding No. 11 District Belfast 1910–14, joined army 1880, served S. Africa 1900–2, Suvla Bay and France 1914–18.

summoned by him, who had tendered resignations, were prepared to go back & assume their duties on the understanding we were not going to coerce Ireland, but our policy was to maintain law & order, protect our ammunition, property & lives, & support the civil authority to keep the Peace.

Seely summoned to Buckingham Palace to report position to the King was absent from cabinet, when paper arrived containing draft statement to be given Gough. This statement intended by Seely to satisfy Officers they had resigned on a false issue was redrafted by the Prime Minister & handed to Seely on his return as the cabinet was breaking up, Seely noticing it did not carry out his intention & undertaking to Gough, revised it behind the back of the cabinet, added 2 paragraphs one of which made our policy & principle of not enforcing Home Rule on Ulster as a condition of military service, Morley who was being coached by ? Birrell at the cabinet table, as to what he should say in the Lords that afternoon, edited the 2 peccant paragraphs & Seely gave it French to give to Gough.

That evening the Prime Minister & Lord Haldane after speaking in both Houses in ignorance of Seely's additions, found to their horror that Gough had been given the memorandum with conditions secured for the seditious officers at the Curragh.

On Tuesday it was found out that Seely had been sent as he was writing the 2 peccant paragraphs a letter from Gough demanding conditions, — & that therefore the fat was in the fire. Under Pressure by question, the Govmt promise to produce documents.

The statement as revised by HHA read:

'You are authorized by the Army Council to inform the officers of the 3rd Cavalry Brigade that the Army Council are satisfied that the incident which had arisen in regard to their resignations has been due to a misunderstanding.

It is the duty of all soldiers to obey lawful commands given to them through the proper channel by the Army Council, either for the protection of public property and the support of the civil power in the event of disturbances, or for the protection of the lives and property of the inhabitants.

This is the only point it was intended to be put to the officers in the questions of the General Officer Commanding, and the Army Council have been glad to learn from you that there never has been and never will be in the Brigade any question of disobeying such lawful orders.'

The 'peccant' paragraphs added by Seely were:

'His Majesty's Government must retain their right to use all the forces of the Crown in Ireland or elsewhere, to maintain law and order and to support the civil power in the ordinary execution of its duty.

But they have no intention whatever of taking advantage of this right to crush political opposition to the policy or principles of the Home Rule Bill.'

(PP, 1914, Cd. 7329, lii, 15)

Margot Asquith adds to JAP's account of what happened after the Cabinet on 24 March:

First McK

M. well I hope Seely has gone?

McK No he is staying. We are all in an awful hole! He ought to go.

M. Good gracious what people you all are! I know between you all my man with his unlicensed kindness will be sacrificed & take the blame for everything .... Henry is badly served! You sd have all threatened resignation if Seely is kept.

McK. I agree with every word but what a man not to go.

McK. shrugging his shoulders. I wish I cd tell you all but I must fly.

M Oh of course run off. I'll see H. & ask him. I went down the lobby & met Pease & Haldane. I accosted them by saying that I hear Seely is being kept. Do you honestly think any one will believe one word we say now when H. forgives Seely cooking a Cabinet document on his own?

Haldane No they won't believe a word we say. I almost spat I was so angry but at that moment Birrell joined me & taking my arm said I'm coming up to lunch with you. When I asked how they could be such fools as to keep Seely he said

Mr B My dear Margot rightly or wrongly Gen French Ewart[11] & the whole Army council will resign if Seely goes as they initialled the document thinking it was the P.M's last word...

(Margot Asquith diary, [24] Mar. 1914, Bodl. MS.Eng.d.3210, ff.183–5)

The Asquiths' domestic routine was unruffled by the crisis. The presence of DLG at lunch on the 24th was unusual; Geoffrey Howard's less so. The 'tiresome' Howard 'talked all the time & no-one could get a word in edge-ways', as one of Clementine Churchill's close friends reported to her mother (Horatia Seymour–Lady Seymour, [25 Mar. 1914], Seymour MSS).

Wed. March 25 Cabinet. We found that French had attached initials to another memorandum of Gough's asking for explanations.

The Prime Minister in strong but necessary terms criticised Seely's conduct. He admitted to the full the fault, & could only give as his excuse his blindness in seeing the conditional character of the peccant paragraphs in his anxiety to keep the officers & army from wholesale rebellion & resignation.

[11] Lt-Gen. Sir John Spencer Ewart (1861–1930); Adj.-Gen. 1910–14; Director, Mili. Ops 1906–10; Mili. Sec. 1904–6; GOC Scottish Command 1914–18. 'Time was when I used to pose as a Liberal, but now all patriotic men should combine to oppose the growth of Socialism as propounded by His Majesty's present Government' (Ewart diary, 6 June 1909, Ewart MSS).

The statements to be made in both Houses were discussed & are on record see Hansard for March 25th debates.

The situation remained critical until Seely & P.M. explained their action, & the Party supported the Govmt in consolidated Fund Bill Division by majority of 92.

French & Ewart who had promised cabinet on the 23rd to remain if Seely did, resigned on the 26th, and although pressed on the 27th decided not to come back.

March 27 Cabinets on 27th at 12.0 & 3.0; P.M. saw French between these occasions & arranged for statement on Friday to House at 5 o'clock. If they resigned it was obvious Seely must go too.

On the evening of 27 March 'Joe' Jeffries of the Daily Mail *camped outside French's house determined to ask if the Inspector-General had maintained his resignation. French, 'with the brevity of his profession', indicated that he had not withdrawn his resignation nor had it been accepted. The telephoned story was 'inserted with due italicised prominence into a heavy-leaded column which led the main page' (J.M.N. Jeffries,* Front Everywhere, *Hutchinson, [1935], p.51).*

For the generals on Sunday 29 March in conclave with Haldane drafting a letter for French, vetted by Morley, conveyed by Bonham Carter to HHA at the Wharf, and Bonham Carter's return in the early hours of Monday morning with a letter from HHA and the conclusion that 'the Generals must go', and French at Downing St the next day, see E. Haldane diary, 5 Apr. 1914, Elizabeth Haldane MSS, MS. 20240, f.39r, NLS.

Monday March 30 French & Ewart decided to adhere to resignations and P.M. undertook to take War Office. House taken by surprise by this masterly & plucky stroke of our great leader.

Seely made his statement. Simon wound up debate in great speech.

March 31 Tuesday's cabinet. The discussion recalled incidents, & the small discrepancies of statements made by different ministers — all anxious to be accurate. It was admitted how impossible it was for the same incidents to be seen by 20 men, & yet inconsistencies in views were always to be found.

Edward Grey made great speech on Home Rule & necessity of Opposition to meet Govmt, & avoid the Army & People issue. He pointed clearly to force being used to suppress an Ulster Provincial Govmt.

Speech allayed temper & tone of the debates which had for 10 days been at fever heat, under crisis through which the Govmt had passed.

Some attributed to Bonar Law filling up holes we had made for burying ourselves, others to luck but more to the consummate quiet master hand of our great Prime Minister who never lost his temper & kept his head, & his judgement cool & collected throughout an exciting period.

I dined quietly with him on the 27th. We discussed certain aspects but chiefly of a non party character (Vienna embassy youths being present[12]) & played Bridge the P.M. winning 3 rubbers.

Friday April 3 The P.M. journeyed to E. Fife to address great meeting at Ladybank of his supporters & delegates. He had an ovation at Kings X Grantham & York & Newcastle.

HHA was setting off for the by-election consequent on his surprise assumption of the War Office. The secret had been kept from his Cabinet colleagues until fifteen minutes before it was announced in the House. Charles Trevelyan told his mother the next day 'I found our three chief officials in Pease's room immediately afterwards. They are all good politicians. Even though I told them that the new War Minister was in the Cabinet, they guessed 13 names and had got down to Aberdeen in despair, before they hit on Asquith' (Trevelyan MSS, Newc. U. Spec. Coll.).

'Half the government and a large crowd of MPs and supporters had been on the platform to see the P.M. off…'. On 4 April there was an anti-Home Rule demonstration in Hyde Park with an estimated 300,000 in attendance, including an unprecedented procession of more than 200 Carlton Club members (Orde-Powlett diary, Bolton MSS, ZBO IV 5, N. Yorks CRO). Believing that WSC had planned to provoke Ulster resistance, Unionist leaders continued to gather evidence for a dossier 'corroborating the existence of a plot'. Midleton furnished a lengthy typescript secret narrative for Lansdowne on 3 April (Lansdowne MSS, BL, uncat. when seen at Bowood, courtesy of the 8th Marquess of Lansdowne).

Ap. 6 announced he wd not be opposed.

'Father is heart broken at not being opposed' (Violet Asquith–A. Ponsonby, 8 Apr. 1914, Ponsonby MSS). At the Wharf with the family for the Easter weekend, HHA wrote to Lady

[12] We cannot be certain of the identities of the 'Vienna embassy youths'. The two youngest Austrian diplomats in London, hardly youths, were the attachés, Count Elemér Pejácsevich (b. 1883) and Count George Festetics (b. 1882), both with the rank of "Legationssekretär II. Kategorie" (legation secretary, 2nd category). Festetics's mother was Lady Mary Douglas-Hamilton, dau. of the Duke of Hamilton and Brandon (William D. Godsey Jr, *Aristocratic Redoubt: The Austro-Hungarian Foreign Office on the Eve of the First World War*, Purdue UP, 1999, esp. pp.24,44). The ambassador, Count Mensdorff, had no children but had a 15-year-old nephew, Alexander (b. 1899), and other relatives who might have been present. We are grateful to Dr Helga Fichtner of the Austrian State Archives for information about the embassy staff and the ambassador's family.

Diana Manners on 12 April after a 'good appearance' at morning church: 'time slips along, and my hands have not been idle enough for Satan to find them mischief' (Lady Diana Cooper MSS, BL Add.MS. 70704, f.12).

Tuesday 21 April — 29 April[13] P.M. took his seat — amid very hearty cheers from a thin House. I saw P.M. on the Friday 24th morning & he chatted to me about Ireland & the Plural Voting Bill for the Tuesday 28th. He told me we must settle somehow. He could not rely on force in Ulster if we tried to force bill through House & riots began. I told him I agreed & the Irish Nationalists must see they must exclude Ulster till it was ready to come in without coercion. I told him I thought all was going smoothly, but great consternation created on the Saturday 25th,[14] owing to Ulster Carsonites gun running, keeping shut up police, customs officers, & coastguard men.

The Tory press loud in praise of the success of the effort. 27,000 rifles supposed to have been landed & motored inland from various places. The P.M. came back to confer with Birrell & arranged for Birrell to go to Ireland. Cabinet summoned for Monday evening.

We discussed situation, & all agreed we could not stand this breach of the law, & proposed to proceed by laying information & so avoid arrests & provocation of civil war.

Tuesday we agreed to send gun boats to patrol the waters to prevent repetition. The Party anxious for Govmt to take strong line, but we realised tact & patience, if we were to successfully call on army to help civil authority if occasion arose.

Crewe dealt with coercion act for India — Cabinet opposed to drastic steps.

The Governments of India and Bengal sought powers to act against increasing political terrorism, particularly assassination (four officials had been killed in four months). The Indian government wanted to use the 1818 preventive detention regulations to have suspects summarily examined by a judicial tribunal; those found wanting were to be given indefinite prison sentences. Crewe's predecessor at the India Office, Morley, argued that the proposals were too drastic and would alienate Indian sympathies (TNA: CAB 37/119/54,56).

[13] JAP misdated this entry 'Tuesday 22 April'. There was a Cabinet meeting on 22 Apr., which he did not mention. HHA's Cabinet letter survives only in draft in the Asquith Papers (Bodl. MS. Asquith 7, f.113; *The Times*, 23 Apr. 1914).

[14] JAP misdated the Larne gunrunning 'Saturday 26th'. Coastguard, police, and Irish Administration reports, correspondence with the Prime Minister, and HHA's notes on contemplated further action are in Bodl. MS. Asquith 41, ff.3–86. The account of this episode in Stewart, *The Ulster Crisis*, has stood the test of time.

Wednesday we expected to talk budget all the time, but Hobhouse's vote & what to do with Post Office grievance & other subjects intervened.

The debate on the Post Office vote was to take place a week later. The Post Office was the largest employer in the country. The Postal Telegraph Clerks' Association and the United Kingdom Postal Clerks' Association had refused to accept wage increases proposed by a committee chaired by the Liberal MP Richard Holt. Strike action was threatened and an independent committee was set up to look at their complaints (Gregory Anderson, Victorian Clerks, *Manchester UP, 1976, p.113; HC Deb 30 April 1914 vol 61 cc1887–2000).*

April 23 Thursday we deferred [*sic*] owing to character of Irish debates day before not to proceed with prosecutions for the time being. George finished unfolding his Budget proposals but we had 2 hours in morning & 1½ hours in evening. We all felt it was too late to take much objection, but the general view was George had not consulted us soon enough, too much money was being raised, but the education demands were not regarded as unjustified.[15]

P.M. Had chat with Churchill Thursday night both of us unhappy in regard to budget prospects.

The Cabinet met on the following Monday, Tuesday, Wednesday, and Thursday: 27, 28, 29, and 30 April (HHA Cabinet letters, 27 Apr. and 2 May 1914, Bodl. MS. Asquith 7, ff.15–20). The principal business was a review of the Budget. JAP had reason to be pleased that, in HHA's words on 2 May, 'the time has come when the Government can no longer postpone the long promised relief to the ratepayer in respect of local expenditure which is of a national character e.g. Education, Main Roads, Lunatics and many items which fall under the general head of Public Health' (Bodl. MS. Asquith 7, f.119). But he had to swallow the rejection of his private bid to be supported for the extended work of the Board of Education by both Christopher Addison as Parliamentary Secretary and Charles Trevelyan as Financial Secretary (JAP–DLG, 24 Apr. 1914, Lloyd George MSS, LG/C/4/12/5, PA). And it would have been more galling to know that behind his back Haldane briefed DLG on 26 April with points in the education

[15] In a pioneering and otherwise admirable article, Bentley B. Gilbert appears to confuse this meeting, of which he says JAP wrote 'bitterly', with a meeting on 24 Apr. of a 'cabinet budget committee' ('David Lloyd George: The Reform of British Land-holding and the Budget of 1914', *HJ*, vol.21, no.1, 1978, p.131). This account is silently superseded by Gilbert in *David Lloyd George: A Political Life. Volume 2: Organizer of Victory, 1912–1916*, p.82. The Cabinet budget committee meeting and the enquiries and action that followed are referred to in Nathan's 'Memorandum of Interviews, 24. 4. 14', TNA: IR 63/46.

programme that might be useful for the budget and urged the Chancellor to 'take the fullest credit for a great reform which the country will owe to your courage & imagination' (Lloyd George MSS, LG/C/4/17/5,6, PA).

Over the next two weeks JAP had a reason to be even less pleased, this time of his own making. After his return from Germany he had given a number of speeches outlining his impressions of the German education system, and the role of employers in supporting continuing education for young employees. In an interview with a Morning Post *journalist on 28 April he was also reported as commenting on some schools for mothers that he had visited, especially one at Charlottenberg designed to reduce infant mortality:*

> This will probably be a rather controversial topic in this country in the immediate future. There is an opinion here that all matters connected with health ought to be in the hands of the Local Government Board, which is the central sanitary authority. But I take the view that, as we have established now at the Board of Education a medical department, as the medical inspection and treatment of children are now run by education authorities who are making arrangements for the treatment of children either in clinics or hospitals, as the Government are responsible for children of school age, we ought also to be responsible for children below the compulsory school age. I am out for looking after them before they come into the schools. If our money has to be spent wisely in looking after children from three to fifteen it seems to me absurd that we should have to hand over to another Department the inspection of children who will suffer from exactly the same ailments and require similar treatment before three years of age.

The story looked very much like a kite. Perhaps the reporter had not realised that some of what he had been told was meant to be on background or off the record. But, with a headline 'The Government's Intentions', the President of the Board of Education's ambition was bound to attract attention. It did not help to be quoted as saying: 'At the same time I want to be loyal to the Local Government Board' or for the idea to be picked up in a Morning Post *editorial a few days later. The retreat was swift and comprehensive. There was some 'misapprehension' possibly arising from his mention of the 'great institution at Charlottenberg'. The new President of the Local Government Board, Herbert Samuel, had to be placated:*

> I wish to say, however, in the plainest possible terms that I never contemplated the transference to the Board of Education and the Local Education Authorities of any work which at present devolves upon the Local Government Board or the Sanitary Authorities. I regard medical care and advice for women during pregnancy and maternity and for them and their babies during the neo-natal period as lying outside the province of the Education Authorities.
>
> Nor have I ever entertained the idea which, I understand, has been attributed to me, of establishing a new Health Authority for children.

JAP professed himself satisfied that the Education and Sanitary Authorities could, with the 'necessary co-operation', do all that was needed, given the powers and the financial assistance that the Chancellor of the Exchequer had announced (JAP–Editor, 9 May 1914, Morning Post, *11 May 1914). In an open letter to the Liberal MP and Barclays Bank director Sir John Bethell Bt on 11 May JAP explained that £515,000 of 'new money' announced in the Budget would provide £92,000 for expenditure on meals and £423,000 for distribution to necessitous areas, defraying elementary education expenditure exceeding a 1s. 9d. rate, and half the spending in excess of a 1s. 6d. rate by 34 authorities that had not previously participated in the Necessitous Areas Grant. For the operation of the provision of meals legislation up to 1914 see J.S. Hurt,* Elementary Schooling and the Working Classes 1860–1918, *Routledge & Kegan Paul, 1979, pp.144–51; and for the clash between the Local Government Board and the Board of Education over maternity and child welfare see Frank Honigsbaum,* The Division in British Medicine: A history of the separation of general practice from hospital care 1911–1968, *Kogan Page, 1979, pp.26–9, and Honigsbaum's monograph,* The Struggle for the Ministry of Health, *Occasional Papers on Social Administration, no. 37, G. Bell, 1970. For Haldane's arbitration of the dispute on overlapping responsibilities for educational and medical services for children see Eyler,* Sir Arthur Newsholme and State Medicine, *pp.316–27.*

Thurs. April 30—May 6[16] Cabs. My big education bill strangled — ordered to bring in Single School area. Cabinets each week — Irish Problem still under consideration.

2 or 3 more letters from Redmond to the Prime Minister which he has read to the cabinet, but attaches very little weight to them, as they are always written from one point of view, namely his difficulty with his own people to settle on any terms which would give the Protestants any rope.

Two letters from Redmond to HHA around this time survive in the latter's papers: on 28 April he expressed concern about WSC's speech asking Carson to propose amendments to the Home Rule Bill; and on 5 May he commented on proposals for federalism (Bodl. MS. Asquith 36, f.47, and 39, ff.167–71). By now the police estimated that the Irish Volunteers numbered 25,000, and Redmond moved to bring them into the Irish Party fold (Colin Reid, 'The Irish Party and the Volunteer Crisis: Politics and the Home Rule Army, 1913–1916', in Caoimhe Nic Dháibhéid and Colin Reid eds, From Parnell to Paisley: Constitutional and Revolutionary Politics in Modern Ireland, *Irish Academic P., Dublin, 2010, pp.33–55).*

[16] JAP misdated this entry 'Wed. 30 April. May 6'. This and the entries for 20, 21, 23, and 25 May were written on 25 May.

In the lobby on 27 April WSC was overheard saying: 'We are near the cataract at last; I can hear the roar of the waters...'. William Ormsby-Gore, Conservative MP for Denbigh Boroughs, told his mother the next day: 'I really think civil war is now inevitable. The Government will stick at nothing' (Harlech MSS, Brogyntyn Estate and Family Records, PEC10/1, NLW).

HHA recorded a talk with Bonar Law and Carson for the best part of an hour on 5 May. They agreed that if a settlement could be reached it should be effected by an amending or Supplemental Bill to be enacted at the same time as the Home Rule Bill. Law expressed fears that his party was growing averse to any kind of settlement and would 'kick over the traces', making subsequent negotiations impossible. The record of the talk was sent to the King (Bodl. MS. Asquith 7, ff.123–4; MS. Asquith 3, ff.223–4). Two days later, with a small deputation of Liberal members who had been working across party lines for a peaceful settlement, a sympathetic HHA 'was very much interested and talked over federalism thinking it out in detail obviously for the first time' (Ponsonby diary, 7 May 1914, Ponsonby of Shulbrede MSS). On the other side, Jim Garvin made no secret in conversation with C.P. Scott of being 'eager for a settlement, especially now that the passage of the Army Annual Bill has struck the last weapon out of the Opposition's hand, was chiefly anxious to develop a federal solution' (Scott 'diary', 4 May 1914, Scott MSS, BL Add.MS. 50901, f.122).

In his consolidated report on two Cabinet meetings JAP makes no mention of an emphatic memorandum by the Chief Whip on 6 May, which explains why the Education Bill was strangled. Illingworth warned ministers that an autumn session would be impossible. 'There is a point of exhaustion beyond which it is impossible to drive the House of Commons...'. More than 5,000 meetings were being organised over the next two months on the Land Question alone. To ensure full value from the heavy expenditure, MPs needed to take up the issue in their own constituencies. Most Liberals had to earn a living from business or a profession and by keeping Parliament in session throughout the year they would be 'driving out of the Party its best and most reliable Members...'. After the end of August the Chief Whip could not 'undertake to secure the attendance of enough Members to ensure the safety of the Government' (Illingworth MSS). The Budget revenue decisions taken by Cabinet on 30 April were reported by DLG to Nathan, who recorded them the next day. Additional decisions and alterations were made at a conference at Walton Heath on Sunday 3 May (TNA: IR 63/46).

I missed cabinet Wed. 13 May — discussion on budget finance Bill.

JAP says nothing of the acrimonious proceedings in the Commons on 12 May, when HHA brought the committee stages of the Home Rule, Welsh Church, and Plural Voting legislation to an end, foreshadowing the introduction of an amending or supplemental bill to the Home Rule

Bill (HC Deb 12 May 1914 vol 62 cc948–1082). At the Cabinet that JAP missed, as Morley told Beauchamp the next day, 'not a word was vouchsafed' about these proceedings. 'The maxim about waiting and seeing can hardly be said to have turned up trumps so far' (Beauchamp MSS).

The always sensitive question of closer relations between Britain, France, and Russia brought an insistence that, if there were to be conversations with Russia, the Russians needed to be informed of Grey's letter to Cambon in November 1912 explaining that military staff talks did not entail any commitment to action (Harcourt Cabinet note, 13 May 1914, Bodl. MS.Eng.c.8269). More importantly for JAP, there was discussion of the necessity for some education legislation. 'Mr Pease was instructed to prepare & circulate alternative proposals in regard to the best way of dealing with the Single School areas in England and Wales' (HHA Cabinet letter, 14 May 1914, Bodl. MS. Asquith 7, f.126).

On the morning of 15 May DLG saw the King telling him that, at the Prime Minister's wish, he was continuing to carry on conversations with Redmond, Dillon, and 'others', including Carson, whom he had seen on 13 May. Carson was preparing a map with a plan to resolve the 'geographical' difficulty of the boundaries of Fermanagh and Tyrone by separating the Roman Catholic districts. Redmond was angry with the Prime Minister for announcing the amending bill without first informing him. DLG 'thought he had explained this to Mr R. But he will soon recover from his temporary ill-humour…'. Believing it best to introduce the amending bill in the Lords, DLG suggested it could be 'amended to any extent even say to the exclusion of the whole Province for an unlimited time; this would then give the Commons something definite upon which to debate and negotiate'. If the Lords refused to discuss the bill and threw it out, 'there would be no alternative but civil war'.

The King told DLG of an offer by the Speaker to HHA to try to bring the party leaders together to seek agreement on 'some points'. According to Stamfordham's report of the meeting, DLG thought it an admirable idea that might be tried 'before too long'. But he warned that the Liberal Party as a whole was against any concessions and did not realise the danger of the situation. At the last Cabinet meeting he had said, echoing WSC's vivid metaphor several weeks earlier: 'We have got into the rapids & are getting very near the cataract' (Stamfordham memorandum, 15 May 1914, GEO. V. K2553 (5), RA).

'On the whole,' HHA told one of his young female friends, Viola Parsons, on 18 May, 'a week teeming with embryo crises has gone off well particularly as regards the Treasury' (BL Add.MS. 59,895, f.29). In fact the embryo crises were still maturing. As the Financial Secretary to the Treasury warned: 'the opinion seems to be growing that the Treasury is losing control over Spending Departments, but competing with Spending Departments for its own projects, and the majority of the party are uneasy about this' (Montagu–HHA, 27 May 1914, copy, Montagu MSS, transcript courtesy of Judy Gendel and the Hon. Randolph Churchill). For Montagu's submission of schemes to remove anomalies and

improve the prospects of the Finance Bill see his two letters to DLG, 19 June 1914, and HHA, 29 June 1914 (copies, Montagu MSS).

Wed. May 20 Cabinet. Procedure.

JAP seems not to have heard, or to have taken less seriously than Harcourt, Grey's confession that he would like 'to retire from the European concert & leave Austria & Italy to settle Albania by themselves' (Harcourt Cabinet note, 20 May 1914, Bodl. MS.Eng.c.8269).

Thurs. 21 Home Rule 3d Rdg. Scene in House. Tories shouted down the Debate on Campbell[17] rising. Speaker asked Bonar Law if he would help him to maintain order. Bonar Law was pert, 'I know my duty; it is not to answer your question'. House adjourned by Speaker.

Angry at HHA's refusal to give any hint of the details of his promised amendment bill to the Home Rule Bill, the Tories had moved an adjournment motion. James Campbell rose after the motion had been defeated, and the scene, fomented by Lord Winterton, George Parker, and Harry Croft, began (Winterton diary, 21 May [1914], Bodl. MS. Winterton 12). The Speaker later apologised to Bonar Law for his error of judgement, having first consulted the Government Chief Whip on wording that would allow the Prime Minister to clear up 'the uncertainty as to the amending bill and its contents' (Lowther–P. Illingworth, 22 May 1914, Illingworth MSS).

Cabinet called *Sat. May 23d.* We agreed the P.M. on Monday should adhere to statement previously made, that we proposed to introduce into House of Lords bill to carry out our concessions named on March 9th if in meantime no terms agreed upon for an agreed amending bill.

Writing on 26 May to Venetia Stanley's sister-in-law, Lady Stanley, in Melbourne, HHA noted that the Home Rule Bill had been read a third and last time in the Commons the day before: 'the end of a chapter if not of a book. There is a lot of rowdiness in the House on the part mainly of the well born and ill bred among the younger Tories, and a certain amount of social friction & boycotting' (Stanley of Alderley MSS, IWM).

[17] James Henry Mussen Campbell (1851–1931); Con. MP Dublin U. 1903–16, Dublin (St Stephen's Green) 1898–1900; Irish barrister 1878; Irish QC 1892; QC 1899; Solr-Gen., Ireland 1901–5; Atty Gen., Ireland Dec. 1905 and 1916; Irish PC 1905; Ld Chief Justice of Ireland 1916–18; Bt 1917; Ld Chancellor of Ireland 1918–21; Baron Glenavy 1921; Irish Free State senator 1922–8; Chmn, Irish Free State Senate 1922–8. W.B. Yeats, a fellow senator, described him as 'handsome, watchful, vigorous, dominating, courteous, he seemed like some figure from an historical painting' (*DNB 1931–1940*, p.141).

Monday 25th P.M. dignified, & shown up to be big man he was. Bonar Law showed he had not the instincts of a gentleman & when Speaker apologised to him he merely accepted it, & did not admit to his own error & insult to the chair given on previous Thursday.

A very different judgement of the Opposition leader's performance that day came from his own back bench: 'Bonar Law did very well.' (W. Anstruther–Gray diary, 25 May 1914, Kilmany MSS, NRAS 3363/145.)

JAP's diary gives no hint that he might have been thinking, as he would once have been, about political currents beyond the parliamentary drama. Charles Masterman, recently defeated in Ipswich, and believing himself a casualty of the government's poor fortunes and misjudgements, saw it differently:

> The Cabinet are living in a dream world apart from the rank and file: the Whips' Office is blindly optimistic about each election and prophesies big majorities: we have nothing to offer positively to attract enthusiasm: and everything we have done since 1910 has cost us a certain number of votes. L.G. is jumpy, irritable, overworked and unhappy: disturbed at the unpopularity of Insurances & the failure of the Land Campaign to beat up a great emotional wave (though I believe it is going well in the country districts): now at the failure of his Budget to command any measure of enthusiasm. Also he is very disturbed about the Irish question where his sympathies are necessary largely with Protestant Ulster...the most difficult problem I hear is Labor...I think an understanding with them is equally imperative and impossible.
>
> *(Masterman–Ponsonby, 30 May 1914, Bodl. Ponsonby of Shulbrede MSS, MS.Eng.hist.c.660)*

On the increasingly tense Irish stand-off, the King's advisers were not hiding their frustration. 'I cannot understand what is going on,' Stamfordham confessed to Hopwood on the day Cabinet was to meet again after a break of several weeks. 'The K. had an important talk with the P.M. on Thursday last...nothing was done in the recess except a letter written to Carson asking for a map which he had promised to give Asquith...Meanwhile the Opposition seem obsessed with the idea that the Govt is wobbling & that it is only necessary to hammer them a little bit more to bring them toppling over—a dangerous game so far as the King is concerned' (Southborough MSS, Bodl. MS.Eng.c.7362). In an untitled Cabinet paper on 15 June Birrell began:

> The whole position is still governed, and consequently dislocated, by the firm conviction in the Unionist mind throughout Ireland that, before anything of political consequence happens with regard to the Home Rule Bill or Act there must be a General Election...They have of course been told by the British members of their

> Coalition that a General Election which may get rid of this Home Rule Bill altogether, is a likely event, and until this contingency is removed from the realm of probability it is impossible to measure the full fighting force of the Covenanters.
>
> *(Birrell MSS, Liverpool U.; TNA: CAB 37/120/70)*

Alternative scenarios were actually exercising a Conservative leadership privately acknowledging that the avoidance of civil war was 'the first necessity'. They are articulated in a letter from Bonar Law to Lord Midleton on 17 June (Bonar Law MSS, copy, BL34/2/80, PA), and for Carson's analysis see Selborne to Lady Selborne, 17 June 1914, Boyce ed., The Crisis of British Unionism, *pp.111–12.*

June 17[18] Debated Irish situation. Education. India Bill.

June 24 Education. Housing Bill. Ireland.

The Education Bill he had recommended to Cabinet on 5 May having been 'strangled', JAP was once again, as 'instructed', developing proposals for a single school areas bill that would 'probably be acceptable to Nonconformists'. On 24 June he presented a draft to the Cabinet affecting about 5,700 schools and 12,000 teachers. 'After much debate', it was decided to recast the bill to give managers of schools in single school areas two options: (1) allowing the local authority to appoint and dismiss teachers who would be empowered to give undenominational instruction, with managers free to provide denominational teaching for children whose parents wanted it, and the local authority undertaking the burden of maintenance, repair, heating, lighting, etc. (2) handing over the school to the local authority to rent or buy on negotiated terms (HHA Cabinet letter, 26 June 1914, Bodl. MS. Asquith 7, f.135).

Cabinet was presented with three options in a paper printed in July ('Education (Single School Areas) Bill', MS. Gainford 127/B, pp.27–30). Option 1: all schools in single school areas would become Council Schools on 1 September 1916; owners/trustees must inform LEA whether they want to close or transfer with/without any valuable consideration. LEA and owners to agree consideration but LEA to have absolute control at all times, including Saturday and Sunday. Additional expenditure: 2/5 from Block Grant plus additional grant dependent on attendance. Option 2, not circulated, less favourable to Nonconformists: all teachers appointed by LEA but existing managers could give denominational teaching to

[18] The entries from 17 June to 8 July were written on 8 July. JAP does not mention the Cabinet meeting on 22 June, which decided on changes to the content and title of the Irish Amending Bill, and the splitting of the Finance Bill in response to 'the exigencies of time' and objections by 'influential supporters of the Government' (HHA Cabinet letter, 23 May 1914, Bodl. MS. Asquith 7, ff.133–4). The difficulties coyly described by Asquith are best explained in Ian Packer, 'The Liberal Cave and the 1914 Budget', *EHR*, vol.CXI, no.442, June 1996, pp.620–35.

children whose parents requested in writing. LEA would keep up repairs but no capital expenditure. Option 3 was a compromise: schools would remain voluntary schools, and could give denominational teaching on premises in school hours, with managers paying (TNA: CAB 37/120/79,83).

Provision had been made in the Finance Bill for an additional £2,750,000 for elementary education in England and Wales, with all local authorities empowered to spend £3 per child (Peden, The Treasury and British Public Policy, *pp.62–3). In fact the formula for calculating the 'block grant' (the first use of the term for legislative purposes, as Selby-Bigge would point out) was rather more complicated. Selby-Bigge's brief description of the local authority grants scheme of the Finance Bill of 1914 highlights its inherent flaws (*The Board of Education, *G.P. Putnam's Sons, London & New York, 1927, pp.95–7).*

July 1 Guillotine finance bill sanctioned. India Bill.

The Council of India Bill, whose preparation had been largely overseen by Montagu, required the appointment of two Indian members and was designed to turn the Council in Whitehall into a quasi-administrative rather than an advisory body. Each India Office department was to have a Council member attached to it. The Bill had not been approved by, or even communicated to, the Government of India. It was rejected by the Lords by 96 votes to 38 on 7 July.

JAP's sparse notes for the previous fortnight are puzzling. The military correspondent of The Times *visited the War Office on 17 June 1914 and shared with his editor 'the conclusion that the P.M. means to do nothing in his department and is merely playing out time. He is rarely there, does nothing, and does it extremely well' (Repington–Robinson, 18 June 1914, in Morris ed.,* The Letters of Lieutenant-Colonel Charles à Court Repington, *p.224). While appearing to do nothing, HHA was opening new lines of communication over the Irish impasse with Alick Murray and Lord Rothermere as the intermediaries (Montagu note, 29 June 1914, Record of Negotiations over Ireland June/July 1914, Montagu MSS; Murray–DLG, 6, 14 July 1914, LG/C/6/5/14,16, PA).*

The Prime Minister had a host of other matters requiring his attention. Walter Runciman, writing to Sir Robert Chalmers, the former Permanent Secretary at the Treasury, on 24 June, said that gun-running and budget drafting had kept his colleagues 'pretty busy. Now in this very week L-G has met with a staggering rebuff over his financial plans... our programme and legislation are horribly upset, and our Chief Whip, the honest Illingworth, is able to give us little or no help...'. For the rest of this letter and the stymieing of the Chancellor's plans to make undefined subsidies to local authorities see Hazlehurst, Politicians at War, *pp.106–7.*

Runciman was not exaggerating. As Edwin Montagu summarised the crowded legislative agenda for Venetia Stanley: 'it is now 25th June. We have to pass a budget, House of Lords resolutions, revenue bill, housing bill, education bill, and possibly devote weeks to Ireland . . .'. The Financial Secretary to the Treasury thought it could not be done, and the Cabinet would not contemplate an autumn session. A despairing Montagu typically blamed himself for the fact that DLG was 'as untrammelled now as ever he was when he wouldn't speak to Hobhouse or Masterman wouldn't try to control him' (Montagu MSS, II 81/80, Wren Lib. TCC). The particular problems of the interrelated Revenue and Finance Bills are explained in John H.N. Pearce, 'The Rise of the Finance Act 1853–1922', Studies in the History of Tax Law, *vol.9, pp.93–9.*

Amid the cares of state there was a private matter that the Asquith family could not ignore. Early in the morning of 3 July, Raymond and Katherine Asquith, Diana Manners along with Duff and Sybil Cooper, Iris Tree, Nancy Cunard, and other revellers from the Asquith circle had witnessed the foolhardy young baronet Sir Denis Anson perish in the Thames after diving from the steam launch on which their already notorious Coterie was enjoying a midnight party given by Count Constantin Benckendorff and Raymond Asquith's brother-in-law, Edward Horner. Venetia Stanley and Maurice Baring had been 'havering' on the jetty (Diana Cooper, The Rainbow Comes and Goes, *Penguin Books, 1961 [1st edn Rupert Hart-Davis, 1958], p.98). Lady Horner had told Anson's mother of her son's death (Elizabeth Haldane diary, 20 May 1914, Elizabeth Haldane MSS, MS. 20240, f.67, NLS). The ensuing press speculation, allegations that Anson had been inebriated and dived in as a result of a wager, were only partly quelled by the inquest jury's finding of accidental death. The Central London Coroner would recall being considerably taken aback to find an array of distinguished counsel appearing at the inquest: F.E. Smith (for whom Edward Horner was devilling), Ernest Pollock, and William Jowitt (J. Ingleby Oddie,* Inquest, *Hutchinson, 1941, p.129).*

July 8 Lords amendment to H.R. bill Crewe instructed. Business of House. Owing to guillotine motion, majority falling to 23, as a protest against closuring finance situation discussed. General feeling to close down as soon as we had considered Home Rule amendment bill.

The government majority fell to 23 in the debate on 7 July on the allocation of time for the Finance Bill. HHA said that ten and a half days had already been spent on the bill. He was proposing a further four in committee, two on the report stage, and one on the third reading. Bonar Law argued that this was the first time the guillotine would be used on a finance bill. Many Liberals sympathised with Bonar Law's arguments and abstained; only 181 Liberals supported the government.

July 13[19] Cabinet. H.R. Amendment Bill from Lords considered. Somewhat short massacre of innocents arranged. Talk on Ireland — time — arrangement made to end Parly Session as soon as may be, meet again in Nov or Dec. Position of negociation with Carson explained. Not apparently by direct interview. The situation being that appointment of Judges & other matters were possible to settle, but Carsonites not prepared to give up Tyrone as in H.R. area. Nationalists equally strong. We all recognised we could not press any arrangement unless we had the acceptance of Nationalists even though it might be reluctantly given. The issues so far reaching not only civil war, but interests in India, industrial world & throughout empire might be broken up by catastrophe in Ireland. Whilst Tories would be in impossible position if they came in — & General Election could not in any case better the situation but would promote collision of forces in Ireland.

July 17 Friday morning at H. of C. The position was: Carson & Bonar Law (the P.M. had seen the latter) said they could not give way.

The P.M. said he had mentioned the possibility of a conference to the King, at supper at the Court Ball the night before, & he the King was quite prepared to invite the parties to Buckingham Palace with a view to bringing them together. The idea generally approved by Cabinet, would Redmond accept such an invitation. We adjourned for 2 hours to find out. Bonar Law & Redmond seen by George & P.M. saw Bonar Law, & at 3.0 we met again & decided to ask the King to invite 8, 2 from each party to the Conference.

P.M. reported at opening of cabinet Max Aitken saw Murray who wrote to the P.M. that Bonar Law was prepared to accept an invitation to a conference if forthcoming.

A few days earlier DLG had acquired some alarming intelligence. Arthur Ponsonby had encountered the King's private secretary in the lobby and had been 'horrified' when Stamfordham said that the government's action in introducing the Home Rule amending bill 'had vitiated the Parliament Act and if it did not bring a settlement the K did not see that he

[19] JAP misdated this entry 15 July; his account matches the Prime Minister's Cabinet letter of 14 July, referring to a meeting on 13 July (Bodl. MS. Asquith 7, f.141). The Cabinet met again on 16 July and twice on 17 July, but there are no Cabinet letters for these meetings. HHA saw the King on the 16th and 18th. Hobhouse referred on the 18th to a meeting on 'Wednesday' (15 July), but HHA, reporting copiously to Venetia Stanley, did not mention a Cabinet on that day (HHA–Venetia Stanley, 15, 17, 18 July 1914, *Asquith Letters*, pp.104–7; Hobhouse diary, 18 July 1914, Hobhouse MSS, and David ed., *Inside Asquith's Cabinet*, p.173).

was under any obligation to give his assent to the Bill'. At DLG's request Ponsonby repeated the conversation to John Redmond, who said that he suspected that this was the King's attitude, and did not think a settlement probable. A week or so later Ponsonby had 'a somewhat ticklish talk with Stamfordham', who apparently had 'completely forgotten saying what he did'. By then Ponsonby had himself begun to have doubts: 'I may be wrong in thinking he mentioned the King though I still think in his last sentence to me he did....' Stamfordham's 'own opinion was very clear' and, while he was friendly to the younger brother of one of his fellow courtiers, 'he showed a completely Tory bias without realising it' (Ponsonby diary, 12–17 July, 27 July 1914, Ponsonby of Shulbrede MSS).

In the House of Lords on 14 July Lord Beauchamp had alluded to a possible conference of the parties. Noticing this, and a call in the Daily Citizen *for Carson and Redmond to meet, the King wrote to HHA: 'You know for how long I have advocated this. You will I am sure appreciate my anxiety, as the time draws near, for the settlement of this momentous question.' On 17 July the King asked HHA to write a short memorandum stating the reasons why he was advising the calling of a conference of leaders of the various parties, and suggesting who they should be. The King would respond with 'a most cordial letter' approving the proposal (Bodl. MS. Asquith 3, ff.233–8). HHA duly submitted a memorandum to the King outlining the impasse over the Home Rule Amending Bill and recommending that the King intervene 'with the object of securing a pacific accommodation'. Suggesting that the King convene a conference of all parties concerned, HHA admitted that a conference might not 'attain a definitive settlement, but it will certainly postpone, & may avert dangerous & possibly irreparable action'. The Prime Minister concluded that in his opinion it was 'not only within the competence, but at such a time part of the duty, of a Constitutional Sovereign to exert his authority in the best interests of the United Kingdom & of the Empire' (Bodl. MS. Asquith 7, ff.143–5). HHA wrote the same day to Speaker Lowther, who had been active for weeks behind the scenes with Carson, canvassing the question: 'what do you mean by Ulster & what wd R[edmond] mean by Ulster?': 'the King is of opinion & I concur with him, that the utility of such a conference wd be rendered more likely if you wd be good enough to preside over it.' (Lowther–Carson–Lowther–Carson, 29, 30 June, 2 July 1914; HHA–Lowther, 17 July 1914, Transcripts from Ullswater MSS by Shane Leslie 1945, Leslie MSS, 30/44, Georgetown U. Library.)*

Neither the King nor the Cabinet was told that HHA had held a 'most secret' meeting with Lord Northcliffe at Alick Murray's flat in Ennismore Gardens after the 13 July Cabinet. Northcliffe, who was preparing his staff to cover a civil war in Ulster, had asked for the meeting. HHA 'talked over the question of areas & c & tried to impress upon him the importance of making The Times *a responsible newspaper' (HHA–Venetia Stanley, 13 July 1914,* Asquith Letters, *pp.100–1).*

I went down to the *Enchantress* with Churchill that evening for the review at Spithead. He told me that F.E. Smith said they were giving up such a lot, the chance of a general Election, the plural voting bill, & we had power, & Home Rule principle established, & we were fools not to meet the Tories in regard to allowing Tyrone to be in excluded area.

I pointed out that it was folly from party point of view to allow a few parishes in Tyrone to stop a settlement, that they would help hereafter to lever Orange Ulster to come into their own country's Government, but without the bills for which we had slaved on the statute book our prestige would be broken & we should be regarded as futile legislators by the country.

Speaker Lowther having agreed to preside over a conference, Stamfordham wrote to him, 'the King directs me', on 18 July conveying the sovereign's belief that Carson was in a very difficult position, 'partly because of the unyielding attitude of his people & partly as a consequence of his own speeches'. One of 'the duties' of the conference the King thought was to 'find means of relieving Sir E. Carson of responsibility for some of the details of settlement. e.g. as regards delimitation of parts of counties'. The controversy had narrowed down to 'what is to become of Tyrone?' Was it to be included or excluded? Or 'as an alternative, how can it be fairly divided?' What was obvious was that 'Civil War cannot be permitted on the subject of the delimitation of a county!' Lowther was left in no doubt of the King's expectation that he would 'not allow the Conference to break off without finding a solution'. At the worst he must have a record of what was agreed, such as taking off the time limit for exclusion, thereby fining down the controversy to 'any one point unsettled ...'. Stamfordham closed with the scarcely comforting assurance that the King is 'most sanguine that under your guidance there should be at any rate the happy result of ending all prospect of Civil War.' (Ullswater MSS, HA47/B3/396, Suffolk Archives.)

July 19 On Sunday morning, Churchill & I went on board the *Victoria & Albert* & saw the P.M. in his cabin. He read us a nice homely letter which the King was addressing to the 8 men to be summoned to the conference, asking them to come to 'my home' (not Palace).

The King was in good spirits, but was anxious about his speech to the members of the conference, He said to Churchill the Prime Minister says only a few words are wanted, but I shall want [to] use words which will be of service & I can't say nothing & must start the conference. The P.M. said the King had asked for the Speaker to preside and he had accepted, & he thought it would help.

'The King's letter was bad grammar but quite intelligent & keen,' Margot Asquith observed, 'Henry says he "is enchanted" and for the first time in his life feels himself a real monarch' (Margot Asquith diary, c.23 July 1914, Bodl. MS.Eng.d.3210, f.237). Rosebery had made a few alterations to the speech, presumably not degrading the syntax. The Opposition had been given no opportunity to discuss the part the Speaker would play in the Conference deliberations and were irked by the fact that the story was in the Harmsworth press (Lord E. Talbot–P. Illingworth, 20 July 1914, Illingworth MSS). Lansdowne and Bonar Law had written to Stamfordham, as he told Hopwood, 'regretting that no basis of discussion had been laid down & expressing grave doubts as to any good results!' Stamfordham then wrote to HHA 'assuming that some terms of reference or agenda—or something wd be given to tomorrow's meeting'. HHA himself was furious at the Northcliffe press (The Times and Daily Mail) getting hold of the secret. Suspicion that DLG was responsible for the leak was dismissed by Bonham Carter, who pointed out that the Liberal papers did not get the story and were 'indignant at the neglect' (Southborough MSS, Bodl. MS.Eng.c.7362).

DLG told Robert Donald of the Daily Chronicle on the day of the leak that it came from 'the other side'; it was understood that announcements concerning the King were never given publicity until he chose to do so. Donald said Bonar Law was responsible (Lloyd George MSS, LG/C/4/8/6,7, PA). Carson told R.D. Blumenfeld, the editor of the Daily Express, on 21 July that it was through 'no fault of the leaders of our Party who received the summons from the King' (Blumenfeld MSS, seen by courtesy of Sir John Elliot before deposit in the Beaverbrook Library, later transferred to the Parliamentary Archives).

July 20 On Monday July 20 the P.M. made his statement to the House which accepted it coldly, The Times having given away the knowledge of proposed conference that morning.

July 22 Cabinet H of C. 5.30. The Prime Minister proceeded in calm mood & with clear words to tell us what had passed at the conference at Buckingham Palace.

Immediately after his return from the palace HHA had joined at lunch his son Raymond, Lady Diana Manners, Rosalind Lyell, Count Harry Kessler, Count d'Haussonville, Lady Paget, Paul Cambon, Feodor Chaliapin (who was heard by a late arriving DLG at the opera on the 24th), 'and a little Indian lady in Indian costume... Despite the serious situation in Ireland', Kessler wrote in his diary, HHA 'seemed so cheerful, as if he hadn't a care in the world' (Laird M. Easton ed. and trs, Journey to the Abyss: The Diaries of Count Harry Kessler, 1880–1918, Alfred A. Knopf, New York, 2011, p.632; The Brocks' 'Mrs Lyall' in HHA's letter to Venetia Stanley that day was Rosalind Lyell, his PPS's wife, described by HHA on 2 September as 'sensible & rather attractive' (Asquith Letters, pp.109,215)).

No official record was kept of the conference, though several participants made their own notes. John Redmond, who was cheered by the Irish Guards at Buckingham Palace, dictated memoranda daily; they are preserved in his papers and were extensively quoted in Denis Gwynn, The History of the Partition (1912–1925), *Browne & Nolan, Dublin, 1950, pp.116–31. His account agrees with JAP's. Bonar Law also kept detailed notes, which tally fairly closely with Redmond's: Robert Blake,* The Unknown Prime Minister. The Life and Times of Andrew Bonar Law 1858–1923, *Eyre & Spottiswoode, 1955, p.215; and see HHA's account to Venetia Stanley in Jenkins,* Asquith, *pp.320–1, and* Asquith Letters, *p.109. John D. Fair,* British Interparty Conferences: A Study of the Procedure of Conciliation in British Politics, 1867–1921, *Clarendon P., Oxford, 1980, pp.103–19, summarises the conference and the parleys that preceded it.*

The Total exclusion of Ulster was first discussed, Carson making a most moving & eloquent speech in its favour, in the interest of Irish unity, apparently under a belief that, if the exclusion was strictly limited to those portions where plantation protestants existed in a large majority, there would remain a constant source of friction for generations. Redmond quite unable to concur. The feature of the discussion was the agreement between Carson & Redmond. They both saw each other's stand point & agreed that in regard to Tyrone they neither could give way, & that if they did, the agreement would not be worth the paper upon which it was written. The difficulty was historical in origin & insurmountable. Lloyd George & I said the Prime Minister tried to secure an assent to exclusion on Unions in Tyrone, counties other than Tyrone not meeting with real difficulty. The Nationalists with 55,000 R.Cs to 45,000 Protestants said they could not give it up as a whole, the Carsonites replying ¾ths the rates were paid by the 45,000 & they must have the whole excluded. Redmond was prepared for sake of Peace to divide Tyrone into Parliamentary Divisions — Carson would not listen to this. The Speaker suggested the Division as the rational solution when 2 parties asked for same area. Carson said no area should be included in H.R. unless there was a real predominance of R.Cs — & it was agreed Time Limit might go if other questions settled. Redmond, & he was prepared to give up Down, as Rostrevor was watering place for Belfast, also South Fermanagh. Derry City not mentioned but the P.M. said he knew he would give that too. Capt Craig[20] urged that the Nationalists

[20] Capt. James Craig (1871–1940); Con. MP Down (E) 1906–18, N. Down 1918–21; Carson's chief lieutenant and organiser of plans for resistance to Home Rule; Treasurer of the Household 1916–19; Bt 1917; Parl. Sec., Min. of Pensions 1919–20; Parl. and Fin. Sec., Admy 1920–1; leader Ulster Unionist Party 1921–40; first Prime Minister of N. Ireland 1921–40; Vt Craigavon 1927.

should remember they gave up 350,000 scattered protestants to HR. Redmond replied & we give up 300,000 R.C. in a small corner. Craig replied but they are safe under the Imperial Parliament.

We then discussed what alternatives we could suggest — one being one I pressed. Tyrone should be exempted from settlement, brought in on poll if a certain percentage agreed.

We then turned our attention to possible contingencies if conference broke up, as Bonar Law was not apparently prepared to go on discussing & adjourning & the P.M. thought it was probable no agreement would be come to. Provisional Govmt might be set up. Customs attached & collared.

It was thought army would move to prevent Belfast disturbances & that Pirrie would close his works, 27,000 men being then at large.

Churchill spoke up in favour of British interests forcing 2 hostile factions in Ireland to agree. It was pointed out that British parties were so closely allied with factions that this course impossible. Grey urged our taking own course but I pointed out that unless we had nationalist [*sic*] with us to press H.R. amending bill with our own proposals was futile as our people would side with Redmond & against our solution, & I urged we might say what we thought or advised but not introduce it into a bill.

I appealed to P.M. not to allow conference to break up. Time was on side of settlement, and a break up might mean violence & shattering of all our aspirations & Imperial interests & that we should only adjourn — to allow violence to be let loose because ¾ of Tyrone was at stake seemed to me a wicked course, & that both parties should retire & come together again. Simon urged that the Speaker should report progress made. Crewe thought the 2 sides would resist this, though at first meeting of conference, this course had been agreed to.

After the discussion on Ireland WSC 'remonstrated' with Harcourt for taking notes of Cabinet proceedings. Harcourt desisted and wrote about this meeting from memory (Harcourt diary, 22 July 1914, Bodl. MS.Eng.c.8269). He reverted to surreptitious note taking soon afterwards.

HHA gave a garden party at 10 Downing St on 23 July. 'It swarmed with Liberal Members and journalists of all shades of opinion,' Francis Hirst of The Economist *wrote. 'Churchill is supposed to be "verting". His difficulty is, according to the story, that "there is no precedent for a statesman ratting twice"' (F.W.H., 'My Journal in July 1914 [continued]',* Common Sense, *vol.VI, no.26, 28 June 1919). To an enquiry from the German Ambassador, Prince Lichnowsky, about how it would all end, WSC was said to have responded: 'Blood, blood' (Kessler diary, 23 July 1914,* Journey to the Abyss, *p.632).*

Friday July 24 3.45 Downing St. Cabinet summoned for the Prime Minister to report that the conference at Buckingham Palace had broken up, & that all they could agree to was to announce that in principle & detail they had failed to agree upon the boundary for excluded area.

The possibility of disclosing how close the parties came to [agreement] could not be revealed — both parties were limited to disclosures by attitude of their public clients. Carson & B. Law refused to accept any basis of settlement, other than exclusion of 6 counties. Lansdowne never tried to settle.

The Speaker suggested exclusion Tyrone for 2 years — but as Carson knew Tyrone would vote themselves in then, he would not have it. I suggested 2 registers & a repres. to both Houses, one from Unionist register to H of C, 1 Nationalist register to H.R. But Prime Minister said they did not mean to settle & all expedients had failed. Redmond & Carson in tears at end, remarkable agreement between them all through — had its comic side. Craig shook hands with Dillon & so it broke up.

The King saw each member & told Redmond he knew Home Rule was inevitable. Discussed European crisis, & Grey's attitude.

The Prime Minister's second private secretary, responsible for foreign affairs, wrote to his wife: 'One doesn't know what might happen at any moment... I don't like this Servian business either at all—the Austrian note as published in the "Times" is very like a declaration of war & one doesn't know how Russia will take it.' (Eric Drummond–Angela Drummond, 26 July 1914, Perth MSS, Stobhall 7/3/2/3, courtesy of Vt Strathallan.) Harcourt, who had already left London when the Friday Cabinet was called, drove to Sutton Courtenay to find out what had happened. Learning of the 'probable Austro-Servian War', which, he said, he could not be a party to, he warned HHA that WSC should be instructed not to move any ships without instructions from the Cabinet. 'I believe that if the German fleet moved out into the Channel (agst. France—not us) he would be capable of launching our fleet at them without reference to the Cabinet...'. HHA 'pooh poohed the idea' (Harcourt note, 26 July 1914, Bodl. MS.Eng.c.8269).

July 27 Cabinet. 5.30 H of C. Row in Dublin — K.O.S.B.160 having fired under provocation volley 31 shots. Position one in which Govt cd only have an inquiry to fully ascertain facts. Asst Commissioner to be suspended.

A cargo of guns and ammunition for the Irish Volunteers had been brought into Howth, near Dublin, by Erskine Childers and some friends. The yacht was met by a detachment of

Volunteers, who marched back to the city with their weapons. When the Assistant Commissioner of Police, William Harrel (not his father, Sir David Harrel, with whom the path-breaking scholar, A.T.Q. Stewart, uncharacteristically confused him), was notified by the Howth police, he telephoned Dublin Castle for instructions. His chief, Sir John Ross, was absent. He was told to go to the castle for instructions. Instead, Harrel summoned out both the police and the military (the King's Own Scottish Borderers), confronted the Volunteers, and demanded that they hand over their weapons. The Volunteers refused and slipped away into the crowd. After a great loss of face, the troops were marched back to their barracks followed by a taunting crowd. The troops lost their nerve and fired on the crowd, killing three and wounding 38 (Stewart, The Ulster Crisis, *pp.230–1).*

Grey had announced our policy in H of C. He said he had little to add — except to criticise Austria's attitude which was most uncompromising & unreasonable — Grey anxious not to disclose we intended keep out of all war, lest his influence as mediator might be thereby diminished.

This and most of the subsequent entries dealing with the outbreak and first few weeks of war were extensively revised on several occasions by JAP some years later. The text given here is the original, without any of JAP's amendments, glosses, or amplifications, unless these are specifically noted. For a version in which more later additions are included see K.M. Wilson, 'The Cabinet Diary of J. A. Pease 24 July–5 August 1914', Proceedings of the Leeds Philosophical and Literary Society, Literary and Historical Section, *vol.XIX, part III, Mar. 1983, pp.39–51. We discovered the existence of this publication by accident four years after it appeared. When Lord Gainford learned that the Leeds society had claimed copyright in the published extract, he wrote: 'I have no recollection of doing anything so drastic' (letter to Cameron Hazlehurst, 24 Aug. 1987). Wilson made use of the Gainford collection in several essays included in his* The Policy of the Entente: Essays on the Determinants of British Foreign Policy 1904–1914, *Cambridge UP, 1985, and* Empire and Continent.

For a detailed account of the decisions for war, drawing on all the then newly discovered sources, see Hazlehurst, Politicians at War, *pp.49–117. Douglas Newton,* The Darkest Days: The Truth Behind Britain's Rush to War, 1914, *Verso, 2014, reviews additional evidence and synthesises more recent scholarship. Simon Heffer,* Staring at God: Britain in the Great War, *Random House, 2019, pp.5–88, is a sound and insightful modern summary. Clark, 'Sir Edward Grey and the July Crisis',* IHR, *vol.38, no.2, 2016, pp.334–8, teases out the ambiguities and contradictions in the Foreign Secretary's behaviour over the next week. John W. Young, 'Emotions and the British Government's Decision for War in 1914',*

Diplomacy & Statecraft, *vol.29, no.4, 2018, pp.543–64, claims to be a 'new view about why the Cabinet decided to go to war on 4 August in defence of Belgium'. See the critical literature review on the European July crisis in James Joll and Gordon Martel,* The Origins of the First World War, *Taylor & Francis Group, 2022, pp.51–97.*

July 29 Cabinet. Ireland. Ross[21] & Harrel[22] having respectively resigned & been suspended. The Prime Minister said he proposed to place Nathan[23] at head of the R.I.C. He had patriotically accepted post knowing how undisciplined & untrustworthy some of them were. Lord Shaw the P.M. suggested should be asked to hold the inquiry into Dublin shooting case.[24]

Amending Bill to be taken on Thursday — P.M. to say we would withdraw time limit, & give county ballot for exclusion.

European situation

Grey criticised Austria's conduct as 'brutal recklessness'. He read telegrams showing an indisposition on Austria's part to listen to Russia & obviously regarded situation as very grave. Our treaty obligations were then considered.

[21] Sir John Foster George Ross-of-Bladensburg (1848–1926); Chief Commissioner, Dublin Metropolitan Police 1901–14; KCB 1903; ADC to two Lds Lt; KCVO 1911. Ross resigned in protest over what he felt was the unjust suspension of Harrel.

[22] William Vesey Harrel (1866–1956); Asst Commissioner of Police, Dublin 1902–14; after removal from office and grant of a pension based on years of service, joined the navy and worked in naval intelligence; son of Sir David Harrel: District Inspector, Royal Irish Constabulary 1886–98; Inspector-Gen. Prisons 1898–1902; CBE 1919. Having previously served John Morley as his PPS when Morley was Irish Secretary, JAP knew of Sir David Harrel and his son (not 'Harril' as transcribed in Keith Wilson, 'The Cabinet Diary…', whose footnote 7 transposes the ranks of Harrel and Ross). Sir David Harrel was known to A.F. Pease as an independent member of the Durham Conciliation Board. 'One of the best heads in Ireland' and a 'strong Protestant', he had at Birrell's request provided advice to the Cabinet in Feb. 1912 on 'Reports on probable resistance to Home Rule' (TNA: CAB 37/109/23). There is a summary of his career in Patrick Long, 'Harrel, Sir David Alfred', in James McGuire and James Quinn eds, *Dictionary of Irish Biography: From the Earliest Times to the Year 2002*, Vol. 4, G–J, Royal Irish Academy and Cambridge UP, 2009, pp.472–3.

[23] Sir Matthew Nathan (1862–1939) was going to replace Sir James Dougherty as U.-Sec. for Ireland not to replace the Inspector-Gen. of the Royal Irish Constabulary, Sir Neville Chamberlain, who served until 1916; Nathan was chmn, Bd of Inland Revenue 1911–14; entered Royal Engineers 1880; Sec., Colonial Defence Committee 1895; administrator, Sierra Leone 1899; Gov., Gold Coast 1900–3; KCMG 1902; Gov., Hong Kong 1903–7, Natal 1907–9; GCMG 1908; Sec., Post Office 1909–11; U.-Sec. of St. for Ireland 1914–16; Irish PC 1914; Sec., Min. of Pensions 1916–19; Gov. Queensland 1920–5. Travers, *The Last Years of Dublin Castle*, pp.168–70, downplays the 'distinguished' nature of Nathan's previous career. Crewe thought there was 'everything to say for him' for the Governorship of Bombay in Aug. 1912 but for the fact that he was a Jew (Bodl. MS. Harcourt 443, f.18). WSC's wild cousin Clare Sheridan praised his 'transcendent idealism', austerity, and 'uncompromising directness' (*Nuda Veritas*, Thornton Butterworth, 1934 [1st edn 1927], p.116). Graham Dominy, '"Not a Position for a Gentleman": Sir Matthew Nathan as Colonial Administrator: From Cape Coast Castle to Dublin Castle via Natal', *Journal of Imperial and Commonwealth History*, vol.46, no.1, 2018, pp.93–120, is a balanced overview.

[24] Thomas Shaw, Baron Shaw (1850–1937); life peer and Ld of Appeal 1909–29; Ld Advocate 1905–9; Lib. MP Hawick Burghs 1892–1909; Scottish Solr-Gen. 1894–5. Baron Craigmyle 1929. A royal commission under Shaw (with his son Alexander as secretary) was appointed on 5 Aug. 1914; and in a scathing report a month later stated that 'the proceedings of the police and military were tainted by fundamental illegality' (Cd. 7631 para. 30, in Bodl. MS. Asquith 41, f.116).

In 1839 Austria, France, Russia, Prussia & England by Art. 17 recognised Belgium as a neutral state, but by subsequent treaty, it was agreed by same parties that same force & validity should be guaranteed to Belgium by their said Majesties, as if the words had been textually inserted in the Treaty on 1839.

In 1870 Collier, Twiss & Coleridge[25] gave it as their opinion each Power to the Treaty would be bound by it even if one power refused or was unable to respect obligation, and if one power was made responsible by Belgium, the power concerned could recover from other signatories, so that the powers were really jointly & severally responsible for the fulfilment of the Treaty. Mr Gladstone in 1870 entered into another treaty with France & Prussia respecting undertaking not to intervene in their quarrel so long as Belgian territory was respected.

Lucy Masterman, admittedly reporting at second-hand and in retrospect, wrote of 'the unfolding of the original neutrality pact, old and yellowed, with notes by Gladstone during the war in 1870' (Lucy Masterman, C.F.G. Masterman, *p.265). For the historical context of Belgian neutrality and the Cabinet's discussion of British treaty obligations, an excellent modern guide is Hull,* A Scrap of Paper, *pp.33–43. There is 'A Counterfactual Analysis of the Regime of Permanent Neutrality, 1839–1914', in Michael F. Palo,* Neutrality as a Policy Choice for Small/Weak Democracies, *Brill|Nijhoff, 2019, pp.15–41. Foreign Office advice to Grey following Eyre Crowe's 1908 'Memorandum respecting Belgian Neutrality and Great Britain's Obligation to Defend it' is summarised in Patricia Lynn Pillsworth, 'Security, Prestige, and Realpolitik: Sir Eyre Crowe and British Foreign Policy 1907–1925', Ph.D. dissertation, U. at Albany, State U. of New York, 2013, pp.88–94. The story is told from the Belgian side in Mario Draper, '"Are We Ready?": Belgium and the Entente's Military Planning for a War Against Germany, 1906–1914',* IHR, *vol. 41, issue 6, 2019, pp.1216–34.*

For the sudden and intense review late in 1911 of strategic options relating to the violation of Belgian neutrality see Keith Wilson's chapter on 'The War Office, Churchill, and the Belgian Option—August to December 1911' in his Empire and Continent, *pp.126–40. In correspondence with Haldane, WSC had written on 2 September 1911: 'we must not lose Belgium &*

[25] *Sir Robert Porrett Collier* (1817–86); barrister 1843; Lib. MP Plymouth 1852–71; QC 1854; Judge Advocate of the Fleet and Counsel to Adm. 1859–63; Solr-Gen. 1863–6; Kt 1863; Atty Gen. 1866–71; puisne judge 1871; judge, judicial committee of privy council 1871–86; PC 1871; Baron Monkswell 1885. *Sir Travers Twiss* (1809–97); Oxford don in international law 1830–63; Prof. of International Law, King's College, London 1852–5; Regius Prof. of Civil Law, Oxford 1855–70; QC 1858; Adm. Advocate-Gen. 1862–7; Queen's Advocate-Gen. 1867–72; Kt 1867. J.M. Robertson in *DNB* pronounced 'his scholarship was as inaccurate as his style was diffuse'. *Sir John Duke Coleridge, 1st Baron Coleridge* (1820–94); barrister 1846; QC 1861; Lib. MP Exeter 1865–73; Solr-Gen. 1865–71; Kt 1865; Atty Gen. 1871–3; last Ld Chief Justice of Common Pleas 1873–80; Baron Coleridge 1874; first Ld Chief Justice 1880–94.

its fine strategic opportunities if we can help it. I am afraid however they will have been tampered with already. Perhaps they have granted a "way leave"' (Ewart MSS). *When Grey received information on 10 October 1912 that the Belgian government seriously contemplated the possibility that England might occupy Belgium in the event of war and was planning legislation to enable it to raise an army of at least 400,000, he annotated a minute from Lord Onslow to Sir Arthur Nicolson: 'We shall not violate Belgian neutrality unless a power with whom we are at war violates it first & if the object of the increase of the Belgian army is to resist violation of its neutrality we shall welcome the increase' (Onslow MSS, 173/21, Surrey History Centre).*

Grey said at any moment the French Government might ask us whether we would support them, & if we said NO, whether we would renew the 1870 treaty to prevent violation of Belgium. The P.M. said the Germans, if they attacked France would go through Belgium & hesitate in attack in any other way, & therefore our reply to France might if in affirmation to 2d question be almost equally provocative as if we said NO to the 1st question.

We were urged by France & Russia to come out with them to establish Peace. Germany & the triple alliance urged our neutrality & said this would alone preserve Peace. Evidently we could do nothing right, & that we should be held liable for anything that happened. The cabinet agreed we must do the best for our own interests, & that the cause of Peace & was the course to be promoted. All the Powers were now building on were their hopes of our participation or abstention as suited them best. Grey said if it had not been for his intervention, they were hopelessly drifting into war, & none had any suggestion to make. He would continue to urge mediation by as many Powers as he could and restrain Russia who was mobilising from doing so opposite German frontier.

The complexities and uncertainties about Russian mobilisation are set out in Joshua A Sanborn, Imperial Apocalypse: The Great War and the Destruction of the Russian Empire, Vol. 1, Oxford UP, 2014, pp.21–31, *and by Bruce W. Menning in important essays based on Russian archives: 'Russian Military Intelligence, July 1914: What St. Petersburg Perceived And Why It Mattered',* The Historian, vol.77, *no.2, 2015, pp.213–68; 'The Russian threat calculation, 1910–1914', in Geppert, Mulligan, and Rose eds,* The Wars before the Great War, *pp.151–75; and 'The Mobilization Crises of 1912 and 1914 in Russian Perspective: Overlooked and Neglected Linkages', in Andreas Gestrich and Hartmut Pogge von Strandmann eds,* Bid for World Power? New Research on the Outbreak of the First World War, *German Historical Institute London/Oxford UP, 2017, pp.223–62.*

We discussed the situation from our selfish point of view. Churchill said we were now in a better than average condition, & the Fleet was at war strength — 24 to 16 battleships in the N. Sea, & 3 to 1 in the Mediterranean. The 2nd fleet could be ready in a few days. Our magazines were now being protected, & Flotillas placed on the North sea. Coal & oil supplies were ready.

The next step, in case Germany made a surprise attack, was to man our coast defences, & issue orders to commanders to be ready against a surprise attack & to have men ready to examine ships coming into port.

I urged that there should be nothing done of a 'provocative' character, by examining Germans on their ships. Churchill agreed reserving rights in case of suspicious landings or movements.[26]

The next step was to be mobilised if circumstances arose.

Grey said he must tell Cambon that our people thought the Austro Servian quarrel did not concern us, that he would say to Cambon Don't count upon our coming in, & to Lichnowsky don't count on our abstention — & neither could then regard our inaction or action respectively as an Act of Treachery. This was assented to. Morley said I shall not be a party to any intervention between Austria & Servia. France may be a different thing. Churchill explained his preparations. Churchill pointed out how if Belgium was taken, how powerful would be the possession of these ports by the Germans — Rhine Scheldt & Ems &c & how serious would be the menace to Grt Britain. & Harcourt wrote me: 'It is very unlike the Admiralty talk where estimates are being considered...'.

Churchill however added it was an appalling calamity for civilised nations to contemplate & thought possible sovereigns could be brought together for sake of Peace.

The P.M. retorted the Austrian Emperor[27] is bitter, by the loss of his heir,[28] & we hear the Czar is violent & they are far apart — no help can be looked for in this direction.

Telling his wife of the 'long and grave Cabinet' that day, Herbert Samuel foreshadowed: 'We nineteen men around the table at Downing St may soon have to face the most momentous

[26] The mobilisation and disposition of the navy in home waters are lucidly summarised in Goldrick, *Before Jutland*, pp.5–15.

[27] Emperor Franz Josef I (1830–1916); succ. uncle 1848.

[28] Arch-Duke Franz Ferdinand (1863–1914); nephew of Emperor Franz Joseph; heir presumptive to Austro-Hungarian throne after suicide of Crown Prince Rudolph at Meyerling in 1889. He and his wife had been assassinated on 28 June 1914 in Sarajevo.

problem which men can face'. 'Each must be led by his own conscience, and none can put the responsibility on his neighbour,' he wrote late the next night at the Royal Palace Hotel to his mother after castigating the 'wicked recklessness of Austria' (Samuel MSS, SAM/A157/69, ff.29–32, A157/467, ff.1087–8, PA). Harcourt had concluded that Grey's position was 'sound, strong & honest... so long as we in Cabinet do not commit ourselves to a decision. When (and if) we do, Grey's position will be hopelessly weakened' (Harcourt diary, 29 July 1914, Bodl. MS.Eng.c.8269). Grey spent three hours as chief guest at the Sessional Dinner of the Welsh Party, confiding to one of his hosts 'he had had a very anxious worrying day, incessant calls from ambassadors, conversations with whom had to be carefully recorded'. DLG had persuaded him to attend 'but a slight illness had prevented L.G. from coming himself' ('Typed Reminiscence of Ll.G.', Wednesday, 29 July 1914, J.H. Lewis MSS (1943), Group 10 231, NLW).

On 8 August the wife of the Parliamentary Under-Secretary for Foreign Affairs wrote of her husband's return home on Thursday 30 July 'with a black face... Francis said "Things have taken a much worse turn. Germany has made a most dishonourable proposal to us." He said he couldn't even tell a soul, and he would give anything not to have seen the telegram himself... that Sir Edward's secretary told him that never before had he been seen in a white heat of passion...'. After they had gone to bed, Francis Acland told his wife the gist of the telegram: 'Germany had proposed that we should undertake to be neutral while she snapped up the French colonies.... Sir Edward's reply had shown his disgust so clearly that Germany would probably explain away her telegram & so the matter would never see the light of day' (Eleanor Acland, 'A Diary of What We Thought and Did During the European War of 1914 written for my children & their children', Acland of Killerton MSS, lent by Sir Richard Acland Bt, current whereabouts unknown).

We don't know how JAP spent most of Thursday 30 July. But the busy and self-important Harcourt says: 'Simon, J. Morley, Hobhouse, Beauchamp, Pease, Runciman, Montagu, Birrell all been in my room this afternoon—all with me, but Hobhouse with some reservations as to Belgium. (he was of course a soldier)...'. In another scrappy note, Harcourt writes: 'Simon sd. to me pointing to Pease "my views are those of his forebears"' (Harcourt note, 30 July 1914, Bodl. MS.Eng.c.8269).

July 31: Friday. Cabinet 11.0.

The P.M. alluded to ingenuous part Bethmann Hollweg had played — how he had written a letter through German Ambassador suggesting that we should abstain from the war if Germans at end of war left Belgium intact & their independence. Grey told him that without cabinet sanction he could not bargain treaty obligations away, & if Germany wanted peace we were working for same end & believed if we could jointly bring it about it would do more to cement good feeling than any abstention now from war, & that he Grey would use his best offices to bring about a more permanent understanding & thought it would be then possible that the better relations which had been established cd take definite form.

In what Sean McMeekin calls a 'diplomatic blunder of the first order', Bethmann had reportedly told Sir Edward Goschen, the British Ambassador in Berlin, that, as regards Belgium, he 'could not tell to what operations Germany might be forced by the action of France, but he could state that, provided that Belgium did not take sides against Germany, her integrity would be respected after the conclusion of the war' (July 1914: Countdown to War, *Basic Books, New York, 2013, p.278). Although Germany was left in no doubt about Britain's commitment to Belgium, a series of ambiguous messages from an exhausted Grey and his principal adviser, Sir William Tyrrell, would be construed in some quarters in Germany as proposing conditional neutrality or hinting at the possibility, 'in the event of a Russian war', that the German and French armies might 'remain facing each other without either side attacking'. This 'misunderstanding', on which there is a substantial literature, was quickly dispelled (Clark,* The Sleepwalkers, *pp.527–37; McMeekin,* July 1914, *pp.348–9; Stephen J. Valone, '"There must be some misunderstanding": Sir Edward Grey's Diplomacy of August 1, 1914',* JBS, *vol.27, no.4, 1988, pp.405–24; and for a more recent interpretation that largely concurs with Valone and suggests 'it is very likely that there was no misunderstanding at all', see T.G. Otte,* July Crisis: The World's Descent into War, Summer 1914, *Cambridge UP, 2014, pp.480–5; there is a useful compilation and commentary in Kenneth Alan Miller, 'England and the Origins of the First World War: Selected Documents', Ed.D. thesis, Columbia U., 1970). Jérôme aan de Wiel collates the information influencing German decision-makers in '1914: What Will the British Do? The Irish Home Rule Crisis in the July Crisis',* IHR, *vol.37, no.4, 2015, pp.2–25.*

Grey, who had never met Bethmann Hollweg, would later say that 'I found out afterwards, & I had some suspicion of it at the time, that I was not discussing with the principals at all. Neither Bethmann Hollweg nor Lichnowsky really represented German policy. The General Staff did. Even the Kaiser was powerless against them' (A.L. Kennedy journal, 27 Apr. 1933, Gordon Martel ed., The Times and Appeasement: The Journals of A. L. Kennedy, 1932–1939, *Cambridge UP, 2000, p.88). For a more nuanced and copiously documented analysis of the Kaiser's role see John C.G. Röhl, 'The Curious Case of the Kaiser's Disappearing War Guilt: Wilhelm II in July 1914', in Holger Afflerbach and David Stevenson eds,* An Improbable War? The Outbreak of World War I and European Political Culture before 1914, *Berghahn Books, 2012 [1st edn 2007]. And for Grey saying in August 1914 that on each of the four occasions he had met the Kaiser the Emperor had said to him: 'I can be at Paris in twelve days whenever I like' see John Bailey diary, 21 Aug. 1914, [Sarah Bailey ed.],* John Bailey 1864–1931, Letters and Diaries, *John Murray, 1935, p.151.*

Policy we agreed to: British opinion would not now enable us to support France — a violation of Belgium might alter public opinion, but we could say nothing to commit ourselves. I urged that we should do nothing provocative, & that our precautionary steps should not be misdirected. After our free expressions & Churchill once or twice bellicose & aggressive Harcourt wrote to me in pencil. 'It is clear that this cabinet will not join in the war…'.

Harcourt claimed in his diary that after the Cabinet on 27 July he started 'talks with several colleagues in order to form a Peace party which if necessary shall break up the Cabinet in the interest of our abstention'. He thought then he could 'count on' ten to join him: Morley, Runciman, McKinnon Wood, Pease, McKenna, Beauchamp, Burns, Simon, Hobhouse, Birrell, 'probably also Samuel and Masterman'. But not, conspicuously, DLG. By 29 July the count had shrunk. He had misjudged McKenna and Masterman, who would explain his justification for supporting the war to Edmund Harvey a few days later (undated letter, Harvey MSS, Friends Lib.). 'I am certain now I can take at least 9 colleagues out with me on resignation viz. Morley, Burns, Beauchamp, McK Wood, Pease, Samuel, Hobhouse, Runciman, Simon…'. The next day, when Harcourt tallied those who had visited him, Samuel's name was no longer on the list. Runciman, if his testimony to the historian Harold Temperley is to be believed, aligned himself with WSC and Crewe, as holding the 'Grey–Asquith view'. His memory that JAP shared this view suggests a subtler understanding of JAP's position than Harcourt's (Response to Temperley's questionnaire, 4 Nov. 1929, Spender MSS, BL Add.MS. 46,386). Harcourt's list was down again on the afternoon of 30 July: Simon, J. Morley, Hobhouse, Beauchamp, Pease, Runciman, Montagu, Birrell, and Hobhouse 'with some reservations as to Belgium'. But he was under the delusional impression, as he told Simon, 'L.G. is now entirely with us!' (Bodl. MS.Eng.c.8269).

Prominent though he was in ushering colleagues into talks about keeping Britain out of a war, Harcourt, the diarist with an eye to history, exaggerated his own influence. He gave the appearance of 'organising opinion', as Morley later put it (Memorandum on Resignation, *p.4). But he was not, as Douglas Newton has characterised him, 'the leading neutralist minister'* (The Darkest Days, *p.4). He was no leader. He mistook posture, wavering, curiosity, and acceptance of hospitality for the settled intentions of many of the Cabinet who were certainly not his 'pledged disciples', as Newton describes them ('Hard Truths about Britain's Entry into World War I', http://historynewsnetwork.org/article/157821), accessed 27 Nov. 2022).*

Nor, evidently, did he realise how appalled some of his colleagues were at his attitude. On the evening of 31 July Haldane told his friend Edmund Gosse: 'The German fleet will sail down the Channel bombarding [Le] Havre and Cherbourg, and smashing the northern coast of France. But people like Harcourt say, "What business is it of ours? Let us be benevolently neutral!"' ('Cabinet Journal of Lewis Harcourt', 26–9, 30 July 1914, Mike Webb ed., From Downing Street to the Trenches: First-Hand Accounts from the Great War, 1914–1916, *Bodleian Library, 2014, pp.29,32; Edmund Gosse, 'What I Saw and Heard: July–August 1914', revised and completed 16 Oct. 1914, BL Ashley 5738, quoted in Mark Bostridge,* The Fateful Year: England 1914, *Viking, 2014, p.187).*

Captain Maurice Hankey, behind the scenes as Secretary of the CID, had told his wife late on 31 July: 'Everything has happened exactly as we expected—War Insurance unobtainable; an attempt to deplete our stocks of gold for the Continent; a consequent reply on our part by raising the bank rate to 8%—unparalleled in our life time, in order to draw gold back here. I expect we shall have a mild run on our banks in a day or two.' Both Hankey and Simon, as Attorney General, furnished advice on 1 August that, although there was no statutory authority for doing so, the export of gold bullion or coin could be prohibited 'if national necessity requires it' (Bodl. MS. Asquith 25, ff.201–4). Hilton Young, City Editor of the Morning Post, *'by a prodigious feat', raised for his brother, the mountaineer Geoffrey Young, who was about to travel to France for the* Daily News, *'the only golden sovereigns allowed out of London during the moratorium'. Charles Trevelyan, on the brink of resignation, farewelled Young with some Napoleon crown pieces kept in the family since the French wars (Geoffrey Winthrop Young,* The Grace of Forgetting, *Country Life Ltd, 1953, p.156). Hankey, custodian of the 'War Book', calculated that Britain had 'enough wheat for 4 months or more, and enough meat for longer—at a price'. If war broke out, he thought, there would be a panic and very high prices, 'and all our ships will bolt to port'. Hankey had walked with the Prime Minister from Downing Street to the Admiralty: he was 'very pressed but cheerful' (Lady Hankey MSS, AHKY 1/2/7, typed transcript, CAC).*

Later that day Eric Drummond was telling his wife that he did 'trust' that, if war came between the great Powers, Britain may not be involved. Working at the Prime Minister's side at 10 Downing Street, Drummond admitted that: 'The only absolute engagement we have in black & white is to maintain the independence & neutrality of Belgium & that itself is serious enough, as the general idea is that the German line of attack on France is through Belgium.' He was to return to Downing Street that evening: 'I rather hope it may be to play bridge & not to work. The P.M. is very fit & well... It must be awful for him & Edward Grey all this responsibility...'. In the event he dined at the Prime Minister's table, and played 'a little bridge. I succeeded in collaring 30 /-... [from Roderick Meiklejohn] paid in gold too'.

> Then about eleven the rush began & Tyrrell arrived here about 12 with a telegram on which we drafted a message from the King to the Tsar & the P.M. & he went off to wake up the King & get his approval to it, while I went off to Queen Anne's Gate & woke up poor Edward Grey to get his approval. We succeeded in doing all these things, but the result was I didn't get home till 2 — however the F.O. staff are worse, poor chaps, they were nearly all working at full strength till about one, then about 12 sat up till ¼ to 5, & they were at it again first thing this morning [Saturday].
>
> *(Drummond–Angela Drummond, 1 Aug. 1914, Perth MSS, Stobhall 7/3/2/3)*

In the diary entries that follow, especially after the nation was at war from 4 August, JAP struggles from time to time to keep up with the flood of subjects that came to Cabinet for decision or information. An unexpectedly colourful and candid description of the emergency legislation flowing in 'a rapid and copious stream ... Acts of Parliament, Orders in Council orders and regulations having the force of law' was provided by Sir Courtenay Ilbert and C.E.A. Bedwell: 'These trod on each other's heels, jostled each other, amended, supplemented, or superseded ... Measures so framed were necessarily experimental, tentative, imperfect, often transitory' (Journal of the Society of Comparative Legislation, *vol.16, 1916, pp.6–10). In the same edition of the journal E. Manson provided a compendium and summary of the war emergency proclamations issued on 1 August and immediately afterwards on the Defence of the Realm, wireless telegraphy, bank holidays, aerial navigation, calling out the men of the Royal Naval Reserve and the Royal Fleet Reserve, RNVR, and the Army Reserve and embodying the Territorial Army, Orders in Council re the takeover of the railways, treatment of enemy shipping, etc. Pre-war deliberations between the civil and military authorities on emergency powers are documented in Andrew G. Bone, 'Beyond the Rule of Law: Aspects of the Defence of the Realm Acts And Regulations, 1914–1918', Ph.D. thesis, McMaster U., 1994, ch. 1.*

August 1 Saturday cabinet called at 11.0 Aug. 1. I was in N. of England. Germany had issued ultimatum to Russia to demobilise in 12 hours — (i.e. to force war) late Friday. It was realised France would assist but Germans had been mobilising secretly.

At 2.0 in the morning early Saturday Grey & the P.M. went to Palace, got the King up & induced him to send a message to the Czar offering his own mediation bet. Russia & Germany, & asking him to avoid steps which would precipitate European conflagration. Cabinet Committees saw financiers — materials arranged 4 months supplies, another 2½ months ready to come.

JAP later interpolated notes explaining that the Cabinet Committees dealt respectively with a financial moratorium and food supplies. WSC had instructed his Chief of Staff and Captain

Richard Webb, Director of the nascent Trade Division of the Admiralty War Staff, to attend a Cabinet committee at 2.00 p.m. prepared to give details of the threat to shipping from German destroyers. 'They shd take with them a chart & explain fully the anxieties & dangers by showing the position of potential German Commerce Destroyers' (Note signed 'WSC' and dated 1 Aug. 1914, Sotheby's catalogue 19 Dec. 1981, p.19). Captain Webb's pre-war policy papers on trade defence are summarised in Matthew Seligmann, 'A Service Ready for Total War? The State of the Royal Navy in July 1914', EHR, vol.CXXXIII, no.560, Feb. 2018, pp.113–14. For an exposition of the supposed danger of German commerce raiders see Seligmann's The Royal Navy and the German Threat, 1901–1914: Admiralty Plans to Protect British Trade in a War Against Germany, Oxford UP, 2012, Jon Tetsuro Sumida's critical review in JMH, vol.85, no.3, 2013, pp.671–3, and the reservations of Dirk Bönker in First World War Studies, vol.5, no.3, 2014, pp.343–5.

Hankey, sustained by daily exercise, swimming, and half hours on a bed in his room, told his wife that night: 'Today has been a day of panic. The bankers are in a panic and are trying to stampede the Government into National War Insurance of Shipping. The grain merchants. are doing ditto but their motives are by no means above suspicion.' (Lady Hankey MSS, ADHY 1/2/7, typed transcript, CAC; Ralph Hawtrey's Treasury account of 'The Emergency Financial Measures of 1914', undated typescript but possibly early 1915, is in Hawtrey MSS, HTRY 1/10, CAC.)

Within days the government had committed to provide 80 per cent reinsurance to any British underwriter who insured a British ship that was part of an existing British shipping association. A State Insurance Office set up in London offered a flat rate for all cargo on merchant voyages on British ships. Apart from the obvious safety net for the insurance industry, keeping the merchant navy afloat, and minimising the interruption of food supplies, the schemes had the critical benefit of denying intelligence from the re-insurance market to the enemy (Luis Lobo-Guerrero, Insuring War: Sovereignty, Security And Risk, Routledge, 2012, ch.3). Insurance of overseas commerce in wartime had been the subject of 'acute controversy' in the CID between WSC and Runciman in February 1913 (Harcourt diary, 6 Feb. 1913, Bodl. MS.Eng.c.8268). Captain Hankey proudly informed the Palace after two weeks of war that the insurance scheme had made a profit for the state of £1½ million (Stephen Roskill, Hankey: Man of Secrets, Vol. I 1877–1918, Collins, 1970, p.132).

A brief overview of pre-war planning on war risks insurance is given by David French in his important study British Economic and Strategic Planning 1905–1915, George Allen & Unwin, 1982, pp.60–7,88. The volume in the Carnegie Endowment for International Peace series provides an excellent overview by contemporaries: Sir Norman Hill et al., War & Insurance, Oxford UP/Yale UP, London, New Haven, 1927. Previous accounts of the *financial measures taken at the beginning of the war are superseded by the meticulous research of Richard Roberts,* Saving the City: The Great Financial Crisis of 1914, *Oxford UP, 2013. But there is much of value in Teresa Seabourne, 'The Summer of 1914', in Forrest Capie and Geoffrey E. Wood eds,* Financial Crises and the World Banking System, *Macmillan, 1985, pp.77–116. The typescript in the Asquith MSS of a speech on 'the maintenance of our overseas trade in time of war', prepared for DLG to deliver to the House on 4 August, is annotated: 'There are differences between this and that in Hansard' (Bodl. MS. Asquith 26, ff.5–11).*

War declared Saturday afternoon by Germany on Russia.

The diplomat J.D. Gregory, who was 'a daily and nightly witness of all the communications that led up to the war', told the new Pope Benedict XV five months later that, if a poll of the British population had been taken on 1 August on the propriety of going to war, 90 per cent would have voted against it. If the same poll had been taken on 4 August, 90 per cent would have voted for it, 'simply and solely on moral grounds, because a sacred treaty had been violated'. Gregory's report to the Prime Minister's private secretary, Eric Drummond, on his interview with the Pope, was shown to Asquith and to Sir Edward Grey, who pencilled: 'I doubt the figure, but it is true that Belgium made us a united Govt, Parliament & Nation. We should otherwise have been divided.' (Gregory–Drummond, 17 Jan. 1915, Grey's comment [?28] Jan. 1915, Perth MSS, Stobhall 7/3/2/5.)

With the Cabinet still divided, Asquith wrote to the Chief of the Imperial General Staff on 1 August putting it on record that the government had never decided to deploy the Expeditionary Force in the event of a European war (IWM Documents.24336). Believing that the Cabinet had 'finally decided to run away, and to desert France in her hour of need', Sir Eyre Crowe, Assistant Under-Secretary of State for Foreign Affairs, wrote to his wife Clema on 1 August of the feeling in the office: 'practically everyone wants to resign rather than serve such a government of dishonourable cowards. I have myself prevented 5 resignations from going in. Of course the supreme duty is not to Sir E. Grey and his cabinet, but to the State, and to desert one's post at this hour would be worse dishonour.' (Bodl. MS.Eng.e.3020, f.1.) Crowe, his Foreign Office colleagues, and the incorrigibly conspiratorial and agitated Henry Wilson at the War Office were not alone in their anxieties as rumours spread. The Conservative MP for Andover, Walter Faber, a supernumerary captain in the Royal Wilts Yeomanry, despatched a telegram to Bonar Law on the morning of 1 August: 'Reliable information yesterday's cabinet council Grey and certain others against helping France Churchill for it says that labour resolution can be ignored if Unionist support firm' (Bonar Law MSS, BL34/3/1, PA).

Lord Charles Beresford, enlisted by fellow backbencher George Lloyd, had gone with Lloyd by train to Reading and then by motor to Ned Goulding's Wargrave Hall near Henley to persuade Bonar Law to return to London ([Lord Charles Beresford], 'Notes on European War', unsigned undated typescript, Maxse MSS, 471/486–7, West Sussex RO, transcript courtesy of Dr John Stubbs; and Beresford's account as told to Alick Murray and recorded in the diary of his brother Arthur Murray MP, 5 July 1916, Elibank MSS, MS. 8815, ff.9–10, NLS). Geoffrey Robinson, editor of The Times, *had 'heard enough from Beauchamp & others' on 1 August 'to know that a large part of the Cabinet were for leaving France in the lurch'. 'Robin' Dawson (as Robinson had become in 1917 after inheriting the Yorkshire estate of his aunt Margaret Dawson) recalled for Leo Maxse that his principal memory of Saturday 1 August was 'that I was constantly bumping into Beauchamp... I found him both lunching at the Travellers' Club and dining at the Beefsteak, on which occasion he was holding forth to a paralysed circle on the importance of strict neutrality whatever happened' (Dawson–Maxse, 13 Aug. 1918, Bodl. MS. Dawson, Box 9 when seen).*

On Saturday night, Wilson and Lloyd briefed a Conservative front-bench group at Lansdowne House on distressing interviews at the French embassy. George Lloyd's droll depiction of the scene found its way into his wife's 'diary': 'The Duke of Devonshire sat on a sofa & slept! Lord Lansdowne listened silently & very attentively—(but at the end said "You must ask Lloyd—he knows the whole of these matters at his finger-tips & I don't!")—while Bonar spouted, but at the end had nothing better to say than "but what are we to do?"' Lloyd told Leo Amery that 'none of them showed the slightest conception of the fact that war was on or that it signified anything' (Amery diary, 1 Aug. 1914, John Barnes and David Nicholson eds, The Leo Amery Diaries, Volume I: 1896–1929, *Hutchinson, 1980, p.104). The meeting dispersed at 3.00 a.m., with agreement to reconvene in the morning (Blanche Lloyd undated narrative, Lloyd of Dolobran MSS, GLLD 28/6, CAC).*[29] *The somnolent Devonshire had caught the essence of the briefing. The French were 'dreadfully sore at us for not sending the military force... it will soon be too late for us to do anything on land' (Devonshire diary, 1 Aug. 1914, Devonshire MSS, DF7/1/17).*

Devonshire together with Sir Cecil Spring-Rice had earlier heard Balfour tell Jasper Ridley, the Russian Ambassador's son-in-law, that the Tories' position was that, 'if it was purely a

[29] This document, catalogued as a 'diary of events from 31 July 1914', and footnoted by Heffer (*Staring at God*, pp.839,841) as a diary, refers to 'Sir H. Wilson'. As Wilson was not knighted until 1 July 1915, the entry could have been transcribed and corrected, or even written, a least a year or so after the events described. We are grateful to Tom Davies, Sophie Bridges, and Katharine Thomson for aid in examining the text. Many writers have awarded Wilson his knighthood up to four years early. A conspicuous example is the title of chapter 17, 'Brigadier General Sir Henry Wilson's Plan', in Paul Ham's monumental *1914: The Year the World Ended*, William Heinemann Australia, N. Sydney, 2013, pp.167–75.

question of Servia, they were against war; if it was the... European issue, they were for it to a man'. Balfour had insisted that there were no obligations, notwithstanding the strong views of Russia and France. That, he said, was what had sometimes made him feel that 'real obligations would be wiser'(Jasper Ridley diary, 1 Aug. 1914, quoted in Marina Soroka, Britain, Russia and the Road to the First World War: The Fateful Embassy of Count Aleksandr Benckendorff (1903–16), *Ashgate, Farnham, 2011, p.254). Geoffrey Robinson walked across Smith Square early the next morning to call on McKenna and 'found him at least on the fence': 'the Govt could do nothing unless the people were behind them, & the people were against war' (Geoffrey Robinson, 'Notes of some critical Sundays July August 1914', n.d. [c.10 Aug. 1914], Bodl. MS. Dawson, Box 8 when seen).*

August 2 I saw Harcourt, George, Simon, Runciman at No. 11 Downing Street at 10.15 — we discussed our attitude & all agreed we were not prepared to go into war now, but that in certain events we might reconsider position such as the wholesale invasion of Belgium. Harcourt not prepared to rely on treaty of 1839, as now binding. Simon arguing too that 80 years had created wholly different circumstances.

JAP's careful statement of the position reached at this gathering is at odds with Harcourt's diary note of what happened next. Harcourt has McKinnon Wood at this meeting as well. He wrote: '11.0 a.m. Before Cab. Ll. Geo. & I went to P.M. & sd we represented 8–10 colleagues who wd. not go to war for Belgium. P.M. listened, sd. nothing. Birrell added his name to others before Ll. G. & I went up.' (Harcourt note, 2 Aug. 1914, Bodl. MS.Eng.c.8269; Webb ed., From Downing Street to the Trenches, *p.33.)*

Cabinet at 11.0. Grey said the time had come for plain speaking & he had made up his mind that we must tell the French — & he must see Cambon at 2.30. He had appealed that morning very pathetically for a decision & we must give one. What we should do to help them in war. The Germans were already in Luxembourg. They, the French, had relying on the entente kept their Northern coast undefended, & might be crushed if we did not come to their assistance. Cambon had twice wept over our statement that we were not committed & that up to the present the French could not rely on our definite help. He Grey regarded our obligation to Belgium neutrality as binding, but if the German Fleet menaced our position down the Channel & attacked the French coast in those waters he could not stay unless we blockaded the German Navy into the Baltic.

I said, if we tell the Germans they may not move their fleet & come out is not that tantamount to a declaration of war. NO, said Grey 'but I believe war will come

& it is due to France they shall have our support'. We discussed the extent to which German Fleet might be left access to the North Sea, & generally agreed that destroyers & cruisers were entitled to protect their own commerce.[30]

The P.M. said he had seen Lichnowsky that morning & he broke down at the conduct of Germany, & Grey said Yes he said things to me against his own Government which would not stand repetition. The P.M. told Lichnowsky there were 2 points that were dangerous, & our abstention largely depended on the non violation of Belgium territory, & the non use of their Navy off the North coast of France.[31] Harcourt wrote to [me] when Grey urged we must protect the Channel 'I can't decline this'.[32]

We all tried to get Grey to seek the neutrality of France in our home waters also, as if the Germans could be assured of food & trade supplies, they might be bought off. Grey thought he could not do this — & we must come to a decision. After an hour & a half Grey became more pro-war — Winston also — & threatened he could not stay if Germans crossed into Belgium. Morley replied he would go, if we went to war, & at end of Cabinet Churchill was adversely criticised for mobilising Fleet late Friday night.

It was agreed to adopt Huth Jackson's committee's recommendations re food supplies.[33]

[30] JAP told Grey's secretary Sir William Tyrrell on 1 Oct. 1914: 'My impression is that Grey had also in his mind the importance of preventing not merely the German Navy coming into the English Channel and devastating the French coast, but that an assurance should be given of a binding character which would prevent the North Sea being utilised to harass the West Coast of France as well as the Northern Coast of France on the South side of the English Channel' (TNA: FO 800/89; and, with some minor errors of transcription, in Wilson, 'The Cabinet Diary…', p.13n.44).

[31] Reporting that day to the German Foreign Office on his meeting with HHA, Lichnowsky wrote: 'Tears repeatedly stood in the eyes of the old gentleman, and he said to me "A war between our two countries is quite unthinkable".' (*Heading for the Abyss*, p.419; Harry F. Young, *Prince Lichnowsky and the Great War*, U. of Georgia P., Athens, GA, 1977, pp.12–26.)

[32] On 5 Aug. Harcourt explained his support for the war by reference to 'three overwhelming British interests' not 'any obligation of Treaty or honour' (Hazlehurst, *Politicians at War*, p.114). Harcourt's embarrassed attempts to justify his own slide towards war are captured in the diary of Percy Molteno, who saw him frequently between 29 July and Sunday 2 August. From insisting that, as long as he remained in the Cabinet, Britain would not go to war, on 2 August he 'modified his statement to the extent that, if the Germans would not agree not to attack the Channel ports of France, and would not respect Belgian integrity and independence in return for our neutrality, then he might be disposed to go to war' (Hirst, *A Man of Principle*, p.437).

[33] Frederick Huth Jackson (1863–1921); London merchant banker and Bank of England director since 1902; contemplated buying a newspaper in 1909 as 'a daily organ of central opinion' (George Boyce, 'The Fourth Estate: the reappraisal of a concept', in George Boyce, James Curran, and Pauline Wingate eds, *Newspaper History from the seventeenth century to the present day*, Constable, 1978, p.34); on list of prospective peers in event of Lords' rejection of Parliament Bill; PC 1911; b.-in-law of Adrian Grant Duff; chaired sub-comm. of CID, whose recommendations on war risk insurance were

WSC had first asked for the Huth Jackson recommendations to be implemented two days earlier. Harcourt enjoyed what happened next: 'Cabinet (not membs. of C.I.D.) never heard of this & wd. not adopt it blindfold. Asq. and I also agst. immediate adoption. Winston very angry—overwrought & excitable.' (Harcourt note, 31 July 1914, Bodl. MS.Eng.c.8269.)

Burns then announced his retirement as any such message as Grey was directed to give Cambon meant war. He was asked to come back to 6.30 cabinet as circumstances might be altered.

Grey told Cambon: the assurance was that if the German Fleet came into the channel or thro' the North Sea to undertake hostile operations against French coasts or shipping the British fleet will give all the protection in its power, subject to the support of Parliament and we were not prepared to bind ourselves to war if it broke out otherwise between France & Germany. That we were not now prepared to land troops.[34]

I had lunch with the P.M. As we walked upstairs he said Jack we have turned many awkward corners but I don't see how we are to get round this. I replied that I thought Germany might see it was to her interest to keep us out of war on our conditions, but everything depended on the way it was put. At luncheon there was a forced effort at cheerfulness — Montagu, Bonham Carter all the 3 Asquith women Puffin & the clever son (No. 3) Beb[35] — Birrell came in too.

Asquith was most natural & chaffed Elizabeth — we discussed word derivation & the soundness of Dryden's English as an example of what words we could well use. [When the ladies withdrew[36]] P.M. asked me to see Burns to see what I could do with him. He also told me he proposed to relieve himself by a War Minister (? Seely).[37] I got a summons to meeting at Beauchamp's where I found

adopted after protracted late night discussion on 1 Aug. 'Better an imperfect plan than none at all,' DLG reflected (*War Memoirs of David Lloyd George*, Vol. III, Ivor Nicholson & Watson, 1934, pp.1210–12). JAP appeared to have written 'Routh' Jackson. Wilson omits the forename and provides no identification (Wilson, 'The Cabinet Diary…', p.9). Jackson's wife, believing that 'the cult of Apollo was best suited to her spiritual needs', had a statue crowned with flowers in a small pool in her London back garden until the effect was spoiled by 'smoke and smuts' (Marie Carola Galway, *The Past Revisited*, The Harvill P., 1953, p.100).

[34] A later interpolation indicates that Grey was reporting at the 6.30 p.m. meeting what he had told Cambon.

[35] 'Puffin' was Anthony Asquith (1902–68), HHA's second child with his second wife Margot, from whose possessive clutches he escaped to become a film director. 'Beb', HHA's second son Herbert, was with the Royal Marine Artillery brigade, which was awaiting delivery of its guns.

[36] Words in square brackets here, and in the rest of the entries to 5 Aug. inclusive, are later amplifications by JAP. There were other additions, but we have inserted only those that clarify the meaning.

[37] Seely, already arranging to serve as a Special Service Officer attached to Sir John French, said he turned down the invitation to return to the Cabinet, although John W. Young argues that the evidence

Morley, McKinnon Wood, Runciman, Samuel, Harcourt, Simon & George.[38] It was agreed we should meet again at 6.0 at George's with Birrell & Crewe. We went over all the ground again. Simon & I went [on] a drive to Lambeth, left Peckham & tried to find Burns at Clapham Common, but he had left.[39] Simon once said I think I may have been slow & ought to have joined Burns. I replied I believed we shd stick together as long as we could.

We all met at George's at 6.0. I went to Board of Trade [found JB in at 4.0] — urged Burns not to retire, on ground it [disunion amongst us] might precipitate war, & if we held together we might preserve peace — for the majority of the Cabinet to now leave meant a ministry which was a war one, & that was the last thing he wanted. He told me he had loyally done everything in his power to meet the situation, but could not declare war on Germany as Grey was doing by his message to Cambon.

At 6.30 — we had a friendly cabinet for 1½ hours & no discordant note struck & we agreed on line of policy, subject to the morning's news & arranged to meet 11.15. Burns adamant. The P.M. said he wanted to see him alone. Grey had had a satisfactory meeting with Cambon. He urged we should land two brigades — but Grey was quite definite No. We discussed food, £1 note issue &c.

that he was offered the post is ambiguous ('Lord Kitchener's Appointment as Secretary of State for War in 1914', *BJMilHist*, vol.7, no.3, 2021, pp.24–5; and see J.E.B. Seely, *Adventure*, William Heinemann, 1930, p.173; Brough Scott, *Galloper Jack: A Grandson's Search for a Forgotten Hero*, Macmillan, 2003, p.168; George H. Cassar, *Kitchener's War: British Strategy from 1914 to 1916, Brassey's Inc, Washington D.C.*, 2004, pp.20–1,299).

[38] This is probably the 'lunch at Beauchamp's' to which Morley recalled being driven with Simon and DLG. According to Morley, the others present at Halkyn House were Harcourt, Samuel, Pease, and McKinnon Wood. He was not sure about Runciman (Morley, *Memorandum on Resignation August 1914*, pp.14–15; and draft in Morley of Blackburn MSS, Bodl. MS.Eng.d.3585). Morley, Beauchamp, Stamfordham, and Fitzroy were at Buckingham Palace for a Privy Council meeting on the afternoon of the 2nd. On the 'Fateful Sunday', Runciman and Masterman lunched with McKenna, 'not amongst the Peace Palaverers and not amongst the War Desirers — with solitary determination to keep the old machine united' (Masterman–Runciman, 14 Feb. 1915, Runciman of Doxford MSS). McKenna averred to the historian Harold Temperley in 1929 that he 'took little part in the discussions because of my firm conviction of the inevitable outcome in the event of war being declared. Such proposals as there were for a mitigated participation as for instance limiting the action of the German Fleet, were so obviously futile that they could have had no reasonable purpose but to avoid a decision until some members of the cabinet were satisfied about public opinion' (Spender MSS, BL Add.MS. 46,386).

[39] Burns had moved in Apr. 1914 to a free-standing fourteen-room house at 110 North Side Clapham Common, in the Borough of Battersea (Kent, *Labour's Lost Leader*, p.235). Nicholas Lambert suggests that a rendezvous might have been planned at The Plough, an old coach inn at 518 Wandsworth Road, at the apex of Clapham Common, a major road junction and opposite the landmark clock tower. We had noticed an earlier occasion when Burns 'left Plough at Clapham in taxi' (Burns diary, 11 June 1911, Burns MSS, BL Add.MS. 46,333, f.112). JAP's letter to his wife that night mentions 'going out to Battersea' with Simon and running Burns to ground at the Board of Trade.

In a speech at an informal meeting of Conservative Party constituency chairmen and agents at the Hotel Cecil on 14 December 1914 Bonar Law divulged that on 2 August, 'when resignations had taken place in the Government, and when rumours of further resignations were in the air', he had written to the Prime Minister 'on the joint authority of Lord Lansdowne and myself', declaring that: 'in our opinion, as well as in that of all the colleagues [with] whom we have been able to consult, it would be fatal to the honour and security of the United Kingdom to hesitate in supporting France and Russia at the present [moment] juncture.'[40] *The letter, partially drafted by Austen Chamberlain, concluded with an offer of 'unhesitating support' in any measures the government 'may consider necessary for [to] that object'.*

Conspicuously absent from the letter was any mention of Belgium (although, writing soon afterwards in the letter quoted below, Lansdowne seems to have thought it was France and Belgium not France and Russia that were to be supported). Writing to Lansdowne at 11.00 p.m. on 2 August, Chamberlain suggested that Asquith be asked 'whether it is true that Germany has refused to pledge itself to observe the neutrality of Belgium' (Lansdowne MSS, BL Add.MS. 88,906/25/2). In the version of the speech released to the press the reference to ministerial resignations was replaced by 'when the decision of the Government was still in doubt'. The Unionist leaders did not disclose that before they had foregathered at Bonar Law's house they had been alerted to the uncertainty and divisions in the Cabinet by WSC. As Lansdowne wrote in a 'secret' letter to his wife:

> I had meant to breakfast late this morning but was woken by an urgent message from Winston C. begging me to see him as soon as possible. He arrived at 9.30 and, after I had bolted my breakfast, we went on to Bonar Law's house, which he couldn't leave as all sorts of people were ringing him up.
>
> I got back at 11 and found A.J.B. just arriving—more talking—in the midst of which Austen arrived with more news, and then Victor [Cavendish, Duke of Devonshire].
>
> We have sent Asquith an intimation that in our opinion this country should support France & Belgium, & that we will support H.M.G in this policy.

[40] There are several versions of the letter with minor variations in wording: the original in Bonar Law's hand on Pembroke Lodge notepaper is in the Lloyd George MSS, LG/C/6/11/20, PA; Newton cites the 'final version of the note (according to the handwritten copy in Lloyd George's papers)' and draws attention to other copies (*The Darkest Days*, pp.158,345n.7). McDonough, *The Conservative Party and Anglo-German Relations, 1905–1914*, p.133, quotes the copy in the Bonar Law MSS, BL37/4/1, PA, which has the words in square brackets. Simon Kerry (*Lansdowne: The Last Great Whig*, Unicorn, 2017, pp.245,380n.3) cites the undated version in the Austen Chamberlain MSS, AC14/2/2, U. Birm., which is printed in Sir Austen Chamberlain, *Down the Years*, Cassell, 1935, p.99, where it is described as 'a draft which ran, I think, almost verbally, as follows', and accompaned by a footnote. 'I have printed the actual text. The version in my memorandum is not exact . . . '. A pencilled copy of the letter in the Cave papers written on an 'Admissions Order Office' paper hand dated '16.3.15' is annotated 'A. Ch's draft not G.C's' (Cave MSS, BL Add.MS. 62,495).

> Winston & Grey are believed to be in favour of it, and perhaps Asquith—Lloyd George against. The Cabinet is sitting this morning, & Bonar Law and I are to see Asquith this afternoon. We offered to see him late last night.
>
> Things may end in a split, and on our being approached—but a change of Govt would be deplorable at such a moment.
>
> *(Lansdowne–Lady Lansdowne, 2 Aug. 1914, Lansdowne MSS, BL Add.MS. 88906/25/21/1, uncat. when seen)*

*Scholars have disagreed about the impact on the Cabinet of the Conservative leaders' intervention. Robert Blake was unimpressed by the Tory claims of decisive influence (*The Unknown Prime Minister*, pp.23–4). The argument of* Politicians at War *(pp.41,114–15) was that the letter was relatively unimportant. There is abundant evidence that the Prime Minister and other Liberal ministers acknowledged among themselves that loss of office, or even sharing power with the Opposition, would be politically disastrous. What the great majority of the Cabinet needed was the predicted invasion of Belgium as a casus belli.*

*Keith Wilson's contention (*The Policy of the Entente*, pp.135–47) that the letter from Bonar Law significantly influenced the Cabinet's decision for war is conjectural, resting on circumstantial evidence. Frank McDonough echoes Wilson but adds no relevant documentation (*The Conservative Party and Anglo-German Relations, 1905–1914*, palgrave macmillan, 2007, pp.132–5). More recently, Samuel R. Williamson Jr has concluded that Law's letter was the 'deciding action' that 'deeply affected many of the hesitant Liberal ministers' ('July 1914 revisited and revised: The erosion of the German paradigm', in Jack S. Levy and Jon A. Vasquez eds,* The Outbreak of the First World War: Structure, Politics, and Decision-Making*, Cambridge UP, 2014, pp.54–5). Williamson had earlier said that the effect of the letter which arrived 'in the midst of two long Cabinet sessions…cannot be overstressed' ('General Henry Wilson, Ireland, and the Great War', in Wm. Roger Louis ed.,* Resurgent Adventures with Britannia: Personalities, Politics and Culture in Britain*, I.B. Tauris/Harry Ransom Center, 2011, p.100).*

When he first wrote about the letter, Williamson did not ascribe great significance to it (Samuel R. Williamson, The Politics of Grand Strategy: Britain and France Prepare for War, 1904–1914*, Harvard UP, Cambridge, MA, 1969, p.354). But a change of mind is marked in Samuel R. Williamson Jr and Ernest R. May, 'An Identity of Opinion: Historians and July 1914',* JMH*, vol.79, no.2, 2007, p.382: 'Though domestic politics had not shaped diplomacy, they had [a] decisive effect on the intervention itself, the Conservative letter of August 2 serving as the turning point.'*

Williamson's evolving views command respect; nevertheless there is no conclusive evidence that the message from the Unionist leaders did more than confirm the predictable position of their party. WSC and F.E. Smith had tried on 1 August to get Bonar Law, HHA, Grey, and

Lansdowne to dine together on the 2nd. HHA was 'engaged elsewhere', and the plan seems to have been overtaken by events (WSC–Grey, 1 Aug. 1914, Elibank MSS, MS. 8805, f.36, NLS). WSC had told the Cabinet of advice from F.E. Smith, written on 31 July that, on the assumption that Germany invaded Belgium, 'the Government can rely on the support of the Unionist party in whatever manner that support can be most effectively given'. HHA had seen a letter from Lord Robert Cecil to WSC on 1 August expressing confidence that 'if the Government decide to take action whether by the despatch of an expeditionary force or otherwise they may count on the support of the whole of the Unionist Party' (Harcourt note, 31 July 1914, Bodl. MS.Eng.c.8269; Churchill ed., Winston S. Churchill, Vol. II, Companion, Part 3, pp.1990,1995; Cecil of Chelwood MSS, BL Add.MS. 51,073 f.99).

There was nothing in these Conservative messages that would have surprised WSC, who had been assured by Balfour in the international crisis three years earlier 'I earnestly hope there will not be war, but, if come it must, the Opposition will certainly not cause you any embarrassment'. WSC's response, quoted by Balfour, was: 'If it comes, you will have to join us…'. This exchange had occurred at Balmoral, where Grey and DLG were also in attendance, and was mentioned to Sandars because it showed that DLG 'had not yet wholly given up' his coalition policy of the previous November (Balfour–Sandars, 21 Sept. 1911, Sandars MSS, Bodl. MS.Eng.Hist.c.764, f.57a).

Nigel Keohane adds a rhetorical flourish but no additional evidence in asserting that 'Keith Wilson is surely right to point to the fact that Asquith brandished the Conservative letter in front of Liberal "waverers" as a veiled threat that the appalling outcome of any irresolute response would be a Conservative coalition' (The Party of Patriotism: The Conservative Party and the First World War, Ashgate, Farnham, 2010, p.12). A reconstruction by John W. Young of the movements of the Opposition leadership and their communication with WSC before the letter of 2 August affords no support for the amplified conjecture about the impact of their letter on the Cabinet. Young assembles evidence to show widespread awareness of the possibility of coalition if there was a substantial defection from the ministry ('Conservative Leaders, Coalition, and Britain's Decision for War in 1914', Diplomacy & Statecraft, vol.25, no.2, 2014, pp.214–39). While he is appropriately sceptical of several self-serving accounts, Young's distrust of Lord Beaverbrook as a source would have been more persuasive but for the assertion that Max Aitken (one of the founding members of The Other Club in 1911) 'barely knew the First Lord' in 1914. More recently Young gives greater credence to Aitken ('"By God, I will make them fight!" Winston Churchill and Britain's decision for war in 1914', in B.J.C. McKercher and Antoine Capet eds, Winston Churchill: At War and Thinking of War Before 1939, Routledge, 2019, pp.81–101).

In much the best narrative of the July/August 'darkest days', Douglas Newton provides an excellent account of the feverish activity of the Unionist leadership but does not suggest that *their letter weighed heavily with the Cabinet: 'taken together with Churchill's contacts with the Tories, and open talk of resignation' by HHA and Grey, 'the letter threatened the insubordinate ministers'. But the threat was neither surprising nor compelling. As Lucy Masterman long ago recorded her husband's report, the message was 'hurriedly read and laid down without comment' (Newton,* The Darkest Days, *pp.158–9,180–1,349nn.19,20,21; Masterman,* C.F.G. Masterman, *p.265). The Masterman version echoes that of Grey, who remembered the letter as affirming that 'the Conservative front Opposition benches were ready to support a decision to stand by France... at a moment when they had not before them, as we had before us, the compulsion of the imminent menace to Belgium'. The message, Grey wrote, 'was first read and laid aside; it could have no influence then on our discussion' (Viscount Grey of Fallodon,* Twenty-Five Years 1892–1916, *People's Library Edition, in three volumes, Vol. Two, Hodder & Stoughton, 1928, p.211).*

JAP's failure to mention something supposedly so important is particularly notable. Neither he, nor any of his like-minded colleagues, would have considered themselves 'insubordinate'. Runciman's memorandum about the first Cabinet meeting on Sunday 2 August mentions that 'the P.M. read letter from Bonar Law in which [he] & Lansdowne promise that they will support us in going in with France'. Then the memo. concluded: 'P.M. reads his summary of considerations to weigh with Cabinet & proposed to say in Parlt that we cannot allow the Channel to be violated. We must come to a decision on neutrality of Belgium now...'. Evidently there was some comfort in the assurance that the Opposition would support joining with France but it does not seem to have had an immediately determining impact (Runciman of Doxford MSS). Writing to the Prime Minister later that day to resign, Simon even conceded: 'It may be that a Coalition Government will be best (and one of your colleagues, I think, intends it)...' (typed copy, Simon MSS).

No wonder then, as the Conservative businessman and publicist F.S. Oliver heard five months later, 'the Unionist idea that the Lansdowne–Law letter did the trick is bitterly resented' (Oliver–A. Chamberlain, 30 Jan. 1915, Austen Chamberlain MSS, AC14/6/30, Cadbury RL, Birmingham U.). Moreover, it can hardly have escaped HHA's notice that Bonar Law and his colleagues showed no desire to join hands with those with whom they had been in bitter confrontation for several years. WSC's overtures notwithstanding, they were offering support to the Liberal government, not bidding to undertake a share of responsibility.

Lord Morley would tell Lord Esher six months later that, faced with the prospect of multiple resignations at the Sunday afternoon Cabinet meeting, Asquith said that he had several alternatives: 'One was to tell the King that he would have to find other Ministers; this course he dismissed, as, in his opinion, the Opposition were not in a position to carry on the Government. He added that there was the alternative of a Coalition, which he personally did not favour, and finally he hoped that his colleagues would reconsider their determinations' (*Esher journal, 17 Jan. 1915, Esher MSS, ESHR 2/13, CAC*).

Bonar Law's amended transcript of the widely publicised December 1914 speech is in Sir Malcolm Fraser's papers (Bodl. MS.Eng.c.4790, ff.73–101). Asquith's recollection of this episode had so far faded by mid-1919 that he wrote to Harcourt asking for 'your memory to refresh mine viz. whether & if so at what time, I communicated to the Cabinet B. Law's letter from himself & Lansdowne' (Asquith–Harcourt, 4 July 1919, Bodl. MS. Harcourt 421, f.220). A year earlier, provoked by a 'ridiculous story' in Leo Maxse's National Review, *HHA's memory had evidently been a little better. As he told a friendlier journalist, St Loe Strachey, on 11 August 1918: 'it had absolutely no influence on the course of events or on the mind of the Cabinet. Indeed I doubt whether I read the letter to them' (Stephen Koss,* Asquith, *Allen Lane, 1976, p.158); and for his letter on the same day to Crewe mocking Maxse's self-importance see Heffer,* Staring at God, *pp.65,839n.228.*

Late on 2 August at 8 Hertford Street, their Mayfair home, JAP sat down to write to Elsie about the day's events and his own feelings. The letter covers much of the same ground as the diary but provides more context, a more coherent and nuanced narrative, and greater insight into his own thinking:

Private
Aug. 2 14

My darling
We have had a strenuous day.
I met Loulou and Simon at George's at 10.15 (after a Turkish Bath & a night journey) at 11 Downing Street.

The position is very serious. The Germans through Lichnowsky to Grey, and through the German Emperor to the King, have been playing a double game. With an outward profession of peace have secretly been preparing for war, mobilising & invading French territory, committing a breach of Treaty in regard to violation of Luxemberg [*sic*] territory, & Grey naturally resents his efforts of mediation having been only utilised to gain time.

I still believe Germany, squeezed between France & Russia, are anxious to avoid war with us and I have consequently stuck to the ship, in the hope that if Germans do not violate Treaty in regard to any substantial invasion of Belgian territory & undertake not to attack defenceless coast of Northern France, we may pull through without going to war ourselves — our interests in English trade, protection of food supplies are such that we can't afford to allow Germans to occupy French coast on channel. If our condition will not be observed we may get into war. I am no use in a warlike policy, but I have honestly believed that to let Germany know where we are may make peace possible & it was due to France they should know our position. The situation otherwise is awful. We shan't in any case land troops as at present advised.

After 3 hours Cabinet this morning, I had lunch with Asquiths — everyone rather strained except P.M who threw off his worries for half an hour. He sent me to see John Burns who is for neutrality at any price (& Morley is rocking), but after going out to Battersea with Simon to see him, I ran him to ground at Board of Trade, but I made little impression on him. Cabinet been in groups all day but anxious to agree.

We had happier Cabinet this evening — an hour & a half — & nothing extreme said. The Tories are out for war at any price. The Labour party will be against it & for neutrality, come what may. I think we have adopted the right course, but the situation may change at any moment, by some overt action — but our fleet is ready.

We have another Cabinet at 11.15 Monday & then have to face Parliament with a statement.

Lovingly
Jack

P.S. [on 10 Downing St paper]

Since writing we have had another Cabinet & I feel more strongly anti-German — they mean to crush Belgium, & their ultimatum to the Belgians is brutal.

Norway will come our way — but neutrality may be possible.
Sweden may side with Germany.

(MS. Gainford 189/13–16)

WSC told HHA and Grey on 3 August: 'Norway, if relieved of Russian fears, appears thoroughly friendly to us' (Gilbert ed., Winston S. Churchill, Vol. III, Companion Part I, *p.13). Assurances of respect for Norwegian neutrality were delivered by the British, French, and Russian ambassadors on 8 August. On the same day both Norway and Germanophile Sweden pledged 'to exclude the possibility that the state of war in Europe shall under any circumstances lead to the taking of hostile measures by either kingdom against the other'. Russian fear of a war against Sweden ensured that the Swedes were not subject to the stringent blockade policies applied to other neutrals (Pillsworth,* Security, Prestige, and Realpolitik, *p.129; Olav Riste,* The Neutral Ally: Norway's Relations with Belligerent Powers in the First World War, *Universitetsforlaget, Oslo, Allen & Unwin,1965, pp.32–41).*

Showing they were serious about neutrality, the Norwegians quickly passed legislation criminalising espionage by foreign powers irrespective of the nationality of the perpetrator and whether or not it was against Norwegian interests (Nik. Brandal & Ola Teige, 'The secret battlefield: Intelligence and counter-intelligence in Scandinavia during the First World War', in Claes Ahlund ed., Scandinavia in The First World War: Studies in the War

Experience of the Northern Neutrals, *Nordic Academic P., Lund, 2012, p.88; Wilhelm Agrell, 'Intelligence and Espionage (Sweden)', in Ute Daniel, Peter Gatrell, Oliver Janz, Heather Jones, Jennifer Keene, Alan Kramer, and Bill Nasson eds,* 1914–1918-online. International Encyclopedia of the First World War, *issued by Freie Universität Berlin, Berlin 2017-11-14. DOI: 10.15463/ie1418.11182, accessed 27 Nov. 2022); Karl Erik Haug, 'Norway', in* 1914–1918-online. International Encyclopedia of the First World War, *Berlin 2016-01-19. DOI: 10.15463/ie1418.10809, accessed 27 Nov. 2022). There are fresh insights in Michael Jonas,* Scandinavia and the Great Powers in the First World War, *Bloomsbury Academic, 2019. Michael Smith,* SIX: A History of Britain's Secret Intelligence Service, Part I: Murder and mayhem 1909–1939, *Dialogue, 2010, pp.35–40, tells of a coast-watch network being set up around Norway and Denmark in 1912–14.*

*'It is very difficult to sit down calmly in the middle of a crisis and to record events as they fly by…', Beauchamp wrote on the morning of 3 August. 'But the decision wh. was taken at yesterday's Cabinet—in the morning—to promise France defence of her coast & shipping against Germany was so momentous that I wish to fix it.' The objections of Beauchamp and others to Grey's proposal, 'a definite step in favour of France', could not withstand 'the overwhelming argument that we had tacitly allowed France to concentrate in the Mediterranean in virtue of those unfortunate naval conversation wh. were to pledge no one to anything'. At the end of the meeting Burns protested and said he must resign. After a 'chorus of dissuasion' Burns agreed to return for the evening Cabinet, when a great fight over Belgian neutrality had to be faced. Exercising the privileged private entry of a Fellow of the Royal Zoological Society, Grey had taken Tyrrell with him to the Bird House at the zoo to prepare his speech for the next day (*Seventy Years Young: Memories of Elizabeth, Countess of Fingall Told to Pamela Hinkson, *E.P. Dutton, New York, 1939, p.359). The rupture that Beauchamp feared did not eventuate. Grey had 'gained his point & avoided a conflict. A form of words was agreed to—we were all jaded & exhausted. Burns renewed his protest & was to see the PM this morning' (Jane Mulvagh,* Madresfield: One home, one family, one thousand years, *Doubleday, 2008, pp.235–6).*

Beauchamp would write to the journalist M. Philips Price three months later that what Grey had written to Cambon in November 1912 was carefully worded 'to make it clear that no amount of colloguing between the Staffs shd in any way commit us without the opportunity to discuss each case on its merits…The most meticulous care for our plighted word cd not after that have demanded any participation in a French war unless for other reasons we thought it wise.' (Beauchamp–Philips Price, 15, 13 Nov. 1914, Philips Price MSS, Glos. Arch.)

Burns, as JAP found, was holding firm 'against the war'. Sitting alone in the President of the Board of Trade's magnificent Adam room in Whitehall Gardens, as 'bands heralded the marching of troops along the Embankment…he would hurry down to the garden and peer over the wall, walking sadly back to the gloom of his lonely splendour' (Sir Charles Rey, Men, Women and Places, Rey MSS, Bodl. MS.Eng.c.7191, f.89). Burns had lunched with Grey, Haldane, and Runciman on Saturday 1 August, talking on with Grey (Burns appointment diary, 1 Aug.1914, Burns MSS, uncat., accession no. B04/019, London Metropolitan Archives). On Sunday evening, when he drove away from Downing Street with Charles Hobhouse, the latter 'hoped that . . . you would be able to stay with your colleagues' (Hobhouse–Burns, 7 Aug. 1914, Burns MSS, BL Add.MS. 46,303, f.71). The former Conservative MP for Leominster, Henry Fitzherbert Wright, recalled in January 1943 being told by Burns in the House of Commons cloakroom after a Cabinet meeting on Sunday that he had resigned because the government was resolved to fight only by sea rather than on land as well. JAP wrote to The Times (29 Jan. 1943) repudiating the story.

The view that Burns's resistance to the moves towards war 'sprang not from any pacifist conviction, but from his belief that Britain was being dragged in . . . mainly in the interests of France and Russia' is thoughtfully argued in Kenneth D. Brown, John Burns, Royal Historical Society, 1977, pp.176–80. For Burns resigning the day before Morley, 'when he thought (rightly) that Asquith's Cabinet had made an irrevocable decision to join France and Russia before the German invasion of Belgium' and bursting into tears with Frank Hirst on the day war was declared, see Francis W. Hirst, In the Golden Days, Frederick Muller, 1947, p.238. Kent, John Burns: Labour's Lost Leader, pp.237–40,249, has selections from the Burns diary and anecdotal evidence of explanations he gave privately in 1915 and 1916 but never publicly.

While the Cabinet moved closer to decisions that would lead to resignations, the strain was beginning to tell on those close to the Prime Minister. At 4.00 p.m. on Sunday Edwin Montagu told his mother that he had hardly been outside the Treasury since Thursday. 'My position is really that of scullery maid to the Govt and the city. Panic follows panic, foreign telegrams come hourly, hopes vanish and revive only to be dashed again—nothing but blackness ahead' (Montagu MSS). Next morning, Monday 3 August, while Cabinet was sitting, Eric Drummond reported that he had got to Downing Street at 10.30 a.m. on Sunday and stayed until 11.30 p.m. He could not get away 'any distance' for dinner as this was unfair on his colleague 'Bongy' Bonham Carter, who 'won't go to bed early a little'. Drummond assured his wife that he thought there was no need to lay in stocks of provisions 'except in the ordinary way. I don't think it is right either. There will be a very important statement made in Parliament this morning & a great deal depends on that . . . I don't think there ought to be any difficulty about money really unless people lose their heads; the financial position is quite sound' (Drummond–Angela Drummond, 3 Aug. 1914, Perth MSS, Stobhall 7/3/2/3).

After dinner with Haldane on Sunday night, Grey and Crewe accompanied their host to Downing St, where they found 'the P.M. and ladies playing bridge. Lord Crewe said it was like playing on the top of a coffin. They waited till they had finished—about an hour.

Then E.G. wrote to the French Ambassador a note to say he would hear from him after the Cabinet next day…He read the note to those present, and the P.M. agreed to sending it' (E. Haldane diary, 8 Aug. 1914, Elizabeth Haldane MSS, MS.20240, f.44, NLS). Crewe's presence with Asquith, Grey, and Haldane shows that Harcourt was wrong to conclude after the Sunday morning Cabinet that he seemed to be with 'us' (Harcourt diary, 2 Aug. 1914, Webb ed., From Downing Street to the Trenches, *p.34).*

11.15 Monday Aug. 3 We discussed what Edward Grey should say [to Cambon] urging him to allude to British interests in addition to moral obligation to support France conditionally at sea.[41] News not very reliable as to war operations.

Prime Minister then alluded to Cabinet resignations. He had failed to alter Burns's decision, & now Morley & Simon had written their resignations. Beauchamp then chipped in that he had been unhappy all Sunday & would like to go too. That is 4 said the P.M. out of our number, others have found it difficult to remain, God knows I should like to be relieved of all this. Then he alluded to personal attachment & his indebtedness to Morley and broke down.

Morley said little, & gave no adequate reasons except that at times he differed from his friends, & a cabinet undecided was a weakness to a Govmt. Simon broke down in saying he would do his utmost outside to secure unity.

I then said I had worked for Peace whole heartedly, for unity in the cabinet, if anyone ought to go on a/c of his views it was myself.[42] I placed myself in the P.M's hand, war was so hateful to me that I might be a weakness in a cabinet at war, & I nearly broke down and paid a tribute to Grey that he had I knew done his utmost, that circumstances & difficulties were too much for even his ability to surmount, & no one could have done more for peace. Grey said he felt some responsibility for the resignations & felt it acutely & broke down.

George kept his voice & said how he had differed from Grey, but the invasion of a neutral State made all the difference to him with our treaty obligations too to Belgium. Harcourt said ditto, an appeal was made for Morley & Simon not to go

[41] Keith M. Wilson notes that 'in his first attempt to expand and clarify his account, [Pease] inserted the word "alleged" before "moral obligation", then crossed it out and ended with "our moral obligation justifying our giving support to France"' (*The Policy of the Entente*, pp.185–6). Here and elsewhere we have generally omitted JAP's later glosses and amplifications; but see the following footnote.

[42] Years later, while reviewing the diary for passages to include in a volume of memoirs, JAP added: 'but the nation's honour was at stake & I saw no alternative but to declare war…'. In the next sentence he prefaced his assertion that war was hateful to him 'As a Quaker & Pres. of the Peace Society'. In an undated diary entry [28 July–10 Aug. 1914?], Hobhouse wrote that 'Pease and Runciman were strongly against war but not for unconditional neutrality' (David ed., *Inside Asquith's Cabinet*, p.179).

at once & it was responded to, but they said their decision to go was not affected thereby.

Beauchamp thought apparent but not real unity now in the cabinet might give a wrong impression outside & anyone remaining who dissented from his colleagues was to be deprecated.

6.0 p.m. — we met to consider our reply to Germany's ultimatum to invade Belgium at 12 hours notice which was up. Owing to the incomplete mobilisation here we decided to postpone until Aug. 4 what might be said to Germany, as our reply might be used as a justification for a surprise invasion by Germany.

Dined with the P.M. — he was much as usual — & we played bridge [to stay the strain Bongie & Margot P.M. & me]. He told me privately when the ladies had gone, that he had believed in a German rapprochement, & thought the anti-German note in Grey's speech was the only adverse criticism to a great speech which could possibly be made. He had believed in Germany's friendship & played up for it but this war they had not only precipitated it, but intended it, & were not working for or anxious for peace.

Our own civil strife might be one cause for the present moment having been selected but the one bright spot in this hateful war was the settlement of Irish civil strife, & the cordial union of forces in Ireland in aiding the Government to maintain our supreme National interests & he added: [nearly breaking down: 'Jack'] God moves in a mysterious way his wonders to perform [& in an emotional voice 'Good night Jack'].

While HHA was dining and playing bridge, Crewe was discharging his 'humble duty' to inform the sovereign about the Cabinet meeting that evening (from 6.30 p.m. according to Crewe) (Bodl. MS. Asquith 7, ff.154,157). The King, responding to cheering crowds, would go out on to the balcony at Buckingham Palace with the Queen three times that evening, at 8.15, 9.00, and 9.45 (Heather Jones, 'The Nature of Kingship in First World War Britain', in Michael Glencross, Judith Rowbotham, and Michael D. Kandiah eds, The Windsor Dynasty 1910 to the Present: 'Long to Reign Over Us?', *palgrave macmillan, 2016, p.197).*

HHA's confidence about 'the cordial union of forces' bears out Harcourt's account of the Cabinet's incredulity at remarks by Carson conveyed to them by the Prime Minister. 'Asq. met B Law & Carson in someone else's house on Tues. ~~Wed.~~ to agree to the postponement on that day of the Amending bill and Carson sd. he thought that if the l[ar]ge no. of Brit. reserve officers now in Ulster Volunteers were called up to rejoin on War they wd. decline to leave Ulster! We suppose he thought this might intimidate Asq. which it did not! It wd. destroy the public respect for the "loyal"(!) volunteers & all these officers wd. be liable as deserters during war to be shot!!' (Harcourt diary, 31 July 1914, Bodl. MS.Eng.c.8269).

Austen Chamberlain had been 'gravely surprised & disturbed by Carson's language about the Ulster Volunteers'. He warned Lansdowne late on 2 August that 'any public expression of the thoughts Carson uttered tonight or any failure of the Ulstermen to do their duty in this crisis will in my opinion absolutely ruin the cause of the Union' (Lansdowne MSS, BL Add.MS. 88,906/25/2). Carson did make it clear that the Ulster Volunteer Force would be available for home defence and would also be able to send a unit overseas. Redmond gave a similar pledge in relation to the defence of Southern Ireland. One of Kitchener's first actions at the War Office was to send Lt-Gen. Sir Bryan Mahon to investigate recruiting prospects in Ireland. Mahon reported favourably but said that declaring the Ulster Division as a separate entity was a grave political error ('The Irish Welter As I Found It: An Indictment of British Methods', in William G. Fitz-Gerald ed., The Voice of Ireland: A Survey of the Race and Nation from all Angles, *Virtue and Co., Dublin and London [1923], pp.125–7).*

It was not until 17 September that Irish Nationalists were encouraged to enlist in the British armed forces (Tim Bowman, 'The Irish Recruiting and Anti-Recruiting Campaigns, 1914–1918', in Bertrand Taithe and Tim Thornton eds, Propaganda: Political Rhetoric and Identity 1300–2000, *Sutton Publishing, Stroud, 1999, p.224; Catriona Pennell,* A Kingdom United: Popular Responses to the Outbreak of the First World War in Britain and Ireland, *Oxford UP, 2012, pp.177–89; James McConnel, '"Après la guerre" John Redmond, the Irish Volunteers and Armed Constitutionalism, 1913–1915',* EHR, *vol.131, issue 553, 2016, pp.1445–70; Ben Novick,* Conceiving the Revolution: Irish Nationalist Propaganda during the First World War, *Four Courts P., Dublin, 2001). Timothy Bowman, William Butler, and Michael Wheatley,* The Disparity of Sacrifice: Irish Recruitment to the British Armed Forces, 1914–1918, *Liverpool UP, 2020, is the standard work now augmented from French diplomatic sources in Emmanuel Destenay,* Conscription, US Intervention and the Transformation of Ireland 1914–1918: Divergent Destinies, *Bloomsbury Academic, 2022, pp.26–34.*

HHA wrote to Venetia Stanley of a 'scratch dinner party' at which JAP was joined among others by Alice and Violet Keppel, Lt-Col. Sir Matthew ('Harry' 'Scatters') Wilson Bt (Lord Ribblesdale's son-in-law, who had defeated Masterman at Bethnal Green in February 1914) and his wife Barbara ('Barby', Margot Asquith's niece), Anne (Lady) Islington, and Polly Stapleton Cotton, soon to be working with the YMCA in France (Maureen Emerson, Escape to Provence: the story of Elisabeth Starr and Winifred Fortescue and the making of the Colline des Anglais, *Chapter and Verse, Cuckfield, 2008, p.65). The Premier was a little more subdued about Ireland. Bonar Law had called to say that his followers suspected that the government might seize the opportunity to prorogue and enact the Home Rule and Welsh Church Bills. HHA assured the Unionist leader that there would be no 'thimble-rigging... the best thing of course wd. be a deal between Carson & Redmond wh. is far from impossible' (HHA–Venetia Stanley, 4 Aug. 1914,* Asquith Letters, *p.150). To Redmond, who feared that a party truce might endanger the Home Rule Bill, he wrote: 'to prorogue at this moment would in all the circumstance be widely regarded as a piece of sharp practice' (copy enclosed with HHA–J.A. Spender, 6 Aug. 1914, Spender MSS, BL Add.MS. 46,388, vol.III, f.125). For HHA's conversations with Redmond, Carson, and Bonar Law through July and August 1914 see James Doherty,* Irish Liberty, British Democracy: The Third Irish Home Rule Crisis, 1909–14, *Cork UP, 2019, pp.187–221.*

After what he called Edward Grey's 'magnificent speech' to the Commons on 3 August, JAP went upstairs to his room at the House to try to sort out his own thoughts in writing again to his wife. His 'one criticism' of Grey echoed HHA's:

> he has shown an anti-German bias, but he is smarting under a sense of unfair dealing by Germany — Lichnowsky is beside himself with indignation at his own Govt & would like to be reasonable but obviously the Germans have laid their plans to attack France through Belgium, & through it they mean to come.
>
> I don't feel I am any help to a Cabinet at war, my heart is not in this kind of work, I hate it all so. I think war so stupid & wrong, & I can't help my Quaker blood — on the other hand to resign at this moment only adds to the necessity of finding more warlike instruments & colleagues, who may go further than we are prepared to go & might urge our troops being sent abroad & so extend the field of our troubles. Of course whilst I am in the Cabinet, or even if I left it, I should do what I could to see the war through — so that from that point of view however there is nothing in staying or leaving.
>
> I feel to leave on the outbreak of war may look rather like cowardice & I can't do so because I honestly think Grey is wrong. On the other hand not to retire now really requires courage.
>
> The Prime Minister is anxious we should see this thing through as a Party, and does not want a coalition & says he wants as many of his colleagues to stay with him as he can get so as not to go outside the Party.
>
> Official Labour will protest against our getting into the war, but many in Labour ranks will realise that we have been driven in to it, under circumstances over which we had no control & have done our utmost to preserve peace.
>
> Give me your advice Darling. I expect some of my colleagues will go, in the course of the next few days, & if I remain I shall have to assume a new role & chuck my Peace Society chairmanship, & I suppose my membership of Friends, & be taunted with sticking to office and changing my convictions to do so! What I want is guidance &

I am torn between loyalty & a desire to be rid of responsibility for this thing which is so horrible to contemplate.

Lovingly Jack

We were nearly all in tears at Cabinet this morning

(MS. Gainford 189/17–18)

Elsie's response blended sympathy with warning: 'You poor thing. I am sorry for the strain & worry. What do you mean by "sticking to the ship"? Did you intend resigning? You could not do it now in a moment of difficulty & no business prospects to look forward to.' (EP–JAP, 4 Aug. 1914, MS. Gainford 85/84.)

Tuesday Aug. 4 Cabinet. We discussed what was to be said in Parliament, & what telegrams we should announce. I urged as much as possible should be conveyed so that those who were hesitating to come to the support of the Government should not make up their minds & take a hostile view now, without a full understanding of the German intention to force war on Belgium & run the risk of our internal differences preventing our support being given to France & in the interest of small independent States. The telegrams seemed to us forcible & impressive & would help to unite us all & were as follows:

JAP included in his diary at this point a telegram from Sir Edward Grey to Sir Francis Bertie, 2 August 1914, no. 487, pp.274–5, in G.P. Gooch and Harold Temperley eds, British Documents on the Origins of the War 1898–1914. Vol. XI. Foreign Office Documents June 28th–August 4th 1914, *collected by J.W. Headlam-Morley, HMSO, 1926; henceforth* BD XI.

We decided to withdraw the Irish Proclamation dealing with the importation of arms — it was no longer required, & the action of Irishmen made its operation now valueless. Simon & Beauchamp were present but not Burns or Morley.

The prevailing policy on arms importation and the thinking behind the change is thoroughly set out in Ben Novick, 'The arming of Ireland: gun-running and the Great War, 1914–16', in Adrian Gregory and Senia Pašeta eds, Ireland and the Great War: 'A war to unite us all'?, *Manchester UP, 2002, pp.95–112.*

Morley's private secretary George Cunningham, a long-serving aide to Lords President of the Council, noted the following day that his chief's line was: 'France & ourselves take no interest in Serbia or in the Balkans... France will be dragged after Russia and ourselves after France. All for the aggrandisement of Russia.' John Burns telephoned Cunningham to ask his views. For Cunningham, an unabashed Liberal Imperialist, the naval situation and agreement convinced him that war was right. Burns 'bluntly' said that he could not agree (Cunningham diary, 5 Aug. 1914, Miller-Cunningham MSS). Burns told Sir Edward Cook a few weeks later: 'I am strongly pro-French, but I am British all the time. I don't think the neutrality of Belgium good enough and I am opposed to our being involved in Continental affairs' (Cook diary, 21 Aug. 1914, Cook MSS).

On 4 August Morley wrote to his old friend Andrew Carnegie 'I cannot imagine men showing loftier temper and tone than our cabinet yesterday: not a single unkind or wounding word' (Bodl. Carnegie MSS, MS.Film569). The next day he told Francis Hirst, an editor of the Carnegie Trust project on the causes and prevention of war, as well as editor of The Economist, *that he was 'going into pretty strict retreat. War is war, and no talk will stop it. I have done all I could, and now have washed my hands of a dire piece of folly.' (Bodl. MS. Hirst, B.1.1.36.) In a letter to J.A. Spender on 6 August he was 'firm in my conclusion as to my personal line, whether the general "policy" is right or wrong' (Spender MSS, BL Add.MS. 46,392, f.163). By April 1915 Morley was arguing with some vehemence that the Cabinet had been deceived about the extent of the commitment to the Entente: 'Belgium was only a pretext — we shd have to have backed up France anyhow' (Violet Asquith diary, 22–3 May 1915 referring to 18 Apr. 1915, in Mark Pottle ed.,* Champion Redoubtable: The Diaries and Letters of Violet Bonham Carter 1914–1945, *Phoenix Giant, 1999 [1st edn, Weidenfeld & Nicolson, 1998], p.39).*

*In an article on 'John Morley's Resignation in August 1914', Morley's biographer Patrick Jackson attempts to answer two questions: 'Why did he fail to ensure that the cabinet explored the key issues before reaching its precipitate decision? Why did he refuse to speak out publicly against the war?' (*J.Lib.H.*, issue 87, 2015, pp.26–33). Jackson underestimated the extent to which the Cabinet had in fact canvassed the 'key issues'; and he had already effectively answered the second question in* Morley of Blackburn: A Literary and Political Biography of John Morley, *Fairleigh Dickinson UP, Madison & Teaneck, 2012, pp.449–57.*

Explaining his own adherence to the ministry after dallying for days with Morley, Beauchamp wrote on 4 August:

> Little did I think when last we met of the divided lines we shd follow today.
>
> But then yesterday afternoon just when I thought the struggle was over — the pressure became most acute.
>
> It is so difficult as events fly by to fix their exact sequence. I am chiefly conscious through all this strain of the appeals to one's loyalty to the party. It seems so presumptuous to set up my own opinion against that of one to whom I owe so much allegiance as to the Prime Minister. To me he is the chief figure in my political life. Always kind and considerate, how difficult to resist a personal appeal!
>
> *(Beauchamp–Morley, 4 Aug. 1914, Morley of Blackburn MSS, Bodl. MS.Eng.d.3585, f.90)*

Morley, it seems, was surprised to discover after he had withdrawn to his Wimbledon home that Beauchamp, along with Simon and Runciman, had not resigned. Geoffrey Dawson told Leo Maxse four years later of learning from Morley a few days after war began that he had 'left the Cabinet under the full impression that they were all pledged to go together' (Dawson–Maxse, 13 Aug. 1918, Bodl. MS. Dawson, Box 9). That was also the understanding of WSC, who told Lord Derby in 1922 that when the Cabinet met on Monday 4 August 'he did not know who had or had not resigned and he quite believed that after Edward Grey had made his speech that at least half the Cabinet would go and it was a great surprise to him to find that only three went one of whom was that very pompous and negligible person Lord Beauchamp' (Derby diary, 16 May 1922, Derby MSS, 920 DER (17)). WSC's memory might have been faulty, but Beauchamp's wavering had clearly damaged his credibility with many of his colleagues though it was unlikely to have surprised the Prime Minister, who dubbed him 'Sweetheart' to Venetia Stanley (Asquith Letters, *p.43).*

Simon, who had yielded to the Prime Minister's entreaties and vague allusions to future preferment, explained to C.P. Scott in the afternoon of 4 August that he 'saw no hope of action within the Cabinet which could avail to change the now destined course of events'. He had thought as late as that morning about the possibility of carrying on an agitation in the country along the lines of the opposition to the Boer War. But he agreed with Scott that the stakes were too great. Scott was 'impressed with his utter prostration. Morally and physically he was like a man half-dead though his mind was as keen as ever' (Scott 'diary', [4] Aug. 1914, Wilson ed., The Political Diaries of C. P. Scott 1911–1928, *pp.97–8).*

By late on 4 August JAP had made up his mind unequivocally not to resign. The British Ambassador would leave Berlin that night, he reported to Elsie, 'and war will reign at sea tomorrow. May God defend the right.'

It is awful to think that possibly 10,000 of our brave boys who I recently saw cheering their King as they passed at Spithead may be at the bottom of the sea in the course of a few days, & all owing to the wickedness & stupidity of a war party in Germany who control the Emperor.

Today we at Cabinet arranged the ultimatum read by the Prime Minister — to delay now meant German strategy overcoming ours & as Belgium is invaded we had to move.

We also undertook to withdraw the arms proclamation in Ireland, as all there are uniting in common actions in support of their common country. I am proposing to stay in the Govmt & am sending a letter to Jonathan Hodgkin…

I dined at No. 10 last night & had a rubber with the P.M. — it did him good. Trevelyan has resigned — impetuously.

(MS. Gainford 189/19)

JAP had talked at length with George Newman about how he would explain his position to fellow Quakers and discussed a draft letter about his decision to remain in the Cabinet. The letter would be addressed to the esteemed evangelical Quaker, Jonathan Backhouse Hodgkin (Newman diary, 4 Aug. 1914, Newman MSS, TNA: MH 139). Like JAP, to whom he was related by marriage, Hodgkin had been mayor of Darlington. JAP had always valued the good opinion of this highly respected Friend and had been heartened by a sympathetic telegram on Sunday morning. Writing confidentially on Tuesday 4 August, JAP said Sunday had been 'a day of the most extreme anxiety' through which he had ever passed:

We had news that Germany, without any declaration of war, was invading or about to invade at different points the territory of France and Luxemburg. Grey pointed out to us that France, relying on our friendship had thought it no longer necessary to protect her northern coasts against British invasion, and had concentrated her own sea power in the Mediterranean. I believe that just as she would have been ready if called upon to come to our assistance in the event of an unwarranted invasion of our coasts by Germany, so she looked to us for support when an attempt was about to be made to crush her to her very knees, and on Sunday we thought it was only fair to France to inform her whether we were in favour of absolute unconditional neutrality, whether we were prepared to adhere to our Treaty obligations in regard to the neutrality of Belgium, and do our best to protect her northern undefended coasts from bombardment and destruction at the hands of the German Fleet.

It was seen that not only was the very independence of Belgium, Holland, Denmark, and other smaller states liable to be sacrificed, but that the possible occupation or possession of Antwerp, Dunkirk, Calais, Boulogne, Cherbourg by the German Navy would create a new situation which would involve this country in even greater expenditure on naval armaments, if we were to retain the control of the English Channel for our trade and for the importation of food materials necessary for our own population.

If Germany was prepared to abstain from using her fleet to attack the North and West Coast of France, and also to respect the neutrality of Belgium I thought it still possible, even on Sunday last, that Peace could be preserved, and it was in that belief that I agreed with my colleagues that we might intimate the terms of our conditional support to France. We had already conveyed to Germany our views on these two points in friendly confidence and had officially asked both Powers if as in 1870 they would respect the neutrality of Belgium. France gave us an assurance, but Germany declined to give us any satisfactory reply.

If Germany would not undertake to respect our two conditions and thereby insure Peace with us, her Fleet might at any moment come down the Channel, and I felt that then such a feeling of apprehension would be aroused in England that war must become inevitable. I therefore assented, though reluctantly, to the message being given to the French Government in the hope that German interests would enable us to remain at Peace, but I did not for a moment hide from myself the possible prospects of war with all that it means, its horrors, its terrors, its suffering, and its misery.

Looking back upon the past it seems to me that we could not possibly have foreseen events, or in any way by anticipation have prevented the crisis of the past ten days. On Sunday week, Austria suddenly declared war on Servia and declined all intervention although the strongest pressure was being placed on her by ourselves and others.

It does seem to me that Germany has premeditated the War and did not wish to prevent Austria's attack on Servia, or intervene to secure a cessation of hostilities, for when Grey suggested that She, Italy, and France should mediate with us in the interests of Peace, France and Italy readily consented but Germany declined, giving a trivial excuse, and then would not herself even make any other suggestion to promote Peace. While she publicly tries to justify her action in declaring War against Russia, by alleging that Russia mobilised her force first, yet as a matter of fact we know that Germany was given an assurance by Russia that Russian troops would not be moved during mediation and that Germany has been carefully making her preparations for this war for some time past. The German Emperor has been I believe overborne by military forces behind him, and whilst the Sovereign, the German people and ourselves are friendly, war has been intentionally made inevitable. Plans have been prepared in advance to secure so far as possible the acquiescence of other smaller Powers so that these — to nominally save their own integrity — may actually be forced in some instances to come to Germany's assistance.

Having laid out the sequence of events, JAP moved to explaining his own course of action, doing what he could to pre-empt the taunts he expected about sticking to office and changing his principles to do so:

I honestly feel we cannot in honour escape from our Treaty obligations, and that the Treaty we entered into to secure the neutrality of Belgium is open to only one interpretation, and that we are as Nations both separately and collectively bound to respect the Treaty and that in this crisis it is binding on us, and that to repudiate our undertaking to preserve Belgium's neutrality would be dishonourable and discreditable.

I recognised that in regard to the quarrel between Servia, Austria–Hungary, and Russia, there would have been no justification for our intervention.

You know me well enough to realise how hateful war is to me in any form and how strongly I believe that there is a much better way of settling international disputes and that all Powers should rely on reason not force, but even in these days if a Nation wilfully declines arbitration or conciliation and invades the country of another, it is impossible to expect Peace to be maintained.

The easiest course for me would undoubtedly have been to say:— 'I hate War so much that I will not make myself responsible for its conduct' — but having carefully thought the whole question over for some days I have come to the conclusion that

Friend as I am by conviction it would be a cowardly and selfish act on my part to seek my own rest of mind and leave to my colleagues the distasteful and hateful work.

The Prime Minister knows that if I am a weakness with my Peace views in the Cabinet I am ready at any moment to leave and that it will make no difference to my loyalty to him, but whether I am in or out of the Government I should now feel bound to vote Supplies and to see the War through.

I know that I cannot expect all Friends to share my views, but there are some things in which one is obliged to come to a decision for one's self under such Guidance as one is given.[43]

I have always used my influence within the Cabinet in the greatest of all causes, and I hope I assisted in the decision that we should not now send an expeditionary force on to the Continent and I hope that during the various Balkan Crises the expression of my Peace views may have been some use in the policy that was pursued in Europe. You may rest assured that if I now remain in the Cabinet I shall always do my utmost to prevent the field of War being extended and to circumscribe its operations, and to lose no opportunity to bring about a cessation of hostilities at the earliest possible date.

There remained one sensitive matter that could not be avoided. 'I have been very frank in telling you my views, and if, under all these circumstances, my remaining in the Government seems to you to place me in a false position as a Member of the Society of Friends, please let me know what step I should take in order that I may do what is right with regard to resigning my Membership if, on consideration, it is thought necessary.' JAP would of course resign as chairman of the Peace Society, 'not because my views on Peace principles have altered a tittle but because I might be regarded as in a false position' (MS. Gainford 85/111–16; Newton, The Darkest Days, *pp.258–9, glosses JAP's letter unsympathetically; John W. Young, 'Every Neutral State within Reach': exaggerations of German aggression and British entry into the First World War',* IHR, *vol.43, no.2, 2021, pp.438–52, refers to it as a letter to JAP's 'brother-in-law').*

What JAP could not say, if indeed he had known, was the truth about the final hours of peace. Francis Acland, at Grey's side throughout the crisis, would tell Percy Molteno a story which Molteno committed to his diary on 25 August 1914:

On Friday August 7th I saw Mr. Acland, the Under–Secretary of State for Foreign Affairs, at lunch. I said to him: 'How is it that you have not published the German reply to our ultimatum, which the White Paper states is unsatisfactory?' He replied that there really was no reply, and then gave the following account of the position:

The Cabinet were meeting on Tuesday night expecting to get the German reply. Eventually a message came in code for the German Ambassador telling him to

[43] In the typescript copy of the letter quoted in JAP's 'Reminiscences' Chapter VIII, (MS. Gainford 36/1), the phrase 'all Friends' has the word 'all' hand-written above 'my' which is deleted.

declare war. This the British Government had interrupted and deciphered. Immediately thereupon Sir Edward Grey wrote a letter accepting the German declaration of war, which was sent to the German Ambassador, Prince Lichnowsky. As a matter of fact that German Ambassador did not get the message from his own Government that night because he had gone to bed; nor did he open the letter from Sir Edward Grey for the same reason.

As no declaration of war came officially from the German Ambassador, and our declaration that we were in a state of war with Germany had been issued at 11 p.m., a messenger was sent over to the German Ambassador to ask for the return of Sir Edward Grey's letter. This was next morning, Wednesday. The German Ambassador had not opened it, and gave it back unopened, so that, as matters stood then, no reply was received to our ultimatum from the German Government.'

(Hirst, A Man of Principle, p.438)

An alternative story of the German Ambassador being aroused from 'a premature slumber' and declining to take delivery of his passports is told in J.D. Gregory, The Edge of Diplomacy: Rambles and Reflections 1902–1928, *Hutchinson, [1929], pp.69–70. For the recollections of Sir Harold Nicolson, Sir Lancelot Oliphant, Lord Drogheda, and Sir Robert Vansittart, then clerks in the Foreign Office, see Vansittart–Sir Oswyn Murray, 14 May 1930, Graham Greene MSS, GEC/13(f), NMM. Colin Davidson, Harcourt's 25-year-old private secretary, had been left by his 'absolutely exhausted' chief, 'who could hardly walk or stand', to await the expiration of the 11.00 p.m. deadline. Having confirmation, from the collarless Foreign Office Resident Clerk with two days' growth of beard, that no reply had been received, he set off up Whitehall then through side streets to the Strand post office to lodge the telegrams to the Colonies advising that war had been declared. By the time he and his escort, the Colonial Office Resident Clerk and an army major, had made their way back through a boisterous crowd to Downing Street, the first acknowledgement had arrived, from Fiji (Robert Rhodes James,* Memoirs of a Conservative: J.C.C. Davidson's Memoirs and Papers 1910–37, *Weidenfeld and Nicolson, 1969, pp.20–1).*

JAP's account of the Cabinet's deliberations and his letters in July and August 1914 give no hint that ministers thought, as Keith Wilson has argued, that Russian Foreign Minister Sazonov 'was effectively able to blackmail Grey by saying that Britain must either support Russia or forfeit her friendship in Asia... peace on the Indian frontier trumped everything' (Wilson's view expressed at an FCO/LSE Symposium on 7 Nov. 2014, as paraphrased by Iain Sharpe in 'Among the Fallodonistas: Sir Edward Grey and the outbreak of the First World War', J.Lib.H., *issue 87, 2015, p.53; and see also Wilson, 'Grey and the Russian Threat to India, 1892–1915',* IHR, *vol.38, no.2, 2016, pp.275–84). For the fears of senior officials see Keith E. Neilson, 'Wishful Thinking: The Foreign Office and Russia 1907–1917', in B.J.C. McKercher and D.J. Moss eds,* Shadow and Substance in British Foreign Policy 1895–1939: Memorial Essays Honouring C.J. Lowe, *U. of Alberta P., Edmonton, 1984, p.158. Thomas Otte's conclusion (*J.Lib.H.*, issue 87, p.22) is convincing: 'The cabinet did not decide to enter the war in Europe as a lesser evil when compared with the recrudescence of the Anglo-Russian Asiatic antagonism…'. There is a comprehensive assessment in Otte's chapter 'A "formidable factor in European politics": Views of Russia in 1914' in Jack S. Levy and John A. Vasquez eds,* The Outbreak of the First World War: Structure, Politics, and Decision-Making, *Cambridge UP, 2014, pp.87–111. For the underpinning of Russian military policy and a literature review see Peter Gatrell, 'Tsarist Russia at War: The View from Above, 1914–February 1917',* JMH, *vol.87, no.3, 2015, pp.668–700.*

*With the decisions taken and forced upon the government, by the late evening of 4 August it was time for the irrevocable formalities. Asked by Asquith to convene a Privy Council without delay, at 10.35 p.m. Sir Almeric FitzRoy brought together the King and one Cabinet minister, Beauchamp, who had preceded Morley as Lord President of the Council and was reinstalled as Lord President the next day. They were joined by the Catholic Lord Granard, Master of the Horse, JAP's friend Lord Allendale, a Lord-in-Waiting, and the courtier Sir William Carington, Keeper of the King's Privy Purse. War was to be declared on Germany from 11.00 p.m. (*The Daily Citizen, *5 Aug 1914; Newton,* The Darkest Days, *pp.5,316n.18,363–4n.64, where the 69-year-old Carington, who died two months later, is described as 'a guardsman', and Sir Charles Cust Bt, Equerry to the King, who was not a Privy Councillor, is described as one of two 'Privy Councillors in Attendance').*

Wednesday Aug. 5 Cabinet. This is the 10th cabinet since 27th July. We were very businesslike. Agreed to a lot of matters without discussion. Teachers service in territorials to count for superannuation; more money should be provided for provision of meals if distress occurred; the withdrawal of importation of Arms proclamation in Ireland; issue & printing of £1 & 10/- notes. What telegrams we could read to House of Commons.

Churchill explained course to be pursued to carry on trade routes convoys — the work of getting German ships & shipping &c.

Grey told some of us quietly that he had had a very harrowing goodbye scene the previous night with Lichnowsky. They had both wept — & he had told Lichnowsky he would find us at any moment prepared to enter into negociations for Peace — & possibly economic forces might quickly work in that direction. If he saw his way at any moment to promote peace he should know we would respond, & anxious to bring the war to an end [consistent with honour].

JAP's letters to his wife and to Jonathan Hodgkin show how hard he found it to reconcile himself to being a member of a Cabinet at war. In conversation with fellow Quaker MP and provincial newspaper owner Arnold Rowntree after lunch on 5 August he said that he had decided to stay 'to urge settlement at the earliest opportunity and to help to feed 9 million children if this is necessary' (Rowntree–M. Rowntree, 5 Aug. 1914, Packer ed., The Letters of Arnold Stephenson Rowntree to Mary Katherine Rowntree, *p.156). But he had committed himself to staying at his ministerial post before the despatch of an expeditionary force was decided. Francis Hopwood, immersed in preparations at the Admiralty, wrote to his 17-year-old son Frank at 8.15 p.m. on Sunday 2 August conveying 'no hope that war will be averted... The war, as far as we are concerned is to be a naval & not a military war, that is, no military force will be sent to the Continent which is something' (Southborough MSS, courtesy of the 3rd Lord Southborough, not found in Bodleian collection). Harcourt had elicited from Asquith on 3 August an assertion in writing about whether he contemplated sending an expeditionary force to France: 'No, certainly not' (Note attached to Harcourt diary, 3 Aug. 1914, Bodl. MS.Eng.c.8269, cited, without reference details added here, in Keith Neilson, 'The Teleology of 1914: British Foreign Policy or the Origins of the War?', Keynote Lecture, The British International History Group, 21st Annual Conference, U. of Salford, 4 Sept. 2009, copy courtesy of Nicholas Lambert).*

Late on 6 August JAP told Elsie: 'I hope we need not send an expeditionary force abroad — but the military will do all they can to get to work somewhere' (MS. Gainford 189/23). His fellow Quakers were unaware of the sure touch with which the Prime Minister had led his Cabinet through a sequence of decisions from which few of them felt able to dissent or resile. As the nature of the conflict became clearer, Friends were far from unanimous in their attitudes. Jonathan Hodgkin left no doubt in a letter on 7 August that he could not imagine himself responsible for carrying on a war. But JAP's 'influence for peace in the past, in the present, and, I feel sure, in the future, is a comfort to many, and in this we desire to support you to the utmost of our power'. As for membership of the Society, he counselled laying the situation before the Darlington Monthly meeting, feeling sure they would look at it 'sympathetically and prayerfully'. They did. (MS. Gainford 85/111–12.)

A document entitled 'Our Testimony for Peace' had been approved by London Yearly Meeting in 1912, enjoining Friends 'to take their stand for peace and righteousness, wherever their lot may be cast'. War, the resolution continued, was 'contrary to the Spirit of the God whose name is Love'. On 7 August 1914 the Friends Meeting for Sufferings reaffirmed this idea with a message to 'Men and Women of Goodwill in the British Empire', reminding Friends: 'Our testimony loses its efficacy in proportion to the want of consistency... amongst us...'. Jonathan Hodgkin, whose son had drafted it, wrote to JAP that he was 'much pleased that you care for the "Goodwill" document'. But there was no disguising the tensions and lack of consistency among Friends, described by Martin Ceadel as a 'partial retreat from pacifism', especially as the war expanded and the struggle against conscription intensified (Martin Ceadel, 'The Quaker Peace Testimony and its Contribution to the British Peace Movement: An Overview', Quaker Studies, *vol.7, no.1, 2003, pp.9–29; and see Brian David Phillips, 'Friendly Patriotism: British Quakerism and the Imperial nation, 1890–1910', Ph.D. thesis, U. of Cambridge, 1989).*

By the spring of 1915 more than 245 Quakers had enlisted in the armed forces, and a Committee on Friends and Enlistment discovered that fifteen Friends were engaged in recruiting activities (Thomas Kennedy, 'Many Friends do not know "where they are": Some Divisions in London Yearly Meeting During the First World War', Quaker Theology: A Progressive Journal and Forum for Discussion and Study, *Issue 11, vol.6, no.2, 2005; and for a more wide-ranging account incorporating the substance of earlier articles see Kennedy's superb* British Quakerism 1860–1920, *pp.236–367; by the end of the war approximately one third of Quakers of military age had enlisted).*

From Elsie Pease came a blunt response to JAP's request for guidance. She wrote on 4 August:[44] *'I feel you have decided rightly. When you became a member of the Cabinet you undertook to share its difficulties & responsibilities & the possibility of war is one of the latter.' JAP's concerns about his fellow Quakers were swept aside: 'Modern Friends seem to me to be very timid people, fearful of censure & the opinion of their fraternity. I don't care a button for the opinion of such inbred anaemic creatures. If we are not good enough for them lets join the Presbyterian Scotch Church—they have plenty of backbone.' As for the decision to stay in the Cabinet, it had never occurred to her that his mind was disturbed by the thought of resigning, 'only on account of the horror & hatred of war'.*

The fact that others were leaving the Cabinet awakened Elsie's barely dormant ambition for her husband: 'Burns & Morley are no loss. I thought Loulou might threaten resignation as he did once before through not seeing eye to eye with E. Grey so May [Harcourt] told me, if it would ease the situation...':

> Lancashire is selfishly opposed to war tho' I don't see how our being involved can further affect her trade—Loulou would not quit—on account of the Colonies it would be an ill compliment to them after their offers of help....
>
> I shan't think much of the PM unless he offers you Board of Trade. You have promise of money for Education & the machinery is in order—& Seely wd not do it so badly—or Masterman.
>
> I'm sorry about Trevelyan. I like him...It's no use thinking of the appalling work which may be taking place now. Miriam wanted to howl this morning [her cousin

[44] The letter is dated 4 Aug. but it might have been completed in the early hours of 5 Aug.

> Spencer Havelock-Allan was about to join his regiment]. I told her I'd done that yesterday & she'd better get to work & help me to save labour—fetch eggs from the village instead of sending Foster who was wanted in the garden. Had you quitted the Cabinet you would have had to organize nursing & field hospital work. I'm not sure we should not be doing so now. I've sent to say we can provide one 2 roomed cottage with 2 beds in answer to appeal.
>
> No flour to be got here in Darlington & what arrived yesterday...was ordered back to Hull—the poor will suffer if people collar supplies like this. Is this letter wanting sympathy—because I am not. I had a wretched evening & night & early morning reading your letters again & again & trying to see the way clear.
>
> *(MS. Gainford 85/84)*

On the same day Miriam Pease displayed a sympathetic understanding of the decision her father faced: 'from your letter to mother this morning I imagine you will sacrifice yourself & your ideas to what you feel to be the need of your country & no man, however great, can do more than this' (MS. Gainford 85/117).

Elsie had not underestimated the Colonial Secretary's love of office. Harcourt would tell Morley on 6 August that he had stayed 'not because of any obligation actual or implied to France' or of 'emotional honour'. He was 'fighting with but not for France except so far as certain elements in her defeat would affect ultimate British interests' (Bodl. Morley MSS, MS.Eng.d.3585, ff.122–3). Simon's volte face *earned the particular contempt of Hobhouse: 'almost despicable because he pretended to a special and personal abhorrence of killing in any shape' (Hobhouse MSS, [? Aug. 1914],* Inside Asquith's Cabinet, *p.180).*

JAP had worked closely with Charles Trevelyan, whom he inherited as his Parliamentary Secretary at the Board of Education. He might not have sensed the depth of his colleague's concern about Anglo-German relations. As early as October 1912 Trevelyan had told his wife that he was becoming 'more and more definitely opposed to Grey and his whole outlook and policy, his reticence and his sympathies'. He had, he said, 'practically made up my mind that if we begin verging towards war, or seriously quarrelling to uphold either the Russian or the French alliance, I will not be a party to it'. As war broke out on the Continent he sought to persuade his closest friend in the Cabinet 'not to allow us to be dragged into war for the sake of preventing Germany making a limited strategical use of Belgium however irritating it may be'. On 3 August, with Britain manifestly 'verging towards war', he submitted his resignation (Trevelyan–Runciman, n.d [?2 Aug. 1914], Runciman of Doxford MSS; A.J. Anthony Morris, 'C.P. Trevelyan's Road to Resignation 1906–14: The Odyssey of an Anti-war Liberal', in Solomon Wank ed., Doves and Diplomats: Foreign Offices and Peace Movements in Europe and America in the Twentieth Century, *Greenwood P., Westport, CT, 1978, pp.85–108; Hazlehurst,* Politicians at War, *pp.70–1,122–3).*

JAP did not conceal his mixed emotions in appealing to Trevelyan to reconsider.

5/8/14
8, Hertford Street, Mayfair.

My dear Charlie,

I had hoped that however much you hate war, you would have waited until you knew all the facts, before you deserted your colleagues, & if not too late I would urge you to recall your resignation, & pluckily face with our Great Prime Minister the responsibilities forced on the Government. I enclose you copy of a letter I am sending to the head of my own society in Darlington. Surely if I a Quaker with more peace blood in my veins than any man in the House, can bring myself to associate myself with the hateful & bloody war, you might also make some sacrifice of your personal feelings too in a National Emergency & help me in our Department to organise the feeding of school children which during coming months maybe an immense work. If we all chucked as you have done, the alternative Government must be one much less anxious for a peace policy than ourselves. If I make my appeal in vain, then may I without delay reciprocate the kind reference to our work together. No man could have had a more loyal & charming colleague to work with than I have had in you, I shall never forget this, & I thank you from the bottom of my heart.

Yours ever
Joseph A. Pease
(Trevelyan MSS, Newc. U. Spec. Coll.)

Dear Jack,

Thank you for your very nice letter. My objection to the whole course of Grey's diplomacy is much too great to allow me to retract my resignation. I could not remain in a government with him.

Yours ever,
Charles Trevelyan
(MS. Gainford 85/58)

Thursday Aug. 6 Cabinet. Procedure — The Prime Minister told us that when Redmond met Carson with the Speaker present the previous afternoon, Carson was in a most uncompromising mood, & insisted upon an adjournment, & not on prorogation, so that his people would remain in their present mood & even threatened opposition to the Appropriation Bill, if H.R. came on Statute book. The P.M. said he had strong letters from Bonar Law & Redmond each asserting they could not look at Prorogation & an adjournment respectively. He was proposing to adjourn for a month but Redmond would not even accept that, but Illingworth would again see him.

Campion's primer for new MPs explains: 'The effect of a prorogation is to pass a sponge over the parliamentary slate… An adjournment leaves uncompleted business unaffected i.e. capable of being carried on from the stage it had reached before the adjournment' (An Introduction to the Procedure of the House of Commons, *pp.80–1). Under the Meeting of Parliament Act 1870, if both Houses stood adjourned for more than fourteen days, they could be called by proclamation to meet within six days (Arthur Berriedale Keith,* The Constitution of England from Queen Victoria to George VI, Vol. I, *Macmillan, 1940, pp.331–2). A fine guide to the Irish deadlock and its resolution is David and Josephine Howie, 'Irish Recruiting and the Home Rule Crisis of August–September 1914', in Michael Dockrill and David French eds,* Strategy and Intelligence: British Policy During the First World War, *Hambledon P., 1996, pp.1–22.*

The P.M. then told us that at the conference of big experts, Roberts, Ian Hamilton, French, Kitchener, the previous day, they all urged an expeditionary force should be landed & kept on our right hand of naval force [*sic*] — not on left of French force necessary — they would not be wiped out, if they could always retire to the sea, even in event of French being overwhelmed. But Kitchener wanted only 4 Divisions sent instead of 6. It would harass & delay German right. It was acquiesced, that this force might go as soon as possible via Calais or Boulogne, Churchill could promise & arrange for safe convoy & transport by Saturday (8th) to commence.

Crewe could get 2 Divisions from India. Dominions prepared to send 20,000 men. Canada 1 million barrels of flour probably.

The Cabinet Committee on Food Supplies had accepted an offer of one million barrels of flour from the Canadian Government. 'No form of contribution by the Dominion could be more welcome to us…', The new President of the Board of Trade told the Colonial Secretary: 'Its effect upon prices, which may otherwise be raised to levels entailing dreadful hardship on our working classes, will be inestimable, and all the more helpful if it reaches us at an early date.' (Runciman–Harcourt, 5 Aug. 1914, Bodl. MS. Harcourt dep.adds.73/28–30.)

JAP, like others who had thought that they were not committed to sending an expeditionary force, seems to have 'acquiesced' without protest in the face of advice from Kitchener (newly appointed as Secretary of State for War) and the nation's senior military commanders. His summary of what he thought Asquith had told the Cabinet should be compared with the minutes of the 'conference of big experts' (the embryo War Council) on 5 and 6 August 1914. See TNA: [CAB] 42/1/4 and 42/1/3, printed in Annika Mombauer ed. and trans., The origins of the First World War: Diplomatic and military documents, *Manchester UP, 2013, pp.582–90. The minutes themselves are complemented by several inside accounts. Douglas Haig's appalled delineation of the views expressed by French and the CIGS Sir Charles Douglas concludes that the meeting in the afternoon of 6 August was told that the Cabinet had decided 'on [sic] principle to send the Expeditionary Force' (Haig diary, 6 Aug. 1914, Robert Blake ed.,* The Private Papers of Douglas Haig 1914–1919, *Eyre & Spottiswoode, 1952, p.70).*

Among less-known 'inside' accounts, that by Sir Ian Hamilton, written five years later, has a ring of authenticity, although undermined by an implausible and inaccurate assertion about Kitchener. When asked by the Prime Minister what military action should be taken, Hamilton said that Amiens was the most important railway junction outside Paris in the west. The Expeditionary Force should at once cross the Channel, concentrate at Amiens, and await developments. 'Henry Wilson (although he has forgotten it) who was sitting beside me at the side of the room and opposite the door, thereupon said, quite loudly, "Hear, hear!"' One point that Hamilton wanted to make clear was that 'Kitchener did not say anything at that first conference... on the contrary, he avoided committing himself to any opinion at all' (Hamilton, 'Note on First Meeting of War Council'–Vt French, 13 Aug. 1919, Ypres MSS, 75/46/11, IWM). Hamilton was wrong about Kitchener, who had 'plumped for Amiens' as well as eliciting agreement that Indian divisions should be transferred to Egypt. Henry Wilson's contemporary record does not confirm his own verbal applause for Hamilton (Wilson diary, 5 Aug. 1914, Wilson MSS, kindly lent by Major Cyril Wilson, now in the IWM).

We then talked of German Colonies, leaving to New Zealand to take the German Island of Yap & German New Guinea & to seize Samoa & Nauru. To leave to India to take Dar-es-Salaam in German E. Africa but not to encourage Dutch to take S.W. Africa. This might not be made a counter in Peace settlement, if Dutch took it & we were victorious & the same might be said of Yap & Guinea we thought Togoland might be taken & so used [possibly later on as a Counter].[45]

[45] The words in square brackets are a later interpolation.

The Cabinet was considering recommendations submitted by a CID subcommittee on offensive operations against German colonies. Immediately after the meeting, Harcourt, as Colonial Secretary, despatched telegrams to the Dominions requesting action on specific targets, and sent instructions to the governments of Sierra Leone and the Gold Coast to eliminate the German wireless stations in Togoland (Phillip G. Pattee, At War in Distant Waters: British Colonial Defense in the Great War, Naval Institute P., Annapolis, 2013, pp.133–7). 'Little more than a sandy coastal sliver, Togoland was pocketed easily by the Allies' (Bill Nasson, 'Africa', in Jay Winter ed., The Cambridge History of the First World War: Vol. I Global War, Cambridge UP, 2014, p.435). The ambitions of the Dominions were in conflict with British desires to use captured German colonies as bargaining chips in post-war peace negotiations. Hermann Joseph Hiery tells how the story played out in The Neglected War: The German South Pacific and the Influence of World War I, U. of Hawai'i P., Honolulu, 1995.

The South African government had been a particular worry for Harcourt, who reminded Crewe on 2 December: 'I warned the Cabinet early in August, when they decided (rather against my inclination) to ask the Union Government to take German South-West Africa, that we could never take the bone out of the dog's mouth. Nor can we, when he gets it.' (Crewe MSS, C/10, CUL, in Ronald Hyam and Peter Henshaw, The Lion and the Springbok: Britain and South Africa since the Boer War, Cambridge UP, 2003, p.71.) How the dog got the bone is described in Bill Nasson, 'British Imperial Africa', in Robert Gerwarth and Erez Manela eds, Empires at War 1911–1923, Oxford UP, 2014, pp.130–51. See also Anne Samson, 'South Africa Mobilises: The First Five Months of the War', Scientia Militaria, vol.44, no.1, 2016, pp.5–21.

'By July 1915, as Denys Reitz noted, Botha and Smuts "had added to the Union a territory larger than Germany, and they had done it with fewer casualties than the cost of an average trench raid in France".' (Ian van der Waag, 'The Battle of Sandfontein, 26 September 1914: South African military reform and the German South West Africa campaign, 1914–15', First World War Studies, vol.4, no.2, 2013, pp.141–65; Colin Newbury, 'Spoils of War: Sub-Imperial Collaboration in South West Africa and New Guinea, 1914–20', Journal of Imperial and Commonwealth History, vol.16, no.3, 1988, pp.83–106; William R. Louis, Great Britain and Germany's Lost Colonies 1914–1919, Clarendon P., Oxford, 1967, pp.11–36.)

Yap, in the Caroline Islands, was ceded to Japan in 1919. It had an important wireless station. The German radio stations in the Pacific such as Nauru were critical for naval operations by the German East Asiatic Squadron based in Tsingtao (Qingdao) (Peter Overlack, 'The Force of Circumstance: Graf Spee's Options for the Cruiser Squadron in August 1914',

Journal of Military History, *vol.60, no.4, 1996, pp.657–82; Peter Overlack, 'The Struggle for the Australian Airwaves: The Strategic Function of Radio for Germany in the Asia-Pacific Region before World War I', in David Stevens ed.,* Naval Networks: The Dominance of Communications in Maritime Operations: 2007 King-Hall Naval History Conference Proceedings, *Sea Power Centre–Australia, Canberra, 2012, pp.111–30).*

JAP seems to have been confused about the respective tasks of New Zealand and Australia. Pre-war planning for the capture of German Pacific colonies discussed in 1912 during the Balkans War had divided responsibilities so that New Zealand would take Samoa and Australia take New Guinea (John Connor, 'Coronation conversations: The Dominions and military planning talks at the 1911 Imperial Conference', in Peter Dennis and Jeffrey Grey eds, 1911 Preliminary Moves, *pp.41–55). Neville Meaney has an excellent chapter on 'The Competition for Germany's Pacific Empire' in* Australia and World Crisis 1914–1923: A History of Australian Defence and Foreign Policy 1901–23: Volume 2, *Sydney UP, 2009, pp.56–76.*

The Royal Australian Navy had the only modern British warships in the Pacific. Because the location of the German cruiser squadron was unknown, the battle cruiser HMAS Australia *escorted both the New Zealand force to Samoa and the Australian force to New Guinea. Samoa had been divided between Germany and the USA in 1899, when British interests were compensated by being given dominion over Tonga. New Zealand captured the island in August 1914 and was granted a mandate over it in 1919 (Ian McGibbon, 'The Shaping of New Zealand's War Effort, August–October 1914', in John Crawford and Ian McGibbon eds,* New Zealand's Great War: New Zealand, the Allies and the First World War, *Exisle Publishing, Auckland, 2007, pp.49–69; Sandra Barkhof, 'The New Zealand Occupation of German Samoa during the First World War, 1914–18: Enemy Aliens and Internment', in Stefan Manz, Panikos Panayi, Matthew Stibbe eds,* Internment during the First World War: A Mass Global Phenomenon, *Routledge, 2020, pp.205–16).*

Nauru, in the Bismarck archipelago, had valuable phosphate deposits. Urged by the Colonial Secretary by telegram on 18 and 19 August, the Australians captured it on 6 November, and were given a mandate over the island in 1919. The Australians also took German New Guinea in September 1914 and kept a mandate over it (Hiery, The Neglected War: The German South Pacific and the Influence of World War I, *pp.21–9; John Connor, 'The capture of German New Guinea', in Craig Stockings and John Connor eds,* Before the Anzac Dawn: A military history of Australia to 1915, *New South Publishing, Sydney, 2013, pp.283–303; David Steven, '"The sea is all one": The dominion perspective, 1909–1914', in Greg Kennedy ed.,* Britain's War at Sea, 1914–1918, *pp.165–82). The pre-war Australian background is explored in Meaney,* Australia and World Crisis

1914–1923, *chs3,4; and reappraised with flair by Douglas Newton,* Hell-Bent: Australia's leap into the Great War, *Scribe, Melbourne, 2014, ch.3.*

The East Africa campaign was controlled from the India Office until the disastrous battle of Tanga and the failed attack on the German colony of Longido in November 1914. The Indian Expeditionary Force B had been poorly led at Tanga by Sir Max Aitken's brother, Maj.-Gen. Arthur Aitken, who was relieved of his command. The War Office then assumed control over operations (Anne Samson, World War I in Africa: The Forgotten Conflict Among the European Powers, *I.B. Tauris, 2013, pp.60–5; Edward Paice,* World War I: The African Front, *Part One 1914, Pegasus Books, New York, 2008,* passim*; Ross Anderson,* The Forgotten Front: The East African Campaign 1914–1918, *Tempus, Stroud, 2007 [1st edn 2004], pp.51–5; Corey W. Reigel,* The Last Great Safari: East Africa in World War I, *Rowman & Littlefield, Lanham, MD, 2015, pp.19–20).*

I dined at 10 Downing St — a family gathering — all depressed except P.M. who was natural.

After dinner he had a long talk with Bonar Law & Ll. George over Prorogation & he also saw McKenna who called Appropriation bill, and adjournment of House postponed again until Monday. The P.M. told me he thought of appointing Dr Addison as my assistant at B. of E. I told him he would be useful but there were difficulties, but I would acquiesce readily if he wished it. We had one game of Bridge. We heard half crew had been saved from *Amphion* which had hit an open floating mine & gone down.

Around 6.30 a.m. on 6 August, the light cruiser HMS Amphion *had steamed into a minefield for which it had been searching and sank about 60 miles off the Suffolk coast. One officer and 150 men were lost (including twenty German sailors saved after their mine-laying vessel was sunk the previous day). Accompanying destroyers of the 3rd Flotilla rescued the survivors, sixteen officers and 125 men.* Amphion *had earlier seen the ship carrying the German Ambassador Prince Lichnowsky home, and warned it about the minefield.*

The next morning, Asquith's third son, Arthur, who was on leave from his job in Argentina and had been at the family dinner along with 28-year-old Nathalie Ridley (wife of the Conservative banker Jasper Ridley, daughter of the Russian Ambassador, Count Aleksandr von Benckendorff), wrote to JAP. Hoping he had not kept JAP up too late the previous evening, he enclosed an application for work, 'partly civil partly military', and asked for it to be forwarded to the proper quarter. The letter appears to have gone the rounds of Whitehall;

but on 23 September 'Oc' Asquith was commissioned as a Temporary Sub-Lt in the Royal Naval Division (Page, Command in the Royal Naval Division, *pp.23–5). By May 1915 he was in hospital in Alexandria, having been shot in the knee. In October 1916 a trench fell in on him and an explosion burst his ear drums. He was shot in the leg by a sniper late in 1917, resulting in a partial amputation (Mary, Countess of Wemyss,* A Family Record, *The Curwen P., privately printed, Plaistow, 1932, p.273; Sylvia Henley–Anthony Henley, 30 Oct. 1916, Sylvia Henley MSS, Bodl. MS.Eng.lett.c.645, f.153). He was awarded the DSO and two bars for bravery under fire. He died in 1939, aged 56.*

Aug. 7 Cabinet at 11.0. Policy of declaring war against Austria discussed — obviously impossible to clear Mediterranean if her battle ships could any moment attack us. Matter left to arrangement as to time with Grey & Churchill, but as Germany's ally, & our forces on land and sea facing Germany, impossible to withstand the logic.

Kitchener present also Emmott & Lord Lucas for first time — in lieu J. Burns' seat.

Burns and Morley had both resigned. Beauchamp stayed, as did Simon, with 'a heavy heart' and an assurance from HHA to 'fully safeguard' his future (Simon–HHA, 4 Aug. 1914, typed copy, Simon MSS). Burns was replaced as President of the Board of Trade by Runciman.[46] *Lucas replaced Runciman at the Board of Agriculture and Fisheries. Beauchamp became Lord President in place of Morley. Emmott replaced Beauchamp at the Office of Works. A disappointed Montagu remained at DLG's side at the Treasury. JAP, still at the Board of Education, was assigned responsibility for coordinating official and voluntary efforts to prevent and relieve distress (JAP–Editor,* The Times, *10 Aug. 1914). As he told Elsie on 5 August, he had thought that Harry Verney or Charles Lyell might join him at Education (MS. Gainford 189/20). But Christopher Addison was appointed to the Under-Secretaryship from which Trevelyan had resigned. An antidote to the difficulty that JAP had foreseen was provided by George Newman, who wrote: 'if A was apptd it would be necessary to explain the positn to Ins Commn & LGB & I promised definitely that… they need have no fear of a "combine"—P said the Med Dept might become too powerful for the Pres & Sec.' JAP admitted that he*

[46] Runciman had given up his partnership in the family shipping company and resigned all his directorships when he joined Campbell-Bannerman's govt in 1905. He told HHA he would prefer to stay at the Bd of Agriculture if he was required to divest himself of his shares in order to take the Bd of Trade. He was assured this would not be necessary. He later put on record that he had never had direct or indirect contact or influence over the wartime requisitioning of steamships, and he did not permit his father's firm to do any business with the govt. He received dividends on his shares of 25% in 1913, 12½% in 1914, 25% in 1915, and 30% in 1916 (Runciman–W.M. Crook, 12 July 1917, Bodl. Crook MSS, MS.Eng.hist.d.393 f.42).

wished it to be powerful but not so powerful that it controlled the Board (Newman diary, 4 Aug. 1914, TNA: Newman MSS, MH 139).

We discussed expeditionary force, & agreed to begin to send it on Sunday to be all over channel in a fortnight. Agreed not to announce it, or to censor the press. F.E. Smith in charge. No argumentation or differences of views discussed. Rest of meeting, discussed food & food prices.

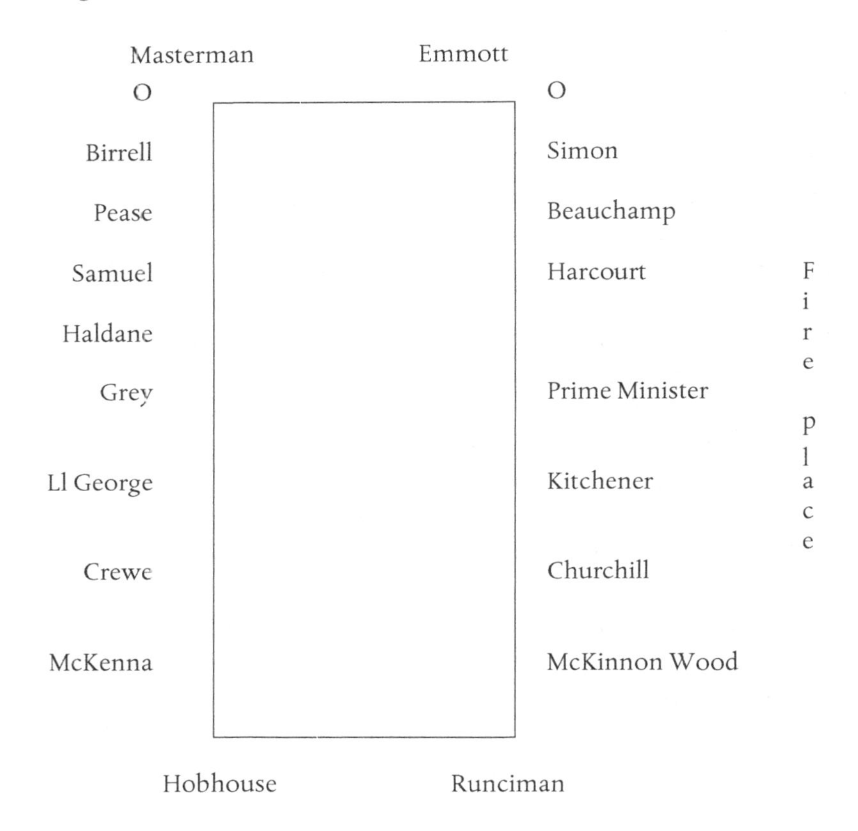

In a rare reproach to Elsie, JAP wrote from Hertford Square on 7 August: 'This is no time to grumble about promotion & I am glad, with all that this war means, & with a lot of work to do, I have not got to listen to denunciation of the greatest statesman of the age who I admire & with whom it is a privilege to be associated. There!' He went on to give his wife a more revealing account of the Cabinet's consideration of proposals for an expeditionary force than he gave in his diary:

we discussed the proposals for an expeditionary force put forward by French, Kitchener, Roberts, & Ian Hamilton. They regard our coast defences adequate, & Bobs admits all his platform gas was on the assumption all circumstances were against us & that now they are favourable.

I think 4 Divisions may go soon but not to penetrate into France, but to be a right wing to our fleet on Belgium seaboard. We hope Holland may come in too — & Italy, but they may wait to see how the cat jumps.

(*MS. Gainford 189/25*)

Aug. 10 Kitchener rather too talkative in urging us to leave Home Rule & Welsh Disestablishment alone. He did not appreciate what the Parliament Act had done & he was out for playing the Tory ticket, & allowing the war to be exploited to stay the passages into law of these controversial measures. I ventured to point out, no Govmt could stay in power which followed such a course, & that supply prevented our carrying on the same session year in & year out, but it was obviously all Greek to him. He thought somehow in war time home controversies could be obviated.

We decided to say that Parliament would meet again in a fortnight & meanwhile we must hope arrangements would be arrived at but if not we would then have to bring session to an end.

Our idea being the postponement of the date when the H.R. Bill should come into operation, & the postponement of the Disendowment part of the Welsh Bill until after the War.

Churchill argued in favour of Japanese coming to our aid. Harcourt asked to ascertain colonial opinion.

Eyre Crowe reported to his wife the next day: 'After much battling with Grey we have got the govt to bring in the Japanese, to deal with Kiao-chau... It looks as if Turkey are definitely going with Germany. That means the whole Balkans and Egypt ablaze' (Bodl. MS.Eng.e.3020, f.30).

The SMS Goeben, *a new German battle cruiser which was to have been the fastest, most powerful ship in the German navy, had put to sea with problems with her boilers, incapable of steaming at full speed. The SMS* Breslau *was its companion light cruiser. At the outbreak of the war, they had been in the Mediterranean and were thought to be a great threat to shipping, particularly to French troop ships from North Africa. The German ships were shadowed but were still able to fire on two ports and take refuge in Constantinople. Eventually the ships were 'sold' to Turkey—there had been rumours of a sale as early as January 1914 and the Turks had deflected the British demand to surrender them or forfeit neutrality by dressing the crews in Ottoman naval uniforms. Renamed the* Jawuz Sultan Selim *and the* Midilli, *the ships were of little use to the Turks. By August 1915 they were out of action. Refitted by the French 1927–30, the* Jawuz *(renamed* Yavuz *in 1936) was the flagship of the Turkish navy until 1950. Decommissioned in 1973, she was scrapped in 1974 having been offered for sale in 1966 at $2,800,000 but failing to find a buyer (Geoffrey Miller,* Superior Force: the conspiracy behind the escape of Goeben and Breslau, *U. of Hull P., 1996; Zisis Fotakis,* Greek Naval Policy and Strategy, 1910–1919, *Routledge, 2005, pp.10–95; Mustafa Aksakal,* The Ottoman Road to War in 1914: The Ottoman Empire and the First World War, *Cambridge UP, 2008, p.35; Redmond McLaughlin,* The Escape of the Goeben. Prelude to Gallipoli, *Seeley Service, 1974; http://www.battleships-cruisers.co.uk/goeben.htm, accessed 16 Apr. 2014; Paul G. Halpern,* The Naval War in the Mediterranean 1914–1918, *Naval Institute P., Annapolis, 1987, pp.12–26).*

If so whether Greek Minister's suggestion (Zouloukos?)[47] (Who Asquith said was the ablest of all the men in the near East) could be brought about. Servia to get Bosnia, Roumania get portion of Bulgaria. Russia Constantinople, Bulgaria give up some territory to Roumania & get a slice of Turkey, Greece part of Albania & Turkey, Montenegro, Herzegovina & part of Albania. Winston gassed eloquently on the advantage of all this for 10 minutes. Edward Grey said, what you have been saying is 'God bless you' — the abrupt synopsis produced a laugh all round to W.C's discomfort.

Some of the issues over which WSC had 'gassed eloquently' (and on which, according to Emmott's diary that day, DLG's imagination had caught fire) are elucidated in B. Kondis, 'The Problem of the Aegean Islands on the Eve of World War I', in Greece and Great Britain During World War I, First Symposium, *Institute for Balkan Studies, Thessaloniki, 1985, pp.49–63, and Lynn H. Curtwright,* Muddle, Indecision and Setback: British Policy and the Balkan States, August 1914 to the Inception of the Dardanelles Campaign, *Institute for Balkan Studies, Thessaloniki, 1986, pp.24–31.*

Aug. 12 (16th cabinet in 16 days). Short cabinet — all present.

Japan. Grey read telegrams showing our readiness to cooperate & work with our allies if they would help us between Japan & Malacca Straits. Austria. A vessel was detained in Devonport, without declaration of war we could not prevent her

[47] HHA was referring to the Greek Prime Minister, Eleuthérios Venizélos (1864–1936).

going on. The Austrian divisions were up against French frontier. Their ships & ours might meet in the Mediterranean. Foodstuffs could go through Austria into Germany. It was essential that war should be declared. France hesitated as such 'aggressive' action she thought might enable Italy to be pressed into activity under her alliance. We felt sure Italy's neutrality might be relied upon, as any act of so called aggression now was the direct consequence of Germany's aggressive act in the 1st instance.

Kitchener told us where the troops were, the character of turning movement to the North the Germans were trying to make, the concentration of troops of our allies in front of German advance. Churchill told us the Turks had bought the *Breslau* & *Goeben* & the crews would be sent over Austria back to their country. & care must be taken the ships were not bought back.

Austria–Hungary had declared war on Russia on 6 August. France declared war against Austria–Hungary on 11 August. Britain did so on the 12th. Austria–Hungary declared war on Belgium ten days later. The ship that had been brought to the Cabinet's attention was the Austrian steamer Mediterraneo. *Caught that morning in the Channel, with a contraband cargo of barley* en route *to the River Weser from the Russian port of Toganrog, she was ordered into Plymouth. There, as the* Western Weekly Mercury *reported on 15 August, she became 'the first prize of war captured from the Austrians since the official commencement of hostilities with that Power'. (We are indebted to Graham Naylor, Plymouth City Council, for details of the* Mediterraneo *story.)*

Aug. 13 A short cabinet — discussed food supplies, trade conditions, finance, & George reported his committee had agreed with Bankers to guarantee their bills of exchange. Loss may be £40M on[?or?] £3½ million — it may save whole trade of country. Nothing said.

Grey thought that the war declaration by France against Austria would make no difference to Italy — who might come over to us — but she Turkey & other small powers waiting to see result of 1st big battle & if Germany could be checked, early opportunities then would be seized to join the allies.

Cabinet was informed that the Americans were seeking to buy the large fleet of Norddeutscher Lloyd steamers. JAP's reference to discussion of food supplies is notably bland given that Emmott's diary and Harcourt's notes make it clear that there was heated argument over Grey's proposal of distant blockade, and treating food sent via Rotterdam as conditional contraband liable to seizure if destined for the German armies. An interdepartmental committee (the Enemy Supplies Restriction Committee) chaired by Hopwood at the Admiralty was being set up (Emmott diary, 13, 17 Aug. 1914, MS. Emmott, I/2, Nuffield Col.). Maurice Hankey took it upon himself to assure Arthur Balfour on 13 August that 'there is no call for anxiety about food supplies, even in the event of some temporary interruption of supplies due either to the armed forces of the enemy or to economic circumstances' (Balfour MSS, BL Add. MS. 49,703, f.40). The debate would continue over the next week until agreement was reached on an order-in-council falling short of declaring a blockade but making it easier to seize cargoes presumed to be en route *to the enemy. The legal complexities and political divisions are summarised in Hull,* A Scrap of Paper, *pp.158–61, and Lambert,* Planning Armageddon, *pp.216–31.*

On 3 August the government had proclaimed a 30-day moratorium on the payment of bills of exchange. Ten days later Cabinet, with the concurrence of the Governor of the Bank of England, had accepted that the Bank should discount all bills dated pre-4 August at the bank rate of 5 per cent. The government, as DLG announced, would indemnify the Bank against losses (Martin Horn, Britain, France and the Financing of the First World War, *McGill-Queen's UP, Montreal & Kingston, 2002, pp.30–1; and p.188 for a helpful explanation of the working of bills of exchange). Sir John Bradbury told Austen Chamberlain whose counsel had been sought:*

> I imagine that the Chancellor of the Exchequer's reason for relieving the bankers from liability in respect of the bills was to encourage the psychological conditions necessary for the creation of new credit to traders. I wish we could have got a more substantial quid pro quo from the bankers than a mere assurance of co-operation but it is difficult to see what form it could have taken.
>
> *(Bradbury–Chamberlain, 13 Aug. 1914, Chamberlain MSS, AC113/4/4, Cadbury RL Birmingham U.)*

Edwin Montagu, passing on to DLG the views of Samuel Montagu & Co. and Sir George Paish about the flaws in the arrangements that had quickly become apparent, advised the Chancellor that it would be essential to talk 'pretty straightly' to the banks. 'They do not seem to me to be playing the game on the evidence we have got. They have been treated with great liberality; they will probably make large profits during the war, and I think we have a right to expect more from them than they seem willing to do...'. DLG turned to Lord Rothschild for advice on the moratorium and the difficulties of some of the Accepting Houses in doing new business (Montagu–DLG, 15 Aug. 1914, TNA: T.170.28 X 1.1261; DLG–Rothschild, 21, 28 Aug. 1914, TNA: T.170.25). On the involvement of George Paish with Huth Jackson, the bankers, and DLG from 'the last Wednesday in July' in stopping the panic in the City and saving the eight accepting houses, see Sir George Paish, 'My Memoirs', (unpublished typescript), c.1950, *kindly lent by Professor Frank Paish, subsequently deposited in the LSE*

Library Archives and Special Collections, COLL MISC 0621. For the Midland Bank's Sir Edward Holden's characterisation of 'Huth Jackson and that other gang round the table of the Bank of England who have put the Chancellor in their pocket' see David Kynaston's richly documented The City of London Vol. III: Illusions of Gold 1914–1945, *Chatto & Windus, 1999, p.8.*

From the ingratiating but always useful chemicals magnate on the back benches, Sir Alfred Mond Bt, the Chancellor was hearing another point of view. Mond had warned as early as 7 August: 'The word "moratorium" conveys no meaning to ordinary persons...could you not get yourself interviewed by some leading newspaper or agency and explain the exact significance of what you have done and arrange to do. People want first to be assured that the banks will not call in their overdrafts and secondly that the banks have promised to assist them in finding wages.' A fortnight later he had more advice:

> I learn that grave dissatisfaction exists among the Managers of the Joint Stock Banks at the extraordinary method adopted by the Bank of England in carrying out your magnificent scheme for dealing with the accumulation of Bills which have for so long stopped the credit market. Apparently this business is being done in a small back room with three or four clerks...proceeding at a ridiculously slow pace...The Bank of England has apparently refused the co-operation of the Joint Stock Banks who are quite ready to lend members of their staffs in order that the work might proceed more expeditiously....any possibility of discounting any bills is being defeated, employment checked and the results of all the intense work of yourself and others is being seriously endangered.

With the moratorium due to expire on 4 September, the Chancellor explained that the bills

> have to be examined and approved by the Bank of England, otherwise you might find the Joint Stock Banks dumping all their rubbish upon the Government, and taking this advantage of getting rid of bad debts for good money...I am now looking into the question of the extent to which financial facilities are affecting the industries of the country. There has been an almost sudden stoppage of orders, and I am afraid that this has far more to do for the moment with the stoppage of mills and factories than any financial trouble over which the Government has control.
>
> *(Sir Alfred Mond Bt–DLG, 7, 21 Aug. 1914 (copies); DLG–Mond, 21 Aug. 1914, Melchett MSS, AP 3/1, courtesy of the 3rd Baron Melchett)*

Austen Chamberlain offered further thoughts on the proposed extension of the moratorium including a suggestion that Lord Reading should 'put in writing...the brief exposition which he gave to us the other day and for you to read to the House—of course as your own...' (Chamberlain–DLG, 30 Aug. 1914, copy; DLG–Chamberlain, 1 Sept. 1914, Chamberlain MSS, AC 11/13/29, AC 13/4/30, Cadbury RL Birmingham U.).

In a widely publicised speech on 19 September DLG admitted that he knew much more about the world of finance and trade than he had six weeks earlier: 'we discovered that the machinery of commerce was moved by bills of exchange. I have seen some of them—wretched, crinkled, scrawled over, blotched, frowsy, and yet those wretched little scraps of paper move great ships laden with thousands of tons of precious cargo from one end of the world to the other.' (Through Terror to Triumph: A speech delivered at the Queen's Hall, *London on September 19th, Liberal Publication Department, 1914.)*

A state of war existed between England and Austria–Hungary from midnight on 13 August (Grey–de Bunsen, 12 Aug. 1914, BD XI, *no.672, p.354). For Italy's declaration of neutrality on 3 August and her wariness about the choice of partners until the final decision in April 1915 to enter the war on the side of the Triple Entente, Richard Bosworth,* Italy and the Approach of the First World War, *Macmillan, 1983, pp.121–41, is a helpful guide. A more comprehensive account is William A. Renzi's* In the Shadow of the Sword: Italy's Neutrality and Entrance Into the Great War, 1914–1915, *Peter Lang, New York, 1987. Modern studies of developments in Italy from July 1914 to May 1915 are referenced in Williamson and May, 'An Identity of Opinion:...',* JMH, *vol.79, no.2, 2007, pp.371–4, and the divisions over entering the war are elucidated by Antonio Gibelli (trans. Paul O'Brien), 'Italy', in John Horne ed.,* A Companion to World War I, *Wiley-Blackwell, Oxford, 2010, pp.466–8. Recent Italian scholarship is reviewed in Roberta Pergher, 'An Italian War? War and Nation in the Italian Historiography of the First World War',* JMH, *vol.90, Dec. 2018, pp.873–88.*

Aug. 14 Discussed Japanese situation & Italian. International points of law in connection with trade into Rhine at Rotterdam, & American views.

The cornering of merchant vessel fleets and the complications this caused for relations with the United States are documented in Lambert, Planning Armageddon, *pp.237–51. With British ships deployed around the globe in multiple time zones 'the Admiralty windows blaze like a Brocks benefit half the night' (Charles Lyell–Maurice Headlam, 14 Aug. 1914, Bodl. Headlam MSS, MS.Eng.hist.c.1103, f.67).*

Although they did not concede that their alliance with Britain obliged them to do so, the Japanese Cabinet had decided on 8 August to enter the war. They did not declare war on Germany until 23 August (and Austria–Hungary on the 25th), by which time it was clear that Germany would give no assurances about the future of the important port city of Tsingtao (Qingdao). Apprehensive about Japanese territorial ambitions, Britain had unsuccessfully sought Japanese agreement to restrict her activities to destroying German naval ships in Chinese waters. As Tatsuji Takeuchi put it 21 years later, 'the embarrassing subject of delimiting the Japanese sphere of warlike operations...was settled by unilateral declarations by both parties' (War and Diplomacy in the Japanese Empire, *Russell and Russell, NY, 1967 [1st edn Doubleday, Doran, 1935], p.174; see also Ian T.M. Gow, 'The Royal Navy and Japan, 1900–1920: Strategic Re-evaluation of the IJN' and Yoichi Hirama, 'The Anglo-Japanese Alliance and the First World War', in Ian Gow, Yoichi Hirama with John Chapman eds,* The History of Anglo-Japanese Relations 1600–2000, Vol. III: The Military Dimension, *Palgrave Macmillan, 2003, pp.35–70; Nish,* Alliance in Decline, *pp.115–31; and Phoebe Chow,* Britain's Imperial Retreat from China, 1900–1931, *Routledge, 2017, pp.101–13).*

An unconstrained Japanese government seized the opportunity to advance plans to eliminate German influence from China and occupy, at least temporarily, German territory in the Pacific (Xu Guoqi, Asia and the Great War: A Shared History, *Oxford UP, pp.25–37, is an excellent summary of events from August to late November 1914. See also J. Charles Schencking, 'Navalism, naval expansion and war: the Anglo-Japanese Alliance and the Japanese Navy', in O'Brien,* The Anglo-Japanese Alliance, *pp.128–35; Jonathan Fenby,* The Siege of Tsingtao: The Only Battle of the First World War to be Fought in East Asia, *Penguin China, 2014). The subsequent British attempts to limit Japanese action and protect the interests of Australia and New Zealand are described in Peter Lowe, 'Great Britain and Japan's entrance into the Great War, 1914–1915', in O'Brien,* The Anglo-Japanese Alliance, *pp.159–75, and Nish,* Alliance in Decline, *pp.132–57.*

Aug. 17 Monday at 12.0.

Prime Minister looking well, said the news from Constantinople indicated that the *Goeben*'s & *Breslau*'s crews had not left their ships, & Turkey was playing a double game. Grey thought Turkey at any moment might declare war with us, & we must be prepared to regard the ships as hostile. It was thought advisable to wire to Mallet[48] at Cn'tople to ascertain if Dardanelles was safe for our Black Sea traffic. Churchill would in 48 hours be able to run gunboats, or torpedo destroyers in to Sea of Marmora & take the 2 ships or sink them. He was not anxious for the French fleet to have a hand in this business.

We discussed effect of action — if it came in advance of an act of war on the part of Turkey (her attitude to ships being itself a breach of neutrality but not sufficiently marked to warrant our action) might have on Mahommedan population in Egypt & India.

[48] Sir Louis Mallet (1864–1936); Amb., Constantinople 1913–14; p.s. to Sir Edward Grey, 1905–7; Asst U.-Sec. of State, in charge of Near and Middle Eastn affairs, 1907–13. PC 1913, GCMG 1915.

The Prime Minister that day, in his regular bulletin of intelligence for Venetia Stanley, identified Crewe and Kitchener as counselling against anything 'which could be interpreted as meaning that we were taking the initiative against Turkey. She ought to be compelled to strike the first blow. I agreed to this' (Asquith Letters, *pp.170–2). Nicholas A. Lambert's important new study,* The War Lords and the Gallipoli Disaster: How Globalized Trade Led Britain to Its Worst Defeat of the First World War, *Oxford UP, New York, 2021, provides a detailed account of Cabinet and Foreign Office responses to the news from Constantinople. The British had intercepted signals but were unable to decipher them and thus were unaware of the fact that a small group of Young Turk leaders had negotiated a secret pact with Germany from late in July to 2 August, pledging their neutrality in any Austro-Serbian conflict and that, if Germany were forced into war by Russia, the Ottoman Empire would join the central powers (Kieran West, 'Intelligence and the Development of British Grand Strategy in the First World War', Ph.D. thesis, U. of Cambridge, 2010, pp.43–4; Sir William James,* The Eyes of the Navy: a Biographical Study of Admiral Sir Reginald Hall, *Methuen, 1956, pp.60–1). What the Turks had not appreciated was that German strategy would inevitably draw France and Britain as well as Russia into war. By 5 November Turkey was at war with all three (Fotakis,* Greek Naval Policy and Strategy, *pp.102–3; Hew Strachan,* The First World War, Vol. I To Arms, *Oxford UP, 2001, pp.644–93; Erik J. Zürcher,* Turkey: A Modern History, *I.B. Tauris, 2004, pp.110–13; Rogan,* The Fall of the Ottomans, *pp.39–41).*

The South African Troops Kitchener said would be here on Sept 15. The Indian Troops in Egypt on the 28th. & he did not want ructions before that date — the 20th — they sailed.

Runciman explained he had tried to secure cornering merchant service of other Powers through Inchcape,[49] Pirrie, Sanderson[50] &c & thought for 3 millions we would only risk 1½ millions.

[49] James Lyle Mackay, 1st Baron Inchcape (1852–1932); described by M.M.S. Gubbay in the *DNB 1931–40* (p.575) as 'the most prominent figure of his time in British shipping'; merchant in India trading in jute, tea, coal, cotton 1874–97; Pres., Bengal Chamber of Commerce 1890–3; member, Bengal legislative council 1891–3; influential in reform of Indian currency; head of British India company 1893–1914; KCIE 1894; member, Sec. of St. for India's Council 1897–1911; negotiated Treaty of Shanghai 1901–2; GCMG 1902; Baron Inchcape 1911; negotiated Pacific & Orient's purchase of British India Company 1914; served on many govt committees 1914–22, and chaired committee on rates of hire for vessels chartered by British govt; Vt Inchcape 1924; Earl of Inchcape 1929.

[50] Harold Arthur Sanderson (1859–1932); mgn dir., White Star Line; partner in many other shipping concerns; appointed pres., International Mercantile Marine Co. 1913. Sanderson's role in the shipping world is documented in Bryan Dyson, 'The End of the Line: Oswald Sanderson, Sir John Ellerman and the Wilsons of Hull', in David John Starkey and Alan G. Jamieson eds, *Exploiting the Sea: Aspects of Britain's Maritime Economy Since 1870*, U. of Exeter P., 1998, pp.59–78.

Simon suggested that the Declaration of London might preclude American purchases of German ships during the war; but matters might be settled with the United States by letting them have much of the shipping when the war was over (Emmott diary, 19 Aug. 1914, MS. Emmott I/2, Nuffield Col.).

I had a talk to Kitchener about horses [& how to get them from America].[51] He said he was buying quietly in Canada.

Kitchener's quiet operation in Canada came unstuck with allegations of corruption against a British agent operating under the authority of Sam Hughes, the Canadian Minister of Militia, 'a bounder of the first order' (HHA–Venetia Stanley, 28 Oct. 1914, Venetia Montagu MSS, transcript courtesy of Judy Gendel and the Hon. Randolph Churchill, passage omitted by the Brocks). The Canadian Cabinet 'successfully countered' the agent's activities (Basil Blackett–Sir John Bradbury, 'Purchase of War Supplies in the United States', 27 Nov. 1914, Bodl. MS. Asquith 26, ff.166–74). For the confusion arising from Hughes's authorisation of his 'business cronies' to pursue contracts in the United States see Keith Neilson, 'Russian Foreign Purchasing in the Great War: A Test Case', S&EER, vol.60, no.4, Oct. 1982, pp.572–90, and '"The work of the F.O. is nauseous in war time—a mess of questions of contraband & kindred subjects that don't exist in time of peace and are a disagreeable brood spawned by war" the foreign office and maritime war, 1914–1915', in Greg Kennedy ed., Britain's War at Sea, 1914–1918, *pp.26–7.*

It had been realised during the Agadir crisis in 1911 that the army would be short of horses if war came (Ewart Memoirs re 9 Nov. 1911, Ewart MSS). Fears that American neutrality would restrict the buying of horses in the USA proved unfounded, and by November 1914 British remount delegations were operating in Kansas City, Denver, St Louis, Chicago, and Fort Worth (John Singleton, 'Britain's Military Use of Horses 1914–1918', Past & Present, *vol.139, issue 1, May 1993, pp.178–203). In late November 1914 it is estimated that the BEF had over 148,000 horses: more than 61,000 for the eleven infantry divisions and 4,000 for the infantry brigade; 49,000 for five cavalry divisions plus 1,800 for the cavalry brigade; 23,000 for the field artillery; 11,600 for the horse artillery brigade; and 1,500 for the heavy batteries. (Exact numbers derived from Adjutant-General's war diaries are listed in Brown,* British Logistics, *pp.67,73n.89). Pre-war planning by Henry Wilson for horse mobilisation is discussed in Allan Mallinson,* 1914: Fight the Good Fight: Britain, the Army and the Coming of the First World War, *Bantam P., 2013, pp.132–7. The most comprehensive study of pre-war planning, mobilisation, and expansion of 'horsing' is Graham Winton,*

[51] The words in square brackets are a later interpolation.

'Theirs Not To Reason Why': Horsing the British Army 1875–1925, *Helion & Co., Solihull, 2013, pp.213–314.*

Aug. 18 Cabinet 11.30 Tuesday. The Prime Minister drew attention to a telegram from Cairo, in which an indication was given the authorities feared an armed force of Turks from Palestine, who would arouse Mohammedan population to revolt — & until Indian contingent arrived force in Egypt was insufficient to cope with attack or revolt. Kitchener thought that from Jerusalem knowledge would be conveyed if such a force was on its way, meanwhile Churchill should convoy any troops of Turkish origin along the canal & sink them if they proposed to land. It was resolved no act of aggression should be perpetrated on our part, in Sea of Marmora or elsewhere to precipitate hostilities with Turkey.

Kitchener seemed pleased at way in which he could tell us our forces were now in their position. He obviously thinks war may last 2 years, & Churchill suggested the cost might reach 1000 millions addition to the debt, this flash was not accepted as accurate.[52] Churchill informed us that a German cruiser the *Rostock* had been sighted that morning in the North Sea & our destroyers were in pursuit;[53] that the *Kaiser Wilhelm der Grosser* [*sic*] was at large off Los Palmas, but not able to do much with ships she overtook. She was after gold but apparently was being hunted down. Runciman reported progress of his negociations to purchase neutral merchant shipping, with a view to place economic pressure on Germany — estimated cost £5,000,000.

Aug. 19 Churchill explained the *Rostock* had evaded us. The *Fearless* came across some 4 other cruisers but kept out of their way. Two of our submarines *E7* & *E5* had got in among the German ships, been seen & chivied, they fired one torpedo which missed its target at a Destroyer. They then submerged 60 feet & came away. It may have caused consternation among the German fleet. Fielmann & ? made very plucky voyages. Discussion on food in neutral vessels & how to deal with ships going into Rhine under Neutral flags to help Germany — food stuffs were going in. Churchill reported we had taken 35 vessels since war opened in

[52] An article in *The Times* on 15 Aug. 1914 hinting that Kitchener was preparing for a three-year war had prompted an expostulation from a former Sec. of the CID that the people of Britain would not stand for it. 'I should myself put the duration of the war at about 9 months, & I can easily conceive circumstances which would shorten that period…'. The editor agreed 'in thinking it unlikely that the war can be a very long one' (Ld Sydenham of Combe–Robinson and reply, 15, 16 Aug. 1914, Times Newspapers Ltd Archives).

[53] The *Rostock* was mistaken for the cruiser *Stralsund*.

open seas. They had taken none of ours. The *Zurindra* — an Austrian ship sunk off Ciltinci ? same as *Aspern*. Decided we should warn U.S.A. if they took over German liners, we should hold ourselves free to take them — neutral power no right to pay for & help a belligerent.[54]

Aug. 20 Kitchener reported that he proposed to send another Division off on Sunday bringing up force of our troops to about 125,000. He still hoped the move into Brussels which had been entered that morning might enable the Germans to be cut off & another Sedan created.

In a letter to Elsie that day JAP admitted that the German progress had to be stopped 'by the French & ourselves if at all between Mauberge & Lille — the enemy are coming in force but we have no knowledge where the French are — but they will move North we presume, & have reliefs behind coming up' (MS. Gainford 189/27).

A protracted discussion on neutral ships, what was & was not contraband of war, & how we could stop ships going into Rotterdam with supplies possibly pretended for Dutch but would find their way into German hands.

Grey, WSC, and others believed that interruption of food supplies might discomfit the advancing German armies. Following a conference of ministers and officials convened by Grey on the 19th, the Admiralty had issued orders at 3.15 a.m. on 20 August that neutral ships carrying conditional contraband, including food, should be detained even if they were proceeding to a Dutch port. In an Order-in-Council drawn up by the Attorney General after the Cabinet on 20 August, British naval officers and prize courts were authorised to seize contraband

[54] Lt-Cdr Ferdinand Feilmann (d. 1956) was the commanding officer of HMS *E7*. In May 1916, in command of *E31*, he shot down a Zeppelin. For his earlier misadventures see Michael Wilson, *Destination Dardanelles: The Story of HMS E7*, Leo Cooper, 1988. The missing name is probably Lt-Cdr Charles Benning (d. 1924) of *E5*. Benning was court-martialled in 1917 for running *K1* aground. Damage was slight and, accepting his excuse that rats had eaten his chart of the anchorage, the board dismissed the charges (Barrow-in-Furness Branch, Submariners Association: http://www.rnsubs.co.uk/index.php, accessed 31 Jan. 2014); Benning was censured late in 1917 when *K1* under his command collided with another submarine and sank off the Danish coast (A.S. Evans, *Beneath the Waves: A History of HM Submarine Losses 1904–1971*, Pen & Sword Maritime, Barnsley, 2010, pp.102–8; Edwin Gray, *A Damned Un-English Weapon: The Story of British Submarine Warfare 1914–18*, Seeley, Service, 1971, pp.196–7,221). JAP seems to have been labouring with the foreign names. A sister ship of the Austro-Hungarian light cruiser *Aspern* was allegedly sunk by mine off Lussin on 14 Aug. The Austrian cruiser *Zenta* was sunk by the French off Antivari in the Adriatic on 16 Aug. We are grateful to Nicholas Lambert for assistance here. See also Lawrence Sondhaus, *Naval Policy of Austria–Hungary, 1867–1918: Navalism, Industrial Development, and the Politics of Dualism*, Purdue UP, Lafayette, IN, 1993.

on 'any sufficient evidence' that its ultimate destination was Germany. It was not until 23 August that the Foreign Office learnt that the navy's orders were unqualified by any requirement about 'sufficient evidence'. For British maritime rights policy, with particular emphasis on American reactions, see Greg Kennedy, 'The North Atlantic Triangle and the blockade, 1914–1915', Journal of Transatlantic Studies, *vol.6, no.1, Apr. 2008, pp.22–3; John W. Coogan,* The End of Neutrality: The United States, Britain, and Maritime Rights 1899–1915, *Cornell UP, Ithaca, 1981, pp.148–93; Arthur Marsden, 'The Blockade', in Hinsley ed.,* British Foreign Policy under Sir Edward Grey, *pp.48–515; Nicholas Lambert's* Planning Armageddon, *pp.210–78, and Coogan's animated critique, 'The Short-War Illusion Resurrected: the Myth of Economic Warfare as the British Schlieffen Plan',* J.Strat.S., *vol.38, no.7, 2015, pp.1045–64.*

We discussed the Greek position. The Grk minister offered us help — unconditionally. Our reply was very carefully considered. We agreed we must not accept if it meant driving Turkey & Bulgaria into arms of Germany. We wanted confederation of the States. We had told Turkey if she remained neutral we would respect her present boundaries but Greek action might precipitate Turkey's hostility. If Turkey opposed us we would then accept Greek help — Churchill pointed out it might be too late. I supported him in view we should accept, but postpone time for operation of Force until we knew Roumanian, Bulgarian & Turkish attitude.

Bulgaria and the Ottoman government had signed a 'treaty of friendship and alliance' on 19 August. The diplomatic dance in August and September 1914 involving Germany, Bulgaria, Turkey, and Roumania, with Greece committed to support Serbia if it were to be attacked by Bulgaria, is summarised in Aksakal, The Ottoman Road to War in 1914, *pp.102–52. On the Austro-Hungarian attacks on Serbia in the autumn of 1914 see James Lyon,* Serbia and the Balkan Front, 1914, *Bloomsbury, 2015.*

Aug. 21 I was absent [at P. & P.'s meeting in the North] from this cabinet. They apparently referred to Irish & Welsh Bills & the moratorium in regard to the date when they should come into force, but the assent of the King to the passage of the Bills under Parliament Act was not questioned.

As well as his meeting of Pease and Partners, JAP was able to fit in two days' shooting at Allenheads, Lord Allendale's 20,000-acre estate in Northumberland, with Allendale himself, Lord Chesterfield, and 22-year-old Captain Guy Allgood of the Northumberland

Fusiliers, heir to the nearby Nunwick Hall (hunting diary, MS. Gainford 75, f.142[v]*). Meanwhile the Allies—some 70,000 British and two French armies of 120,000 each as well as what was left of the Belgian forces—were in retreat as the Germans captured the fortresses of Liège and Namur. The German strength had been estimated at 400,000, but the invasion force was in fact some 700,000 (Clayton Donnell,* Breaking the Fortress Line 1914, *Pen & Sword, Barnsley, 2013, pp.98–101).*

On the evening of 23 August, Johnny Baird MP, now in uniform as an intelligence officer attached to the Adjutant-General and liaising with the General Staff, was at Le Cateau:

> saw General Wilson, who said today's reverse was entirely due to our having only four Divisions instead of six. If we had had six, as asked for by soldiers, we should have advanced next day; instead of which we were going to retire. It was the difference between victory and defeat, and might change the character of the whole campaign.
>
> *(Baird diary, 23 Aug 1914, Stonehaven MSS, vol.128, Aberdeen U, courtesy of the 13th Earl of Kintore)*

Aug. 24 Met at 12.0 & sat until 1.55. Kitchener explained on map what the position was. The serious effect produced in military situation by fall of Namur. The P.M. read out the telegram from French giving very scant information. Kitchener read long letter from French he had received the previous evening, in which he thought the position of the allied troops was satisfactory — but Namur was weaker than he had supposed, the trees had probably protected the Germans who had rushed it & might now be following up rearguard actions on both British & French, & dividing the forces & Army Corps 3d and 4th to their detriment.

We discussed the possibilities & what further steps we could take. Kitchener outlined his own scheme for Army. By April next he hoped to complete 30 divisions

4 had gone abroad as 1st expeditionary force
5th was across (Saturday Aug. 19 crossed) & joining French
6th would be ready by Sept 12
7th " " " Sept 30
8th was in China, & would come to India & relieve another
9th was Colonial, ? regulars in Egypt, Malta & S. Africa mostly on high seas or making preparations to start
10th was Colonial which he hoped would follow

11th Territorial – the best trained men 75% had
12th " " volunteered
13th–17th 5 more Territorial would train on for the front
18–24 6 more special reserve 1/3 competent
1/8 guarding bridges
1/3 useless — over 55 yrs of age
1 cavalry — Yeomanry
30[55] He might get another Division fr. New Zealand
20000
1,000,000

To equip them with artillery, 700,000 men would require more than this country could manage but works more fully occupied — cartridges we were buying from America through Canada. He told me at end he had got more than the 100,000 new recruits for the regulars but it was best not to say what he had got.

One of those who had answered the call to arms was the Peases' 25-year-old son Joe. 'If there's no stopping him', Elsie wrote, then Gordon Wilson, commander of the Royal Horse Guards ('the Blues'), would look after him '& he wd see something of life & gentlemen'. The problem was money: 'it costs 1,000 a year at least in normal times & the other cavalry regiments, 12th Lancers & &c nearly as expensive' (EP–JAP, 23 Aug. 1914; this and subsequent letters about Joe Pease's military future are in MS. Gainford 85/73–107). In 1912 the enormously rich Harold Wernher was guided by the King into the 12th Lancers, a regiment where, as the family historian put it, 'there was no chance of junior officers exploiting his wealth and encouraging extravagant tastes' (Raleigh Trevelyan, Grand Dukes and Diamonds: The Wernhers of Luton Hoo, *Secker & Warburg, 1991, pp.258–9). Contemporary estimates of the private income necessary for officers in the Guards, cavalry, infantry, and artillery are provided in Timothy Bowman and Mark Connelly,* The Edwardian Army: Recruitment, Training, and Deploying the British Army 1902–1914, *Oxford UP, 2012, pp.11–12.*

With detailed knowledge about to be imparted by Kitchener on the success of recruiting, and a telegram from Elsie on 26 August saying she had heard that Joe had applied for a commission in the 18th Hussars, JAP sat down to write:

[55] JAP calculated in the margin that 30 divisions of 20,000 men each was a total of 600,000 men.

My dear Joe

A week ago I was congratulating myself I had a son who had kept his head when so many others were losing theirs & rushing about trying to do something for their country without regard to their capacities or the emergency.

If I have any qualities — & I am conscious of my limitations — it is the possession of cool judgement, & the more people lose their heads the less I am likely to lose mine, & it is in a spirit of calm thought I write to you this morning.

I could of course dwell on your not thinking it necessary to consult either your mother or me before taking a step such as you contemplate — but I shan't do so, though I should have been glad to have seen you yesterday or Saturday to talk the matter over, if you had given me a chance. I can't do so now, as we have cabinets today & tomorrow, & the House sits the next 2 or 3 days. So I must content myself with my pen.

In the first place, you have had no training for the army & you are not therefore the kind of man preferred by the War Office for regular army recruiting. You would start 9 years later than the raw recruits they want & in 3 years time you would find your work in life gone & you had missed your mark. You have not in the second place the figure for a cavalry officer & you would never look one. You would hate the life. You would be sent to the riding school for six months to bump hour after hour round a hot dusty building being sworn at every day by a drill serjeant. You would have to sit hours at work, in studying strategy, ballistics, history, signalling and a lot of stuff which would be no use to you.

In the third place if you went into a decent regiment you would find you were handicapped for money. No officer can live on his pay. If you went into a bad regiment you would hate your companions & it would be still a struggle even if P. & P. [paid a] dividend on your few shares, & after all that is all you would then possess.

Those that have joined the regulars, and there are still plenty coming forward from occupations in which they are doing little good for their country, are already grumbling at the life they have to lead at Aldershot! There is no prospect of their reaching the front before a year is over. The trained Territorials would no doubt be taken first — & new regulars would probably later on sent to India to do routine duty.

From therefore that point of view I beg you to take my advice and recognise that you will only make your life a failure if you join now.

From the point of view of your duty to your country I would say you are of more value than to go into a profession which if even it lead to your going on active service, would only mean you let yourself be put into a position, not to fight, but to be mown down by concerted machine guns for that is what scientific war is more & more coming to.

We have plenty of recruits without you. Although an Island Power depending on the Navy rather than the Army for our position in the world, we have now got 1 million men under arms, all but 100,000 more or less trained. We have some 50,000 trained colonials now on their way to go to the front, if they are wanted.

If we were short of land forces, I would speak very differently, but for men in the field we are not in the need of services such as yours.

What we are in need of? Men to carry on the great industries and productions of this country, to employ the people & to secure for them the necessities of their very existence. If young men trained to business, engineering, chuck their work for arms our country must sink.

There was more in the same vein, leading to an appeal to stay and play a part in running the Pease & Partners business and 'resuscitating the fortunes of the family'. The plea 'in the most urgent way a Father can' to cancel any steps Joe had taken to join the regulars, and wait until men of his 'calibre' were needed, was ill-judged. 'I am returning your letter,' his son replied, 'as in my opinion it is a most cowardly and selfish one and the less said about it the better.' It would not be playing the game if he were to stop at home while others were responding to his father and the government when they were calling for recruits. He was waiting for the War Office's instructions to report for six months' training and then take his part in 'protecting our friends abroad; and when all has been settled for the cause of peace I will be ready again to take up my position in Industrial life'. Signing himself 'Your devoted son', Joe softened the confronting message (MS. Gainford 85/126–7, courtesy of the Hon. Matthew Pease).

There was no stopping Joe. But Elsie, the famous General's daughter, continued to try to steer. 'As inevitable get Kitchener to give commission in good Cavalry Regiment. Why not first Life Guards Blues or Scots Greys. Joe has contemporaries in all of these . . .'. Not only were some of Joe's contemporaries in the 1st Life Guards, and probably the Royal Horse Guards as well, more than a third of their officers in 1912 had inherited titles (P.E. Razzell, 'Social Origins of Officers in the Indian and British Home Army: 1758–1962', The British Journal of Sociology, *vol.14, no.3, 1963, p.255). The quest for the right regiment continued for weeks, with Elsie increasingly agitated: 'You had really better see Sir Alfred Codrington. Write to him 160 Eaton Square. I think I know him...'. She might have known the former commander of the Brigade of Guards now recalled as Kitchener's Military Secretary, but she had little confidence in her husband's influence. 'Don't let the boy go into a rotten regiment—unless you do something I'll wire Lord Lovat...' (EP–JAP, 7 Sept. 1914, MS. Gainford 85/98). And it was to the Lovat Scouts Joe went, serving throughout the war on Home Defence, at Gallipoli, in Egypt, and in Salonika. A collection of his papers is held by the IWM (Documents.10945).*

Joe's cousin Christopher, son of Sir Alfred Pease Bt, had been given a commission on 23 September 1914 in the 1/1st Yorkshire Hussars Yeomanry (Alexandra, Princess of Wales's Own). In August 1917 his regiment was converted to infantry and sent to the 9th Battalion, West Yorkshire Regiment, re-designated 9th (Yorkshire Hussars Yeomanry) Battalion. Captain Pease was killed in May 1918. His older brother Edward Pease was severely wounded in Flanders in 1915 but survived to inherit his father's title in 1939. For the impact of the war on other Quaker business families see Deborah Cadbury, Chocolate Wars: from Cadbury to Kraft—200 Years of Sweet Success and Bitter Rivalry, *Harper P., 2011 [1st edn 2010], pp.229–30,235–6, and David Rubinstein,* A Quaker Dilemma: The Rowntree Family and the Great War, *Quacks Books, York, 2015.*

Aug. 25 Kitchener read out French's telegram 5.0 p.m. & 12 o'clock midnight of previous day — & his reply that morning after consultation with Prime Minister.

JAP might not have heard of HHA's exasperation on learning that the second deciphered telegram from French had been sent to Kitchener, who could not be found. What Kitchener appears to have described as a 'midnight' telegram had actually come in at about 10.30 p.m. but did not reach Downing Street until nearly 1.00 a.m. As Eric Drummond told his wife, 'we were all rather jumpy by then'. The Asquiths had dined and played bridge with Harcourt. It was 4.00 a.m. before an angry Prime Minister, at last assured that the British army had not been cut off, went to bed (Drummond–A. Drummond, 25 Aug. 1914, Perth MSS, Stobhall 7/3/1/3; Harcourt diary, 24 Aug. 1914, Webb ed., From Downing Street to the Trenches, *p.47;* The Autobiography of Margot Asquith, *Vol. II, Thornton Butterworth, 1922, pp.206–7; and, for the more colourful contemporary account,* Margot Asquith's Great War Diary 1914–1916, *pp.25–6).*

'We were rather upset at cabinet this morning by the position of the French...', JAP told Elsie on the 25th, 'they seem to have their worst men in the places where they ought to have their best'. Cabinet did not know if Namur had fallen. 'The Belgians say they are still there, & we can only imagine the French have fallen away from supporting them, & have assumed that

Namur would then fall... we are short of knowledge & facts, & could only state to the public what is the gist of French's telegram this morning' (*MS. Gainford 189/30*).

French asked for 6th Division to be sent. Reported retirement to line Valenciennes Mauberge effected better than anticipated but casualties over 2000. Men could not have done better — he would have to withdraw further to keep in contact with the allies — but he would do his best to obey instructions

Kitchener wired French to use his own discretion as to whether it was best to adhere to course discussed before his departure — he must be guided by circumstances. The supports that he asked, 10,000 men, on previous day, to make good deficiencies should be sent.

K. told the cabinet he thought he ought to keep 6th Division at home for eventualities & emergencies; we did not want to send our last complete division away from our own coasts.

The P.M. read a letter from F.E. Smith urging leaders of both sides to step out into open and urge the people to recruit. Churchill harangued us for half an hour on the necessity of compulsory service. Pointing out the importance of young unmarried men going to the front rather than the territorial, a married man who had trained with a limited obligation, & now his patriotism was being exploited by being pressed into going abroad, & almost compelled to agree to do so, whilst others were loafing & cheering & doing nothing for their country &c. &c. &c.

We all sat and listened, much bored. The P.M. took it with impatience — the matter he said was not urgent. George said we need not be in a panic — the people would not listen to such proposals. The P.M. asked how many of our own men in the H of C. would now assent, such a proposal would divide the country from one end to the other. I chipped in & said if he thought the men of the North would respond to such legislation he did not know them. If they knew a necessity had arisen they would come forward voluntarily, but conscription would not be listened to or acquiesced in. K. said it might come to this later on. He made no appeal for compulsion yet. He had got his 120,000 men & recruiting was still going on although he had only asked for 100,000. He could not arm more before April.

Kitchener asked then that the re-export of meat into this country could be stopped. Runciman pointed out that this meat went to France under contract, to stop its re-export not merely hit the French but would check supplies into this country. The French would pay as high a price for it as we would. We would be deprived of handling it, & trade was so sensitive it would stop ships coming here to bring us provisions. If an emergency occurred we should possess it for the time being but to divert trade & provisions from our coast was bad policy. Poor K. could not see it. He does not understand trade or politics one iota!

Sir Charles Harris, Director of Finance at the War Office, was making no secret of his concern about 'K. of Chaos'. He was also perturbed by Runciman, who, apparently having caught a 'noble Briton... collaring the meat market', merely threatened him with exposure (Eleanor Acland diary, 30 Aug. 1914, Acland of Killerton MSS). The Commission Internationale de Ravitaillement had been created on 17 August with French representatives sitting with Admiralty, War Office, and Board of Trade officials, to coordinate Anglo-French purchasing of frozen and tinned meat, flour, grain, and forage for the two armies. In late October, instructed by the Cabinet Committee on Food Supplies, the Board of Trade appointed the Queensland Agent-General and former shipping manager, Sir Thomas Robinson, to secretly organise the purchase for the army of 15,000 tons of frozen meat a month in Argentina. Robinson's proposal that he should negotiate for the supply of frozen beef with Argentina, Uruguay, Australia, and New Zealand on behalf of both the British and French governments was accepted in January 1915. The standard account of the initial responses to war and the focus on supply is L. Margaret Barnett, British Food Policy During The First World War, *George Allen & Unwin, Boston, 1983, pp.20–47; and see John Connor,* Someone Else's War: Fighting for the British Empire in World War I, *I.B. Tauris, 2019, pp.38–9.*

Wed. Aug. 26 We commenced by the usual collection of ministers round the Map, whilst Kitchener explained the movement of troops. Obviously French was retiring near Amiens to force the Germans an extension of their communications, & to keep in touch with the French. He knew where the 1, 3, & 5 French Army corps were, but had no knowledge of the 2 & 4 which should be very strong. He had wired to our military attaché[56] with Joffre[57] to tell us. He read telegrams from French telling us little more than he had given us the day before. There seemed little more we could do but to ask for more recruits so as to be ready for future emergencies.

[56] Col. the Hon. Henry ('Yardie') Yarde-Buller (1862–1928); military attaché, British Embassy, Paris, attached to Joffre at Kitchener's request. Disliked by the Amb., Sir Frank Bertie (Lord Bertie of Thame June 1915), he was unable to win Joffre's confidence; succeeded by Major Sydney Clive (Keith Hamilton, *Bertie of Thame: Edwardian Ambassador*, Boydell & Brewer, 1990, pp.345,352).

[57] Gen. Joseph Joffre (1852–1931); Chief of Staff, French Army, 1911–16; effectively dismissed and made Marshal of France Dec. 1916; head, French military mission to USA 1917; pres., Supreme War Council 1918.

Ostend was to be occupied by 3000 marines today protected by ships & transports drawing little water.

I urged in appeals for recruits, we should not devastate the industrial workers but keep on giving employment, & making good wastages & supplying materials.

Aug. 27 Kitchener asked whether we should make 20 million rounds of Mauser ammunition for Belgians at Antwerp & reduce our own when we might need it all ourselves. We agreed to take the risk.

He then read French's wire telling us that he had met Joffre, was satisfied now with disposition, & spirit of French troops & their officers. We would take up line from Amiens to Rheims — & the southern French army must [work] with the [N.] French [command],[58] if we then could not hold this much stronger line in the open retire together on Paris, move our supplies across country from Paris to Loire, & keep our base on the sea on Bay of Biscay.

We discussed problem of recruiting in all its phases, & agreed to go on on voluntary system so long as necessary recruits were coming in.

Recruiting was about to peak. Nearly 300,000 enlisted in August. Numbers were never higher than between 31 August and 11 September (Peter Simkins, Kitchener's Army: The Raising of the New Armies, 1914–16, *Manchester UP, 1988, ch.2; Ian Beckett, Timothy Bowman, and Mark Connelly,* The British Army and the First World War, *Cambridge UP, 2017, p.89). Jack Gulland told the Scottish lawyer J.H. Balfour Browne on 1 September that the War Office had more recruits than they could manage and the recruiting campaign was to be slowed down (Letter paraphrase,* John Wilson Autograph Letters & Historical Documents Catalogue, *No.85, item 6184). Some of the extensive literature on voluntary recruiting to May 1916 is critiqued in David Silbey's study of* The British Working Class and Enthusiasm for War, 1914–1916, *Frank Cass, 2015. The story in a part of the country JAP knew well is meticulously analysed in Edward M. Spiers, 'Voluntary Recruiting in Yorkshire, 1914–15',* Northern History, *vol.LII, no.2, 2015, pp.295–313; and a niche market is discussed in Cameron McKay, '"Likely to make good soldiers": mobilizing Britain's criminal population during the First World War',* Historical Research, *vol.94, issue 265, 2021, pp.578–600. Peter Doyle provides a 'more nuanced' class and regional interpretation in '"Kitchener's Mob": myth and reality in raising the New Army, 1914–15', in Kevin Linch and Matthew Lord eds,* Redcoats to Tommies: The Experience of the British Soldier from the Eighteenth Century, *Boydell & Brewer, Martlesham, 2020, pp.58–81.*

[58] The words in square brackets are a later interpolation. Kitchener's role in the last week of August 1914 can be followed in Cassar, *Kitchener's War*, pp.81–91.

Knowing that Alfred Pease had been critical of the Liberal government's foreign policy, JAP wrote for his brother's eyes alone an explanation of the Cabinet's position on recruiting and the way Britain should fight the war.

> The possibility of a war with Germany was carefully considered by the Defence Committee, even if we had no other help than France and we decided we could win through by holding the sea maintaining our credit, keeping our people employed & our industries going. By economic pressure, destroying Germany's trade cutting off her supplies we would gradually secure victory. This policy is being steadily pursued. We have never thought we could successfully afford to compete with her by maintaining also a continental army on her scale. Our Navy, finance & trade was our life's blood, & we must see to it that these are maintained.
>
> *(JAP–Alfred Pease, 28 Aug. 1914, MS. Gainford 176/33)*

28 Aug. Friday 35 minutes desultory talk as to how much information should be given the Press, Churchill arguing that anything the Germans knew could be given, L. George arguing we should plainly state when we met with disaster. Kitchener urging no names of places should ever be mentioned on principle, that it was a pity to make people anxious about their relatives, & that he would never give anything which might add to the enemies' information. Ultimately the P.M. read French's telegram announcing at Cambrai–Le Cateau a very heavy loss had been incurred, the shrapnel playing havoc on our men when retiring in front of an overwhelming force, 3 to 1 opposed to us. The withdrawal had at last been effected without French support. But now French were in front of us on both sides & an army corps at Amiens, & the 1st Army corps had come up to Laon–Rheims line.

The impact of the losing Battle of Le Cateau on 26 August and the broader 'Failure of the Battle of the Frontiers' on French strategic planning and Entente cooperation is outlined effectively in Roy A. Prete, Strategy and Command: The Anglo-French Coalition on the Western Front, 1914, *McGill-Queen's UP, Montreal & Kingston, 2009, pp.94–106. The artillery battle at Le Cateau is analysed in Sanders Marble,* British Artillery on the Western Front in the First World War: 'The Infantry cannot do with a gun less', *Ashgate, Farnham, 2013, pp.44–7. Citing the tone of French's diary for 22 and 28 August, Ian Malcolm Brown has ventured that 'one might say that Sir John left the control of the BEF in the hands of his CGS during the battles and that Haig, Smith-Dorrien, and Allenby actually fought the battles with little higher direction'* (British Logistics on the Western Front 1914–1919, *Praeger, Westport, 1998, p.59).*

Very early in the morning of 28 August Major-General Henry Wilson gave Johnny Baird a rather more coherent picture than JAP had gathered from the briefing by Kitchener and HHA.

'The Battle of Le Cateau and the Retreat from there', he said, 'would probably turn out to be one of the finest things, from private soldiers' standpoint, that had ever been done':

> We had stood up 2½ Divisions, only 2 of which had full complement of artillery, against 5 German Divisions with overwhelming artillery, and had extricated ourselves from the position. The whole of the fighting of the last four days had been magnificent performance on the part of the men, company officers, regimental officers and Brigadiers, and he was not prepared to say the same of the Staff work. Trouble originally arose out of Mons position, which he (General Henry Wilson) did not consider a satisfactory one. When forced to retire our two Armies fell back on either side of a wood and thus lost touch. Consequently Germans were able to concentrate their 4 or 5 Divisions on our 2 (2nd Army). French were much ashamed, he said, of their failure to help us, either at Mons or Mauberge; their cavalry apparently did come up on our left at Le Cateau, and greatly assisted our retirement. General Henry Wilson has been working at this scheme of co-operation with the French for many years. His disappointment at its failure cannot be described.
>
> *(Baird diary, 26–8 Aug 1914, Stonehaven MSS, vol.128, Aberdeen U.)*

Research in German regimental histories and tactical manuals calls into question histories which appear to exaggerate German casualties and the extent to which the British were outnumbered (Terence Zuber, The Mons Myth: A Reassessment of the Battle, *History P., Stroud, 2011, pp.209–59; and see David Hutchison, 'The Effectiveness of German Field Artillery at Mons and During the Retreat in August 1914',* JSAHR, *vol.95, no.384, 2017, pp.331–7.*

Churchill told us that 4 o'clock that morning our submarines had appeared off Heligoland our destroyers were waiting off the coast of Denmark & would try & cut their destroyers off & cruisers would be ready to help.

I played a rubber between 10.30 & 11.30 at No. 10 with Bonham Carter & Drummond (the P.M's secretaries) & Illingworth. The P.M. looked in, he of course had received at about 8 o'clock the news of the successful sea fight off Heligoland, 3 cruisers & 2 destroyers of the Germans being sunk. He made no comment.[59] We told him our gossip from Paris through a Mr May (his brother married the Speaker's sister[60]) that 600,000 Germans had been killed, 150,000 French &

[59] Goldrick, *Before Jutland*, pp.111–38, for the Heligoland Bight battle; for the background and aftermath see Jan Rüger, *Heligoland: Britain, Germany, and the Struggle for the North Sea*, Oxford UP, 2017, pp.133–43; and Jan Asmussen, 'Heligoland and the Great War: A Major Theatre of War That Never Was', in Jaroslaw Suchoples and Stephanie James eds, *Re-Visiting World War I: Interpretations and Perspectives of the Great Conflict*, Peter Lang, Frankfurt, 2016, pp.385–419. For a summary of naval dispositions in the North Sea and Channel, Steve R. Dunn, *Securing the Narrow Sea: The Dover Patrol, 1914–1918*, Seaforth Publishing, Barnsley, 2017, pp.27–8.

[60] None of James Lowther's sisters married a Mr May, but his third sister, Mabel Cecily, had married James Bey in 1912 and lived in Paris. It is possible that JAP misheard the name. James Bey (d. 1941) was

35,000 English! We asked him to play with us he said Oh NO I've won 33/-s so you think I'm going to lose it to you. I called on Churchill at Admiralty & he was in great heart & showed me on the map where the battle was.

Aug. 29 Kitchener explained the retiring lines taken up from Amiens to Rheims with Fr. corps & cavalry on our left. He thought this could be well held. We discussed recruiting & how to raise a steady stream of men — he was getting more than enough at the moment.

Telling his wife, the daughter of a retired CIGS, what had happened at the Saturday Cabinet, Charles Masterman said 'K appealed to the rest to find some means of steadying the stream... he simply hasn't the machinery to register & examine & drill them all at once' (Lucy Masterman–Lady Lyttelton, 31 Aug. 1914, Lyttelton MSS, LM/KL 248b, Queen Mary U. of London Archives).

On Sunday August 30 The Times *shocked its readers with a dramatic account of British losses at Mons and Cambrai. F.E. Smith, in charge of the Press Bureau, had not only passed the story but embroidered it. What became known as the 'Amiens Dispatch' is the subject of an informative essay by Stephen Badsey, 'Strategy and Propaganda: Lord Kitchener, the Retreat from Mons, and the Amiens Dispatch, August–September 1914' in Mark Connelly, Jo Fox, Stefan Goebel and Ulrich Schmidt eds,* Propaganda and Conflict: War, Media and Shaping the Twentieth Century, *I.B. Tauris, 2019, pp.21–38. Hazlehurst,* Politicians at War, *p.149, has a capsule version drawing on the diary of E.T. Cook.*

Aug. 31 Monday We had an extraordinary telegram from French, in which he told us he proposed for 8 days to march & retire W. of the Seine from Noyen, leaving the French to do their own fighting. We could not explain its real meaning. Kitchener read his own reply telegram in which he asked for full explanation & the cabinet suggested in another to French that we ought to support the French & fill up gap if wanted but we had confidence in him & troops, but the cabinet were anxious 'Whatever the cost' were suggested but these 3 words I insisted on should be expunged that we should support the French in line of battle if reqd. The reply came at 11.0 at night whilst I was playing Bridge with the P.M., Margot & Elizabeth. It was to the effect that 2d army corps had been 'shattered' required 'reorganising' that he could not face the 'disaster' wh. wd ensue to the Fr. troops of facing German troops again against 3 army corps, & find himself unsupported

the eldest son of Elias Pasha Bey. Mary Eleanor Rose, eldest sister of Vt Ullswater (as Lowther became on his retirement as Speaker in 1921), married Paul Vieugué of the French Diplomatic Service.

by the French. If they closed in & made an offensive attack he would stay at Nanteuil & be guided by circumstances. [The P.M. suggested I should go quietly across that night & find out the true position from French & come back at once & report. K. insisted on going himself.[61]] Kitchener & Churchill came across to see P.M. & me & we decided there & then that Kitchener would leave at once. Evidently Joffre & French were not cooperating & situation was critical. Kitchener wired he was anxious to respond to appeal made by President of Republic & would see him that afternoon. Churchill arranged

1. Special to Dover
2. Convey K. to Havre
3. Special take K to Paris
4. Embassy to receive message from French
5. Bertie to send K. on to French.

George, Simon, McKenna came in & approved course we had taken. George said K was a plucky old boy. Asquith said well I'm nearly his age & I would think nothing of it. Churchill said K. that evening said he was feeling very tired, but he is a bit of hard stuff.

I went off to Haldane's house, got Grey out of bed & at 1 o'clock we sent a telegram to Bertie at Embassy to tell him Kitchener's movements.

Sept. 1 Cabinet. A letter dated 29th was read from General French to Kitchener, in which he said the cabinet failed to realise the shattered condition of his troops, & we must be given time to reform & reorganise. We all felt when he had told us their spirit was excellent & they could encounter any force again when called upon, & that the casualties were approximately 4–5,000 men (3 per cent of the men he had) and that his units had been made good, that we were not to blame for failing to realise the shattered condition. It was however decided in spite of Churchill trying to press his own views as to what had happened & what we should do, to postpone any further discussion until after we had heard from Kitchener. Grey wanted Indian troops to be stopped landing Marseilles. This too was thought premature, they had not yet got through Egypt. We discussed moratorium, & how to try & secure credit & circulation among foreign traders of payments. Hobhouse authorised to lay submarine [cable] to La Rochelle.

[61] The words in square brackets are a later interpolation. HHA made no mention to Venetia Stanley of the idea that JAP might go to see French (*Asquith Letters*, pp.212–13).

WSC would later write of the momentous events which had so shaken French: 'hideous and measureless miscalculation of almost every factor present at the outbreak of the War was made by General Joffre and his officers. In consequence the two armies of the Allied Left were placed in positions of inconceivable peril' (Foreword, Major-General Sir Edward Spears, Liaison 1914: A Narrative of the Great Retreat, Eyre & Spottiswoode, 1968 [1st edn 1930], p.ix). French actions in 'the war of movement' are described in Robert A. Doughty, Pyrrhic Victory: French Strategy And Operations In The Great War, Harvard UP, Cambridge, MA, 2008, pp.46–104. For a piquant narrative by Richard Holmes see Riding the Retreat: Mons to the Marne 1914 Revisited, Jonathan Cape, 1995.

Kitchener's secret Paris meeting with French was to be one of the most controversial events of the early months of the war. JAP revealed to Elsie on 1 September: 'K. came back 7.15 last night direct from Havre & Portsmouth in khaki. He came into the cabinet direct from the station. He was not able to throw very much light on the French military strategy, as he did not get to see Joffre or his generals.' JAP gathered that Sir John French 'did not much care for his coming', thinking it was some reflection, and did not want him to show himself to the British troops. 'No one knows about K having been out of the country except those who may have secretly recognised him at Dover, Portsmouth, Charing X, & Waterloo' (MS. Gainford 189/41).

Kitchener's personal private secretary recalled that during the next 36 hours 'to preserve the secret of the hurried historical journey, I told more innocent fibs than in all the rest of my life' (Sir George Arthur, Not Worth Reading, Longmans Green, 1938, p.218). A greatly discomfited French complained to the Prime Minister that the Secretary of State for War's arrival, in the uniform of a Field Marshal, appeared to be an assertion that he could exercise the power and authority of a Commander-in-Chief in the field. Colonel Victor Huguet, the French liaison officer at GHQ, later described the C-in-C of the BEF as 'a spoilt child on whom Fortune had smiled prodigiously but who, the day she left him, seemed abandoned and forlorn' (General [Victor] Huguet, Britain and the War: A French Indictment, Cassell, 1928, p.84).

The Kitchener–French telegrams, their background and aftermath are reviewed in Stephen Badsey, 'Sir John French and Command of the BEF', in Spencer Jones ed., Stemming the Tide: Officers and Leadership in the British Expeditionary Force 1914, Helion & Co., Solihull, 2013, pp.27–50; on the Kitchener–French relationship see Richard Holmes, 'Sir John French and Lord Kitchener', in Brian Bond ed., The First World War and British Military History, Clarendon P., Oxford, 1991, pp.113–39. The significance of the high command reliance on face-to-face consultation is evident from Brian N. Hall, 'The "Life-Blood" of Command? The British Army, Communications and the Telephone, 1877–1914', W&S, vol.27, no.2, 2008, pp.43–65, and 'The British Army and Wireless Communication, 1896–1918', War in History, vol.19, no.3, 2012, pp.290–321. The activities of Bonar Law's former PPS, Captain Baird, exemplify the informal channels by which he, Freddie Guest,

Arthur Lee, Charley Castlereagh, Ned Goulding, and other parliamentarians in uniform, kept their political leaders informed. On 1 September, Baird wrote:

> I learnt that Lord Kitchener was coming over to see Sir John French in Paris today, and obtained leave to take our Records into Paris Embassy for transmission to War Office...owing to our attitude since we took the knock at Le Cateau we are running very grave risk of breaking up the Entente, and that we are within measurable distance of shouts of 'Vive l'Angeterre' being changed to 'A bas les Anglais! Nous sommes trahis'. Lord Kitchener arrived at 4 and I gave Fitzgerald, his Military and Personal Secretary, the fullest account of events.
>
> ...French's reply to General Joffre's telegram...was couched in language which showed a great deal of temper. This had greatly perturbed the whole Cabinet, owing to danger it implied of breaking the Entente and of deplorable effect that would thus produce in Italy, Turkey and elsewhere. Fitzgerald said close co-operation between British and French Commanders-in-Chief was, of course, indispensable, and question had been discussed whether Sir John French ought to be ordered to act under orders of Joffre.

Baird was pleased when told on 6 September that 'our C. in-Chief had been definitely placed under the orders of the French C-in-C' (Baird diary, 1, 7 Sept. 1914, Stonehaven MSS, vol.128, Aberdeen U.).

Sept. 2 Anniversary of Sedan.[62]

The P.M. read a telegram from Kitchener who had seen Sir John French at 4 o'clock in the English Embassy in Paris previous evening. He said the English force would support the French a little in arrear rather than in advance — NO great difference between French & Joffre & he (K.) would be back again this evening.[63]

Hobhouse reported he was taking up 300 miles of a German cable, & would put it down in 8 days to La Rochelle — cost £70,000 with the 300 miles of new cable.

Post Office officials would boast that in concert with the Admiralty they 'did a smart thing in Aug. Lifting & cutting of 180 M of the only cable that went direct from Germany to USA which was promptly used to improve communication with France for the Germans had cut 33 out of the 37 wires across the Channel' (Lord Ebrington diary, 19, 24 Jan.1915, Richard Batten

[62] The Prussian Army under von Moltke had encircled and defeated the French at Sedan on 1 Sept. 1870; Napoleon III surrendered his sword to Bismarck, and a few days later a popular uprising in Paris led to the fall of the Second Empire.

[63] HHA conflated the gist of two telegrams from Kitchener ('Private & Secret', and 'most urgent'), drafted in his own hand, sent to the Foreign Office for the Prime Minister 7.30 p.m, and 7.55 p.m. 1 Sept., printed in facsimile in Lady Algernon Gordon Lennox ed., *The Diary of Lord Bertie of Thame 1914–1918, Vol. I*, Hodder and Stoughton, 1924, p.25.

ed., A Lord Lieutenant in Wartime The Experiences of the Fourth Earl Fortescue during the First World War, *Devon and Cornwall Record Society/The Boydell P., Woodbridge, 2018, p.73). Hobhouse recorded on 3 September that the cable was to replace those likely to be lost in northern France. The German cable from Emden to Vigo would be picked up, 30 miles then added to it in the Channel, before being led into Newhaven and the new naval base in La Rochelle. Four days later Hobhouse learned that St Nazaire, favoured by French, was to be the 'sea-base', not Kitchener's choice of La Rochelle (David ed.,* Inside Asquith's Cabinet, *pp.187,189).*

The Post Office Engineer-in-Chief Sir William Slingo's 200-page 'Report on Work of the Engineering Department During the Five Years Covering the War Period 1914–1919', 10 June 1919, contains a full narrative of cables cut and provided, with a schedule of cables laid, their length and cost, etc. (POST 30/4304A, BT Archives). Cables listed as laid in September and October 1914 were Dunkerque–Cherbourg, Cherbourg–Brest, Dartmouth–Jersey; St Margarets–Dunkerque; Jersey–St Malo; and Birling–St Nazaire. There is no mention of La Rochelle. British cable strategy and censorship planning 1902–18 are summarised in Daniel R. Headrick, 'Strategic and Military Aspects of Submarine Telegraph Cables, 1851–1945', in *Bernard Finn and Daqing Yang eds,* Communications under the Seas: The Evolving Cable Network and Its Implications, *MIT P., Cambridge, MA, 2009, pp.194–7. The War Office Directorate of Military Operations' MO5 role in cable censorship in 1914–15 is examined in Jonathan Clay Randel, 'Information for economic warfare: British intelligence and the blockade, 1914–1918', Ph.D. thesis, U. of North Carolina, 1993, pp.144–55.*

We discussed what we could do to bring Turkey in to submission if she came out against us, Churchill in favour of landing Greek force on isthmus of W. side of Dardanelles & controlling sea of Marmora. Ships were now at Besika Bay. Troubridge[64] was being court–martialled for not firing & taking *Goeben* & *Breslau* at Messina — he funked losing his ships at outbreak of war.

Vice-Admiral Ernest 'Tom' Troubridge had sighted the Goeben *in open waters. He was advised by his Flag Captain, Captain Fawcet Wray, a gunnery expert, that it was impossible for the squadron to catch up with the* Goeben *and that the squadron was at risk from the* Goeben's *longer-ranging guns (for his advice Wray was later ostracised in the navy). Both 'knew' that the* Goeben *was the fastest, most powerful battle cruiser afloat; no one knew that the* Goeben *had left Germany with boiler troubles. HHA reported to Venetia Stanley*

[64] Ernest Charles Thomas Troubridge (1860–1926); Vice-Adm. commanding Mediterranean Cruiser Sqn 1913–14; entered navy 1875; naval attaché, Vienna, Madrid, and Tokyo 1901–5; p.s. to First Ld 1910–12; Chief, Admy War Staff 1912; head, British naval mission to Serbia 1915–19; Pres., International Danube Commission 1920–4; Kt 1919; Admiral 1919.

on 29 September that a court of inquiry of two admirals had found Troubridge's conduct 'deplorable and unworthy' and recommended a court-martial (Martin Gilbert ed., Winston Spencer Churchill, Vol. III, Companion, Part 1, *Heinemann, 1972, p.144). 'The way in which the Admiralty search for a scapegoat is both pitiful and contemptible' (Rear Adm. A.L. Duff diary, 10 Nov. 1914, Duff MSS).*

The court-martial found that the enemy's force had been superior and gave Troubridge an honourable discharge on 14 November. Nonetheless, Troubridge was never employed afloat again. The minutes of the court of inquiry and court-martial, and other relevant documents, are in E.W.R. Lumby ed., Policy and Operations in the Mediterranean 1912–14, *Navy Records Society Publications, Vol. 115, 1970. Geoffrey Miller,* Superior Force, *rests on a wider range of sources. A summary, drawing on more recent research, is Andrew Gordon, 'The Transition to War: The* Goeben *debacle, August 1914', in Ian Speller ed.,* The Royal Navy and Maritime Power in the Twentieth Century, *Cass, 2005, pp.13–32; and see the discussion at http://www.gwpda.org/naval/goebresl.htm, accessed 27 Jan. 2016. For the unhappy aftermath see Lovat Dickson,* Radclyffe Hall and the Well of Loneliness: A Sapphic Chronicle, *Collins, 1975, pp.60–2.*

George authorised to see Bankers & arrange for Govmt thro Bank of England taking 50 per cent of liability on bills of exchange & postponing prewar bills to end of war.

2d Cabinet 7.0 p.m. Kitchener came in in his Khaki uniform straight from Havre & Portsmouth. He admitted French seemed rather annoyed to see him — did not want him to see troops. The position was much as we thought. By retiring General French hoped to force Joffre to take up position & hold it. He now wanted Joffre to go to the Marne & *stand*. Joffre & French Army staff thought their views should predominate more than Sir John French & he should do what they asked but there was no real friction — but lack of power to understand & talk French was partly cause of slight differences of view. Our troops were scattered rather than shattered, French required another Division to come up & take the fighting line — & more time to make up units. Our supports had not been brought up but were on lines of communications some even at Havre. French's staff not too strong but K. had no one better to send. They would leave Paris & retire & wait for opportunity to attack later.

Indian troops might wait a little in Egypt.

Sept. 3 A general conversation on recruiting, arming, at home. Organisation of supplies abroad. K. reported 278,000 recruits up to date. Grey complained of military censorship of P.M's & his own speeches which were sent & not sent to America.

Grey would have expected that, if his or the Prime Minister's speeches had been cleared for release, they would not be held up by military censors. Arrangements for international dissemination of news and propaganda were about to be clarified, with responsibilities distributed between the News Department of the Foreign Office, the Press Bureau headed by F.E. Smith, and a new War Propaganda Bureau under Charles Masterman (Gary S. Messinger, British propaganda and the state in the First World War, *Manchester UP, 1992, pp.33–40). For the government planning a campaign to influence public opinion in neutral countries, especially the USA and Italy, see Sir Claud Schuster–Sir Edward Cook, 4 Sept.1914, Cook MSS; for the continuing difficulties faced by Masterman's Wellington House propagandists in getting cooperation from the War Office over interviews with generals and use of the 'cinematograph' see Schuster–Harcourt, 20, 31 Mar. 1915, and Sir Gilbert Parker–Harcourt, 26 Mar. 1915, Bodl. MS. Harcourt 445, ff.59–61,108–9,99–104.*

Over the next month a row broke out between the Foreign Office and the Central Committee for National Patriotic Organisations run by Harry Cust, his wife, and a team of volunteers. The festering dispute led Hubert Montgomery (Foreign Office assistant clerk and former assistant p.s. to Campbell-Bannerman and précis writer to the Foreign Secretary) to write to Bonham Carter on 23 November asking him to invoke the Prime Minister's name to impress on Cust that he should take no steps to ignite his 'far-reaching scheme' of disseminating pamphlets to influential individuals in neutral countries without the approval of the Foreign Office or 'the Masterman Committee': 'Sir Edward Grey is anxious that we should not appear in any way to emulate what has been described as "the orgy of second-rate publicity" in which the Germans have indulged' (Bodl. MS. Asquith 26, ff.50–79).

Churchill raised questions as to being able to clear North Sea of trawlers unless licensed by ourselves. They were flying false flags & continually putting down mines. Zeppelin & aeroplanes & how to meet German intentions to bomb us were considered. Agreed to place torpedo nets over vulnerable spots at Portsmouth & Chatham.

WSC stood high in the esteem of some of his fellow ministers at this time, something few of them were to bring to mind in later years. Haldane wrote to him on 3 September: 'Asquith said to me this afternoon that you were the equivalent of a large force in the field & this is true' (Lady Spencer-Churchill MSS, CSCT 3/15, CAC). It was on 3 September (not the 2nd as JAP has it) that Hobhouse says 'W.S.C. elaborated a plan for combining with the Greeks to seize Gallipoli, and thus dominate Constantinople before the Germans have armed the forts' (David ed., Inside Asquith's Cabinet, *p.187).*

From 3 November 1914 the English east coast ports were closed to neutral fishing vessels and the North Sea was declared a 'military area'. Any vessels found inside the area would be treated as suspicious. German mine laying and the British response are the subject of F.J. Jim Crossley, The Hidden Threat: The Story of Mines and Minesweeping by the Royal Navy in World War I, *Pen & Sword Maritime, Barnsley, South Yorkshire, 2011, pp.45–95.*

I saw the King at 7.0. P.C. meeting — but he only referred to the shortness of this business meeting.

JAP along with the Lord President of the Council (Beauchamp), Lord Islington (U.- Sec. of State for the Colonies), and Sir William Carington (Comptroller and Treasurer of the Household), had been 'collared' by Sir Almeric Fitzroy to deal with the submission of 'a Proclamation entirely recasting the Moratorium arrangements'. The Clerk of the Council explained that the drafters of the original Proclamation, which was due to expire the next day, had overlooked that many debtors ready and willing to meet their obligations would be prevented from doing so by the further postponement of all bill-accepting for another month. Officials worked through the night to ensure that the Proclamation would be on the walls of the Mansion House by 8.00 a.m. (FitzRoy diary, 3 Sept. 1914, FitzRoy, Memoirs, Vol. II, *p.569).*

Sept. 4 To an audience of some 5 to 6000 men at the Guild Hall, the P.M. made a fine appeal to the Nation to come forward. The delivery was not so brilliant as his tribute to the Belgians in the H of C. of 10 days earlier, but his speech was regarded by everyone as the right note. B. Law, Balfour & Churchill also did well.

At 3 o'clock cabinet which lasted to 4.45. We discussed the control of the N. sea & how we could get over the mine laying strategy of our opponents, bombs in Zeppelin, aliens & refugees, & what limit we were to place on French Belgians & neutrals coming in.

Left with McKenna to check the former at port of embarkation, & Samuel at port of arrival.

Refugees, being aliens, were the responsibility of the Home Office. McKenna proposed sending them to camps in southern Ireland. Samuel was horrified. When he protested, McKenna handed over responsibility to him. On 9 September Samuel announced in the House of Commons that all refugees would be welcome. He gave official blessing to Lady Lugard's War Relief Committee and called for voluntary local reception committees to be set up. Earl's Court and the Alexandra Palace were used as reception and distribution centres. In using the language of 'hospitality' and 'guests of the nation', the government was signalling that philanthropy rather than official funds would be expected to provide for those who came.

By the autumn of 1914 some 2,000 Belgian Relief Committees had been established; and the Board of Education was encouraging local authorities in their efforts to provide schooling for thousands of Belgian children (Tony Kushner, 'Local Heroes: Belgian Refugees in Britain during the First World War', Immigrants & Minorities, *vol.18, no.1, 1999, pp.1–28; Katherine Storr,* Excluded from the Record: Women, Refugees and Relief 1914–1929, *Peter Lang, Oxford, 2010, pp.58–9; Kevin Myers, 'The Hidden History of Refugee Schooling in Britain',* Hist. Ed, *vol.30, no.2, 2001, pp.153–62; for the wider context, Pierre Purseigle, 'The Reception of Belgian Refugees in Europe: A Litmus Test of Wartime Social Mobilisation', in John Crawford and Ian McGibbon eds,* New Zealand's Great War, *pp.69–84, and Peter Grant,* Philanthropy and Voluntary Action in the First World War: Mobilizing Charity, *Routledge, 2014, p.27 and* passim*). For the interaction between atrocity stories and attitudes to the fleeing Belgians: Paul Dominick Hodges, 'The British infantry and atrocities on the Western Front, 1914–1918', Ph.D. thesis, U. of London, 2007, pp.48–56; for other insights see Nicoletta Gullace, 'Sexual Violence and Family Honor: British Propaganda and International Law during the First World War',* American Historical Review, *vol.102, no.3, 1997, pp.714–47.*

Victoria Wemyss, wife of the admiral commanding the 12th Cruiser Squadron, had driven around London a few days earlier with Lady Lugard, Edith Lyttelton, and Lady Gladstone, whose husband Herbert was already playing a leading role with their War Refugees Committee (Brown, The Unknown Gladstone, *pp.210–14):*

> from Victoria station to St George's Road thence to Dulwich we flew & oh how different from what I had expected...They have made the hugest preparation enormous wards with hundreds & hundreds of beds but up to now the number of refugees has been very small—twenty in one place & about fifteen to thirty in another—mostly comfortable looking people of the bourgeoisie class, looking quite content & apparently having undergone very little privations...They were all evidently very much pleased to be the object of so much attention & rather inclined to magnify their sufferings but none of them had apparently witnessed any atrocities, it is all hearsay.
>
> *(V. Wemyss diary, 31 Aug. 1914, Wester-Wemyss MSS, WMYS 9/1, CAC)*

A similar story was told by the Duke of Norfolk, who wrote to Wilfrid Ward on 14 October: 'I cannot talk Flemish, but have mixed with some thousand Belgians during the last six weeks and have talked French with some and through interpreters, Priests and others, with others, and I have not heard a single allusion to atrocities except as to the burning of houses and the shooting of civilians, the latter cases are mentioned very rarely and brutal as they are it is possible there may have been reasons which technically may have given cause' (B.H. Holland, typescript biography of 15th Duke of Norfolk, Norfolk MSS, Arundel Castle Archives).

But for a modern historian's analysis of the German method of waging war in 1914 see Isabel V. Hull, Absolute Destruction: Military Culture and the Practices of War in Imperial Germany, *Cornell UP, Ithaca, 2005, pp.208–13. Adrian Gregory,* The Last Great War: British Society and the First World War, *Cambridge UP, 2008, pp.40–69, has a balanced chapter on 'Defining the enemy: atrocities and propaganda 1914–1915'. For a powerful review of evidence, John Horne and Alan Kramer,* German Atrocities, 1914: A History of Denial, *Yale UP, New Haven, 2001, and Horne's overview 'Atrocities and war crimes', in Jay Winter ed.,* The Cambridge History of the First World War, *Vol. 1 Global War, pp.561–84.*

In response to concern that 'enemies might come in under the guise of Belgians', Samuel assured the House on 14 September that a 'careful scrutiny' was being made. At the same time depositions were being taken to establish the veracity of 'accusations of inhumanity and outrage' by German soldiers (Horne and Kramer, German Atrocities, *p.231). From November 1914 registration of Belgian refugees and changes of address were mandatory. The General Record Office statistical branch maintained the records. By the end of the war a quarter of a million Belgian refugees and 19,000 wounded soldiers had come to Britain at a cost of £3.5 million in public money and £6 million in private money. Colin Holmes cites analyses of where the arrivals came from, their occupations, and wartime employment in Britain (*John Bull's Island: Immigration and British Society, 1871–1971, *Macmillan Education, 1988, pp.87–8, 90–1), and for the recollections of friction between Walloons and Flemish Belgians, stiff class distinctions, and the behaviour of some 'who seemed to combine the acquisitiveness of the Scot with the cunning slimness of the Red Indian' see Laurence Housman,* The Unexpected Years, *Jonathan Cape, 1937, pp.299–305. Samuel went on to become President of the Anglo-Belgian Union in 1918 and British Special Commissioner to Belgium 1919–20 (Audrey Collins, 'The General Register Office and the First World War',* GOV.UK, History of Government Blog, *10 Nov. 2017; Bowle,* Viscount Samuel, *pp.121–3; Peter Calahan,* Belgian Refugee Relief in England during the Great War, *Garland, New York, 1982).*

K. reported the German troops were concentrating East of Paris. We discussed the terms of the compact which we should enter into with Russia & France as to not leaving off war by the inaction of anyone of us without securing the assent of each other. We did not want to put ourselves in the position of having to avoid a peace settlement because of one power being unreasonable, & if we were agreed Peace might be arranged, we thought it was safe to say we must not negociate without the assent of each other.

The pact of Paris, under which Britain, France, and Russia agreed not to make a separate peace or unilaterally to define peace terms came into force on 5 September 1914. HHA and his wife were on their way that day to Lord Curzon's Hackwood Park in Hampshire, there to dine and sleep with the Queen of the Belgians and her three children, Bonar Law, and Lord and Lady Lansdowne (Anne de Courcy, Margot at War, *pp.211–12).*

Sept. 7 Kitchener explained to us how Joffre by placing 3 army corps behind Paris (S.W.) was now making a move towards Compiégne to cut through German communications, whilst they were attempting to force a passage between the allies between Rheims & Verdun. The Germans he thought must retire now but possibly direct later their attack again effectively. But for the allies to take the offensive might alter the situation for the better. K. told us the allies ought to have in the fight.

50 French Divisions (3 brigades in each of 4000)
5 British
45 Germans.

We would send another the sixth beginning at 3.0 this afternoon. 7th was ready but not safe to allow it to depart. We had now at home

28,920 regulars left
306,000 territorials[65]
300,000 recruits.

by the 12th } he would have ready colonial help
13th }
by 17th } other brigades to go abroad

There was an offer in from Samuel? Canada[66] to obtain 60,000 recruits *in* Canada from friends in U.S.A. who volunteered to help us. We all agreed we

[65] Peter Simkins, *Kitchener's army: The raising of the New Armies, 1914–16*, Manchester UP, 1988, p.18, writes of 268,777 members of the Territorial Force in July 1914. Many Territorial units, although not obliged to serve outside the United Kingdom, had indicated their willingness to do so. Twenty-two Territorial Battalions had joined the BEF in France by Christmas 1914 (Hugh Cunningham, *The Volunteer Force: A Social and Political History 1859–1908*, Croom Helm, 1975, p.148).

[66] Colonel Sam Hughes (1853–1921); Canadian Min. of Militia and Defence 1911–16; Kt 1915; driving force behind raising, training, and equipping the 1st Canadian Contingent at Camp Valcartier. The Canadian volunteers, together with a newly created cavalry brigade, arrived in England on 14 Oct., attested as 'Imperials', integrated into the British army. Hughes's continual meddling in military appointments and procurement exasperated Prime Minister Laurier and led to his forced resignation in Nov. 1916. A month earlier DLG and Bonar Law had incurred the King's wrath by offering Hughes the rank of Hon. Lt-Gen. without prior royal approval (Desmond Morton, *A Peculiar Kind of Politics: Canada's Overseas Ministry in the First World War*, U. of Toronto P., 1982, pp.19–23,86–91; Ronald G. Haycock, *Sam Hughes: The Public Career of a Controversial Canadian 1885–1916*, Wilfred Laurier UP, 1986, pp.180–312; Stamfordham–Bonham Carter, 4, 6 Oct. 1916, Bodl. MS. Asquith 4, ff.229–36).

could accept such troops but we left it to Grey to draw up letter for K. to privately send as a confidential message.

K. drew attention to exportation of meat to French army again — when we needed it here — Runciman was to look again into question.

K. reported he was getting 2 territorial Divisions ready for foreign service, the 3d best he would send to Egypt (the Lancashire).

The East Lancashire Division had been told on 5 September that it was to go to Egypt. The Manchester Guardian *reported on 7 September that unconsumed battalion rations in Burnley were being sent for distribution to needy families. The first transports left three days later. Arriving on 25 September, they were concentrated around Cairo with the Manchester Brigade remaining in Alexandria, where they disembarked. A battalion was sent to Khartoum and half a battalion to Cyprus, to protect key military installations. But their main objective was to defend the Suez Canal against the expected Turkish attack from Palestine. They were poorly organised, and sickness was rife in their camps around Cairo and Alexandria (Frederick P. Gibbon,* The 42nd (East Lancashire) Division, 1914–1918, *[1920], ch.1; Jeffrey Grey,* The War with the Ottoman Empire: The Centenary History of Australia and the Great War, Vol. 2, *Oxford UP, Sth Melbourne, 2015, p.28). The East Lancashires' mobilisation from the beginning of August is documented in Mitchinson,* England's Last Hope, *pp.201,221–30.*

I raised question of Germans communicating through Holland by letters. McKenna undertook to open all letters going there — business was being done this way with our enemies, but no spy messages were being sent. The Attorney was requested to draft a bill to stop business men here doing business with our enemies.

A Proclamation on Trading with the Enemy had been issued on 5 August. A Trading with the Enemy Act was passed on 18 September.

Sept. 8 We occupied most of our two hours in discussing how we might occupy Holland or use the Scheldt to advantage for saving Antwerp. Churchill suggested that we should be better at war with Holland, & blockade all supplies to Germany, that we could not go to Ghent & maintain a route from Ostend with a small army. We must concentrate our forces. He could come up the Rhine with big guns & keep access to Antwerp. I pointed out that Germans could attack a small force on a river as affectively [*sic*] as on land, & Ll. George pointed out that we might find ourselves opposed by 250,000 Dutch troops if we invaded territory or territorial waters. Hobhouse pointed out that we might be said to be invading a small state with just as much force as we alleged Germany for her own ends was proceeding to do in Belgium. Churchill modified his tone to going there by Dutch assent — & Grey said he would look into the Powers & treaties as to the use of the Scheldt.

Pre-war Dutch planning had envisaged the scenarios now being debated by the British Cabinet (Hubert P. van Tuyll, 'The Dutch Mobilization of 1914: Reading the "Enemy"'s Intentions', Journal of Military History, *vol.64, no.3, 2000, pp.711–37). With the Dutch determined to preserve their neutrality, and concern that Holland could be a back door for contraband into Germany, it was imperative to define a blockade and trading regime that would be both effective and agreeable to the Dutch. The innovative but flawed scheme of using a private trading agency to manage imports on behalf of Dutch traders came into force early in 1915 (T.G. Otte, '"Between Hammer and Anvil": Sir Francis Oppenheimer, The Netherlands Overseas Trust and Allied Economic Warfare, 1914–1918', in Christopher Andrew and Andrew Stewart eds,* Diplomats at War: British and Commonwealth Diplomacy in Wartime, *Martinus Nijhoff, Leiden, 2008, pp.85–107; and Otte, '"Allah is great and the NOT is his prophet": Sea power, diplomacy and economic warfare. The case of the Netherlands 1900–1918', in Greg Kennedy ed.,* Britain's War at Sea, 1914–1918, *pp.38–69).*

For the big issues of blockade policy and the Netherlands, Lambert's Planning Armageddon, *especially pp.216–31,463–70,474–5, and 491–6, is an indispensable guide. Marc Frey, 'Bullying the Neutrals: The Case of the Netherlands', in Roger Chickering and Stig Förster eds,* Great War, Total War: Combat and Mobilization on the Western Front, 1914–1918, *Cambridge UP, 2000, pp.227–44, draws on German and Dutch sources; Dutch archives are also used in Samuël Kruizinga, 'NOT Neutrality: The Dutch government, the Netherlands Overseas Trust Company and the Entente blockade of Germany, 1914–18', in Johan Den Hertog and Samuël Kruizinga eds,* Caught in the Middle: Neutrals, Neutrality and the First World War, *Amsterdam UP, 2011, pp.87–103; and the wider context is canvassed in Herman de Jong, 'Between the devil and the deep blue sea: the Dutch economy during World War I', in Stephen Broadberry and Mark Harrison eds,* The Economics of World War I, *Cambridge UP, 2005, pp.137–68, and Maartje Abbenhuis,* The Art of Staying Neutral: the Netherlands in the First World War, 1914–1918, *Amsterdam UP, 2006. On Dutch efforts to thwart British consular officials spying on German shipping movements see Wim Klinkert,* Defending Neutrality: the Netherlands Prepares for War, 1900–1925, *Brill, Leiden, and Boston, 2013, pp.165–228.*

K. gave us some information. We were on the East of Paris, with the 6th Fr. army corps on our left & 5th corps on our right. On the Banks for the Marne with 4th German Reserve opposite the 6th.

2d German Corps opposite us
3 & 9 German Corps opposite the 5th.

With 4 & 10 in the background.
We were told that the 2. 4. 6. 7. 8 German corps & 2d Bavarian had been transferred to East Prussia.
We had sent 26,790 drafts to make good the losses of 16,000.
We had 4 Divisions at Aldershot.

We sh have 6 " of new recruits (coming in at 30,000 p. day)
3 " raised by local patriotism
Manchester, Leeds, B'ham, Glasgow
3 from India 2 were at Suez

French had written account of war to 28th & would send it through — pressure work prevented more.

*HHA told Venetia Stanley of the Cabinet that morning 'rather cheered by French's telegrams' (*Asquith Letters, *p.226). It is not clear whether Cabinet was cheered that French had wired Kitchener on 6 September saying that he had received only 13,000 reinforcements to offset the loss of 488 officers and 19,532 men since the battle of Mons (Nikolas Gardner,* Trial by Fire: Command and the British Expeditionary Force in 1914, *Praeger, Westport, CT, 2003, p.74). There seems to have been a deal of confusion about troop replacements; recruiting numbers of course grew every day. Maj-Gen. Sir Henry Rawlinson, Director of Recruiting at the War Office, noted in his diary on 9 September 'we have now 417,000 men for K's armies'; and the next day he recorded '438,000 recruits today!!' (Rawlinson MSS, RWLN 1/1, CAC.)*

Holger H. Herwig's The Marne 1914: The Opening of World War I and the Battle That Changed the World *(Random House, New York, 2009, pp.240–306) recounts the ensuing events until 11 September when Gen. Joffre informed the French War Minister, Alexandre Millerand: 'La bataille de la Marne s'achève en victoire incontestable.' The failure of the Schlieffen–Moltke plan and German hopes for a short decisive victory are explained in Annika Mombauer, 'German War Plans', in Hamilton and Herwig eds,* War Planning 1914, *pp.48–79. The emerging roles of aerial reconnaissance and radio intercepts as sources of information on German movements are well told in Terrence J. Finnegan,* Shooting the Front: Allied Aerial Reconnaissance and Photographic Interpretation on the Western Front—World War I, *National Defense Intelligence College P., Washington, DC, 2006, pp.7–38.*

Cabinets

Wed. Sept. 9 Press Bureau — McKenna told to take responsibility

Two days earlier, at a meeting described by Sir Edward Cook as the 'Masterman Conference', DLG's friend Sir William Robertson Nicoll, editor of the Nonconformist journal the British Weekly, *'pitched into Press Bureau & said it was absurd to have it run by F.E. Smith, his brother and no journalist' (Cook diary, 7 Sept. 1914, Cook MSS). WSC passed on to Smith DLG's view that the constitution of the Bureau was 'unduly Tory'. Smith told DLG on 9 September that he had already suggested Elibank, Riddell, and another Liberal for the Neutral Press Department. 'You know me too well to suppose I want political capital out of the damned office' (Lloyd George MSS, LG/C/3/7/5, PA). The subsequent development of the 'machinery of censorship' is summarised, with valuable bibliographical notes, in Tania Rose,* Aspects of Political Censorship 1914–1918, *U. of Hull P., 1995, pp.10–41, and Colin Lovelace, 'British press censorship during the First World War', in Boyce, Curran and Wingate eds,* Newspaper History from the seventeenth century, *pp.307–19. The evolution under Reginald McKenna in 1914–15 of a postal and press censorship regime designed to protect military secrets into a Home Office mechanism for surveillance and subduing domestic dissent is the theme of Brock Millman,* Managing Domestic Dissent in First World War Britain, *Frank Cass, 2000, pp.30–48.*

Thurs. 10 discussed recruiting, & grievances. J.A.P. absent recruiting speech Rotherham

Fri. 11 p.m. outlined H.R. proposals. Food stuffs again.

Mon. Sep. 14 K. told us that French pressed for more officers. He would look closely into position French thought he had 85 too few — War Office figures showed he had 70 in excess of number to which he was entitled.

We had sent out 213,700 men. He was only entitled to 161,715 with 6 Divisions. He had 57,600 horses 56,000 baggage wagons & 80,000 tons of materials & we had done him well.

We discussed German East African situation. Grey's brother Charlie had lost his arm & was in hospital — position serious.[67] Harcourt asked K. & Churchill to send & convoy Indian Division. Discussed how to transport quickly contingents of territorials to India, & secure Regular artillery from India to France.

Hobhouse placed cost of Marconi installation before us —

we had incurred	40 }	£
must be liable for	120 }	[1,060,000?]
to complete [?]	500 }	
Marconi asking for	400 }	
conjectural	250 }	

By cancelling contract we would save nearly a million. K. & C. thought with our having taken German stations, & developments, expenditure might be avoided. Hobhouse must make best case he cd.

The German wireless stations at Dar-es-Salaam and Yap in the Caroline Islands had been destroyed in the first two weeks of the war. The Germans had themselves blown up the station at Kamina, Togoland, on 24 August. New Zealand troops had seized Samoa on 29 August. The Royal Australian Navy battle cruiser HMAS Australia, *the light cruiser HMAS* Melbourne, *and the French armoured cruiser* Montcalm *linked up at Nauru with New Zealand troop transports and some ageing British cruisers. On 11 September, the Australian Naval and Military Expeditionary Force landed on the island of New Pommerne (New Britain), overwhelmed the German forces, and captured the station at the capital Herbertshöhe. It was not until 12 May 1915 that the powerful Windhoek station in German East Africa was captured by Union of South Africa military forces. The Admiralty had taken over the Marconi works at the beginning of the war. In November 1914 the government contracted with the Marconi Company to install and man thirteen long-range rotary discharger stations around the world, starting with Ascension Island in the South Atlantic (W.J. Baker,* A History of the Marconi Company, *Methuen, 1970, pp.158–61; for an able summary of pre-war international cable and wireless developments see Jonathan Reed Winkler,* Nexus: strategic

[67] Charles Grey (1873–1928); big game hunter, travelled on foot and by boat for several days to a British camp and went into action before enlisting; wounded, an arm was amputated; recovered and commissioned into the King's African Rifles, he took 'his remaining arm back to his regiment' (Michael Waterhouse, *Edwardian Requiem: A Life of Sir Edward Grey*, Biteback, 2013, p.355); MC 1917; killed by a buffalo in Tanganyika, https://www.europeansineastafrica.co.uk/_site/custom/database/default.asp?a=viewIndividual&pid=2&person=7201, accessed 28 Nov. 2022). Telling the Chief Whip about his brother, Edward Grey added that his nephew had been missing since 26 Aug.. We do not know what Grey had in mind in saying: 'The general news of the war is almost too good to be true' (Grey–Illingworth, 14 Sept. 1914, Illingworth MSS).

communications and American security in World War I, *Harvard UP, Cambridge, MA, 2008, ch. one).*

What the government wanted to do was cancel the original Imperial chain contract, but this proved difficult (Harcourt's note, Bodl. MS.Eng.c.8270). Hobhouse told Marconi on 30 December that the contract was to be cancelled. Within weeks Godfrey Isaacs, the Marconi managing director, wrote claiming compensation for breach of contract. The matter was still unresolved when JAP became Postmaster General in 1916. Godfrey Isaacs wrote alleging that Hobhouse had gone to Paris in the summer of 1914 to hatch a plot with Telefunken to compete against Marconi for the second part of the contract. On negotiations towards a settlement of Marconi's claims against the government for not proceeding with the 1913 contract for four stations see Godfrey Isaacs–Attorney General (Sir F.E. Smith), 2 Aug. 1917, Birkenhead MSS (courtesy of Lady Gilbert). Marconi brought a breach of contract case in March 1918 and were awarded £600,000 compensation in 1919. Isaacs sued Hobhouse for libel and lost. 'The Imperial Wireless Scheme and the Marconi Enquiry, 1911–23' can be explored in the Marconi Archives: Bodl. MSS. Marconi 219–29. For papers and transcripts of proceedings in the cases of Isaacs *v.* Hobhouse, *1918, and v.* H.M. Postmaster General, *1918–19, Bodl. MS. Marconi 540–2; and see R.P.T. Davenport-Hines, 'Godfrey Charles Isaacs', in Jeremy and Shaw eds,* Dictionary of Business Biography, *Vol. 3, pp.446–52.*

Tues. Sep. 15 short cab. — shipping — insurance.

The P.M. in House explained why Govmt were introducing suspensory bill in connection with H.R. & Disestablishment. He spoke quietly & deliberately not effectively [*sic*] & for over an hour sought to vindicate placing H.R. on the statute book now. His strongest point was the response of the Irish to the country's need as soon as this was done.

Bonar Law made the speech of a cad in reply & was offensive as to breaches of faith & so on & most of our best men left the House as protest, but ended up by saying the Tories would support the Govmt during war. It was a horrid debate because we could not retort & show how divided the parties were, & yet we were forced to sit still & hear Billingsgate[68] & vituperative & vindictive charges against

[68] Billingsgate: 'coarsely abusive language; foul-mouthed vituperation', originally supposedly typical in the Billingsgate fish market, below London Bridge (Eric Partridge, *Name into Word: proper names that have become common property, a discursive dictionary*, Secker and Warburg, 1949, p.55). Illingworth and McKenna did not sit still; they left 'lest they should be unable to over come their impulse to throw books, paper knives, and other handy missiles' at Bonar Law's head (*Asquith Letters*, pp.239–40). It looked different to Willie Bridgeman, who told his wife that Bonar Law 'made his enemy look very much ashamed & Winston & McKenna turned very pale and went out in the middle of his speech' (Bridgeman MSS).

the greatest man in the Public eye of the world. I was glad when the Tories dramatically ? [sic] left to listen to a Speech of Redmond which struck a high note.

HHA, who had been under pressure from the King to be more conciliatory, argued that he was not taking advantage of the national emergency to pass controversial matters; he claimed that in the normal course of events both bills would have passed into law. Bonar Law compared HHA's own promises to those of Germany promising peace. He declared that he would support Ulster in maintaining its rights without any conditions. He went on to say that debate was pointless and wounding, and that he and his party would take no further part in it. The Unionists had assumed that, if the amending Bill was to be postponed, so would the Home Rule Bill itself, and on 6 August Bonar Law had warned HHA that the suspensory bill would be seen as a breach of honour. Bonar Law's first major biographer, Lord Blake, commented: 'It is difficult to avoid the conclusion that the Unionist leaders — Bonar Law not the least among them — had lost all sense of proportion over this question' and that this was 'possibly the most bitter of Bonar Law's speeches' (Blake, The Unknown Prime Minister, *p.229).*

Bonar Law's bitterness is understandable. He had for weeks been telling uneasy party colleagues that they were 'unnecessarily anxious'. He was in communication with the Prime Minister and he was certain that HHA 'meant to deal fairly with us'. HHA's behaviour was now seen by the Opposition as 'elaborate play-acting' (Lord R. Cecil–Sir E. Grey, 11 Sept. 1914, Cecil of Chelwood MSS, BL Add.MS. 51,073, f.73). Bonar Law had told Unionist Members of Parliament at the Carlton Club on 14 September that they 'cannot fight the Government now. They have tied our hands by our patriotism.' (Transcript from Shorthand Notes of G. Moore & Co., Sir Malcolm Fraser MSS, Bodl. MS.Eng.c.4790, f.51.) The course of events in August and September, with particular attention to interventions by the Archbishop of Canterbury, is well told in Scot M. Peterson, 'The Establishment and Disestablishment of Religion in Great Britain, 1906–1936, A Comparative Historical Study', D.Phil. thesis, U. of Oxford, 2009, pp.97–104.

Wed. Sep. 16 Proposals as to contribution to be made by Govmt to families of soldiers & sailors.

Thurs. Sept. 17 Cabinet, nothing exciting said.

The next day Maurice Bonham Carter reported to his fiancée, Violet Asquith: 'When the business of the House of Commons was over and the Prorogation message read, Will Crooks asked Harry Whitley if it would be in order to sing God Save the King & started off in a high croak which was gradually taken up an octave down by the rest of the House. Illingworth came out of the House with tears in his eyes. I hope the King will appreciate the lesson, it is perhaps too much to expect it from the Unionist Party' (Bodl. MS. Bonham Carter 256, ff.29–30). As for the King, he wrote confidentially in his own hand on 19 September to thank Francis Hopwood for the 'wise, patient & unprejudiced spirit' in which he had provided advice (and draft letters to the Prime Minister) over the last twelve months. 'I do not conceal from you my regret at having to give my assent to the Home Rule Bill' (Southborough MSS, Bodl. MS. Eng.c.7362).

Monday Sep. 21 Cabinet ditto, except Kitchener asked for Indian Army to be given him, so that he could control all the Imperial troops during war. Crewe assented. Kitchener told us he did not like the situation on the R. Aisne, the battle had gone on for 10 days & stalemate might enable the Germans to concentrate & pierce the allies front at one point. If he was Joffre, he would retire at the East side so as to get the Germans moving out of their entrenched position, a move he thought was imperative.[69]

Churchill informed us where our ships were in the open seas, & how he hoped to get the *Emden* — at Rangoon — the position of the *Dantzig* — *Königsberg* & other German cruisers which we were hunting.

He proposed to land 3000 marines at Dunkirk to strengthen the 18,000 French territorials there, & the Oxfordshire Yeomanry (with F.E. Smith) to scout & find out where Germans were on their lines.

The Indian troops of the Lahore Division landed at Marseilles on 26 September. Sent to replace losses in the BEF, they found their khaki drill uniforms gave poor protection as winter advanced, and blankets were in short supply (Vedica Kant, 'If I die here, who will remember me?' India and the First World War, *Lustre P./Roli Books, New Delhi, 2014, p.41). The Queen's Own Oxfordshire Hussars (the Oxford Yeomanry), among whom Winston and Jack Churchill as well as F.E. Smith had served, left for France on 20 September: 24 officers, 447 other ranks, and 455 horses. They were the first Territorial unit in action (Jane Cotter with soldiers of Oxfordshire Museum,* Great War Britain: Oxfordshire Remembering 1914–18, *The History P., Stroud, 2014, p.82).*

Tuesday 22 Sept. French reported little change. The Algerian troops on his right were not steady & wanted to come out of their trenches. Kitchener said he wanted to admit he had been mistaken in his war office staff — the purchase department

[69] For the stalemate at the River Aisne: Jerry Murland, *Aisne 1914*, Pen & Sword Military, 2013; Paul Kendall, *Aisne 1914: The Dawn of Trench Warfare*, Spellmount, Stroud, 2012; and for first-hand accounts, Adrian Gilbert, *Challenge of Battle: The Real Story of the British Army in 1914*, Osprey Publishing, 2014, Part Three.

had been mismanaged by (? De la Touche[70]) & he had arranged with Baker to supersede him — we all concurred & that new organisers like Burridge[71] or Selfridge[72] would be brought in to advise. Runciman ordered to see them.

The Cabinet ordered the removal of Henry De La Bere, the Director of Army Contracts (HHA Cabinet letter, 22 Sept. 1914, TNA: CAB 41/35/46). The sidelining of De La Bere was allegedly precipitated when Ulick Wintour of the Board of Trade, who was leading the Anglo-French Commission Internationale de Ravitaillement, contrived to obtain a large consignment of blankets over his head. When asked who the new Director should be, Kitchener said: 'Why Wintour, of course... He must be a very capable man' (Arthur, Not Worth Reading, *p.203). The Board of Trade had already taken the initiative in seeking advice from Richard Burbidge, managing director of Harrods, who met Ulick Wintour on 21 and 29 September (Burbidge diary, 21, 22, 29 Sept. 1914, Burbidge MSS, 4218/1/10, Wilts & Swindon Archives).*

At the same time Kitchener and Hubert Llewellyn Smith had drawn in the leather manufacturer and shipowner George Macaulay Booth for advice and asked him to confer with Wintour. Booth suggested a small advisory committee of businessmen only to be told by HHA that he did not like the idea of industrialists in such positions, as the government could not afford another Marconi scandal. Wintour told Booth to disregard the Prime Minister's objections, and went ahead enlisting the men they needed. A month later Booth would tell Maurice Headlam, one-time Treasury official and now Treasury Remembrancer in Ireland, that he had been brought in to 'put some sound sense into the W.O. Contracts department. "My! but what a curious thing. The War Office had no War Office scheme. They planned to

[70] JAP meant Henry De La Bere (1861–1937); Director, Army Contracts 1907–14; Director, Army clothing factory 1898; Asst Accountant Gen. 1900; Asst Director, Army Finance 1905; Commissioner, Inland Revenue 1914–16; Commissioner, Chelsea Hospital 1915–20.

[71] JAP might have misheard: the name was Burbidge. We are grateful to Sir Peter Burbidge Bt and Lady Burbidge, the family genealogist, for confirming that the pronunciation is phonetic (email to CH, 13 Dec. 2015). Richard Burbidge (1847–1917); creator of Harrods as gen. man. then man. dir. 1891–1917; gen. supt, Army and Navy Auxiliary, Victoria Street, then William Whiteley's grocery business, and West Kensington Stores; member, advisory bd, Min. of Munitions; chmn, committee on Royal Aircraft Factory; established Richard Burbidge Staff Benefit Fund for wounded Harrods staff and widows, and built rehab. hospitals in Belgium and England. Bt 1916: the draft printed recommendation of his baronetcy to the King noted that he had 'rendered suspicious services in connection with the war'. A vigilant Prime Minister substituted 'conspicuous' (Bodl. MS. Asquith 83, f.158). For Burbidge's 'romantic life story': Mrs Stuart Menzies, *Modern Men of Mark...*, Herbert Jenkins, 1921, pp.43–108.

[72] Harry Gordon Selfridge (1858–1947); American-born owner of Selfridge's 1909–39; closely connected to press and financial circles through Sir Max Aitken, Sir Edward Holden, R.D. Blumenfeld, editor of the *Daily Express*, and the financier Sir Ernest Cassel; entered Marshall Field & Co. (then Field Leiter & Co.) as clerk 1879; junior partner 1890; rtd 1904; arrived in London 1906; naturalised 1937. Selfridge acted as purchasing agent for underwear and socks for the French army (Reginald Pound, *Selfridge. A Biography*, Heinemann, 1960, p.127; Lindy Woodhead, *Shopping, Seduction & Mr Selfridge*, Profile Books, 2012, p.136). When visiting Germany in the spring of 1915, using his US passport, it is possible that he undertook a mission for British intelligence.

send X troops to France etc. etc. but never thought about the Ordnance, Ammunition, Clothes, Food, etc. for additional men. It's inconceivable but true"' (Duncan Crow, A Man of Push and Go: The Life of George Macaulay Booth, *Rupert Hart-Davis, 1965, pp.68–79; Booth–Headlam, 21 Oct. 1914, Headlam MSS, Bodl. MS.Eng.hist.c.1103, f.97).*

McKenna reported that sugar was coming in here from Holland grown in Germany — it was agreed to stop its importation.

Grey informed us the Portuguese were prepared to sell arms to the French & convoy them, this was an act of war, the Germans might retaliate and Harcourt was apprehensive about Lourenco Marques & what terms the Portuguese might subsequently ask when peace was in the air.

Under pressure from Britain, Portugal had declared itself neutral in August. Portuguese East Africa had a Colonial Army garrison of about 1,500 African troops led by European officers. Portugal sent reinforcements on the outbreak of war, fearing that fighting in the neighbouring German African colonies might spread over the border. The ensuing German incursion in Angola, and their withdrawal when it seemed that the South Africans would resume their German South West Africa campaign, are sketched in Samson, World War I in Africa, *pp.76–8. For references on Portugal's involvement in East Africa and its eventual alignment with the Entente see Bruce Vandervort, 'New Light on the East African Theater of the Great War: A Review Essay of English-Language Sources', in Stephen M. Miller ed.,* Soldiers And Settlers In Africa, 1850–1918, *Brill, Leiden, 2009, pp.299–302. Portugal's path to war with Germany in March 1916 through 'selective belligerency' is set out in http://encyclopedia.1914-1918-online.net/article/diplomacy_portugal, a brief essay based on Portuguese sources with bibliography by Pedro Aires Oliveira, accessed 21 Aug. 2016. By a royal charter granted in 1889, but expiring 29 October 1914, the British South Africa Company controlled the Rhodesias and large swathes of other territory on the border of Portuguese East Africa. There was opposition to the extension by advocates of responsible government.*

We agreed to allow the S. African charter to be extended for 10 years more.

We wired New Zealand — after seeing Admiral Sir Henry [*sic*][73] that we could not convoy troops from Wellington to Adelaide for 6 weeks. Only Australian troops could be convoyed to Ceylon as arranged, & if N.Z. troops were not prepared

[73] Admiral Sir Henry Bradwardine Jackson (1855–1929); pres., CID subcomm. on seizure of German colonies Aug. 1914; entered navy 1868; pioneer of wireless telegraphy; FRS 1901; 3rd Sea Ld and Controller 1903–8; KCVO 1906; KCB 1910; director, Royal Naval War College 1911–13; Chief, Admy War Staff 1913–14; Adm. 1914; chmn, CID subcomm. on German colonies; 1st Sea Ld 1915–16; Pres., Royal Naval College, Greenwich 1916–19; Adm. of the Fleet 1919; rtd 1924.

to take the risk, we could not bring the first contingent together. Harcourt was authorised to wire Liverpool[74] to tell him the troops might not be prejudiced as to the time for their continental expedition as K. would train on the Australian troops after their arrival here before sending them to the front.

The N.Z. cabinet were on the point of breaking up, if we declined convoy.

The New Zealand government had mobilised an expeditionary force of over 8,500 with more than 3,800 horses but declined to despatch it without an adequate naval escort. Two transports actually left Auckland on 24 September, planning to rendezvous with eight ships from Wellington, but were recalled when the Australian Governor-General warned that German warships were probably in New Zealand waters. New Zealand's Governor-General, Lord Liverpool, suggested that he could order the whole force to sail, invoking his authority as Commander-in-Chief. But Prime Minister William Massey, under pressure from a divided Cabinet, threatened to resign if this happened. Liverpool backed down and the British agreed two weeks later to send an acceptable escort (Ian McGibbon, 'The Shaping of New Zealand's War Effort, August–October 1914', in John Crawford and Ian McGibbon eds, New Zealand's Great War, *pp.65–7).*

The news came in about 4 o'clock that 3 big cruisers 1900 vessels *Hogue Cressy* & *Aboukir* had been sunk off Lowestoft by German submarines.

Aboukir *was the first to be torpedoed.* Hogue *and* Cressy *came to its rescue and were themselves torpedoed. Over 1,400 men were lost, 800 saved. 'The way in which Hogue & Cressy stopped their engines & asked the submarines to torpedo them was most foolish. Rule has been issued to stop mistaken humanity acting thus in future' (JAP–EP, 23 Sept. 1914, MS. Gainford 189/42). Francis Hirst brought Morley to 'laugh immensely' about the* Daily Express *headline on the sinking of the three cruisers: 'Sinking of two German submarines' (Hirst, 'Conversation at Flowermead Sunday Sept. 27 1914', Bodl. MS. Hirst, B.1.1.36).*

I dined with the Prime Minister, my son Joe, being present. I thought it might be an experience but he had a dull dinner. The Parsons were there, Ernley Blackwell,[75]

[74] Arthur William de Brito Savile Foljambe, Earl of Liverpool (1870–1941); Gov. (Gov. Gen. from 1917) and C-in-C, New Zealand 1912–20; soldier; State Steward and Chamberlain, Ld Lt of Ireland 1906–8; 2nd Earl 1907; Comptroller of Household 1909–12; PC 1917.

[75] Ernley Robertson Blackwell (1868–1941); Legal Asst U.-Sec. of St., Home Office 1913–33; barrister 1892; Asst U.-Sec. of St., Home Office 1906–13; KCB 1916. He had told the Prime Minister's wife that WSC had sworn before Home Office officials that he could prove 'to a hair how poorly off Germany wd be for ships compared to us & how he intended with every power he had in the world to cut down McK's ridiculous ship-building schemes' (Margot Asquith diary, 21 May 1912, Bodl. MS.Eng.d.3210, f.34).

& Montagu & Lady Sheffield & her married daughter.[76] The P.M. after alluding to the worst news we had had during the war did not again refer to the disaster & was quite himself — & full of going to Ireland & Anglesey for Sunday.

23/9 Wednesday Cabinet. Winston Churchill back from Dunkirk where had met Col Seely by accident, Winston wanting to see for himself position with a view to landing marines and Oxfordshire Yeomanry, Genl French wanting to know thro' Seely the extent to which 18,000 garrison of French territorials were reliable. Seely reported the men at the front were in good heart, but the German Howitzers were not liked.

Learning from Seely of the chance meeting with WSC in Dunkirk, their mutual friend Lord Castlereagh wrote to his wife on 24 September: 'Winston I suppose came over to get a medal; he is entitled to one if he sets foot on French soil I believe' (H. Montgomery Hyde, The Londonderrys A Family Portrait, *Hamish Hamilton, 1979, p.118). Castlereagh's cynical surmise was a widely shared opinion. Brig. Gen. Henry Horne at HQ I Corps wrote to his wife on 29 September 1914: 'Winston Churchill appeared here two days ago...They say he was dressed as a "Trinity Elder Brother". It is said that he came to get the clasp for the Aisne!' (Simon Robbins ed.,* The First World War Letters of General Lord Horne, *The History P. for the Army Records Society, Stroud, 2009, p.52). Later in the month WSC was witnessed by a Marine in Antwerp 'up and down the road amongst the shells' (S. Macnaughtan,* My War Experiences in Two Continents, *John Murray, 1919, p.16) and was seen nearby by a fellow Other Club member within 800 yards of rifle fire: Waldorf Astor MP wrote: 'I was walking up and down by the side of the car and, to my relief, I saw the First Lord of the Admiralty take cover behind a tree. So I said to myself "If you take cover behind a tree, I may" So I did' ('My Personal Experiences with the Royal Marine Brigade', n.d., Astor MSS 41/772, Reading U.).*

We discussed convoying N.Z. & Australian troops together, & the shorter postponement of 3 weeks now found possible, decided upon subject to N.Z. acquiescing.

Position at front unchanged.

The siege of Antwerp began on 27 September. British troops were despatched there on October 4.

29 Sept.[77] *Monday* — absent — discussion on Turkey's attitude & Army chaplains.

[76] Three of Lady Sheffield's surviving four daus were married; the dau. in question was the Hon. Blanche Pearce-Serocold (1885–1968), m. 1912 Brig.-Gen. Eric Pearce-Serocold (HHA–Venetia Stanley, 22 Sept. 1914, Venetia Montagu MSS, partly quoted in *Asquith Letters*, pp.253–4).

[77] Cabinet met on Mon. 28 Sept. Kitchener provided the number of allied and enemy divisions at the front. Hobhouse noted them in his diary on 29 Sept. (Hobhouse MSS, not quoted in David ed., *Inside*

At the beginning of the war there had been 117 chaplains: 89 Anglicans, 11 Presbyterians, and 17 Roman Catholics (http://www.chaplains-museum.co.uk/further-reading, accessed 26 Jan. 2017). Peter Howson, Muddling Through: The Organisation of British Army Chaplaincy in World War One, *Helion & Co., Solihull, 2013, p.20, has slightly differing figures that seem to overlook the informal arrangement with the Admiralty and War Office whereby the Congregational and Baptist Unions jointly nominated chaplains and officiating clergymen to minister to their own members (Alan Ruston, 'Protestant Nonconformist Attitudes towards the First World War', in Alan Sell and Anthony Cross eds,* Protestant Nonconformity in the Twentieth Century, *Paternoster P., Carlisle, 2003, pp.259–60).*

*Tom Johnstone and James Hagerty quote an answer to a House of Commons question on 17 September 1914 that there were twelve Catholic chaplains with the BEF (*The cross on the sword: Catholic Chaplains in the Forces, *Geoffrey Chapman, 1996, pp.85–6). Over the resistance of a bemused Kitchener, Cabinet had decided on 28 September that the Army should have commissioned Nonconformist chaplains as well as Anglicans. DLG and Percy Illingworth had taken the lead in pressing the case for their Nonconformist brethren (Howson,* Muddling Through, *p.46; Shepherd,* John Howard Shakespeare and the English Baptists, 1898–1924, *p.174). The first chaplains were gazetted and left for France in October. A United Army and Navy Board, representing the main non-Wesleyan denominations (with Baptists and Congregationalists joined by Primitive Methodists, United Methodists, Welsh Baptists, and Independents) was formed in March 1915 (J.H. Thompson, 'The Nonconformist Chaplain in the First World War: The Importance of a New Phenomenon', in Michael Snape and Edward Madigan eds,* The Clergy in Khaki: New Perspectives on British Army Chaplaincy in the First World War, *Ashgate, Farnham, 2013, pp.22–3). See also Robin Barlow,* Wales and World War One, *Gomer P., Llandysul, Ceredigion, 2014, pp.64–87, and Harold Walker, 'Saving Bodies and Souls: Army Chaplains and Medical Care in the First World War',* Postgraduate Journal of Medical Humanities, *no.3, 2016, pp.24–38, and the bibliographical guidance in Clive Field, 'Keeping the Spiritual Home Fires Burning: Religious Belonging in Britain during the First World War',* W&S, *vol.33, no.4, 2014, pp.244–68.*

Sept. 30 Churchill reported *Emden* had got away out of Bay of Bengal was being hunted by our *Hampshire* & by Jap. *Chakime.*[78]

Asquith's Cabinet). HHA sent a similar tabulation to Venetia Stanley, 'of course Secret', as soon as the Cabinet dispersed (Venetia Montagu MSS, not included in the Brocks' edition of the HHA–Venetia Stanley letters).

[78] The Japanese light cruiser was the *Chikuma*; see 11 Nov. 1914. In fact another Japanese cruiser, the *Ibuki*, played the major role in pursuit of the *Emden* (Tim Gellel, 'Unlikely Partners: The Destruction of *Emden* and the Paradox of Japanese Naval Cooperation with Australia during World War I', in David Stevens ed., *Naval Networks: The Dominance of Communications in Maritime Operations*, pp.309–30); Timothy D. Saxon, 'Anglo-Japanese Naval Cooperation 1914–1918', *Naval War College Review*, vol.53, no.1, 2000, pp.62–92.

The *Königsberg* being hunted by *Chatham Weymouth & Dartmouth*. We discussed how to stop ore going into Baltic via Scheldt & agreed to meet U.S.A. in allowing food stuffs through. Harcourt reported Germans had retired from Duala in Cameroons. A mishap in S.W. Africa surrender of 200 men &c which Kitchener thought would wake up S. Africans.

Thurs. October 1 We discussed Turkish situation, Enver Bey's[79] strength.

K. informed us that the

Germans had	22 army corps East.
	18 " " West

86 Divisions. We decided to send division to Antwerp.

We discussed policy of exchanges names of prisoners, & doing anything we could to induce the Germans to surrender easily.

Treasury Bills. Gl French reported he proposed to move and get round to N.E. with Joffre's consent. Australian expedition & dates of arrival.

P.M. spoke at Cardiff — recruiting speech.

'The Turkish situation' now confronting the Cabinet was the closing of the Straits of the Dardanelles to British and imperial shipping. 'At a stroke,' Kristian Coates Ulrichsen writes, 'this wiped out more than half of Russia's export trade and exhausted London's patience with Constantinople' (The Logistics and Politics of the British Campaigns in the Middle East, 1914–22, *palgrave macmillan, 2011, pp.29–30). The power struggle in Turkey preceding the decision to enter the war on 29 October is summarised in Ian F.W. Beckett,* The Making of the First World War, *Yale UP, New Haven, 2012, pp.30–49, and more fully covered from Turkish sources in Michael A Reynolds,* Shattering Empires: The Clash and Collapse of the Ottoman and Russian Empires, 1908–1918, *Cambridge UP, 2011, pp.107–23.*

'Both from strategical reasons and tactical reasons', French had said on September 29, 'it is desirable that the British Army should regain its position on the left of the line. There remains the question of when this move should take place. I submit that now is the time…'. Joffre's response did not come until 5 October: 'the C-in-C has the honour to state that he will

[79] Enver Bey or Enver Pasha (1881–1922); Turkish Min. for War 1914–18; a leader in the 1908 Young Turk revolution; fled to Russia 1918, fought the Bolsheviks, and was killed in 1922. WSC had met Enver in 1909 when Enver was Turkish Attaché in Berlin, concluding after a long conversation that he was 'a very able, sincere, and spontaneous man' (WSC–Grey, 22 Sept. 1909, TNA: FO 800/89/124).

endeavour to satisfy this request, but... the movement of the British troops can only be carried out in succession...'. (See Christopher Phillips, Civilian Specialists at War: Britain's Transport Experts and the First World War, *U. of London P., 2020, p.101).*

Monday Oct. 5 Harcourt wrote to me that Churchill was back from Antwerp with amazing story but the position was getting better. But no material change in position.

Secret
Treasury Chambers,
Whitehall, S.W.

5.10.14

My dear Jack

No change in Turkey, Bulgaria, Roumania, Italy. On our front in France things are much the same but our troops gradually disentangling with a view to the move to the new position of which you know.

Antwerp has been very bad, but is better now. Winston has been there with good result — it is a marvellous story but I dare not write it.

German S.W. Afr. — no fresh news of importance. I hope the Un. Govt. are pulling things together.

Nothing new in North Sea, but sub-marines have been in to the Forth (Rosyth) and fired 9 torpedoes, which hit nothing! All this is very secret.

There is a Cabinet tomorrow but none on Wednesday as we have a Comm. of Imp. defence that day.

I expect you are having a splendid shoot. I envy you.

Yours
Loulou H.
(MS. Gainford 85/4)

JAP was shooting at the famed Warter Priory in East Yorkshire with Lord Chesterfield, son-in-law of the matriarch of the estate, the widow of the 1st Lord Nunburnholme, shipping magnate and former Liberal MP for Hull. The bag recorded for 5–7 October in JAP's hunting diary was more than 2,000 — birds, hares, and rabbits. Five years earlier there had been a celebrated day when 3,824 pheasants were bagged (John Martin, 'British Game Shooting in Transition, 1900–1945', Agricultural History, *vol.85, no.2, 2011, p.206). After a shoot at the Priory many men retired upstairs with splitting headaches leaving the women at tea, 'hot buns and jam with delicious cream from the Nunburnholme herd of pedigree Jerseys' (Mrs Hwfa Williams,* It Was Such Fun, *Hutchinson, 1935, p.121). Harcourt's secret story of nine torpedoes might have correctly embodied what the navy thought had happened. But the German official history shows that, when U19 and U22 got into the Firth of Forth on 25 September, each managed to fire only one torpedo. We are grateful to Rear Adm. (rtd) James Goldrick RAN for guidance on the frequency of 'false sightings and imaginary reports'.*

Tuesday Oct. 6 no material change.

Wednesday [Oct. 7] I came south from Warter Priory wrote to P.M. about Barker[80] & Lord Lieutenancy of Herts.

The Lord Lieutenant of Hertfordshire, Edward Villiers Hyde, 5th Earl of Clarendon (1846–1914) had died on 2 October. The candidature of the retail magnate Sir John Barker Bt, whose home was in Bishop's Stortford, was also supported by DLG and Illingworth; but Barker was, in HHA's words, 'opportunely removed', dying on 16 December (HHA–Venetia Stanley, 26 Dec. 1914 (Asquith Letters, *p.340). The new Lord Lieutenant was Thomas Walter Brand, 3rd Vt Hampden (1869–1958).*

Oct. 8 Thursday's Cab. We had sent into Antwerp six 4.7 guns now being used, six 6.0 guns, 2 9:2 would be there, 2,600 marines, 40 maxims, 16 field guns & aeroplanes make up 8,000 marines.

The Chikuma	}	
Hampshire	}	were pursuing Emden
Yarmouth	}	
Australia	}	Scharnhorst
Man[81]	}	
Jap	}	Gneisenau

[80] Sir John Edward Barker, Bt (1840–1914); Lib. MP Penryn and Falmouth 1906–10; draper, founder John Barker & Co Ltd, Kensington; a leader of the movement for early closing of shops; JP Herts; Bt 9 Nov 1908. On becoming Chief Whip, JAP asked Barker if he would accept a knighthood. 'He said NO, he has volunteered to do what was right by party, but wanted a baronetcy and went into reasons and past creations.' Barker did what was right and got his baronetcy five months later (JAP diary, 4–6 June 1908, MS. Gainford 38, in *A Liberal Chronicle…1908–1910*, p.36). Barker confessed to G.R. Tweedie, a former Lib. agent, that he had spent 'thousands of pounds in excess of the maximum' electoral expenditure during his two contests (Kathryn Rix, '"The Elimination of Corrupt Practices in British Elections"? Reassessing the Impact of the 1883 Corrupt Practices Act', *EHR*, vol.cxxiii, no.500, Feb. 2008, pp.87–8).

[81] Possibly JAP meant the *Montcalm* and the *Empress of Japan*; both were involved in the long search for the *Scharnhorst* and the *Gneisenau*.

Churchill had been in Antwerp for 4–5 days, only just returned. When there he had wired to ask to be allowed to take charge of all the forces, & to hold Antwerp with forces. He proposed to place in trenches between forts which might fall, the cream of our forces the 7th Division with 20,000 French (territorials) & 60,000 Belgians, & to keep Antwerp in this way against computed 60,000 besieging Germans.

When I reached London the Cabinet had overcome their surprise at this extraordinary request, they had decided on the Monday or Tuesday to recall Churchill, & he came into the Cabinet moody sulky, but explained the position. He made out a poor case for shutting up our troops. The 7th Division had been landed and stopped by Kitchener at Bruges. Churchill wanted them to be sent on. Kitchener was away that day at Salisbury saying goodbye to territorials going to India, so we wired for him to come back, & left the decision to Grey, the P.M. Churchill, Haldane & Kitchener, as to whether the troops should be moved. Sir J. French wanted them to help him. The French had been stopped at Poperinghe, just over the Dunkirk border, but we had no knowledge why. The one thing we knew which the public did not was that the Belgians would not fight, their nerve was gone, they wanted to run away, & could not be relied upon. It was abundantly clear we must retire our 8000 marines at night & get away as best we could & save men.

[This was done & Seely did much to secure the return of 6700 of them — 1260 got into Holland & were interned.[82]]

JAP might not have realised that his friend Seely was now 'the laughing stock of the Army; his vanity really has become a form of madness' (Baird diary, 3 Oct. 1914, Stonehaven MSS; Lt-Gen. W. Pulteney–Lady Desborough, 27 Oct. 1914, Anthony Leask, Putty: from Tel-el-Kebir to Cambrai: The Life and Letters of Lieutenant General Sir William Pulteney 1861–1941, *Helion & Co., 2015, p.227). 'It is an outrage that Churchill should be allowed to play around with troops', Lord Newton told Lord Curzon on October 14 'but I suppose that Asquith never thinks of keeping him in order. It was bad enough to let that ass Seely go on French's staff.' (Curzon of Kedleston MSS, BL: A & AS, MSS.Eur.F.112 E/3/7.) Willie Bridgeman told Leo Maxse that he had been refused permission by the clerks to ask the Solr-Gen. why the Press Bureau had allowed Seely's appointment as Brig.-Gen. to leak out in view of the statement that 'no intelligence likely to encourage the enemy ought to be published' (9 Feb. 1915, Maxse MSS, 490, f.76, West Sussex RO). WSC would incur considerable mockery*

[82] The words in square brackets were a later interpolation.

and opprobrium for his role in Antwerp. 'The verb "to be Antwerped" is now in common use throughout the Army to signify being sent to war without arms, accoutrements, transport, guns, or any of the essential necessaries' (Maj.-Gen. Ivor Maxse–Leo Maxse, 20 Nov. 1914, Maxse MSS 469/615, West Sussex RO).

'Can you imagine,' the King's private secretary asked his confidant Sir Francis Hopwood in a 'secret' letter on 5 October, 'that until I went to see "K" yesterday at 1.00 pm the King was absolutely ignorant of what had occurred at Antwerp or that W. had gone off there Friday night... It strikes me that W & K are running the show' (Southborough MSS, Bodl. MS.Eng.c.7362). Hopwood, disloyal to his political masters as ever, responded the next day: 'the Cabinet is both distracted & helpless' (RA: George V, G.775). But Haldane, DLG, and Edward Grey were lavish in their praise; and on 7 October Grey would write to Clementine Churchill: 'I am sitting next Winston at the Committee [of Imperial Defence], having just welcomed his return from Antwerp. And I feel a glow imparted by the thought that I am sitting next a Hero. I can't tell you how much I admire his courage & gallant spirit & genius for war. It inspires us all.' (Spencer-Churchill MSS, CSCT 3/15, CAC.) The capitulation of Antwerp was signed on 9 October. The Royal Naval Division withdrew. Britain had lost 57 killed, 193 wounded, and 936 captured. HHA railed to Venetia Stanley on 13 October about the '<u>wicked</u> folly of it all' (Asquith Letters, *p.275).*

The expected French marines, whose objective had been to cover the withdrawal of the Belgian field army, had been diverted by General Joffre to Poperinghe and Ghent, the Belgians having already been evacuated. On 10 October Kitchener made known to the French Ambassador, Paul Cambon, his unhappiness about the French failure to turn up. To Sir John French he asserted that Joffre was 'to a considerable extent responsible' for the fall of Antwerp. Sir Edward Grey had a similar view (Elizabeth Greenhalgh, Victory through Coalition: Britain and France during the First World War, *Cambridge UP, 2005, pp.20–1; William James Philpott,* Anglo-French Relations and Strategy on the Western Front, 1914–18, *Macmillan in assoc. with King's College London, 1996, pp.31–50). The ongoing resistance of the Belgians in October 1914 is sympathetically chronicled in Paul Van Pul,* In Flanders Flooded Fields: Before Ypres there was Yser, *Pen & Sword, Barnsley, 2006; and placed in the context of British and French operations in Beckett,* The Making of the First World War, *pp.12–30.*

9th/12th October

Friday's cabinet } absent
Monday's cabinet } (see Harcourt's Report.)[83]

[83] Harcourt's report has not been located. There are entries in Harcourt's diary notes, 7, 8, 9, and 12 Oct. 1914, Bodl. MS.Eng.c.8284; see below. HHA's Cabinet letters cover 8–9 Oct. and 12–13 Oct., 9 Oct. and 13 Oct. 1914 (TNA: CAB 41/35/51–2).

JAP was at Hutton Castle, Berwick-on-Tweed, after attending a recruiting meeting with Jack Tennant. There was a record bag of partridges (230 brace) on 11 October, total bag over 1,000. Cabinet met on the 8th, 9th, 12th and 13th. Hobhouse, Haldane, Birrell, and Simon as well as JAP, were absent on 12 October. Harcourt's notes show DLG complaining on the 8th about the War Office not ordering enough guns; and Grey expressing disquiet over foreign reservists being forcibly removed from ships on the high seas while there was difficulty in declaring copper, petroleum, and rubber as absolute contraband. Italy was sitting on the fence and expected to sit tighter when Antwerp fell. Kitchener advised that fourteen fully equipped divisions (400,000 men) would be in, or ready for, the field by January.

The expected return of WSC from Antwerp prompted Asquith to exclaim that they must kill a fatted calf. But a decision on what was to be done about Antwerp was to be settled by WSC, Kitchener, and the Prime Minister. WSC wanted to mine the mouth of the Scheldt and the Rhine, thus blocking the port of Rotterdam. He had circulated a paper showing an overwhelming naval preponderance over Germany, 'actual and immediately accruing' (Harcourt diary notes, 7, 8, 9, and 12 Oct. 1914, on back of Foreign Office telegrams and rewritten and reworded later, not 'transcribed litterally' as Harcourt's header says, Bodl. MS.Eng.c.8284).

The majority of the Cabinet, including JAP, were increasingly being excluded from the strategic direction of the war. 'The military position... is more for expert executive officers than for politicians & whilst I have my views as to what is good strategy & tactics, yet as a minister one is bound to accept French & Joffre's views... I feel bound to leave to K home matters. I dont think my absence from 2 or 3 cabinets matters' (JAP–EP, 8 Oct. 1914, MS. Gainford 189/43–5). Towards the end of November the creation of a War Council—albeit technically a subcommittee of the CID without executive authority—formalised the separation of responsibilities. HHA invited Balfour to join Grey, Kitchener, WSC, and DLG at a 'consultation' at Downing Street on 25 November. Ministers 'may bring with them one or two experts. Naturally, I don't wish this to be known.' Lord Fisher and the CIGS Sir James Wolfe Murray came (HHA–Balfour, 24 Nov. 1914, Balfour MSS, BL Add.MS. 49,692, ff.146–7). For more on the meeting see the commentary following JAP's entry on the Cabinet meeting of 24 November 1914. Crewe, Haldane, McKenna, retired Admiral Sir Arthur Wilson, and Harcourt were progressively added to the original invitees.

JAP kept silent on matters on which his opinion was not sought, and does not seem to have been aware of the frustration driving the Financial Secretary to the Treasury to plead with HHA on 1 October to do something about the very large problems that were never dealt with by the War Office 'because they never seem to occur to the plain, simple hero who is at the helm' (Levine, Politics, Religion and Love, *p.262,).*

Oct. 13 Tuesday we discussed scheme for pensioning widows of soldiers killed in war, & agreed after a division which the P.M. took 6/6 for all widows, 3/6 for the 1st child, & 2/6 for next. Those who wanted 5/- only for childless widows were Wood, Lucas, Hobhouse, McKenna, Grey, George, Samuel, Runciman, Beauchamp, whilst the P.M., K., Churchill (7/6), Crewe, Haldane, J.A.P., Masterman, Emmott, Simon & Harcourt voted for 6/6.

A leading article in The Nation *a month earlier had drawn attention to the inadequate provision for the dependants of serving men. WSC, given a galley proof by the editor, had sent it on to DLG on 9 September: 'The 5/- pension is a scandal. No soldier's wife shd be dependent on charity. Your large outlook shd be turned to this' (Lloyd George MSS, LG/C/3/16/9, PA). JAP's tally of the voting differs from HHA's, given in his Cabinet letter to the King (TNA: CAB 41/35/52). HHA said there was one vote for 7/6, nine for 6/6 (JAP gave nine) and eight for 5/- (JAP gave nine). In writing to Venetia Stanley, HHA gave the same totals as he had given the King; but an appended list of names has Samuel in a column of ten for 6/6, not in the 5/- column. HHA appears not to have counted his own vote when calculating the total for the King. The King himself had weighed in, hoping that Cabinet would accept 7/6 for a widow, 2/6 for the first three, and 2/- for the rest.*

*HHA told Venetia Stanley that he had only twice before in seven years taken a division. The matter was revisited the next day and again on 4 November when Cabinet settled on 7/6 (HHA–Venetia Stanley, 13 Oct. 1914 (*Asquith Letters*, pp.276–7); Stamfordham–Bonham Carter, 11 Oct. 1914, Bodl. MS. Asquith 4, f.24).*

We discussed how to meet invasion by Germans. K. said he would try it if he was them, & strike at us by landing force of 120,000, have air ships, transport & fleet all out. The P.M. said he hoped they would try. K. urged more mine laying. Ch. replied he had only 10,000, 300 miles of them. The German could always sweep a channel through them & if he exhausted his supply he could not get more than 5000 & that not before Jany & the Admiralty wanted to be in bight of Heligoland themselves with submarines to see what Germans were doing. If mined it would be shut to us, & our information delayed & invasion moved concealed. [We discussed landing of Canadians on Monday at S'ton in 3 days or Devonport in 6 — decided latter, as a submarine was seen off I. of W.][84]

Wed. Oct. 14 K. reported that the troops were now with French on the left wing — Headquarters moved from Abbeville to St Omer. The cavalry were engaged east of Hazebrouck, & the Germans must be realising we had come up from

[84] The words in square brackets were a later interpolation.

Soissons. We had opposite to us the XIX, & XII German army corps, & there would be a forward move from Ypres (Rawlinson[85] & 7th Div.) with Haig's[86] (2d & 1st Div.) joining the III Army Corps at Hazebrouck, & our other troops occupying Fietre to Mervis almost immediately.

JAP probably meant Fletre, four miles west by north of Bailleul, which was ten miles SWW of Ypres; and Merville, eight miles north of Bethune.

K. reported we found we could get

68 big guns by April 1		
450	"	May 1
630	"	June 1
1420	"	July 1

It was computed

Opposite the allies in the West 2,000,000 enemies' forces in field.

There were now	20 German Corps	
	15 " "	reserves
& some Landwehr	1	
opposite Russians	8 German Corps in the South	
	3 Landwehr in North	
	47 = 2,800,000 men	
with Austrians.	1,800,000 Total 4,000,000 [sic]	

At Hendon we had 3 air ships

	nearly ready	2	would ready to take on
?	Teaching craft	4	Zeppelins Graham White[87]
	Building	1	in Govmt employ.
	Brookland	3	
	Elsewhere	3	

[85] Maj.-Gen. Sir Henry Rawlinson (1864–1925) tmpy GOC 4th Div. 21 Sept. 1914; tmpy Lt-Gen., GOC IV Corps 5 Oct. 1914; tmpy Gen., GOC 1st Army 22 Dec. 1915; Gen. 1 Jan. 1917; briefly British Mili. Rep. Supreme War Council, then various Army commands to end of war; GOC Nth Russia, Aldershot, 1919–20; C-in-C India 1920–5; KCB 1915, KCMG 1918, GCB 1919, Baron Rawlinson of Trent 1919 (Ian F.W. Beckett, 'Henry Rawlinson…', in Beckett and Steven J. Corvi eds, *Haig's Generals*, Pen & Sword, Barnsley, 2006, pp.164–82; Robin Prior and Trevor Wilson, *Command on the western front: the military career of Sir Henry Rawlinson, 1914–18*, Basil Blackwell, Oxford, 1992; Rodney Atwood, *General Lord Rawlinson: From Tragedy to Triumph*, Bloomsbury Academic, 2018).

[86] Lt-Gen. Sir Douglas Haig (1861–1928); GOC 1st Army 1914–15; GOC Aldershot 1912–14, C-in-C BEF 1915–19, C-in-C Forces in Great Britain 1919–20; KCVO 1901; Field Marshal 1917; Earl 1919.

[87] Claude Grahame-White (1879–1959); Flt-Cmdr Royal, Royal Naval Air Service 1914–15; aviator and aircraft designer; patrolled over London 5 Sept. 1914 looking for a falsely reported Zeppelin; first

Long discussion details of how to treat dependents of those killed in war.

Hobhouse, who said that he was absent from the 13 October meeting, recorded 'a long discussion as to the rate of payment for soldiers' widows and for the second time in my 3 years, a formal division of the Cabinet by votes was taken. Ten including the P.M, Haldane, Pease, Churchill, Beauchamp, Kitchener voting for 6/6 pension per week; 8 including Ll.G, Lucas, McK. Wood, McKenna and myself for 5/-. Birrell and Runciman were away.' (Hobhouse diary, 14 Oct. 1914, David ed., Inside Asquith's Cabinet, *p.198.) If WSC had shifted into the 6/6 camp overnight, it appears that the whole Cabinet moved to the more generous 7/6 on 4 November. For the report considered by the Cabinet see Robin Betts,* Dr Macnamara 1861–1931, *Liverpool UP, 1999, pp.282–3, and for the ensuing agitation for more adequate pensions and separation allowances see Pedersen,* Family, Dependence, and the Origins of the Welfare State, *pp.108–15, and Gill Thomas, 'State Maintenance For Women During The First World War: The Case of Separation Allowances and Pensions', D.Phil. thesis, U. of Sussex, 1989; and for the controversy over payment of allowances to unwed mothers see Susan R. Grayzel,* Women's Identities at War: Gender, Motherhood, and Politics in Britain and France during the First World War, *U. of North Carolina P., Chapel Hill, 1999, pp.90–103. Angela Smith's analysis brings out the link between separation allowances, pensions, and recruitment (*Discourses Surrounding British Widows of the First World War, *Bloomsbury, 2013, pp.60–3). The story is carried forward in Ingrid H. James, '"To keep me all my life": policy, provision and the experience of war widowhood, 1914–1925', Ph.D. thesis, U. of Cambridge, 1999.*

Thurs. Oct. 15 Cabinet.

Churchill reported that up to date 4800 mines were ready in stock, 1860 had been laid, 3090 were being converted at Woolwich from Heneage type to pendulum at rate of 100 p. wk. 130 were on mine layers, 200 p. wk could be made by Vickers &c by Elswick, 1400 girls loadg.

He could have by	Jany	3,000
	Ap.	3,000
	July	5,500
ready 8 months hence		15,000

Englishman to receive French Aero club pilot licence 1910; set up London Aerodrome at Hendon 1911; organised first airmail delivery (Hendon–Windsor) 1911; Flt-Cmdr, Royal Naval Air Service 1914–15; resigned to manage aircraft construction business whose staff had increased from 20 to 1,000 because of war contracts. Took Violet Asquith on her first flight, 'the most thrilling experience of my life' (Violet Asquith–Venetia Stanley, 22 Aug. 1912, Bodl. MS. Bonham Carter 155, f.32).

After considering the likely reaction of the United States to any flouting of the Declaration of London, HHA had written secretly to WSC on 29 September that the time had come to start mining, and to do it without stinting, and if necessary 'on a Napoleonic scale'. Not knowing what supply of the 'infernal machinery' was in hand, the Prime Minister felt sure 'you can't do better than make the most ample provision, and use it freely & even lavishly' (Churchill MSS, C 13/44, CAC). Prompted by the 'temerity' of German submarines that had shown themselves in the Straits of Dover, the Cabinet concluded that they should mine the North Sea. 'It is the only effective answer we can make', Venetia Stanley was advised on 30 September, 'as they refuse to come out & have a fight in the open' (Venetia Montagu MSS, passage omitted from the Brocks' edition). Tracing the debates within the government and Admiralty over the first six months of the war, Richard Dunley concludes that 'the bellicose attitude of the Liberal Cabinet forced the navy into accepting a mining strategy' (Britain and the Mine, 1900–1915: Culture, Strategy and International Law, *Palgrave Macmillan US, 2018, pp.226–56).*

The Directorate of Naval Operations had long been concerned about the dangers of explosion from the accidental firing of the Heneage type pistol during the priming of contact mines. Hurried priming by inexperienced crew was thought to have caused the destruction of the minelayer HMS Princess Irene *in the River Medway on 27 May 1915,* http://www.rainham-history.co.uk/articleslist/363-the-hms-princess-irene-disaster-of-may-1915, accessed 27 Nov. 2022.

Churchill reported (airguns) 213 were required, 175 were mounted & in position on fleet all had 2 of a kind 46 required of this type 38 mounted already round London. 11 had bn mounted reqd 4 more.

Runciman reported in Hamburg

220,000 tons of German shipping could be used to transport armies across N. Sea.

136,000 tons of British

400,000 " of all other nationalities.

We discussed the difficulties increasing of transport across English channel owing to risk of submarines one having been seen off Isle of W., others may be in Channel & as one had been seen at Loch Ewe no knowing where our battle ships were safe.

Churchill alluded to intended raids to be made by our aeroplanes — & pointed out how by diving submarines could penetrate without great risk mine laid areas of the sea.

We discussed spies & whether non Germans were on the coast of Belgium, & communications wireless were so easy & cheap. We should export all Germans.

There is no record of what Cabinet might have been told about the potential for wireless communication between Britain and Belgium; but a cogent summary of information about developments that some of them could have known is in Kapil Subramanian and Graeme Gooday, 'British Telecommunications History in the First World War', in Peter Liddle ed., Britain and the Widening War, 1915–16: From Gallipoli to the Somme, *Pen & Sword Military, Barnsley, 2016, pp.213–30.*

Some, if not all, Cabinet ministers might have been aware that MI5 had secretly accessed the manuscript records of the 1911 Census and compiled an unofficial register of some 80,000 resident aliens, including those who were naturalised British: Germans, Belgians, Danes, Dutch, Norwegians, Swedes, Swiss, and Austro-Hungarians but not Italians and Turks (Andrew, The Defence of the Realm, *pp.48,872; Edward Higgs,* The Information State in England: The Central Collection of Information on Citizens since 1500, *Palgrave Macmillan, 2004, p.110). According to the official history compiled in 1921 (TNA: KV 1/35 Prevention of Espionage 1914–1918), the police, at the request of the Special Intelligence Bureau, had listed by July 1913 28,380 names on a register of aliens begun in 1910. The work of the Secret Service Bureau in gathering and disseminating intelligence on enemy aliens up to the outbreak of war is best followed in Martin John Farrar, 'The Illusory Threat: Enemy Aliens in Britain during the Great War', Ph.D thesis, King's College London, 2016, pp.29–66. There is a useful summary of lists of espionage suspects and arrests, and MI5's 'Special War List' in Nigel West,* Historical Dictionary of World War I Intelligence, *Rowman & Littlefield, Lanham, 2014, pp.296–8,355–94.*

Three years later Reginald McKenna would reminisce to Basil Thomson, then headquartered at New Scotland Yard: 'Do you remember how in the first six months of the War a hundred thousand stories were investigated and not one of them led to a prosecution?' (McKenna–Thomson, 19 Oct. 1917, copy, McKenna MSS, MCKN 9/9, CAC). For the evidence on German covert operations and the limited success of British counter-intelligence see Thomas Boghardt, Spies of the Kaiser, *and Bostridge,* The Fateful Year, *p.382; the invaluable research of Nicholas Hiley ('The Failure of British Counter-Espionage against Germany, 1907–1914',* HJ, *vol.28, no.4, 1985, pp.835–62; 'Entering the Lists: MI5's great spy round-up of August 1914',* I&NS, *vol.21, no.1, 2006, pp.46–76; 'Re-entering the Lists: MI5's Authorized History and the August 1914 Arrests',* I&NS, *vol.25, no.4, 2010, pp.415–52); and the more focused study by Chris Northcott,* MI5 at War 1909–1918 How MI5 Foiled the Spies of the Kaiser in the First World War, *Tattered Flag P., Ticehurst, 2015. Haia Shpayer-Makov ranges more widely than the title suggests in 'Close Encounters of an Unprecedented Kind: Police and German Enemy Aliens in Britain during the First World War',* JBS, *vol.61, no.2, 2022, pp.422–49. Compare J.C. Carlile,* My Life's Little Day, *Blackie & Son, 1935, p.204: 'The Secret Service was very busy in*

Folkestone, and not infrequently I would speak to a man one day and the next learn that he had been shot...'. Among the thousands of Belgian refugees making landfall at Folkestone, spies were both caught and recruited. McKenna, under attack from ill-informed newspapers, told Ralph Blumenfeld of the Daily Express *on 29 September: 'I don't write in deprecation of your criticism of me. On the contrary, I think the charges of ignorance and apathy directed against me by your and another newspaper have materially contributed to the success of our operations by lulling the enemy in our midst into a false sense of security' (Blumenfeld MSS, BLU/1/McK 1, 2, PA).*

I dined at night with Harold Baker, met Prime Minister, Benckendorff[88] & McKenna (& their 3 wives). When ladies left the room, the P.M. said enough credit had not been given Haldane for expeditionary force & that Haldane & McKenna deserved any credit for position we might secure for ourselves in war. The fleet was McKenna's & only Churchill's opposition (when at Home Office) to McKenna's demands for more cruisers, prevented our possessing the necessary craft to sink the roaming German cruisers around the world. We discussed the impossibility of stopping all spies even if we got rid of Germans, & we discussed possibilities of German raid into this country. Benckendorff argued ably, it would be the despairing effort of German Navy but the P.M. pointed out this week was the German best opportunity we had no regulars at home, in 3 weeks we would have two divisions, & McKenna thought it might be a risk & so did the P.M. for the Germans to take, if a long battle occurred say for 6 weeks & stalemate existed.

'I think we are not far off the stale mate that Lord K. spoke of. Sir John French's movement seems to be encountering a good deal of opposition and the Russian news is not as yet very stimulating...', Hankey confided to Balfour on 15 October (Balfour MSS, BL Add.MS. 49,753, f.56). JAP told EP that night: 'We are not very happy about the war prospects. The Germans are very cock a hoop about Antwerp & Ostend & getting so near us—& their airships aeroplanes & submarines can or may play havoc with our shipping & coasts & London, & we cannot retaliate with much effect.' (MS. Gainford 189/48.)

[88] Count Aleksandr Konstantinovitch Benckendorff (1849–1916); Russian Amb., London 1903–16; previous postings in Vienna and Copenhagen; Countess Sofia Petrovna Shuvalova (1859–1928) m. Benckendorff 1879; her husband's close confidante and adviser, 'a brilliant woman, bursting with Slavonic vitality, and the best of company, with the one reservation that her utterance was torrential' (Edward Marsh, *A Number of People: A Book of Reminiscences*, William Heinemann in assoc. with Hamish Hamilton, 1939, p.168).

As British losses mounted and coastal defences seemed vulnerable, the arrival of the Canadian First Contingent on 14 October brought some comfort. A Second Contingent of twelve battalions had been approved on 9 October. By the end of the year the Canadian Expeditionary Force had grown to 56,584 (Desmond Morton and J.L. Granatstein, Marching to Armageddon: Canadians and the Great War 1914–1919, *Lester & Orpen Dennys, Toronto, 1989, pp.8–30).*

Friday Oct. 16 Cabinet. In reply to demand by Churchill Kitchener reeled out a lot of figures of our army. He read them fast frequently corrected himself, & they were difficult to take down. K. did not mean us to have them. Apart from expeditionary force of about 220 M

The Canadian force were	31,941
The regulars at home	26,000
The territorials	492,234
The New Army	673,215

The enlisting had been each week

	Aug. 10	15,000		Sept.	28	25,000
	17	47 "		Oct.	5	19,000
	24	49 "			12	16,000
	31	83 "			17	
back to)	Sept 7	188 "				
[?Marne])	14	108 "	standard raised			
	21	39 "	height & chest			

Churchill told us now 33 seaplanes 45 air planes we could have 177 air planes 141 seaplanes 318 in all; not available 10; pilots 78, training 50, [total] 138.

HHA spent the weekend with Lord and Lady Sheffield at Alderley Park. Henry Dickens KC, a guest at Alderley the next weekend, asked Lady Sheffield if the Prime Minister had given her any idea about the probable duration of the war. 'Oh yes!' she said. 'He thought it would be over in the spring!' (The Recollections of Sir Henry Dickens, KC, *William Heinemann, 1934, p.302). A few days after his Alderley weekend, talking to George Macaulay Booth about Booth's new assignment to assist the War Office with contracts, HHA said: 'I believe you are a shipowner…'. Booth said he was. 'Well', HHA continued, 'this war is going to be over in a few months. Ships aren't going to play an important part in the war, so you go on helping Lord Kitchener' (Crow,* A Man of Push and Go, *p.69). A few months later, admitting he was not a prophet, the Prime Minister was writing from Alderley to*

Venetia Stanley's sister-in-law in Melbourne that 'the daily & weekly wear & tear is so terrific that I take a shorter view than most people of the duration of the war' (HHA–Lady Stanley, 11 Dec. 1914, Stanley of Alderley MSS, Document 1456, IWM).

After the 16 October Cabinet meeting a CID subcommittee considered the enemy aliens problem. Foreshadowing proposals he would bring to Cabinet the following Tuesday, McKenna told Kitchener it recommended that male Germans and Austrians not of military age should be deported along with 'suspected females'. The whole of the East Coast should be declared a prohibited area; the 'military authority' should be empowered to remove any persons from a defended harbour and further powers should be taken to deal with any person not of British parentage. An 'indispensable preliminary' was completing the existing policy of interning all Germans and Austrians of military age. Nearly 10,000 were already held, but there were 'possibly 20,000 for whom accommodation has to be found'. With the public being 'worked up to a state of frenzy', he feared 'we may have disturbances'(McKenna–Kitchener, 16 Oct. 1914, Kitchener MSS, TNA 30/57/75).

In his advice for the Cabinet McKenna gave more precise figures: there were 9,000 Germans and Austrians of military age in confinement and some 23,000 still at large. The 23,000 would be confined, 'instalment by instalment', as soon as the War Office authorities could provide for them (HHA Cabinet letter, 22 Oct. 1914, Bodl. MS. Asquith 7, f.222; J.C. Bird, Control of Enemy Alien Civilians in Great Britain 1914–1918, *Garland Publishing, New York, 1986, pp.38–40; Panikos Panayi,* Prisoners of Britain: German civilian and combatant internees during the First World War, *Manchester UP, 2012, pp.43,48).*

Tuesday Oct. 20 @ 3.0. We discussed the whole progress & position of war in France — the system of entrenching as seen on Sunday by Lloyd George, Lord Reading & Simon who were at Paris & at the front. George saw Foch & Castelnau[89] & liked them both, they seemed confident that they could hold their own now but quite unable to see how they could get across the German entrenched positions.

Simon had been consulting the French artillery expert, General Sainte Claire Deville, on gun manufacturing techniques ('J.A.S', holograph notes, 18 Oct. 1914, TNA: MUN/4/7069/1; Extract from Lord Reading's diary, 18 Oct. 1914, Lloyd George MSS, LG C/14/3/9b, PA). DLG and his companions (who included Jean de Castellane as interpreter, and the wealthy Australian Jewish MP Sir Charles Henry Bt with whose wife Julia he was thought to have had

[89] Noël Joseph Edouard de Courières de Castelnau (1851–1944); GOC French Second Army; commanded Army Group Centre 1915; Joffre's Chief of Staff at Verdun; career stalled with Joffre's dismissal in 1916; recalled autumn 1918 to command Army Group East in Lorraine.

a dalliance) met Foch at the Tenth Army HQ at St Pol on 17 October. Years later DLG would remind Foch: 'You are the man of the Saint-Pol programme'. 'Saint Pol?' 'Yes... You said to me; "We are going to dig trenches... They shall not break through (ils ne passeront pas)" And they did not...'. Foch told his ADC after the war that DLG 'saw everything clearly. He invented me' (Commandant Bugnet [trs. Russell Green], Foch Talks, *Gollancz, 1929, p.218).*

The attack on England was then discussed, the distance of the main fleet for safety. Churchill reported that 20 torpedo attacks had already been made, 5 of our ships were sunk, & we must expect more. Ours would do what they could & were with destroyers shelling the Germans near Ostend. The 3 monitors had been there since Saturday. The *E.3* was said to be sunk off the Elbe by the Germans. She was there, so that it was probably true.

The E.3 ('a submarine of the best class' [HHA–Venetia Stanley, 21 Oct. 1914, Gilbert ed., Churchill, Vol. III, Companion, Part 1, *p.210]) ran foul of a U-boat while on patrol on 18 October and sank with all hands. Stung by public criticism of his Antwerp expedition, WSC was talking of leaving the Admiralty. Haldane wrote to dissuade him on 19 October: 'Do not pay the least attention to the fools who write & talk in the press. It is the real thing that counts, & the nation thoroughly believes in you' (Lady Spencer-Churchill MSS, CSCT 3/15, CAC).*

It was obvious that if stalemate arose on land, the Germans who had their transport, cement laden vessels to sink in the Thames, Zeppelins, aircraft, bombs, mines, landing rafts, submarines & fleet ready might attack us in force — & that submarines having driven off our fleet & feint made, a sudden raid in force might be successful. All counter methods for guarding against submarines were being considered & made. It was rather depressing to have to realise the absence of safety, & our [in]ability to rely on our 1st line of defence with certainty. We decided to arrest 25,000 Germans in the country of military age (set them to dig trenches).

At night I dined with the McKennas, the P.M. & K. were there — we talked about the War Office & their ways. K. admitted their extraordinary & unaccountable procedure due to some Major as a rule, who decided policy for himself.

The way in which the arrest of Germans had been stopped by War Office, without K's knowledge & against his & McKenna's wishes was a case in point. McKenna said at Harwich a large gun stand built on cement in a commanding position had been found. The P.M. at Bridge afterwards was in a very chaffing mood. I revoked & tried to hide it — he regarded it as a hellish Jermyn St dodge!

The dinner party, at which Violet Markham, Margot and Elizabeth Asquith, were also present, carried on into Wednesday morning. 'We had a rubber that went on for nearly 2 hours, the P.M. sent me home in his car at 1 o'clock' (JAP–EP, 21 Oct. 1914, MS. Gainford 189/51–2). HHA told Venetia Stanley on 21 October the bridge was 'pretty dull, except when Jack Pease, who is not a bad player, revoked twice in the same hand!' (Venetia Montagu MSS, passage omitted by the Brocks). For an understanding of JAP's misdemeanour see Ernest Bergholt, Royal Auction Bridge The Laws and Principles: Under the English Code of 1914, *George Routledge & Sons, [1916], pp.30–3.*

The association of Jermyn St with the 'dodge' was possibly an allusion to Cox's Hotel at 55 Jermyn Street: 'the most discreet private and luxurious hotel; with an entrance you could only find if you knew exactly where to look' (Tim Coates, Patsy: The Story of Mary Cornwallis West, *Bloomsbury, 2012, p.79). Evidently Alick Murray and Charles Hobhouse knew where to look (David ed.,* Inside Asquith's Cabinet, *p.97). Another possible venue for a Jermyn Street dodge was the celebrated cook Rosa Lewis's Cavendish Hotel at No. 81–83, a few steps from Turnbull & Asser, where HHA's widower brother-in-law, Lord Ribblesdale, lived; and, as the 5-year-old Timothy Bevan remarked when told the name of the street in which he was walking, 'Ah! That's where the unmarried ladies live.' (George Leveson Gower,* Mixed Grill, *p.147.)*

'Those who did not know the Cavendish imagined it was altogether louche, a den of iniquity, the scene of orgies; but in reality it was often very dull and respectable' (Daphne Fielding, The Duchess of Jermyn Street: the Life and Good Times of Rosa Lewis of the Cavendish Hotel, *Eyre & Spottiswoode, 1964, p.100; Evelyn Waugh,* Vile Bodies, *Chapman and Hall, repr. 1965, pp.37–9; and, for Mrs Lewis's uncorroborated testimony that her clients included DLG, McKenna, and HHA himself, Michael Harrison,* Rosa, *Corgi, 1977, pp.233,239). Lord Winterton recorded dining with Ribblesdale at the 'delightful cosy little hotel, with a perfect gem of a cook', on 1 July 1912, and playing baccarat with Lady Essex and others (Bodl. MS. Winterton 11). The young Foreign Office clerk Duff Cooper and his fun-loving friends would occasionally lunch or dine there, although it was thought not entirely suitable for some of their female companions (Duff Cooper diary, 1915* passim, *Norwich MSS, DUFC 15/1/5, CAC).*

Wed. & Thurs. Oct. 21 & 22 We discussed without much variation how to circumvent the Germans if they tried to or landed, what the home forces could do, & how long it would take the navy to reach the point aimed at by the enemy's forces. We also discussed how to act so as to protect the civil population. Churchill & I argued that the people should not be restrained in making the invaders life a hell, by concealed attack behind any hedge or window, & that to now create panic by issuing circulars would be folly, when we trust the naval experts to know their business.

In a 'secret & private' letter to Balfour on 3 October Hankey had warned of a state of confusion over home defence. At the Admiralty, Hankey was told that naval policy was to allow the enemy to land 'though I think this was an exaggeration'. The General Staff intended to await the enemy in a prepared position round London with the Territorials and bring back part of the Expeditionary Force from France 'in order finally to finish the enemy off'. A disturbed Hankey then talked to Sir Ian Hamilton, commander of the Central Force, who revealed that he had contradictory orders in an official letter from the Army Council conveying the General Staff view. But Kitchener's personal instructions, which Hamilton preferred, were to meet an enemy at the beach immediately he landed, deploying all available forces, and 'worry him at every moment until he was utterly crushed'. Hankey had 'laid the whole matter before the Prime Minister', who decided to call a meeting of the CID. The meeting was deferred when Kitchener sent for Hankey and told him 'the whole question was in a muddle which he had to disentangle'. Hankey said he did not fear invasion at the moment but that they ought to get the house in order 'before invasion or attempted invasion comes within the bounds of reasonable probability' (Balfour MSS, BL Add.MS. 49,703, ff.47–50).

The premise of the discussion on 22 October was Kitchener's view that, if there were a stalemate in the 'two military fields', the Germans might contemplate invasion with 150,000 to 200,000 men. The Cabinet had seen a pessimistic paper by Hankey of 14 October on the likely consequences of invasion; and Kitchener had written to WSC on 19 October that it might be a good thing to have some of the more powerful modern ships from the grand fleet in the Eastern ports, so that they could act quickly in case of emergency in the North Sea or Channel. WSC had responded immediately that there could be no question of 'dividing or dispersing the fleet' (Howard Roy Moon, 'The Invasion of the United Kingdom: Public Controversy and Official Planning 1885–1918', Ph.D. thesis, U. of London, 1968, pp.499–503). The probability and likely scale of invasion and how best to counter it had been the subject of recurring debate in the navy and CID. The immediate pre-war period is illuminated by David G. Morgan-Owen, The Fear of Invasion: Strategy, Politics, and British War Planning, 1880–1914, *Oxford UP, 2017, ch.8.*

The First Lord thought an operation on more than an insignificant scale was doomed to disaster. Flotillas of torpedo destroyers and submarines had the primary duty of preventing a landing. But he was also planning a line of torpedo proof harbours for battleships and cruisers not immediately needed by the main fleet to 'safely lie'. His 'general outlines' of a scheme to close the whole of the northern sea area up to 30 miles north of Shetland to all except licensed British ships was accepted in principle (HHA Cabinet letter, 22 Oct. 1914 [re meetings of 20,

21, 22 Oct.], Bodl. MS. Asquith 7, ff.220–21). When Samuel presented proposed regulations for the East Coast in the event of a landing, he said that the War Office view was that the retreating population should take horses but leave cattle. Kitchener, evidently unaware of the recommendations of his officials, offered his personal view that 'everything should be swept away' (Hobhouse diary, 22 Oct. 1914, David ed., Inside Asquith's Cabinet, *p.201).*

The chaotic planning got worse before it got better. On 24 October, draft instructions 'For the Guidance of the Civil Population in the event of a Landing by the Enemy in this Country' were printed by the CID. They were circulated to Lords Lieutenant before Balfour, who was responsible for briefing them, was consulted. Balfour was perturbed to discover an instruction that 'all other food supplies [apart from livestock which were to be driven off or slaughtered] and forage should be removed or destroyed unless the police or the military authorities should otherwise direct'. The effect of the order was to require the whole civil population to evacuate at once. As Balfour recognised, this was a direct contradiction of another instruction to keep the roads clear. Revised printed instructions stressed that no attempt to 'burn and/or destroy' food supplies should be made except under orders from the military authorities (Balfour–Hankey, 27 Oct. 1914; Balfour–Lord Harris, 27 Oct. 1914, Balfour MSS, BL Add.MS. 49,703, ff.59, 60–2).

Brett Holman, 'Constructing the Enemy Within: Rumours of Secret Gun Platforms and Zeppelin Bases in Britain, August–October 1914', BJMilHist, *vol.3, no.2, 2017, pp.22–42, is a sober appraisal of the rumours fuelling spy scares, their 'sudden and brief plausibility', and the government's actions.*

Churchill told us he was afraid *E.3* had gone under as she was 48 hours late — & that we had lost at sea as many men as Nelson lost in all his naval engagements! One submarine had reached Libau in the Baltic, the other 2 were possibly engaged.

At the beginning of the war Britain had 77 submarines and France 60. Germany's 28 included several that were obsolete but the latest ten (U-19 to U-28) were much superior, and sixteen were under construction (Jan S. Breemer, Defeating the U-Boat: Inventing Antisubmarine Warfare, *Naval War College P., Newport, MD, 2010, p.16). Three British submarines (E.1, E.9, and E.11) had been ordered to penetrate the Baltic and attack the German High Seas Fleet. If necessary they had permission to refuel at Libau, a Russian naval port. Unfortunately the Admiralty did not know that the Russians had abandoned Libau as a naval port and that the Germans had blockaded it with mines. Two of the submarines got through to Libau safely but without causing any damage to the German fleet. The captain of E.11 (Lt-Cdr Martin Nasmith (1883–1965), VC for conspicuous bravery in the Sea of Marmora, May–June 1915, adopted surname Dunbar-Nasmith 1923, Adm. 1936) thought he was being attacked by a U-boat but found, after it had returned fire, that the attacking vessel was a neutral Danish submarine. No damage had been done. Spotted by a German seaplane,* E.11 *was attacked by destroyers but returned safely to its base.*

We had (from one ship — Monitor class — at Ostend) fired 1100 rounds of 4 inch shell. We agreed to help the starving Belgians, whom the Germans declined to feed thro' philanthropic agencies who could buy food in Holland & as neutrals distribute it so as to reach those starving & prevent the Germans getting it. K of K had seen French officer who said 2 guns in each battery were proved sufficient if they had plenty of ammunition. He advocated a ricochet shell. The French had 4000 guns great rush had occurred.

Oct. 22 Thursday With assent of Lord K. & under direction of the P.M. I had called meeting together to arrange for occupation of men in camps during winter evenings; in accordance with arrangements entered into with Dawson[90] & Heath Caldwell[91] of War Office. They did not turn up but a letter came from K of K. to say no such committee was required & the men would be occupied by him 5 nights out of the 6.

War Office,
Whitehall,
S.W.
22nd October 1914

Dear Pease,

I am sorry that I cannot agree to your proposals. The men must be at work at cockcrow and be kept hard at it during the day so that they only have between 6 o'clock and 7 o'clock free; it will be far better for them to turn in early than to attend elaborate entertainments. So far as evening occupation is necessary, I intend to provide for it by means of lectures on several evenings of the week on Military subjects, such as Military Duties, Musketry, Instruction by Specialists,

[90] Col. Sir Douglas Frederick Rawdon Dawson (1854–1933); Asst Director Personnel Services, War Office 1914–15; entered army 1874; mili. attaché, Vienna 1890–5, Paris 1895–1901; Master of Ceremonies for the King 1903–7; Sec., Order of the Garter 1904–33; Comptroller, Lord Chamberlain's Dept 1907–20; KCVO 1907; GCVO 1911; KCB 1924. The incident is not mentioned in his memoirs, *A Soldier-Diplomat*, John Murray, 1927.

[91] Maj.-Gen. Frederick Crofton Heath-Caldwell (1858–1945); Director Mili. Training, War Office 1914–15 and proponent of machine gun corps; entered Royal Engineers 1877; took additional surname Caldwell as condition of uncle's will; A/g Adj.-Gen. Royal Engineers, Army HQ 1906–8; Inspector Royal Engineers 1908–13; GOC Scottish coastal defences 1913–14; GOC Portsmouth 1916–18; GOC S-E Area RAF 1918–19, https://jjhc.info/heathcaldwellfc1945, accessed 28 Nov. 2022.

and sanitary and hygienic questions affecting the soldier. I am sure you will be ready to help, if necessary, with lecturers, but the object is military instruction and this is what the men desire.

A Committee has been formed at the War Office for making all necessary arrangements. Such a Committee as you proposed would not, I feel sure, meet the requirements above stated, although I fully recognise the kind intentions of yourself and those associated with you.

I think on Saturday evenings some form of entertainment would be appreciated and would not interfere with military instruction. Could not this be arranged without such a committee?

As regards the newspaper cuttings you sent me, they do not affect the matter so far as I am concerned. I cannot allow the military preparations of the Army for war to be guided by such stupid effusions.

I regret that I was not made aware of the preparations that were being made in time to inform you of my views before matters had gone so far as they appear to have done.

Yours very truly,
Kitchener
(MS. Gainford 89/39)

JAP's Parliamentary Secretary, Christopher Addison, recorded that everyone at the meeting sympathised with his chief, who 'took it very well'. It seemed to be 'generally agreed that it was the most insulting performance any of them present had ever met with... another of the many examples we have had lately of the woeful lack of imagination on the part of K.' (Addison diary [original typescript], 22 Oct. 1914, Bodl. MS. Addison, dep.d.1.) JAP had been criticised by the Daily Chronicle *for not organising education classes to occupy recruits in the evenings. He had told his wife on 11 October that he was already doing so and was going to 'work a committee to look after this & recreative work... They are tired at night & want entertaining rather than educating or studying French as the Chronicle suggested' (MS. Gainford 189).*

It was a humiliating position so I went across & saw the P.M.

He wrote to K. to say my committee had been thought by him an excellent one & he hoped he would see me again.

I dined with P.M. on Oct 22: Sir Ernest Cassel, Mrs Darrell (Miss Emerson Bainbridge née),[92] John Morley, Crewe, McKenna.

[92] (Eva) Jeffie Darell (not Darrell) (d. 1966); dau. Emerson M. Bainbridge (1845–1911), mining and railway engineer, Lib. MP Lincs (West Lindsey or Gainsborough) 1895–1900; she m. 1907 William

Addison had spoken to JAP on his return from seeing HHA and found him 'in uncommonly good form'. 'What an extraordinary man,' HHA had said when told what Kitchener had done. 'K's dictatorial attitude won't go down in a democratic country', JAP told Elsie on 22 October, '& he can't send the men to bed at 7.0 — or expect them to respond to a life of no leisure or recreation' (MS. Gainford 189/53–5). There was a 'very stormy interview with K.' the next day.

A face-saving retreat by Kitchener saw the appointment of a War Office committee with the Board of Education invited to cooperate; and JAP's proposal of local camp committees with laymen on them was accepted. But the issue dragged on, aired in the press, until the Treasury approved regulations enabling reimbursement of up to two-thirds of expenditure by Local Education Authorities in organising courses and recreation (Addison diary [original typescript], 23 Oct., 3 Nov. 1914, Bodl. MS. Addison, dep.d.1). The allocation of grants to the YMCA, the Salvation Army, and the Church Army to assist their work in army training camps was still under negotiation between the Board of Education and the Treasury in the second week of November. HHA and DLG had privately agreed that £15,000 might be allocated to the YMCA (JAP–Sir Thomas Heath; Selby-Bigge–Heath, 10, 11 Nov. 1914, MS. Gainford 85/133–4; HHA–Lord Glenconner, 30 Oct. 1914, Glenconner MSS).

Friday Oct. 23 K. said he would not be interfered with & had told the P.M. he would resign! & after the cabinet the P.M. said he never saw a man so angry, and we must give him a few days 'to cool down'. We discussed position in S. Africa, De Wet's rebellion.[93]

'The news from South Africa is quite bad...', Venetia Stanley was told after the Cabinet, 'threats of further outbreaks in the Transvaal & Free State...and a most inopportune dearth of rifles, which can only be supplied in existing circumstances from America' (Venetia Montagu

Harry Verelst Darell (1878–1954) 2nd son of Sir Lionel Darell, 5th Bt. Major Darell was Dep. Asst Quartermaster Gen., 17th Division, BEF 1914. Jeffie Darell, a friend of Lord Basil Blackwood (p.s. to Ld Lieut. of Ireland but now serving in the Intelligence Corps after being wounded with the 9th Lancers) and her husband, a career soldier, moved in the same circles as Cynthia Asquith. Horatia Seymour, whose brother Ralph was serving as Adm. Beatty's Flag Lt, commented in her diary (29 Nov. 1916) 'there is an atmosphere of second rateness about her & her friends' (Seymour MSS). William Darell had won the Sword of Honour at Sandhurst, and the Diamond Sculls at Henley in 1907, and served in the Coldstream Guards in S. Africa 1899–1902 before entering the Staff College in 1913. A short biography of Brig.-Gen Darell by John Bourne (http://www.birmingham.ac.uk/research/activity/warstudies/research/projects/lionsdonkeys/d.aspx, accessed 27 Nov. 2022) details his war and post-war service.

[93] Christiaan Rudolph de Wet (1854–1922); Boer general and politician; member, Transvaal Volksraad 1885; protested against use of railways and vehicles on Sundays. Boer general and guerrilla leader 1899–1901; MP, Orange River Colony 1906–9; delegate, Union of S. Africa convention 1908–9; supporter of Hertzog against Botha and advocate of declaring Orange Free State and Transvaal republics. Found guilty of high treason and sentenced in 1915 to six years' imprisonment and a £2,000 fine, de Wet was released that year on parole. He spent the rest of his life farming.

MSS, passage omitted by the Brocks). In September de Wet was among the leaders of a revolt against the government of the Union of South Africa, some 11,000 Afrikaner men refusing to be called up for national service and then rising in rebellion. Harcourt suggested that Australian and New Zealand troops en route *to England might be diverted to the Cape to be used against the rebels. An alternative to the Colonial Secretary's idea, offered by Hobhouse, was to send the troops first to Colombo; if they were needed in South Africa, they could be sent there via Mauritius rather than proceed to England through the Suez Canal.*

At the Cabinet on 30 October HHA and Crewe cautioned that sending Australians might not be wise in view of their role in the South African war. This was good thinking in more ways than one, as khaki uniforms that had been mandated for South African troops were a hated reminder of the British enemy. The plan was abandoned when the South African Prime Minister Botha indicated on 4 November that he did not want Australian or any foreign troops unless it proved absolutely necessary. Using de Wet's own tactics against him, Botha defeated and captured him in December (Bill Nasson, Springboks on the Somme, *Penguin, Johannesburg and New York, 2007, pp.35–59; Sandra Swart, '"A Boer and his gun and his wife are three things always together": Republican masculinity and the 1914 rebellion',* Journal of Southern African Studies, *vol.24, no.4, Dec. 1998, pp.737–51; Antonio Garcia,* The First Campaign Victory of the Great War: South Africa, Manoeuvre Warfare, the Afrikaner Rebellion and the German South West African Campaign, 1914–1915, *Helion, Solihull, 2019, ch.4).*

Oct. 26 Travelled with Crewe from Postwick, Norwich.[94]

We concurred in all our views regarding situation. No feature at the cabinet. We decided to send Australian troops by Mauritius, in case reqd in S.A.

Crewe's summary view of the situation was conveyed to Lansdowne the next day: 'The wastage from the original expeditionary force has been terrific on the army, as in the others, altogether beyond the rate contemplated by experts, and this though transport and organization have in the main stood the test well, though there has been no epidemic, and no business conditions of hardship' (Lansdowne MSS, Bowood).

Oct. 28 We discussed recruiting. George let fly at K. of K. because he had taken Welsh regiments into his new army & prevented a Welsh Division or corps being formed. He let him have it straight. K. said he would resign. P.M. said that was not practical.

[94] Postwick in Norfolk was a Rosebery family estate. The Manor House in the village was a shooting lodge of Lord Rosebery's younger son, the Hon. Neil Primrose, MP for Wisbech. Capt. Primrose, who had spent several months there each year since 1910, was, as JAP noted in his hunting diary, 'out

According to Margot Asquith, her husband related in a midnight conversation that: 'They both lost their tempers. LlG was ill-mannered and insolent, and they both resigned. After lunch Ll.G. was quite normal.' The story given to Venetia Stanley was more consistent with JAP's: 'it looked as if either or both of them wd resign... K. is much the most to blame' (Asquith Letters, *p.291). Margot Asquith records (28 Oct. 1914) Edwin Montagu adding that he was 'too glad K. was sat on! He richly deserves it after snubbing Jack Pease in his admirable plan of amusing the new army in the evening...'* (Margot Asquith's Great War Diary *1914–1916, p.45).*

In a speech at the Queen's Hall on 19 September, DLG had called for a 'Welsh Army in the Field'. Official sanction had been given on 10 October 1914 for a Welsh Corps of two Divisions to be raised by public subscription. The 'Welsh Army Corps' was never formed, but two months later, the 43rd Division was created, originally part of the Fifth New Army. When the Fourth New Army was broken up in April 1915, the Division was renumbered 38th (Welsh), and assigned to the Fourth. By late 1916 the Welsh character of the 38th Division had been heavily diluted. Robin Barlow suggests that around 20 per cent of the volunteers into the Welsh Regiment might have been English (http://www.walesonline.co.uk/news/wales-news/new-history-wales-dr-robin-1889475, accessed 23 May 2014). DLG was said to have declared that it was a 'Nonconformist Division' notwithstanding, according to Anglican sources, 'the overwhelming evidence to the contrary' (Michael Snape, God and the British soldier: religion and the British Army in the First and Second World Wars, *Routledge, 2005, p.145).*

In a path-breaking analysis of 'Taffs in the trenches: Welsh national identity and military service 1914–1918', Chris Williams concludes that 'quantitative evidence points strongly towards ethnic heterogeneity as being a very common characteristic of Welsh regiments' (Matthew Cragoe and Chris Williams eds, Wales and War: Society, Politics and Religion in the Nineteenth and Twentieth Centuries, *U. of Wales P., Cardiff, 2007, pp.156–7). Barlow,* Wales and World War One, *pp.107–17, gathers what is known of the geographic, occupational, and religious backgrounds of 'the Welsh soldier'. On the 'sense of detachment' affecting Welsh recruiting see Pennell,* A Kingdom United, *pp.154–6; and for the creation of a national uniform consequent on a shortage of khaki and equipment for the new Welsh units see Clive Hughes, 'The Welsh Army Corps 1914–15',* Imperial War Museum Review, *no.1, 1986, pp.91–100.*

John Pollock, Kitchener, *Robinson, 2002 [1st edn Constable 2001], ch.18, is a well-documented account of the Secretary of State's difficulties with DLG in October 1914. One of the problems all Kitchener's Cabinet colleagues had with him was described by JAP:*

at war' with the Royal Bucks Hussars. JAP, Crewe, Montagu, Jack Tennant, and Lord Annaly (MFH Pytchley Hunt) had shot partridges over the Rosebery estate on 24–5 Oct. (JAP's hunting diary, MS. Gainford 75; Anne Carter, *Postwick — The History of a Norfolk Village*, 1987).

> In counsel I always found it difficult to know... whom Lord Kitchener was particularly addressing, and at whom he was looking; one eye seemed to be following the other, and he was apparently incapable of concentrating his attention on any one particular person. The result was, frequently, that two or more of his colleagues desired to reply to him at the same moment.
>
> *(War Reminiscences, ch.VIII, p.78, MS. Gainford 36/1)*

Oct. 30 K. asked for more pay for officers promoted out of ranks, George fell on his neck & gave him whatever advance he asked. They had the day before met & patched up their difference by some compromise in a transfer of Welsh battalions recruited into new units into a new Welsh Division.

Position with Turkey very strained, & ships authorised to hold or fire on Turkish gunboats outside Alexandria & prevent their passing into Red Sea.

A telegram from the Secretary of State for India to the Viceroy was despatched at 4.05 p.m. on 31 October: 'Russian Amb^r Constantinople having asked for his passports yesterday Mallet and French Amb^r followed suit & Mallet hopes to leave tonight. Cable communication with Constantinople is interrupted, & a state of war exists...'. A correction followed two days later: 'Although warlike operations have been undertaken war has not been formally declared and declaration may be delayed for a time. No official statement should therefore refer to declaration of war, but operations sd of course continue' (Draft telegrams, 31 Oct., 2 Nov. 1914, Crewe MSS I/19 (2), CUL).

While DLG and Kitchener were patching up their differences, the BEF's I Corps was fighting for its life in the Ypres sector. This would have been a shock to Cabinet ministers, who had been told that day by Kitchener of messages from Sir John French that were 'satisfactory in substance and confident in tone. The enemy makes no way, and is being slowly but steadily pushed back' (HHA Cabinet letter, 30 Oct. 1914, Bodl. MS. Asquith 7, f.224). 'Saturday 31 October was to be one of the most critical days fighting, not merely of 1914, but of the whole war.' (J.P. Harris, Douglas Haig and the First World War, *Cambridge UP, 2008, p.100.) The British were in retreat. They had lost part of Messines in the morning and Gheluvelt on the Ypres-Menin road, temporarily, in the afternoon. An emotional French, stiffened by an accidental meeting with Foch, ordered Haig to follow Foch's instructions and 'hold the ground you are now on'. Consequently, as Roy Prete comments, French had 'signified his full acceptance of Foch's right to lead' (*Strategy and Command...1914*, p.166). See also B.H. Liddell Hart,* Foch: The Man of Orleans, *2 vols, Penguin, 1937 [1st edn 1931], Vol. One, pp.149–52; Elizabeth Greenhalgh,* Foch in Command: The forging of a First World War general, *Cambridge UP, 2011, pp.65–7. HHA's private news bulletins at midnight on 31 October and the next morning indicate* *he had no appreciation of the gravity of the situation (Venetia Montagu MSS, passages omitted by the Brocks).*

'It was a regular touch & go business' on 31 October and 1 November, Lord Newton learned in a letter from the front, and the British force were only just saved in time by the French:

> you can judge of the situation by the fact that they had to use their last reserves in the trenches, and that Haig had personally to rally the fugitives close to the firing line. The 1st Division is reduced to 3000: the 7th Division to 2300 and certain battalions were wiped out. The 1st Coldstreams are commanded by the Quarter Master.
>
> *(Newton–Curzon, 1 Nov. 1914, Curzon of Kedleston MSS, BL: A & AS, MSS.Eur.F.112 E/3/7)*

Nov. 2 We were told the result of K's meeting with Joffre & Foch & Belgian General & the President at Dunkirk. K. did not realise why he had been sent for on Sunday unless it were to strike up an acquaintance. He thought Joffre lethargic. Foch a soldier. Our losses had been great, our men were tired, the Kaiser was throwing his legions still at us at Messines to take Ypres, the Kaiser being at Courtrai. Joffre promised battalions at once & an army corps forthwith in support.

At the inter-allied conference in Dunkirk on 1 November Kitchener was joined by the French President Raymond Poincaré, Alexandre Millerand, Alexandre Ribot, Paul Cambon, and Generals Joffre and Foch. The Belgian Chief of Cabinet (Prime Minister) Baron Charles de Broqueville was also present. We have found no record of a Belgian general. But it is possible that Colonel (later Lieutenant-General) Félix Maximilien Eugène Wielemans, Head of de Broqueville's Military Cabinet as Minister of War (1913–15); Deputy Chief of the General Staff of the Army Sept 1914–15 (the Chief of Staff post was unfilled) could have attended. A number of French officers (Generals Duparge and Bidon, Colonel de La Panouse, Commandants de Galbert and Muller) joined the party for dinner. We are indebted to Rob Troubleyn of the Royal Military Museum, Brussels, and Mario Draper of the U. of Kent for information about the known attendees; and to John Keiger for information from Poincaré's diary on the 1 November meeting.

*There was more to Kitchener's contribution to the meeting at Dunkirk than JAP's report suggests. He was, according to Foch, 'very anxious. He accosted me with the words: "well, so we are beaten!"' Kitchener subsequently asserted that there would be one million trained English soldiers in France by 1 July 1915, and conveyed to the French and Belgian ministers and generals the conviction that the war would last a very long time (*Memoirs of Marshal Foch*, pp.183–4; Charles d'Ydewalle [trs. Phyllis Mégroz],* Albert King of the Belgians*, Methuen, 1935, p.143). 'In imagined privacy', as Liddell Hart wrote, 'Kitchener mooted his intention of recalling Sir John French and replacing him by Sir Ian Hamilton.' Foch and Joffre,* *who themselves wanted French's recall, would not accept Kitchener's ageing friend 'Johnnie' Hamilton. They would have liked to see French's Chief of Staff, Maj.-Gen. Henry Wilson, in French's place. But Wilson's role in the Curragh incident was a stumbling block to significant preferment by the Asquith government. For Wilson's role as principal liaison officer with French Army Headquarters (GQG) see Gary Sheffield and John Spencer, 'Soldiers and Politicians in Strife: The Case of Henry Wilson in 1915', in Liddle ed.,* Britain and the Widening War, *pp.83–99.*

Content with the effective liaison arrangements Wilson had established, Joffre shifted his support back to French. Foch disclosed to French via Wilson that Kitchener had wanted Hamilton to command the BEF. French's position was secured when he sought an assurance of support from the government, and HHA said there was not a word of truth in a story he attributed to 'that poisonous fellow' Wilson (Prete, Strategy and Command…1914, *pp.172–5; Liddell Hart,* Foch, *Vol. One, pp.157–8; Esher journal, 24 Dec. 1914, Esher MSS, ESHR 2/13, CAC). For Col. Tom Bridges's report of HHA's fear that Wilson was 'capable of leading a revolution' see Wilson diary, 6 Feb. 2015, Wilson MSS.*

The discussions at Dunkirk are reconstructed from other sources (the memoirs of the French leaders, the HHA–Venetia Stanley correspondence, Hobhouse's diary, and a report in the Asquith MSS) in Cassar, Kitchener's War, *pp.112–13. The Kaiser's presence at Courtrai was known from intercepted wireless messages. 'The intercepted messages were circulated to the troops of the B.E.F., and the places through which the Kaiser was expected to pass were shelled, if within range, and bombed by our aircraft' (Brig. General J.E. Edmonds,* History of the Great War…Military Operations France and Belgium 1914, *Vol. II, Macmillan, 1925, p.349).*

Churchill told us the *Königsberg* was now in an East African River, & the *Pelham* & *Fox* were ready to deal with her.

The Königsberg *had been lost since 20 September, when it sank the* Pegasus *off Zanzibar. It was discovered by the light cruiser* Chatham *on 30 October in the delta of the Rufiji River. It had mined the river and entrenched its troops so an immediate British attack was out of the question; a blockade was begun. The old light cruiser* Fox, *waiting off Mombasa for the Indian Expeditionary Force to arrive in East Africa, took part in the blockade. We have found no trace of a ship called* Pelham. *WSC was perhaps referring to the* Chatham.

With his eyes on actual battlefields, JAP made no mention of Grey's report on the obscure situation in Turkey and the Cabinet's opinion that Britain ought to take 'a vigorous offensive', and make every effort to bring in Bulgaria, Greece, 'and above all Roumania'. The Cabinet decided the next day that the time for an official declaration of war against Turkey had come. 'Britain', Lyn Curtwright notes, 'had been waging war against the Turks for three days without the sanction of the Cabinet' (Muddle, Indecision and Setback, *p.47; and HHA's reports to the King, TNA: CAB 41/35/56, 57).*

Wed. Nov. 4 Whilst French wired 'Foch & I agree in thinking that the enemy cannot now possibly succeed in the Ypres or Calais direction' yet we knew that our casualties in these prolonged battles from Nieuport to La Bassie had killed off an enormous number of our men, though insignificant to the hosts slaughtered by the oncoming solid phalanxes of the enemy.

For the turning point reached at the beginning of November, and the role of the 'man who saved Calais' see Spencer Jones, '"The Demon": Brigadier-General Charles FitzClarence V.C.', in Spencer Jones ed., Stemming the Tide, *pp.240–62. On casualties, the figures as they were officially known are in* Statistics of the Military Effort of the British Empire During the Great War. 1914–1920, *HMSO, 1922, Part IV; Beckett* et al., The British Army, *p.89.*

The news from Chile was bad. The *Monmouth & Cape of Good Hope* were sunk, apparently with all lives, owing to some mistaken enterprise by Cradock[95] in taking on the *Scharnhorst & Gneisenau* with 16 8 inch guns with the support of the old *Canopus* with her big guns. Churchill showed how all our losses had occurred through folly on part of trusted naval officers. In clearing himself of blame he went further in the Cabinet than was necessary, as no one ought to hold him responsible for tactics at sea but he just longs to be in command.

JAP had learned about this 'very black day' while lunching at 10 Downing Street (JAP–EP, 5 Nov. 1914, MS. Gainford 189/65). WSC's sensitivity over the 'sore disappointment' of the fight off Coronel lingered for months (WSC–Walter Long, 12 Dec. 1914, BL RP2175). Yet, so far from blaming WSC, the Cabinet concluded on 4 November that 'this incident, like the escape of the Goeben, *the loss of the* Cressy *& her two sister-cruisers & that of the* Hermes[96] *last week, is not creditable to the officers of the Navy'* (Bodl. MS. Asquith *7, f.228). Robin Prior excoriates the breakdown of Admiralty staff work that created confusion about*

[95] Rear-Adm. Sir Christopher George Francis Maurice Cradock (1862–1914); cmdr, Nth America and West Indies station 1913–14; entered navy 1875; Rear-Adm. 1910; KCVO 1912. He went down with his ship, HMS *Good Hope* not HMS *Cape of Good Hope*. For a brief study of Cradock's fate: Jack Sweetman, 'Coronel: Anatomy of a Disaster', in Gerald Jordan, *Naval Warfare in the Twentieth Century 1900–1945: Essays in honour of Arthur Marder*, Croom Helm, 1977, pp.70–89. A memorial in York Cathedral was unveiled by Balfour in June 1916.

[96] *Hermes*, an old cruiser converted into a seaplane tender, was sunk by a submarine off Calais on 31 Oct., 'lost by neglect of orders', according to Churchill (Emmott diary, 2 Nov. 1914, MS. Emmott, I/2, Nuffield Col.).

Cradock's orders (Conquer We Must: A Military History of Britain 1914–1945, *Yale UP, New Haven, 2022, pp.57–9. Attending a memorial service for Cradock, the wife of a fellow admiral noticed: 'no uniforms & nothing naval about it... nobody from the Admy who are trying to hush up the whole matter in a most disgraceful way...'. Why, she asked Lord Charles Beresford, did he not as an MP stand up in the House of Commons and 'try to clear the memory of an admiral whom he & all the navy looked upon as a gallant officer...?' Beresford told her he had considered doing so, but desisted on advice from party leaders that it might be harmful to party interests (Victoria Wemyss diary, 13 and 24 Nov.1914, Wester-Wemyss MSS, WMYS 9/1, CAC).*

Friday Nov. 6 Churchill told us he was proposing to send the *Carnarvon, Cornwall, Kent* & *Defence* (with 4 9.5 guns) to assist the *Canopus* & *Glasgow*, who were now at the Falkland Islands.

He asked permission to build *Albion* & *Goliath* Monitor class. He would have the *Minotaur, Warrior* & *Black Prince* off Ascension.[97]

To order from U.S.A. £1.800,000 ? rifles or shells from Steel Trust, & guns for monitor class 14.8" to be delivered in 6 mos; 20 new sub. to deliver in 7. mos. in addition to 8 now building; 100 field guns (18lb shell) for army; 100 field guns for navy.

The American State Department had released advice to the press on 15 October saying that it had no authority to prevent the sale of goods, including munitions, to belligerents. This cleared the way for British purchases. The War Office had already sent agents to assess the capacity of American companies, and a Cabinet Committee on Munitions decided on 21 October that at least 400,000 more rifles than could be provided by British firms would be needed by July 1915. A two-man negotiating team had been despatched on 24 October (Kathleen Burk, Britain, America and the Sinews of War, 1914–1918, *George Allen & Unwin, Boston, 1985, pp.14–15). Charles Schwab of Bethlehem Steel met Jacky Fisher and WSC at the Admiralty on 3 November. Large orders were placed for monitors and submarines (Gaddis Smith,* Britain's clandestine submarines, 1914–1915, *Yale UP, New Haven, 1964).*

Report made of disaster on German E.A & Indian troops cut up & failing to stand against entrenched Germans.

[97] *Carnarvon* was a Devonshire class armoured cruiser; *Cornwall*, a Monmouth class armoured cruiser; *Defence*, a Minotaur class armoured cruiser; *Albion* and *Goliath* were Canopus class battleships. Two Erebus class Monitors were laid down by Harland and Wolff in Oct. 1915. Both the British and German fleets were slow in approaching the Falkland Islands at the beginning of Dec. But, as Graham Pascoe writes, 'it was the Falklands' good luck...that at the vital moment, von Spee out-dawdled [Admiral] Sturdee'. The British battle cruisers arrived less than a day earlier than von Spee—trapping and overwhelming him with a greatly superior force (*The Battle of the Falklands, 1914: A Falklands perspective*, p.28).

JAP's note about 'Indian troops' was a reference to the Indian expeditionary forces in Tanga, which had been repulsed in a few days with many casualties (S.D. Pradhan, Indian army in East Africa, *1914–1918, National Book Organisation, New Delhi, 1991, pp.56–71; Strachan,* The First World War, *Vol. I, pp.579–84). It might also have reflected the situation on the Western Front. Reports were cascading in of the disintegration of Indian units whose British officers were being killed at an alarming rate. The BEF Adj.-Gen. Sir Nevil Macready had wired the War Office on 5 November that regiments that had lost British officers were 'useless'. The casualty figures suggested that well over half of the wounds to Indian soldiers were self-inflicted. The American surgeon Harvey Cushing was told in May 1915 of a 'disproportion' between the left-hand wounds of Indian and other troops 'too great to be a mere accident of figures' (*From A Surgeon's Journal *1915–1918, Constable 1936, p.59). Col. Arthur Osburn RAMC wrote of many Indians with a single penetrating wound in the right hand (*Unwilling Passenger, *Faber & Faber, 1936). However, a secret analysis of 1,000 cases carried out the same year by Col. Sir Bruce Seton Bt, commander of the Kitchener Indian Hospital at Brighton, concluded that there was 'no evidence of self-infliction of wounds that could be supported by statistical examination'. The contrast between Seton's more relaxed regime at the Kitchener Hospital and the Pavilion and Dome hospitals is highlighted in Joyce Collins,* Dr Brighton's Indian Patients December 1914–January 1916, *Brighton Books Publishing, 1997. Andrew Tait Jarboe shows what the government wanted to be believed in 'Propaganda and Empire in the Heart of Europe: Indian Soldiers in Hospital and Prison, 1914–1918', in Andrew Tait Jarboe and Richard S. Fogarty eds,* Empires in World War I: Shifting Frontiers and Imperial Dynamics in a Global Conflict, *Bloomsbury Academic, 2020, pp.107–35. For the difficulties in replacing the Indian Army officers who were being transferred into the Home Army, there is a well-researched account in Adam John Prime, 'The Indian Army's British Officer Corps, 1861–1921', Ph.D. thesis, U. of Leicester, 2018, pp.62–9; and, for logistics and combat deployment, Graham Winton, 'British–Indian Cavalry: From Mobilisation to the Western Front 1915', in Spencer Jones ed.,* Courage Without Glory, *pp.146–79.*

Denied his request for two British brigades to strengthen the Indian Corps, the Corps commander Lt-Gen. Sir James Willcocks had executed two soldiers who had self-inflicted hand wounds, and announced on 14 November that soldiers with such wounds would be returned to the front lines rather than, as they evidently had hoped, repatriated to India. A year later, there having been no perceptible improvement in morale or effectiveness in the field, the Indian Corps was withdrawn from the Western Front (Santanu Das, 'The Indian sepoy in the First World War', http://www.bl.uk/world-war-one/articles/the-indian-sepoy-in-the-first-world-war, accessed 23 Jan. 2016; George Morton-Jack, The Indian Army on the Western Front: India's Expeditionary Force to France and Belgium in the First World War,

Cambridge UP, 2014, passim*; Vedica Kant,* 'If I die here, who will remember me?': India and the First World War, *pp.39–49; Rob Johnson, '"I Shall Die Arms in Hand, Wearing the Warriors' Clothes": Mobilisation and Initial Operations of the Indian Army in France and Flanders', in Alan Jeffreys ed.,* The Indian army in the First World War: new perspectives, *Helion & Co., Solihull, 2018, pp.40–51). More comprehensive is Shrabani Basu,* For King and Another Country: Indian Soldiers on the Western Front 1914–18, *Bloomsbury, New Delhi, 2015. For the sunny perception of Sir Walter Lawrence, formerly of the Indian Civil Service and private secretary to Curzon as Viceroy, on the conditions of convalescent Indian troops in France ('they are comfortable, contented and grateful') see Lawrence–Keogh, 15 Dec. 1914; Lawrence–Kitchener, 31 Dec. 1914,* RAMC 446/7, CMAC, *Wellcome I).*

Discussed how to attack *Königsberg* in Harbour *Chatham* next day.

Churchill & Kitchener to arrange what should be done. No minister seems responsible for attack of G. E. Africa. Criticism on Defence Comtee Staff having arranged this attack.

The Königsberg *saga would continue until July 1915, when two shallow draft river gun boats, HMS* Mersey *and* Severn, *were towed out from Malta, brought six-inch guns to bear from a range of five miles, and disabled the cruiser. The British retired, leaving the Germans to strip the ship of its guns and other fittings (Kevin Patience,* Königsberg: A German East African Raider, *Zanzibar Publications, 2nd edn, 2001).*

Nov. 9 Monday King's Speech. Desultory conversation re recruiting. I was asked to get out statement as to result of recruiting, K. to raise 500,000 more men. Now got

274,000 at front, less losses
206,000 reserve
700,000 new army
1,180,000 men under arms with territorials at home
1,250,000
P.M's Guild Hall Speech (he dealt with Turkish situation & declaration of war).

Nov. 11 Wednesday Churchill reported the loss of the *Emden* & 200 men on board in the Cocos Islands.

On 9 November the Emden *had attacked the wireless station on Cocos Island but had been caught by the Australian light cruiser* Sydney. *The* Emden *had sailed into Penang Harbour on 28 October disguised with a false extra funnel, painted British battleship dark*

grey, and flying what was taken to be a White Ensign. A Russian light cruiser and a French destroyer were lost.

K. reported Dixmude had been taken by the Germans, that it was not much value as it could not be effectively occupied by either side, as it had been demolished. Newspapers Bureau debate & how to deal with the Press flouting the S.G. We discussed action to counteract Turkey in Egypt &c. Edward Grey never spoke, & slept soundly, dead beat. Hobhouse brought up case against Churchill of having placed under arrest — 40 men in Sutherland Postal Service. I said compensate — Churchill had acted arbitrarily under provocation, a letter had been opened & the private flag signal having been discovered.

Hobhouse records the incident:

> On the 11th, I brought up a stupid act of W.S.C. for which I could in private get no redress. Last Friday his Admiral, Stanley Colville, arrested & imprisoned in the local gaol without warning the whole of the postal staff of Lerwick, on the ground that some of his letters had been tampered with. They were kept in prison for 7 days and then released, a committee of experts having decided that the wiseacre of an Admiral had accidentally cut open his own letter which was enclosed in 3 envelopes. The Cabinet decided that the Admiralty must pay compensation, but Churchill would not consent to consider such cases jointly with the P.O. until I threatened to cut off all his own & the Fleet's postal or telegraphic communication. He behaved like an untruthful & spoilt schoolboy, which leavened by genius for speech is what he really is.
>
> *(David ed., Inside Asquith's Cabinet, p.206)*

Thursday Nov. 12 I dined with the P.M. at Downing Street. I played with him afterwards against Lytton[98] & Lady Helen Vincent.[99] No news came in. I gave the

[98] Victor Alexander George Robert Bulwer-Lytton, 2nd Earl of Lytton (1876–1947); 3rd Bt Bulwer, 3rd Baron Lytton of Knebworth, and 2nd Earl of Lytton 1891; Civil Ld Admy 1916–1917, 1919–20; British Commissioner of Propaganda in France 1918; PC 1919; Gov. Bengal 1922–7; KG 1933. A long friendship with WSC foundered when WSC would not support women's suffrage legislation (Lyndsey Jenkins, *Lady Constance Lytton: Aristocrat, Suffragette, Martyr*, Biteback Publishing, 2015, pp.174,258).

[99] Lady Helen Vincent, Lady D'Abernon (1866–1954); dau. 1st Earl of Feversham, 'one of the loveliest, if not the loveliest, lady of my time' (Sir Lionel Earle, *Turn Over the Page*, Hutchinson, 1935, p.47), m. 1890 Sir Edgar Vincent (1857–1941); younger son Sir F. Vincent, 11th Bt. She had ceased to be Lady Helen Vincent in July 1914 when her husband became Baron D'Abernon. He was Fin. Adviser to Egyptian Govt 1883–9; KCMG 1887; Gov. Imperial Ottoman Bank 1889–97; Con. MP Exeter 1899–1906; chmn Central Control Bd (liquor traffic) 1915–20; GCMG 1917; Amb. to Berlin 1920–6; PC 1920; GCB and Vt D'Abernon 1926 (R.P.T. Davenport-Hines and Jean-Jacques Van Helten, 'Edgar Vincent, Viscount D'Abernon, and the Eastern Investment company in London, Constantinople and Johannesburg', in R.P.T. Davenport-Hines ed., *Speculators and Patriots: Essays in Business Biography*, Frank Cass, 1986, pp.35–61).

P.M. the figures of recruitment up to date: 897,186 = Territorials 236,000 Regulars 661,186. England 13.8 per cent Scotld 16.7 per cent Ireland 5.7 per cent of those available age. If we recruited another million 15 per cent more wanted = 28.2 per cent.

Details of recruiting can be seen in JAP's Cabinet memorandum, 'Recruiting in proportion to population', 12 Nov. 1914 (TNA: CAB 37/122/164). His figures were tentative, as recruiting returns showed only a man's place of recruitment, not his place of residence. Nor was he able to make any allowance for the presence of special industries or reserved occupations, which would depress the figures for their localities. Naval figures were unavailable. The figures for England are the figures for England and Wales.

There was nothing in JAP's figures to suggest the need for any revision to the assurance given by Crewe to Lord Bryce in asking him to second the address when the Lords next met: 'I do not anticipate any invitation by the Government to the country to contemplate anything in the nature of compulsory service. The recruiting returns have been curiously patchy, and some districts and some classes seem still to be apathetic... But it seems as though the required force will be forthcoming; and it would only be in a desperate necessity, which we do not contemplate, that public opinion would oblige us to have recourse to any measure of the sort' (Crewe–Bryce, 5 Nov. 1914, copy, Crewe MSS, C/3, CUL). Public opinion might not yet have been stirred by desperate necessity, but, as Lord Newton noted in his diary on November 7: 'Everyone, press included, talking of compulsion. Daily News & other Radical papers repudiating the idea' (Newton MSS). Shortages of men were being masked by a haphazard reinforcement system (Thomas E. Davies, 'Sustaining Britain's First "Citizen Army": the Creation and Evolution of Reinforcement Policy for Kitchener's New Armies, 1914–1916', BJMilHist, *vol.8, no.1, 2022, pp. 20–39).*

In fact, as Robertson Nicoll told the editor of The Spectator *on 11 November, DLG and Kitchener already had an understanding about how to advance towards compulsory service. DLG had taken a first step in a public speech the night before in which he said: 'I should like to see each county called upon for its quota... to see every town, every city, every area know what is expected of it...'. He had put the idea before Kitchener, who said that it meant that every district that did not contribute its quota would be liable to conscription. 'I know that very well...', was the Chancellor's response. 'Then I can have no objection...', Kitchener had said. The Cabinet, on the other hand, rejected the idea (Robertson Nicoll–J. St Loe Strachey, 11, 18 Nov. 1914, Strachey MSS, courtesy of the editor of* The Spectator, *now in the Parliamentary Archives).*

In response to an overwhelming number of volunteers, a large proportion of whom were deemed unfit for service, Kitchener announced on 11 November that the minimum height for army recruits was raised from 5'3" to 5'6". From 136,160 in the week ending 12 November, enlistment dropped to 44,679 in the next seven days (David Silbey, 'Bodies and Cultures

Collide: Enlistment, the Medical Exam, and the British Working Class, 1914–1916', Social History of Medicine, *vol.17, no.1, 2004, pp.61–76).*

On Irish recruiting Edwin Montagu wrote to the Prime Minister on 12 November about the War Office's 'irritating deliberate obstruction' of attempts to form distinctive Irish units: 'The Secretary of State for War told Redmond that he was not trying to raise English Scottish, or Irish Armies, but a British Army . . .'. In spite of the impediments, 34,000 men had volunteered for the new armies, 13,000 of them from Ulster, of whom '10,000 are Carson's men, and 3,000 are Roman Catholics' (Bodl. MS. Asquith 41, ff.180–4).

For recent research on recruitment trends in the first three months of the war see Bostridge, The Fateful Year, *pp.246–60. On Irish recruiting 1914–15, L.W. Brady has a thoughtful discussion in* T.P. O'Connor and the Liverpool Irish, *Royal Historical Society and Humanities P., New Jersey, 1983, pp.220–3. For an exemplary analysis see David Fitzpatrick, 'The Logic of Collective Sacrifice: Ireland and the British Army, 1914–1918',* HJ, *vol.38, no.4, 1995, pp.1017–30, and Fitzpatrick's extended chapter, 'Ireland and the Great War', in Thomas Bartlett ed.,* The Cambridge History of Ireland, Vol. IV, 1880 to the Present, *Cambridge UP, 2018, pp.223–57. James McConnel, 'Recruiting Sergeants for John Bull? Irish Nationalist MPs and Enlistment during the Early Months of the Great War',* WiH, *vol.14, no.4, 2007, pp.408–28, is valuable; an updated review of the literature is Richard S. Grayson, 'Ireland', http://encyclopedia.1914-1918-online.net/article/ireland (accessed 21 Aug. 2016), which should be read in conjunction with Keith Jeffery,* Ireland and the Great War, *Cambridge UP, 2000, pp.5–36, which suggests Fitzpatrick overestimates Irish recruiting; and Beckett* et al., The British Army, *pp.108–12. Nicholas Hiley carries the story further into 1915 in 'Sir Hedley Le Bas and the Origins of Domestic Propaganda in Britain 1914–1917',* European Journal of Marketing, *vol.21, no.8, 1987, pp.30–48.*

Education department files contain evidence of JAP's response to a young school teacher seeking guidance on where his duty lay:

Albert Villa,
Barton Road,
Ely.
Nov. 12th 1914

The Rt. Hon. J. Pease, Esq., M.P.

Dear Sir,

I venture to write to you on a personal matter hoping that you may be able to tender me some advice.

I am anxious at this time to render the utmost possible service to my country but the path of duty is not clear to me.

I am an Assistant-Master in a boys' school here. There is no other Assistant, and of course there is the Headmaster, who is an elderly man.

I feel the call to military service but special circumstances have deterred me from offering my services.

In the first place, I am far from strong although it is possible that at the present time I might pass the required medical test, but I fear that the hard rigorous military duties would soon impair my health. But of course there is the possibility that I should be able to stand the rougher mode of life.

My headmaster thinks it is my duty to remain in the school. My leaving the school would undoubtedly make things very much harder for him and he regards it as unlikely that he would be granted a man in my place. He was good enough to speak in an appreciative manner of my work in the school & my influence with the boys. I quite realise that, for myself, the classroom is more my place than the Training Camp, but the call for Men has unsettled me.

What is my Duty? & am I, in your opinion, best serving the interests of my country by continuing my scholastic work—work to which I am very much attached?

I have the honour to remain.

Your obedient servant,
H. W. Benjafield.
(TNA: ED 24/1683/8157)

COPY
PERSONAL
13th November, 1914

Dear Sir,

Thanks for your letter of November 12th. I sympathise with your difficulties and would gladly assist you with any advice in my power, but at the same time I feel that you must be guided largely by your own personal feelings in deciding whether the balance of public advantage lies on the side of volunteering for military service or on the side of continuing in the public service of Education. Speaking as a fellow member of the Educational Service of the Country, there seems to me so much to be done by all of us in bringing home to the generation passing through our schools the lessons of the war, in keeping before them the principles for which we are fighting, in preparing them for the struggles that may be before them as a result of the sacrifices which the war entails, and in teaching our duty towards those whom the war had plunged into distress, whether our own kinsmen or aliens, that in my opinion the public service which a Schoolmaster can render by sticking to his post is quite comparable in importance and value with military service in the field. I do not think, therefore, that if you decide to continue your work as a Schoolmaster you need fear that you will not be playing a man's part. But it is impossible for me to judge in which capacity you can best serve your Country.

Yours faithfully,
(Sd.) JOSEPH A. PEASE.
(TNA: ED 24/1683/8157)

Harry Wilfred Benjafield (1890–1949) had been appointed as a trained certificated assistant at Needham's School in Ely on 5 September 1910. On 20 July 1915 he was granted leave of absence to enlist (Isle of Ely County Council Education Committee Minutes). He served in the 6th Divisional Signal Company, Army Service Corps (https://livesofthefirstworldwar.org/lifestory/5005869#facts, accessed 24 May 2014) and ended the war as Private, Acting Sergeant.

Friday Nov. 13 Cabinets at 12.0 to 1.50, & from 4.0 to 5.45. We discussed for over an hour—Buckmaster attended, made out his case. K. declined to prosecute at present. I urged a warning, my suggestion not accepted but no other made. K. undertook to court martial *Times* (Ld Northcliffe on first good case).

Harcourt, 'suffering from a good deal of heart weakness', told Morley on 13 November he was spending all his time in bed except when he was allowed to attend Cabinet meetings. A week earlier JAP had cancelled a visit to Nuneham because of Harcourt's indisposition (Bodl. MS. Harcourt 427, f.259; JAP–EP, 5 Nov. 1915, MS. Gainford 189/64). Charles Hobhouse's account of what happened after Sir Stanley Buckmaster, Director of the Press Bureau, had made his case portrays some more colourful exchanges:

Ll.G. & W.S.C. had some high words. Buckmaster had attended to explain he could not maintain the authority of Press Censor unless the W.O. and Admiralty supported him fully. K. as usual tried to control the exercise of censoring the press, but would not incur the odium of restraining much less prosecuting the press. Churchill

> supported him in what Ll.G. truly called a mean & shabby attack on Buckmaster. W.S.C. became white (or green) with anger, denounced Ll. G.'s 'insolence' which he would not tolerate from anyone; Ll.G. responded equally hotly, & the P.M. intervened.
> *(David ed., Inside Asquith's Cabinet, pp.206–7)*

Buckmaster told McKenna on 14 November that the only conditions on which the Press Bureau could operate were that it should be given information as soon as possible and that the press should be given harmless news immediately. The Bureau must have the final decision on publication. Delayed permission to release news of the capture of the Emden *had led to public complaints (Buckmaster MSS, copy courtesy of the Hon. Barbara Miller). That the system continued to run less than smoothly was illustrated by the Press Bureau's handling of a Central News story early in December which Sir Reginald Brade at the War Office had said did not need to be referred to them. Brade knew nothing of the report (that Lord Esher was to lead a committee to inquire into Admiralty and War Office contracts) but he saw no harm in publication. When the story appeared in several newspapers as 'officially' announced, Brade asked the Press Bureau what the authority was for this, instancing the* Daily Express, *'that being the paper I read with a morning cup of tea'. The Bureau then demanded an explanation of what the Express meant. As Brade explained to the* Express *editor Ralph Blumenfeld, this was not what he intended. 'I am afraid the Press Bureau misunderstand their functions' (Brade–Blumenfeld, 6 Dec. 1914, Blumenfeld MSS).*

*A month later it was rumoured that Buckmaster 'seldom now goes to the Press Bureau, and... the Press generally has formed a very bad opinion of him and of the spirit which he has introduced into the Press Censorship' (Charles Ed. Jerningham–Sir William Bull, 14 Jan. 1915, Bull MSS, BULL 4/11, CAC). Buckmaster's biographer, R.F.V. Heuston, wrote that for 'a man of Buckmaster's meticulous habits and sensitive cast of mind' the Press Bureau task was 'something of a nightmare'. Buckmaster was well aware that the 'proper execution of my duties' was impeded by the support and encouragement that the Northcliffe press in particular enjoyed from within the government (*Lives of the Lord Chancellors 1885–1940, *Clarendon P., Oxford, 1964, pp.262–3). He had lamented to Riddell on 9 October: 'How would you like to control an office staffed by men whom you have not appointed, whom you cannot dismiss, and most of whom have been appointed in order to find them jobs at £300 or £400 per annum?' (McEwen ed.,* The Riddell Diaries, *p.92).*

At the War Council on 28 January 1915 a discussion of the indiscretions of the Daily Mail *elicited Crewe's opinion that most of the trouble was with the 'Harmsworth press'. The* Daily Chronicle *had been indiscreet; the* Daily Telegraph *had been 'a model of discretion'. WSC pointed out how difficult it was to maintain an effective censorship: 'no country had nearly so large or such an influential press as our own...'. Suggestions that Buckmaster might be replaced by Field Marshal Lord Nicholson or General Sir Neville Lyttelton were not taken up. Balfour characteristically contributed that it was extremely difficult for the Censor to keep the secrets unless he knew the secrets. To Balfour's rumination that 'something might be done by approaching Lord Northcliffe', a realistic DLG was quick to point out that Northcliffe was 'above all things a journalist and could not help putting his journalistic influences before everything else' (TNA: CAB 42/1/26). Bone,* Beyond the Rule of Law, *ch.2, has more on Buckmaster's frustrations.*

We then were given George's budget proposals & agreed to raise price of beer p. glass by ½d & to give back something to Brewers for diminished sales — 25/- p. barrel less 7/- for reduction sales; Tea to be up 3*d.* to 8*d.* p. lb; Income Tax to be doubled all round: estimate to meet deficiency of 206 millions, 28M this year, next year £68,000,000 new taxes to meet Estimated War Expenditure of £500,000,000 to March 31; Loan to be raised at 95 bearing 3½% repayable in 13 years.

*In the first entry of the second volume of his diary (MS. Gainford 40), under the heading '1915', JAP set out the 'particulars given by the Chancellor of the Exchequer to the Cabinet when he issued the war loan'. The estimate of expenditure to 31 March 1915 was £538,483,000, of which £331,550,000 was 'expenditure on war'. Interest on war expenditure was estimated at £3,750,000; army £191 million; navy £83,450,000; civil £7,800,000; loans £3 million; colonies £31,750,000 (Canada £12 million; 'Cape' £7 million; Australia £7,500,000; New Zealand £5,250,000). The expected deficit, after allowing for normal revenue, was £342,687,000. The increased yield from income tax would be £46 million; from the ½*d. *on beer £2,150,000. The proposed loan was of £350,000,000 issued at a generous 95, and yielding approximately four per cent.*

For a distillation of the modern literature on 1914–15 war finance see Martin Horn, 'War Finance (Great Britain and Ireland)', in Ute Daniel, Peter Gatrell, Oliver Janz, Heather Jones, Jennifer Keene, Alan Kramer, and Bill Nasson eds, 1914-1918-online. International Encyclopedia of the First World War, *Freie Universität Berlin, 2016-1024. DOI: http://dx.doi.org/10.15463/ie1418.10986, accessed 29 Dec. 2016. The huge concealed shortfall in the 1914 war loan, first revealed by R.S. Sayers in* The Bank of England 1891–1944: Vol. 1, *Cambridge UP, 1976, p.81, is told in detail in Michael Anson, Norma Cohen, Alastair Owens, and Daniel Todman, 'Your country needs funds: The extraordinary story of Britain's early efforts to finance the First World War' (bankunderground.co.uk/2017/08/08, accessed 13 Aug. 2017).*

K. would not discuss my paper on recruiting as he had not read it.

Nov. 16 Lord Roberts' funeral.

Nov. 17 Cabinet — desultory war talk.

HHA, Grey, DLG, and Balfour were attending a French War Cabinet meeting on the 17th (J.F.V. Keiger, Raymond Poincaré, *Cambridge UP, 1997, p.223). Cabinet met on 16 and 18 November, not the 17th, and discussed army pay; Bulgaria and Roumania; Egypt; and proclaiming a protectorate over Egypt (HHA Cabinet letter, 18 Nov. 1914, TNA: CAB 41/35/60). On the 17th Harcourt told Kitchener he was 'staggered' by the Secretary of State's statement at the Cabinet the previous day that he agreed with Harcourt's suggestion that the Australian and New Zealand contingents should be stopped in Egypt and train there until the spring. He had immediately denied making such a suggestion, and had determined that the idea had not come from anyone in the Colonial Office. 'Perhaps you had in your mind my suggestion, which you adopted, that the Maoris should go to Egypt or the Sudan' (Bodl. MS. Harcourt 464, f.150).*

The 'desultory war talk' would have interested the GOC First Army, Sir Douglas Haig, who wrote to Sir Charles Harris at the War Office that day:

> We have had terrible hard fighting. I thought on the 3rd Nov. the fatigue had got beyond the limit of physical endurance for the troops! But somehow we have managed to keep things going.
>
> The truth is that our little army has been placed on too large fronts so that there are no reserves available for resting troops in the front line... These French will drain the last drop of blood from the British soldier if we allow them.
>
> *(Harris MSS A30 1, Balliol Col.)*

Nov. 20 [Cabinet] suppression of Irish Papers.

HHA kept no letter to the King describing a 20 November meeting, but the Cabinet was probably discussing the regulations to be applied under the Defence of the Realm Act, which were published 28 November 1914. They appeared in the Dublin Gazette *on 2 December, and seven newspapers were warned that they contained articles that were seditious. Copies of the December issue of* Irish Freedom *were seized. Three of the papers warned ceased publication, two changed their content, and two were 'dealt with' (B. Mac Giolla Choille ed.,* Intelligence Notes 1913–16, *Government Stationery Office, Dublin, 1966, p.116).*

Nov. 24 [Cabinet] discussed Toluol & Aniline dyes.[100]

[100] HHA Cabinet letter, 25 Nov. 1914, TNA: CAB 41/35/6. HHA had on 25 Nov. held a 'consultation', which as he told Balfour on the 24th 'can be technically called a meeting of a sub-committee of the

The War Office had appointed an Advisory Committee on Explosive Services chaired by Lord Moulton. Moulton was already working with a Committee on the Supply of Chemical Products headed by Lord Haldane. Before the war 80 per cent of dyes used in Britain were imported from Germany. Much of the other 20 per cent relied on German 'intermediates' derived from petroleum. Critical shortages threatened the viability of the textile industries. A German monopoly controlled the dwindling supplies of dye for the army's khaki uniforms. With the growing demand for explosives, the government was subsidising the production of picric acid and trinitrotoluene (TNT). Two tons of toluene were needed for every three tons of TNT, which was displacing Lyddite for shells. Cabinet appears to have had some forewarning of Moulton's report on 27 November that 'the only safe line of action therefore is to develop the production of these explosives to the utmost in every direction until the danger of shortage is removed' (William Van Der Kloot, 'Lord Justice of Appeal John Fletcher Moulton and Explosives Production in World War I: "The Mathematical Mind Triumphant"', Notes and Records, The Royal Society Journal of the History of Science, *vol.68, 2014, pp.171–86; Guy Hartcup,* The War of Invention: Scientific Developments, 1914–18, *Brassey's Defence Publishers, 1988, pp.44–9).*

Dr Emile Bucher, owner of a Jamaican dyewood factory whose views had been publicised in the British press, convinced Moulton that increased official involvement in the dye industry was essential. In July 1915 a new company, British Dyes Ltd, was formed and bought the leading dye manufacturer, Read Holliday & Sons of Huddersfield. The government contributed £1.7 million of the capital, and granted £100,000 for research, to be repaid in ten years. It had earlier decided to mount training programmes in the expectation that within six months Britain would be making 30 per cent of the previous normal consumption of dyestuffs (Harcourt diary, 16 Mar. 1915, Bodl. MS.Eng.c.8270). In 1926, British Dyestuffs merged with Nobel Industries, United Alkali, and Brunner, Mond, to form Imperial Chemical Industries (ICI). See H. W. Richardson, 'The Development of the British Dyestuffs Industry Before 1939', Scottish Journal of Political Economy, vol.9, issue 2, 1962, pp.110–29.

On 26 November, HMS Bulwark*, a London class pre-dreadnought with the 5th Battle Squadron attached to the Channel Fleet, was destroyed by an internal explosion while anchored near Sheerness. Among the 736 men killed, as the Cabinet learned the next day, was one of Walter Runciman's nephews, a Dartmouth naval cadet. The cause of the disaster was thought to be overheating of cordite charges left near a boiler room bulkhead: 'the vessel had been destroyed by the exploding of a magazine or magazines—it was not certain which—and it was probable that some loose ammunition or cordite may have been detonated by some*

C.I.D.', with WSC, Kitchener, DLG, Grey, Balfour and attendant experts to take 'a full survey' of the 'critical' military and naval situation (Balfour MSS, BL Add.MS. 49,692, ff.146–7).

means that caused the explosion' (Coroner's conclusion at http://www.wessexwfa.org.uk/articles/hms-bulwark.htm, accessed 25 Apr. 2018).

Nov. 27[101] [Cabinet] H. of C. Churchill told us how he proposed to deal with torpedo submarine craft in harbours, net in ships — use nets again — also sink enemy if she came up with guns to merchant men, concealed guns. House of Commons adjourned.

Dec. 1, 3, 8 Discussions on how to secure Bulgarian & Roumania, support Greece & Italy.

Grey took the view that Bulgaria would not be influenced by offers from the allies, that she was not anxious to fight, that she had better offers from Germany & Austria, who if on top would be able to give her terms she liked better than those we could offer with the assent of Greece & Servia. By making our offers more attractive, we might do no good but have all the Balkan states in opposition, & a clear road from Germany thro' Constantinople to Bagdad. Everything turned on the result of the arms of the allies being successful. Masterman took the view that Bulgaria was in sympathy with the allies, & could be brought in. We discussed loans to Denmark (£8M), France, Belgium (£10M). We agreed to give France a loan at 5 per cent to be raised here, not to finance Germany thro' Denmark or Belgium, but to restrict our help to Belgians outside area occupied by Germany in Belgium. Samuel thought it could be ear marked for food for the starving Belgians anywhere. We decided to decline Italy's attempt to borrow money unless Imperiali[102] could give us satisfactory information as to Italy joining the allies. It was thought the French were endeavouring by financing the Belgian army trying to secure a claim on her after the war.

Denmark did not get the loan but remained neutral throughout the war. Tage Kaarsted, Great Britain and Denmark 1914–1920, *Odense UP, 1979, p.104 and* passim, *is a good guide utilising Danish archival sources and publications as well as British diplomatic correspondence. On Danish efforts to bring about a negotiated peace early in the war see Wilhelm E Winterhager,* Mission fuer den Frieden europ. Maechtepolitik u. daen.

[101] Neither in the Asquith papers nor the Royal Archives is there a report to the King of a Cabinet meeting on 27 Nov. JAP's date and summary of the subject discussed are confirmed by Harcourt's diary (Bodl. MS.Eng.c.8269), which is also the source for the fate of Runciman's nephew. That evening the House of Commons was adjourned until 2 Feb. 1915 (HC Deb 27 November 1914 vol 68 cc1593–5).

[102] Marquis Guglielmo Imperiali (1858–1944); Italian Amb. London 1910–20; Italian Rep. to Council of League of Nations 1921–3.

Friedensvermittlung im ersten Weltkrieg; vom August 1914 bis zum italien. Kriegseintritt Mai 1915, *Steiner, Wiesbaden,1984. For WSC recurrently advocating the invasion of the island of Borkum, thereby to bring Denmark into the war on the Allied side, see Nicholas Duncan Black, 'The Admiralty War Staff and its influence on the conduct of the naval war between 1914 and 1918', Ph.D. thesis, University College, U. of London,* 2005, *pp.110–15.*

The Cabinet was puzzled by the French request for money, a relatively small sum, 'little more than, if as much as, the cost of the war for a single week'. The explanation, as provided to the King on 4 December, was that if a small loan could be successfully floated 'it would go some way to restore the confidence & to open the pockets of their own people' (Bodl. MS. Asquith 7, f.238). The British sought to attach conditions which were resisted until agreement was reached on 15 January 1915 for an issue of £10 million of French treasury bonds discounted by 5 per cent by the Bank of England, thereby yielding £9.5 million for the French (Horn, Britain, France, and the Financing of the First World War, *pp.44–5).*

The British view of 'pooled resources' for war finance and French reluctance to comply, which 'partly mystified, partly annoyed Treasury officials', is explained by J.A. Hemery, 'The Emergence of Treasury Influence in British Foreign Policy 1914–1921', Ph.D. thesis, U. of Cambridge, 1988, p.40. In a rare compliment to DLG, Charles Hobhouse wrote to Sydney Buxton in South Africa on 4 Dec. 1914: 'the Belgians are asking us to finance the entire Govt of Belgium, even that part of it which is in German occupation. I am glad to say that Ll.G. has stuck at this last demand' (Buxton MSS). Financing Belgian government would be a recurring topic at Cabinet over the next few months. There is helpful context in Dirk Luyten, 'War Finance (Belgium)', in 1914-1918-online. International Encyclopedia of the First World War, *Berlin 2014-10-08. DOI: 10.15463/ie1418.10411, accessed 27 Nov. 2022.*

K. reported that on Dec. 8. there were:

East Germany theatre	56	German Divisions	
	30	Austrian "	86
no more available for 5 wks but now Russian had			95
W. Germany theatre	84	German Divisions	84
no more to be put }	73	French "	
into the field but }			
only kept up }			
(1 more shortly) –	11 English		
	2 to 3 Belgians		86

As various voluntary groups of men over military age or engaged in important civil occupations sprang up around the country, in mid-November 1914 a Central Association of

Volunteer Training Corps was recognised by the War Office with Lord Desborough as President and General Sir O'Moore Creagh VC, former C-in-C in India, as Military Adviser. Uncertainty continued to surround the legal status of individual battalions; and JAP was concerned to ensure that school teachers and training college students who joined them should be regarded as having 'genuine reasons' for not enlisting.

Following the Cabinet meeting on 8 December, of which there appears to be no record made for the King, JAP wrote to his wife:

> No news, stalemate continues, 'all quiet and no change' is French's daily communique.
>
> Since my row with K. I am getting my way on other points & he has agreed to allow civil servants (e.g. officers of B. of E.) and all teachers in public and grant earning secondary schools, and all certificated teachers in elementary schools to be allowed to have a 'genuine reason' for not serving in the regulars, and can, therefore, enrol themselves in the volunteer training corps created by Lord Desborough. This will enable the War Office to enlist them later on (in the case of civil servants with the consent of their department) if the need arises.
>
> It will ease the mind of those who are wobbling & who still want to serve their country in the profession of teacher as well as in arms that they have undertaken to serve if the emergency is such as to need them.
>
> *(MS. Gainford 189/170)*

JAP wrote to the Secretary of the War Office, Sir Reginald Brade, to consolidate the agreement with Kitchener:

> COPY
> 8th December, 1914
>
> My dear Sir Reginald,
>
> Last night I wrote to Lord Kitchener and reminded him that the Army Council had consented to regard Training College students who have not completed their first year's training as having a 'genuine reason' for not enlisting at once and for joining a Volunteer Training Corps out of which they could be enlisted later on if the need arises. I asked him if he could extend the same privilege to —
>
> (a) Certified Teachers serving in Public Elementary Schools.
> (b) Teachers serving in State-aided or Public Secondary Schools.
>
> He has written across the top of my letter:— 'I have no objection to this, but all that can should join the Regular forces either as Officers or men'.

I have thought it better to inform you at once that Lord Kitchener would recognise (a) and (b) as possessing a 'genuine reason' for not joining the Regular Forces now if they cannot see their way to do so, and I am proposing to write to Sir John McClure, the President of the Incorporated Association of Headmasters, to tell that in the event of Masters not being able to join the Regular Forces at once, I am under the impression that if he appeals on their behalf to the War Office, their educational service might be accepted as a 'genuine reason' for their joining a Volunteer Training Corps with a view to their enlistment later on if the need arises.

I enclose a copy of a Confidential Circular which I sent to the Cabinet to-day, and in connection therewith it was decided that Civil Servants should also be permitted to join the Volunteer Training Corps with a view to their subsequent enlistment provided the War Office secured the consent of the Heads of their Department. Lord Kitchener left the Cabinet before this matter was discussed but he told me that he had no objection to this latter condition though he did not place, apparently, much value upon the Volunteer Training Corps.

Perhaps you would kindly arrange that in the event of any Civil Servants actually joining the Volunteer Training Corps arrangements should be made by the War Office in these cases to consult the Heads of the Departments before enlisting them so that the work of the Civil Departments shall not be disorganised to a greater extent than the circumstances at the time justify.

I am,

Yours faithfully,
(Signed) JOSEPH A. PEASE
(TNA: ED 24/1683/8157)

Dec. 10 Cabinet debated advances to Roumania, France.

[Dec.] 15 Belgium, Russia.

The Cabinet was unimpressed by the requests for aid from Russia and France. They were considered too vague to be discussed on 10 December. The Russians asked for an astonishing £100 million. After overcoming their incredulity, the government offered Russia £40 million at 5 per cent and required the deposit of 25 per cent in gold for all expenditure outside the United Kingdom. France was to be invited to guarantee half and 'to be informed that we are spending more on the war than either Russia or herself'. The British estimated their own monthly expenditure at about £45 million and that of their allies at less than

£40 million each (HHA's Cabinet letters to the King, 10, 18 Dec. 1914, Bodl. MS. Asquith 7, ff.240,242). The Roumanian, Russian, and French requests were taken up in a discussion of 'The Finance of the Allied Powers' at a meeting of 'A War Council' on 16 December (TNA: CAB 42/1/6). The British deliberations over the Russian financial demands and scepticism within the Cabinet over pleas of imminent military disaster are described in Chapters 4 and 6 of Nicholas Lambert's The War Lords. *HHA had written to Lady Stanley, Venetia Stanley's sister-in-law, on 11 December: 'I am not a prophet, but the daily & weekly wear & tear is so terrific that I take a shorter view than most people of the duration of the war.' (IWM Spec. Misc. J.6.)*

[Dec.] 17 Bombardment on 16th Scarbro. Whitby & Hartlepools.

The German naval bombardment of the north-east coastal towns was seized on by the press as an atrocity. The Times *had sold out by 9.15 a.m. on 17 December. The* Daily Mail *devoted three pages to the story, leading with 'Damage to Churches, an Hotel and Private Houses', and going on to note that the police had named seventeen dead. Among the wounded a 'considerable proportion... are, after the German heart, women and children' (Adrian Gregory, 'A Clash of Cultures: The British Press and the Opening of the Great War', in Troy R.E. Paddock ed.,* A Call to Arms: Propaganda, Public Opinion, and Newspapers in the Great War, *Praeger, Westport, CT, 2004, pp.34–5; Adrian Gregory,* The Last Great War: British Society and the First World War, *Cambridge UP, 2008, pp.54–5).*

There is an exhaustive account in Mark Marsay, Bombardment: the day the east coast bled: accounts of the German naval raids on Scarborough and Whitby on Wednesday, 16th December 1914, (with details of the raid on the Hartlepools), and the German submarine attack on Scarborough on Tuesday, 4th September 1917, *Great Northern Pub., Scarborough, 1999. For the navy's failure to track and intercept the German ships see Goldrick,* Before Jutland, *pp.196–222. The Metropolitan Police Commissioner, Sir Edward Henry, issued a warning to the civil population to stay under cover, preferably in basements, if they heard gunfire or explosions. The Board of Education and the London County Council educational authorities, and the management of the London Underground, were advised on measures to be taken in the event of an aerial attack (Susan R. Grayzel,* At Home and Under Fire: Air Raids and Culture in Britain from the Great War to the Blitz, *Cambridge UP, New York, 2012, pp.24–5). But leading Opposition figures were unimpressed: 'We have been assured that elaborate preparations have been made to deal with the Civilian population whenever a raid occurs...yet so far as we can learn the Lords Lieutenant issued no instructions in the areas affected' (Earl of Crawford &*

Balcarres, 'Memorandum: Subjects for discussion on January 5th and 6th', 28 Dec. 1914, Curzon of Kedleston MSS, BL: A & AS, MSS.Eur.F.112 D/3/10).

[Dec.] 22 We decided to help & pay for genuine damage to property & to compensate in case of dependents — if bread winner killed — over 600 civil casualties.

K. told us we had now in France 287,000 men. In a day or two another Division would make over 304,000. He was going to divide the forces into armies. At the front, Sir Douglas Haig and [*sic*] 150,000 each,[103] At home Rundle[104] — Ian Hamilton, Bruce Hamilton[105] & another[106] Plumer[107] in Northern Command would be replaced by Paget.[108] Methuen[109] would go to Malta.

K. told us if Germans took Warsaw as seemed not improbable (they had only 3 round p. man p. day to our 20) they might at the worst bring to the West 41 divisions & bring their force from 85 to 126 to face the French & British. We decided to ask Joffre for a conference, so as to decide strategy, & as to whether the loss in troops by our offensive was justified. It would be better if the Germans attacked us in our trenches & suffered losses as they must do.

[103] Haig was GOC, I Army; the other commander was Gen. Sir Horace Lockwood Smith-Dorrien (1858–1930); GOC, II Army Dec. 1914–Apr. 1915; Adj.-Gen., India 1901–3; GOC, 4th Division 1903–7; KCB 1904; GOC, Aldershot 1907–12; GOC, Sthn Command 1912–14; GCB 1913; GOC, II Army Corps (following death in train of Lt-Gen. Sir J.M. Grierson) Aug.–Dec. 1914; GOC, 1st Army Home Defence June–Nov. 1915; GCMG 1915; Gov., Gibraltar 1918–23. His active service was brought to an abrupt end on 27 Apr. 1915. His army had suffered heavy losses trying to maintain the Ypres salient. Smith-Dorrien's request to withdraw two miles was answered by an order to return to England and give up his command to Herbert Plumer, whom French had wanted in Aug. 1914 (Steven J. Corvi, 'Horace Smith-Dorrien…', in Beckett and Corvi eds, *Haig's Generals*, pp.202–4).

[104] Gen. Sir (Henry Macleod) Leslie Rundle (1856–1934); Gov., and C-in-C Malta 1909–15; GOC Nthern Command 1905–9, Eastn Command 1915; rtd 1916. He had been Kitchener's first choice to command at Gallipoli (Violet Asquith–Rupert Brooke, 12 Mar. 1915, in Mark Pottle ed., *Champion Redoubtable*, p.32). But F.S. Oliver told Austen Chamberlain on 30 Jan. 1915 that he was 'gaga' even in the Sth African War (Austen Chamberlain MSS, AC 14/6/3, Cadbury RL Birmingham U.).

[105] Gen. Sir Bruce Meade Hamilton (1857–1936); cmdg 2nd Division 1st Army Corps 1914–17; served numerous wars, Sth Africa and Boer War, Lt-Gen. 1907; Gen. 1913; Army Command Home Defence 1914–18; GOC-in-C Scottish Command 1909–13; KCB 1902; GCVO 1911; GCB 1915. 'A ridiculous appointment, it only has one redeeming point that he is too deaf to hear even a shell' (Leask, *Putty*, p.255).

[106] Gen. Sir Archibald Hunter (1856–1936); GOC Aldershot 1914–17; Egyptian Army 1884–99; Gov., Red Sea littoral and Suakin 1892–4; Maj.-Gen. 1896; KCB 1898; led defence of Ladysmith; GOC Scottish District 1900–3; GOC Westn Command, India 1903–7; Gen. 1905; GOC Sthn Command, India 1907–9; Gov. and C-in-C Gibraltar 1909–13; GCB 1911; ADC to George V 1917–19; Con. MP Lancs (Lancaster) 1918–22.

[107] Lt-Gen. Sir Herbert Plumer (1857–1932); GOC V Corps 8 Jan. 1915, GOC Second Army 7 May 1915; Gen. June 1915; C-in-C Italy Nov. 1917; GOC Second Army Mar. 1918, British Army of the Rhine April 1919; Gov. and C-in-C, Malta 1919–24; KCB 1905; GCMG 1916; GCVO 1917; GCB 1918; GBE 1924; Baron Plumer of Messines and Bilton 1919, Vt 1929.

[108] Paget, still out of favour with the govt over the Curragh incident, was passed over. He was given the Sthn Army in Apr. 1916.

[109] Field Marshal Paul Sanford Methuen, 3rd Baron Methuen (1845–1932); Gov. and C-in-C Natal 1910–15; appted Gov. and C-in-C Malta Feb.1915. His dau. Ethel ('Kitty') m. Geoffrey Howard.

We were making 25,000 shells p. wk, the French 25,000 p. day, it would be in Jan 30,000 p. wk. We had ordered from U.S.A. 1¼ million.

Kitchener seems to have been unduly pessimistic about Warsaw. The Germans did not take it until August 1915 (Jesse Kauffman, Elusive Alliance: The German Occupation of Poland in World War I, *Harvard UP, Cambridge, MA, 2015, pp.29–30). He was gloomy about Russia as well. Hobhouse noted: 'K said his news about Russia was disastrous' (Hobhouse diary, 22 Dec. 1914, David ed.,* Inside Asquith's Cabinet, *p.214). There are succinct analyses of what Kitchener could not have known about French, Russian, and German armed forces and armaments in essays by Douglas Porch, David R. Jones, and Holger H. Herwig in Allan R. Millett and Williamson Murray eds,* Military Effectiveness Volume I: The First World War, *Allen & Unwin, Boston, 1988.*

Churchill was authorised to circulate paper as to wireless chain & a committee to consider it.

The Postmaster General Hobhouse crisply records:

> W.S.C. sprang a scheme of wireless stations round the world, worked by the Navy and *essential* to it...He puts its cost at about £840,000. As it gave me a pretext for getting rid of H. Samuel's wretched Marconi scheme I offered no objection beyond warning the Cabinet the new proposal would cost £1½ millions.
>
> *(David ed., Inside Asquith's Cabinet, p.214)*

The P.M. in Percy Illingworth's illness sent for me at 5.0 to ask me to try & settle Swansea district representation. T. J. Williams[110] was intending to stand, but he could not have Masterman splitting the vote now. I saw Williams, but could not arrange for him to withdraw — though he talked of what would happen if he did. I think I left him unhappy in his mind — I arranged truce until he heard again.

In November, Auguste Rodin had given eighteen of his sculptures, mostly bronzes, to the Victoria & Albert in honour of the French and British soldiers killed in the war. With the New Year's honours recommendations being compiled, JAP had proposed that Rodin should be

[110] Thomas Jeremiah Williams (1872–1919); barrister; tin plate manufacturer; his father (William Williams) had been MP Swansea (District) 1893–5; Lib. MP Swansea (District) 1915–18 and Swansea (E) 1918–19.

recognised. The O.M. and G.C.B. were ruled out and Rodin went 'empty away' (Stamfordham–Bonham Carter, 23, 24 Dec. 1914, Bodl. MS. Asquith 4, f.536).

Dec. 30 Cabinets.

Agreed to reply to U.S.A. on contraband & right of search.[111]

[111] HHA Cabinet letter, 31 Dec. 1914, TNA: CAB 41/35/65, covers the 30 Dec. meeting. A Foreign Office paper on British treatment of neutral ships on the high seas, and US protests, was circulated on 31 Dec. (TNA: CAB 37/122/199).

Chapter 5
1915

Early in December the Government Chief Whip, Percy Illingworth, had been taken ill with high and fluctuating temperatures. Doctors initially thought he might have malaria but eventually in mid-December diagnosed typhoid, allegedly from a bad oyster. On 26 December his wife told JAP 'the attack has been just about as severe as it could have been but... so far no complications have set in' (MS. Gainford 97). Illingworth died on 3 January 1915. With his death, JAP found himself drawn back into some of the party work for which he had been responsible in the first years of HHA's government. 'A great rush today — seeing Freddie Guest, Lloyd George, Gulland, [Harold] Storey (Yorkshire Liberal Association)[1] *St Davids*[2] *and Welsh Secretary*[3] *re Swansea District, Masterman...', he told Elsie on 5 January. 'And now I am going to see L.G. again. Bigge, Newman, Fass [JAP's p.s.], files, etc. have filled the interstices' (MS. Gainford 190/1).*

He collaborated with Jack Gulland in drawing up a scheme of parliamentary work down to Easter (JAP–Montagu, 12 Jan 1915, copy, MS. Gainford 86/57). The most pressing issue was finding a seat for Charles Masterman, whose half-hearted fight for a vacancy at Swansea infuriated DLG. HHA had summoned JAP and made it clear that he did not want a contest for the Liberal nomination, and he did not want Masterman to stand. Masterman compliantly produced a succession of excuses to avoid nominating against the determined local Liberal, T.J. Williams.

DLG had expended considerable political capital to ensure that Masterman had local support. But, faced with the threat of an independent Liberal candidacy, Masterman withdrew. Within weeks he had made an enemy of DLG, exasperated JAP, and was forced to resign his Cabinet post when HHA was advised by the new Chief Whip, Gulland, that no constituency

[1] (Edwin) Harold Storey (1869–1956); sec., Yorkshire Lib. Fedn 1908–19; Congregational minister 1896–1906; sec., Lib. Publications Dept 1919–36; *The Liberal Magazine* (vol.XLV, no.52, Feb. 1937, p.41) called Storey 'the best political pamphleteer of his time'. JAP thought him 'a capable fellow' (JAP–HHA, 24 Oct. 1910, Bodl. MS. Asquith 23, f.300).

[2] John Wynford Philipps, Baron St Davids (1860–1938); Lib. MP Pembrokeshire 1898–1908, Lanarkshire (Mid) 1888–94; barrister then financier; Ld Lt, Pembrokeshire 1911–32; Baron St Davids 6 July 1908, Vt 1918; PC 1914. His younger brothers, Ivor (later Lord Treowen, commanded the 38th Welsh division 1915–16) and Owen (shipowner, ennobled as Lord Kylsant), were both elected as Lib. MPs in 1906.

[3] John Thomas Davies (1881–1938); succeeded John Rowland as DLG's Welsh p.s Apr. 1912; B.Sc., school teacher; shared a room with Frances Stevenson, whom he took under his wing; principal p.s. to DLG as Min. of Mun., Sec. of St. War, and PM; KCB 1922; director Suez Canal Co. 1923 (Frances Lloyd George, *The Years that are Past*, Hutchinson, 1967, pp.57–8,210).

would have him. (The story was told in Cameron Hazlehurst, 'Masterman–Lloyd George Split', New Outlook, *no.72, July–Aug. 1968, pp.33–9, elaborated in E.I. David, 'Charles Masterman and the Swansea District By-Election, 1915',* WHR, *vol.V, no.1, 1970, pp.31–44, revisited in Hopkins,* Charles Masterman, *pp.131–49, and revived in J. Graham Jones, 'C.F.G. Masterman and the Swansea District Vacancy of 1914–15: some new evidence',* Morgannwg, *vol.XLVI, 2002, repr. in Jones,* David Lloyd George and Welsh Liberalism, *pp.158–72.) JAP's long letter to DLG on 1 January 1915, explaining all he had done between Christmas and New Year to dissuade Jeremiah Williams from standing, is in Lloyd George MSS, LG/C/4/12/8, PA.*

Jany 6[4] — saw the P.M. before cabinet, explained Swansea situation & asked if Birrell wd retire. P.M. said yes later, & I've thought of you for his successor.

> I had a few minutes chat alone with the P.M. this morning about recruiting, & K's speech & I asked him if Birrell was going & he said not yet but if he went later he might &c, but he wanted B. to stay on for a time with his new L.L. & was anxious to avoid changes at this moment.
>
> I asked if I might go to America in March to see some experiments in Education with 2 or 3 of my staff...but the P.M. said my staff could go, but he did not want me to go.
>
> I am dining with Edward Grey for a bridge party tomorrow to meet the P.M. & another.
>
> *(JAP–EP, 6 Jan. 1915, MS. Gainford 190/2–3)*

On *Jany 7th* dined with Edward Grey to meet the P.M. & Montagu at 33 Eccleston Sq. After the parlourmaids left, the P.M. asked our views as to how to fill places. He told us he had asked Whitley to be Chief whip. He thought Cecil Harmsworth[5] might succeed Dr Addison, & Addison succeed Ellis Griffith[6] at the Home Office. He said Birrell wanted to retire, & it was his intention to put me in his place.

With his ailing wife living in an 'imaginary world', Birrell was talking privately of his desire to 'bid the world of politics Goodnight—but the opportunity never comes' (Birrell–T.P. Le Fanu,

[4] JAP slightly muddled the Cabinet chronology for early Jan., misdating this entry 'Jany. 5'. Although there is no Cabinet letter to the King, the Cabinet did meet on 6 Jan. (HHA–Venetia Stanley, 6 Jan. 1915, *Asquith Letters*, p.362; Harcourt notes, 6 Jan. 1915, Bodl. MS.Eng.c.8270).

[5] Cecil Bisshop Harmsworth (1869–1948); Lib. MP Bedfordshire (Luton) 1911–22 and Worcestershire (Droitwich) 1906–10; younger brother of Lords Northcliffe and Rothermere; newspaper proprietor; PPS Pres. Bd of Ag. and Fish. 1911–14; PPS Pres. Bd of Trade 1914–15; Parl. U.-Sec. of St. for Home Affairs 1915; member Prime Minister's secretariat 1917–19; Parl. U.-Sec. of St. for Foreign Affairs 1919–22; acting Min. of Blockade 1919; Baron Harmsworth 1939.

[6] Ellis Jones Griffith (1860–1926); U.-Sec. of St. for Home Affairs 1912–15; barrister 1887; Lib. MP Anglesey 1895–1918 and Carmarthen 1923–4; Recorder, Birkenhead 1907–12; KC 1910; PC 1914; Bt 1918 as Sir E.J. Ellis-Griffith.

21 Feb. 1915, Birrell MSS, 8. 3. (3), Liverpool U.). JAP later added the following note: 'Birrell afterwards asked to be left in office & so I never went to Ireland…'. HHA had asked Venetia Stanley on 11 October 1914: 'What do you say to sending Jack Pease (!) to Ireland (it doesn't want a clever man just now)' (Asquith Letters, *p.273). Elsie Pease's response to the idea was less than enthusiastic: 'So the PM intends to make an April fool of you! A stop gap office, the last Chief Secretary of Ireland—with Larkinism & treason added to the existing problems.' She wanted the Speakership for him. 'The peaceful atmosphere of Speaker's House & prospective pension Why not!' (EP–JAP, 10 Jan. 1915, MS. Gainford 86/39).*

When the Irish idea was broached to Montagu, he wrote to the Prime Minister that JAP was a good example of the success of character 'unaided by any intellectual or interesting qualities'. As *HHA told Venetia Stanley on 9 January 1915, it followed that JAP 'therefore & thereby' would be unequal to coping with potential parliamentary difficulties. Further objections according to Montagu were 'Mrs Pease in Dublin' and the 'almost certain suicide of Simon'* (Asquith Letters, *p.366). Bonham Carter expressed similar concerns in writing to Violet Asquith on 10 January 10 but concluded 'I am not so certain that your father is wrong as is Montagu, who naturally takes the blackest view of it' (Bodl. MS. Bonham Carter 256, ff.100–1). The matter hung fire for some months: JAP was still being considered for Ireland in April. HHA wrote to Montagu on 7 March:*

> Birrell's case in any event will have to be provided for. There is much truth in your mordant thumb-nail sketch of J.P. But he has some sterling merits, and is so much pressed by the pinch of poverty that a rise from 2 to 5 thousand a year is to him a matter of great moment. Would it be too much of a scandal to put him at the L.G.B. if Samuel were sent to Ireland? And then who is to do Education?
>
> *(Montagu MSS II A4/1–3, Wren Lib. TCC)*

Birrell wrote to Elsie 11 March 1915 (in reply to her letter of condolence on the death of his wife):

> Had I known the P.M. had ever mentioned his idea (which I favoured and fostered) I would have spoken to Jack, but as I did not know I felt bound to hold my tongue. For long months past I have been convinced that it was my duty to go—being too upset to do my job properly. But I found the P.M. disinclined to move, & also Redmond & Dillon most anxious I should remain.
>
> *(MS. Gainford 86/70)*

Edward Grey said yes its an excellent appointment. I said nothing — but said if Whitley wouldn't take the Whip, Sir Harry Verney[7] might.

[7] Sir Harry Calvert Williams Verney Bt (1881–1974); Parl. Sec., Bd of Ag. 1914–15; asst p.s. to Sec. of St. for Colonies 1907–10; 4th Bt 1910; Lib. MP Buckinghamshire (Buckingham) 1910–18; PPS to Ch. Sec. for Ireland 1911–14. T/Lt-Col., DSO 1918; convicted of indecent assault on under age boys 1937, 1954.

There was considerable public speculation that Whitley had been offered the post of Chief Whip in succession to Percy Illingworth. 'A good many names are mooted . . .', Edwin Montagu told Geoffrey Howard on 15 January:

> including Whitley, Seely, Wedgwood Benn, you, Freddie [Guest], Neil [Primrose], and, ye gods, me! Up to date the only firm move has been to offer the job to Whitley, who, I understand, is not at all keen to take it. I am not surprised. Neil's name is a jest, I think, possibly due to Alick [Murray] . . .
>
> Meanwhile the Chief Whip work there is to do seems to be in the hands of Jack Pease, who is driving me frantic by his inability to master straightforward statements as to what the Treasury requires in the way of estimates &c, and Parliamentary time. Have you heard it reported that he is going to Ireland . . .? The choice of Pease does not make a very vivid appeal to my imagination: imagine a debate between Carson, Healy and Jack!
>
> *(Howard MSS, Castle Howard Archive, J30, courtesy of Dame Christian Howard and the Howard Family)*

An old story was revived: that it had been Campbell-Bannerman's intention to appoint Whitley as Chief Whip in 1906 but that George Whiteley had been asked by mistake (Whitley MSS, JHW/2/6/56 et seq.*, Huddersfield U.). In the end, Whitley declined the post: he 'objects to be again regarded as a controversialist I suppose' (JAP–EP, 18 Jan. 1915, MS. Gainford 190/14). Jack Gulland—whose name had not occurred to the gossip-gathering Montagu—was appointed in his place. JAP wrote: 'Whitley declined on ground of being high strung and unable to stand the job on grounds of health. Gulland does H. of C. work well. His obvious failing as to being "class" enough is not of his own making, but he is a good sort' (JAP–EP, 20 Jan.1915, MS. Gainford 190/16–17). JAP's qualified esteem of the new Chief Whip appears to have been no secret to Gulland's wife, Edith:*

> If he had been passed over it would have been a terrible slight, a clear case of mere pandering to birth & snobbery . . .
>
> There has been a good deal of wire-pulling. I believe it is quite true . . . that Seely was approached to become Chief Whip by Pease (who has done a great deal of fussing). Curiously enough when he should have been elected Chief Whip straight away, when his turn came, a delay was caused & Jack remembers they got up a Round Robin for him!!!

Edith Gulland told her sister on 2 February 1915 that it was practically certain that Whitley had been offered the Chief Whipship 'with the intention of Seely's taking his place & being in direct line for the Speakership. Jack thought this was a frightful insult to Whitley' (Gulland MSS, courtesy of John Gulland Osborne). Whitley told Samuel on 15 January that 'for me, or anyone, to step out of the Chair for the Chief Whipship would be to some extent to lower the position...The increasing power & responsibility given in recent years to the Chair makes it the more important not to do this' (Samuel MSS, SAM/A/155 IV, ff.128–30, PA).

Gulland was worried about his own deficiencies, but, as he told his family on 21 January, 'it is a great position and I could not refuse. The very harassing work of English candidates & constituencies is to be in the hands of Wedgwood Benn. Fortunately one begins in a comparatively easy time.' Gulland had not expected the 'hard & busy week' that followed. 'My first job (very private)', as he wrote home on January 31, 'was to sack a Cabinet Minister in some very unpleasant interviews.' (Gulland MSS.) HHA's displeasure about Masterman could hardly have been more pointedly expressed than by leaving Gulland to break the bad news. Benn in fact turned down what amounted to the joint Chief Whipship, electing to stay with his cavalry regiment, the Middlesex Yeomanry (Duke of Cambridge's Hussars).

In the aftermath of Masterman's unhappy exit, a minor ministerial reshuffle occurred on 3 and 4 February bringing Montagu to the Duchy of Lancaster. Montagu's place at the Treasury was taken by Francis Acland, who had been acting as head of the news department at the Foreign Office, meeting correspondents three times a week for two hours (Philip Taylor, 'Publicity and Diplomacy: The Impact of the First World War upon Foreign Office Attitudes towards the Press', in David Dilks ed., Retreat from Power: Studies in Britain's Foreign Policy of the Twentieth Century, Vol. One 1906–1939, *Macmillan, 1981, p.49). Neil Primrose followed Acland as Parliamentary Under-Secretary for Foreign Affairs.*

At the Home Office, Cecil Harmsworth succeeded Ellis Griffith as McKenna's Under-Secretary. Griffith had resigned. According to DLG, he was unable to live on his pay; on 3 January Margot Asquith had besought Illingworth and DLG to help, perhaps by getting Alfred Mond to pay his debts (Lloyd George MSS, LG C/6/12/1, PA), and Dr Addison remained with JAP at the Board of Education until the coalition government was formed in May 1915 (Addison diary, 3 July 1914, Bodl. MS. Addison, dep.d.1). Macnamara, Financial Secretary at the Admiralty and certainly senior to Montagu, as HHA acknowledged to Venetia Stanley, was once again passed over (Betts, Dr Macnamara, *pp.278–9).*

We had 3 pleasant rubbers, & walked together to Victoria Station at 12.45 at night where a taxi was found for the P.M.

I went abroad to Calais St. Omer Dunkirk Dixmude Ypres & St. Omer on the 8th 9th, returned on Sunday 10th. Drove from Folkestone with Freddie Guest to Walmer Castle[8] when I saw the P.M., explained to him how Sir John French

[8] HHA had considered becoming Lord Warden of the Cinque Ports in 1913 but decided that the upkeep of the official residence, Walmer Castle, would be too expensive, a decision he later said he regretted (E.T. Cook diary, 20 Jan. 1915, Cook MSS). Lord Beauchamp was appointed; after the war began, Beauchamp agreed to let the Prime Minister use Walmer as a sort of halfway house to the front.

was unhappy about not getting more troops & disliked them coming out in armys & not in battalions — & that the Typhoid outbreak at Dunkirk should be arrested.

There was in fact no typhoid outbreak at Dunkirk. The sufferers there were wounded French soldiers from around Ypres and Poperinghe. Effective segregation and adequate treatment were lacking and it was feared that Dunkirk would become an 'infected area'. The Friends' Ambulance Unit and the British Red Cross were keen to set up a typhoid hospital. They had the resources to meet current expenditure. According to George Newman, Sir Alfred Keogh, head of the Royal Army Medical Corps, was 'very favourably disposed' to the idea. After some early friction between the Red Cross and the R.A.M.C., newly promoted Colonel Arthur Lee MP had reported confidentially to Lord Kitchener in October 1914 that the two organisations were working harmoniously. Relations broke down again in December but were improving by Christmas under a new Red Cross Commissioner (Lee–Kitchener, 12 Oct., 25 Dec. 1914, RAMC 446/7, CMAC, Wellcome I; for Lee's work as Kitchener's 'Commissioner' see A Good Innings, *Vol. I, pp.586–9,979–86; Ian R. Whitehead,* Doctors in the Great War, *Pen & Sword Military, Barnsley, 2013 [1st edn Leo Cooper, 1999], p.35). Keogh suggested approaching Kitchener via the Prime Minister for* ad hoc *funding for capital and equipment; and made it clear that 'preventive and sanitary measures' should be undertaken by the R.A.M.C. But, as there were no British forces in Dunkirk, the R.A.M.C. required an express invitation from the French military authorities to operate there. If the British did come, Keogh's administration would take over the voluntary hospital (Newman–JAP, 13, 17, 19 Jan. 1915; 'Typhoid Fever in Dunkirk and Neighbourhood' Preliminary Report by Dr E.W. Goodall, Special Medical Officer for Typhoid Purposes, c.18 Feb. 1915, MS. Gainford 86/52–6). JAP had half an hour on 20 January with Kitchener on the Friends' Ambulance Unit and Dunkirk, telling Elsie 'he is responding all the extent I can expect, and helping us to deal with Typhoid' (MS. Gainford 190/17).*

Very private

The P.M. last night was quite definite after dinner as to his intention in regards to Ireland about April he thought. Edward Grey heartily approved.

(JAP–EP, 8 Jan. 1915, MS. Gainford 190/5)

In a long letter to Elsie on 10 January from the Turf Club, Piccadilly, JAP wrote up his adventures in France with the generals and the Duke of Marlborough (who crossed the Channel twice a week as a King's Messenger, being seasick every time):

Sir George Newman and I and about 20 refugee Belgians (men sent back because they are in the prime of vigour) took the Calais boat…

Jack Seely met me at Calais Pier, and after a cup of tea in the curiously looking deserted restaurant George Newman went with one of the ambulance units to Dunkirk, and I with Seely some 40 kilometres to St Omer.

...I delivered two letters personally to Sir John French, which Winston & Guest had asked me to deliver...

Jack Seely makes no secret to me that he thinks new armies now would be much better than new men being contaminated with the grousing of old men, reservists etc., who are sick of their work...

Things at the front have been so beastly, with mud, that men could not scramble out of trenches without such mud clinging to them as to choke & jam their rifles, & as French said to me, we can't go forward at this moment, not only does the mud pull the men's boots off, but it gives the enemy three times as long to fire at them when changing from one trench to another...

Rifle sniping was going on but as it was getting dark we were not picked up by any of the outlook men of the enemy in the mist & rain.

(MS. Gainford 190/7–13)

With German shells occasionally falling just beyond them and at the roadside, and French artillery firing over their heads from 30 yards back, it was as close as JAP would get to the war the soldiers were fighting. Delivering personal letters from WSC and Freddy Guest to the C. in C. in France was as close as he would (unwittingly) come to an alleged conspiracy against HHA.

Jany 12[9] Discussed attitude to U.S.A. in regard to S.S. *Dacia*. If she was transferred fr. German to U.S.A. flag agreed to explain in advance we could not regard it as a purchase & must on technical rights insist on detention.

The SS Dacia *had been transferred from the ownership of the Hamburg–Amerika line to that of a US citizen of German extraction and sent to Bremen with a cargo of cotton. On 20 January Grey declared that the* Dacia *would be refused passage and the British Ambassador in Washington claimed that the transfer of ownership was not valid under international law. A confrontation was avoided by allowing the French to capture the* Dacia *and apply the stricter rules of the French prize courts. We are indebted to Nicholas Lambert for the information that the businessman and Conservative MP for Plymouth, Arthur Shirley Benn, had suggested the use of the French, calculating that the Americans would not challenge them. Benn's letter to Sir Francis Hopwood on 18 January was passed to the Foreign Secretary via Sir William Tyrrell. Grey told Hopwood on 23 January that he had already suggested to WSC,*

[9] JAP headed this entry 'Jany. 5' as well as 12 Jan., but it refers only to the Cabinet discussions on the 12th (HHA Cabinet letter, 13 Jan. 1915 TNA: CAB 41/36/1). It ends the second volume of his diary (MS. Gainford 39). It was written at the same time as the entries starting 30 Dec. 1914. The first entries (Jan.–10 Feb.1915) in the next volume of diary (MS. Gainford 40) were all written at the same time.

partly for the reasons Hopwood gave, that the ship should not be seized off the American coast (TNA: FO 800/88, ff.295–6; Southborough MSS, Bodl. MS.Eng.c.7346).

P.M. raised question of rates & how to ease freights by releasing ships for our own commerce.

Loulou Harcourt's notes on that day's proceedings make clear that the issue was thought to be the 'immense charters of ships by the Admiralty', which was driving up the price of corn and coal. HHA told the King that the Admiralty's taking-up of more than 1,000 merchant ships had led to 'a violent rise on freights' (Bodl. MS.Eng.c.8270; MS. Asquith 8, f.1). Montagu had sent a memorandum to Runciman and other colleagues that day asserting that

> the main cause of the rise in wholesale prices of the necessaries of life—wheat, coal &c, is the question, it is alleged, of freights ... even if ships are very scarce, I do not see that it necessarily follows that shipowners should be allowed to make as big profit as they can get on the usual economic or competitive terms. Nor ought they to be able to recoup themselves for their losses on passenger traffic by their gains on the needs of the nation. It might be necessary to take by force any ships we want, allowing the owners there-of a reasonable percentage on their outlay.
>
> *(Montagu–McKenna, Runciman, Lucas, 12 Feb.1915, Runciman of Doxford MSS and Montagu MSS, A1/6/18/(1))*

With Parliament reassembled, an exhausted Runciman would tell Sir Robert Chalmers secretly on 15 February that the Admiralty had on hire 1,150 cargo steamers besides 350 tugs & trawlers (Runciman of Doxford MSS). But his diagnosis of the cause of rising prices was flawed, as the Admiralty's Graeme Thomson soon demonstrated to the delight of WSC ('Report by the Director of Transports, Admiralty, on the Memorandum on the Shortage of Merchant Shipping Tonnage prepared by the Board of Trade', 16 Jan. 1915, TNA: ADM 116/3486, Lambert, Planning Armageddon, *pp.330–2).*

In mid-March the Admiralty issued a return of 88 British merchantmen lost during the war: sunk by cruisers 54; sunk by submarines 22; sunk by mines 12. To the rear-admiral, 4th battle squadron in the Grand Fleet, the number was 'nothing like what one expected in the first months of the war' (Duff diary, 16 Mar. 1915, Duff MSS; an Admiralty list of British ships sunk on the high seas had been circulated to the Cabinet on 23 Sept. 1914, TNA: CAB 37/121/111).

Cabinets were held on all Wednesdays in Jany[10] & on Feb. 3. & 10. European positions & situations were discussed. Rumanian & Bulgarian attitude. Finance of Belgium &c. &c.

[10] The meeting on Jan. 12 was on a Tuesday. There was a meeting of the CID on the 13th.

Among the subjects on which JAP did not report was that of Imperial wireless stations, on which it was agreed that 'for the moment strategic must be regarded as overriding commercial considerations'; if the government proceeded with repudiating the old contract, they would face a substantial damages claim.

The 'possible expediency' of offering Cyprus to Greece as an inducement to her to join the allies was discussed. Cyprus, occupied and administered since 1878, was annexed on 5 November 1914, when war with the Ottoman empire began (Andrekos Varnava, British Imperialism in Cyprus, 1878–1915: The Inconsequential Possession, *Manchester UP, 2009, pp. 247–71). As those who were privy to War Council proceedings, and high-level Foreign Office, War Office, and Admiralty thinking, knew, the purpose of a generous offer to Greece was originally the hope that she might agree to land a large invading force at Gallipoli concurrently with a British naval attack. JAP was doubtless one of the Cabinet ministers who, as HHA told Venetia Stanley on 9 January, was not informed about the impending attack in the Dardanelles (*Asquith Letters, pp.421–3*). In response to concern about the possible collapse of Serbia and the desirability of bringing in Greece and Roumania, DLG 'argued strongly in favour of despatch of a British supporting force'. On DLG's advocacy for a Balkan bloc and an expedition to Salonika see Curtwright,* Muddle, Indecision and Setback, pp.123–59*).*

*A further loan to Serbia was approved (HHA Cabinet letters, 21 Jan., 3 Feb. 1915, Bodl. MS. Asquith 8, ff.3–6). The King expressed his 'earnest hope' that Grey's proposal to offer Cyprus to Greece would be accepted. 'To be able to offer something of our own without consulting any other Power… gives us a strong position and a powerful asset to bargain with…'. Cyprus was 'an unprofitable possession' and strategically a failure (Stamfordham–HHA, 22 Jan. 1915, Bodl. MS. Asquith 4, ff.7–80). By the end of 21 January, after weeks of indecision, HHA had come to the conclusion that the next major operation should be against Austria not Turkey (*Asquith Letters*, pp.388–9). Before JAP heard about it the Prime Minister had changed his mind again.*

On 27 January WSC said he wanted to stop all trade with and from Germany to neutrals, declaring an effective blockade. In the long argument that followed, JAP agreed with WSC, DLG, and Kitchener. At the next meeting WSC advocated stopping all enemy cargoes of food, partially starving neutrals bordering on Germany and supplying her. The major clash to come over recruiting and manpower was anticipated in the response of McKenna and Runciman to Kitchener's declaration that he was going to take every man between 17 and 35: 'if you do that you won't be able to run the trades manufacturing for war' (Harcourt diary, 27 Jan., 3 Feb. 1915, Bodl. MS.Eng.c.8270). At a meeting of the CID on the 27th to discuss a paper by Balfour on the 'Limits of Enlistment', eight of JAP's Liberal Cabinet colleagues (HHA, DLG, McKenna, Harcourt, Lucas, Runciman, Crewe, and Haldane) had been present when Kitchener declared: 'We could not allow that the limit of recruiting had been reached until we were beyond 3,000,000' (TNA: CAB 42/1/25). M.J. Lewis and Roger Lloyd-Jones, Arming the Western Front: War, business and the state in Britain 1900–1920, *Routledge, 2016, ch.5, 'The rise of the engineer's war and the origins of the Ministry of Munitions', is an important new interpretation of the intertwined issue of munitions and labour supply.*

With public concern about Belgian refugees rising, at the beginning of February, J.H. Whitehouse, a Quaker Liberal MP and DLG's PPS, published Belgium in War A Record of Personal Experiences.[11] *The pamphlet ran into a third impression in ten days. DLG introduced the 'record which enables the reader to realize in part what the war has meant for Belgium ... this brave and much-wronged people'.*

An inconclusive allied financial conference had been held in Paris 3–5 February 1915. On his return DLG told Grey on 7 February it had been 'a great success' but let it be known that he was 'much struck by the ignorance of the French and Russian Finance Ministers' (Lloyd George MSS, LG/6/14/25, PA; Esher journal, 6 Feb. 1915, Esher MSS ESHR 2/14, CAC). Just over a week earlier he had called together representatives of the Dominions to lay before them 'very serious financial position of Empire, its Allied Governments and friends'. As the New Zealand High Commissioner cabled his Prime Minister on 26 January: 'Money already borrowed, Dominions £47,000,000, Allied Governments and Friendly States £118,000,000, Home Government £400,000,000. Above nearly all gone' (Bodl. MS. Harcourt 464, f.183). In Paris, Britain had hoped for the creation of a gold pool but settled for a plan obliging France and Russia to provide up to £12 million in gold—to be repaid by one year after the end of hostilities—if Bank of England reserves fell more than £10 million in the next six months. Britain had also agreed secretly to allow the French to float short term loans on the London money market (Horn, Britain, France, and the Financing of the First World War, *pp.51–6). For the conference of DLG, and the French and Russian Finance ministers, Alexandre Ribot,[12] and Peter Bark,[13] there is an excellent account in Jennifer Siegel,* For Peace and Money: French and British Finance in the Service of Tsars and Commissars, *Oxford UP, New York, 2014, pp.13–44.*

On 4 February the German government announced that a submarine blockade of Great Britain would begin on 18 February. The nature and limited impact of the first few months of

[11] John Howard Whitehouse (1873–1955), former sec. Toynbee Hall, elected for Mid-Lanark in Jan. 1910, was Masterman's PPS before joining DLG in 1913. Later a prominent educationist and Ruskin scholar. Referred to by John Campbell in quoting a DLG letter 30 Sept. 1913 as 'presumably another of LG's secretaries, though there is no other record of him' (*If Love Were All... The Story of Frances Stevenson and David Lloyd George,* Vintage Books, 2007 [1st edn Jonathan Cape, 2006], p.36).

[12] Alexandre Félix Joseph Ribot (1842–1923): French Min. of Finance Aug. 1914–17; four times Prime Minister between 1892 and 1914, and again in 1917.

[13] Peter Bark (1869–1937); Russian Min. of Finance 1914–17; advised British Treasury and Bank of England on post-war Russian finance; banker; hon. GCVO 1929; Kt 1935.

German unrestricted submarine warfare are detailed in Lawrence Sondhaus, The Great War at Sea: A Naval History of the First World War, *Cambridge UP, 2014, pp.136–70.*

On *Feb. 10.* — The Prime Minister said we must decide what we should do to keep Belgium Govmt going, & George reported his interview with Ribot & Bark (Russia) the 2 finance ministers of our allies, & it was decided we should all share in an advance of £20,000,000 — to enable her to pay her army, railway men &c & carry on — otherwise the Belgians would accept the German 'inevitable' occupation as their only alternative.

Kitchener read to us his Intelligence Officers' report on the position — it indicated pressure on the Russians on the Carpathian front — & that the movement of troops to the West were the German troops still training, it being thought advisable to have them near the Belgian frontier, in case of necessity.

For the identity of the first cohort of BEF intelligence officers the essential guide is Jim Beach, '"Intelligent Civilians in Uniform": The British Expeditionary Force's Intelligence Corps Officers, 1914–1918', W&S, *vol.27, no.1, 2008, pp.1–22. Notwithstanding its title and Kitchener's absence from the text, there is also much of value on military and secret service intelligence 1914–15 in Beach,* Haig's Intelligence: GHQ and the German Army, 1916–1918, *Cambridge UP, 2013. On Kitchener's familiarity with signals intelligence see John Ferris, 'Before "Room 40": The British Empire and Signals Intelligence, 1898–1914',* J.Strat.S., *vol.2, no.4, 1989, pp.431–57.*

On *Feb. 11* — The P.M. made a statement on Food supplies, it revealed nothing heroic, but was a masterly exposition. I asked him afterwards on the Bench whether he still proposed to send me to Ireland, as there were domestic reasons which would be determined, he said he had not changed his mind as to my going, that Birrell still pressed to be relieved, but that he did not want Birrell to leave with a new Lord Lieut.[14] & a new permanent Secy. All 3 new men at once at the lead made the further change at the moment undesirable.

Feb. 16. We discussed the note we should publish as the retaliatory message to the German policy of sinking merchantmen they could not capture, without notice by torpedoes — it was deferred pending Simon seeing the French representatives. We discussed what we should do on the Welsh Disestablishment

[14] Lord Wimborne, Churchill's cousin, became Ld Lieut on 19 Feb. 1915. Sir Matthew Nathan had been U.-Sec. for Ireland since Aug. 1914.

amendment bill to be introduced by D. of Devonshire, & decided to confer with opposition.

The Duke's amendment concerned the Welsh Church (Postponement) Bill, which was given its 1st, 2nd, and 3rd readings on 9 March. The government proposed to suspend the Welsh Church Act until six months after the end of the war (HL Deb 9 March 1915 vol 18 cc614–16). 'The Act is a model of precise drafting' (E. Manson in Journal of the Society of Comparative Legislation, *vol.16, 1916, p.2).*

Lord Robt. Cecil D. of D. Lord Lansdowne to meet McKenna, George & Crewe. Churchill told us the result of the air raid, & bomb dropping on Zeebrugge making it impossible as a submarine base. Harcourt reported mutiny in Santiago & Crewe anxiety as to troops being spared from India.[15]

K. told us our loss as from Feb. 3–13 had been over 2000 men & over 100 officers.

The precise figures Kitchener gave were 101 officers and 2,620 men. JAP passed over in silence the news from WSC that the naval bombardment of the forts at and beyond the Dardanelles would begin on 19 February, and Kitchener's advice that the 29th Division would be on its way to Lemnos over the next week, with their reinforcement in case of need being the Australian and New Zealand contingent. Perhaps he heard the same message about the naval action as Hobhouse: 'No risks were to be run. . .'. But for JAP, as for most of his Cabinet colleagues, there was little realisation of the intensity of the debate in the War Council over the previous few weeks about the nature of the Dardanelles campaign (HHA Cabinet letter,

[15] The mutiny was in Singapore, not Santiago. It involved Indian troops who stole weapons and gave them to German prisoners. Its causes were obscure to the Cabinet, which decided to keep it secret. But the situation was soon brought under control by a hastily improvised force of the Sultan of Johore's private army, and British, Japanese, French, and Russian soldiers and sailors. Thirty-seven mutineers of the 5th (Native) Light Infantry were executed (HHA Cabinet letter, 16 Feb. 1915, TNA: CAB 41/36/5; Harcourt diary note, 16 Feb. 1915, MS.Eng.c.8270; Tim Harper, 'Singapore, 1915, and the Birth of the Asian Underground', *Modern Asian Studies*, vol.47, issue 6, 2013, pp.1782–1811; Ian F.W. Beckett, 'The Singapore Mutiny of February 1915', *JSAHR*, vol.62, no.251, 1984, pp.132–53; Leon Comber, 'The Singapore Mutiny (1915) and the Genesis of Political Intelligence in Singapore', *I&NS*, vol.24, no.4, 2009, pp.529–41; Heather Streets-Salter, *World War One in Southeast Asia: Colonialism and Anticolonialism in an Era of Global Conflict*, Cambridge UP, 2017, pp.17–87). On German sponsored revolutionary activity in East Asia see Antony Best, *British Intelligence and the Japanese Challenge in Asia, 1914–1941*, Palgrave Macmillan, Basingstoke, 2002, pp.23–4; and for the introduction of legislation on seditious publications in the Straits Settlements, Mohd Safar Hasim, 'Singapore's Sepoy Mutiny and the Beginning of Press Control in Malaya', in Jarosław Suchoples and Stephanie James eds, *Re-visiting World War I: Interpretations and Perspectives of the Great Conflict*, Peter Lang, Frankfurt am Main, 2016, pp.129–48.

17 Feb. 1915, Bodl. MS. Asquith 8, f.9; Harcourt diary, 16 Feb. 1915, Bodl. MS.Eng.c.8270; Hobhouse diary, 16 Feb. 1915, David ed., Inside Asquith's Cabinet, *p.222; Secretary's Notes of a Meeting of a War Council Held at 10, Downing Street, February 19, 1915, TNA: CAB 42/1/36).*

Der Tag.

Feb. 18 Two cabinets. K. read French's telegrams — fairly quiet. He read the War Office's intelligence report of Russia position — their 'appreciation'. It was very discouraging. They seemed not to have arms or ammunition — they had 900,000 trained men without arms, & could only make them at rate of

45,000 p. month. We were making them at
55,000 " " & altering others.[16]

K. told us he had bought 100,000 mausers with 1000 rounds from a good firm. Harcourt could have 1/10 for S. Africa & Churchill could send 6 4.6 guns.[17] Crewe reported death of Capt Shakespear[18] whom K. eulogised. Position at Basra considered Turks were amassing at Bagdad important 2 brigades shd go — from India — places to be retaken from Egypt.

Basra, a small fort on the confluence of the Rivers Tigris and Euphrates, was 75 miles upriver from the head of the Persian Gulf. Control of the head of the Gulf had assumed strategic importance with the development of the oil installations there. But the occupation of Basra (22 Nov. 1914) had been decided on, not only to protect the Royal Navy's oil supply, but also to meet the Turkish threat to British trade in Mesopotamia and the Gulf, and for fear of the effect on Indian Muslims of a Turkish declaration of a jihad against Britain. The success of this first move led to the extension of the campaign to include the capture of Baghdad. There were British captives in Baghdad; the city was expected to fall easily; it was the terminus for the Baghdad railway; it controlled the irrigation of the Basra vilayet (Mohamed Gholi Majd, Iraq in World War I: From Ottoman Rule to British Conquest, *UP of America, Lanham, 2006, pp.45–97).*

[16] Russian munitions stocks in 1914–15 are analysed in David R. Jones, 'Imperial Russia's Forces at War', in Millett and Murray eds, *Military Effectiveness Volume I: The First World War*, pp.262–9.

[17] The naval guns were 4.7 inches (Ian V. Hogg and L.F. Thurston, *British artillery weapons and ammunition, 1914–1918*, Ian Allan, 1972, p.144).

[18] Capt. William Henry Irvine Shakespear (1878–1915); soldier 1898–1903; lone explorer in Arabia; member, Indian Political Department; consul and assistant to Political Resident in Persian Gulf; killed 24 Jan. 1915 fighting with the Emir Abdul Aziz ibn Sa'ud. He had persuaded ibn Sa'ud to fight the Turks, thereby securing British influence in Kuwait (H.V.F. Winstone, *Captain Shakespear*, Jonathan Cape, 1976; Barbara Bray and Michael Darlow, *Ibn Saud: The Desert Warrior Who Created the Kingdom of Saudi Arabia*, Skyhorse, New York, 2012).

The campaign collapsed, mainly through difficulties of climate and terrain, and the poor organisation of the Indian Expeditionary Force. British troops under General Townshend got as far as Kut in November 1915, but they were besieged there and surrendered 29 April 1916. A good brief account is Rob Johnson, The Great War in the Middle East: A Strategic Study, *Oxford UP, 2016, pp.133–53. For the full story resting on impeccable scholarship: Charles Townshend,* When God Made Hell: the British Invasion of Mesopotamia and the Creation of Iraq, 1914–1921, *Faber & Faber, 2010.*

We considered & agreed upon Flag letter to U.S.A. Punjab was restless owing to price of wheat.

5.0 p.m. we considered our reply to Germany, & statement as to stopping all ships to Germany, & claiming retaliatory steps to Germany in regard to detention of commodities for Germany. Churchill's heard from the Hague 8 submarines of 1,000 tons were leaving this afternoon for English Channel, 10 of 1500 tons tomorrow, & 4 on Saturday for the Shetlands. They would keep the sea for 11 days.

Germany had announced that as from 18 February the waters around the British Isles and the Channel would be a 'war zone' in which only neutral vessels, hospital ships, and Belgian Relief Commission ships would be immune from attack. A note to the Americans on the use of neutral flags to escape capture or scrutiny was drafted. WSC told the Cabinet that he thought Germany had 25 effective submarines (Harcourt diary, 18 Feb. 1915, Bodl. MS. Eng.c.8270). Estimates of the U-boat order of battle vary. Avner Offer, citing a German authority, says that, at the end of January 1915, there were 21 boats available, of which eight were obsolete; all required long periods of maintenance ('Economic interpretation of War: the German submarine Campaign 1915–18', Australian Economic History Review, *vol. XXIV, no.1, 1989, pp.21–41). But most sources indicate that there were more boats available for blockade than WSC's intelligence suggested (Breemer,* Defeating the U-boat, *pp.19,23n.69). 'I cannot tell what the effect of the German SM attack on trade may be…', WSC admitted to the President of the Board of Trade. 'It is quite possible that we shall lose 15 or 20 ships in the first week, when all their submarines are out. But this effort cannot be maintained; & the exertions which can be required of these small craft are limited.' The First Lord's hope was that insurance rates would not be raised until there was 'a proper experience of the new conditions' and that the Admiralty would have the opportunity to express its view before any rate increases were decided (WSC–Runciman, 13 Feb.1915, Runciman of Doxford MSS).*

The difficulties in determining statistics of German submarine numbers are evident in Hans Joachim Koerver ed., German Submarine Warfare 1914–1918 in the Eyes of British Intelligence: Selected Sources from the British National Archives, Kew, *LIS Reinisch, Steinbach, 2010, pp.xii–xx.*

At 10 Downing Street on 22 February, the Prime Minister's luncheon guests included Lady Essex (a vegetarian, celebrated for breaking the taboo on women smoking in public), Victor Lawson (proprietor of the Chicago Tribune*), and Marie Belloc Lowndes, who learned that the American newspaper man had 'come over to see whether news can be less censored'. The table talk, uncensored, 'centred round the Dardanelles and many ships were mentioned'. HHA seemed 'annoyed and surprised' that Mrs Lowndes knew about 'the expeditionary force to Egypt'. But he added to her store of secret news 'the fact that 15,000 marines were going out' (Susan Lowndes ed.,* Diaries and Letters*, p.54). As the former Conservative Whip, Lord Crawford and Balcarres, put it in his journal: 'It has long been a bye word, the freedom of conversation in Downing Street' (Crawford and Balcarres diary, 2 Mar. 1915, vol.xxviii, f.33, Crawford and Balcarres MSS; and for a horrified Marquis de Soveral reporting on a dinner party at which the position and disposition of the fleet were discussed with the financier Sir Edgar Speyer, whose loyalty was widely but, at that time unjustifiably, suspected, and Lady Speyer as well as the Churchills present, Crawford diary, 13 [Nov. 1914], Vincent ed.,* The Crawford Papers*, pp.344–5).*

HHA might have been even more annoyed and surprised to learn that Mrs Lowndes's likely source of information was her brother Hilaire Belloc, whose best Cabinet informant on war news was the Home Secretary. Belloc's magazine The County Gentleman and Land & Water *was infused with confidential advice from McKenna, who counselled him not to give actual figures lest he lay himself open to contradiction or the censor's pen (McKenna–Belloc, 8 Dec. [1914], Belloc MSS, MS2005-02, 120/14–17, John J. Burns Library, Boston College). Belloc was also a friend and regular dining companion of Raymond Asquith, 'Bron' Lucas, and Harold 'Bluetooth' Baker, Financial Secretary at the War Office (Belloc MSS, MS2005-02, 8/11–13).*

Feb. 22 Dined at 12 Downing St. — sat between Francis McLaren[19] & Eddie Marsh[20] (Churchill's Sec) — the latter told me, we were still trying to locate the *Dresden* & *Karlsruhe* off Southern America. The Prime Minister & Violet Asquith were dining out but turned up before our bridge tables broke up.

[19] Francis Walter Stafford McLaren (1886–1917); Lib. MP Lincs (Spalding) 1910–17; younger s. Sir Charles McLaren Bt (1st Baron Aberconway June 1915); PPS to Lewis Harcourt, Sec. of St. for Colonial Affairs 1910–15; commissioned in RNVR Sept. 1914; 'would vanish nightly for bridge with the Asquiths' (Josiah Wedgwood, *Memoirs of a Fighting Life*, Hutchinson, 1940, p.96); saved Josiah Wedgwood's life at Gallipoli (C.V. Wedgwood, *The Last of the Radicals, Josiah Wedgwood, MP*, Cape, 1951, p.109); transferred to RFC; killed in action. His wife Barbara was Pamela McKenna's younger sister; his sister Priscilla (Fay) was married to Sir Henry Norman, Lib. MP Blackburn, JAP's bête noire as sec. of the Budget League 1909 (*A Liberal Chronicle… 1908–1910, passim*).

[20] Edward Hamilton Marsh (1872–1953); p.s. to WSC 1905–15, 1917–22, and 1924–9; entered civil service 1892; asst p.s. to HHA 1915–16; p.s. to successive Secs of St. for Colonial Affairs 1929–37; KCVO 1937; patron of artists and poets; edited the five volumes of *Georgian Poetry* (four with Rupert Brooke).

The Dresden, *a German light cruiser, had been part of Admiral Graf von Spee's Squadron, which had been defeated at the Battle of the Falkland Islands on 8 December 1914. Von Spee had told his three cruisers to scatter and run; only the* Dresden *escaped. She was scuttled after a brief encounter with British ships on 14 March 1915. WSC had ordered two ships to attack her after she was located in a Chilean bay. But HHA and Grey, alerted by Hankey, himself told of it by Captain W.R. Hall of Naval Intelligence, insisted that no attack could occur in neutral waters (Roskill,* Hankey: Man of Secrets, *Vol. I 1877–1918, p.160). The* Karlsruhe *was also a light cruiser, attacking British shipping in the North and South Atlantic on the same lines as the* Emden *in the Indian Ocean. It sank fifteen British ships totalling 68,000 tons before being destroyed by an internal explosion in the Caribbean; its loss was not known until March 1915.*

Feb. 24 — We discussed for over an hour at cabinet, how to deal with Labour at Glasgow; Government orders were being neglected, men were working badly, irregularity was increasing, strikes too. I laid it down that higher wages meant more irregularity more drink among a class of operatives who delayed the work of other steadier men whose work was dependent on the work of each man in the squad, closing pubs early & late might check irregularity, but must be administered tactfully, or the men would rebel. If Govmt intended to intervene, it was thought high profits should be limited & the Govmt take over the contract work given to Vickers, Armstrong &c. I said this was impossible & Churchill agreed, he had no staff. It was left to Simon to consult Thring & submit some bill giving powers.

In a 'violent discussion', DLG was now calling for martial law, and compelling the men to work. WSC offered conscription for work not fighting. The drafting of a bill was to be under the supervision of DLG as well as Simon (Harcourt diary, 24 Feb. 1915, Bodl. MS.Eng.c.8270). A strike on the Clyde led by William Gallacher and the Central Labour Withholding Committee had been called in response to the hiring of American craftsmen at higher rates of pay. The men returned to work on 4 March having been awarded 4s. 6d. *a week on time rates and 10 per cent on piece rates.*

Apparently misunderstanding something he had been told by Sir George Askwith's deputy, Haig Mitchell, DLG was saying that an 'anti-war set' in Glasgow was behind the Clyde dispute. WSC had suggested that Germans might 'be at the back of it'. Askwith assured the Prime Minister on 10 March that Mitchell said there was no such party. As for the German theory, Askwith gave it little credence: 'if the men suspected any one, they would tear them to pieces' (Bodl. MS. Asquith 14, f.17; for the background see Alison Heath, The Life of

George Ranken Askwith, 1861–1942, *Routledge, 2015, ch.14; and Joan Smith, 'Taking the leadership of the labour movement: the ILP in Glasgow, 1906–1914', in Alan McKinlay and R.J. Morris eds,* The ILP on Clydeside, 1893–1932: from foundation to disintegration, *Manchester UP, 1991, pp.96–8). Alistair J. Reid is perceptive on government, union, and employer interactions in* The tide of democracy: Shipyard workers and social relations in Britain, 1780–1950, *Manchester UP, 2010, pp.182–6; and the pre-war background is in William Kenefick and Arthur J. McIvor eds,* Roots of Red Clydeside, 1910–1914: labour unrest and industrial relations in West Scotland, *John Donald, Edinburgh, 1996.*

If DLG appears to have been a little febrile in the last weeks of February and into March, the pregnancy of Frances Stevenson, arrangements for an abortion, the end of her dream of a 'love child', and a prolonged convalescence afford some understanding (Ruth Longford, Frances, Countess Lloyd George: More than a Mistress, *Gracewing, Leominster, 1996, pp.29–31; Ffion Hague,* The Pain and the Privilege: The Women in Lloyd George's Life, *Harper P., 2008, pp.278–85; Campbell,* If Love Were All, *pp.78–87).*

German blockade & our reply

We discussed form of reprisals resolution & agreed to accept one alteration of 2 lines only suggested by the French lawyers.

The question as to what reply should be given to the U.S.A. suggestion, that we should allow foodstuffs into Germany for non combatants that we should neither sow sea mines, or torpedo merchant men was deferred to

Feb. 25 Thursday evening at 5.0. Grey advocated no reply of a committal character, & the course he recommended was approved. It was hoped we should hear what Germany might say, & meanwhile we should consult our allies.

In a paper for the War Council on 25 February Kitchener had said that there were two ways the war might end victoriously for the Allies: a decisive victory or series of victories either inside or outside German territory, or by attrition when Germany could no longer support her armies in the field and must sue for peace. Thinking it would be interesting, he had asked Lord Moulton to furnish 'a mathematical calculation of approximate dates when attrition might force our enemies to sue for peace'. As far as he could judge, this state of affairs might be reached at the beginning of 1917. He had not allowed for the possibility of starvation of the 105 million civilian population of Germany and Austria (TNA: CAB 42/1/45). HHA had been reminded by Hankey the same day that 'if Germany's "Achilles heel" is her food supply it is only common sense that we should devote our efforts to attacking it systematically' (Roskill, Hankey: Man of Secrets, Vol. I 1877–1918, *p.158).*

Monday. March 1 The P.M. introduced the vote of credit for a further sum of £37,000,000 for year to March 31st & a sum of £350,000,000, to carry on the war during the next few months of the new financial year.

He began on a low note, & after reading from a brief supplied by the Treasury passed on to his own material, the notes for which he had scribbled on a sheet of note paper. He read the views of the cabinet on our 'rights & duties' in reply to the German Fleet proposals to 'blockade' our ports by submarines. He proceeded to say we had not replied to the U.S.A. suggestions but were considering them with our allies (the proposal being we should let in & out materials to & from German civil population, if the Germans stopped torpedoing our non-armed merchant men). He laid down our terms for Peace

1. Belgium to recover in full measure all she had sacrificed
2. France secured against the menace of aggression
3. Rights of smaller nations placed on an unassailable foundation
4. Until the military domination of Prussia is wholly & finally destroyed.

It was a magnificent speech, & one of the most stirring & momentous in History.

March 2nd On Tuesday — we had a cabinet. K of K. told us he could move fr. Egypt 39,000 men to the Gallipoli Peninsula without danger to the Canal & Egypt.

A Naval Division of 11,000. A Territorial Division of cavalry from N.East coast of 9000 strong in 10 days time. The Greeks according to their Prime Minister would land 3 Divisions, the Russians an army corps from Odessa, & the French a Division making 150,000.

We discussed taking over armament companies. I suggested high profits being taxed & men induced to accept arbitration of Govmt no decision taken.

Order in Council carrying out the document read to H. of C. day before was discussed, & main lines agreed to.

In the debate on supplementary grants for the cost of the war, HHA had read out the British reply to the German blockade: the British and French governments threatened their own blockade of German ports but promised not to attack neutral ships (HC Deb 1 March 1915 vol 70 cc598–600).

In afternoon in H. of C. by bill we proposed to give Oxford & Cambridge University power to raise money to finance their universities over the war by anticipating revenues, the P.M. was again very eloquent, & paid a high tribute to patriotism of the undergraduates who at the expense of their careers had joined the colours.

J.M. Winter details the enlistment of Oxford scholars and fellows, and the university's war finances in 'Oxford and the First World War', in Brian Harrison ed., The History of the University of Oxford: Vol.VIII The Twentieth Century, *Clarendon P., Oxford, 1994, pp.3–25). JAP does not refer to the information WSC gave his colleagues about progress at the Dardanelles and perhaps might not have heard his buoyant suggestion: 'We should take & occupy all Turkey in Europe' (Harcourt diary, 2 Mar. 1915, Bodl. MS.Eng.c.8270).*

In their excitement about the prospect of Greek participation in the Gallipoli campaign ministers had paid insufficient attention to reservations from Grey about the likely reaction of the Russians. By the end of the week they were reminded of Russia's ambition to acquire Constantinople and informed of their refusal to contemplate Greek troops setting foot there (Ronald Bobroff, Roads to Glory: Late Imperial Russia and the Turkish Straits, *I.B. Tauris, New York, 2006, pp.130–41).*

March 4 Thursday. A cabinet of 2 hours discussing Russian opposition to Greek help. The danger in Mesopotamia & the losses suffered by an outpost. We urged K. & Crewe to send more troops to safeguard our position.

We agreed to the Order in Council terms for reprisals at sea, & agreed to go quietly taking only picked cargoes least annoying to U.S.A. I lunched with Margot met a Doctor — a leading surgeon home from the front (Milne)[21] Lady Wimborne.[22] P.M. not present.[23]

At 6.0 we discussed how we should deal with Italy — if she came in & offered conditions. Grey told us the ambassador had come in all smiles to the F.O. that afternoon — but plans must be kept absolutely secret — as they could not be ready until end of [*sic*].

[21] Robert Milne (1881–1949), general and orthopaedic surgeon; major, RAMC on active service in France; surgical tutor, London Hospital 1914–20; consulting surgeon, Dr Barnardo's Homes, where his father was chief medical officer 1880–1919; consulting orthopaedic surgeon, Royal Navy 1939–45 with rank of rear-adm.; FRCS 1906. Sir Bertrand Dawson, physician in ordinary to the King, wrote in July 1910: 'his record is one of brilliant success' (www.richardfordmanuscripts.co.uk/catalogue/10777, accessed 10 Apr. 2016).

[22] Probably Hon. Alice Grosvenor (1881–1948), dau. of 2nd Baron Ebury, m. Hon. Ivor Guest 1902; her husband cr. Baron St Legers 1910, succ. father as 2nd Lord Wimborne 1914. Possibly Baroness Wimborne of Canford Magna (1847–1927), Lady Cornelia Henrietta Maria Spencer-Churchill, dau. 7th Duke of Marlborough; m. 1868 Sir Ivor Bertie Guest Bt and styled Lady Wimborne on her husband's elevation to the peerage in 1880.

[23] HHA was lunching with Montagu, and seeing Venetia Stanley and McKenna (HHA's miniature diary and engagement book, 4 Mar. 1915, Bodl. MS.Eng.hist.g.24, f.21).

JAP might deliberately have refrained from putting on paper the sensitive information Grey gave the Cabinet that Italy would be ready to enter the war, as the less cautious Hobhouse wrote 'about the middle or end of April' or Harcourt 'towards the middle of April'. JAP would have known that, not only were the Russians opposed to the Greeks entering Constantinople with the British, they were also unenthusiastic about Italy joining the war (Hobhouse diary, 4 Mar. 1915, David ed., Inside Asquith's Cabinet, *p.225; Harcourt diary, 4 Mar. 1915, Bodl. MS.Eng.c.8270). Ambassador Imperiali had submitted a detailed statement of Italian claims which Grey needed to study in English translation. The Foreign Secretary had made it clear that any discussion of peace terms would entail consultation with Britain's French and Russian allies. Renzi's* In the Shadow of the Sword, *pp.202–12, carries the story forward to the signing on 26 April of what would come to be known as the 'Pact of London' between Britain, Russia, France, and Italy. Italy's ambitions are the subject of Richard Bosworth and Giuseppe Finaldi, 'The Italian Empire', in Robert Gerwarth and Erez Manela eds,* Empires at War 1911–1923, *pp.34–51.*

Although the news was leaked almost immediately in the French press, it was not until 20 May that the government's rationale for choosing to side with the Entente was laid out for the Italian Parliament, and another four days before Italy formally entered the war. The strategic and military considerations are elucidated in Nicola Labanca, 'The Italian Front', in Jay Winter ed., The Cambridge History of the First World War Vol. I Global War, *pp.266–77; Gooch,* The Italian Army and the First World War, *pp.53–78, and Filippo Cappellano (trs Noor Giovanni Mazhar), 'Warfare 1914–1918 (Italy)', in Ute Daniel, Peter Gatrell, Oliver Janz, Heather Jones, Jennifer Keene, Alan Kramer, and Bill Nasson eds,* 1914–1918-online. International Encyclopedia of the First World War, *Freie Universität Berlin, 8 Oct. 2008. DOI:* http://dx.doi.org/10.15463/ie1418.10484, *accessed 29 Dec. 2016.*

K. of K. urged we should take over 32,000 men & get them to work on shells. I said you can't force them, but induce employers to liberate, & get men to see profits were not going exclusively to capital! We agreed to allow penalty clauses to be cancelled when contractual obligations had been entered into, when such contract work prejudiced Govmt work being undertaken & proceeded with, & we agreed to indemnify & exonerate the firms. Churchill talked wildly — McKenna George & K out for compulsion — I urged voluntary effort & clear exposition of needs, Samuel, Montagu, Grey & P.M. — spoke same sense.

WSC's wild talk had been foreshadowed in a discursive and muddled essay presented as a Cabinet paper on 'Armament Firms' on 3 March 1915. WSC concluded: 'If a system of compulsory arbitration, gilded by State bonuses to the workmen and sustained by restriction of public house hours, is inaugurated, it will secure almost all the results desired...'. His quasi-philosophical memorandum was followed with 'Seven Practical Steps' (dated 15 March 1915 but apparently circulated on 12 March, Gilbert ed., Winston S. Churchill, Vol. III, Companion Part I, *pp.619–22; TNA: CAB 37/125/17). A Munitions Levy was introduced after the creation of the Coalition ministry; for the levy and the subsequent Excess Profits Duty see Mark Billings and Lynne Oats, 'Innovation and pragmatism in tax design: Excess Profits Duty in the UK during the First World War,'* Accounting History Review, *vol.24(2–3), 2014, pp.83–101. For Treasury views on taxing excess profits see Martin Daunton,* Just Taxes: The Politics of Taxation in Britain; 1914–1979, *Cambridge UP, 2002, pp.55–7.*

March 9 Birrell — very sad on my left. — His wife's life being only maintained by oxygen — she had been unconscious for some days.[24] We discussed the ultimatum from Sazonoff that Russia must have Constantinople and both banks of Bosphoros & Dardanelles. — We were all prepared to acquiesce — if we could arrange with France that we should get Alexandretta.

Samuel raised a caveat in Jewish interest that holy places should not go to the French. Damascus he was willing, but not Jerusalem.

As Admiralty and War Office assessments made clear, Alexandretta (now Iskenderun) was strategically desirable as a potential naval base on the assumption that after the war Britain controlled Mesopotamia and the Persian oil fields, France had Syria, and Russia had Constantinople. Moving troops by railway to Mesopotamia would be two weeks faster than by sea and would permit the holding of Mesopotamia with a smaller garrison (Martin William Gibson, Britain's Quest for Oil: The First World War and the Peace Conferences, *Helion & Co., Solihull, 2017, p.27).*

Samuel, not so much against *French possession of Jerusalem (and Palestine) as* for *British possession, put the Zionist case to the Cabinet in two memoranda: 'The Future of Palestine', 21 Jan. 1915 (TNA: CAB 37/123/43), and 'Palestine', 11 Mar. 1915 (TNA: CAB 37/126/1). His evolving views on the possible 're-establishment of the Jewish State' are traced in David Glover, 'Liberalism, Anglo-Jewry and the Diasporic Imagination: Herbert Samuel via Israel Zangwill, 1890–1914',* Jewish Culture and History, *vol.6, no.1, 2003, pp.186–216.*

Ministerial conflict on the future of Palestine, and Edwin Montagu's withering riposte to Samuel, are authoritatively presented in Jonathan Schneer, The Balfour Declaration: The

[24] Eleanor Birrell (1854–1915); dau. of Frederick Locker Lampson, widow of Lionel Tennyson, the poet laureate's younger son; m. Birrell as his second wife 1888. Long bedridden, she had been critically ill since early Feb. She died the next day, 10 Mar.

Origins of the Arab–Israeli Conflict, Bloomsbury, 2010, *pp.144–7. For the British negotiations with Russia over the Straits issue and Grey's quiet assurance to Count Benckendorff that 'whatever the theatre of war where various powers act, at the time of peace the totality of the rights of each of them will be taken into consideration', followed by the signing of the Treaty of London on 25 April 1915, see Soroka,* Britain, Russia and the Road to the First World War, *pp.262–7. British, Russian, and Greek diplomacy from August 1914 to May 1915 are painstakingly reconstructed in George B. Leon,* Greece and the Great Powers 1914–1917, *Institute for Balkan Studies, Thessaloniki, 1974, pp.16–187.*

The Cabinet reported on by HHA met on the Tuesday morning, 9 March, not the more usual Wednesday. Greek Prime Minister Venizelos had resigned, unable to carry his policy of cooperation in the Gallipoli venture against the veto of the King and army chiefs. Grey reported that a prearranged formal inquiry had been received from Greece about the use of Lemnos as a British naval base. After a discussion about the reply to be given to the Russian 'aide memoire' on the future of Constantinople and the Straits, it was agreed that a meeting of the Foreign Ministers of the three Allied Powers was desirable, 'preferably on board of a British man of war at or near Lemnos' (Bodl. MS. Asquith 8, ff.17–18). The War Council (to which Harcourt had been added on 4 March, and to which Lansdowne and Bonar Law were invited) met on the 10th and again on the 19th to consider the demand for an assurance that Constantinople would go to Russia in a post-war settlement (Keith Neilson, '"For Diplomatic, Economic, Strategic And Telegraphic Reasons": British Imperial Defence, the Middle East and India, 1914–1918', in Greg Kennedy and Keith Neilson eds, Far-Flung Lines, *p.104).*

Hobhouse raised effect on Bulgaria & Roumania. Greece obviously had lost her opportunity of joining allies, & the new cabinet was obviously opposed to carrying out policy the Grk Prime Minister had the week before to carry out [sic] & land 3 Division.

Situation not probably prejudiced as Russia viewed with opposition the entrance of Greek help to the allies, but Churchill wanted use of Tenedos as a base, & Greek naval assistance.

We all thought Grey ought to meet Sazonoff and Delcassé at Salonika on the *Queen Elizabeth* & discuss terms upon which we could all work & whole heartedly without suspicion & mental reservations.

Wed. Mar. 10 Benckendorff reported Sazonoff would not leave Petrograd.

Thursday March 11 Cabinet discussed how to deal with labour, secure regularity of work promote sobriety & remove discontent.

Churchill very voluble & assertive but not convincing or clear, he likes to hear his own voice.

After an hour's discussion we agreed that Lloyd George should with Runciman see what arrangements could be made with private firms doing war work, so as to prevent large profits being made out of war, that if these could be taken over, we should approach labour representatives & arrange with them compulsory arbitration and there should be no laying down of tools. Subsequently we thought we could restrict morning drinking & close all drink shops between 9 at night & 11.0 in the morning.

The question of Grey going to meet Sazonoff was off.

Welsh Disestablishment amendment bill would not be pressed owing to attitude of Welsh members.

Progress in Dardanelles slow owing to fogs, & aviators' work dangerous & difficult.

Kitchener would summon Sir Ian Hamilton, HHA's choice, the next day to give him command of the land forces that might be used at Gallipoli, the 'Mediterranean Expeditionary Force'. The Secretary of State for War had refused to make Royal Flying Corps support available. Struggling with the exiguous reconnaissance from the Ark Royal's *lumbering seaplanes and four other aircraft, Vice-Admiral S.H. Carden had advised the Admiralty on 9 March that he could not make further progress without reinforcement of the air services (Peter Chasseaud and Peter Doyle,* Grasping Gallipoli: Terrain, Maps and Failure at the Dardanelles, 1915, *Spellmount, Staplehurst, 2005, pp.177–82; Hugh Dolan,* Gallipoli Air War: The Unknown Story of the Fight for the Skies Over Gallipoli, *Pan Macmillan Australia, Sydney, 2013, is a well-documented account of the matters the Cabinet had begun to learn about; see also Sterling Michael Pavelec,* Airpower Over Gallipoli, 1915–1916, *Naval Institute P., Annapolis, 2020).*

March 12 Friday I went down to Walmer, arriving at 6.0, the P.M. & Margot appearing at 8.0. Party was Harold Baker, Geoffrey Howard,[25] Violet Asquith — (on Sat.

[25] Hon. Geoffrey William Algernon Howard (1877–1935); son 9th Earl and Countess of Carlisle; Lib. MP Cumberland (Eskdale) 1906–10, Wilts (Westbury) 1911–18 and Luton 1923–4; PPS to HHA 1910; Vice-Chamberlain to Household 1911–15; junior whip 1915–16. Lord Knollys wrote to HHA on Howard's appointment to the Household that he had been told that 'he is out of the way unprepossessing looking, & that in regard to "presence" therefore he would not make a good "Court Official". He [the King] sees however that it would be difficult for him to refuse a man's appointment because he is ugly!! I don't know why he should be so, as his Father is not bad looking & his Mother when I used to know her, years ago, was the prettiest of the Stanley of Alderley Family…'. Howard's glass eye, which he used to tap with a fork at meals, did not enhance his 'presence' (Knollys–HHA, n.d. [5 or 6

Lord & Lady Lytton[26] & Mrs Rupert Beckett[27]).[28] At dinner we discussed who should or could organise a lot of big business Berridge[29] of Harrods, Lord Cowdray;[30] & Margot urged that we should secure Alexandretta, as the only port of any value to us. We should not think of tricking or securing by sly means plural voting. I told her we were all of one mind in regard to former, if it could be done, & the latter had not been discussed at all. Harold Baker told us he had had dinner with K. at St. James's Palace. K. complained that the pictures were wanting. He looks a gift horse in the mouth![31] He said K. had told him that Maxwell[32] wired him from Egypt in regard to transports going to Gallipoli Peninsula 'Contractor let cat out of bag'. K. replied:—'Dangle canard to entice feline (back) at once…'.

Margot Asquith's advice that the British should secure Alexandretta indicates that she was privy to discussions in the Cabinet on 9 March, and possibly the War Council on 10 March. WSC had argued in late January for an operation against Alexandretta. If the Dardanelles operation failed, he said, it could be explained away as a feint to cover the taking of Alexandretta. DLG thought Palestine was a better target. But Kitchener weighed in with a

Feb. 1911], Bodl. MS. Asquith 2, f.122; Deborah Devonshire, *Wait For Me! Memoirs of the Youngest Mitford Sister*, John Murray, 2010, p.83). Rosalind, 'The Radical Countess', might have been the prettiest of the Stanleys. But, according to his great-granddaughter, George Howard had an affair with her sister Maisie; and 'Venetia Stanley…was generally thought to be George's daughter' (Venetia Murray, *Castle Howard: The Life and Times of a Stately Home*, Viking, 1994, p.202; divers family opinions on Venetia's paternity are gathered in Stefan Buczacki, *My darling Mr Asquith: The extraordinary life and times of Venetia Stanley*, Cato & Clarke, Stratford-upon-Avon, 2016, pp.4–5).

[26] Countess of Lytton (née Pamela Frances Audrey Chichele-Plowden) (?1873/4–1971); dau. Sir Trevor Chichele-Plowden: m. Earl of Lytton 1902. WSC was a suitor and lifelong friend.

[27] Muriel Helen Florence Beckett (1878–1941); dau. Lord Berkeley Paget; m. 1896 the Hon. Rupert Evelyn Beckett (1870–1955) Yorkshire banker; chmn, *Yorkshire Post* 1920–50; director, Westminster Bank 1921–55 (chmn of directors, 1931–50). His father, William Beckett, and two brothers, Ernest (later 2nd Lord Grimthorpe, lover of Alice Keppel and reputed father of Violet Keppel) and Sir Gervase, were Con. MPs.

[28] Viola Parsons was also of the party, taken by HHA with Muriel Beckett to Dover to look at submarines (JAP–EP, 14 Mar. 1915, MS. Gainford 190/26–7).

[29] See 22 Sept. 1914 for Richard Burbidge. JAP appears here to be conflating Burbidge (managing director) and Selfridge (owner) of Selfridge's.

[30] Weetman Dickinson Pearson, Baron Cowdray (1856–1927); Lib. MP Colchester 1895–1910; construction contractor; his company discovered oil in Mexico; Bt 1894; Baron Cowdray 1910; Pres., Air Bd 1917; PC 1917; Vt 1917; proprietor, *The Westminster Gazette*; chief source of funds for Asquithian Liberals 1918–27; on his death his estate was worth £4,000,000.

[31] The King had lent St James's Palace to Kitchener, who had previously occupied Lady Wantage's house in Carlton Gardens.

[32] Lt-Gen. Sir John Grenfell 'Jack' Maxwell (1859–1929); C-in-C British forces in Egypt; commanded 14th Brigade, Sth African War, Military Gov., Pretoria and the Western Transvaal (1900); Duke of Connaught's staff 1904–8; Maj.-Gen. 1907; Head British military mission at French GHQ Aug.–Sept. 1914; transferred to UK at own request then despatched by Kitchener as C-in-C and Mili. Gov.of Ireland 28 Apr. 1916, crushed the Easter rebellion; C-in-C Nthern Command 1916–19; Gen. 1919; PC GCB KCMG CVO DSO.

raft of strategic arguments in favour of Alexandretta (TNA: CAB 42/2/10; Halpern, The Naval War in the Mediterranean, *p.66). For Ian Hamilton's 'outlandish scheme', written on 24 April, of turning a failed Gallipoli operation into a feint preceding an attack on mainland Turkey see Robin Prior,* Gallipoli: The End of the Myth, *UNSW P., Sydney, 2009, pp.87–8.*

Andrekos Varnava, 'Imperialism first, the war second: the British, an Armenian legion, and deliberations on where to attack the Ottoman empire, November 1914–April 1915', Hist. Res., *vol.87, no.237, Aug. 2014, pp.533–55, argues with conviction that 'the British and French ... got it wrong with their decision to land forces at Gallipoli in April 1915 instead of at Alexandretta'.*

Sunday March 14 Had a quiet chat with the P.M. for a quarter of an hour. before we dressed for dinner. He walked up & down the drawing room whilst I stood with my back to the fire, it reminded me of my old chief whip's days. The P.M. let himself go, & said I hate the Welsh, no I can't say that but, their pernickety ways, jealous petty ways. I trust McKenna's administration & I have found his work good but I suppose we all make mistakes, he has let me in about Welsh Disestablishment. McKenna says, it is all due to the hatred in the Welsh Party of Lloyd George, they will oppose his power, & dictatorship. George is a man of varied powers, & I have an exception to make in his favour, when I charge the Welsh Nation as a whole. But Ellis Davies,[33] Roch[34] & others will attack tomorrow & Lord Robt Cecil, who is untrustworthy like all the Cecils, & bad in himself, second only to Hugh will attack too.

I suggested that he the P.M. would deprecate any discussion, & say that this was not the time to discuss differences, but to try & agree, but if parties could not, we would withdraw the Bill.

The P.M. said that he had explained in writing his position to Lord Robt & if the H. of C. took a different view to the H. of Lords, he was free to withdraw.

[33] Ellis William Davies (1871–1939); Lib. MP Caernarvonshire (Eifion) 1906–18; Ind. Lib. MP Caernarvonshire (Denbigh) 1923–9; member DLG's Urban and Rural Land Enquiry Committees; joined Lab. Party 1937. He did speak the next day, attacking the govt's bill because it proposed a six months' pause between the declaration of peace and the beginning of disestablishment. He argued that this would mean another general election before the act came into force, thus putting the act at risk. He also attacked the proposal giving to the Church the value of vacancies that might arise before disestablishment was effected (HC Deb 15 March 1915 vol 3 cc1821–2).

[34] Walter Francis Roch (1880–1965); Lib. MP Pembrokeshire 1908–18; 'a wit and fine talker' (*The Times*, 19 May 1965); barrister and landowner; served on Dardanelles Commission; his promising political career foundered when he chose to support HHA after DLG became Prime Minister; author of *Mr Lloyd George and the War* (1920); his two brothers were killed in action in 1918.

When ladies left Dining Room after dinner on Friday night we discussed War Office short comings, promotions in army &c.

On Saturday night Belgian refugees, & their ways & ingratitude & reasons for same — Lytton being the active organiser of their distribution — how to secure the training of those Belgians here of military age. Sunday night, we talked about Dardanelles. Ian Hamilton going out — rapidity of transit — the relative seniority of commands.

Kitchener had informed the War Council on 3 March that the French had agreed that the supreme command of the forces assembled for the Dardanelles should be vested in a British general notwithstanding that the French General Albert d'Amade, although being sidelined by Joffre, was senior to Sir William Birdwood, the British commander. If a larger force was contemplated, Kitchener proposed to nominate Sir Ian Hamilton. With the prospect of the Russians and Greeks sending very senior generals, WSC thought it might be advisable to send a senior man immediately so as to avoid an Allied bidding war over seniority (Secretary's Notes on a Meeting of the War Council, 3 Mar. 1915, TNA: CAB 42/1/45). Hamilton was told on 12 March of his appointment to lead the Mediterranean Expeditionary Force. Millerand and Joffre were soon stunned to realise that the Dardanelles arrangement giving seniority to the commander of the largest army would not be reciprocated in France. Sir John French and the BEF had always been meant to act independently (Elizabeth Greenhalgh, The French Army and the First World War, *Cambridge UP, 2014, p.102).*

On Monday 15 March HHA had 'opened' to Simon about Ireland being 'for the time being a backwater' with a strong civil servant in Sir Matthew Nathan 'therefore, for the moment, a fit place in wh. to put a solid 2nd rate man like Jack Pease'. Two days later the Prime Minister discussed possible successors to Birrell with John Redmond. Presented with a choice between Samuel and JAP, Redmond 'declared himself... strongly anti-Pease' (Asquith Letters, *pp.482,485).*

While HHA was ruminating about JAP and Ireland, WSC and his First Sea Lord were butting heads over fleet tactics in the Dardanelles. At WSC's urging—and against the advice of Fisher and Sir Henry Jackson—Vice-Admiral Carden had agreed to switch from long-range deliberate fire against the forts, to short-range suppressing fire. With the naval attack impending, an apprehensive Fisher was seeking political cover by calling for 'instant action by a collective vote & decision of the War Council with the Opposition joined in'. WSC's rejection on 15 March was swift and secret: 'I don't think we want a War Council on this. It is after all asking a lot of ignorant people to meddle in our business.' (Tom Curran, ed. Andrew G. Bonnell, The Grand Deception: Churchill and the Dardanelles, *Big Sky Publishing, Newport, NSW, 2015, p.109.) JAP records that WSC told the Cabinet in the absence of Fisher that he and Carden were agreed on going into the Dardanelles and directly attacking the forts.*

Tuesday 16 March Cabinet. We discussed labour questions. Runciman reported his interviews with Armstrongs & Vickers, & that they would agree to

1. Retaining their control
2. Govmt taking surplus profits to distribute to Exchequer or as bonus
3. Surplus to mean same dividend left to shareholders, & 15 per cent more to their total profit than prior to the war.
4. Their expenditure to be written against revenue & capital.

1. When capital advanced by Govmt, the govmt to have right to acquire purchases at War end.
2. Capital they spent to be regarded as spread over short period
3. Accountants to examine a/cs. We agreed that Labour must undertake not to down tools & accept arbitration, if surplus profits were taken from firms with govmt contracts.

Churchill reported he & Carden agreed the time was come for us to risk more & go in to the Dardanelles, & attack directly the forts.

Result reported Sat. 20th loss of *Ocean*, *Irresistible* by mines — also *Bouvet* — 3 battle ships lost!

In the attack on The Narrows on 18 March the Formidable class HMS Irresistible *was badly hit by Turkish howitzers. Listing and drifting she struck a mine. A destroyer, HMS* Wear, *and the Canopus class battleship HMS* Ocean *came to her aid. After an unsuccessful attempt to tow by* Ocean, Irresistible *was abandoned.* Ocean, *damaged by gunfire and a submerged moored mine, was also abandoned. Both ships sank; all* Ocean*'s 683 crew and 610 from* Irresistible *were saved, but 200 were lost (http://www.naval-history.net/WW1Battle1503Dardanelles1.htm, accessed 26 Nov. 2022). The French ship* Bouvet *sank within two minutes after 'a huge column of reddish black smoke shot up from under her… followed almost immediately by another, higher and more dense, which seemed to tell a magazine had gone'. According to the official history, it was impossible to tell whether a shell or mine had caused the initial damage. On the role of Ottoman artillery, see Ayhan Aktar, 'Who Sank the Battleship* Bouvet *on 18 March 1915? The problems of Imported Historiography in Turkey',* W&S, *vol.36, no.3, 2017, pp.194–216.*

On 20 March 1915 the United Kingdom and Russia signed an agreement under which in a post-war settlement Russia would annex Constantinople, the Bosporus Strait, and more than half of the European section of Turkey. Russia was also promised future control of the Dardanelles and the Gallipoli peninsula. In return, Russia would agree to British claims on other areas of the former Ottoman Empire and central Persia, including the oil-rich region of

Mesopotamia. David French, British Strategy and War Aims 1914–1916, *Allen & Unwin, 1986, ch.5, is a comprehensive study of the Constantinople Agreement. For the aborted secret mission to bribe the Turks to leave the war see Stafford,* Churchill and Secret Service, *pp.90–1.*

Tuesday 23rd March[35] We discussed the terms of a telegram sent to Bertie in Paris No 610 & to Buchanan[36] at Petrograd No. 406 from Grey giving the proposals of the Italian Govmt conveyed to him by Imperiali, and the conditions reqd. to secure the assistance of Italy on behalf of the allies by the end of April.

We agreed to generally accept the terms as set out, but we thought Spalato should be neutralised or at any rate made an open port for Servia.

The P. Minister spoke of the perfidy of Italy & the necessity to secure a real cooperation & not the mere occupation of the territory she coveted. Churchill & George also pressed Grey to secure a real cooperation with the allies, & to unite with allies on the agreement — as to no separate PEACE.

*HHA knew, as he told Venetia Stanley in the afternoon after the Cabinet meeting, that 'the news from the Dardanelles is not very good' and Rear Admiral John de Robeck (who had just replaced Carden, whose health had collapsed) was nervous about continuing the naval attack. He said that he had withheld the information from the Cabinet (*Asquith Letters, *pp.500–1).*

Friday March 26 Churchill reported a battleship in the North Sea had rammed *U29*, but he did not want the Germans to know about it but the crew had said so much he thought he had better make the fact of the loss known & have the enemy in doubt as to how it had been done.

The U29 had attacked a dreadnought squadron of the Grand Fleet on 18 March and had been rammed by the Dreadnought. *WSC had issued instructions to merchant navy captains on 10 February: if they could not escape they should steer 'at utmost speed' towards the submarine. Although the word 'ram' was not used, the implication was obvious if the submarine failed to dive (Diana Preston,* A Higher Form of Killing: Six Weeks in World War I That Forever Changed the Nature of Warfare, *Bloomsbury P., 2015, p.76, and see Marder,* From the Dreadnought to Scapa Flow, *Vol. II, p.349, for more bizarre methods).*

[35] JAP wrote this entry in red ink.

[36] Sir George (William) Buchanan (1854–1924); Amb. to Petrograd 1910–18; Sec. of Embassy Rome 1900, Berlin 1901–3; Min. Plenipotentiary Sofia 1903–8; Min. at the Hague 1908–10; Amb. to Rome 1919–21. PC, GCB 1915; GCMG 1913; GCVO and KCMG 1909; KCVO 1905; m. 1885 Lady Georgina Bathurst, who typed telegrams and other documents and decoded cypher telegrams (Rey, *Men, Women and Places*, Rey MSS, Bodl. MS.Eng.c.7191, f.153).

Grey reported that on Wednesday he had had a depressing day, Bulgaria, he learned from Jagow the French Fo. Minister,[37] was not going to come in, but on Thursday, he saw the Bulgarian minister[38] who said they were not allowing ammunition to go thro' Turkey. He saw the minister who had come straight from Roumania from Budapest, who said he had authority from his Govmt to say they would definitely come in at the beginning of May & the only condition they made was ammunition from the French, & that Grey was to be allowed to make it known to the allies, meanwhile no munitions of war were being allowed to go through.

Churchill referred to quarrel the Germans were promoting with Holland by sinking her ships. Grey & I thought she wanted to secure free access to the Scheldt but Churchill thought she might insist on taking Holland, & their being in occupation have more to negociate with for Peace.

K. of K. said he would like to put everyman he could into Holland if she joined the allies, & move up French's forces. Grey had assured Netherlands' minister we would not disturb neutrality. We thought Holland should realise her interest was with the allies, & if she thought so too we would like to help her.

We then discussed P.O. advance. Hobhouse wanted £980,000 more, equivalent to the Railway men. We arranged to take Askwith's, Gibb[39] & [*sic*] opinion as to merits.

A strong feeling was expressed that on grounds of rise in prices a case in war did not justify Govmt money — the more wages the workers had & more to spend the more would prices rise & they must be content to make some sacrifice during war.

Hobhouse's scheme, on which there was much difference of opinion—Crewe and Haldane cautiously in favour, DLG and Montagu against—was to give a 'war bonus' to postal servants of two to three shillings a week. Advice was to be sought from the 'Three Wise Knights', Sir George Askwith, Sir George Gibb, and Sir Francis Hopwood (HHA Cabinet letter, 27 Mar. 1915, TNA: CAB 41/36/13; Hobhouse diary, 26 Mar. 1915, David ed., Inside Asquith's Cabinet, *p.233). The three investigated a large number of industrial problems (the Committee*

[37] Gottlieb von Jagow (1863–1935) was the German State Secretary (Foreign Min.) 1913–16; Théophile Delcassé (1852–1923) was French Foreign Min. (1898–1905 and 1914–15).

[38] The Minister whom Grey saw was not Bulgarian but Roumanian: Emanuel (Emanoil) Porumbaru (1845–1921); Min. of Foreign Affairs, Jan. 1914–Dec. 1916 (Bodl. MS. Asquith 8, f.25).

[39] Sir George Stegmann Gibb (1850–1925); member (chmn 1918), govt Arbitration Bd 1915–18; solicitor, Nth-Eastn Railway Co. (NER) 1882–91; gen. mgr, NER 1891–1906; Kt 1904; director, NER 1906–10; mgn dir., Underground Electric Railway Co. and Metropolitan District Railway Co. 1906–10; chmn, Road Bd 1910–19; additional member, Army Council (supervising Army contracts) 1914–15. A member with JAP of the group creating a network of local committees to arrange food distribution and work for the unemployed in the first week of the war (JAP–EP, 6 Aug. 1914, MS. Gainford 189/233).

on Production in Engineering and Shipbuilding Establishments engaged in Government Work) and were frequently chosen to arbitrate disputes. The nine reports of the committee, delivered 12–23 April 2015, are in the Lloyd George MSS, LG/C/21/2/22, PA. After listening to her friend Askwith at lunch four months earlier, Victoria Wemyss recorded that 'he seemed outraged at the way the contractors who are making 100% are trying to grind down the work-people' (diary, 28 Nov. 1914, Wester-Wemyss MSS, WMYS 9/1, CAC).

HHA understandably did not report to the King on the political discussion on 26 March of registration and postponement of the general election. Samuel and JAP, whose silence on the subject in the diary is surprising, brought up the question. Hobhouse wrote that DLG was for postponement, Harcourt against. Crewe mentioned Coalition as the possible price of Opposition agreement. 'The P.M. remarked he could not believe the Opposition wished to have any responsibility for the conduct of the war' (David ed., Inside Asquith's Cabinet, *p.233).*

Tuesday 30 March K. of K. reported that on Sunday 28 March he met Joffre & Sir John French in France — the French said they hitherto had not tried to penetrate German lines, but to keep enemy sufficiently occupied with a view to relieve Russia from overwhelming troops attacking allies on the Eastern theatre. K. was then told on the 18th April the French proposed to penetrate, but they wanted 2 Divisions from us to help them. K. at once responded & said they should have them, although this might somewhat delay our sending out our full strength to Sir John French of 100,000 new army men during April. He proposed to send territorials, he now believed they would have been satisfied with one Division from us & did not expect so ready a response. K. however made it clear, if their proposed advance failed on the 18th, he could not do this again for them.

We were sending across now 4,000 a day & the 2 extra divisions would postpone 10 days our normal additions owing to shortage of small arms.

Churchill told us, we were still clearing the Dardanelles of mines, but the main attack would not begin until after April 7.

Grey reported passage of aide memoires which had crossed between Sazonoff & himself. Grey urged Russia to accept terms with Italy, & to be satisfied if Spalato were made a free port for Servia.

George reported interview with shipbuilders advocating prohibition of all alcohol so as to induce men not to lose time. After ½ hours discussion, we adjourned to see statistics & papers.

That afternoon DLG wrote to Stamfordham about Cabinet's discussion of the 'alarming reports' of excessive drinking from the Admiralty transport and munition directors.

The Cabinet believed that the announcement of a pledge by the King to ban the consumption of wines, spirits, or beer in any of His Majesty's houses would have an excellent effect (Lloyd George MSS, LG/C/5/6/13, PA; for the background see John Grigg, Lloyd George: From Peace to War 1912–1916, *Methuen, 1985, pp.229–33). DLG, reputedly a tee-totaller since the age of 19, but always a moderate drinker, saw no need to take the pledge. Kitchener hesitated but fell in line with the sovereign. Runciman was already a tee-totaller. McKenna, Emmott, Grey, and Haldane joined the abstainers, the last with the caveat, as he told a confidant, that his guests 'will find everything as usual for themselves' and noting that, although he did not like the cure, ten days of abstention had apparently diminished his rheumatism (Haldane–Gosse, 10 Apr. 1915, Gosse MSS, MS. 19c Gosse D, Brotherton Coll., Leeds U.).*

Harcourt, WSC, and the Prime Minister did not sign up for the new regime. 'P.M. sees no reason to change his ways' (E. Haldane diary, 9 Apr. 1915, Elizabeth Haldane MSS, MS.20240, ff.92–3, NLS). Johnny Baird, departing from Windsor after receiving his DSO, was told by Harry Verney 'that Asquith made them all very angry . . . by saying to one of the Household, "I suppose all you fellows have your whack upstairs"!' (Baird diary, 23 Apr. 1915, Stonehaven MSS, vol.129, Aberdeen U.) Margot Asquith was observed at Windsor 'taking copious swigs out of a medicine bottle' (Nicolas Mosley, Julian Grenfell: His life and the times of his death 1888–1915, *Holt, Rinehart and Winston, New York, 1976, p.245). Sir Derek Keppel's instruction to the kitchens as Master of the Household was that no wine or sherry was to be used in cooking (Gabriel Tschumi,* Royal Chef: Recollections of Life in Royal Households from Queen Victoria to Queen Mary, *William Kimber, 1954, p.133). Robert Duncan,* Pubs and Patriots: The Drink Crisis in Britain During World War One, *Liverpool UP, 2013, pp.67–92, is a thoughtful meditation on DLG and the Drink question in March–April 1915. The electoral and parliamentary influence of the liquor trade is assessed in David M. Fahey, 'Brewers, Publicans, and Working-Class Drinkers: Pressure group Politics in Late Victorian and Edwardian England',* Histoire Sociale—Social History, *vol.XIII, no.25, May 1980, pp.85–103.*

On 30 March JAP hosted a lunch for DLG, Haldane, Addison, and Sir William McCormick to present a 'scheme of education' to DLG. In a prearranged statement JAP had told Parliament on 10 March that the government was considering the whole question of the organisation of educational machinery with respect to the relation of science and industry. With DLG's concurrence, Addison was now charged with carrying the scheme forward (Addison diary, 8 Feb.–3 May 1915, Bodl. MS. Addison, dep.d.1, ff.214 et seq.*).*

April 7th George said he proposed to await for further evidence before calling cabinet's attention to drink problem & war munitions. K. & C. had nothing to report. Churchill sparred with K to the amusement of the rest of us, for bagging men into a corps of army workers on munitions when doing naval work under contract. Grey & Birrell away. P.M. reported negociations re Italy coming in with allies, & the difficulty about ownership of Peninsula of C.

Some of the points in dispute were ownership of the Sabbioncello Peninsula and the Curzola Islands and the Serbian interest in Dalmatia (TNA: CAB 37/17/1; HHA Cabinet letter, TNA: CAB 41/36/15. The copy of this report in Bodl. MS. Asquith 8, ff.29–30, appears to have been written, dated, and docketed '8 April 1915'). Keith Neilson sets these matters in context in 'The Foundations of British War Aims in the First World War', in Gestrich and Pogge von Strandmann eds, Bid for World Power?, *pp.313–34.*

From the last week of March HHA had ceased to convene the War Council and was conferring on the higher direction of the war with only two Cabinet colleagues: Kitchener and WSC. A meeting of the three men on 6 April was headed in the Secretary's notes as 'an Informal Meeting of a War Council' (TNA: CAB 42/2/17). Like those of the rest of the Cabinet from this time on, JAP's opportunities to contribute to deliberations on strategic issues were limited. In saying that 'K. and C. had nothing to report' he passes over in silence the information from Kitchener about Ian Hamilton's plan for an amphibious attack at the Dardanelles. Both Hobhouse and Harcourt took the news very seriously (Harcourt Cabinet note, 7 Apr. 1915, Bodl. MS.Eng.c.8270; Hobhouse diary, 7 Apr. 1915, David ed., Inside Asquith's Cabinet, *p.234). Two days later Montagu was moved to write to Grey:*

> There has been no rearrangement, no appointment of any substituted body and therefore the doctrine of Cabinet collective responsibility still exists...we are all liable to be hanged in Palace Yard at the same time for the mistakes of any one of us ....nothing of importance is withheld from the Cabinet when the Cabinet happens to meet so that the amount of material upon which a Cabinet minister can form his judgment depends upon the number of days which have elapsed since the last meeting...and also upon the amount of leisure which he permits himself from the task of listening to Cabinet discussions in order to read telegrams.
>
> *(Montagu–Grey, 9 Apr. 1915, TNA: FO 800/101)*

JAP's mind that day was less on his shared responsibility for decisions he had not influenced than on his personal future, the long term potential for his portfolio, and a fanciful idea that he might visit the United States, improve Anglo-American relations, and even deter premature peace moves.

My dear Prime Minister,

> A few months ago I asked you if I might try & pick up a few educational wrinkles in U.S.A. you did not then favour the suggestion but I did not press the matter, as from what you said I hoped I might be more usefully employed in another sphere of work.

[JAP deleted the following at this point: 'I was & am still disappointed at not getting the promotion you led me to expect . . .'.] I have been giving attention to educational problems & especially the question of how to help home industries by a better application of scientific knowledge to trade processes and by research work. I am circulating tomorrow a cabinet memorandum which is a précis of papers drafted by Addison, & which has been submitted to George, Haldane & Runciman, who favour the scheme.

I hope you and the cabinet may regard the proposals with approval. Money this year is not essential but if the scheme is adopted next yr half a million wd be wanted & occupy [*sic*] the interval in getting the machinery started.

I still think I might do good in running over to the U.S.A. but in this matter I of course am in your hands. My work arising out of the war could now easily be carried on by others, and Addison who has developed into a most valuable colleague can be trusted to deal with any departmental matters in the House.

I suggest that by a visit to America to pick up ideas as to the way in which they take advantage in their industries of their Higher School & University work might be the avowed object, but is it not possible that such a visit now might be politically useful, in promoting cordial relations, interchange of commodities (including munitions of war) and remove apprehensions. As the late President of the Peace Society my visit might deter premature peace efforts being made before there exists any prospect of the terms you defined in your Guild Hall speech being within reach.

The friendly reception given to our notes, & their not unfriendly reply seems to me a not unfavourable moment for a personal & private interchange of sentiments.

If you think it is worth considering, would you cable Spring Rice[40] & ascertain his view. If I went I should suggest going with Selby-Bigge & a private secretary, or with Bruce[41] & Dr Heath,[42] the departmental heads of the Secondary & University branches. If I go I suggest the sooner I went the better.

Yours Ever,
[sgd] Joseph A. Pease
(JAP–HHA, [8 Apr. 1915], draft, MS. Gainford 86/80)

[40] Sir Cecil Spring-Rice (1859–1918); Amb. to United States 1912–18; Foreign Office 1882–6; asst p.s. to Ld Rosebery then transferred to diplomatic service 1886; chargé d'affaires Tehran (1900); Commissioner of Public Debt Cairo (1901); chargé d'affaires St Petersburg (1903); promoted to Sec. of Embassy 1901. Posted to Persia (1906) and Sweden (1908). A poet and translator from Persian, celebrated as lyricist of 'I Vow to Thee My Country'.

[41] William Napier Bruce (1858–1936); 2nd son 1st Lord Aberdare; principal asst sec. Bd of Educ. 1903–21; called to Bar from Lincoln's Inn 1883; asst commissioner, Charity Commission under the Endowed Schools Acts 1886–1900. See Mark Curthoys, 'Bruce, William Napier (1858–1936), civil servant and educationist', *Oxford Dictionary of National Biography*. Retrieved 21 Jan. 2023, from https://www.oxforddnb.com/view/10.1093/ref:odnb/9780198614128.001.0001/odnb-9780198614128-e-90000382398.

[42] (Henry) Frank Heath (1863–1946); principal asst sec. Universities Branch, Bd of Educ. 1910–16; Director, Office of Special Inquiries and Reports 1903–16; Prof. English Literature and Language, Bedford Coll. London 1890–5; Sec. Dept Scientific and Industrial Research 1917–27; KCB 1917. To his successor at DSIR, Sir Henry Tizard, 'he was never a scholar in the accepted sense and rightly abandoned an academic for an administrative career' (*DNB 1941–1950*, p.372).

This letter, annotated by JAP 'turned down verbally', survives only in draft but appears to be the final text. 'I presume', Elsie Pease wrote on 16 April, 'the PM treated your letter with the contempt he usually shows' (MS. Gainford 86/45). Elsie was right.

To my letter of April 8th offering to go to U.S America I received no reply. K. reported rate of recruiting 18,000 p. wk ex-territorials.

April 16[43] Churchill gave us some figures.

He had 180,000 afloat
220,000 with Naval Division[44]
3,200 ships in commission or requisition of wh.
120 were merchantmen, 1600 under white ensign & 500 trawlers.
62 battleships.

K. told us he had

in France	509,779		
in Egypt	121,223		
		630,402	
At home		415,336	1,038,357
Territorials			
abroad	306,403		
at home	139,400		
		446,803 }	
		}	1,926,000
Total at home}	1,480,000	}	
troops}		}	
Total at home & abroad} ?			
Colonials}			
Total with colours			2,115,602
Besides other Canadian & Australian}			
troops on sea.		}	

[43] JAP misdated this meeting 15 Apr. There is no Cabinet letter to the King or Harcourt diary note for the 15th. On 15 Apr. there was a fiery Cabinet committee meeting on the Drink Problem; JAP was not present unless he was one of the 'one or two others' whose names were not mentioned to Venetia Stanley (*Asquith Letters*, pp.542–3). There was a Cabinet meeting on 13 Apr. which JAP did not record (Harcourt diary, 13, 16 Apr. 1915, Bodl. MS.Eng.c.8270).

[44] The figure of 220,000 is hard to understand. The Naval Division had around 11,000 men. Even if shore-based personnel are included, the number cannot be correct. Possibly JAP misheard or mistranscribed his own notes.

to April 15. 1915

We had sent out to France	821,042
casualties had been	186,484
We had now at the front	630,402
in reserve	190,640
unfit	70,133
in hospital }	
recoverable }	88,841
recovered	27,820[45]

*There were Cabinets on 13 and 16 April, neither of which appears to have been reported to the King. There is no mention by JAP of the drama at Cabinet on Friday 16 April when Kitchener railed against WSC and DLG for sharing figures with the Munitions Committee on the number of men at the front. Kitchener threatened to resign, and got up to leave the meeting. According to Harcourt, Kitchener was stopped when Harcourt made the obvious points that the information was unlikely to reach the Germans and, if it did, would be of little use to them. Peace was restored by HHA, with agreement that figures provided by Kitchener should never be disclosed, even to confidential Cabinet committees. Venetia Stanley received two reports on the 16 April Cabinet (*Asquith Letters*, pp.543–6).*

Harcourt was told by Grey that his doctor said he needed six months 'absolute rest' in order to save his eyesight. This was impossible, but the Foreign Secretary would have to retire from public life as soon as the war was over. The other news JAP did not record was:

> Russia now being again troublesome about Italy & Dalmatian coast; but Italy will be in with us by the beginning of May.
>
> Greece again boggling & bargaining; we shall take a strong line with them.
>
> Dardanelles going quietly & well.
>
> *(Harcourt diary, 16 Apr. 1915, Bodl. MS.Eng.c.8270)*

In his letter to the King on 19 April HHA reported WSC's statement on ships: a grand total of 3,927. He gave no details of army numbers (Bodl. MS. Asquith 8, f.31 or TNA: CAB 41/36/16).

April 19 Churchill gave us more figures

500 aeroplanes by July after wastage

180 we had now

Drink debate George put before us scheme of prohibition, but we demurred to placing restrictions on men whose work was not prejudiced by excessive

[45] For the context of the casualty figures see Mark Harrison, *The Medical War: British Military Medicine in the First World War*, Oxford UP, 2012, pp.18–64.

drinking, or to select what they might or might not drink — & George instructed to see Brewers & see if a partial scheme in munitions area would be acceptable under compensation or purchase, Agreed to fine men, if they treated one another, to increase tax on spirits, & alcohol wines.

JAP had been approached privately by his Quaker cousin Jonathan Hodgkin in the earliest days of the war urging the 'almost limitless advantage' of materially lessening the consumption of alcohol. The subject had already been considered by the Cabinet Committee for the Prevention and Relief of Distress. The Committee had jibbed: it would be 'impossible to get any controversial measure through Parliament altering the hours during which public houses are open which appeared to us to be the best one if it could be adopted' (J.B. Hodgkin–JAP–Hodgkin, 13, 14 Aug. 1914, MS. Gainford 85/115–16). Over the following months attitudes had changed. Acknowledging the impossibility of giving adequate compensation if anything like universal prohibition was attempted, Bonar Law told Robert Cecil on 1 April 1915: 'I would not say this except as an obiter dictum, almost the only way of dealing with it is for the State to make a complete monopoly both of the sale and production of alcohol' (Cecil of Chelwood MSS, BL Add.MS. 51161, f.215); and for his further thinking after DLG had explained his plans (Law–Chamberlain, 2 Apr. 1915, Austen Chamberlain MSS, AC 13/3/39, Cadbury RL Birmingham U.).

*Amid the 'animated' discussion on 19 April of the 'great problem of drink' HHA wrote to Venetia Stanley: 'I have never written to you under quite such peculiar conditions: for every 2 or 3 minutes I am constrained to burst or break into the debate….'. Simultaneously Edwin Montagu, who had just learned that Venetia Stanley had agreed to marry him, wrote to her: 'I am not the only member of the Cabinet writing to you during its deliberations….'. HHA himself received the shattering news early on 12 May (*Asquith Letters*, pp.551–3, 593).*

Grey reported his difficulty with Sazonoff in inducing him to accept Italy's terms — Sazonoff stipulating for immediate action & war declaration if Italy's terms were to be accepted.

Harcourt recorded that trouble with Russia over Italy arose from a quarrel between Sazonoff and the Italian Ambassador in Petrograd. Sazonoff had told the Ambassador that Italy was asking too much, to which the Italian Ambassador replied: 'London will make you give way.' (Harcourt diary, 19 Apr. 1915, Bodl. MS.Eng.c.8270.)

K. reported, French was pleased with success of action in taking Hill 60 near St. Eloi, though our casualties were great but not half the German losses — strategic observation position of first importance for accurate fire.

Hill 60, one of three mounds of earth excavated during the cutting of the Comines–Ypres railway, was named after the contour ring for it on the map. The official history of the war noted that the site was of 'very considerable military importance', but it formed an exposed salient for either side. The Germans recaptured it on 5 May after repeated gas attacks. British losses amounted to 100 officers and 3,000 men; four VCs were earned in the fighting. By 20 April, after German and British entrenchment, mining, and bombardment, the hill became 'a medley of mine and shell craters... in this rubbish heap it was impossible to dig without disturbing the body of some British or German soldier' (Brig. General J.E. Edmonds and Captain G.C. Wynn, Military Operations France and Belgium 1915, Vol. 1, *Macmillan, 1927, pp.167,169–70). The background is recounted in Phillip Robinson and Nigel Cave,* The Underground War: Vimy Ridge to Arras: 1, *Pen & Sword Military, 2011, and Peter Barton, John Vandewalle and Peter Doyle,* Beneath Flanders Fields: The Tunnellers' War 1914–18, *Spellmount, Staplehurst, 2003. Will Davies,* Beneath Hill 60 *(Random House, Nth Sydney, 2010) inspired an Australian feature film of the same name, written by David Roach, directed by Jeremy Sims.*

JAP sent an account of the 19 April meeting to Herbert Samuel, absent unwell, who read it several times and then burnt it (Samuel–JAP, 20 Apr. 1915, MS. Gainford 86/28).

April 20 P.M. addressed North Country munition & miners at Newcastle.

The theme of HHA's speech was 'Deliver the Goods'. Denying that field operations were being limited by a lack of ammunition—as was widely believed in Whitehall and Westminster and rumoured elsewhere—he was warmly received.

April 22nd George deprecated any new tax except on drink — it was admitted income tax was now too light on farmers & certain men making money out of war, but time not opportune for one, & impossible to draw line with others — super tax & graduation would touch most of them & the high income tax. Three months bills had a limit, & George thought we might be driven to take bankers' securities in Govmt stock. He reported interview with Brewers. They insisted on purchase where govmt destroyed their trade by setting up canteens to limit consumption. It was agreed we should see bill.

Grey reported progress with Italy & Sazonoff's climb down, & it looked now like a settlement. Churchill spoke of disposition of Italy & French commands in Meditn sea, during our action at Dardanelles.

The invasion of the Gallipoli Peninsula began on 25 April. An Anglo–French–Italian naval convention was signed on 10 May 1915. Details of the negotiations and the outcome are teased out in Halpern, The Naval War in the Mediterranean, *pp.96–101. For the deliberations in the Foreign Office on bringing Italy into the war see Gerald J. Protheroe,* Searching for Security in a New Europe: The Diplomatic Career of Sir George Russell Clerk, *Taylor and Francis, 2004, pp.22–4.*

April 26[46] Cabinet discussed Dardanelles situation &c. Asphyxiating gases — Churchill authorised to prepare materials but not committed to use them yet. Drink proposals — George outlined his proposals — K. & C. only caring about canteen proposals.

HHA reported to the King on 27 April about the enemy resort to 'asphyxiating gases'. As they were apparently stored in and drawn from cylinders rather than projectiles, using them was, the Prime Minister suggested, perhaps not an infraction of the 'liberal terms of the Hague convention'. The loopholes in the Hague Declaration concerning asphyxiating gases and HHA's interpretation are explained in Ulf Schmidt, Secret Science: A Century of Poison Warfare and Human Experiments, *Oxford UP, 2015, pp.24–9.*

Kitchener had despatched the respiratory physiologist J.S. Haldane (brother of the Lord Chancellor) to France to investigate. Haldane's report, identifying chlorine as the chemical weapon, was published on 29 April (Steve Sturdy, 'War as Experiment. Physiology, Innovation and Administration in Britain, 1914–1918: The Case of Chemical Warfare', in Roger Cooter, Mark Harrison, and Steve Sturdy eds, War, Medicine and Modernity, *Sutton, Stroud, 1998, pp.65–6). The press response to the German use of gas, and the Cabinet's deliberations, can be seen in Preston,* A Higher Form of Killing, *pp.113–17. For the earliest British efforts to neutralise the impact of gas attacks see Albert Palazzo,* Seeking Victory on the Western Front: The British Army and Chemical Warfare in World War I, *U. of Nebraska P., Lincoln, NE, 2000, pp.41–77; and Hanene Zoghlami, 'Franco–British responses to chemical warfare 1915–[1]8, with special reference to the medical services, casualty statistics and the threat to civilians',* Med.Hist., *vol.65, no.2, 2021, pp.101–12.*

The Admiralty had been experimenting for some time with the production of large quantities of smoke 'for a screen'. But, in an admission that Cabinet was beginning to consider

[46] Both JAP and Charles Hobhouse dated this meeting 27 Apr. but HHA's Cabinet letter of 27 Apr. refers to a meeting on 26 Apr. (Bodl. MS. Asquith 8, ff.35–6; TNA: CAB 41/36/18 1915). Harcourt and Alfred Emmott also date the meeting 26 Apr. (Bodl. MS.Eng.c.8270 and Emmott diary, 13 June 1915, MS. Emmott, I/2, Nuffield Col.). Writing his diary a week later, JAP did not mention that Grey had announced the signing of a secret agreement bringing Italy into the war. The 'profound secret that Italy has signed an agreement with the Allies' was divulged by Arthur Balfour to his brother Gerald, who passed it on to his lover, who recorded it in her diary on 29 Apr. (Peter Lord ed., *Between two worlds: The diary of Winifred Coombe Tennant 1909–1924*, NLW, Aberystwyth, 2011, p.165). There was a meeting on 28 Apr. which also discussed dealing with asphyxiating gases (HHA Cabinet letter, 29 Apr. 1915, Bodl. MS. Asquith 8, ff.37–8; TNA: CAB 41/36/19 1915).

other dubious methods, HHA told the King that 'a suggested scheme [by Hankey supported by WSC] for destroying the enemies' crops by means of incendiary pellets dropped from balloons or aeroplanes did not meet with much favour' (TNA: CAB 37/127/40, in William Moore, Gas Attack! Chemical Warfare 1915–18 and afterwards, *Leo Cooper, 1987, p.45; Harcourt diary, 26 Apr. 1915, Bodl. MS.Eng.c.8270). Edward M. Spiers provides an introduction in* A History of Chemical and Biological Weapons, *Reaktion Books, 2010, pp.27–46.*

The government proposed to set up canteens next to works where food and 'decent' drink could be obtained in moderate quantities (HHA Cabinet letter, TNA: CAB 41/36/16). HHA, it seems, had been going about 'saying that he knew nothing about the King's letter on the drink question and that he was never consulted'. At Buckingham Palace it was known that: 'Lloyd George wrote to say that Stamfordham's letter had been read out to the Cabinet and that they had unanimously recommended its publication.' Later DLG was anxious that the King should make a more definite announcement and added that he had spoken to the P.M., 'who quite agreed!' (Sir 'Fritz' Ponsonby–Lady Paget, 26 Apr. 1915, Paget Papers, BL Add. MS. 51250, f.161). When wine for the Household staff was rationed, 'one of the servants draped the cellar door with crape' (Fortescue, 'There's Rosemary…', *pp.202–3).*

There is no report by JAP on the meeting held on 28 April when the Cabinet was told all was going well at the Dardanelles where 25 per cent of the troops were casualties; the French in a Flanders battle two days previously had run away without firing a shot, leaving 47 guns behind; and Kitchener was saying he must have powers to 'liquefy all arms of the service i.e. transform Cavalry into Infantry' (Harcourt diary, 28 Apr. 1915, Bodl. MS.Eng.c.8270).

JAP meanwhile was still struggling with the stand he should take in public about the war. He wrote to E. Harry Gilpin[47] on Board of Education letterhead:

April 30th, 1915

DEAR FRIEND,

On receiving your letter I at once drafted a telegram to authorise the addition of my name to the list of those who propose to send a letter to friends who have enlisted, but on second thoughts it seemed to me my name might weaken rather than strengthen the message, as I, myself both morally and legally, am as responsible for taking an active part in the war as any member of the Society who had joined the colours. For years we strove to avoid conflict among the great European Powers, and no one but Sir Edward Grey's colleagues know how great were our

[47] Sir (Edmund Henry) Harry Gilpin (1876–1950); Kt 1949; contested (Lib) Finsbury 1922; chmn Liberal Party National Executive 1943–6.

difficulties during all those months when the Balkan States were at war, to preserve Peace and prevent the Great Powers being drawn in.

Those, too, who know the facts, realise how every possible step was taken to avoid the present war, for which Germany had long made definite preparation. She intended to *force* her own military domination on the world irrespective of her own word or the rights of other Nationalities. As a Friend, and President of the Peace Society, it was for me to do my utmost for principle, but not to cowardly allow principle, honour, good faith, freedom and right to be crushed under militarism and German despotism, and this was our only alternative to war. I have not resigned my membership, and if the Society intend to disown those who are now actively engaged in the Front, who are fighting for the cause of an enduring peace, they should commence with me. Our testimony to Peace principles and their value will, in my judgment, not be promoted by letting others actively work for this cause, whilst we remain content to passively protest against war, knowing all the time that our homes, our children's lives, and the honour of our women are safe-guarded by their efforts.

I associate myself with those who are now in khaki; they are fighting for what they believe to be right, having sought for Divine Guidance in the course they have taken. In these terrible days my sympathy goes out to those Friends who are ready to sacrifice their lives and who have enlisted, and *I should like to join in a message to them,* but it must be as one Who as a member of the Government is engaged with them in carrying on the war, and it is only on account of this that I do not associate myself with other Friends who are writing from a somewhat different standpoint.

I am,

Yours very sincerely,
Joseph A. Pease
(copy, MS. Gainford 86/93)

May 3 George & I saw the P.M. about expend. on research work. He admitted I had made my case out & sanctioned publicity (see my cab mem. on RESEARCH) (also letter to P.M. Ap. 8.15).

JAP's Cabinet memorandum was 'Proposals for a national scheme of advanced instruction and research in science, technology and commerce', 9 April 1915 (TNA: CAB 37/127/18). He argued that the war had revealed British industrial dependence on Germany for many things, particularly dyes, drugs, and X-ray machinery. This, he said, was the result of a great emphasis in Germany on scientific education and research; he claimed that only 1,500 chemists were employed in industry in Britain, compared to 1,000 in one German industry alone. JAP proposed to rectify this by a scheme of bursaries and scholarships through all levels of education to encourage the study of science and the channelling of money from government and industry into scientific research, particularly research dealing with industrial problems. He estimated that this would cost £500,000 in 1916–17. A national research council would coordinate all interested parties.

Although the scheme went forward over JAP's signature as President of the Board of Education, it was largely developed by his Parliamentary Secretary, Christopher Addison, with a small committee, cheered on by Haldane and with DLG's warm support. Approval was promptly given (Daglish, '"Over by Christmas"...', pp.315–31; Ashby and Anderson, Portrait of Haldane, *pp.118–19).*

When I was with the P.M. Grey came in he betted George a box of cigars the war would be over by the end of this year. The P.M. agreed with Grey's view.

*DLG, with both JAP and Edwin Montagu, had called on the Prime Minister 'ostensibly to talk about the next day's Budget'. HHA's account of the day to Venetia Stanley makes no mention of 'research' but dwells on DLG's report that the Tory Party was going to oppose the 'Drink taxes' and the fact that Grey 'talked at length about his eyes' (*Asquith Letters, *p.582). The morning after the meeting with the Prime Minister Addison found JAP in 'high fettle'. HHA had given the scheme (which he admitted he had not read) his blessing after Montagu 'backed it up heartily' (Addison diary, 4 May 1915, Christopher Addison,* Four and a Half Years: A Personal Diary from June 1914 to January 1919, *2 vols, Hutchinson, 1934, Vol. I, p.74).*

May 4 Grey reported difficulties in bringing in Bulgaria & Greece — Kavalla.

Also Japan & China & bullying tactics of former. We again postponed how to retaliate. Amended drink proposals reported.

Bulgaria had proclaimed itself neutral on the outbreak of war. On the Ottoman Empire's entry into the war on 2 November, the Allies and the Central Powers courted her. Bulgaria's principal goal was the return of Macedonia, mostly in Serbian hands after the Balkan Wars. By the autumn of 1915, with Entente setbacks in Galicia and Gallipoli, the Bulgarians were ready to ally themselves with Germany and Austria–Hungary. The Bulgarians had briefly occupied Kavala, an important northern Greek seaport town, during the 1912 Balkan war. But the port had been captured by the Greeks the following year and was retained by them in the subsequent peace settlement (Richard C. Hall, The Balkan Wars 1912–1913: Prelude to the First World War, *Routledge, 2000; Marvin Benjamin Fried,*

Austro-Hungarian War Aims in the Balkans during World War I, *palgrave macmillan, 2014, pp.50–8, 77–85).*

An ambivalent Chinese government had declared itself neutral on 6 August 1914. Japan, determined to exploit the European war by exacting concessions from China, had seized control of Shandong province in Manchuria from Germany. On 18 January 1915, the Chinese president was presented with a humiliating set of 'Twenty-one Demands'. Although they published the demands, in defiance of the Japanese insistence they be kept secret, and sought to enlist the aid of the United States, the Chinese capitulated on 9 May 1915 (Xu Guoqi, China and the Great War: China's pursuit of a new national identity and internationalism, *Cambridge UP, 2005, pp.87–98). Phoebe Chow outlines parliamentary questions and editorial commentary on the 'tepid response' of the British government to Japanese action* (Britain's Imperial Retreat from China, 1900–1931, *Routledge, Abingdon, 2017, pp.104–10); and 'the relatively muted' reaction of the government is explained by Antony Best, 'Britain, Japan, and the Crisis over China, 1915–16', in Oliviero Frattolillo and Antony Best eds,* Japan and the Great War, *Basingstoke, 2016, pp.53–7.*

With the Japanese flag already flying over former German territories in Jaluit, Yap, and Palau Islands, a secret agreement in October 1914 acknowledged the equator as the dividing line between Japanese and British forces. Harcourt's and Grey's surprise and displeasure at the Admiralty proposal to leave the Japanese in Yap are in an exchange of notes on 12 October 1914 (Harcourt MSS, Bodl. MS.Eng.c.8269). The British had asked for a commitment of Japanese troops to the Western Front (Frederick R. Dickinson, 'The Japanese Empire', in Robert Gerwarth and Erez Manela eds, Empires at War 1911–1923, *pp.198–203; and Dickinson's full-length study,* War and National Reinvention: Japan in the Great War, 1914–1919, *Harvard U. Asia Center, Cambridge, MA, 1999, pp.33–116).*

May 5 Dined alone with Asquith Margot & a Secy (Meiklejohn) we discussed recruiting, supplies &c. Margot said the P. of W. had told her at Windsor we could have forgiven our faulty General at Neuve Chapelle (who was Stellen-bosched) if he had admitted to his faults, but he sheltered himself behind Casper [sic] & Bailey.

Someone—the Prince of Wales, the Prime Minister's wife, or JAP—was confused. Margot Asquith had recorded on 17 April (Margot Asquith's Great War Diary 1914–1916, *p.100), the Prince of Wales's comments on this affair, so it is likely that JAP, engrossed in bridge, had misheard. Maj.-Gen. Sir Henry Rawlinson, commanding IV Corps at the battle of Neuve Chapelle, 10–13 March 1915, complained to his chief, Douglas Haig, of the performance of Maj.-Gen. F.J. 'Joey' Davies, the commander of the 8th division. Rawlinson's resort to 'the underhand stratagem of attempting to scapegoat' Davies is described in*

Gary Sheffield, Command and Morale: The British Army on the Western Front, 1914–1918, *Pen & Sword, Praetorian P., Barnsley,* 2014, *pp.37–53. Subsequently, after incurring the wrath of the commander-in-chief, Sir John French, for not accepting responsibility, Rawlinson admitted that the fatal delay in advancing on the first day of the battle was as much his own fault as anyone else's. Although the Prince of Wales had said no one would forgive Rawlinson for allowing the blame to fall on his subordinates, Rawlinson was not 'Stellenbosched'—assigned abruptly, as were commanders deemed incompetent in the 2nd Boer War, to a base where they could do no harm. But Davies was, temporarily. Davies went on to be Military Secretary to the Secretary of State for War 1916–19. The 'Davies affair' is recounted in Prior and Wilson,* Command on the Western Front, *pp.70–3, and Atwood,* General Lord Rawlinson, *pp.116–17. On the lessons of Neuve Chapelle see Robin Prior, 'The Western Front', in Jay Winter* et al. *eds,* The Cambridge History of the First World War: Vol. I Global War, *pp.209–10. The historiography is reviewed in Patrick Watt, 'Douglas Haig and the Planning of the Battle of Neuve Chapelle', in Spencer Jones ed.,* Courage Without Glory, *pp.183–203.*

*Elizabeth Haldane's diary (21 April 1915, referring to the previous week) mentions three generals being called to account but not sent back: 'Davis [*sic*], Capper, Snow?' (Elizabeth Haldane MSS, MS. 20240, f.94, NLS). Maj.-Gen. Thomas D'Oyly Snow had also been under a cloud since August 1914 but was redeemed in leading the 27th Division through the first German poison gas attack and made KCB. On Snow an essential text is Dan Snow and Mark Pottle eds,* The Confusion of Command The War Memoirs of Lieutenant General Sir Thomas D'Oyly Snow 1914–1915, *Frontline Books, 2011.*

Lt-Col. Vivian Telford Bailey (1868–1938) DSO CMG; commanded the King's Liverpool Regiment (Pioneers) 1914–17; Brig.-Gen. 1917, GOC 142nd (6th London) Infantry Brigade, was wounded and captured Mar. 1918.

*The audacious commander of the 7th Division was Maj-Gen. Sir Thompson Capper (1863–1915), who 'had before, at and after the first Battle of Ypres, made for himself a name which will never be forgotten' (*The Times History of the War, *Vol. VI, 1916, p.409). 'Tommy' Capper died from wounds 26 September 1915. The oft-repeated story that he was shot when riding in front of enemy lines brandishing his sword to inspire his troops was reliably contradicted as long ago as 1920 (Gardner,* Trial by Fire, *pp.15–17 for the myth; for the rebuttal see Frank Davies & Graham Maddocks,* Bloody Red Tabs: General Officer Casualties of the Great War 1914–1918, *Leo Cooper, 1995, pp.53–4, and Richard Olsen, 'An Inspirational Warrior: Major-General Sir Thompson Capper', in Spencer Jones ed.,* Stemming the Tide, *pp.189–208). For Rawlinson's displeasure with Capper's disposition of his troops exposed to enemy fire on forward slopes at Ypres in October 1914 see Simon Batten,* Futile Exercise?: The British Army's Preparations for War, 1902–1914,

Helion & Co., Warwick, 2018, p.195; and for his staff's complaint that 'he was far too little at the end of the wire, or rather at the centre *of all wires but miles away in front, practically in the firing line' see Paul Harris,* The Men Who Planned the War: A Study of the Staff of the British Army on the Western Front, 1914–1918, *Ashgate, Farnham, 2016, p.168.*

JAP was almost certainly present (although WSC and Simon were absent) at the Cabinet meeting at noon on 6 May when Kitchener advised that he was going to have gases ready to be sent to French in ten days (Harcourt diary, 6 May 1915, Bodl. MS.Eng.c.8270).

May 11 This was a week of heavy fighting, a heavy pall seems to be hanging over everyone under the sense of coming reports of long drawn out engagements with enormous casualties. Real disaster is not anticipated, but the feeling that Russia is retreating & losing heavily has its effect in adding to the depression. Kitchener at the cabinet today said the Grand Duke[48] tells him they will hold the Germans alright & are only retiring to find a stronger position as they did twice before Warsaw. Joffre is pleased with the effort we are making to engage the Germans on the left of their attacking line. K. thinks & Grey's information confirmed it, that the Germans had knowledge in advance of the attack, & they were able to mass men & make their preparations.

Ian Hamilton's report shown the Turks are well posted & are in strong positions, & he feels he has no great quantity of fresh troops if he meets with anything like heavy losses. K. says in addition to the Division he is sending out in Mauritania &c, he has 4000 men still to spare in Egypt.

Hamilton reported the Navy & he are working daily together, & that the spoon shaped ground makes it difficult for Navy fire even helped with aviators to demolish the Turks positions — but their dead lie thick on the ground before them. Churchill said if the Navy had gone through in Feby as he still thinks in spite of losses they could have done a great object would then have been secured. They did not & he had now to face with us the delay & heavy army casualties.

We discussed invasion here by Germany, & the depletion of forces. Churchill felt the Grand Fleet were ready & nearer than ever before, being protected by nets against submarines.

A German submarine was now in the Med. had been seen near Gib, the Balearic Islands & Malta going West. Nets in the Aegean would be put round our biggest ships by destroyers when in action. He admitted we had got one other

[48] Grand Duke Nicholas (1856–1929); Tsar's 2nd cousin; C-in-C Russian Army from 3 Aug. 1914 until relieved of command and appointed Gov. Caucasus Aug. 1915. Paul Robinson, *Grand Duke Nikolai Nikolaevich Supreme Commander of the Russian Army*, Northern Illinois UP, DeKalb, 2014, pp.219–44, puts the Grand Duke's assurance in perspective.

German submarine (the report from Lord Moulton[49] asserts that by a new method we had collared 32, but if there is any truth in this it is concealed by the 1st Lord from his colleagues).

News of the sinking on 7 May of the Cunard Liner RMS Lusitania *with the death of 785 out of 1,257 passengers, 413 of the 702 crew, and three German agents, had led to a spate of anti-German riots. It was not officially admitted until 1918 that the ship had been carrying a number of cases of munitions (rifle cartridges, shrapnel shells, and percussion fuses). These were contraband and would have justified the enemy in stopping and searching but not torpedoing the vessel without warning. Recent scholarship gives little credence to theories that the contraband cargo might have been the cause of a second explosion that sank the ship (Diana Preston,* Wilful Murder: The Sinking of the Lusitania, *Special Centenary edn, Doubleday, 2015 [1st edn 2002). But for lingering doubts see Savvas Bournelis,* The Truth of the Sinking of the Lusitania: The British Admiralty and The American Entry into The First World War, *Hellenic College Holy Cross Greek Orthodox School of Theology, 2017, https://independent.academia.edu/SamuelBournelis, accessed 4 Apr. 2020; and a critique of recent books (at http://minioceanliners.blogspot.com/2015/05/remember-lusitania.html): 'Remember the Lusitania: A Historiographical Review', by Nick McCormick (U. of Illinois at Chicago), 1 May 2015, accessed 19 May 2020.*

May 12 A cabinet called suddenly to decide on policy of interning more Germans to protect them against mob law & retaliation. McKenna opposed to undertaking duties, I pressed local authorities should be made responsible. P.M. wanted discrimination — McKenna said it was impossible — George & I urged an advisory comtee should assist the Home Office, & the critics made responsible for an awkward & difficult question. K anxious that nothing should lead to reprisals in Germany. P.M. prepared form of words which we accepted & he read it to the House of Commons after questions.

The Cabinet's revived concern about enemy aliens came six months after Hankey prepared a paper for the Prime Minister about the dangers of 25,000 able-bodied Germans and Austrians at large in London. Hankey had rehearsed the argument for Balfour on 4 December 1914: the

[49] John Fletcher Moulton, Baron Moulton (1844–1921); the government's principal adviser on explosives production and former backbench ally of DLG; Chmn Medical Research Council 1912–16; Ld of Appeal in Ordinary 1912–21; Judge Court of Appeal 1906–12; Baron Moulton (life peerage) 1912; Dir.-Gen. Explosive Supplies, Min. of Munitions 1915–18; QC 1885; PC 1906; Kt 1906; KCB 1915; GBE 1917; Lib. MP S. Hackney 1894–5, Cornwall (Launceston) 1898–1906. Senior Wrangler, Cambridge Mathematical Tripos, with highest total marks then known; called to the Bar in 1874: 'he kept no diary and hardly any letters, considering the fire the only trustworthy guardian of confidences' (H. Fletcher Moulton, *The Life of Lord Moulton*, Nisbet & Co., 1922, p.147).

number, 'equal to the infantry of an army corps', exceeded the total number of police in the metropolis. 'They could do a tremendous amount of damage in an emergency by incendiarism (using petrol), destroying railways and telegraphs, and knocking on the head simultaneously most of the Cabinet Ministers and principal Government Officials (!) to say nothing of destroying power stations by short circuits, gas works etc.' (Balfour MSS, BL Add.MS. 49703, ff.108–9). Hankey had taken his concern directly to the Prime Minister on the same Friday afternoon when HHA was setting off for a weekend at the Wharf. The proposed immediate arrest of the 25,000 received 'a rather curt "no"' (Asquith Letters, *p.326). McKenna's period of responsibility for aliens as Home Secretary, the criticism he received as a result of general ignorance of the War Office's 'primacy in the arrest, custody and release of enemy subjects', and HHA's statement of 12 May are ably reviewed in Bird,* Control of Enemy Alien Civilians, *pp.40–91.*

Both Harcourt's and JAP's accounts of the 12 May Cabinet meeting omit that 'much time was given to discussing the latest reports from France & the Dardanelles'. This discussion was a fact adduced two years later in rebuttal of the Dardanelles Commission's contention that the failure of the War Council to meet between 19 March and 14 May was evidence of insufficient political oversight of the campaign. Simon Heffer would say that this was 'another sign of how little Asquith grasped the gravity of events on the Western Front and the deterioration in the Dardanelles, and the active response they required' (Staring at God, *p.193). In fact the Cabinet held twelve meetings between these dates. 'On all but two of these occasions the Dardanelles operations were the subject of report & discussion . . .'. Kitchener's secretary, the punctilious and discreet Herbert Creedy, said there were thirteen 'full Cabinets' (Notes [by Bonham Carter?], n.d. [?1917]; Creedy–Bonham Carter, 17 March 1917, Bodl. MS. Asquith 133, ff.315,326).*

There was another meeting on Thursday 13 May. The Prime Minister's report to the King on the successive meetings was signed on 14 May (Bodl. MS. Asquith 8, ff.43–4). Political turmoil was precipitated that day by the publication in The Times *of an article by their military correspondent alleging that 'the want of an unlimited supply of high explosives is a fatal bar to our success'. The flight from office of Lord Fisher a few days later intensified the instability. Doubtless swept up in the colour and movement, JAP made no mention of his own 'heartily supported' speech on the new research proposals to a 'thin House' on the evening of 13 May (Addison diary, 13 May 1915,* Four and a Half Years, *Vol. I, p.77).*

May 18[50] Cabinet called but rescinded. It appeared that Fisher called to see the P.M. on Sat. 15. & resigned without reason. On being pressed for a reason he stated he declined to serve at the Admiralty under Winston Churchill & nothing would move him.

[50] JAP later headed this entry '1915 Coalition'.

On Monday the P.M. consulted George Crewe & Grey, & decided to call into his cabinet the opposition as he saw no way to avoid a Parliamentary attack on munitions, & he could not reform his ministry from his own side without weakening the Govmt & helping the enemy. He sent round a letter asking us all to place our resignations in his hands. We were told letters were unnecessary. At 12.0 at night another circular letter expressing his great regret that he had felt bound to ask us to respond in this way & pointing out his reluctance. Next day Tuesday — the enclosed circular was received.

CONFIDENTIAL.

I wish to put on record exactly what has happened, and what has led me to resolve on an entirely new departure.

I have for some time past come, with increasing conviction, to the conclusion that the continued prosecution of the War requires what is called a 'broad-based' Government. Under existing conditions, criticism, inspired by party motives and interests, has full rein, and is an asset of much value to the enemy.

The resignation of Lord Fisher, which I have done my best to avert, and the more than plausible parliamentary case in regard to the alleged deficiency of high-explosive shells, would, if duly exploited (as they would have been) in the House of Commons at this moment, have had the most disastrous effect on the general political and strategic situation: in particular, such a discussion might have had the result of determining adversely to the Allies the attitude of Italy.

Upon a full review of all the circumstances, I have come to the conclusion that, in the best interests of the country, the reconstruction of the Government can no longer be deferred.

Neither I, nor any of my colleagues, have anything to regret or to be ashamed of in the steps, legislative and administrative, which we have taken, in the face of unexampled difficulties, since the War began. I am proud to think that we have a record which, when it is impartially appraised by history, will stand the most exacting scrutiny, and be always gratefully and approvingly remembered.

I tender to them, one and all, my warmest and most heartfelt thanks for the inestimable service which they have rendered to the country, and for their unwavering loyalty to myself.

There is not one of them from whom it is not a real pain to me, even temporarily, to part; and no one among them would more readily step aside than I.

But, in the time in which we live, all personal ties and associations must be disregarded, at whatever cost, in the general interest.

And it is for that purpose and in that spirit that, with infinite reluctance, I ask them to help me in the discharge of a most repugnant but most imperative duty.

H.H.A.

May 17, 1915

'Asquith's congé to his colleagues', as JAP annotated it, was printed and circulated on 18 May. In his draft memoirs JAP wrote that the Prime Minister's colleagues all felt that his first request for their resignation was 'curt and tactless and that we, at least, ought to have had explained to us at a Cabinet Council the reasons for the request' (War Reminiscences, *ch.IX, p.117, MS. Gainford 36/2).*

Tuesday May 18 — sitting on the front Bench the next thing I knew was that the P.M. told me to go on appointing my Research Committee & he said 'you will be alright Jack' so I went north for a P. & P meeting the following day.

Wednesday May 19 The House adjourned until June 2d.

In spite of the Prime Minister's assurance, JAP was soon to learn that his position was far from secure. Like other members of the Cabinet outside the inner circle, he would spend a week of anxiety about his future, calling on colleagues closer to the principals in a quest for hopeful information. He wrote to his wife on 22 May in a letter marked 'Private. Please lock up at once after perusal':

> I went across to Crewe House, to ask Crewe for his advice as to what I should do in regard to carrying on my work. He said nothing is yet settled, though it looks like the opposition pressing for more places in the Government, but this can be said for your office that the Tories won't want it now, & our people wouldn't like a Tory in it, — but the Prime Minister may have to vacate more offices now than he intended to, when he spoke to you on Tuesday.
>
> I dined at Brooks's. Haldane was there, & after dinner we had a cigar together. He said 'I have told the Prime Minister not to think of me any more. Bonar Law has pointed out to the P.M. that many of his party regard me as suspect, though he Bonar Law does not share their views. I don't like the Lord Chancellor's duties as Speaker, but the law work interests me & I shall continue that, & go on with a work I am writing.'
>
> He obviously would have liked to have put the War Office civil administration into working order leaving K. to do the military side, but Leo Maxse, & Northcliffe make that impossible.
>
> He talked about his efforts at Berlin to induce the Germans to reduce their ship-building programme & thought that the suspicion & anti German feeling would have subsided if the German staff had only responded, & that war might in that event have been averted.
>
> He had warned Germany that we should come in if they were aggressive & that we were bound to stand by Belgium. I however pointed out that the war was produced by Germany's fear of the Slav on the one side, & the French seeking a revenge on the other, & the German view was that if a war did not take place this year, they would be in a worse position another, & that this reason induced Germany to adopt the

aggressive policy this year. He admitted the force of this; & concluded this part of our talk by saying both countries Germany & ourselves were incapable of seeing each other's standpoint. He alone had been able to do this! & nearly brought off a policy which would have secured a European Peace & that Grey had played up & helped to bring it off, & the 2 foreign offices were never so friendly as a few months before the outbreak.

I gathered posts had not been settled but this sort of shuffling had been under discussion. Winston to be degraded to Duchy of Lancas. Harcourt, Emmott, Beauchamp, Lucas, & Samuel or Hobhouse to quit office. Crewe to give up India to retain Privy Seal & remain Leader of Lords. Montagu to leave the Cabinet & become financial secretary. Bonar Law — a Canadian to go to the Colonies. Balfour to go to the Admiralty, Lansdowne to be President of Council. Henderson to Post Office or L.G.B. Chamberlain to India. Curzon — Office of Works. Long — Board of Agriculture. Carson & F.E. Smith possibly Local Government Board or in legal work, e.g. Law Officers. Simon did not want the woolsack — Findlay[51] [*sic*] did but some-one else might be found. The Speaker would retire if Cave had the reversion, but not for a Liberal. Haldane said the other places had not been discussed — i.e. Home Office Ireland B. of Trade and Education & Scotland. George would remain at the Treasury. It was all rather vague & nothing was finally settled.

... [After lunch] started off to call on A.J.B. to talk to him about his brother-in-law's [Lord Rayleigh] suitability for Research Council Chairmanship, but in crossing Waterloo Place I intercepted George Simon & Montagu who had been lunching at the Carlton Hotel. George said don't call on Balfour yet, as nothing is yet settled & the Coalition may not yet come off, & you had better wait before doing anything. We are going he said to have another Pow ow [*sic*] at Downing Street this afternoon.

He told me he had been to see the King this morning but did not say more, but that if he wanted me to help munitions with North Country firms he hoped he could rely on me but that he very likely would remain at the Treasury. He then went into No. 11, & I came on here [to the Board of Education].

... My impression is that the P.M. is very unhappy, & dislikes the idea of a Coalition, but the Tories by putting a pistol to his head have forced him to give them high office, & they are now pressing for more places & for more colleagues being thrown over so as to square their own party. The Party Irish Labour & Liberals who were returned to support a Liberal Government don't like the outlook & to be suddenly told to support a Coalition & the Experiment to me looks one of doubtful expediency. The rank & file on both sides always resent the leaders working together, & even our common cause in the War, seems hardly likely to induce them to change their view now.

(JAP–EP, 22 May 1915, MS. Gainford 190/31)

[51] Robert Bannatyne Finlay (1842–1929); MP Inverness Burghs (Lib. 1885–6; Lib. Unionist 1886–92, 1895–1906); Con. MP Edinburgh and St Andrews Univs 1910–16; Solr-Gen. 1895–1900; Atty Gen.1900–5; Ld Chancellor 1916–19; Kt 1895; GCMG 1904; Baron Finlay 1916; Vt Finlay 1919.

May 26[52] I heard nothing more — but what I saw in the Press & on Wednesday the 26th the announcement of the new Coalition Govmt with my name excluded. At 2 o'clock I received at the B. of E. the following letter.

10, Downing Street,
Whitehall. S.W.

26 May 1915
CONFIDENTIAL

My dear Jack,

It has been a great grief to me that I could not find myself able, as I had hoped & expected, to keep you at the place where you have done so well. The demands which, as things progressed, had to be satisfied made it impossible.

There is no one from whom I feel the severance more, after so many years of intimate cooperation. But I trust & believe that it will not last long.

There is, if you have any reason for anxiety on that score, a pension at your disposal. And I hope you will be able to continue to do war work, though for the moment outside the Government.

Believe me always,

Affectionately & gratefully yours,
H. H. Asquith

I wrote in reply. I would consider the question of a political pension. That I appreciated the kindly & affectionate tone. That what I minded most was the severance with the P.M. himself.

Board of Education
Whitehall,
London, S.W.

26 May 1915
CONFIDENTIAL

My dear Prime Minister,

After what you said to me last week, I admit the shock was somewhat severe when this morning I opened my newspaper, but I have realised the difficulties,

[52] JAP, writing some weeks after the event, wrote '26th June', but the surrender and receipt of seals took place in May.

and that you have had to face the most awkward and unpleasant task that has ever fallen on any Prime Minister.

May I thank you for all the personal kindness & help you have always given me & for the affectionate letter just received.

If I can struggle along, without resort to a political pension I shall try and do so, but perhaps for the time being you can allow the offer to remain open.

If I can continue to do war work, & help the new government thus, my services are of course at their disposal in any direction.

For the past 8 years I have felt it a privilege & a pleasure to work with you and for you, and it's *this* severance I mind most now.

I am yours always,

affectionately
Joseph A. Pease
(MS. Gainford 86/161)

In one rough, undated, outline of his new Cabinet, HHA kept JAP at Education; Arthur Henderson was proposed for the Office of Works (Bodl. MS. Asquith. 27, f.198). As late as 24 May, after talking to DLG, Simon, and Bonham Carter, Montagu told Venetia Stanley 'Pease is staying!' (Montagu MSS II B1/112, Wren Lib. TCC). In a diary entry of 25 May, Hobhouse wrote: 'Tonight I received a brief letter from P.M. regretting the severance of ties, and thanking for services rendered and hoping for a speedy reuniting. All of which is the purest bunkum. Jack Pease who is also "out" was personally assured by HHA that he at any rate "would be all right"...'. Later, on the morning of 27 May, Hobhouse 'heard from Samuel that he deeply regretted supplanting a colleague, and only did it at the insistence of the P.M. Unfortunately Jack Pease met him yesterday, and asked him how he could take the place of a friend and colleague, to which he had replied "Oh well one must look after oneself"' (David ed., Inside Asquith's Cabinet, *p.247).*

JAP drew his salary as President of the Board of Education until 26 May. He was paid a political pension from 27 May 1915 to 5 January 1916, at the rate of £1,200 p.a. less £300 p.a. deducted because of his salary as an MP (JAP–HHA, draft, undated [8 Nov. 1915], MS. Gainford 87/87–8; PP 1916, [93], xvii, 1; and TNA: T 1/11901/3699/1916). His letter applying for the pension was based on one submitted in 1902 by Sir J.E. Gorst (JAP–Lords Commissioner of the Treasury, 13 June 1915, MS. Gainford 86/169). He resigned the pension when he was offered a £2,000 p.a. directorship by the shipping magnate Lord Furness to help Furness's companies negotiate with government departments. JAP had hardly started with Furness when he resigned in order to accept the Post Office early in 1916. He was able to resume the directorship the following December (JAP–EP, 22 Oct. 1915, MS. Gainford

190/75–6; J.H. Beckington [managing director of Broomhill Collieries Ltd, one of Furness's companies]–JAP, 16 Feb. 1916, and note by JAP, 20 Dec. 1916, MS. Gainford 87/73–7). JAP's political pension under the Political Officers Pension Act 1869 was the first to be awarded by HHA, and the first Liberal pension since 1897 (The Morning Post, *5 July 1915).*

At Buckingham Palace on Thursday 26th May Ll. George just said 'I am sorry'. McKenna also made some remark. Churchill said I want you to know that I am not responsible, & I will let you know more.

A manifestly hurt JAP wrote to Reginald McKenna on 28 May:

My dear Regie

You & Pamela have been such good friends & so kind to me in recent years that I do hope that I shan't lose your friendship now my 18 years of official life has been temporarily or permanently brought to an end.

I don't understand what has been the occasion, or the justification for bringing Henderson in to do my work, or how he at the Board of Education will help to end the war quicker than if I had been left there, but perhaps my friends will tell me some day.

I appreciated your kind grip of the hand yesterday which was perhaps more expressive than words.

You will be happier I think at the Treasury than at the Home Office, and for the country's sake I am glad you are going there. It is horrid saying goodbye to officials who have worked with one well, & whilst you must regret parting with some of them, yet you have been so abominably attacked, & without the slightest justification that you will I hope welcome your promotion, even with the financial anxieties which are to be yours.

Best of luck my dear Regie

Yours ever
Joseph A. Pease
(McKenna MSS, MCKN 9/6, CAC)

McKenna had learned the previous day that he was to go the Treasury, HHA having told him that 'at the last moment the demands of the Unionists had been so insistent that the Cabinet had to be reconstructed and he had to replace Lloyd George as Chancellor of the Exchequer in order to keep Bonar Law out of the Ministry of Munitions'. McKenna's offer to 'vacate his office and serve the country without salary in any capacity' had been rejected, as HHA had wanted him to stay at the Home Office (Basil Thomson diary, 27 May 1915, Sir Basil Thomson, The Scene Changes, *Collins, 1939, pp.243–4).*

Unreconciled to the political imperatives of coalition, JAP told Haldane on 25 May: 'It does seem curious that the man I pulled out of a moulder's job because he was a trades union organiser, & who I appointed as my Father's registration agent, & who possesses no other qualification should be put at the Board' (Haldane of Cloan MSS 5911, f.74, NLS). JAP's friends would not have been able to tell him how Henderson had accepted the Presidency of the Board of Education 'with great reluctance and under protest'. But Henderson did: 'When I told the PM there was nothing appropriate in my accepting such a post he replied there was nothing appropriate in any of the appointments.' (Henderson–JAP, 28 May 1915, MS. Gainford 86/16.) Reminding HHA of this on 26 July 1916, Henderson wrote: 'not only was it inappropriate, but that, from a National standpoint, my acceptance was, as recent Education Debates in both Houses prove, impolitic, if not unwise' (Bodl. MS. Asquith 17, f.27).

*For JAP, saying goodbye to officials who had worked closely with him had been 'the most painful morning in my life'. When it came to the last of the adieus, to the Hon. Maude Lawrence, the long-serving Chief Woman Inspector, 'I made a fool of myself. I could say nothing, so big was the lump in my throat, I gripped her hand, and left the room in tears' (*War Reminiscences, *ch.IX, p.136, MS. Gainford 36/2). Lawrence was the niece of Sir Henry Lawrence, who, unlike JAP's father-in-law, had not survived the siege of Lucknow. Chosen by Morant in 1905, she 'had few academic pretensions, little knowledge of paedagogy or departmental requirements, and above all no feminist axe to grind' (Meta Zimmeck, 'The "new woman" in the machinery of government: a spanner in the works?', in Roy Macleod ed.,* Government and Expertise: Specialists, administrators and professionals 1860–1919, *Cambridge UP, 1988, p.192).*

On *June 3d* — I lunched with him [WSC] at the Admiralty.

He told me Fisher had left on the Friday, 15th May, without a word to him & he had had no difference with Fisher.

He had accepted all that had been done, & when things were going well gloried in their success, but like an old man was very apprehensive when things went wrong. Torpedo work unnerved him, but he not at any time dissented.

On Sat. 16. Fisher saw Ll.G. went into the P.M. and resigned. What influence did G. bring to bear? Churchill thought George meant to be war minister — & by bringing in Tories he would gain his end. The P.M. failed to prevent Fisher's resignation — but could get nothing out of him more than that he would not work with Churchill.

On the Sunday Churchill offered to resign. The P.M. declined it.

18th On the Monday, Churchill brought in his new Board all willing & ready to go on except Fisher, who he replaced by Sir A. Wilson.

The P.M. then said, no you must go, I must bring in the Tories, & he sent round the box.

Churchill, Grey Haldane had not been in the deal & when Grey told Haldane he went deadly white with amazement.

From Hobhouse It appears that Balfour had had frequent meetings with Lloyd George at Montagu's house — a Labour M.P. told him in passing down that St. one or other were constantly going out or going in.

Churchill also told me George never breathed to him his scheme for wrecking the Liberal Party, he did not blame the Tories for pressing home their advantage, when the P.M. had sent for Bonar Law.

Ch. said he would go & fight in France, but afterwards he accepted the P.M's invitation to remain in the cabinet. He seemed sore that George had not consulted him — he had stood by George over Marconis.

Churchill also told me George wanted both munitions & the Exchequer but the Tories stopped it at once, & said he could take his choice.

Balfour was the man he preferred to succeed him, he was a gentleman, & understood him.

Since the fate of the last Liberal government was explored and extensively documented for the first time in Politicians at War (1971), *the events of May 1915 have been reviewed in a succession of articles and in the biographies of the party leaders and their principal associates. Differences of emphasis and interpretation and some colour from previously unavailable sources are offered, but little has emerged to change the chronology of the story. The following studies are notable: Martin D. Pugh, 'Asquith, Bonar Law and the First Coalition',* HJ, *vol.17, issue 4, Dec. 1974, pp.813–36; Peter Fraser, 'British War Policy and the Crisis of Liberalism in May 1915',* JMH, *vol.54, 1982, pp.1–26. In addition the outstanding research of Bruce Ivar Gudmundsson has established that the vital element in hampering the British forces at Neuve Chapelle and Aubers Ridge was not so much a 'shortage of shells' but a shortage of 6-inch howitzers, which alone 'possessed both the accuracy and the power to reliably destroy German trenches…' ('Learning from the Front: Tactical Innovation in France and Flanders, 1914–1918', D.Phil. thesis, Oxford U., 2007, pp.2–3).*

The coalition ministry was announced on 25 May. Of JAP's Liberal colleagues, McKenna became Chancellor of the Exchequer, DLG Minister of Munitions, Simon Home Secretary. Crewe exchanged the Privy Seal for Presidency of the Council and leader of the House of Lords. Grey, Runciman, Birrell, and McKinnon Wood retained their posts. Buckmaster was elevated as Lord Chancellor. Haldane, Emmott, Beauchamp, and Lucas (who turned down the Under-Secretaryship at both the India and Colonial Offices) left the government. Samuel, dropped from the Cabinet, became Postmaster-General. A crestfallen WSC accepted the Duchy of Lancaster, displacing Montagu, whose appointment as Financial Secretary to the Treasury kept him close to the centre of affairs. Making way for Bonar Law, Harcourt left the Colonial Office but stayed in the Cabinet as First Commissioner of Works; his aide memoire on 25 May of HHA's private explanation of Cabinet changes is at Bodl. MS. Dep. 6231. Kitchener held on to the War Office. Balfour succeeded WSC at the Admiralty, Lansdowne, Long, Carson, Austen Chamberlain, and Curzon entered the Cabinet.

A still bewildered JAP continued to try to piece together the course of events that had brought about his ejection from office and replacement by Labour's Arthur Henderson. His former private secretary, George Young,[53] *'who perhaps knew me and the motives which actuated me better than anyone else', wrote appreciatively (*War Reminiscences, *ch.IX, p.134, MS. Gainford 36/2). Young, the future historian of the Victorian age and biographer of Stanley Baldwin, drew a link with what he thought he knew about secret pre-war politics:*

> The story is that in 1909 (I think) there were a series of conferences between Balfour, Winston and Lloyd George with the object of forming a coalition or a new party on a Social-Reform-Imperialist basis.
>
> I am not sure of the date, but the rest of the story may be taken as true. I had forgotten all about it, but it does throw light on the present situation.
>
> *(G.M. Young–JAP, 14 June 1915, MS. Gainford 86/38)*

JAP continued to gather intelligence. From Margot Asquith he heard the surprising nuance that DLG 'never was an intriguer, but has been with his newspaper love of notoriety made the instrument for the purpose by Northcliffe, Dalziel etc.' (JAP–EP, 16 June 1915, MS. Gainford 190/37). JAP was more disposed to believe the implausible and factually inaccurate circumstantial account of ministerial treachery that Hobhouse had been retailing since before the crisis came. Accusing WSC of 'his old game of intriguing all round. First against the P.M. and

[53] George Malcolm Young (1882–1959); p.s. to Arthur Henderson as Pres. Bd of Educ. 1915; sec. Standing Joint Committee for Universities. Prize Fellow, All Souls 1905–16 (re-elected 1948); joined Bd of Educ. 1908; civil sec. to Sir M. Hankey as War Cabinet Sec.; Joint Perm. Sec. Min. of Reconstruction 1917; CB 1917. Established his reputation with *Portrait of an Age: Victorian England* (1936). His *Stanley Baldwin* (1952) 'did less than justice to a misunderstood Prime Minister; and nothing at all to enhance its author's reputation as a historian' (J. Mordaunt Crook, 'G. M. Young: The Last Victorian?', in S.J.D. Green and Peregrine Hordern eds, *All Souls and the Wider World: Statesmen, Scholars, and Adventurers, c.1850–1950*, Oxford UP, 2011, p.311). For 25 years he lived companionably with the civil servant and independently wealthy writer Mona Wilson (L.E. Jones, E.T. Williams, 'Young, George Malcolm (1882–1959)', rev. *ODNB*, 2004, http://www.oxforddnb.com/view/article/37076; Elaine Harrison, 'Wilson, Mona (1872–1954)', *ODNB*, online edn, Jan. 2008, http://www.oxforddnb.com/view/article/70137, both accessed 17 Mar. 2014).

Grey with the strange combination of A.J.B., Garvin, Ll.G. to which they proposed to add "K" — When the latter declined, partly from loyalty, partly from prudence, and partly from distrust the attack was turned on him, and Sir John French was to be substituted for "K"' (Hobhouse–Buxton, 30 Apr. 1915, Buxton MSS).

The Hobhouse suspicions, repeated and expanded in a letter to Buxton on 10 June, and elaborated uncritically by Stephen Koss in 'The Destruction of Britain's Last Liberal Government', JMH, vol.40, no.2, 1968, pp.255–77, and his biography of Haldane, are scrutinised in Hazlehurst, Politicians at War, *pp.240–54, in an allegedly 'belligerent' style that upset Koss's champions Robert Rhodes James and Alfred Gollin. The latter's incorrigible reliance on J.L. Garvin's propagandist version of events is exhibited at its worst in a patronising review of David French's* British Economic and Strategic Planning, 1905–1915, *Allen & Unwin, 1982, in* Albion: A Quarterly Journal Concerned with British Studies, *vol.15, no.3, 1983, pp.259–65.*[54]

Two days later:

> I had 10 minutes chat with Pamela [McKenna] at the back of Mrs. Lowther's[55] Gallery — no one else was in the Gallery last evening. I gathered McKenna was in the Fisher know on the Saturday & Sunday, saw L.G. on the Monday, but did not wait to see Bonar Law with L.G. L.G. went alone (? with Bonar Law) on the Monday to the P.M. & it was after that, the P.M. dismissed his Ministers unceremoniously & sent round a minute box. He ought of course to have called us together & discussed the situation but he hates emotional scenes, & his courage failed him to face us. It is so true that the greatest men have their limitations. George is now suspect in the Party, he will try his wiles, & secure cheers in his munitions speech on Tuesday and much depends on his success. & he will adroitly sway his views to his audience's but he may find us cold! but he had got the Press squared but that's not everything. The P.M. & the Party machine counts most
>
> *(JAP–EP, 17 June 1915, MS. Gainford 190/38)*

June 18 Runciman travelled with Elsie on June 4 — & for an hour gave a detailed account of the comings & going of Ministers & ex-ministers in order to secure the ends they had in view.

Evidently Runciman who had never seen the P.M. — any more than I had between May 12. Wed (our last Liberal cabinet) & Wednesday May 28th. when the

[54] Stephen Koss's review of *Politicians at War* in *Political Scence Quarterly*, vol.87, no.4, Dec. 1972, pp.678–80, speaks of gratuitous and excessively lengthy replies to other historians without disclosing that he was the only historian whose work was closely examined. Unfortunately Kenneth O. Morgan's version of the Koss contretemps is misleading about the critique of the article. Nor does he discern the mischief-making in what A.J.P. Taylor reportedly told him (Kenneth O. Morgan, *My Histories*, U. of Wales P., Cardiff, 2015, pp.72–3).

[55] Mary Frances Lowther (?–1944); dau. Alexander James Beresford-Hope MP and Lady Mildred, granddaughter 2nd M. of Salisbury; m. James Lowther 1886.

new cabinet was announced in the Press — felt he had been treated badly. He told E.P. that the only men who the P.M. fought for to remain were Baker & Jack Tennant[56] — that Ll. George not the Tories had me chucked out.

That Crewe had let himself go to Runciman & let him see how hateful the whole thing had been to him. That Crewe was indignant at Churchill having struggled to oust him from India, to go there when it was necessary for him to leave the Admiralty.

JAP had grounds for feeling hurt by the way he had been treated. For more than three weeks from 18 May when he had been told he would be 'alright' it seemed as though HHA had been purposely avoiding him. He turned to Margot Asquith: 'You are my oldest friend. If I have said anything to annoy the Prime Minister please *tell me quite frankly . . .'. 'Of course,' came the reply, 'you have never vexed Henry in your life'. But in a characteristic free-flowing effusion Margot urged that it was the Prime Minister who deserved sympathy for having to part with friends like Jack and Haldane and 'Bluey' Baker. He had written a letter, and it was Bongy's fault that JAP didn't get it. And it was temporary after all, 'So buck up!' Margot's 'blathering' riled Elsie, who wanted nothing more to do with 'the P.M. who pursues the policy of least resistance' (JAP–Margot Asquith, 10 June 1915, and reply, 11–14 June, EP–JAP, 16 June 1915, MS. Gainford 86/166–8).*

It was not just that JAP had been assured he was safe when the coalition was about to be formed. As he told Hobhouse, with whom he was staying in mid-July, he had been offered a very good industrial appointment some years earlier but HHA had begged him not to accept because 'he relied so much on his (J.P's) judgement'. An exclamation mark at the end of this sentence in Hobhouse's diary makes plain his incredulity (David ed., Inside Asquith's Cabinet, *p.250).*

Loyal as JAP was to HHA, he did not conceal his unabated dismay at the way the change of government had been orchestrated. Writing to JAP on his valedictory speech, the ever hopeful backbencher Alex MacCallum Scott congratulated him for intimating 'that you were not yet apprised of the reasons which led to the political revolution'. John Simon said 'you did a difficult thing so well. Everyone felt this—manly, firm, generous, modest—and I feel more sorry than ever to see the table between us' (3 June 1915, MS. Gainford 86/15,145). JAP, Hobhouse, and other displaced Liberal ministers had declined to sit behind Carson, Bonar Law, and WSC; they joined a handful of Tory ex-ministers on the unofficial front bench.

On 25 July JAP left for France to begin working with the Claims Commission. He had been asked to go by H.W. Forster, Financial Secretary at the War Office. Until his appointment to

[56] Although JAP wrote 'Jack Tennant', his daughter Miriam later amended the text to 'Jack Pease'. In his typed war memoirs JAP wrote 'Jack Pease'.

*the War Office, Forster himself had been civilian member of the commission. He told JAP that it was essential to have a man on the commission with broader experience than army discipline (*War Reminiscences*, ch.X, p.142, MS. Gainford 36/3).*

The Claims Commission assessed claims submitted by French civilians for damage done by British troops. Damage caused during fighting such as trenches and shellfire could not be included in any claim; such damage was classed as faits de guerre *and assessment had to wait for the end of the war. The Commission considered damage caused by the troops or their transport (animal and mechanical) to their billets, and the damage done to standing crops by the erection of telegraph poles. Troops foraging for firewood frequently burnt any wood that they could find, including furniture, flooring, and roof rafters.*

JAP wrote to Pamela McKenna on 17 August 1915 explaining his work:

> The cases are varied, personal injuries e.g. runovers by lorries & despatch riders. Fires e.g. cigarette ends thrown down in barns where soldiers sleep — damage to crops e.g. practice trench-digging & the erection of telegraph poles in standing corn. Injury to trees e.g. horses tied in orchards ringing the bark off pear trees. Billeting e.g. spoons, pans, taken away — glass in windows broken, firewood e.g. shutters & gates broken up! Our Tommies smash things about & are charmingly casual.
>
> I have been once to head quarters to discuss with Maxwell points of policy & twice up to the front to inspect damage. Some extraordinary fraudulent claims are put in, but all the checking possible is being done, & the French peasantry are glad to see the colour of money from the British.
>
> *(McKenna MSS, MCKN 9/7, CAC)*

It was hoped that by meeting fair reasonable claims, Anglo-French relations, at least at the local level, would remain amicable. Not surprisingly, the Commission's work was seen by some French civilians as a golden opportunity: there was no time for detailed inventories to be taken after civilians had been evacuated from an area and before the troops moved in. Moreover, the British paid out cash; the French military authorities merely issued certificates that damage had been done but postponed any settlement to the end of the war. The Commission had to establish a certification scheme to prevent several claims against different units being submitted for the same damage. Where it was impossible to apportion the damage done by different units, a rental scheme was devised. R.H. Mottram's The Twentieth Century: A personal record *(Hutchinson, 1969, pp.63–8), describes the work of a young Claims Commission officer.*

One of the Commission's main problems was the definition of faits de guerre*. For example, trenches were classed as* de guerre*, but the wood taken to prop them up was not, unless it was taken in an emergency. JAP drew up a scheme differentiating 'preventable' damage and* faits de guerre*. His system was based on one adopted after the Franco-Prussian* *war. Unfortunately the memorandum embodying his system has not survived in his papers. After JAP's departure, Brigadier-General Colquhoun Grant Morrison, President of the Commission, wrote: 'Have you heard that we now mark everything Fait de guerre (Pease). The abbreviation is FdeG(P) which some people think means "Provisional" i.e. to be dealt with hereafter; but in reality it all comes from your excellent memorandum...' (Morrison–JAP, 6 Feb.1916, MS. Gainford 94).*

Despite JAP's efforts, the problem of faits de guerre *remained unresolved. Morrison wrote:*

> This question of FdeG must be grappled with somehow. It is not fair upon the old CC to leave it to bear all the brunt of the fray. Forster has secured a splendid victory over the 'litiges' but faits de guerre stand outside that agreement, and action ought now to be taken diplomatically to determine the procedure in regard to FdeG. Nothing will be gained by continued arguments with the French Mission.
>
> *(Morrison–JAP, 4 Jan. 1916, MS. Gainford 88/9)*

Many of the Claims Commission's assessments were performed by teams of British and French valuers who toured the affected districts to assess damage. However, the army was persuaded to appoint officers with each division to assess small claims up to 125 frs and to meet them immediately. Morrison himself, who died in an auto accident in May 1916, came under fire in the spring of 1916 when a fact-finding mission by Capt. Francis Goldney-Bennett MP uncovered complaints about payments considerably less than those claimed, and 25 per cent rejected as faits de guerre *(Craig Gibson,* Behind the Front: British Soldiers and French Civilians, *1914–1918, Cambridge UP, 2014, pp.223–8,242).*

Although JAP occasionally visited the front and came under fire (see his entry for 19 September), his work seems to have been more uncomfortable than dangerous—though he did observe the battle of Cambrai on 13 October. When not on tour, he soon fell into a routine, working from 9.15 to 1.00, 4.30–7.00 and 8.15–10.00. He played golf for two hours from 2.15 and usually had a rubber of bridge in the evening. The Commission was based on Hardelot Plage, so he often took exercise on the sands before breakfast, frequently in the form of building sand forts with a little girl called Marthe. Originally he had started the day with a morning bathe in the sea, but on 31 July, he had collapsed after bathing. It is not clear whether the collapse was caused by tiredness or a mild heart attack. The former seems more likely, since JAP was able to play sixteen holes of golf on 2 August (a bank holiday). Elsie wrote:

My darling,

I won't fuss, if you will treat this fainting fit for what I believe it is—a danger signal. You have been living at great strain since the outbreak of war. Not merely through work & increased effort but your nervous system & mind have had no ease or relaxation—& I have thought that I have never seen you look so badly since before your trip to Mexico...

(EP–JAP, 2 Aug. 1915 [incomplete], MS. Gainford 87/1)

He seems to have continued his rapid recovery without any ill effects and by the end of August was taking part in a tennis tournament. He suffered a similar, though more severe, attack three years later in Italy. Stricken on 30 April 1918, by 4 May he was walking again with no paralysis or loss of power (JAP–EP, MS. Gainford 191; copy of doctor's report, Bordighera General Hospital, MS. Gainford 47/51).

Golf seems to have been JAP's principal form of relaxation; he frequently played with the President of the Claims Commission, Col. Morrison. JAP described Morrison as 'madly keen... but only a moderate performer. His figure was not suited to the game' (War Reminiscences, *ch.X, p.142, MS. Gainford 36/3). Morrison himself would come under fire in 1916.*

JAP's diary entry for 19 September is fairly typical of his tours to assess claims, except for the political conversations with Seely and the visit to the front line. Apart from visits like this one, JAP learned much about conditions at the front through conversations with officers, especially in the mess. For example, Lt-Gen. Sir James Willcocks of the Indian Division offered £100 to anyone who could stay in the trenches for 30 seconds without hearing a shot or two minutes without hearing a shell (JAP–EP, 10 Aug. 1915, MS. Gainford 190/47).

Sept. 19

Went to St. Omer. called on Henry Guest.[57] Went with him to Bailleul Nieppe, Petit Pont & so to Petit Monk under 'Halte' Ploegsteerte wood, where we had luncheon with General Seely, Watts[58] his A.G., & Alec Sinclair[59] his A.D.C. Under heavy firing of 18, 15 & other cannons close by us. S & I had an hour's chat on

[57] Hon. Christian Henry Charles Guest (1874–1957); Lib. MP Pembroke & Haverfordwest 1910–18; serving in France; 2nd son 1st Baron Wimborne; served 2nd Boer War, India 1902–7, staff coll. then instructor, cavalry school; Lib. MP East Dorset 1910, Nat. Lib. MP Bristol N 1922–3, Con. MP Plymouth Drake 1937–45; PPS to Charles Hobhouse as PMG 1914–15.

[58] Capt. Disney Younger Watt, professional soldier; Duke of Cambridge's Own Lancers; Lt 1899; Leics Regiment, 1908; tmpy Lt-Col. commanding a battn, Loyal North Lancashire Reg. 17 Dec 1915. Seely wrote in *Adventure* (William Heineman, 1930), p.244, 'our new Brigade Major Lawson...had replaced Watt, brother of Sir John French's aide-de-camp, now promoted to command a battalion. His promotion was well deserved, but unfortunately shortly afterwards he had his right leg shot off...'. In 1926, Lt-Col. Watt exhibited a picture in an exhibition by soldiers; serving in Kenya 1936.

[59] Capt. Sir Archibald Henry Macdonald Sinclair Bt (1890–1970); ADC to Seely, known as Archie not Alec; commissioned into Life Guards 1910; succ. g'father as 4th Bt 1912; Major, Guards Machine Gun Regiment; served with WSC in 6th Battn Royal Scots Fusiliers 1916; Personal Mili. Sec. to WSC as Sec. of St. for War 1919–21; p.s. to WSC at Colonial Office 1921–2; Lib. MP Caithness and Sutherland 1922–45; Sec. of St. for Scotland 1931–2; Sec. of St. for Air 1940–5; Leader of Lib. Party in House of Commons 1935–45; Vt Thurso 1952.

situation by Seely's tent in paddock — on position, situation at front, Dardanelles, & political situation at home with L.G. in alliance with Harmsworth to out the P.M. on conscription.

Canadian Corps — 1st Canadian Division Nieppe. Seely's view that method of securing recruits by an agitation for conscription is the very way to stop recruiting & the men coming forward of being trained in a spirit to play up. He of opinion war over in 6 weeks that the French would get through if not they would not be able to make any further effort & we would have to take the Germans on single handed but he was very sanguine we could do it, but at heavy loss to men engaged where the general attack began. We were already working up for it. At four o'clock went by River Douve up to corner of trenches 800 yds from shattered Messines. Walked in trenches for 3 hours, peering thro loopholes at barbed wire entanglements & line of German trenches 100–300 yards off, heavy small arm firing going on, whole time bullets whizzing just over one, whistling into trees by which we were standing, & one hit ground by my left foot as I walked home across pasture between La Halte & the Nouveau Eglise & Messines road. Only one big shell fell.

Except when bad weather or submarines intervened, JAP was able to keep up with political events through the newspapers and his correspondence. Though he and Elsie complained of the postal service, she was replying on 2 August to the news of his fainting attack on 31 July. Moreover JAP and his fellow officers were able to censor their own letters and could be fairly uninhibited in their exchanges. Although it was possible for wives to visit France, Elsie herself never crossed the Channel. JAP was able to enjoy two weeks' leave in England in October.

Sept 21 Left on leave for England Sept 21. Tuesday attended Pease & Partners Board Sept 22 went to Nuneham Park on Sept 23. Had talk on Sunday Sept 26 with Edward Grey in the garden, he was harassed about attitude of Bulgaria, & regarded her mobilisation of ill omen. He said, 'since my holiday in June, & you left the cabinet we have had a bad time, not that the new colleagues worked adversely to the policy of the Govmt, but the press was damnable and the agitation for conscription most detrimental to British interests, in diplomacy where things are going badly I have little influence and work is much more severe & difficult, & much will depend upon the result of this week's effort on the West front by the French'. L.L. Harcourt said 'we have I think killed conscription, & Lloyd George is in full flight. Balfour's resistance has been of real help, but we have had no cabinet discussion on it — 2 memorandums by me & one by Balfour...'.

Hobhouse reported his discoveries in France in regard to the French experience of drilled & forged steel shells, & on the Monday Sept 27 he had a talk to the P.M. who was going to see Lloyd George and the result was Le Roy Lewis[60] military attaché in Paris was directed to hold an inquiry.

In London Monday 27th to Thursday 30th spoke against conscription on the Tuesday in unfortunate debate raised by Capt Guest against the appeal of the Prime Minister. On 30th went to Nuneham shot Partridges again on Oct 1 & 2. The bag for 4 days 1807 birds a record for the 4 days. Edward Grey Harcourt, Montagu, Sir F. Ponsonby,[61] Burns, Hobhouse, & the Speaker & I. Returned to Hardelot 2.0 boat on Sunday Oct 3.

Shortly after JAP's return to France, Hobhouse went to Paris to pursue the shells question. He called on JAP on his return and passed on his news: the French had seven million shells in stock for '75 guns', but in a ten-day attack, three and half million shells had been used. Hobhouse had also discovered that the French manufactured a fuse which cost only three francs, compared to the British fuse which cost 15s. The Belgians had tried the French fuse and found that it gave the same result as the British. JAP was back in England ten days later.

Oct. 21 Shot 2 pheasants dined Brooks's & played with Edward Grey. He disappointed at Balkan position. Servians fought out, no use assisting them. German communication to Constantinople assured. Turks would be armed, & their position strengthened. He evidently thought P.M. ill partly through worries. Carson's statement satisfactory but he left because we would not send sufficient forces to

[60] Col. Herman Le Roy-Lewis (1860–1931); appointed military attaché Jan. 1916; businessman; fluent French speaker; 15th Battn Imperial Yeomanry, S. African War, 1900–1; DSO 1901; Col. commanding Hampshire Imperial Yeomanry from 1902; Dep.-Asst-Adj.-Gen., on HQ Staff of Army from 1901. CH, CMG, DSO; chmn executive committee National League for Opposing Woman Suffrage 1911–12; a director of Midland Bank at his death. A letter to *The Spectator*, 13 June 1931, p.18, observed: 'His good looks and debonair manner were most attractive throughout his life. He never needed to care about money, which he spent some-times carefully and sometimes gaily. He had intelligence, wit and taste.' Lord Derby, his ambassador in Paris from April 1918, commented 16 May 1918: 'I suffered in the early part of my time here through having as Military Attaché, Le Roy Lewis, who though he had my confidence was detested and distrusted in French political and military circles.' (David Dutton ed., *Paris 1918: The War Diary of the British Ambassador, the 17th Earl of Derby*, Liverpool UP, 2001, p.4.)

[61] Frederick Edward Grey Ponsonby (1867–1935); Keeper of the Privy Purse 1914–35; known as Fritz; his godparents were the German Emperor Frederick III and Empress Victoria; 2nd Lt, Grenadier Guards 1888; served in Second Boer War, later Major and Brevet Lieut-Col.; served WWI; Equerry-in-Ordinary to Queen Victoria 1894–1901; Asst Keeper of the Privy Purse and Asst PS to Queen Victoria 1897–1901, to King Edward VII 1901–10, and King George V 1910–14; Lt Governor Windsor Castle 1928–35; KCVO 1910; Baron Sysonby 1935. For the Crown's pitiless abandonment of his impoverished widow see Simon Heffer ed., *Henry 'Chips' Channon The Diaries: 1918–38*, Hutchinson, 2021, pp.482–3 (diary, 6 Dec. 1935).

Salonika, & withdraw from Dardanelles — this latter course might be impossible except under heavy fire & enormous loss.

Oct. 22 Breakfast with Tennants. Luncheon with Colebrook[62] who said Cabinet differences had been considerable previous week — position clearer under Derby's[63] voly recruiting scheme. Crossed channel 2.0 — 6.30 — reached by motor Des Raimiers Le Touquet with Williams[64] & Auckland[65] about 8 o'clock.

In September JAP had begun the negotiations with Lord Furness which led to his appointment as a director of Broomhill Collieries (Furness–JAP, 25 Oct. 1915, MS. Gainford 93). By 8 November he was able to write to HHA that he hoped to be able to take up the directorship in the New Year and relinquish the political pension which, as he told Harcourt, 'just kept me going during the last six months' (JAP–Harcourt, 15 Dec. 1915, Bodl. MS. Harcourt 445, f.280). He left France in the middle of December. Gen. Morrison wrote: 'My personal indebtedness to you I have already put on paper in terms which were in no sense a figure of speech' (Morrison–JAP, 18 Dec. 1915, MS. Gainford 87/75).

Keeping a watchful eye on developments at Westminster, JAP saw an opportunity to put his name before the Prime Minister early in November:

Claims Commission,
Boulogne Base
Nov. 8. 1915

My dear Prime Minister,

As the session is now approaching its termination I feel bound as the minister in charge of the P.V. Bill to record my expectation that the Government will see that the prospects of the Bill passing into law under the provisions of the Parliament Act shall not be prejudiced.

[62] Edward Arthur Colebrooke, 1st Baron Colebrooke (1861–1939); Govt Chief Whip in the Lords 1911–22 (whip 1906–11); succ. father as 5th Bt 1890; Baron Colebrook 1906.

[63] Edward George Villiers Stanley, 17th Earl of Derby (1865–1948); director-gen. of recruiting Oct. 1915, the 'Derby Scheme' canvassed men aged 18 to 42 to volunteer immediately or when asked. Lack of sufficient volunteers by Dec. 1915 led to conscription of single men Jan. 1916. U.-Sec. of St., War July–Dec. 1916; Lord Stanley 1893–1908; succ. father 1908; Con. MP SE Lancs. (West Houghton) 1892–1906; Fin. Sec., War Office 1900–3; Postmaster-Gen. 1903–5; Sec. of St., War 1916–Apr. 1918 and 1922–4; Amb. to France 1918–20; he did not speak French. A keen race horse owner (two Derby winners), he had the largest Newmarket stable at the end of 1918.

[64] We have been unable to identify Williams.

[65] William Morton Eden, 5th Baron Auckland (1859–1917); b. Frankfurt-am-Main, Hessen, Germany, succ. father 1890. tmpy Major 6th Service Battn, Dorsetshire Regmt 1914.

Last July I conferred with some leading unofficial members in our own party the labour party & the Irish Nationalists, they all concurred that if Peace had prevailed the majority in the House, no matter what else might have happened, would have insisted upon the passage of the Plural Voting Bill through its third consecutive session & before the General Election.

Last autumn you made it clear that the war should not prejudice the bill's position. The majority in the House do not desire to arouse controversy by pressing its passage this session if we can be assured that its position is safeguarded after the war is over, and I should prefer that no question on the subject should even be asked on the subject; I feel however that it is now up to the Government to safeguard its future passage into law after the war is over and that the country should know that if within say six months after the declaration of peace, — it passes through the Commons for the 3d time it shd. become law.

Could not a clause in the Act, amending the Parliament Act to extend the life of the present parliament, safeguard in also the Pl Voting Bill in the way I suggest.

Yours ever

(JAP–HHA, copy, 8 Nov. 1915, MS. Gainford 87/87)

JAP drafted a covering note to HHA explaining that he hoped this letter would strengthen the Prime Minister's hand. He also said that he would give up his pension at the end of the year as he had been offered work 'in an industrial concern' (JAP–HHA, draft n.d. [8 Nov. 1915], MS. Gainford 87/88).

Dec. 14 to Jan 16 Took up directorate on Broomhill Collieries Board & saw Lord Furness[66] & Mr Fred Lewis[67] at Furness House Billiter Street, & arranged to help them for £2,000 p.a. just as they wanted advice or help with Gov. wages & officials.

[66] Marmaduke Furness, 2nd Baron Furness (1883–1940); chmn Furness Withy, shipowners and builders; substantial interests in collieries and iron and steel works on NE Coast; succ. father 1912; Vt Furness 1918. He was rumoured improbably to have murdered his first wife; his second wife Thelma was the Prince of Wales's mistress 1929–34; his third was the Australian Enid Cavendish (née Lindemann), whose lovers included Vt Castlerosse (who, as the 6th Earl of Kenmare, was, for eight months before his death, her fourth husband), Bernard Baruch, the 17th Earl of Derby, the 5th Earl of Carnarvon, and the 2nd Duke of Westminster (Lyndsy Spence, *She Who Dares: Ten Trailblazing Women*, The History P., Stroud, 2019, pp.35–51; Pat Cavendish O'Neill (ed. Shelley Gare), *a lion in the bedroom*, Jonathan Ball Publishers, Johannesburg & Cape Town, 2004).

[67] Frederick William Lewis (1870–1944); dep. chmn Furness Withy 1914; mgr London office 1890; chmn 1919–44; sometime chmn Royal Mail Lines, Director Cunard White Star, Barclays Bank, Sun Life and Sun Insurance Offices; dep. chmn Ship Licensing Committee appointed by Pres. Bd of Trade, Nov. 1915; member Shipping Control Committee appointed by Prime Minister 1916; Pres. UK Chamber of Shipping 1922; Bt 1918; Baron Essendon 1932.

Chapter 6
Aftermath

JAP's return to business was short-lived. The resignation of Sir John Simon over conscription at the beginning of 1916 resulted in a minor reshuffle and an invitation to return to the ministry as Postmaster-General, outside the Cabinet. If JAP was disappointed that his recall to office left him outside the Cabinet, he could scarcely have predicted the circumstances in which for a few more tantalising days later in the year he might find himself once again intimately involved in headline-making events.

Ireland's Easter rebels had made their headquarters in the Dublin General Post Office. (Keith Jeffery, The GPO and the Easter Rising, *Irish Academic P., Dublin, 2006, is the authoritative study, but Clair Wills,* Dublin 1916: The Siege of the GPO, *Profile Books, 2009, is also useful, as is Claire Fitzpatrick on the symbolic significance of the Post Office: 'The First Step to a Nation? The Irish Postal Service and the Home Rule Crisis',* History, *vol.104, issue 360, 2019, pp.228–44.) Who else but the Postmaster-General would be the right man to go to Ireland and assess the situation? It would not do for the Prime Minister to send a more senior minister, thereby suggesting that the rebellion was more serious than the government was admitting. The Irish administration itself was discredited. And the most delicate part of JAP's mission had nothing to do with re-establishing communications and setting up a temporary GPO and telegraph office. In a rare resumption of his journal he recorded the brief that HHA gave him on Friday 5 May 1916. Apparently it was a spur of the moment decision: 'I called at Downing St at 2.0 to see if the P.M. would like to see me.' He did. He asked JAP to convey to Lord Wimborne, the Lord Lieutenant, 'the view that the Cabinet expected his resignation as head of the Govmt hierarchically speaking & that whilst he did not request him to resign, he thought he would be well advised to do so'. JAP had been around the traps long enough to ask for some clarification:*

5 May 1916

I said did it mean it would be accepted. Yes the P.M. said. If at the inquiry he was found to have been implicated with Birrell's errors of judgment his retention of office would prejudice him, if on the other hand he was white washed he might be re-instated with flying colours.

Wimborne was not going to fall on his sword. 'The Lord Lieutenant sees no adequate reason to justify him in tendering his resignation...', JAP reported to the Prime Minister on 7 May:

> Such action would generally be interpreted as a recognition on his part that he had been guilty of executive mismanagement, and errors of judgement, for which he is not responsible, nor for which he could be held liable.
>
> His assent or dissent to Executive action cannot be called in question. He moreover feels, that had his advice been taken or his suggestions accepted the rebellion would have been averted and he does not see how his position as His Majesty's Representative in Ireland could be strengthened, were he to offer to resign and thereby associate himself with the errors of judgement of which Birrell & Nathan admit themselves to be guilty.
>
> From all I can gather Wimborne has been placed in a difficult position, but by tact & influence done all he could to strengthen the executive, and during the rebellion did all that was possible, and by taking action himself at the critical moment prevented the rebels all over the country from rising, and creating a situation which would have been infinitely more worse than that which has been so quickly dealt with by the Military.

As for his own departmental responsibilities, JAP had conferred with Generals Maxwell (military governor) and Friend (C-in-C Ireland) who 'seemed pleased with the way in which the Post Office staff have restored communications. Postal and telephone facilities will be fully resumed today, the arrears of letter deliveries even in Dublin were cleared yesterday.' A new telegraph office with 130 instruments had been set up. Negotiations were in train to acquire the skating rink attached to the Rotunda, the Rotunda building itself, and two concert halls in the same building to serve as a sorting office, a central post office, and administrative offices. Fires and shelling had caused an estimated £1,000,000 in damage. Thomas Purcell, head of the Dublin Fire Brigade, put the damage at £2.5 million ('Story of the great fires told by Captain Purcell, chief of Dublin Fire Brigade', 1916 Rebellion handbook, *Belfast, 1998, p.29), reference courtesy of Daithí Ó Corráin, whose 'They blew up the best portion of our city and... it is their duty to replace it': compensation and reconstruction in the aftermath of the 1916 Rising',* Irish Historical Studies, *vol.39, no.154, 2014, pp.272–95, is essential reading. The good news was that in the burnt-out GPO the safe containing £7,000 was intact; only £60 in cash was gone. 'The allegation that the Postal service is honeycombed with Sinn Feiners will not I think on investigation prove accurate.'*

JAP had not previously been able to 'understand what could have induced the Sinn Feiners to rebel — but I now realise that given an innate detestation of English rule by a section of Irishmen, a dislike of constitutional means unattractive to a section of an imaginative people, that there was presented on Easter Monday a favourable moment to establish freedom from the English yoke by the creation of an Irish republic.' (Bodl. MS. Asquith 36, ff.154–7; Leon Ó Broin, Dublin Castle and the 1916 Rising: The Story of Sir Matthew Nathan, *Helicon, Dublin, 1966, pp.127–9 summarises JAP's report to HHA, unfortunately attributing it to 'Joseph Alfred Perse'.)*

In the political climacteric of December 1916, JAP left office with HHA and the majority of Liberal ministers. 'If I was to adequately pen my views as to the methods employed by Lloyd George & Northcliffe to unseat Asquith, the words would burn a hole in this paper.' (Diary, 25 Jan. 1917, MS. Gainford 34/4). He was happy to accept the offer of a peerage, to join what his old colleague Lord Buckmaster called 'the tiny band of Liberals in the House of Lords, where Liberalism seems to dissolve like a lump of sugar in hot tea' (Buckmaster–JAP, 18 Jan. 1917, MS. Gainford 90/6).

JAP returned to the Claims Commission between September and December 1917. When his successor, the Conservative MP for Newbury, W.A. Mount, left the Commission, JAP's old colleagues asked him to rejoin them (their letter ends 'S.O.S. Do come'). As JAP was able to cross over to France for frequent short stays, he was able to combine the Commission work with his business obligations.

Taking up his diary fitfully in 1917, JAP recorded some inconsequential conversation and bridge games with the Asquiths (MS. Gainford 34/4). On a weekend visit to the Wharf on 29 May–1 June, 'Asquith seemed relieved not to have the responsibility of office. He appeared very well in health and sat in the garden & in his own room a good deal, reading Shakespeare's England…'.

JAP's ingrained capacity for denial was exhibited in an entry on

November 1

Lord Selborne's speech attacking honours, & giving a case in which it was alleged at the time of the Licensing Bill the Liberal Whip sold an honour to a man in Exeter for £5000. The Westminster Gazette, accepted the statement & denounced it.

I went to see Asquith after dinner at Cavendish Square, & asked him if I should contradict it — my judgement was against taking notice but there was a reflection on us both, & if uncontradicted it might injure him. He said he thought at first, it was worth repudiation, but on 2[d] thoughts he agreed with me, & for me to clear myself might bring counter charges against Whiteley & Elibank whose records were more open to suspicion.

The diary stops on 13 November 1917 but begins again briefly on 30 December 1939 (MS. Gainford 34/3, ff.28–31). Lord Gainford, as he had been since the end of 1916, had commended Neville Chamberlain's journey to Munich as 'one of the greatest achievements of any *statesman'. Major Tommy Dugdale, a junior whip writing on behalf of the Prime Minister, had expressed his appreciation. A few days later, Chamberlain, with Sir John Anderson and Sir Thomas Inskip, received a delegation from the Federation of British Industries (F.B.I.). The delegation included Pease, Sir George Beharrell, Peter Bennett (President of the F.B.I.), Lord Hirst, Sir James Lithgow, and Guy Locock (director of the F.B.I. and former p.s. to Foreign Office U. Secs Francis Acland and Neil Primrose). Apart from the then president and the director, they were all former F.B.I. presidents (*Daily Express*, 18 Nov. 1938, press cuttings book, MS. Gainford 56). Pointing out that a significant amount of vital industrial plant could be knocked out in a single raid—plant which would take years to replace—they asked for emergency arrangements to be formulated and spare plant stockpiled. JAP claimed that as a result £3 million of spare electrical plant was manufactured and two industrialists (unnamed) appointed to the war defence committee.*

On 11 December 1939 a further F.B.I. delegation saw Chamberlain. The group included members of the F.B.I.'s War Emergency Committee: Lord Dudley Gordon, Sir George Beharrell, Sir Joseph Jones, Guy Locock, and Douglas Walker, Secretary of the F.B.I. The delegation had already sent a memorandum urging the appointment of a Cabinet minister to oversee export trade. They argued that the maintenance of a strong economy was as vital a part of the war effort as the manufacture of munitions. Sir John Simon, the Cabinet minister most concerned (he was Chancellor of the Exchequer), replied that he would bear their points in mind. Chamberlain added that he was not yet in favour of such a move but would keep an open mind.

The delegation had been received in the Cabinet room of 10 Downing Street.

On leaving the Cabinet I reminded my colleagues & the P.M. of having stood in front of the cabinet door during the previous war, to stop Kitchener leaving the cabinet in a pet and the PM laughed and said he knew of the incident.

(*MS. Gainford 34/3, f.31*)

JAP's intervention was not mentioned by Harcourt who took credit in his diary for stopping Kitchener (see 16 April 1915).

MANUSCRIPT SOURCES

Citation

Many of the manuscript collections we have cited were first examined before their existence was known outside their families. Some remain in private hands; others have found their way into repositories. Some, such as the (Walter and Hilda) Runciman papers and the (Arthur) Ponsonby diaries, were entrusted to us for extended periods by their owners. At that time they had not been catalogued.

Much of our research in the Gainford papers also occurred before they were organised and listed. As with other collections, such as the Lansdowne papers seen both at Bowood and in the British Library, where possible we have added details that make it easier for items to be traced. Regrettably it has not always been practicable to do this. But provisional catalogue numbers that had been assigned when we saw the file have been included in square brackets.

In some cases, such as the diaries of Lord Balcarres (as he then was), Charles Hobhouse, and Richard Holt, scholars have subsequently edited selections from the originals that are now publicly available. In other cases, biographies, family histories, or collections of correspondence drawing on the papers we saw have now been published, among them those of Sydney Buxton, William Wedgwood Benn (Lord Stansgate), and Francis Acland. Most conspicuous of all are the letters of H.H. Asquith to Venetia Stanley, copies of which, originally provided to Randolph Churchill, were lent to us in the late 1960s by Venetia Montagu's daughter Judy Gendel and Robert Jackson. When we quote from unpublished extracts from these transcripts they are cited as 'Venetia Montagu MSS'.

Where we have seen the original of a document, we refer to the version we have seen; and, if it has been published, the relevant publication is also cited. It will be noted that we customarily refer to collections of private papers by the name of the person at the time of their death: thus Ypres not French. Where a collection has been given the name of a house or estate in which it rests, or a pre-ennoblement family name, or is part of a collection bearing a different family name, these widely varying names are also given.

Permissions

Her late Majesty Queen Elizabeth II graciously allowed us to examine and quote from papers in the Royal Archives.

We are greatly indebted to many people for permission to see and quote from personal papers and privately printed books in their care or now in repositories, and in many cases for warm hospitality and unique recollections. We thank too those who have allowed us to quote from letters and diaries whose copyright they hold. Despite our best efforts to identify, locate, and contact copyright holders, we regret that we have not always been successful. If new information makes it possible to remedy errors or omissions, corrections will be made in any subsequent editions.

As the research began five decades ago, sadly many of those who generously helped us have not lived to see the book completed.

Sir Dominic Acland Bt (Sir Arthur Acland Bt)
Sir Richard Acland Bt (Francis and Eleanor Acland MSS)
The 4th Marquess and Marchioness of Aberdeen and Temair (Aberdeen MSS)
The 3rd Viscount Addison and the 4th Viscount Addison (Addison MSS)
The 7th Marquess of Anglesey (Anglesey and Queenborough MSS)
Christopher Arnander (McKenna MSS)
David Ayerst (Guardian MSS)
The 8th Earl Balfour of Burleigh and the Countess Balfour of Burleigh (Dr Janet Morgan) (Balfour of Burleigh MSS)
The 8th Earl Beauchamp and the Countess Beauchamp (Beauchamp MSS)
The Beaverbrook Foundation (Lloyd George MSS)
Eleanor Bland (Birkenhead MSS)
Juliet Boulting and Lady Margaret Glasse (Miller-Cunningham MSS)
The Hon. Virginia Brand for the Estate of Lord Bonham Carter (H.H. Asquith, the 1st Earl of Oxford and Asquith MSS, Sir Maurice Bonham Carter and Baroness Asquith of Yarnbury MSS)
Sir Felix Brunner Bt (Brunner MSS)
Lady Burke (Norman MSS)
The 5th Baron Burnham (Burnham MSS)
The Hon. Randolph S. Churchill (Churchill MSS)
Elizabeth Clay and Lady Alethea Eliot (Buxton MSS)
Lady Hermione Cobbold (Lytton MSS)
The 3rd Baron Craigmyle (Craigmyle MSS)
The 28th Earl of Crawford and 10th Earl Balcarres and the Countess of Crawford (Crawford MSS)
A.E.W. Crowe (Crowe MSS)
The Hon. Cecilia Dawson (Dawson MSS)
The 18th Earl of Derby (Derby MSS at Knowsley Hall)
The Devonshire Collections, Chatsworth (Devonshire MSS)
Dr Pauline Dower and Newcastle University Special Collections (Trevelyan MSS)
Douglas Duff (E.T. Cook MSS)
Lady Duff (Duff MSS)
Sir John Elliot (Blumenfeld MSS)

Sir Hugh Elliott Bt (Elliott MSS)
The 4th Viscount Esher (Esher MSS)
Campbell Fraser (Elizabeth Haldane MSS)
The 2nd Lady Gainford (Gainford MSS)
Bamber Gascoigne (Crewe MSS)
Judy Gendel (Montagu/Venetia Stanley MSS)
Sir Martin and Lady Gilbert (Birkenhead MSS)
The Hon. Jane Gillies (Kilmany MSS)
The 3rd Baron Glenconner (Glenconner MSS)
A.R.B. Haldane (Haldane of Cloan MSS)
The 2nd Viscount Harcourt (Harcourt MSS)
Sir Geoffrey Harmsworth Bt (Northcliffe MSS)
Vice-Admiral Sir Ian Hogg, Dr Jeremy Hogg (Gwynne MSS)
Anne Holt (Holt MSS)
Dame Christian Howard and the Howard Family (Howard and Lady Carlisle MSS)
Henry Illingworth, Jamie and Tania Illingworth (Percy Illingworth MSS)
The Hon. Betty Miller Jones (Askwith MSS)
The 13th Earl of Kintore (Stonehaven MSS)
Mildred Kirkcaldy (Robertson Nicoll MSS)
The 8th Marquess of Lansdowne (Lansdowne and Fitzmaurice MSS)
The Hon. Laura Lloyd (Lloyd of Dolobran MSS)
Frances, Countess Lloyd-George
The 2nd Baroness Lyell (Lyell MSS)
Anna Mathias (Edwin Montagu MSS)
J.C. Medley (Birrell MSS)
The 3rd Baron Melchett and Cassandra Wedd (Melchett MSS)
Lady Melville and Miss Mary Melville (Melville MSS)
The Hon. Barbara Miller and Sir Hal Miller (Buckmaster MSS)
Robert Molteno (P. Molteno diary)
Baron Monro and Anne Monro (Ewart MSS)
Lady Morrison (Beauchamp MSS)
The 4th Baron Mottistone (Mottistone MSS)
The 4th Baron Newton (Newton MSS)
The 16th Duke of Norfolk and the 18th Duke of Norfolk (Norfolk MSS, Arundel Castle)
The 2nd Viscount Norwich (John Julius Norwich) (Norwich and Lady Diana Cooper MSS)
Christopher Osborn (Margot Asquith, the 1st Countess of Oxford and Asquith MSS)
J. Gulland Osborne (Gulland MSS)
Professor Frank Paish (Paish MSS)
Sir Joseph Gurney Pease Bt (Pease MSS)

The Hon. Matthew Pease (Joseph Pease MSS)
Jonathan Peto and the Hon. Selina Peto (Peto MSS)
Anthony Pitt-Rivers (Sylvia Henley MSS)
The 3rd Baron Ponsonby of Shulbrede (Ponsonby of Shulbrede MSS)
The 4th Baron Ponsonby of Shulbrede [Baron Ponsonby of Roehampton] (Ponsonby of Shulbrede Diary)
The Hon. Caroline Ponsonby (Sysonby MSS)
The Hon. Laura Ponsonby and the Hon. Kate Russell (Ponsonby of Shulbrede MSS)
Andrew Rawlinson (Rawlinson MSS)
The Hon. Sir Steven Runciman, the 2nd Viscount Runciman of Doxford, and Newcastle University Special Collections (Runciman of Doxford and Viscountess Runciman of Doxford MSS)
The 5th Marquess of Salisbury (Salisbury and Cecil of Chelwood MSS)
The 2nd Viscount Samuel and the Hon. Godfrey Samuel (Samuel MSS)
John H. MacCallum Scott (MacCallum Scott MSS)
Russell Scott (C.P. Scott MSS)
The 2nd Viscount Simon and Charles Simon (Simon MSS)
Joan Simon (Emmott MSS)
The 3rd Baron Southborough (Southborough MS)
Viscount Strathallan (Perth MSS)
A.J.P. Taylor (Beaverbrook MSS)
Sir Charles Tennyson (Birrell [Liverpool U.] MSS)
Lady Todd and Wilhelm Feldberg (Dale MSS)
Lucy Chenevix-Trench (Beauchamp MSS)
The 2nd Viscount Ullswater (Ullswater MSS)
Sir Harry Verney Bt (Verney MSS)
The 6th Duke of Westminster (Wyndham MSS)
Major Cyril Wilson (H.H. Wilson MSS)
Peter Wilson (L.O. Wilson MSS)
R.P. Winfrey (Winfrey MSS)
Gwendolen McKinnon Wood (McKinnon Wood and Spicer MSS)

Archives and Libraries

The aid we have received from archival institutions and libraries over some 52 years of intermittent work on this project is incalculable.

For access to collections entrusted to them, provision of copies, and permissions they have been authorised to grant, we thank the following repositories and their staff, too often unsung, but unfailingly helpful:

All Souls College Library, Oxford (Onslow–Malcolm letters)
Army Medical Services Museum
Alnwick Castle Archives (Northumberland MSS)

Arundel Castle Trustees Ltd (Norfolk MSS)
Australian National University Library
Australian War Memorial
Austrian State Archives
Balliol College Archives and Manuscripts (Harris and Mallet MSS)
Barclays Group Archives
The Beaverbrook Library (Beaverbrook, Lloyd George, and Bonar Law MSS before their transfer to the House of Lords Record Office)
Bembridge School, Isle of Wight (J.H. Whitehouse MSS)
University of Birmingham, Cadbury Research Library, Special Collections (Austen Chamberlain and Masterman MSS)
Bodleian Libraries (Addison, Asquith, Margot Asquith, Bonham Carter, Bryce, Carnegie, Crowe, Dawson, Fraser, Harcourt, Headlam, Henley, Hirst, Lincolnshire, Morley of Blackburn, Rey, Sandars, Simon, Southborough, and Winterton MSS; Marconi Archives)
British Broadcasting Corporation Written Archives Centre
British Library (Balfour, Burns, Buxton, Cave, Cecil of Chelwood, Lady Diana Cooper, Gladstone, Lansdowne, Northcliffe, Paget, Riddell, Scott)
British Library Asian and African Studies (Curzon of Kedleston MSS)
British Library of Political and Economic Science (Paish MSS)
Brotherton Collection, University of Leeds (Gosse MSS)
BT Archives
The Syndics of Cambridge University Library (Chiozza Money and Crewe MSS)
Castle Howard (Geoffrey Howard MSS)
Churchill Archives Centre, The Master, Fellows and Scholars of Churchill College, Cambridge (Bull, Churchill and Chartwell, Lady Spencer-Churchill, Grant Duff, Esher, Hankey, Hawtrey, Lloyd of Dolobran, McKenna, Norwich, Rawlinson, and Wester-Wemyss MSS)
Churchill College Library, Cambridge
Devon Record Office, Exeter (Acland of Killerton MSS)
The Devonshire Collections, Chatsworth (Devonshire MSS)
Fryer Library, University of Queensland, St Lucia (Leslie Orme Wilson MSS)
Georgetown University Library, Special Collections Division (Sir Shane Leslie MSS)
Gennadius Library Archives, American School of Classical Studies at Athens
University of Glasgow Library Special Collections (MacCallum Scott MSS)
Gloucestershire Archives (Philips Price MSS)
The Grainger Museum, University of Melbourne (Ella Strom Grainger MSS)
The Grosvenor Estate (Wyndham MSS)
Hampshire Archives and Local Studies, Hampshire Record Office (Portsmouth MSS)
Hatfield House Library and Archives, Hertfordshire (Salisbury and Cecil of Chelwood MSS)

Highland Archive Centre, Inverness
Hoover Institution Archives, Stanford University (P.W. Wilson MSS)
The Trustees of the Imperial War Museums (Ypres, de Chair, Gwynne, Stanley of Alderley, and Sir Henry Wilson MSS)
Isle of Wight County Record Office (J.H. Whitehouse MSS)
The John J. Burns Library, Boston College (Belloc MSS)
The John Rylands Library, University of Manchester (Neilson and Crawford and Balcarres MSS)
King's College London Archives
Labour History Archive and Study Centre (People's History Museum/University of Central Lancashire)
Lambeth Palace Library, London (Archbishop Lord Davidson of Lambeth MSS)
Liverpool Record Office (17th Earl of Derby MSS)
London Metropolitan Archives (John Burns MSS)
Madresfield Court, Worcestershire (7th Earl Beauchamp MSS)
Modern Records Centre, University of Warwick (Sir G. Granet MSS)
The National Archives
National Library of Australia
National Library of Ireland (Redmond MSS)
National Library of Scotland Edinburgh (Haldane of Cloan, Elizabeth Haldane, Elibank, Murray of Elibank, Fife and Kinross Miners' Association, and Steel-Maitland MSS)
National Library of Wales (Lloyd George, Harlech, J.T. Davies, and William Jones MSS)
National Maritime Museum (Sir A.L. Duff MSS and Sir W. Graham Greene MSS)
National Records of Scotland (Ewart MSS)
National Register of Archives for Scotland
Newcastle University Library, Special Collections and Archives (Trevelyan family and Runciman of Doxford family MSS)
North Yorkshire County Record Office (Bolton and Zetland MSS)
Northumberland Archives (Ridley MSS)
Nuffield College Library, Oxford (Gainford, Emmott, and Mottistone MSS)
Parliamentary Archives (previously the House of Lords Record Office) (Lloyd George, Bonar Law, Blumenfeld, and Beaverbrook MSS on behalf of the Beaverbrook Foundation; Samuel, Stansgate, St Loe Strachey, Ashbourne, and Whitehead MSS)
The Postal Museum, London
Public Record Office of Northern Ireland (Carson and Londonderry MSS)
Queen Mary University of London Archives (Lady Lyttelton)
Queensland University of Technology Library, Brisbane
Religious Society of Friends Library, London (T.E. Harvey MSS)
Rotherham Archives and Local Studies Service
Royal Archives, Windsor (King George V and Stamfordham MSS)

Royal Australian College of Physicians Library, Sydney
Royal College of Art
Royal College of Surgeons of England
Royal Military Museum, Brussels
Standing Council of the Baronetage
Suffolk Archives (Ullswater MSS)
Sunshine Coast (Queensland) Library and Community Services
Surrey History Centre (formerly Guildford Muniment Room, Surrey County Record Office) (Onslow MSS)
The Master and Fellows, Trinity College, Cambridge, Wren Library (Montagu MSS)
Tyne & Wear Archives & Museums (Melville MSS)
University of Aberdeen Special Collections Centre (formerly Special Library and Archives) (Robertson Nicoll and Stonehaven MSS)
University of Birmingham, Cadbury Research Library, Special Collections (Chamberlain and Masterman MSS)
University of Bristol Theatre Archive (Tree Family Archive)
University of Huddersfield Heritage Quay, University Archives and Special Collections (Whitley MSS)
University of Keele Library (Arnold Bennett MSS)
University of Liverpool Department of Special Collections and Archives (Birrell MSS)
University of Nottingham Department of Manuscripts and Special Collections (Galway MSS)
University of Reading Library Special Collections (Astor MSS)
West Sussex Record Office (Maxse MSS)
Wellcome Institute for the History of Medicine, Wellcome Library, London, Contemporary Medical Archives Centre
Wiltshire and Swindon Archives (Burbidge MSS)

BIOGRAPHICAL GALLERY

Acland, Arthur Herbert Dyke (1847–1926); Lib. MP W. Riding of Yorks. (Rotherham) 1885–99; succ. brother as 13th Bt 1919; Vice-Pres. of the Council (Minister responsible for Educ.) 1892–5. Sir William Harcourt wanted Acland as Chief Whip in 1892, but Gladstone insisted on Edward Marjoribanks; declined peerage 1908. (Philip W. Evans, 'The contribution of Arthur Herbert Dyke Acland, *c.*1847–1926), to the Education System of England and Wales', Ph.D. thesis, Manchester U., 1989).

Acland, Francis Dyke (1874–1939); U.-Sec. of St. Foreign Affairs 1911–15; Fin. Sec. War 1908–10; son of A.H.D. Acland; m. 1905 Eleanor Cropper, later prominent Lib. and suffragist; Lib. MP Yorks. (Richmond) 1906–10, Cornwall (Camborne) 1910–22, Devon (Tiverton) June 1923–4, Cornwall (N.) July 1932–9; PPS to R.B. Haldane 1906–08; Fin. Sec. Treasury Feb.–June 1915; Parl. Sec. Bd of Ag. & Fish. 1915–16; PC 1915; 14th Bt 1926.

Addison, Christopher (1869–1951); Parl. Sec. Bd of Educ. 1914–15; surgeon, prof. of anatomy U. Coll. Sheffield, Hunterian prof. Royal College of Surgeons; Lib. MP Hoxton 1910–18; Co. Lib. MP Shoreditch 1918–22; Lab. MP Swindon 1929–31, 1934–5; Parl. Sec. Munitions 1915–16; Min. Munitions 1916–17; Min. Reconstruction 1917–18; Pres. LGB 1919; Min. Health 1919–21; Min. w'out Portfolio 1921; Parl. Sec. Min. of Ag. & Fish. 1930, Min. Ag. 1930–1. Baron Addison 1937; leader Labour Peers 1940–51; Vt and Leader H of L 1945; Sec. of St. Dominion Affairs then Cwlth Relations 1945–7; thereafter successively Ld Privy Seal, Paymaster Gen, and Ld Pres. of Council; KG 1946.

Aitken, Sir Max (1879–1864); Con. MP Ashton-under-Lyne 1910–16; Canadian businessman and newspaper owner; Kt 1911; Canadian 'Eye-Witness', Records Officer with Overseas Expeditionary Force, and Mili. Rep. Jan. 1915–Dec. 1916; Bt 1916; Baron Beaverbrook 1917; Chanr Duchy of Lancr and Min. of Information Feb.–Nov. 1918; Min. of Aircraft Production 1940–1; Min. of St. May–June 1941; Min. of Supply 1941–2; Min. of War Production 1942; Ld Privy Seal 1943; controlling owner *Daily Express* 1916–64; part owner *Evening Standard* 1923–64.

Alexandra, Queen (1844–1925); eldest dau. of Prince and Princess Christian, later King Christian IX of Denmark; m. Edward VII (then Prince of Wales) 1863.

Allard, William (1861–1919); sec., chief organiser, Lib. HQ, 1909–13; Lib. League 1902–9; trained as Lib. organiser under Francis Schnadhorst in 1880s; sec. Nottingham and Birmingham Lib. assocs; Mayor Kingston-on-Thames 1893; Lib. agent and sec. Home Counties Lib. Fedn, 'his desertion to the Lib. Imps was…on a purely commercial basis of £1,000 per ann. for 5 years certain' (L. Harcourt–Morley, 10 Nov 1901, copy, Bodl. MS. Harcourt 427, f.175); sec. Lib. Insurance Committee 1912, Home Rule Council, 1913–14.

Askwith, George Ranken (1861–1942); controller-gen. commercial, labour & statistical dept Bd of Trade 1908–11; barrister 1886; worked with Sir Henry James (later Baron James of Hereford); specialist arbitrator in labour disputes; asst sec. railway branch, Bd of Trade 1907–9; chief industrial commr 1911–19; KCB 17 Sep. 1911; Baron Askwith 1919.

Asquith, Herbert Henry (1852–1928); PM 1908–16; Lib. MP Fife (E.) 1886–1918, Paisley 1920–4; Sec. of St. Home Affairs 1892–5; Chanr of Exchequer 1905–8; Sec. of St. War 1914; Earl of Oxford and Asquith 1925.

Asquith, Emma Alice Margaret ('Margot') (1864–1945); m. HHA as his second wife 1894; dau. of Sir Charles Tennant Bt; one of the 'Souls'.

Asquith, Violet (1887–1969); HHA's only dau. by his first wife; m. HHA's p.s. (Sir) Maurice Bonham Carter 1915; Baroness Asquith of Yarnbury (a life peerage) 1964.

Atherley-Jones, Llewellyn Archer (1848–1929); Lib. MP Durham (NW) 1885–1914; barrister 1875; QC 1896; Recorder Newcastle 1906–29; Judge Mayor's City of London Court 1913–29; son of Ernest Jones, Chartist leader; coined phrase 'The New Liberalism' 1889; published several novels anonymously.

Baker, Harold Trevor 'Bluie' or 'Bluetooth' (1877–1960); Lib. MP Accrington 1910–18; PPS to R.B. Haldane, 1910–11; Fin. Sec. War Office 1912–1914; PC 1915; friend of Raymond Asquith; Warden, Winchester College 1933–46. HHA called him 'the most promising of our younger men' (Hilda Runciman diary, 9 Apr. 1913, Runciman of Doxford MSS). Two suitcases of his papers were destroyed by his sister Hilda 'Queenie' Baker (Roger Ellis–CH, 6 May 1971).

Balfour, Arthur James (1848–1930); Leader, Con. Party 1906–11, 1892–5; nephew of 3rd Marquess of Salisbury, and his p.s. 1878–80; Con. MP Hertford 1874–85, Manchester (E.) 1885–1906, City of London 1906–22; Pres. LGB 1885–6; Sec. Scotland 1886–7; Chief Sec. Ireland 1887–91; First Ld Treasury and Leader H of C 1891–2, 1895–1905; Ld Privy Seal 1902–3; PM 1902–5; First Ld Admy 1915–16; Sec. of St. Foreign Affairs 1916–19; Ld Pres. of Council 1919–22, 1925–9; Earl of Balfour 1922.

Banbury, Sir Frederick George, Bt (1850–1936); Con. MP City of London 1906–24, Camberwell (Peckham) 1892–1906; Bt 1903; director and Chmn Great Nthn Railway; member Stock Exchange; Chmn RSPCA; PC 1922; Baron Banbury 1924.

Beauchamp, William Lygon, Earl (1872–1938); First Commr of Works 1910–14; Ld Pres. of Council June–Nov. 1910 and 1914–15; Vt Elmley 1872–91; 7th Earl 1891; Gov. New South Wales 1899–1902; joined Lib. Party 1902; Ld Steward of Household 1907–10; Warden Cinque Ports 1913–34, the appointment declined by the Duke of Connaught largely because of the expense, especially of Walmer Castle (Stamfordham–Bonham Carter, 31 Oct., 5 Nov. 1913, Bodl. MS. Asquith 3, ff.196–8).

Benn, William Wedgwood (1877–1960); Jr Ld of Treasury 1910–15, Lib. MP St George's (Tower Hamlets) 1906–18, Leith 1918–27; PPS Reginald McKenna 1906–10, joined Lab. Party 1927; MP Aberdeen (N.) 1928–31, Manchester (Gorton) 1937–42; Sec. of St. India 1929–31, Air 1945–6; served WWI Middlesex Yeomanry and RNAS, WWII RAFVR; Vt Stansgate 1941. (Alan Wyburn-Powell, *Political Wings: William Wedgwood Benn, First Viscount Stansgate*, Pen & Sword Aviation, Barnsley, 2015.)

Birrell, Augustine (1850–1933); Chief Sec. Ireland 1907–16; Lib. MP Fife (W.) 1889–1900, Bristol (N.) 1906–18; literary critic; Quain Prof. of Law London U. 1896–9; Pres. Bd of Educ. 1905–7.

Bonham Carter, Maurice 'Bongie' or 'Bongy' (1880–1960); principal p.s. to PM 1910–16; asst sec. Min. of Reconstruction 1917–18; m. Violet Asquith 30 Nov. 1915; KBE 1916.

Borden, Robert Laird (1854–1937); Con. PM of Canada 1911–20; lawyer; Con. MP (Canada) Halifax 1896–1904, 1908–17 and Kings County 1917–20; Leader Canadian Con. Party 1901–20; PC 1912; GCMG 1914; first overseas minister to attend British Cabinet meeting (14 July 1915); chief Canadian delegate, Peace Conference 1919.

Botha, Louis (1862–1919); first PM of Union of South Africa 1910–19; member Transvaal Volksraad 1896–9; Commandant-Gen. Boer forces 1900–2; first PM of Transvaal 1906–10.

Buckmaster, Stanley Owen, Baron (1861–1934); Lib. MP Yorks. (Keighley) 1911–15, Cambridge 1906–10; Solr-Gen. 1913–15; Ld Chanr 1915–16; Kt 1913, Baron Buckmaster 1915, Vt Buckmaster 1933; barrister 1884; KC 1902; director Press Bureau 1914–15; increasingly radical on social issues in later life, especially divorce law reform; chmn, political honours scrutiny committee 1929–31; keen fisherman.

Burns, John Elliot (1858–1943); Pres. LGB 1905–14; engineer; member Social Democratic Federation 1884–9; LCC member for Battersea 1889–1907; 'Independent Lab.' MP Battersea 1892–5; Lib. MP Battersea 1895–1918; Chmn TUC Parl. Committee 1883; Pres. Bd of Trade 1914.

Buxton, Sydney (1853–1934); Pres. Bd of Trade 1910–14; Postmaster-Gen. 1905–10; Lib. MP Tower Hamlets (Poplar) 1886–1914, Peterborough 1883–5; U.-Sec. of St. Colonial Affairs 1892–5; Gov. Gen. S. Africa 1914–20; author of *Handbook to Political Questions of the Day* (1880); Vt Buxton 1914, Earl 1920.

Cambon, Pierre Paul (1843–1924); French Amb. London 1898–1920; lawyer; prefect départements of Aube 1872, Doubs 1876, Nord 1877–82; French min. plenipotentiary, Tunis 1882–6; Amb. Madrid 1886–90, Constantinople 1890–8; helped negotiate Entente Cordiale between Britain and France 1904; French rep. at London Conference to resolve Balkan Wars 1912–13; brother Jules Cambon was Amb. Berlin 1907–14.

Carrington, Charles Robert Wynn-Carrington, Earl (1843–1928); Pres. Bd of Ag. & Fish. 1905–11; Lib. MP Wycombe 1865–8; 3rd Baron Carrington 1868; Gov. New South Wales 1885–90; Ld Chamberlain 1892–5; Earl Carrington 1895; Ld Privy Seal

1911–12; Ld Great Chamberlain 1911–28; Marquess of Lincolnshire 1912; close friend of Edward VII and George V. For Carrington's land issue ideas and advocacy see Andrew Adonis, 'Aristocracy, Agriculture and Liberalism: The Politics, Finances and Estates of the Third Lord Carrington', *HJ*, vol.31, no.4, 1988, pp.871–97. Carrington's extensive diaries would be better known if his handwriting was more legible.

Carson, Sir Edward Henry (1854–1935); Lib. Un. MP Dublin University 1892–1918 and Belfast (Duncairn) 1918–21; Irish Solr-Gen. 1892, Solr-Gen. 1900–5; Atty-Gen. 1915; First Ld Admy 1916–17; Min. w'out Portfolio 1917–18; Kt 1900; leading QC defending Ld Queensberry against Oscar Wilde's libel charge 1895; defended *Evening Standard* against libel action (use of slave labour) brought by Cadbury Bros 1908; defended George Archer-Shee against charge of theft 1910 (the trial inspired Terence Rattigan's play *The Winslow Boy*); Ld of Appeal 1921–9. Baron Carson 1921.

Cecil, (Edgar Algernon) Robert (Gascoyne-), Lord (1864–1958); Ind. Con. MP Herts. (Hitchen) 1911–23; Con. MP Marylebone (E.) 1906–10; 3rd son of 3rd Marquess of Salisbury; p.s. to father 1886–8; barrister; U.-Sec. of St. Foreign Affairs 1915–18; Min. of Blockade 1916–18; Asst Sec. of St. Foreign Affairs 1918–19; PC 1915; Ld Privy Seal, in charge of League of Nations affairs 1923; Chanr Duchy of Lancr, in charge of League affairs 1924–7; dep. Leader British delegation 1929–31; Pres. League of Nations Union 1923–45; organiser of Peace Ballot 1934–5; Nobel Peace Prize 1937; Vt Cecil of Chelwood 1923.

Chalmers, Sir Robert (1858–1938); Chmn Bd of Inland Revenue 1907–11; asst sec. Treasury 1903–7; KCB 1908; Perm. Sec. Treasury 1911–13; Gov. Ceylon 1913–16; Joint U.-Sec. Treasury 1916 and 1916–19; U.-Sec. to Chief Sec. Ireland 1916; PC 1916; Baron Chalmers 1919; Master of Peterhouse, Cambridge 1924–31.

Chamberlain, (Joseph) Austen (1863–1937); Lib. Un. MP Worcs. (E.) 1892–1914, Birmingham (W.) 1914–37; son of Joseph Chamberlain, half-brother of Neville; Lib. Un. Jr Whip 1892–5; Civil Ld Admy 1895–1900; Fin. Sec. Treasury 1900–2; Postmaster-Gen. 1902–3; Chanr of Exchequer 1903–5, 1919–21; Sec. of St. India 1915–17; member War Cabinet Apr.–Dec. 1918; Leader Con. Party in H of C 1921–Oct. 1922; Ld Privy Seal 1921–2; Sec. of St. Foreign Affairs 1924–9; Kt 1925; First Ld Admy Aug.–Oct. 1931.

Churchill, Winston Leonard Spencer- (1874–1965); Sec. of St. Home Affairs 1910–11; Con. then Lib. MP Oldham 1900–6 (Unionist Free Trader, crossed floor to Libs May 1904); Lib. MP Manchester (NW) 1906–8, Dundee 1908–22 (Co. Lib. 1918–22); Con. MP Essex (Epping) 1924–45, Woodford 1945–64; U.-Sec. of St. Colonial Affairs 1905–8; Pres. Bd of Trade 1908–10; First Ld Admy 1911–15; Chanr Duchy of Lancr 1915; Min. of Munitions 1917–19; Sec. of St. War and Air 1919–21, Air and Colonial Affairs 1921, Colonial Affairs 1921–2; Chanr of Exchequer 1924–9; First Ld Admy 1939–40; PM and Min. of Defence 1940–5; Leader Con. Party 1940–55; PM 1951–5; (Min. of Defence 1951–2); KG 1953.

Crewe, Margaret, Marchioness of (1881–1967); dau. of 5th Earl of Rosebery, known as Peggy; m. Crewe as his second wife 1899. A leading Lib. hostess. Sometime mistress of Ld Elcho, 11th Earl of Wemyss from 1914.

Crewe, Robert Offley Ashburton Crewe-Milnes, Earl of (1858–1945); Ld Privy Seal 1908–11, 1912–15; asst p.s. to Sec. of St. Foreign Affairs 1883–4; 2nd Baron Houghton 1885; Ld-in-Waiting 1886; Ld Lt Ireland 1892–5; Earl of Crewe 1895; Ld Pres. of Council 1905–8, 1915–18; Sec. of St. Colonial Affairs 1908–10; Sec. of St. India 1910–15; Pres. Bd of Educ. 1916; Amb. Paris 1922–8; Sec. of St. War 1931; Marquess 1911.

Cromer, Evelyn Baring, Earl of (1841–1917); soldier; ADC to Sir H.K. Storks 1858–67; p.s. to Ld Northbrook when Viceroy India 1872–6; first British Commr, Egyptian Debt Office 1877–9; British controller 1879; financial member Viceroy's council 1880–3; KCSI 1883; British Agent and Consul-Gen. Egypt 1883–1907; Baron Cromer 1892; Vt 1899; Earl of Cromer 1901; declined Foreign Secretaryship Dec. 1905 because of Lib. Party 'socialism' and S. African policy; wrote *Modern Egypt* 1907; pres. Dardanelles commission 1916–17 but died before it reported.

Curzon of Kedleston, George Nathaniel Curzon, Baron (1859–1925); Irish representative peer 1908–11; suffering from curvature of the spine, wore a corrective steel corset from 1878; traveller and writer; Con. MP Lancs. (Southport) 1886–98; U.-Sec. of St. India 1891–2; U.-Sec. of St. Foreign Affairs 1895–8; Viceroy India 1898–1905; Baron Curzon 1898 (an Irish peerage, so he might return to H of C); Earl Curzon of Kedleston 1911; Pres. Anti-Suffrage League 1912–17; Ld Privy Seal 1915–16; Pres. Air Bd 1916; 5th Baron Scarsdale 1916; Ld Pres. of Council and member War Cabinet Dec. 1916–18; Sec. of St. Foreign Affairs 1919–24; Marquess Curzon of Kedleston 1921; Ld Privy Seal 1924–5.

Davidson, Randall Thomas, Archbishop of Canterbury (1848–1930); Archbishop Canterbury 1903–28; ordained 1875; chaplain to Archibald Tait as Archbishop Canterbury 1877–82; m. Tait's dau. 1878; Dean of Windsor 1883–91; Bishop Rochester 1891–5, Winchester 1895–1903; Baron Davidson of Lambeth 1928.

Devonshire, Victor Cavendish, 9th Duke of (1868–1938); Con. Chief Whip Lords 1911–15; joint Govt Chief Whip 1915–16; eldest son of Ld Edward Cavendish, 3rd son of 7th Duke; succ. uncle 1908; m. Lady Evelyn Fitzmaurice, elder dau. of Marquess of Lansdowne; Lib. Un. MP W. Derbyshire 1891–1908; Fin. Sec. Treasury 1903–5; Gov. Gen. Canada 1916–21; refused to serve as Sec. of St. India under DLG Mar. 1922; Sec. of St. Colonies 1922–4. One of his ADCs, Harold Macmillan, m. his dau. Lady Dorothy Evelyn Cavendish 1920. PC 1905. Described by ministerial colleague Gerald Balfour as 'a man of plain common sense and great character, but of limited education and information, with the slowest mind of anyone he knew' (Mersey, *A Picture of Life 1872–1940*, pp.218–19).

Drummond, James Eric (1876–1951); asst (2nd) p.s. to HHA 1912–Feb. 1915; p.s. to Grey and Balfour as Foreign Secretary 1915–18; Sec.-Gen. League of Nations 1919–33; KCMG 1916; 7th Earl of Perth 1937. Reassignment to Grey in Feb. 1915 elicited lamentation by Margot Asquith: no one living, she said, understood 'more perfectly' her domestic difficulties of which she had 'only very slightly spoken', 'inevitable, incommunicable & I imagine unchangeable... Your delightful temper, fine spirits, devotion & amazing understanding & quickness has as Henry said been the sunshine of this house' (M. Asquith–E. Drummond, 23 Feb. 1915, Perth MSS,

Stobhall 7/1/5/1). HHA told Venetia Stanley he was 'in some ways far the best Private Secretary I have ever had' (22 Feb. 1915, *Asquith Letters*, p.444).

Elibank, Alexander W.C.O. Murray, Master of (1870–1920); Patronage Sec. Treasury (Lib. Chief Whip) 1910–12; Lib. MP Edinburghshire 1900–5, 1910–12, Peebles and Selkirk 1906–10; Comptroller of Household and Scottish Lib. Whip 1906–9; U.-Sec. of St. India 1909–10; PC 1911; joined Pearson & Sons on retirement from politics; Baron Murray of Elibank 1912.

Emmott, Alfred (1858–1926); Lib. MP Oldham 1899–1911; cotton-spinner; PC 1908; Baron Emmott 1911; U.-Sec. of St. Colonial Affairs 1911–14; First Commr of Works 1914–15; Director War Trade Dept 1915–19; chmn FO committee to collect information on Russia 1920; Anglican but Quaker-educated. Declined Governorship of Bombay Aug. 1912.

Esher, Reginald Brett, Viscount (1852–1930); Perm. Member CID 1905–18; pres. Co. of London Territorial Assoc. 1912–21, confidant of Kitchener 1914–16, liaison between Kitchener and French War Minister, and unofficial head of British Intelligence Service in France; succ. father as 2nd Vt 1899; Sec. Office of Works 1895–1902.

Fisher, John Arbuthnot, Baron (1841–1920); First Sea Ld 1904–10, 1914–15; reorganised fleet distribution with Germany as most likely enemy; principal supporter of the Dreadnought; KCB 1894, OM 1905; GCVO 1909; Baron Fisher 1909 (motto 'Fear God and Dread Nought').

Foch, Ferdinand (1851–1929); GOC French 9th Army Aug.–Oct. 1914; drafted French plan of campaign (Plan XVII) 1913; Cmdr, XX Corps 1913; Dep. C-in-C 1914–15; GOC Nthn Army Group 1915–16; CGS 1917–18; Allied Supreme C-in-C Mar.–Nov. 1918; Marshal of France Aug. 1918.

Forster, Henry William (1866–1936); Con. MP Kent (Sevenoaks) 1892–1919; Jr Ld Treasury 1902–5; Fin. Sec. War Office 1915–19; PC 1917; Baron Forster 1919; Gov. Gen. and C-in-C Australia 1920–5. First-class cricketer; Pres. MCC 1919. Sir William 'Paul' Bull noted on 18 July 1911 that Harry Forster, entrusted with leading the Opposition response to the Insurance Bill, 'was entitled to be Chief Whip by seniority but not being thought good enough he was flattered into going once more on to the Front Bench and talking a little while Balcarres was put in his place' (BULL 4/4, Bull MSS, CAC).

French, Sir John Denton Pinkstone (1852–1925); Field Marshal and CIGS 1913–14; resigned over Curragh incident; C-in-C BEF 1914–15; C-in-C Home Forces 1916–18; Vt 1915, Earl of Ypres 1921.

Furness, Christopher Furness, Baron (1852–1912); shipowner, shipbuilder, and industrialist; Lib. MP Hartlepool 1891–5, 1900–10; Kt 1895; Baron Furness 1910 following offer to JAP to spend £2 million ordering 50 new ships to stimulate trade and employment.

George V, King (1865–1936); reigned 1910–36.

Gladstone, Herbert John Gladstone, Viscount (1854–1930); Gov. Gen. S. Africa 1910–14; Sec. of St. Home Affairs 1905–10; youngest son of W.E. Gladstone; Lib. MP Leeds (W.) 1880–1910; Fin. Sec. War 1886; U.-Sec. of St. Home Affairs 1892–4;

First Commr of Works 1894–5; Lib. Chief Whip 1899–1906; Vt Gladstone 1910. Lawrence Iles re-evaluates his career in 'Organiser Par Excellence: Herbert Gladstone (1854–1930)', *J.Lib.H*, no.51, 2006, pp.24–31.

Glenconner, Edward Priaulx Tennant, Baron (1859–1920); brother of Margot Asquith and H.J. Tennant; m. Pamela Wyndham 1895. Lib. MP Salisbury 1906–10; succ. father as 2nd Bt 1906; Baron Glenconner 1911; Ld High Commr Gen. Assembly Church of Scotland 1911–1914. Generous contributor to Lib. Party funds incl. £4,000 in Dec. 1909 (Glenconner MSS 40).

Glenconner, Pamela Adelaide Genevieve, Lady (1871–1928); one of the Wyndham sisters painted by John Singer Sargent 1899; one of 'The Souls'; friend of Henry James, Oscar Wilde, and Edward Burne-Jones; m. 1895 Margot Asquith's brother Edward Tennant, 2nd Baron Glenconner 1911. Published and edited poems, prose, children's literature; m. widower Edward Grey, becoming Viscountess Grey of Fallodon 1922. Pamela's affair with Grey was an open secret years before she was free to marry him. The Glenconners are most intimately portrayed in Claudia Renton, *Those Wild Wyndhams: Three Sisters at the Heart of Power*, Wm Collins, 2014.

Gorst, Sir (John) Eldon (1861–1911); British consul-gen. Egypt 1907–11; eldest son of Sir John Eldon Gorst; barrister 1885; diplomat 1887–1901; adviser, Egyptian Min. of Interior 1894–8; financial adviser 1898–1904; Asst U.-Sec. of St. Foreign Affairs 1904–7; KCB 1902; GCMG 1911 'long after he had ceased to be conscious' (Ronald Storrs, *Orientations*, Nicholson & Watson, 1945, p.77).

Granard, Bernard Arthur William Patrick Hastings Forbes, Earl of (1874–1948); succ. father as 8th Earl 1889, sitting in Lords as Baron Granard, the earldom being an Irish peerage; Master of the Horse 1907–15, 1924-36; Asst Postmaster-Gen. 1906–9; ADC to Ld Lt Ireland 1896–9; served S. African War and 1915–18; raised and commanded a battn 5th Royal Irish Regiment; Lt-Col. (Reserve) Scots Guards; ADC to GOC 1st Division Aldershot 1904–5; Ld-in-Waiting 1905–7, 1924–36; PC 1907; Senator Eire 1922–34; m. 1909 American heiress Beatrice Mills.

Grey, Sir Edward, Bt (1862–1933); Sec. of St. Foreign Affairs 1905–16; Lib. MP Northumberland (Berwick-on-Tweed) 1885–1916; succ. g'father as 3rd Bt 1882; sent down from Balliol College for incorrigible idleness 1884; U.-Sec. of St. Foreign Affairs 1892–5; director and Chmn North-Eastern Railway; Vt Grey of Fallodon 1916. Grey and JAP were both tutored by Mandell Creighton.

Guest, Hon. Frederick Edward (1875–1937); Jr Ld Treasury 1911–12; asst p.s. to cousin WSC 1907–10; Lib. MP Dorset (E.) 1910–22 (Co. Lib. 1918–22), Gloucester (Stroud) 1923–4, Bristol (N.) 1924–9; Con. MP Plymouth (Drake) 1931–7; commissioned in 1st Life Guards, served White Nile, S. African War, India; ADC to Sir John French 1915, ASO in East Africa 1916–17; Treasurer of Household 1912–15: Jt Patronage Sec. Treasury and Co. Lib. Chief Whip 1917–21; Sec. of St. Air 1921–2.

Gulland, John William (1864–1920); Scottish Whip 1909–15; Lib. MP Dumfries Burghs 1906–18; corn merchant; director, Edinburgh Chamber of Commerce; member Edinburgh School Bd 1900–6, Town Council 1904–6; sec. Scottish Lib. Committee in H of C 1906–9; Joint Parl. Sec. Treasury 1915–16.

Haldane, Richard Burdon, Viscount (1856–1928): Sec. of St. War 1905–12; Lib. MP Haddingtonshire 1885–1911; Ld Chanr 1912–15, 1924; OM 1915; Leader, Lab. peers 1925–8; Vt Haldane 1911. With eyesight seriously deteriorated, diagnosed as diabetic in 1909; badly affected by rheumatism. Ordered to take a complete rest, he missed much of the 1909 session. A legendary walker and cigar smoker.

Halsbury, Hardinge Stanley Giffard, Earl of (1823–1921); barrister 1850; Solr-Gen. 1875–80; Con. MP Launceston 1877–85; Ld Chanr 1885–Jan. 1886, July 1886–92, 1895–1905; Baron Halsbury 1885, Earl of Halsbury 1898.

Hamilton, Lt-Gen. Sir Ian Standish Monteith (1853–1947); C-in-C Central Force, Home Defence, Aug. 1914–Mar. 1915; GOC Mediterranean Cmd, and Inspr Gen. Overseas Forces 1910–14; maj.-gen. and Kt 1900; twice recommended for VC (award considered inappropriate because of his rank); Mili. Sec. at War Office May–Nov. 1901; CoS to Ld Kitchener S. Africa 1901–2; QMG to the Forces 1903–4; GOC-in-C Sthn Cmd 1905–9; Adj.-Gen. to the Forces 1909–10; Cmdr Allied Mediterranean Expeditionary Force to gain control of Dardanelles Straits from Turkey and capture Constantinople Mar.–Oct. 1915. Spoke German, French, and Hindi. Wounded in wrist at Battle of Majuba 1881, leaving left hand almost useless. Left leg shorter than the right, after injury falling from a horse.

Hankey, Lt-Col. Maurice Pascal Alers (1877–1963); Sec. CID 1912–38; Royal Marine Artillery 1897; NID 1902–8; Naval Asst Sec. CID 1908–12; Sec. War Council 1914–16; Sec. War Cabinet 1916–19; Sec. Cabinet 1919–38; Clerk Privy Council 1923–38; British Govt Director Suez Canal Co. 1938–9; Min. w'out Portfolio and member of War Cabinet 1939–40; Chanr Duchy of Lancr 1940–1; Paymaster-Gen. 1941–2; KCB 1916; Baron Hankey 1939, PC 1939, FRS 1942.

Harcourt, Lewis V. 'Loulou' or 'Lulu' (1863–1922); Sec. of St. Colonial Affairs 1910–15; First Commr of Works 1905–10, 1915–16; p.s. to father, Sir William Harcourt, at the Home Office and Treasury, and in Opposition 1881–1904; m. 1899 Mary Ethel 'Molly' (d. 1961), dau. of Walter Hayes Burns, New York banker, and niece of J. Pierpont Morgan. Lib. MP Lancs. (Rossendale) 1904–17; Vt Harcourt 1917. Active in party organisations, particularly the Home Counties Lib. Fedn; a founder of the Free Trade Union. A paedophile, his rumoured suicide in 1922 to avoid imminent scandal was attributed to 'misadventure' by a bromidia overdose.

Hardinge, Charles, Baron Hardinge of Penshurst (1858–1944); Viceroy and Gov. Gen. India 1910–16; diplomatic service 1880; first sec. Tehran 1896, St Petersburg 1898; Asst U. Sec. Foreign Affairs 1903–4; Amb. Russia 1904–6; KCMG 1904; Perm. U. Sec. Foreign Affairs 1906–10 and 1916–20; Baron Hardinge of Penshurst 1910; Amb. France 1920–2. His eldest son, Lt The Hon. Edward Hardinge, died of wounds 18 Dec. 1914.

Healy, Timothy Michael (1855–1931); Irish Nationalist MP Wexford 1880–3, Co. Monaghan 1883–5, Londonderry (S.) 1885–6, Longford (N.) 1887–92, Louth (N.) 1892–1910, Cork (NE) 1910–18; Called to Irish bar 1884, Irish QC 1899. Turned against Parnell, fearing his involvement in a divorce scandal would lose Gladstone's support for the Irish Nationalist cause. Defended employers in Dublin Lockout 1913; Gov. Gen. Irish Free State 1922–8.

Hemmerde, Edward George (1871–1948); Lib. MP Norfolk (NW) 1912–18, Denbighshire (E.) 1906–10; Lab. MP Cheshire (Crewe) 1922–4; barrister; Recorder Liverpool 1909–48; won Diamond Sculls, Henley 1900; for his recurring financial woes and chicanery see David Dutton, '"They were the best of friends; they were the worst of friends": A Tale of Two MPs', *Bulletin of the John Rylands Library*, vol.89, no.2, 2013, pp.33–50.

Henderson, Arthur (1863–1935); sec. Lab. Party 1911–34; trade unionist; agent to Sir J.W. Pease, JAP's father, 1895–1903 at Durham (Barnard Castle); after Sir Joseph's death elected as Independent Lab. MP for the division 1903–18, Lancs. (Widnes) 1919–22, Newcastle (E.) 1923, Burnley 1924–31, Derbyshire (Clay Cross) 1933–5; Chmn Parliamentary Lab. Party (after MacDonald resigned at outbreak of war) 1914–17; Pres. Bd of Educ. 1915–16; Paymaster-Gen. 1916; Min. w'out Portfolio 1916–17; responsible for reorganisation of Labour Party in 1918 and new constitution encouraging constituency organisations; Lab. Chief Whip 1914, 1921–3; Sec. of St. Home Affairs 1924; Sec. of St. Foreign Affairs 1929–31; refused to accept 1931 financial cuts, becoming Leader Lab. Party in opposition; pres. World Disarmament Conference 1932–5; Nobel Peace Prize 1934; Wesleyan lay preacher. See F.M. Leventhal, *Arthur Henderson*, Manchester UP, 1989, pp.9–18, for his association with the Pease family.

Hobhouse, Charles Edward Henry (1862–1941); Fin. Sec. Treasury 1908–11; Lib. MP Bristol (E.) 1900–18, Wilts. (Devizes) 1892–5: asst p.s. to U.-Sec. of St. Colonial Affairs 1892–5; U.-Sec. of St. India 1907–8: PC 1909; Chanr Duchy of Lancr 1911–14; Postmaster-Gen. 1914–15; 4th Bt 1916.

Hopwood, Sir Francis John Stephens (1860–1947); Vice-Chmn Development Commission 1910–12; Addt Civil Ld Admy 1912–17; civil servant and courtier; asst law clerk Bd of Trade 1885–8; asst solicitor Bd of Trade 1888–92; Sec. Railway Dept, Bd of Trade 1892–1901; Perm. Sec. Bd of Trade 1901–7; KCB 1901; Perm. U. Sec. of St. Colonial Affairs 1907–10; PC 1912; secret mission to Scandinavia to investigate Austrian peace feelers 1917; Baron Southborough 1917; Sec. Irish Convention 1918; chmn committee investigating Indian franchise 1918–19. For Hopwood being 'sore' on not being made Treasury Sec. because DLG would not release him from the Development Commission see HHA–WSC correspondence 13 Dec. 1911, CHAR 13/1/53, CAC; and Austen Chamberlain–Hopwood, 18 July 1911, Southborough MSS. For selling all his S. African mining shares on appointment to Colonial Office see Sir Charles Rey, *Men, Women and Places*, unpublished TS memoirs, *c.*1961, Bodl. Rey MSS, MS.Eng.c.7191, f.191.

Illingworth, Percy Holden (1869–1915); Jr Ld of Treasury (unpaid) 1910–12; Patronage Sec. Treasury (Lib. Chief Whip) 1912–15; Lib. MP Shipley 1906–15; Chmn Yorks. Lib. Fedn; p.s. to A. Birrell as Chief Sec. Ireland; barrister 1895; Yorks. Yeomanry in S. Africa 1900; Capt. Westminster Dragoons Imp. Yeo. The Tory Chief Whip thought Illingworth 'unversed in the niceties of parliamentary affairs...the prospect of daily intercourse with the new patronage secretary is somewhat embarrassing' (Balcarres diary, 7 Aug 1912, Vincent ed., *The Crawford Papers*, p.278). As a memorial to Illingworth a recreational institute was erected by the Baptist Union in 1916 on War Office land at Aldershot. See Douglas C. Sparkes, 'Percy Holden Illingworth and the Last Liberal Government', *Baptist Quarterly*, vol.39, no.7, pp.328–46.

Kitchener of Khartoum, Horatio Herbert Kitchener, Earl (1850–1916); HM's Agent and Consul Gen. Egypt 1911–14; C-in-C India 1902–9; soldier and administrator; served Franco–Prussian war 1870; Palestine Exploration Fund 1874–8; surveyed Cyprus 1878–82; Sudan Expedition 1884–5; Gov. Gen. Eastern Sudan 1886–8; Adj.-Gen. Egyptian Army 1888–92; Sirdar Egyptian Army 1892–9; KCMG 1894; Baron Kitchener 1898; CoS S. Africa 1899–1900, C-in-C 1900–2; Vt Kitchener 1902; FM 1909; Sec. of St. War 1914–16; Earl Kitchener of Khartoum 1914.

Knollys, Francis Knollys, Baron (1837–1924); p.s. to King George V 1910–13, to King Edward VII 1870–1910; PC 1910; Baron Knollys 1902, Vt Knollys 1911.

Lansdowne, Henry Charles Keith Petty-Fitzmaurice, Marquess of (1845–1927); leader Con. peers 1903–16; 5th Marquess 1866; Jr Ld Treasury 1869–72; U.-Sec. of St. War 1872–4; U.-Sec. of St. India 1880; Gov. Gen. Canada 1883–8; Viceroy India 1888–94; Sec. of St. War 1895–1900; Sec. of St. Foreign Affairs 1900–5; Min. w'out Portfolio 1915–16. A Lib. till 1880.

Law, Andrew Bonar (1858–23); Con. MP Lancs. (Bootle) 1911–18, Camberwell (Dulwich) 1906–10, Glasgow (Blackfriars) 1900–6, Glasgow (Central) 1918–23; iron merchant; Parl. Sec. Bd of Trade 1902–5; leader Con. Party 1911–21, 1922–3; Sec. of St. Colonial Affairs 1915–16; Chanr of Exchequer 1916–19; member War Cabinet 1916–19; Ld Privy Seal 1919–21; PM 1922–3.

Lee, Arthur Hamilton (1868–1947); Con. MP Hampshire (Fareham) 1900–18; soldier 1888–93; prof. of mili. history, strategy and tactics, Royal Military College, Kingston, Canada 1893–8; *Daily Chronicle* special correspondent in Klondyke Gold Rush 1896; mili. attaché Washington 1898–1900; Civil Ld Admy 1903–5; opposition spokesman on naval affairs 1906–14; special service with BEF 1914–15; Parl. Mili. Sec. to Min. Munitions 1915–16; personal Mili. Sec. to DLG at War Office 1916; KCB 1916; Dir-Gen. Food Production 1917–18; Baron Lee of Fareham 1918; Min. Ag. & Fish. 1919–21; First Ld Admy 1921–2; delegate, Washington Disarmament Conference 1921–2; Vt 1922. In 1921 gave Chequers plus an endowment for upkeep, for use of successive PMs; founded Courtauld Institute of Art 1932.

Lichnowsky, Prince Karl Max von (1860–1928); German Amb. London 1912–14; attaché London embassy 1885; legation secretary Bucharest; German Amb. Austria–Hungary 1902–4; succ. father as 6th Prince and 8th Count Lichnowsky 1901. His deliciously wry story in *Heading for the Abyss: Reminiscences*, Constable, 1928, pp.1–3, of being brought out of retirement and appointed following the early death of Marschal is inconsistent with John Röhl's documented account in *1914: Delusion or Design? The testimony of two German diplomats*, St. Martin's P., NY, 1973, pp.40–3.

Lloyd George, David (1863–1945); Chanr of Exchequer 1908–15; Lib. MP Caernarvon Boroughs 1890–1945 (Co. Lib. 1918–22; Nat. Lib. 1922–3); Pres. Bd of Trade 1905–8; Min. Munitions 1915–16; Sec. of St. War 1916; PM 1916–22; Earl Lloyd-George of Dwyfor 1945.

Long, Walter Hume (1854–1924); Con. MP Wilts (N.) 1880–5, Wilts (E.) 1885–92, Liverpool (W. Derby) 1893–1900, Bristol (S.) 1900–6, Co. Dublin (S.) 1906–10, Strand 1910–18, and Westminster (St George's) 1918–21; Parl. Sec. LGB 1886–92, Pres. Bd of Ag. 1895–1900; Pres. LGB 1900–5 and 1915–16; Chief Sec. Ireland 1905; creator, Union Defence League 1907–14; aspired to Tory party leadership on Balfour's resignation 1911; Sec. of St. Colonial Affairs 1916–19; chaired cab. cttee on Ireland and responsible for Government of Ireland Act (1920); First Ld Admy 1919–21; Vt Long of Wraxall 1921.

Loreburn, Robert Threshie Reid, Baron (1846–1923); Ld Chanr 1905–12; Lib. MP Hereford 1880–5, Dumfries Burghs 1886–1905; Solr-Gen. 1894; Atty-Gen. 1894–5; Kt 1894; Baron Loreburn 1906. Earl 1911. Keen racquets player; played cricket for Oxford for three seasons, noted wicket-keeper; pres. MCC 1907. David Dutton, 'Liberalism's Radical Lord Chancellor Robert Threshie Reid, Lord Loreburn, 1846–1923', *J.Lib.H.*, issue 90, 2016, pp.14–23, is the best short account of Loreburn's career.

Lowther, James William (1855–1949); Speaker, H of C 1905–21; Con. MP Rutland 1883–5, Cumberland (Penrith) 1886–1921; U.-Sec. of St. Foreign Affairs 1891–2; Chmn Ways and Means Committee and Dep. Speaker 1895–1905; PC 1898; Vt Ullswater 1921.

Lucas, Auberon Thomas Herbert ('Bron'), 8th Baron Lucas, 5th Baron Dingwall (1876–1916); succ uncle 1905; p.s. to Haldane at War Office 1905–6; Parl. Sec. Bd of Ag. 1911–14; U.-Sec. of St. War 1908–11; U.-Sec. of St. Colonies Mar.–Oct. 1911; Pres. Bd of Ag. & Fish. 1914–15; RFC 1915–16; missing in action, presumed dead. Wounded as correspondent for *The Times* in Boer War, leading to amputation of leg below the knee. Close friend of HHA. Admiringly portrayed in Maurice Baring, *Flying Corps Headquarters 1914–1918*, Wm Heinemann, 1920, pp.193–5; described as 'an extremely energetic and domineering host' in Count Constantine Benckendorff, *Half a Life: The Reminiscences of a Russian Gentleman*, The Richards P., 1954, pp.95–6. For Lucas's greatly criticised performance as Ag. minister, and Charles Hobhouse's tasteless diary comment in Mar. 1915 that he had not 'found his legs', see L. Margaret Barnett, *British Food Policy During The First World War*, George Allen & Unwin, Boston, 1985, pp.26–7.

Lyell, Hon. Charles Henry (1875–1918); PPS to HHA 1911–16, Grey 1906–11; Lib. MP Edinburgh (S.) 1910–17, Dorset (E.) 1904–10; severely wounded as artillery officer; asst mili. attaché, Washington 1918 where he d. of pneumonia; eldest son of 1st Baron Lyell.

Macdonald, John Archibald Murray (1854–1939); Lib. MP Falkirk Burghs 1906–18, Tower Hamlets 1892–5, Stirling and Falkirk Burghs 1918–22; PC 1916.

MacDonald, James Ramsay (1866–1937); Chmn Parliamentary Lab. Party 1911–14, 1922–31; Lab. MP Leicester 1906–18, Glamorganshire (Aberavon) 1922–9, Durham

(Seaham) 1929–31; National Lab. MP Durham (Seaham) 1931–5, Scottish Universities 1936–7; sec. Labour Representation Committee 1900–12, treasurer 1912–24; member LCC 1900–4; Chmn ILP 1906–8; PM and Sec. of St. Foreign Affairs 1924; PM 1929–35; Ld Pres. of Council 1935–7.

McKenna, Pamela (1889–1943); m. Reginald McKenna 1908; younger dau. of Col. Sir Herbert Jekyll KCMG (1846–1932) and Dame Agnes Jekyll (1861–1937). Her relationship with the Asquiths, especially the PM, drew her husband into their social circle. Niece of noted landscape gardener Gertrude Jekyll.

McKenna, Reginald (1863–1943); First Ld Admy 1908–11; Lib. MP Monmouthshire (N.) 1895–1918; Fin. Sec. Treasury 1905–7; Pres. Bd of Educ. 1907–8; Sec. of St. Home Affairs 1911–15; Chanr of Exchequer 1915–16; Chmn Midland Bank 1919–43.

Marchamley, George Whiteley, Baron (1855–1925); Patronage Sec. Treasury (Lib. Chief Whip) 1905–8; Con. MP Stockport 1893–1900; Lib. MP W. Riding of Yorks. (Pudsey) 1900–8; PC 1907; Baron Marchamley 1908.

Masterman, Charles Frederick Gurney (1873–1927); U.-Sec. of St. LGB 1908–9; journalist and author; Lib. MP West Ham (N.) 1906–11, Bethnal Green (SW) 1911–14, Manchester (Rusholme) 1923–4; U.-Sec. of St. Home Affairs 1909–12; Fin. Sec. Treasury 1912–14; PC 1912; Chanr Duchy of Lancr 1914–15.

Maxse, Leopold James 'Leo' (1864–1932); journalist and political activist; editor *National Review* 1893–1929. His sister, Violet, Lady Milner, succeeded him as editor. An imperialist and Germanophobe; uncompromising advocate of Joseph Chamberlain's tariff reform programme; member Imperial Maritime League, which criticised Fisher's naval economies; editor, *The Globe*, 1917–21 until merged with the *Pall Mall Gazette*. Remained a Germanophobe after 1918, defending increased armaments spending. Keen amateur tennis player.

Metternich zur Gracht, Paul Count Wolff (1853–1934); German Amb. London 1901–12, Constantinople 1915–16. Prominent opponent of Turkish actions in the Armenian Genocide. 'Afflicted with a nervous twitch' (Consuelo Vanderbilt Balsan, *The Glitter and the Gold*, George Mann, Maidstone, 1973 [1st edn, William Heinemann, 1953], p.116).

Midleton, (William) St John Fremantle Brodrick, Viscount (1856–1942); leader, Irish Unionist Alliance 1910–18; 9th Vt 1907; member Irish Convention 1911–18; cr. Earl of Midleton 1920. Con. MP Surrey W. 1880–5, Surrey (Guildford) 1885–1906; Fin. Sec, War 1886–92; U.-Sec. of St. War, 1895–8; Parl. U.-Sec. of St. Foreign Affairs, 1898–1900; Sec. St. War, 1900–3; Sec. St. India, 1903–5.

Milner, Alfred Milner, Viscount (1854–1925); barrister 1881; journalist under Morley and W.T. Stead; greatly influenced by S.A. Barnett, a co-founder of Toynbee Hall; p.s. to G.J. Goschen 1883–5 and Dec. 1886–8 when Goschen was Chanr of Exchequer; active with him in founding Lib. Unionist Association 1886; Dir.-Gen. Accounts Egypt 1890; U.-Sec. Finance Ministry, Egypt 1890–2; Chmn Bd of Inland Revenue 1892–7; KCB 1895; High Commr S. Africa 1897–1905; Baron Milner 1901, Vt 1902; ardently opposed 1909 Budget, the Parliament Act and Home Rule;

member War Cabinet 1916–18; Sec. of St. War Apr.–Dec. 1918; Sec. of St. Colonial Affairs 1918–21.

Mond, Sir Alfred Moritz, Bt (1868–1930); Lib. MP Swansea (later Swansea, W.) 1910–23, Chester 1906–10, Carmarthen 1924–8; Bt 1910; PC 1913; First Commr of Works 1916–21; Min. Health 1921–2; managing director and Chmn Imperial Chemical Industries Ltd and its fore-runners; Zionist; joined Con. Party 1926; Baron Melchett 1928.

Montagu, Hon. Edwin Samuel (1879–1924); U.-Sec. of St. India 1910–14; PPS to HHA 1906–10; Lib. MP Cambridgeshire (Chesterton) 1906–22; Fin. Sec. Treasury 1914–Feb. 1915, May 1915–16; Chanr Duchy of Lancr Feb.–May 1915, 1916; Min. Munitions 1916; Sec. of St. India 1917–22. Described his feeling for HHA as 'hero-worship', though his engagement and marriage in 1915 to the Hon. Venetia Stanley (1887–1948) was one of HHA's greatest emotional blows.

Morant, Sir Robert Laurie (1863–1920); Perm. Sec. Bd of Educ. 1903–11; tutor to Siamese royal family; devised Siamese public education system 1886–94; asst director special enquiries and reports, Bd of Educ. 1895; p.s. to Sir John Eldon Gorst (Pres. Council Committee on Educ.) 1899–1902; asst p.s. Duke of Devonshire (Ld Pres. of Council) 1902, and principal architect of 1902 Educ. Act; KCB 1907; Chmn National Health Insurance Commission 1911–19; first Sec. Min. of Health 1919–20.

Morley of Blackburn, John Morley, Viscount (1838–1923); Ld Privy Seal 1910–14; Sec. of St. India 1905–10; Vt Morley May 1908; editor, *Fortnightly Review* 1867–82; editor, *Pall Mall Gazette* 1880–3; Lib. MP Newcastle-upon-Tyne 1883–95, Montrose Burghs 1896–1908; Chief Sec. Ireland 1886, 1892–5 (JAP was his PPS 1892–5); author of official life of Gladstone (1903).

Murray, Sir George Herbert (1849–1936); Perm. Sec. Treasury 1903–11; civil servant 1872–1911; p.s. to W.E. Gladstone 1892–4, Ld Rosebery 1894–5; KCB 1899; GCB 1908; PC 1910; GCVO 1920. 'His wife is a rabid Ulsterwoman & G. M. himself is bitten by it' (Harcourt diary, 9 May 1916, Bodl. MS.Eng.c.8271).

Nash, Vaughan (1861–1932); p.s. to HHA 1908–12; journalist, *Daily Chronicle* 1893–9; *Manchester Guardian* 1900, *Daily News* 1901; p.s. to Campbell-Bannerman 1905–8; Chmn Development Commission 1912–29; Sec. Min. Reconstruction 1917–19.

Newman, Sir George (1870–1948); first Chief Medical Officer, Bd of Educ. 1907–35, responsible for setting up school medical service; kt 1911; first Chief Med. Officer, Min. of Health 1919–35. His annual reports were widely regarded as authoritative monographs. MD (gold medallist) Edin. and Dipl. Public Health (Cantab.) 1895; Med. Officer of Health Finsbury 1900–07; his *Infant Mortality: a Social Problem* (1906) highlighted the unchanged infant mortality rate over the preceding 50 years, identifying social causes and potential methods of prevention; birthright Quaker; (anonymous) editor *Friends' Quarterly Examiner* 1899–1939; GBE KCB FRSE.

Nicoll, Sir William Robertson (1851–1923); editor the Nonconformist *British Weekly*, with a peak readership of 100,000+; ordained Scottish Free Church minister 1874; editor *The Expositor* for Hodder & Stoughton from 1884; rtd from pastoral ministry with lungs impaired by typhoid 1885; moved to London founding *British Weekly* 1886 and *The Bookman* 1891, acting as chief literary adviser to Hodder & Stoughton; kt 1909 reflecting his sustained support for the Liberal Party and close friendship with DLG, CH 1921. (Roisin Higgins, 'William Robertson Nicoll and the Liberal Nonconformist press, 1886–1923', Ph.D. thesis, U. of St Andrews, 1996).

Norfolk, Henry Fitzalan-Howard, 15th Duke of (1847–1917) Premier Duke and Hereditary Earl Marshal; most prominent Roman Catholic layman; Unionist politician and philanthropist; Capt. later Lt-Col. 2nd Sussex Rifle Volunteers; KG 1886; Postmaster Gen. 1895–1900; Lt-Col. Imperial Yeomanry in second Boer War; ch. Royal Commission on Militia and Volunteers 1903 which influenced the creation of the Territorial Force 1908. His philanthropy concentrated on Roman Catholic causes and the city of Sheffield where he was Mayor then first Ld Mayor 1895–7.

Northcliffe, Alfred Charles William Harmsworth, Baron (1865–1922); journalist and newspaper proprietor; bought derelict *Evening News* 1894; started *Daily Mail* 1896; Bt 1903; Baron Northcliffe 1905; chief proprietor, *The Times* 1908–22; chmn British Mission to USA May–Nov. 1917; director of propaganda to enemy countries Feb.–Nov. 1918; Vt Northcliffe 1918.

Pease, Ethel ('Elsie') (1867–1941); m. JAP in 1886. Her g'father, Sir Henry Havelock, relieved Lucknow in 1857. Her father was Sir Henry Marshman Havelock-Allan, 1st Bt, VC for his conduct at battle of Cawnpore. Her mother, Lady Alice Moreton, was 2nd dau. of the 2nd Earl of Ducie. EP was such a good horsewoman her father said he would not permit her to marry anyone who could not outride her; JAP did.

Pease, Joseph (1889–1971); JAP's only son; Lovat Scouts 1914–18; m. 1921 Veronica Margaret Noble (1900–95) dau. of Sir George Noble Bt; 2nd Baron Gainford 1943.

Pease, Miriam Blanche (1887–1965); JAP's eldest child; great friend of Harcourt's daughters; Inspector of Factories, Home Office 1916–38 (initially unpaid); Supt Inspector West Midland Division 1938–42.

Pirrie, William James Pirrie, Baron (1847–1924); shipbuilder and shipowner; apprenticed to Harland & Wolff 1862, partner 1874, Chmn after Harland's death in 1895; Ld Mayor Belfast 1896–7; Baron Pirrie 1906; Comptroller-Gen. Merchant Shipbuilding 1918; Vt 1921. Described by Ld Inverforth as 'probably the richest man in England' (Arthur Pound and Samuel Taylor Moore eds, *They Told Barron: Conversations and Revelations of... Clarence W. Barron*, Harper Brothers, NY, 1930, p.167). Michael S. Moss, 'Pirrie, William James, Viscount Pirrie (1847–1924)', *ODNB*, 2004, http://www.oxforddnb.com/view/article/35534, accessed 22 June 2017.

Ponsonby, Arthur Augustus William Harry (1871–1946); Lib. MP Stirling Burghs 1908–18 (succeeding Sir Henry Campbell-Bannerman); p.s. to PM 1905–08; leading radical MP; Lab. MP Sheffield (Brightside) 1922–30; U.-Sec. of St. Foreign Affairs, Jan.–Nov. 1924; U.-Sec. of St. Dominion Affairs June–Dec. 1929; Parl. Sec. Min. Transport 1929–Mar. 1931; Chanr Duchy of Lancr Mar.–Aug. 1931; cr. Baron Ponsonby of Shulbrede 1930; founder member Union of Democratic Control, opposing war; ran Peace Letter campaign 1927–8; founder member Peace Pledge

Union; resigned from Lab. Party when it joined Churchill coalition 1940. Son of Sir Henry Ponsonby, p.s. to Queen Victoria; younger brother of 'Fritz' Ponsonby; m. Dorothea, dau. of Sir Hubert Parry: their family is portrayed in *Shulbrede Tunes*. Duncan Marlor, *Fatal Fortnight: Arthur Ponsonby and the Fight for British Neutrality in 1914*, Frontline Books, 2014.

Primrose, Hon. Neil James Archibald (1882–1917); Lib. MP N. Cambs. (Wisbech) 1910–17; 2nd son Ld Rosebery; U.-Sec. of St. Foreign Affairs Feb.–May 1915; PC 1917; MC; died of wounds.

Reading, Sir Rufus Daniel Isaacs, Baron (1860–1933); Atty-Gen. 1910–13 (first Atty-Gen. in Cabinet 1912–13); Lib. MP Reading 1904–13; early years in family fruit merchandising business; barrister 1887; QC 1898; specialised in commercial and trade union cases; Solr-Gen. Mar.–Oct. 1910; Kt 1910; PC 1911; Ld Chief Justice 1913–21; Baron Reading 1914; led Anglo–French mission to USA for American credits, Sept. 1915; Vt Reading 1916; High Commr to USA and Canada 1917; Earl of Reading 1917; Amb. USA 1918–19; Viceroy India 1921–6; Marquess of Reading 1926; Sec. of St. Foreign Affairs 1931.

Redmond, John Edward (1856–1918); Chmn Irish Parliamentary Party 1900–18; Clerk H of C 1880; close friend of Parnell even after Irish nationalists split in 1890; Irish Nationalist MP New Ross, Co. Wexford 1881–5, N. Wexford 1885–90, Waterford 1890–1918.

Riddell, Sir George Allardice (1865–1934); newspaper proprietor; solicitor 1888–1903; legal adviser and Chmn *News of the World*; Kt 1909; liaison officer between British government and press 1914–18 and British delegates and press at Paris Peace Conference; Bt 1918; Baron Riddell 1920; benefactor of Royal Free Hospital and Eastman Dental Hospital. First divorced peer to enter the Lords 1920. 'He has an H "where other beasts have none" underneath a heart of gold…and a passionate admiration of success' (P. McKenna–H. Belloc [*c.*Sept. 1914] Belloc MSS).

Rosebery, Archibald Philip Primrose, Earl of (1847–1929); succ. g'father as 5th Earl 1868; U.-Sec. of St. Home Affairs 1881–3; Ld Privy Seal 1885; First Commr of Works 1886; Sec. of St. Foreign Affairs 1886, 1892–4; Chmn LCC 1889–90, 1892; PM & Ld Pres. of Council 1894–5; pres. Lib. League 1902–9.

Runciman, Walter (1870–1949); Pres. Bd of Educ. 1908–11; Lib. MP Dewsbury 1902–18, Oldham 1899–1900, Swansea (W.) 1924–9, Cornwall (St Ives) 1929–31; Nat. Lib. MP Cornwall (St Ives) 1931–7; Parl. Sec. LGB 1905–7; Fin. Sec. Treasury 1907–8; Pres. Bd of Ag. & Fish. 1911–14; Pres. Bd of Trade 1914–16, 1931–7; Ld Pres. of Council 1938–9; 2nd Baron Runciman 1937; Vt 1937.

Salisbury, James Edward Hubert Gascoyne-Cecil, 4th Marquess of (1861–1947); ADC to George V 1910–29; Vt Cranborne 1868–1903; Con. MP Lancs. (Darwen) 1885–92, Rochester 1893–1903; U.-Sec. of St. Foreign Affairs 1900–3; Ld Privy Seal 1903–5, 1924–9; Pres. Bd of Trade 1905; ADC to Edward VII 1903–10; Ld Pres. of Council and Dep. Leader, Lords 1922–4; Chanr Duchy of Lancr 1922; Leader Lords 1925–31. An ardent and vigorous churchman and a 'Die-Hard' in 1911; continued agitating for Lords' reform through 1930s.

Samuel, Herbert Louis (1870–1963); Postmaster-Gen. 1910–14; U.-Sec. of St. Home Affairs 1905–9; Lib. MP N. Riding of Yorks. (Cleveland) 1902–18, Lancs. (Darwen) 1929–35; Chanr Duchy of Lancr 1909–10, May 1915–16; Pres. LGB 1914–May 1915; Sec. of St. Home Affairs 1916, 1931–2; High Commr Palestine 1920–5; C-in-C Palestine 1922–5; prominent Zionist; Leader, Lib. Party in H of C 1931–5, in Lords 1944–55; Vt Samuel 1937.

Sandars, John Satterfield (1853–1934); p.s. to A.J. Balfour 1895–1915; barrister 1877; p.s. to Sec. of St. Home Affairs 1885–92; PC 1905.

Sazonov, Sergei Dmitrievich (1860–1927); Russian Foreign Min. 1911–16; previously Dep. Foreign Min. and diplomat in London and the Vatican; popular with Foreign Office as a supporter of the Entente (Keith Neilson, '"Only a d…d marionette?" The influence of ambassadors on British Foreign Policy, 1904–1914', Michael Dockrill and Brian McKercher eds, *Diplomacy and world power: Studies in British Foreign Policy, 1890–1950*, Cambridge UP, 1996, p.70).

Scott, Alexander MacCallum (1874–1928); Lib. MP 1910–18, Co. Lib. 1918–22 Glasgow Bridgeton; barrister and author; sec. League of Libs against Aggression and Militarism and New Reform Club; Lewisham borough councillor 1903–6; first biographer of WSC 1905–16; Scottish nationalist, radical, ardent anti-suffragist; p.s. Ld Pentland Sec. for Scotland 1909-10; PPS to WSC 1917–19; govt Scottish whip 1922; joined Lab. Party 1924; died with wife in aircraft crash in Puget Sound.

Scott, Charles Prestwich (1846–1932); owner (from 1907) and editor (1872–1929) *Manchester Guardian*; Lib. MP Leigh 1895–1906; powerful advocate and candid critic of DLG and Liberal policies; supporter of female suffrage but not suffragette 'misguided fanaticism'.

Seely, John Edward Bernard (1868–1947); U.-Sec. of St., War 1911–12; Con. then Lib. MP Isle of Wight 1900–6 (Unionist Free Trader, crossed the floor to the Libs Mar. 1904), Liverpool (Abercrombie) 1906–10, Derbyshire (Ilkeston) 1910–22; U.-Sec. of St. Colonial Affairs 1908–10; Sec. of St. War 1912–14; Special Service Officer with Sir John French 1914–15; Cmdr 1st Canadian Cavalry Bde 1915–18; U.-Sec. of St. & Dep. Min. of Munitions 1918–19; U.-Sec. of St. Air 1919; Baron Mottistone 1933.

Selborne, William Waldegrave Palmer, Earl of (1859–1942); High Commr S. Africa and Gov. and C-in-C Transvaal and Orange River Colony 1905–10; p.s. to Ld Chanr, to Sec. of St. War, and to Chanr of Exchequer 1881–5; Lib. MP Hampshire (Petersfield) 1885–6, Lib. Un. MP 1886–95, Edinburgh (W.) 1892–5; Lib. Un. Whip 1886–95; 2nd Earl 1895; U.-Sec. of St. Colonial Affairs 1895–1900; First Ld Admy 1900–5; Pres. Bd of Ag. & Fish. 1915–16; Warden Winchester College 1920–5; High Steward Winchester 1929–42; m. dau. of 3rd Marquess of Salisbury. Edward Grey was his fag at Winchester.

Selby-Bigge, Sir Lewis Amherst (1860–1951); Principal Asst Sec. Bd of Educ. 1907–11; barrister 1891; Asst Charity Commr 1894–1902; Asst Sec. Bd of Educ. 1903–07, Perm. U. Sec. 1911–25; KCB 1913; Bt 1919.

Simon, Sir John Allsebrook (1873–1954); Solr-Gen. 1910–13; Lib. MP Essex (Walthamstow) 1906–18, W. Riding of Yorks. (Spen Valley) 1922–40; barrister 1899;

KC 1908; Kt 1910; PC 1913; Atty-Gen. 1913–15; Sec. of St. Home Affairs 1915–16, 1935–7; Chmn Statutory Commission to investigate development of Indian government 1927–30; formed Lib. Nat. later Nat. Lib. Party and supported National Government 1931; Sec. of St. Foreign Affairs 1931–5; Chanr of Exchequer 1937–40; Ld Chanr 1940–45; Vt Simon 1940.

Smith, Frederick Edwin (1872–1930); Con. MP Liverpool (Walton) 1906–18, Liverpool (W. Derby) 1918–19; barrister 1899; Solr-Gen. June–Nov. 1915; Atty-Gen. 1915–19; Ld Chanr 1919–22; Sec. of St. India 1924–8; PC 1911; Kt 1915; Bt 1918; Baron Birkenhead 1919, Vt 1921, Earl of Birkenhead 1922.

Stamfordham, Sir Arthur Bigge, Baron (1849–1931); p.s. to King George V 1910–31; p.s. to Prince of Wales 1901–10; asst p.s. to Queen Victoria 1880–95, p.s. 1895–1901; KCB 1895; PC 1910; Baron 1911.

Stanley, Hon. Beatrice Venetia (1887–1948); Violet Asquith's intimate friend and complicit object of HHA's infatuation; received torrent of HHA's letters 1912–15 totalling some 300,000 words, frequently revealing Cabinet secrets. Unenthusiastically tolerated Edwin Montagu's prolonged suit, finally agreeing to marry him, delivering the shattering news to HHA 12 May 1915, adopting the Jewish faith and marrying 26 July 1915. Her later life of 'conjugal carnage' and 'flings' floridly portrayed in Stefan Buczacki, *My Darling Mr Asquith*, 2016.

Tennant, Harold John (1865–1935); Fin. Sec. War 1911–12; Lib. MP Berwickshire 1892–1918; Margot Asquith's brother; asst p.s. to HHA as Home Sec. 1892–5; Parl. Sec. Bd of Trade 1909–11; U.-Sec. of St. War 1912–16; PC 1914; Sec. Scotland 1916.

Tennant, Margaret Mary ('May') (1869–1946); dau. of G.W. Abraham; sec. to Lady Dilke; treasurer Women's Trade Union League; asst commr royal commission on labour 1891; first woman factory inspector 1893, resigned on marriage to widower H.J. Tennant 1896; member, Central Unemployed Body for London; member, royal commission on divorce 1909–12; welfare adviser at War Office then director, women's section, Dept of National Service 1917. (Helen Jones, 'Women Health Workers: The Case of the First Women Factory Inspectors in Britain', *Social History of Medicine*, vol.1, Aug. 1988, pp.165–81; Mary Drake McFeely, *Lady Inspectors The Campaign for a Better Workplace 1893–1921*, Basil Blackwell, NY, 1988, *passim*. For the Tennants as Lib. Imperialists see Eliza Riedi, 'Options for an Imperialist Woman: The Case of Violet Markham 1899–1914', *Albion*, vol.32, no.1, 2000, pp.59–84.

Thring, Sir Arthur Theodore (1860–1932); First Parliamentary Counsel 1903–17; barrister 1887; Clerk of the Parliaments 1917–30; KCB 1908.

Trevelyan, Charles Philips (1870–1958); Parl. Sec. Bd of Educ. 1908–14; Pres. Bd of Educ. Jan.–Nov. 1924 and 1929–31; Lib. MP W. Riding of Yorks. (Elland) 1899–1918; Lab. MP Newcastle-upon-Tyne (Central) 1922–31; p.s. to Ld Lt Ireland 1892–5; Parl. Charity Commr 1906–8; brother of historian G.M. Trevelyan; a founder of the Union of Democratic Control; succ. father as 3rd Bt 1928.

Tyrrell, Sir William George (1866–1947); p.s. to Sir Edward Grey 1907–15 then transferred to Home Office after breakdown; Foreign Office civil servant 1889–1928;

p.s. to Perm. U. Sec. of St. Foreign Affairs 1896–1903; p.s. CID 1903–4; Second Sec. British embassy Rome 1904–5; précis-writer 1905–7; KCMG 1913; head of Political Intelligence Dept 1916–19; Perm. U. Sec. 1925–8; Amb. France 1928–34; PC 1928; Baron Tyrrell 1929; Pres. British Bd of Film Censors 1935–47. Both his sons were killed in WWI.

Wedgwood, Josiah Clement (1872–1943); Lib. MP (Lab. from 1919) Newcastle-under-Lyme 1906–42; naval architect; resident magistrate, Transvaal 1902–4; advocated land valuation taxes; Chanr Duchy of Lancr 1924; PC 1924; Baron Wedgwood 1942. Publicity following his 1919 divorce helped divorce law reform.

Whitley, John Henry (1866–1935); Chmn of Ways and Means (Dep. Speaker) H of C 1911–21; Jr Ld Treasury 1907–10 (unpaid till June 1908); Lib. MP Halifax 1900–28; cotton spinner; PC 1911; chmn various H of C committees incl. relations of employers and employed 1917–18, which led to consultative machinery incl. Whitley Councils; Speaker, H of C 1921–8; Chmn, BBC 1930–5. (Clyde Binfield, 'J.H. Whitley A Model for Free Churchmen', in John A. Hargreaves, Keith Laybourn, and Richard Toye eds, *Liberal Reform and Industrial Relations: J.H. Whitley (1866–1935), Halifax Radical and Speaker of the House of Commons*, Routledge, 2018, pp.50–66.)

Wilson, Sir Arthur Knyvet (1842–1921); First Sea Ld 1910–11; VC for gallantry at battle of al-Teb 1884; Kt 1903; adm. of the fleet 1907; OM 1912; returned to Admy w'out official position or salary Oct. 1914–18; succ. brother as 3rd Bt 1919.

Wilson, Henry Hughes (1864–1922); director of mili. operations, War Office 1910–14; brig.-gen. and commandant, Staff College, Camberley 1907–10; close friend of Gen. Foch from 1909; maj.-gen. 1913; sub-CGS BEF Aug. 1914; lt-gen. 1914; chief liaison officer French HQ 1915; KCB 1915; Cmdr 4th Corps Dec. 1915–16; Anglo–French mission to Russia, Jan.–Feb. 1917; chief liaison officer French HQ Mar.–Sept. 1917; Cmdr Eastern Command Sept.–Dec. 1917; British permanent mili. rep. Supreme War Council Dec. 1917–Feb. 1918; CIGS 1918–22; Field Marshal July 1919; Bt, thanks of Parliament, and grant of £10,000 1919; Con. MP N. Down Feb. 1922; assassinated 22 June 1922.

Wimborne, Hon. Ivor Churchill Guest, Baron (1873–1939); Paymaster-Gen. 1910–12; Lib. Un. then Lib. MP Plymouth 1900–6, Cardiff 1906–10; a Unionist Free Trade Trader, crossed the floor in Apr. 1904; Baron Ashby St Ledgers 1910; PC 1910; Ld-in-Waiting 1913–15: succ. father as 2nd Baron Wimborne 1914; Ld Lt Ireland 1915–18; Vt Wimborne 1918; 1st Pres. Nat. Lib. Party 1931; m. 1902 Hon. Alice Katherine Sibell Grosvenor (d. 1948).

Winterton, Edward 'Eddie' Turnour, Earl Winterton and Baron Turnour (1883–1962); 6th Earl (Irish peerage) 1907; Con. MP Sussex NW (Horsham) 1904–18, Horsham and Worthing 1918–45, Horsham 1945–51; Sussex Yeomanry and Imperial Camel Corps Gallipoli and Palestine 1915 then Arabia; U.-Sec. of St. India 1922–4, 1924–9; PC 1924; Chanr Duchy of Lancr 1937–9; member Cabinet 1938–9; Baron Turnour (UK peerage) 1952; succeeded DLG as 'Father' of H of C 1945; a founding member of The Other Club.

Wood, Thomas McKinnon (1855–1927); U.-Sec. of St. Foreign Affairs 1908–11; member LCC 1892–1907 (Chmn 1898–9); Lib. MP Glasgow (St Rollox) 1906–18; Parl. Sec. Bd of Educ. 1908; Fin. Sec. Treasury 1911–12; PC 1911; Sec. Scotland 1912–16; Chanr Duchy of Lancr and Fin. Sec. Treasury 1916. Considered but not chosen as Chief Sec. Ireland on resignation of Birrell; 'his Parly manner is thought to be too bad' (Harcourt diary, 4 May 1916, Bodl. MS.Eng.c.8271).

Wyndham, George (1863–1913); Con. MP Dover 1889–1913; p.s. to A.J. Balfour 1887–92; U.-Sec. of St. War 1898–1900; Chief Sec. Ireland 1900–5; soldier, tariff reformer, poet, a 'Soul'; m. 1887 Sibell, Countess Grosvenor. His mistress, the Countess of Plymouth, and her dau., Lady Phyllis Windsor-Clive, were with him in Paris when he died. Family tradition has him dying of a heart attack in a brothel (Gerald Gliddon, *The Aristocracy and the Great War*, Gliddon Books, Norwich, 2002, p.419); Simon Blow suggests it was a male brothel (Michael Bloch, *Closet Queens: Some 20th Century British Politicians*, Abacus, 2015, p.301); Nancy W. Ellenberger, 'Constructing George Wyndham: Narratives of Aristocratic Masculinity in Fin-de Siécle England', *JBS*, vol.39, no.4, 2000, p.501; Caroline Dakers, *Clouds: The Biography of a Country House*, Yale UP, New Haven, 1993, pp.189–90).

INDEX

We are grateful to Marian Aird for her expeditious compilation of the index to this complex work.

Personal names are arranged under the name by which a person was known when last mentioned in the text. Hyphenated names are arranged under first name. JAP has been used to signify Jack Pease. Entries in bold indicate a biographical note.